The Cambridge Encyclopedia of
Latin America and the Caribbean

The Cambridge Encyclopedia of

LATIN AMERICA

AND THE CARIBBEAN

General editors

Simon Collier
Reader in History, University of Essex

Harold Blakemore
Secretary, Institute of Latin American Studies
Reader in Latin American History, University of London

Thomas E. Skidmore
Director, Ibero-American Studies Program
Professor of History, University of Wisconsin–Madison

*The right of the
University of Cambridge
to print and sell
all manner of books
was granted by
Henry VIII in 1534.
The University has printed
and published continuously
since 1584.*

CAMBRIDGE UNIVERSITY PRESS

Cambridge London New York New Rochelle
Melbourne Sydney

100369

Published by the Press Syndicate of the University of Cambridge
The Pitt Building, Trumpington Street, Cambridge CB2 1RP
32 East 57th Street, New York, NY 10022, USA
10 Stamford Road, Oakleigh, Melbourne 3166, Australia

© Cambridge University Press 1985

First published 1985

Text setting by Wyvern Typesetting Ltd, Bristol
Colour origination by Anglia Reproductions, Witham
Printed in Great Britain by W. S. Cowell Ltd, Ipswich

Library of Congress catalogue card number: 84–19886

British Library cataloguing in publication data

The Cambridge encyclopedia of Latin America
    and the Caribbean.
    1. Latin America – Dictionaries and
    encyclopedias
    I. Collier, Simon   II. Blakemore, Harold
    III. Skidmore, Thomas E.
    980'.003'21   F1406

    ISBN 0 521 26263 1

wv

Contributors

AEA   **Alan Angell**
       Latin American Centre, St Antony's College, Oxford

GA-B   **Dr Gertrud Aub-Buscher**
       Language Teaching Centre, University of Hull

GHAB   **Dr George Bankes**
       Manchester Museum, University of Manchester

HB   **Dr Harold Blakemore**
       Institute of Latin American Studies, University of London

RB   **Dr Richard Boulind**

JBHB   **Dr Ben Box**

WB   **Dr Warwick Bray**
       Institute of Archaeology, University of London

GB   **Professor Gordon Brotherston**
       University of Essex

PARC   **Professor Peter Calvert**
       University of Southampton

RC   **Robin Chapman**
       Lloyds Bank International

CMC   **Dr Chalmers Clapperton**
       University of Aberdeen

CC   **Dr Colin Clarke**
       Jesus College, Oxford

SC   **Dr Simon Collier**
       University of Essex

FC   **Dr Frank Colson**
       University of Southampton

GC-S   **Professor Gordon Connell-Smith**
       University of Hull

PEBC   **Dr Peter Coy**
       University of Stirling

EC   **Eduardo Crawley**
       Latin American Newsletters

MDD   **Malcolm Deas**
       Latin American Centre, St Antony's College, Oxford

MD   **Professor Marco Díaz**
       Universidad Nacional Autónoma de México

JPD   **Dr J. P. Dickenson**
       University of Liverpool

EFE   **Edwin Early**
       Portsmouth Polytechnic

JF   **Jan Fairley**

JVF   **Dr J. Valerie Fifer**
       Goldsmiths' College, University of London

JRF   **Dr John Fisher**
       University of Liverpool

DF   **David Fox**
       University of Manchester

VF   **Dr Valerie Fraser**
       University of Essex

DG   **Professor Douglas Gifford**
       Centre for Latin American Linguistic Studies, University of St Andrews

TFG   **Professor Thomas F. Glick**
       University of Boston

RNG   **Dr R. N. Gwynne**
       University of Birmingham

JH	**Jonathan Hakim** *The Economist*		IR-U	**Professor Ina Rosenthal-Urey (formerly Dinerman)** Wheaton College, Mass.
AH	**Professor Alistair Hennessy** University of Warwick		SBS	**Professor Stuart B. Schwartz** University of Minnesota
HAH	**Hugh Holley** Lloyds Bank Group Economics Department		DLS	**Professor Donald L. Shaw** University of Edinburgh
PH	**Dr Peter Hulme** University of Essex		TES	**Professor Thomas E. Skidmore** University of Wisconsin–Madison
PJ	**Dr Peter Janke**		CTS	**Professor Clifford T. Smith** University of Liverpool
JPK	**Dr John King** University of Warwick		RS	**Professor Robert Stevenson** University of California at Los Angeles
AK	**Dr Alan Knight** University of Essex		EMT-H	**Dr Elizabeth M. Thomas-Hope** University of Liverpool
FL	**Dr Francis Lambert** Institute of Latin American Studies, University of Glasgow		DW	**David Winder** Ford Foundation, Mexico City
JCL	**J. C. Langley**		JTW	**James Winpenny**
RLeP	**Professor R. B. Le Page** University of York			
WL	**Dr Walter Little** Centre for Latin American Studies, University of Liverpool			
JL	**Professor John Lynch** Institute of Latin American Studies, University of London			
JSMacD	**Professor John MacDonald** Chelsea College			
AMcF	**Dr Anthony McFarlane** University of Warwick			
GM	**Professor Gerald Martin** Portsmouth Polytechnic			
KM	**Professor Kenneth Medhurst** University of Stirling			
NM	**Professor Narciso Menocal** University of Wisconsin–Madison			
TM	**Tony Morrison**			
DRM	**Professor David Murray** University of Guelph, Ontario			
LAN	**Dr Linda Newson** King's College, London			
DN	**The Reverend David Nicholls**			
JJN	**Professor John J. Nitti** University of Wisconsin–Madison			
FN	**Felicity Nock**			
MN-M	**Sister Mary Noel-Menezes, RSM** University of Guyana			
JO-S	**Professor Juan Orrego-Salas** Latin American Music Center, University of Indiana			
AMAP	**A. M. A. Palaus** Latin American Service, British Broadcasting Corporation			
GP	**Dr George Philip** London School of Economics			
DP	**Dr David Preston** University of Leeds			
LSR	**Dr L. S. Rebelo** King's College, London			
MRR	**Dr Michael Redclift** Wye College, University of London			

Contents

Maps

Select glossary

AIFLD	American Institute of Free Labour Development
Altiplano	extended high plateau (Bolivia, Peru)
Ancom	Andean Pact Countries
AP	Acción Popular/Popular Action (Peru)
APRA	Alianza Popular Revolucionaria Americana/ American Popular Revolutionary Alliance
ARENA	National Renovation Alliance (Brazil)
cacique	see p. 305
CACM	Central American Common Market
campesino	country-person or peasant
CARICOM	Caribbean Community
caudillo	see p. 305
CECLA	Special Latin American Co-ordinating Commission
civilista	political supporter of civilian as opposed to military rule
CLAT	Latin American Confederation of Workers
comercio libre	open trade
conquistador	conqueror
CORFO	Corporación de Fomento de la Producción/ Production Development Corporation (Chile)
coronel, coroneis	literally 'colonel', 'colonels', i.e., local political boss(es) (Brazil)
ECLA	Economic Commission for Latin America; also known as CEPAL, Comisión Económica para la América Latina
EEC	European Economic Community
ejido	communal landholding (Mexico)
encomienda	see p. 182
engenho	sugar mill (Brazil)
ERP	Ejército Revolucionario del Pueblo/People's Revolutionary Army (Argentina)
estancia	ranch
estanciero	rancher
FSLN	Frente Sandinista de Liberación Nacional/ Sandinista National Liberation Front
gaucho	semi-nomadic cowboy of Argentine pampa (seventeenth century to late nineteenth century)
GSP	US Generalized System of Preference
hacienda	landed estate
IDB	Inter-American Development Bank
IMF	International Monetary Fund
junta	committee
LAFTA	Latin American Free Trade Association (Spanish acronym: ALALC)
LAIA	Latin American Integration Association
latifundio	large estate
licenciado	holder of the academic degree of *licencia* (Spanish America)
llano	plain
MDB	Brazilian Democratic Movement (Brazil)
mestizo	of mixed Spanish/Indian blood
minifundio	smallholding or subsistence plot
MNR	Movimiento Nacionalista Revolucionario/National Revolutionary Movement (Bolivia)
mulatto	of mixed European/African blood
OAS	Organization of American States
obraje	textile workshop (Spanish America)
ODECA	Organisación de Estados Centroamericanos/ Organization of Central American States
OECD	Organization for Economic Co-operation and Development
OLAS	Organization for Latin American Solidarity
OPEC	Organization of Petroleum Exporting Countries
ORIT	Inter-American Regional Organization of Labour
pampa(s)	plain(s) (Argentina)
PAN	Partido Acción Nacional/National Action Party (Mexico)
PDC	Partido Demócrata-Cristiano/Christian Democratic Party (Chile)
PRI	Partido Revolucionario Institucional/Institutional Revolutionary Party (Mexico)
PSD/PDS	Social Democratic Party (Brazil)
PTB	Brazilian Labour Party (Brazil)
ranchero	smallholder
SELA	Latin American Economic System
selva	jungle
serrano	mountain-dweller
sertão	the hinterland of north-east Brazil
sierra	mountain range
UDN	National Democratic Union (Brazil)
UNCTAD	United Nations Conference on Trade and Development
UP	Unidad Popular/Popular Unity (Chile)

LATIN AMERICA – the expression first came into use in France just before 1860 – refers to the eighteen Spanish-speaking republics of the western hemisphere, together with Portuguese-speaking Brazil (which is by far the largest Latin American country) and French-speaking Haiti.

SOUTH AMERICA is the big southern land mass of the American continent, which is really a double continent.

CENTRAL AMERICA – the area lying between, and linking, North and South America – is normally taken to include the small republics of Guatemala, Honduras, El Salvador, Nicaragua, Costa Rica and Panama, together with Belize.

MIDDLE AMERICA (or *MESOAMERICA*) is a term sometimes used to denote the area covered by Central America and Mexico together. It should be noted that Mexico is geographically a part of the North American land mass.

THE CARIBBEAN usually refers to the islands of the Caribbean Sea, but sometimes also to the adjacent mainland countries.

THE WEST INDIES are the Caribbean islands, especially (in Anglo-American parlance) those of the non-Latin Caribbean.

THE PHYSICAL ENVIRONMENT

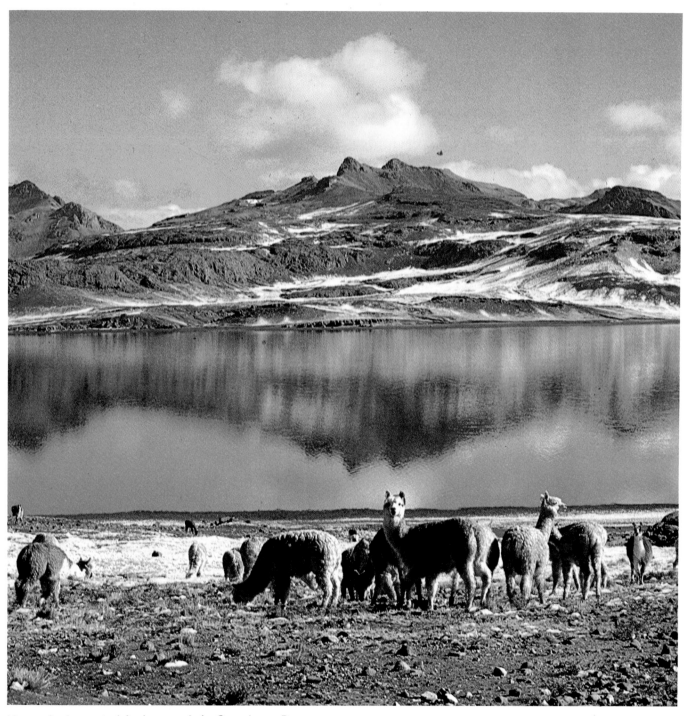

Llamas in the central Andes near Lake Orcochoca, Peru

Main tectonic and structural features

NORTH AMERICAN PLATE

Mexican Plateau

Yucatan block

Neovolcanic Axis

Balsas Depression

Crystalline highlands

Mexican Trench

COCOS PLATE

Plate segments

Galapagos Is.

NAZCA PLATE

Peru–Chile Trench

Plate segments

ANTARCTIC PLATE

OLD ANTIIIIA

CARIBBEAN PLATE

Mid-Atlantic

Spreading Centre

Amazon cone

Guyana Shield

Amazon Basin

Brazillian Shield

Parnaíba–São Francisco basin

SOUTH AMERICAN PLATE

Paraná Basin

Great eastern escarpment

0   1000 miles

0   1600 Km

Key

Pre–Cambrian Shield; ancient massif

Sedimentary basin

Plains

Intermontane basin: basin and range

Young mountains: main ridges

Volcanic areas

Plateau basalts

Tectonic history and structure

Latin America and the Caribbean are a mosaic of distinct structural units varying considerably in age and size and linked together by tectonic movements of recent geological time. The main composing units are the South American continent, the Caribbean ocean basin, the Lesser Antilles island arc, Old Antillia (Greater Antilles islands and parts of eastern Central America), western and southern Central America and Mexico north of the Balsas depression. The evolution of these units can best be understood by applying the modern concept of Plate Tectonics which states that the Earth's crust is composed of discrete slabs or plates that are continuously in motion with respect to each other. Six crustal plates have been involved in the tectonic and structural evolution of Latin America and the Caribbean.

Main structural trends: description

Beginning in Mexico and moving through Central America and the Caribbean into South America, the main structural trends are as follows.

1. Mexico north of the Balsas depression consists mainly of the Mexican Plateau, a tilted block of upland defined on its eastern, southern and western sides by prominent fault zones. Declining from 2500 m in the south to 1200 m in the north, the plateau is an area of low mountain ridges and shallow intermontane basins bearing two dominant structural trends; a north-west–south-east alignment in the eastern (folded limestone) and western (volcanic) cordilleras is one trend and this is sharply truncated in the south by the younger west–east Neovolcanic zone. The latter is typified by large active and inactive central volcanoes like Popocatapetl (5500 m), Colima (3900 m) and Ixtaccíhuatl (5250 m).

2. The Balsas depression and structure lines dominating mountain ranges in eastern Guatemala and Nicaragua and in the Greater Antilles also have a west–east alignment and may be tectonically related to the Neovolcanic zone.

3. Southern Mexico and Yucatán are two independent blocks of ancient crystalline and Mesozoic limestone respectively and lack clear structural lineation. They appear to be plate fragments moved into their present positions by fault dislocation and shearing.

4. The Central America volcanic axis extends south-eastwards continuously for 1300 km from the Guatemala–Mexico border to western Panama. It cuts across and partially mantles the adjacent and older west–east structures of Old Antillia. Constant volcanic activity for more than 20 million years has constructed volcanic uplands and chains of volcanoes in Guatemala, El Salvador, Nicaragua, Costa Rica and western Panama. More than thirty active volcanoes lie along this axis.

5. The Lesser Antilles is an 800 km arc of young volcanicity, having grown during the last 10 million years at the eastern edge of the Caribbean crustal plate where it is being underthrust by a portion of the Atlantic plate. The arc includes the highly dangerous volcanoes of Mont Pelée, Martinique, and La Soufrière, St Vincent.

6. Along the Pacific coast of Costa Rica and both coasts of eastern Panama mountain ranges seldom exceeding 1000 m altitude curve to the Andean system of north-west Colombia. Distinct from the volcanic axis of central Costa Rica and western Panama, these appear to share a common origin with the Colombian Andes and result from subduction processes at the complex junction of three crustal plates – the Cocos, Caribbean and South American.

7. The Gulf of Mexico is an abandoned ocean basin which has become isolated by the development of the Caribbean plate and has remained tectonically quiescent for about the last 40 million years; it has been an immense sediment trap since that time.

8. The Caribbean Sea occupies an ocean basin developed by sea floor spreading between 40 and 10 million years ago; floored by basaltic rock, it forms an independent crustal plate bounded on the east and west by the volcanic arcs of Lesser Antilles and Central America respectively and on the north and south by the Balsas–Greater Antilles zone of crustal shearing and the Caribbean coast ranges and shear zones of Venezuela respectively. The plate seems to be moving slowly towards the east.

9. South America is the continental part of the large crustal plate presently being created along the mid-ocean ridge of the South Atlantic. It has a much longer history of structural evolution than most of Central America and the Caribbean and is a complex assemblage of many different formations developed over more than 3000 million years. Basically, the continent is dominated by three major types of structure: up-warped and faulted massifs composed of pre-Cambrian crystalline rocks thinly covered with some Palaeozoic and Mesozoic strata; down-warped basins in the same pre-Cambrian basement filled with more than 4000 m of Palaeozoic, Mesozoic and Cainozoic sedimentary rocks; and great chains of folded and thrust rocks composing the Andean cordilleras and Caribbean coast ranges. The up-warped ancient massifs are largely composed of metamorphic and igneous rocks like gneiss, schist and granites which crop out extensively in areas known as the Guiana and Brazilian shields; such rocks form the pre-Cambrian basement that probably underlies the entire continent and which developed over almost 3000 million years. The ancient massifs of the shields have been deeply weathered and dissected due to prolonged exposure to the elements, giving rise to spectacular residual topography in granitic areas such as eastern Brazil and the Guianas where sugar-loaf inselberg landforms occur. The shield areas are dominated by dissected plateau country in which tributary streams draining to major river basins have become deeply incised as a result

of geologically recent uplift, but impressive structurally controlled scenery includes the fault line escarpment of east-central Brazil and the extensive plateau basalt terrain masking the southern edge of the shield in southern Brazil, northern Uruguay and north-east Paraguay; the Iguassú Falls plunge over the edge of this formation. Smaller ancient massifs forming uplifted plateaux are present in the southern hills of Buenos Aires and in Patagonia.

Down-warped portions of the continental pre-Cambrian basement are occupied by the immense sedimentary basins of the Amazon, Paranaíba–São Francisco and Paraná. Originating more than 600 million years ago, these have been periodically inundated with marine and terrestrial sediments which now exceed 4000 m depth in places. The most recent pulse of sedimentation and subsidence was during the last 15 million years as the Andes formed, resulting in a thick cover of late Tertiary and Quaternary sediments on top of older strata. The present course of the Amazon became established between 15 and 8 million years ago as the Andes were elevated across drainage routes to the Pacific and the Gulf of Guayaquil; this river system has not only deposited over 3000 m of sediment in the basin but has also built out an immense sedimentary cone over the continental shelf and slope; the computed rate of sedimentation during the last 2,200,000 years is 50 to 115 cm/10^3 yr. The majority of exposed strata in the basins and the thin sedimentary cover rocks fringing the shields show signs of only gentle tectonic disturbance, mainly in the form of large-scale warping, and hence are typical of the relatively quiescent tectonic environment of continental interiors. In South America such little disturbed strata extend west of the shield massifs and sedimentary basins as gently sloping plains. These stretch as a belt parallel to the Andes for almost the entire length of the continent from the llanos of Venezuela to the steppes of Patagonia and form an intermediate structural–topographical zone before the Andean province. The multiple ranges of the Andes continue for more than 6500 km from the shores of the Caribbean to the tip of Tierra del Fuego. This remarkable mountain barrier is much narrower (*c.* 300 km) and higher than the mountains of western North America. Aconcagua (6960 m) is the highest peak in the western hemisphere and the Cordillera Blanca of Peru and the Cordillera Real of Bolivia each contain many peaks exceeding 6000 m in altitude. The geological structure and history of the Andes is quite complex and to describe them as a single continuous unit is incorrect. There are distinct lithological, structural and age differences along their length and across their breadth. In general, the Andes are composed mainly of folded, thrust and faulted sedimentary and volcanic strata extensively intruded in places with immense linear masses (batholiths) of granitic rock; zones of metamorphic rock are also present. The number of structurally distinct ranges varies along the length of the Andes. In Colombia there are three principal ridges, the western,

central and eastern cordillera and a minor range of coastal hills; the eastern cordillera swings eastwards into Venezuela and the western can be traced into Panama. Southwards the Andes are continued in Ecuador by only two principal ranges, although the low coastal hills may be structurally linked with those of Colombia. A change in alignment occurs at the Peruvian frontier, south of which three closely spaced principal ranges extend south-eastwards as far as the latitude of Lima. South of here the eastern cordillera swings farther inland away from the central cordillera but continues southwards in Bolivia and Argentina while the central and western cordillera extend parallel with the coast into Chile and Bolivia. The immense down-faulted basin of Lake Titicaca and the Bolivian Altiplano occupies the unusually wide gap between the eastern and central cordillera. The basin has been filled with more than 5000 m of fluvial, volcanic and glacial deposits. The three-fold structural assemblage of cordillera continues into Chile and Argentina but by latitude 28°S the eastern cordillera becomes more diffuse and splits into faulted basin and range topography; south of 34°S only two cordillera compose the Andes, the most westerly of which is lower and becomes an archipelago of coastal islands before curving south-eastwards to terminate in Tierra del Fuego.

Other important differences in the structure of the Andes include the predominance of Palaeozoic sedimentary strata in the eastern cordillera (although granitic intrusions of Mesozoic age occur in places), the predominance of Mesozoic volcanic, sedimentary and igneous rocks in the western cordillera and the abundance of Cainozoic to present-day volcanic rocks, sediments and igneous intrusions in the central cordillera. The distribution of active volcanoes is also not uniform; they occur in southern Colombia and Ecuador, southern Peru and along the Bolivia–Chile border and in the southern part of middle Chile; in other segments of the Andes volcanicity has either become recently extinct or has been extinct for a few million years.

Structural evolution: explanation

Although the structural evolution and tectonic history of Latin America and the Caribbean has been a continuum it is perhaps helpful to consider it in two sections: from the Cambrian to Triassic period and from the Jurassic to the present. At the end of pre-Cambrian times South America was part of an assemblage of 'southern' continents (nowadays referred to as Gondwanaland) and lay on the opposite side of the globe from its present location in an 'upside-down' position; the 'northern' continents lay some distance away across an ocean basin. Central America and the Caribbean did not exist at this period.

TECTONIC HISTORY: CARBONIFEROUS–PERMIAN TIMES TO THE END OF THE JURASSIC PERIOD

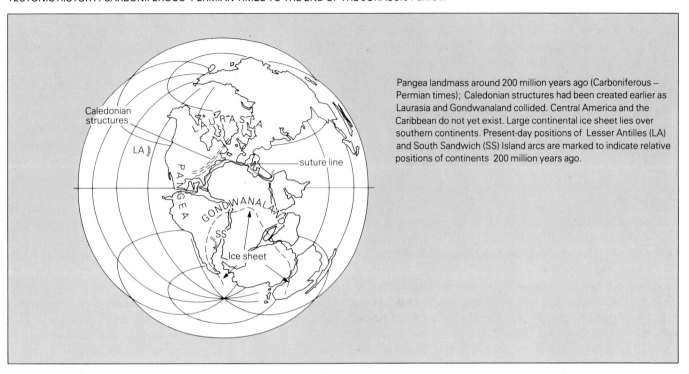

Pangea landmass around 200 million years ago (Carboniferous – Permian times); Caledonian structures had been created earlier as Laurasia and Gondwanaland collided. Central America and the Caribbean do not yet exist. Large continental ice sheet lies over southern continents. Present-day positions of Lesser Antilles (LA) and South Sandwich (SS) Island arcs are marked to indicate relative positions of continents 200 million years ago.

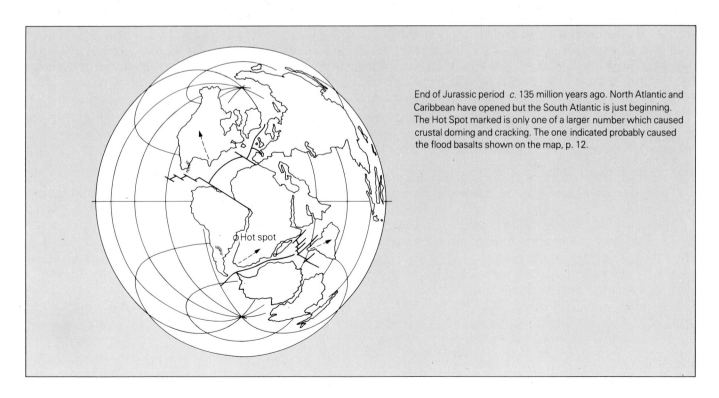

End of Jurassic period c. 135 million years ago. North Atlantic and Caribbean have opened but the South Atlantic is just beginning. The Hot Spot marked is only one of a larger number which caused crustal doming and cracking. The one indicated probably caused the flood basalts shown on the map, p. 12.

Developments in the Cambrian–Triassic period (600–200 million years ago)

Major structural events affecting South America during this period may be summarized as follows.

1. Periodic marine sedimentation along the western margin of the land mass and a Pacific ocean connection into down-warped basins of the interior.

2. Development of large ice sheets during the Silurian and Carboniferous–Permian periods as Gondwanaland moved across south-polar latitudes from one side of the globe to the other.

3. Gondwanaland collided with the northern continent Laurasia in Silurian times, forming the Caledonian mountain system extending from south-west North America to north-west Europe.

4. Subduction of Pacific ocean floor along western South America in Permian times with volcanism, folding and faulting of palaeozoic rocks, creating early Andean structures. Subduction and probable continental collision at the southern margin of Gondwanaland (South America/Africa with India/Antarctica/ Australia) during the upper Triassic period, producing folded structures exposed in the hills south of Buenos Aires and the Drakensbergs of South Africa. Most of the Earth's continental crust was now joined up to form the Pangea super-continent.

5. During the upper Triassic period massive plumes of heat rising from the mantle bulged up the crust of the quasi-stationary continental mass, cracking open the surface to release vast quantities of basaltic lava and beginning the break-up of Pangea which continues in today's movements of continents and ocean basins.

Jurassic period to the present day

Stresses set up by prolonged up-doming of the Pangea continental crust at the end of the Palaeozoic era began a period of active tectonic disturbance which continues to the present day. By the late-Jurassic period (150 million years ago) the lithosphere broke all along the western side of Pangea as parts of the Pacific ocean basin began to subduct beneath the super-continent. Heat generated at depth by this activity produced masses of molten magma that rose upwards to form arcs of volcanic islands, the roots of which partly compose the western cordilleras of South America. The northern margin of South America/Africa separated from North America as crustal fracturing and then ocean-floor spreading opened up the Gulf of Mexico and the southern North Atlantic. Thus a proto Caribbean and Central American domain came into existence for the first time. By early Cretaceous times (100 million years ago) North and South America had widely separated and, although Africa remained joined to northern South America, a great dome in the crust had developed and split in the region of eastern Brazil and a

gulf like the Red Sea opened up to form an incipient South Atlantic ocean basin. During the late Cretaceous period (90–60 million years ago) subduction of the Cocos plate beneath the Caribbean basin and adjacent parts of the North and South American plates produced the Greater Antilles arc across the position of present-day Central America. Meanwhile, subduction of the Nazca plate formed a second volcanic arc in the Andean province, the roots of which are now exposed in places as great granitic batholiths in the western cordilleras. By the Eocene period (c. 40 million years ago) considerable tectonic developments had occurred in the Caribbean. The Greater Antilles arc had migrated eastwards and widened south-eastwards, shearing past the Yucatán escarpment until it collided with the Florida–Bahama limestone mass; ocean-floor spreading moved part of the arc south-eastwards to collide with northern South America, forming the Caribbean coast ranges. Meanwhile, subduction beneath the southern North American plate produced volcanic activity and fold structures with the north-west to south-east trend now exposed in the Mexican Plateau.

By the mid-Miocene period (about 15 million years ago) the present-day geometry of the Caribbean plate and hence of most of Central America began to finalize. As the Greater Antilles arc complex collided and extinguished against Florida, convergence of the Pacific and North American plates produced master shear faults which sliced Cuba from Haiti-Dominican Republic and also defined the Caribbean plate edge along northern Venezuela; jostling between the Cocos, North American, Caribbean and South American plates ignited two new subduction zones, resulting in the volcanic arcs of the south Mexican Plateau, Central America and the Lesser Antilles.

While such events occurred in the Caribbean domain, even more violent tectonics were unfolding along the western side of South America. About 15 million years ago in the mid-Miocene period there began a third major phase of magmatic activity which affected not only the Andean zone but also much of the whole continent, causing substantial warping and elevation. Remarkable volcanic activity burst out in the Andes as uplift and folding disturbed the rock sequences; immense volumes of acidic magma, rich in silica, poured out of fissures and spread mobile incandescent flows of ash over wide areas of terrain to depths exceeding 500 m, particularly in Peru, Bolivia and Chile. The ash eruptions continued until about 4 million years ago when they ended and were replaced by the growth of large andesitic central volcanoes, indicating a change in the magmatic chemistry. This was accompanied by the main pulse of regional uplift that created the present mountainous topography; prior to this time only low mountains rose above a widespread rolling plain close to sea level. Magmatic swelling of the crust uplifted the gentle plain by 3500–4000 m, forming the Altiplano; it also caused extensive folding and thrust faulting which compressed

TECTONIC HISTORY: EOCENE TIME TO THE PRESENT

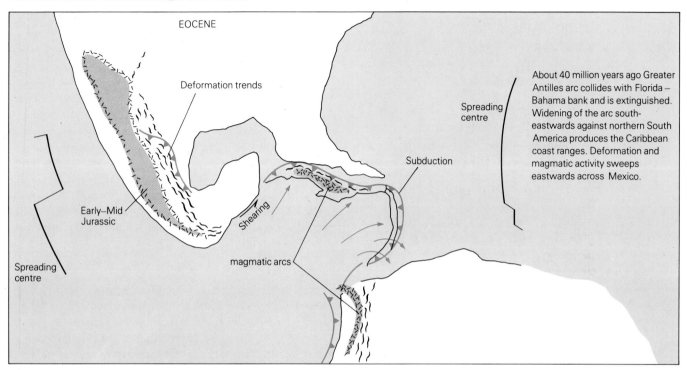

EOCENE

Deformation trends

Spreading centre

Subduction

Early–Mid Jurassic

Shearing

Spreading centre

magmatic arcs

About 40 million years ago Greater Antilles arc collides with Florida – Bahama bank and is extinguished. Widening of the arc south-eastwards against northern South America produces the Caribbean coast ranges. Deformation and magmatic activity sweeps eastwards across Mexico.

PRESENT (almost)

North American plate

Caribbean plate

Cocos plate

South American plate

The pattern initiated soon after Eocene time: Subduction of Cocos plate forms land-bridge in Central America. Crystalline highlands of Southern Mexico and Yucatán sheared and moved into position. New Caribbean plate moves eastward with respect to a slightly convergent North America and South America igniting the Lesser Antilles volcanic arc – trench system.

| 0 | | 750 km |
| 0 | | 465 miles |

CROSS SECTION THROUGH SOUTH AMERICA FROM THE PACIFIC TO THE AMAZON BASIN IN THE LATITUDE OF SOUTHERN PERU

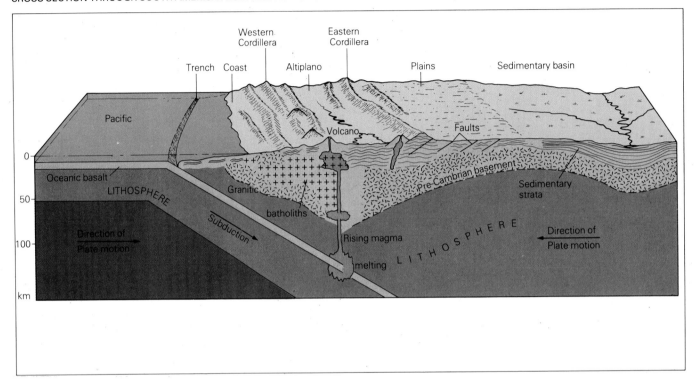

strata into anticlinal-synclinal structures, and formed the parallel ranges of the eastern cordillera. Some units of terrain, formerly part of the low-lying denudation plain, were differentially uplifted along major fault systems to form the most scenically spectacular ranges of the Andes, such as the Sierra Nevada de Santa Marta in Colombia, the Cordillera Blanca in Peru and the Cordillera Real in Bolivia. As the central and western cordillera were elevated, intense erosion removed huge volumes of sediment, exposing the great plutonic intrusions (batholiths) and in-filled down-faulted intermontane troughs with vast quantities of sands, gravels and conglomerates. Although the basic structural pattern and high elevation of the Andes had probably become established by 6 to 4 million years ago, with final details developing since then, it is perhaps worth emphasizing that the evolution was probably differential along the various structural segments of these mountains. The present uneven distribution of active volcanoes indicates that this still characterizes tectonic activity in the Andes. East of the active tectonic edge of South America much of the continent has remained tectonically quiescent but not quite immobile. Broad-scale warping and localized faulting has occurred during the last few million years, perhaps as a response to disturbance of underlying thermal circulation by deep (c. 700 km) penetration of the relatively cool slabs of Pacific ocean crust, their inclination down the subduction zone taking them far eastwards beneath the continent. This possibly accounts for the widespread late Cainozoic uplift which affected the shield massifs, basins and plains as well as the Andean region; together with lowering global sea level related to growth of the Antarctic and other ice sheets, this has produced a condition of geocraty – a time of much land above sea level.

CMC

Further reading
W. F. Jenks, ed., *Handbook of South American Geology*, Geological Society of America, Memoir 56 (1956)

W. Zeil, *The Andes: a Geological Review*, Beiträge zur Regionalen Geologie der Erde (Stuttgart, 1980)

Climate

There is a great diversity of climate in Latin America and the Caribbean, varying in type from tropical to cool temperate. Principal reasons for such diversity include the latitudinal range, the pattern and movement of atmospheric pressure cells and related wind systems, the influence of adjacent oceans and seas and the altitude and alignment of mountains.

Latitude

The location of more than three-quarters of Latin America and the Caribbean within tropical latitudes means that the climate is predominantly tropical at low altitudes. This ensures high average annual temperatures (over 20°C) and abundant rainfall in most places; but most characteristic is the relatively small annual *range* in temperature, that is the difference between the average temperature of the warmest and coldest months. Since this is usually less than 1°C there are no distinct summer and winter seasons with respect to temperature. The diurnal range (commonly 15–20°C in tropical mountains) is normally much greater than the annual range, hence the expression, 'Night is the winter of the tropics.' Outside tropical latitudes, in much of northern Mexico and south of Paraguay, the annual temperature range increases markedly poleward, demarcating definite summer and winter seasons. With increasing latitude there is also a higher number of days in the year with killing frosts. The high southerly latitudes of southern South America are in the cool temperate zone where mean annual temperatures may be less than 10°C and where mountain ice caps exist.

Pressure systems and air masses

Weather patterns in Latin America and the Caribbean are fundamentally influenced by pressure systems at three scales. At the largest are the four vast high-pressure cells at mid-latitudes in the neighbouring oceans and the zone of low pressure along the inter-tropical convergence. Anticyclonic circulation of air around those in the Atlantic directs trade winds towards the Caribbean and eastern South America from the north-east, east and south-east; winds associated with the Pacific cells trend more parallel with the coasts of Mexico and most of South America. As the inter-tropical convergence zone moves slightly northwards and southwards seasonally with the sun, the strength and location of the pressure systems also change. This influences the second scale of pressure system which involves cyclonic depressions originating along the zone of convergence of polar and tropical air. When these develop, mainly in the respective winter seasons north and south of the equator, they bring outbursts of cooler polar air into the Caribbean and the South American continent. South of latitude 40°S travelling depressions generated along the polar front in the south-east Pacific bring notoriously stormy weather into southern Chile and Patagonia. At the smallest scale are the tropical hurricanes which develop mainly over the warm waters of the Caribbean; intense thermal convection and very low atmospheric pressure over a localized area cause violent circulation of air and, accompanied by extremely high winds and torrential rain, the hurricanes may travel over long distances.

Water masses and ocean currents

Since the temperature and moisture characteristics of air masses are derived from the surfaces over which they originate and since most air masses affecting Latin America and the Caribbean come from oceanic source regions, the nature of the seas and oceans surrounding the area are of critical importance in understanding the climate.

The Caribbean Sea and the Gulf of Mexico are warm, practically inland seas fed by warm off-shoots of the Atlantic north-equatorial current. With surface water temperatures ranging from 22–28°C, these water masses are like hot cauldrons over which air travelling with the north-east trades becomes hot and moist. On the Pacific side of Central America are two contrasting water bodies: a northern extension of the equatorial counter current provides warm, moist air for the southern part of Central America, whereas the relatively cold southward flowing Californian current ensures cool year-round temperatures in western Mexico. A similar situation occurs down the west coast of South America from Chile northwards to the Peru–Ecuador border where the cold Peru current exerts a cooling influence on the coastal air masses. Because mild oceanic air from the Pacific Ocean passes over a cooler surface it is not able to absorb moisture and hence becomes a stable and dry air mass, inducing arid conditions immediately onshore. East of the Andes tropical regions are affected by hot, moist air masses moving in from the equatorial Atlantic with the north-east and easterly winds and, since moderate ocean temperatures persist as far south as the Plate estuary, southern Brazil, Paraguay, Uruguay and northern Argentina all experience sub-tropical to warm temperate conditions. South of the River Plate the cool Falkland current exerts an influence and moderates the temperatures of southern Argentina.

Altitude

Since air temperature decreases with altitude at the rate of about 1°C per 165 m of elevation, it follows that even on tropical mountains there will be an altitudinal zonation of weather and climate. This fact is keenly recognized by people living in mountainous parts of Latin America and the Caribbean where altitudinally distinct climatic belts have long-established Spanish names – the *tierra caliente*, *tierra templada* and *tierra fría*, meaning the hot, temperate and cold land respectively; in particularly high areas a fourth zone, the *tierra*

Climate

MEAN ANNUAL PRECIPITATION, OCEAN CURRENTS, TRACKS OF POLAR AIR AND HURRICANES

California Current

Gulf of Mexico

North Atlantic Ocean

Caribbean Sea

South Equatorial Current

Equatorial Counter Current

Peru Current

Brazil Current

Falkland Current

KEY

2000 mm
1000
500

0   1000 km
0   1600 miles

→ Polar air mass track
→ Hurricane track
→ Warm ocean current
→ Cold ocean current

helada or icy land, may be present. In an environment like the Andes with such a relief amplitude there may be three or four types of climate within a horizontal distance of only 40 km.

Tierra caliente lies between sea level and 800 m altitude and thus covers all the coastal lowlands, large plains and interior basins and low mountain and foothill areas. The zone is characterized by high daytime temperatures (30–33°C) and cool night-time conditions (20–24°C) for most of the year with only small differences between the summer and winter months. Frosts are unknown and rarely do night temperatures descend below 15°C.

Tierra templada lies roughly between 800 and 1000 m altitude and constitutes the tropical highlands of Central America and northern South America; the term could also be applied to parts of the Guiana and Brazilian shields. Warm daytime temperatures (24–27°C) prevail, although hot afternoons with temperatures rising to 32–35°C sometimes occur in the summer months. The difference between summer and winter temperatures increases polewards so that in the Mesa Central of Mexico and in the southern Brazilian escarpment periods of cold and occasional night frosts are not uncommon during mid-winter months.

Tierra fría lies above 1800–2000 m and is thus widespread throughout the Andes but in Mexico occurs only in the higher basins and mountain slopes. This is a zone of warm pleasant days (24–27°C) and cold nights (10–12°C). Frosts are common during the winter months and at the upper limit of the zone.

Tierra helada lies above 4000 m and extends over the higher cultivable slopes of much of the Andes and higher parts of the Altiplano. Daytime temperatures during the dry season may often exceed 15°C but, because of the altitude and clear night-time skies, temperatures plummet below freezing most nights.

Climate types

These main climatic variables have produced a variety of distinctive climatic types in Latin America and the Caribbean, classified in detail by the Köppen system which has been generalized for the figure on p. 22 and the following description.

Tropical wet climates have high temperatures all year round, the average for each month being above 18°C and there is no pronounced dry season; this corresponds with the *tierra caliente* or hot tropical lowlands. Such conditions pertain to the north-eastern (windward) side of the Caribbean Islands, most of the eastern half of Central America and southern Mexico, the north-east coast of South America, upper Amazonia and the interior valleys of Colombia. Many of these areas experience a short drier period during cooler

MEAN JANUARY TEMPERATURE

KEY
- < 26°
- 22–26°
- 15–22°
- 10–15°
- 5–10°
- > 5°

MEAN JULY TEMPERATURE

months. Annual precipitation usually reaches over 2000 mm and relative humidity is frequently high (over 75 per cent).

Tropical wet-and-dry climates have temperatures similar to the tropical humid types but are distinguished by a definite dry season of four to six months during the cooler part of the year; this dry season may not be entirely rainless but is sufficient to induce a seasonal rhythm to vegetation growth. In the Caribbean and Central America this type is characteristically developed in the lee of the trade winds along southern and western coasts and in interior basins lower than 1000 m; it also covers the biggest portion of South America, extending across most of the Guiana and Brazilian shields and into eastern Bolivia and northern Argentina. Annual rainfall varies from 750–1500 mm in this zone.

Tropical highland climates correspond generally to the *tierra templada* and *tierra fría* – tropical highland zones. There are only scattered patches in the Caribbean Islands, and in Central America

they are confined to the mountain ranges of the Mexican Plateau and volcanic highlands. They occur throughout the Andes and in parts of the great eastern escarpment of Brazil. Because of the altitude at least one month in the year averages below 18°C. Within the tropics seasonal temperature differences are slight but they increase with increasing latitude, as in Mexico where the northern half of the Sierra Madre Occidental has cold winters, often with snow, followed by warm summers. Throughout parts of the central and eastern cordillera of the tropical Andes this zone is characterized by a wet season and is known as *invierno* (winter) even though it is in the southern summer. Increased cloudiness induces lower temperatures and above 4000 m snowfall commonly occurs.

Subtropical climates are typified by mild winters, hot summers and either no dry season or a short, dry summer season. They occur in a small area of north-east Mexico and over a much larger area of south-east South America where they comprise the humid pampa of Argentina, Paraguay and Uruguay. This is a truly temperate climate in which the average summer temperature is around 28°C and the winter average seldom drops below 10°C. During the winter season, however, occasional outbursts of cool polar air from North America and from Antarctica may cause spells of more bitter weather in Mexico and south-east South America respectively. Rain normally falls each month but the total amount is relatively low at 500–1000 mm.

Warm temperate climates are characterized by mild, rainy winters and cool, dry summers or by mild winters, cool summers and no dry season; they are restricted to the so-called 'Mediterranean' part of central Chile and to the part of Argentina south of the Plate estuary around Mar del Plata. At Valparaiso on the coast of Chile the coldest

CLIMATE TYPES

KEY

- ◼ Tropical wet climate
- ◼ Tropical wet-and-dry climate
- ◻ Subtropical climate
- ◼ Tropical highland climate
- ◼ Warm temperate climate
- ◻ Dry climate
- ◻ Cool temperate
- ◼ Cold climate

Amazon rainstorm

months (June and July) average 11.25°C and the warmest months average 17.6°C. Santiago is more extreme because of its location in the Central Valley and averages 7.6°C and 20.4°C for those periods. Rainfall increases steadily southwards from the Atacama Desert until by the latitude of Santiago it totals 350 mm and is produced by the interaction of cold polar air with warm Pacific maritime air.

Dry climates are the semi-arid and arid types. They are absent from the Caribbean but occur in the northern interior and north-west of Mexico where they are related to the persistence of dry, stable air from the Pacific and rain-shadow effects of the mountains. In South America, however, beginning at the Peru–Ecuador border, arid and semi-arid conditions affect much of the coastal cordillera and some interior basins of the Andes continuously southwards to central Chile. The Andes are an effective barrier preventing moist Atlantic air masses reaching the Pacific coast. Warm, moist air moves over the cold Peru current and becomes chilled in its lower layers; during the southern winter months this cool, damp air moves slightly onshore from a south-westerly direction as a coastal mist and brings rather unusual and miserable conditions to the Peruvian desert. During the rest of the year and for most of the time in northern Chile the air movement is more parallel or offshore in alignment and this leads to clear, dry conditions which reach their greatest intensity in the Atacama Desert. This is one of the driest places on earth, where so little rain falls that average precipitation figures are meaningless; in some places east of the coastal plateau no rain has ever been recorded. Nevertheless, there are temperature and humidity differences between the coast and the interior, the former having higher humidity and greater cloudiness and hence lower temperature range.

Atacama Desert, Chile, after a rainstorm nine months before

Cold montane climates are characterized by continuously cool or cold weather with no warm season and are caused either by exceedingly high altitudes (above 4500 m) or by exposure to polar cyclones in the high latitudes of southern Chile and Argentina. In the tropical Andes the abundance and warmth of diurnal sunshine is offset by the effect of altitude and shade; many of these climatic types are close to or above the regional snowline. A low altitude type occurs in southern Chile where south of 40°S the climate deteriorates progressively until it has become one of the stormiest and most unpleasant in the world. At Chiloé island, for example, almost 40 per cent of the weather is classified as stormy and may average little more than 50–60 days each year with sunshine. The regional snowline descends rapidly southwards until it is at 700 m in Tierra del Fuego; in Patagonia the Andes are able to support two large ice caps and in places glaciers terminate in the Pacific Ocean. Precipitation reaches 5000 mm, summer temperatures average little more than about 8.3°C and winter months 3.8°C, there are few hours of sunshine and few hours when wind is not blowing. Drier lee-side sites, such as Punta Arenas, may have only 490 mm rainfall, however.

The climatic types described above indicate the variety that exists in Latin America and the Caribbean. These are extremely generalized and simplified, however, and it should be emphasized that a much greater range of climates actually exists and at various scales; this is particularly significant when attempting to understand soils, natural vegetation and especially land use.

CMC

Natural disasters

Because of their tectonic and climatic setting, the high amplitude of relief and dense concentrations of population, Latin America and the Caribbean are subject to a variety of natural processes that often have disastrous consequences. They can be grouped into three main categories, tectonic, meteorological and geomorphological.

Tectonic disasters
Interaction between six crustal plates in the tectonic domain of Latin America and the Caribbean results in a great deal of seismic (earthquake) and volcanic activity distributed in distinct linear belts. Earthquakes occur because the energy of frictional stress between sections of crustal rock being forced past each other is periodically released by a sudden slip, causing a violent shaking of the Earth's crust. The 'stick-slip' points may be at shallow (<100 km), intermediate (100–300 km) or deep (300–700 km) levels (focal points) within the crust. Latin America and the Caribbean count for approximately 17 per cent of the world's total

Natural disasters

VOLCANOES AND SEISMICITY

North American plate

Popocatapetl

La Soufrière
Mt Pelée

Caribbean plate

Cocos plate

Arenal
Irazú

Coseguina

Cotopaxi

Sangay

South American plate

Nazca plate

El Misti

Antarctic plate

KEY

▲ Active volcano

Zone of high seismicity

Subduction trench

0		1600 km
0		1000 miles

seismicity. In Central America the Cocos plate and the overriding Caribbean plate are broken to eight discrete segments 100–200 km long. Transverse breaks in the crust separate segments of overriding lithosphere that have greatly differing volcanoes, topography, structure and geologic history. Structural depressions infilled with volcanic and alluvial sediments typically mark the transverse breaks in the volcanic axis. Dense rural settlement, urban development and many large cities have developed in such apparently prime localities which unfortunately lie exactly above the zones of most active crustal slippage and the generation of what are termed 'large shallow' earthquakes. The cities of San José (Costa Rica), Managua (Nicaragua), Santa Ana and Ahuachapan (El Salvador) and Guatemala City and Quezaltenango (Guatemala) are located near the intersections of transverse and longitudinal depressions, the loci of moderate-size shallow earthquakes; such earthquakes have repeatedly destroyed Guatemala City (9 times) and San Salvador (14 times) as well as razing most of Managua to the ground in 1972.

In South America the subducting Pacific plates are also broken by transverse shear zones into discrete segments which behave differentially in space and time. At present the most tectonically active segments are indicated by the coincidence of higher seismicity and active volcanicity, although no part of the Pacific coast can be deemed entirely free from earthquakes. In the northern Andes (Colombia and Ecuador) most earthquakes occur in a belt along the Pacific coast from the Panama–Colombia border to the mouth of the Guayas River, but others may occur inland where prominent shear faults (e.g. the Bocono fault) and graben occur. That which took place on 12 December 1979 at Tumaco in south-west Colombia (magnitude 8) was the largest in South America since 1942; it had been forecast that one would occur to fill the seismic gap detected for that plate segment. In the central Andes (Peru and Bolivia) major seismicity is concentrated along the coast of southern Peru, destructive shallow-intermediate tremors frequently occurring in Arequipa province. More northerly parts of Peru also suffer periodically as in 1970 and 1974 when the Chimbote and Lima areas were respectively shaken. In the southern Andes north of Antofagasta intermittent but extremely large earthquakes at intermediate depths (120 and 220 km) offshore produce destructive tidal waves (*tsunami*) and in central Chile activity along the Coast Range fault is the cause of infrequent but very destructive earthquakes. Southern Chile is another region where large earthquakes offshore severely shake the landward area and produce devastating tidal waves.

Earthquakes have three main damaging effects; they cause buildings to collapse, killing people inside or in the streets; they generate rock-falls and landslides in mountainous areas, causing considerable destruction and death on roads and in settlements; and at the coast the displacement of the sea bed offshore creates tidal waves which devastate low-lying coastal areas.

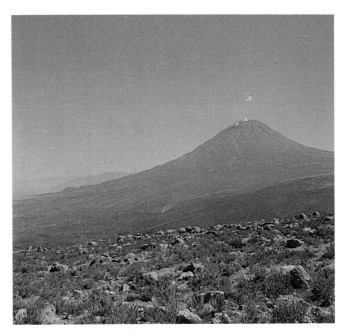

El Misti, volcano and fumarole in 1971

Volcanic disasters are relatively infrequent in Latin America and the Caribbean despite the number of active volcanoes. There are six well-defined zones of present volcanicity, Lesser Antilles, Mexican volcanic axis, Guatemala–Costa Rica, southern Colombia–Ecuador, southern Peru–northern Chile and south Central Chile. Most activity is characteristically explosive because of the chemical make-up of the molten rock (magma). Generally known as Andesitic (intermediate) and Rhyolitic (acidic), magma generated in these regions normally contains much silica (more than 50 per cent) which, together with other compounds makes the magma viscous, slow moving and relatively cool (750–850°C) at the surface. Because of this, magmatic volatiles escape out of solution only with great difficulty and gas bubbles develop extremely high confining pressures as the magma approaches the surface. Thus, when the magma erupts, pent-up gases escape explosively, pulverizing lava into incandescent fragments (tephra) and throwing out masses of large blocks and dense glowing clouds of magmatic froth. The most devastating eruptions in Latin America and the Caribbean have involved activity of this nature. For example, in 1835 Coseguina on the Gulf of Fonseca in north-west Nicaragua erupted with explosions that were heard as far away as Kingston, Jamaica, and Bogotá, Colombia. The exploded debris partially buried villages and farmland in the surrounding area over a radius of 160 km. A great loss of life resulted from powerful eruptions of three volcanoes during 1902 when a total of approximately 37,500 people were killed. In that year the volcano Mont Pelée on Martinique (Lesser Antilles) burst open and discharged a dense emulsion of incandescent lava droplets and hot gases which raced downslope and over the town and harbour of St Pierre, instantly suffocating 30,000 inhabitants. Twenty-four hours later La Soufrière volcano on the neighbouring island of St Vincent, 150 km distant, erupted in a similar fashion killing over 1500 people. During the same year an eruption of Santa Maria (Santiaguito) volcano in Guatemala took 6000 lives. Elsewhere in Central America only two other volcanoes have been a major problem in recent decades. In Costa Rica, Arenal exploded exceptionally violently in 1968 after prolonged quiescence and threw bombs on to a nearby village, killing 64 people; and from 1963 to 1965 Irazú volcano just south-east of San José discharged so much tephra that the nation's coffee crop and economy were seriously affected. Six volcanoes in Nicaragua are currently in various states of activity: Concepción, Santiago, Momotombo, Las Pilas, Cerro Negro and Telica; ranging from vigorous emissions of gas to explosive discharges of ash with minor lava flows, the activity is seldom destructive and is more an inconvenience.

In South America the majority of volcanoes that have erupted in historical times are too remote from densely settled areas to have caused major calamities. However, eruptions of Cotopaxi (Ecuador) in 1877 and Villarica (Chile) in 1963 melted ice and snow which mixed with tephra to produce large mud flows that descended rapidly downslope to overwhelm considerable areas of settled and cultivated land. Probably one of the potentially most dangerous volcanoes in the whole of South America is El Misti in southern Peru which has not had a major eruption in historical recollection but which appears to be a young volcano in a state of temporary dormancy. Rising above the large and beautiful city of Arequipa, the volcano could cause an appalling loss of life and property if it were to erupt explosively.

A much milder form of eruption has been typical of the Mexican volcanic axis. Eruptions at Jorullo between 1759 and 1774 and at Paricutín between 1943 and 1952 produced new volcanoes that developed and became extinct after fifteen and nine years duration respectively. The products built up cinder cones 380 m and 410 m high respectively and thick (245 m) lava flows which buried farmland and, in the case of Paricutín, the villages of Paricutín and San Juan de Parangaricutiro. Such activity does not have the sudden devastating explosiveness of the more acidic volcanoes and no lives are normally lost, but El Chichon exploded in 1981 and killed 2000 people.

Meteorological disasters

Because Central America and the Caribbean are located at the poleward margin of the tropics, they are vulnerable to atmospheric disturbances originating in both low and middle latitudes and invasions of frost-producing polar air from higher latitudes.

Prolonged droughts occur in central Mexico, flood-producing excesses of rainfall periodically occur throughout Central America and the Caribbean and summer hailstorms damage crops in the highlands of Mexico and Guatemala. Much more destructive, however, are the tropical hurricanes and mid-latitude cyclonic storms. Caribbean hurricanes develop between July and October, when there may be five to twelve affecting areas shown on the map, p. 20. Originating over warm waters of the Atlantic, Caribbean and Gulf of Mexico, hurricanes (c. 150 km across) move slowly westward or north-westward and eventually re-curve to the north and north-east to be dissipated in mid-latitudes. High winds cause enormous destruction of life and property, both directly and through the creation of large tidal waves along coasts, while torrential downpours frequently flood large areas of land. Pacific hurricanes are much less dangerous but cause destruction along the west coast of Mexico, as in November 1961. Mid-latitude cyclonic disturbances commonly develop between November and March when incursions of northern polar air into the tropics are common. Along the polar front heavy rain storms are followed by cold northerly winds and accompanying destructive frosts. They affect the Gulf coast of Mexico and the Caribbean coast of Guatemala and Honduras where extensive sections of banana plantations may be destroyed.

South America is much less susceptible to extreme meteorological events than other continents, suffering less from drought and floods than Africa and India, but problems occur at local and regional scales, for example mid-latitude polar fronts bring cold frost-producing air to affect parts of Brazil and Paraguay, where much of the coffee crop can be lost, as in July 1981. The Brazilian north-east has suffered recurrent severe droughts over the past century, prompting mass migration to the coast and southern Brazil. Such a drought struck in 1977 and was still holding in early 1984. The year 1963 can be taken here to illustrate climatic disasters which may occur in any one year in South America. During the winter months, May–October, serious droughts affected southern Brazil, Paraguay and northern Argentina; crop yields were greatly reduced and there were water shortages and power cuts in Rio and São Paulo. Dry conditions allowed fires to spread and in Paraná state, Brazil, around 30,000 people were made homeless. Exceptionally severe frosts afflicted the same general region and some 650 million coffee trees were destroyed. Frosts destroyed up to half the vine harvest in central Chile, storms and heavy rain caused damage farther south; floods in south coastal Peru affected several towns, droughts impaired rice crops farther north while exceptionally heavy rains caused problems in the Andes. The Caribbean area was swept by hurricane Flora which caused the loss of several thousand lives and the destruction of tens of thousands of homes (mostly in Haiti), the destruction of half of the cocoa crop in Tobago and most of the bananas in several of the smaller British islands. In 1982–3, the

Destruction wrought by hurricane Allen in Barbados in 1980

Debris of the 1941 avalanche near Huaras, Peru

periodic El Niño climatic phenomenon of the central Pacific caused floods and landslides in coastal Ecuador and northern Peru, killing 600; it also produced severe droughts in Central America and Mexico.

Geomorphological disasters

Much destruction can result from large-scale falls of rock and ice and from the slumping or flowing of large masses of soil and rock; both phenomena may be triggered off by earthquakes and torrential rains. Because such disasters involve the downslope mass displacement of debris, they occur mainly in areas of steep slopes and high relief such as the Andes and some highland areas of the Guiana and Brazilian shields. As precipitous rock faces in the Andes experience stress release, rock expansion may periodically cause the loosening of very large slabs which crash destructively into the valleys below. Should these be accompanied by overlying ice and snow then highly mobile debris avalanches develop, covering long distances very rapidly and devastating everything in the way. The Cordillera Blanca in Peru is notorious for such events; one in 1941 ripped through part of the town of Huaras, killing over 4000 people; one in 1962 obliterated small settlements and part of Ranrahirca village, killing 3500 people; and that triggered by the 1970 earthquake took 5000 lives in the same area. Another process leading to large-scale slumping and/or flowage involves the presence of steep unstable slopes and the build-up of high pore-water pressure in unconsolidated overburden and along less permeable beds in underlying strata. Destructive mud flows can result from prolonged torrential rainfall as around Rio and other regions of steep relief in Brazil and

in many parts of the Andes. The sudden downslope discharge of large volumes of mud and/or wholesale rotational slumping of large sections of mountainside can devastate wide areas of terrain, taking many lives. Scars left by two gigantic prehistoric landslides are present at the edge of the Altiplano in southern Peru (at Chuquibamba north of Arequipa) and in Bolivia (at the southern outskirts of La Paz); these cover thousands of square kilometres and may have occurred during a period of late Quaternary climatic change when more rain fell in these regions. Should an event of such magnitude take place in a settled area today, thousands of lives would be lost.

CMC

Further reading

T. Y. Canby, 'El Niño's III Wind', *National Geographic*, Feb. 1984, pp. 144–83
C. M. Clapperton, 'The Glaciation of the Andes', *Quaternary Science Reviews*, 2 (1983), 83–155
J. P. Cole, *Latin America* (London, 1970)
P. James. *Latin America* (New York, 1969)
R. C. West and J. P. Augelli, *Middle America* (New York, 1966)

Flora and fauna

Central and South America, tropical Mexico and the Caribbean islands constitute the Neotropical realm, one of the major zoo-geographical regions of the world. Within these limits and touching adjacent areas including the southern United States, particularly Texas and Florida, the animal and plant life is rich in species. Many of the families are unique to the New World, and of these a large proportion are exclusively South American. The diversity stems from the wide range of habitats in a land of rivers, tropical forest, mountains and grasslands coupled with the unique geological history of the isolation of the subcontinent.

About 200 million years ago the enormous continent of Pangea began to divide into two super-continents of which the southern part, Gondwanaland, was made up of South America, Africa, India, Antarctica and Australia. Then, about 130 million years ago, South America began to move away from Gondwanaland and its marsupials and extraordinary early mammals evolved in total isolation. North America, on the other hand, remained part of the northern continent, Laurasia, for perhaps as long as another 50 million years. Resulting from this prolonged connection, the northern hemisphere mammals, including monkeys, some rodents and the large carnivorous cat predators, evolved separately and only reached South America when the land masses were linked.

Two-toed sloth (*Choloepus*)

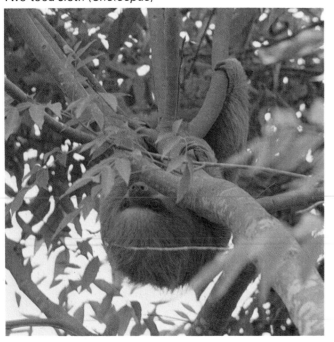

The isolation of South America and its subsequent re-connection to North America produced some remarkable animal types. Some orders of mammals are exclusively South American: three of these are now extinct, including the Litopterna or hoofed herbivores, some of which resembled horses or camels. The other order, the opossum rats, includes survivors such as the little-studied rat-sized marsupials of the dense Andean forests and southern Chile. While Neotropica offers a large variety of obscurely evolved curiosities, many of the mammals are among the most unusual in the zoological world, none more so than the Edentates, an order including armadillos, sloths and anteaters. These peculiar animals form part of the relic fauna of South America which, as the fossil record reveals, included ancestors on a much grander scale than modern types. A glyptodont of a million years ago was a massively armoured armadillo-like beast; some possessed heavy club-like tails, and their remains are commonly found in the southern part of South America, particularly in the recent sedimentary deposits of the pampas and Patagonia; their beautifully patterned carapaces have survived well. Likewise, in the same places, the remains of bear-sized ground sloths are not uncommon. One of these sloths, the *Megatherium*, was massively built and reached a length of 6 m. *Megatheria* were browsers, standing on their hind feet to reach branches and leaves of the trees that once clothed this now desolate place.

By contrast, modern sloths are much smaller, and renowned for their agonizingly slow movements. They usually live in the forest upper level or canopy, seldom venturing to the ground. When they do, they manage a slow crawl, of little more than 1 km per hour. As they are well camouflaged and their coarse grey hair is often tinged green with microscopic algae, sloths are relatively safe from predators. Armadillos, on the other hand, are ground dwellers, but are good burrowers, digging into even hard earth in a rapidly accomplished defence that complements the hardened bony scutes of their shell. The third Edentate family, the anteaters, comprises both arboreal and ground-living forms. A typical, though hard-to-find rainforest inhabitant is the 25 cm-long pygmy or silky anteater with a strongly prehensile and gripping tail which it can use as a fifth limb. This rare animal is almost defenceless and seeks safety in the higher levels of trees. Inhabiting the open plains and forest edges, a giant anteater up to 5 m long is armed with powerful claws on its forelimbs which it uses for ripping open termite nests. Less spectacular, medium-sized and equally at home on the ground or in the trees, is the *Tamandua* anteater, also equipped with a nearly hairless prehensile tail.

Many Neotropical mammals have evolved with similar prehensile tails, a clear indication of their long arboreal ancestry. Some New World monkeys have tails with a powerful, almost hand-like grasping ability, while spider monkeys have tails equipped with highly developed special pads resembling a soft palm. Among the other groups of mammals, one rodent, the prehensile-tailed porcupine, is a good climber; so too is the kinkajou, one of the two living carnivores with a prehensile tail.

Of all South American mammals, the Edentates are probably the best known of those that evolved during the isolation of the subcontinent and began to spread northward as the isthmus and Central Americas formed. Sloths now occur as far north as Costa Rica and Honduras; anteaters, the pygmy species especially, as far north as Mexico and the nine-banded armadillo to the south United States including Texas and Oklahoma.

Also of the ancient fauna, the marsupials, including opossums, flourished during the isolation of South America and many different forms evolved. Some, like the common opossum (*Didelphis*), have survived, and this species has reached far into North America with a none too specific habitat. The meat-eating marsupials, many of them hyaena- or wolf-like, with short legs and large skulls – at least one had large stabbing canine teeth – were the only carnivorous mammals in ancient South America and are now extinct. Others, like the tiny mouse opossums, are some of the least conspicuous members of the Didelphidae and different species inhabit forests, arid places and even houses.

When the land connection was formed with North America, the movement southward was suddenly far stronger with bats, deer, tapirs and particularly predators, including bears, otters, dogs and cats moving into every part of the diverse southern land which was already well stocked. The incoming predators met the established marsupial carnivores, and being more successful in evolutionary terms they have occupied their place in the ecology.

Among the most successful of the newcomers were the Cricetid rodents: the hamster family, and rats and mice of the Old World. Once these mammals found their way into the rich and complex habitats of South America, a remarkable evolutionary explosion occurred, which is probably unparalleled in any other part of the world. Now, at least fifty genera can be identified with countless species and subspecies of Cricetids occupying many habitats from the swamp lands bordering the Amazon to high, cold and arid plateaux in the Andes; some even occur in the barren south as far distant as the Straits of Magellan. Not all are hamster- or rat-like. The forests are well populated with Cricetid climbers, endowed with specially adapted paws. And there are many marsh dwellers with webbed feet or jumpers that have well-developed kangaroo-like thighs. All these, and there are many more, highlight the evolution of species to fill many ecological niches or an adaptive capacity which has reached record proportions.

More than 3500 species of birds have been recorded and described in the Neotropical region and that amounts to more than two-fifths of all the known bird species of the world. South America

Nine-banded armadillo (*Dasypus novemcincus*)

alone has over 2900 species, making it outstanding as the 'bird continent'. The reason is perhaps two-fold. An influx of tropical northern families, including barbets, thrushes, motmots and wrens added to those already enjoying the existing variety of habitats. Then a factor that strongly influenced speciation was a changing climate brought by the ice ages, creating near-arctic conditions in the north and severely cooling the southern part of the globe.

Particularly in the warm and humid Amazon region, where rich forests were flourishing much as they had done for millions of years, the cooling induced clear ecological change. As the rainfall was reduced, the forests shrank to patches restricted within a grassland vegetation something akin to savanna. The effect of this change is most noticeable among birds and some butterflies, and recently these have drawn the attention of researchers. Within these so-called Pleistocene refuges, many species evolved in isolation, each becoming significantly different from species of the same genus in another refuge. When the ice retreated and the humid conditions returned, the forests spread once again, and when the populations mixed again interbreeding was impossible. The result is obvious in an abundance of species. Now the Neotropical forests are virtually unbroken from southern Mexico to northern Argentina.

Many species of birds followed the spreading forest, though in a few areas where the original isolation has been maintained, some original refuge species are strongly represented. On some isolated mountains of Venezuela, Colombia and Brazil, species occur many hundreds of kilometres from the mainstream of their distribution in the Andes, as they were cut off when the climate changed, leaving wide expanses of savanna. (Pleistocene refuges are becoming increasingly important for researchers and conservationists, and Brazil has selected some of these unusual areas as national parks or forestry reserves.)

Neotropical habitats are immensely varied, ranging from dry tropical forests of Mexico southward to the ice-bound mountains of Tierra del Fuego, or mangrove-fringed Atlantic shores of Brazil to the desert coast of Peru. Between these limits are the many specialized habitats of the largest tropical rainforest in the world. The Amazonian and Guyanan forests contain the most diverse ecological communities with the largest collection of plant and animal species in the world. Altogether about 900 tons of living plants per acre have developed in these regions as the result of constant high temperature and rainfall. Though by no means uniform in character for the vast area of the Amazon region, the rainforests tend to have certain well-defined characteristics. The number of species of trees is immense: as many as 117 in a square kilometre; most frequently encountered are Brazil nuts, rubber trees (*Hevea*), species of myrtles, laurela, acacias, bignonias and palms. Strongly characteristic too of many of these are odd flange-like structures or buttresses which perhaps may have a supportive function, though such an assumption is by no means certain. Some palms though, including *Iriartea*, have numerous stilt roots while other trees have multiple smaller buttresses.

Of the ancient flora the only survivors are a few gymnosperms, like the rare podocarpus found in some higher montane forests, or the climbing *Gnetum*. Otherwise the tropical forests abound with the more recent angiosperms that evolved in the same period as the insects. Often the pollination of these plants is closely tied to insect visitors.

With all-year-round near unchanging conditions, the tropical rainforest offers unparalleled evolutionary possibilities. Plants in the tropics do not flower in regular seasons, and so there is a constant supply of nectar, fruits, young shoots and other foods to be exploited by animals of every form. The temperature is ideal for cold-blooded animals (those unable to regulate their body temperature). Insects are especially abundant and have become the food supply for many birds. Some, like the ant-birds, or certain woodcreepers, follow the hordes of army ants, carnivorous ants

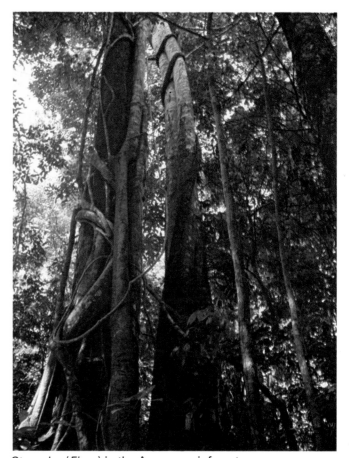

Strangler (*Ficus*) in the Amazon rainforest

moving slowly through the forest. These ants, descended from wasps, feed largely on other arthropods such as crickets and spiders.

The presence of large numbers of birds and insects increases the possibilities of cross pollination, and insects naturally help to recycle the forest debris. Thus the rainforest can be reckoned as a powerhouse of life where the number of species seems boundless. Adding to the already diverse habitats within such a forest are the various levels, perhaps as many as five between the ground, where decomposition is rapid, and the canopy exposed to the sky where sunlight induces rich growth and where photosynthesis occurs. In this carbon cycle oxygen is produced, to be used again by the same plants.

Between the two extremes are lower, shade-loving trees including the palms, mauritia and euterpe, and below them at the next level are many herbacious plants. Calliandras, heliconias and hirtellas are typical of the Amazon region. Growing in the crowns of the tallest trees are stranglers such as *Ficus* or *Clusia* species, their seeds deposited there by birds. As a seed develops, the young plant sends

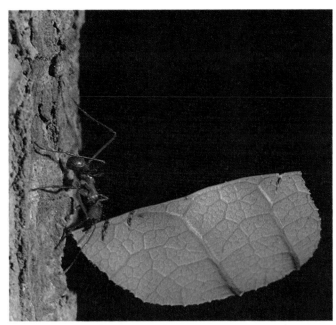

Leaf-cutting ants (*Sauba* g. *Atta*)

Giant spider (fam. Theraphosidae) on the forest floor

out aerial roots to descend (by geotropism) to the ground. (Once the root has a firm hold, the plant grows rapidly in the crown and its bulky roots may ultimately envelop and 'strangle' the tree.) Sometimes the strangler fills the entire crown and the host eventually dies. Lianas, on the other hand, are more like weak-stemmed trees: they find a hold on the rainforest trees, and, by a variety of biological means, hoist themselves to the sunlight. Some have sharp, recurved spines and the plant can jack its way up the tree. A few of these plants have stems as bulky as a man's thigh, others are flattened and ribbed, and, like stranglers, their flowers and seeds usually form high in the canopy, out of normal sight.

Animal life has a foothold at every level, even subterraneously. An ever growing wealth of plant material supports countless millions of insects. Butterflies may be eyecatching, but the less gaudy sauba or leaf-cutting ants can defoliate a tree, taking all the leaves, bit by bit, to an underground nest that may occupy many cubic metres. Nothing escapes their ravages, so even flowers are cut into tiny pieces to be turned into a mulch in which the ants grow a fungus to be eaten by both young and mature ants. Similarly, ants in the grasslands cut grass and build underground gardens, the only visible sign on the surface being a small entrance.

The floor of a tropical forest is an arthropod world, with termites, scorpions, spiders, isopods, millipedes, centipedes – some almost 25 cm long – sheltering beneath decomposing wood. There is a clear trend towards gigantism, and some spiders, notably the Theraphosidae or 'bird eaters', can reach a span of 25 cm, with a body over 9 cm long. Beetles such as *Dynastes* can be the size of a child's clenched fist and butterflies, like the spectacular blue morphos with a span of 15 cm, flash brilliantly and can be seen from more than a kilometre away. Sometimes for no obvious reason hundreds of thousands of butterflies gather in moist places on river banks or occasionally migrations of what must be millions of a single species take days to pass one point. American naturalist William Beebe reported such migrations during his work in the Guianas early this century.

Frogs and toads are well represented by many species, the tree frogs being particularly well adapted to the forest. Other frogs live among the debris on the forest floor, or within the natural reservoirs of rain water captured in the tight leaf rosettes of certain bromeliads. Other amphibians, the curious caecilians, have a burrowing habit and are rarely seen. Similarly snakes and other reptiles are not immediately obvious, though there is an abundance of species. Some, like the vine snakes (*Oxybelis*), are bootlace thin and beautifully adapted to a life among spindly climbing plants. At the other extreme, the largest water boas or anacondas may attain a girth of a man's body or more, and live in swampy places. Other snakes, particularly the brightly coloured coral snakes and the false corals, are adapted to life underground, with their flattened heads and small eyes.

South American rivers and lakes are richly endowed with fish, and as many as 2000 species occupy niches in the immense Amazon, itself with one-fifth of the world's fresh water. Others have adapted

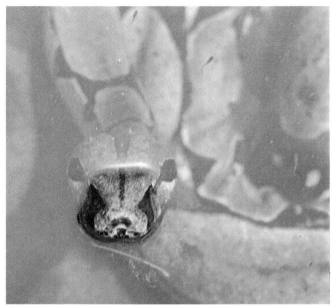

Water boa (*Constrictor constrictor*)

to survival in places baked dry by intense sun (for example, killifish in the Chaco). Catfish species are numerous and often taken as an important food source: the larger specimens attain gargantuan proportions. One species of the Amazon and Orinoco can weigh as much as 180 kg, so a fully grown specimen needs two men to carry it. These monsters, living on the river bed, have the reputation of attacking swimmers, though perhaps they are doing no more than scavenging. At the other extreme, a tiny 5-cm-long near transparent catfish, the candirú, is a danger as it may enter the urethra, its backward-facing spines preventing simple removal. Many of the catfish are heavily and grotesquely armoured, others are beautifully coloured with leopard-like spots or a variety of dark bands. The reputation of the piranha as a man-eating fish is exaggerated, though, as a carnivore, it is always potentially dangerous.

The important food fish, the pirarucú (arapaima or paiche are other names), is a relative of salmon and trout, measuring 3 m in length. This superb fish provides such high-quality meat that its numbers are declining everywhere and it has disappeared totally from some places. It is easily caught (by harpoon) as it comes to the surface to gulp air. But the trade in pirarucú simply underlines the importance of the tropical rivers as a resource, and as more access roads open, refrigerated or ice-packed trucks are hauling tons of fish to urban centres. Particularly rich fishing times are during the seasons of low water; at these times some tributaries of the Amazon are so densely packed with fish (charachoids) that local fishermen can scoop them with pails and plastic bowls. Man is not the only predator: the giant catfish follow the mass upriver.

Top: *Puya raimondii*, a gigantic bromeliad, in the Bolivian Andes. Above: Andean condor *(Vultur gryphus)*

The life of the lakes, rivers and estuaries is everywhere diverse and extraordinary. Numerous species of freshwater turtle were abundant a hundred years ago, but their numbers have declined as they are much used as a food; there are now plans to farm some of the larger types. Reptiles related to crocodiles – in South America the caimans and a variety of curious and seldom seen denizens, among them manatees or sea cows – are relatively common, though hunting has reduced both size and numbers of individuals. River dolphins occur far upriver, even at the foot of the Andes over 3000 km from the Amazon mouth; another species exists in the Plate system.

The same pattern of variety and high proportion of endemic families is repeated throughout Neotropica. Both the number of species and individuals is limited by geographical and climatic conditions. Along the Andes, in the cooler heights of the mountains or in the far south, there are fewer species; for example, at the equator as many as 163 hummingbird species have been listed, though in Tierra del Fuego only one, the Green-backed Firecrown, is resident. With such limiting factors, the vegetation changes too, with species of plant families becoming dwarfed and assuming a compact alpine form. One outstanding exception to the rule is the bromeliad, *Puya raimondii*, with its flower spike reaching to 6 m. This is the world's largest flower spike, and bears many thousands of individual flowers. Growing in the barren plateaux, the *Puya raimondii* is a micro habitat occupied by many species of birds and insects. This plant is a native of only a few places in the central Andes and may be a relic of the ice-age flora that has survived as it is well adapted to the semi-arid environment of the cordilleras.

Among the other arid lands, pure deserts are numerous in Neotropica. None are large but some, like the Atacama of northern Chile (and parts of Bolivia and Argentina), are exceptionally dry. Plants have adapted and among the numerous cacti there are a few remarkable species. One from the Atacama grows beneath the surface and gets enough light through the opalescent sand for its photosynthesis. Occasionally the desert is itself modified by local conditions: on the west coast, within sight of the Pacific, condensing fog can induce rich plant growth in certain places. These *lomas* are tiny oases of fertility and attract many species of birds and insects not commonly occurring in the desert. Man, too, is there, using the *lomas* for small patches of farmland, growing corn or grazing cattle.

Of the major habitats, though, grasslands have a special economic importance, especially the pampas of Argentina or llanos of Colombia and Venezuela. These open seas of grass were once home to specialized mammals including armadillos and many rodents. The pampas have long been turned into ranch and farmland, so only pockets of the endemic flora and fauna survive. Within the other grasslands north of the Amazon and across the Orinoco drainage there is a fauna very much reflecting the closeness of the Amazon

region. Gallery forests along the rivers contain many monkeys, parrots and toucans, many of which have circum-Amazon distribution. The rivers here once contained many turtles and caiman, but their numbers have declined sharply with the opening up of the region. On a broad front, almost all the way across South America, development plans clearly mean that great changes are occurring all the time. But so, too, are attitudes and new national parks and forestry reserves have been established in recent years.

TM

Further reading

M. Bates, *The Land and Wildlife of South America* (New York, 1965)

J. Dorst, *South America and Central America: a Natural History* (London and New York, 1967)

R. J. A. Goodland and H. S. Irwin, *Amazon Jungle: Green Hell to Red Desert* (New York, 1975)

T. Harper Goodspeed, *Plant Hunters in the Andes* (London, 1961)

Geography

The importance of the physical environment to the people who live in it hardly needs to be underlined. It limits the range of feasible activities which may be altered and reassessed by changing technologies and capital investment. Resources and their possibilities are continually reappraised in the light of technological, social and economic change, as becomes abundantly apparent where there have been repeated adjustments over a long history going back far beyond the impact of Europeans on the Americas, as in parts of Mexico and the central Andes. Colonial empires which once gave direction to geographical change – in the nature and distribution of economic activities and population – were replaced in the nineteenth century by export economies. In the twentieth century, however, urbanization and industrialization have tended to shift the growth points of spatial organization to the urban-dominated regions which are, in Latin America, most frequently, though not always, the capital cities of old colonial administrations and their republican successors. This is partially a geographical consequence of the shift from outward-directed development, characteristic of the nineteenth and early twentieth centuries, to inward-directed development of more recent decades. It is often possible, within the Latin American countries, to see at least three categories of region in this sense: advancing areas of urban and industrial growth with a good network of communications, an agriculture vitalized by urban markets, and above-average levels of literacy, welfare and income. South-east Brazil, the Puebla–Mexico City–Guadalajara axis in Mexico, the Buenos Aires–Córdoba axis in Argentina and Greater

PRINCIPAL PHYSICAL FEATURES

Metres
5000
3000
1000
500
200
Sea level

Lima and the coastal region of Peru are examples of this kind of area. Secondly, there are relatively stagnant or depressed areas, often quite densely populated but remote from the advancing areas, which may have experienced a former prosperity or levels of development adjusted to a local rather than a national economy, which have been by-passed by growth elsewhere: the south-central sierra of Peru, parts of southern Mexico, north-east Brazil are examples. Thirdly, there are the sparsely populated regions in which potential resources exist to be developed, exploited (and sometimes, perhaps, destroyed) and which offer hopes for expansion as yet unrealized. The interior lowlands of South America and the Brazilian west seem to offer such possibilities. But the form which such development is taking, in terms of its social and ecological consequences, is very often a matter of grave concern. Latin America still has vast areas for potential settlement.

The Andean region and coastal margins

Though not the oldest geological feature of the South American continent by any means, the Andes are the framework around which the geography of the continent is moulded. Relief is complex, reflecting a varied geological and geomorphological history, and general statements are difficult to make. Between Chile and Argentina there is a single, continuous range, rising to Aconcagua (the highest peak of South America), and presenting a difficult barrier for modern communications; in Bolivia and southern Peru, western and eastern branches diverge to enclose within them the high plateau generally known as the Altiplano and constituting the only substantial area of inland drainage to Lake Titicaca at 3812 m above sea level and Lake Poopó in Bolivia. In Ecuador, well-defined western and eastern ranges of the Andes are separated by intermontane basins, but in northern and central Peru this clarity is absent, and although the western cordillera is massive and continuous, intermontane basins, fault-guided troughs and discontinuous high massifs follow no single orientation and make it difficult to identify a single eastern range. Structure and drainage define a simpler general pattern of relief in Colombia, however, with a clear division of western, central and eastern ranges, the latter continuing into northern Venezuela.

Towards the Pacific margins, fragments of ranges older geologically than the main Andean front – in northern and southern Peru and in northern and central Chile – give shape to the coastal zone and define the western limits of relatively low basins filled or partially filled with the debris of erosion from the main Andean chain, as, for example, in the neighbourhood of Ica in southern Peru, or on a grander scale in the Central Valley of Chile. But elsewhere the low-lying coastal fringes of the Pacific are largely composed of alluvial or fluvio-glacial materials derived from the erosion of the Andean chain.

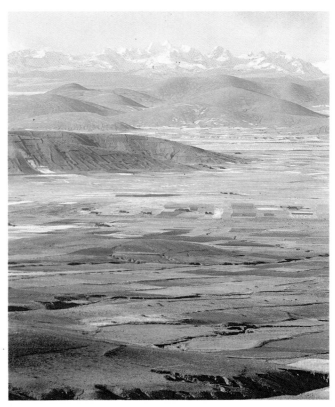

Altiplano, with the Cordillera Real in the distance

At a very general level, the characteristic landforms of the Andes fall into five groups. Glaciated landforms characterize the highest massifs in the tropical Andes, with features of Pleistocene glacial deposition reaching down to 3500 m in northern and central Peru (where modern glaciers are to be found at 5000 m). Modern snow levels and glaciers reach their maximum low-point in southern Bolivia and northern Chile, but south of this point glaciated features (and modern glaciers) are to be found at steadily lower levels to reach sea level itself in southern Chile. Volcanic landforms – active and recently extinct volcanoes, calderas, associated lava flows and deposits of volcanic ash – are characteristic of northern Chile, Bolivia and southern Peru and reach classic proportions in Ecuador. These are the most dramatic manifestations of Andean landforms, but in the central Andean region as a whole, and particularly in Bolivia and southern and central Peru, one of the most universal features is the existence of high-level erosion surfaces (at c. 4500 m in southern Peru), occasionally warped and at times overlain by volcanic ash or lava. Complex erosion surfaces such as this, and others at lower levels, mark stages in the uplift and warping of the Andean region. Structural troughs and intermontane basins, partially filled with alluvial and lacustrine deposits and sometimes excellent examples, again adding to the difficulties of communications across the Andean region, particularly where they lie parallel to the high ranges.

One most important consequence of these patterns of relief is the tendency for nuclei of population to be highly concentrated in the agriculturally productive valleys, intermontane basins and on alluvial or erosional benches at intermediate altitudes. Small, but densely populated zones tend, therefore, to be separated from each other by high-level surfaces, high ranges, or deep river troughs. There is a degree of local isolation and a need for self-reliance in basic food and raw materials which were certainly not broken down by the railway, and have not been totally broken down by modern road-building.

Secondly, given the enormous variety of local and regional climates within the Andean region as a whole, together with the implications this variety has for natural vegetation and for potential crop production, it is not surprising that one of the enduring features of the Andean region as a whole is its capacity for producing a wide variety of products from relatively small areas which offer complementary ecological riches. The territory of single communities, or single landowners, may commonly include land with an altitudinal range of 1500 m, and sometimes much more than this. Complementary production of irrigated maize, subtropical crops, temperate grains such as wheat or barley, rootcrops such as potatoes, and high-level pasture can take place within a few kilometres. Different plots of land within the same holding may sometimes cover this range, though more commonly traditional mechanisms of exchange between neighbouring communities secure a variety of products for consumption from very different ecological zones. In the Inca empire ethnic groups with their 'core' area at intermediate altitudes had 'colonies' at both higher levels (to

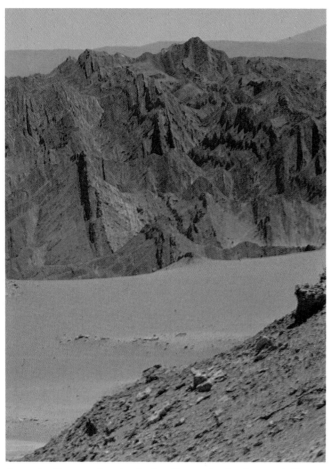

A vertically standing bed of sediment in the Atacama Desert

with deposits of volcanic ash, vary in size and altitude from the Altiplano to relatively small areas like those which are strung out between the east and west ranges of Ecuador, but their importance in the human geography of the central Andes is immense, for unlike the high-level erosion surfaces, they are below the upper limits of arable agriculture and are generally densely populated, supporting nuclei of rural settlement and major provincial towns or cities such as Quito, Cuenca, Huancayo or Ayacucho. In the humid areas of the Andean region, notably in Venezuela, Colombia, Ecuador, and in eastern Peru and eastern Bolivia, the landforms are those of tropical weathering and erosion, with intricately dissected steep slopes of bewildering complexity, rapid erosion and frequent landslips, tending to make communications much more difficult to build and maintain than in the arid Andes or where erosion surfaces and intermontane basins provide more uniform surfaces. Finally, there are the river valleys, often deeply and spectacularly incised into the surrounding landforms. The Upper Marañón or the Apurimac are

KEY

1 Mountain vegetation
2 Conifer forest (*pine, spruce and larch*)
3 Mixed forest, mid-latitudes (*broadleaf and conifer*)
4 Prairie (*long grass*)
5 Steppe (*short grass*)
6 Savannah (*grass and scrub*)
7 Tropical rain forest (*selva*)
8 Monsoon forest (*moist deciduous*)
9 Dry tropical forest (*semi-deciduous*)
10 Dry tropical scrub and thorn forest
11 Desert vegetation (*xerophytic shrub, grass and cactus*)

VEGETATION

An almond orchard in the Chilean Central Valley

produce salt, animal products, high-level arable crops and especially potatoes) and at lower levels (for coca, maize, manioc and forest products). High-level groups around Lake Titicaca (the Lupaca, for example) had 'colonies' at lower levels both in the Bolivian *yungas* and on the Pacific slope of southern Peru.

Viewed on a larger scale, it is evident that different ecological zones within the Andes have been given different social and economic values at different times and in different areas. In pre-Colombian times the sub-humid intermontane basins at intermediate altitudes from Venezuela through Colombia to Peru and northwest Argentina, together with the arid, but irrigable coastal zone of Peru, supported intensive irrigated and terrace agriculture focused on the cultivation of maize, chief among a whole repertoire of indigenous crops adapted to various ecological levels. Dense agricultural populations in the Andean region were associated with the most developed of the South American cultures, including of course that of the Inca empire. It is indeed within the heart of that empire, in the sierra regions of Ecuador, Peru and Bolivia, that ethnic Indians still form a majority of the population. The Spanish colonial empire, relying as it largely did on Indian labour, did relatively little to change the pre-existing general distribution of population except in a few areas where African slave labour was used in plantation agriculture. But the expanding commercial world of the nineteenth century ultimately saw a significant reassessment of ecological zones with the downward shift in Colombia, Venezuela and Ecuador for

the cultivation of coffee and cacao. Since the 1940s the movement down from the mountains has, at least in relative terms, accelerated with the conquest of malaria. In Venezuela the Andean region of the north-west is the poorest and most depressed region of the country and a region of out-migration. In Ecuador, the balance of population is steadily shifting towards the coastal zone in spite of the capital's location in the sierra. In Peru the sierra as a whole is a region of out-migration both to the coast and, to a much lesser extent, to the eastern regions. And in Bolivia, too, growth of population has been much less rapid on the Altiplano than in the eastern regions, even though, as in Ecuador, the capital city is on the edge of the Altiplano itself.

In part, this trend reflects the fact that in some areas Indian peasant-farming communities have pressed traditional methods of cultivation to and even beyond their limits in order to sustain the increasing rural population over the last generation. Farms are fragmented, pastures overgrazed and cultivated land pushed to apparently impossible slopes. Soil exhaustion and soil erosion are all too evident. Except for Bolivia and Chile, each of the Andean countries possesses a share of the coastal margins, the Andean ranges, and a share of interior lowlands. Bolivia was bereft of its narrow coastal section as a result of its defeat by Chile in the War of the Pacific (1879–83); the Andean crest-line constitutes, effectively, the eastern boundary of Chile except in the south.

In the Andean region the major motif is of high contrast between adjacent micro-regions. On the coastal margin, the pattern is simpler, reflecting in the main the regional contrasts of climate. In Chile the gradation is from a wet, cool climate and broad-leaved evergreen and deciduous beech forests of the south, through the cool temperate, almost West European conditions of south-central Chile to the favoured 'Mediterranean' climate of the Central Valley, grading northwards into semi-aridity and then to the arid coastal zone of the Atacama and of Peru. In northern Peru and southern Ecuador there is, however, a sharp transition to hot and humid equatorial climate supporting rainforest under natural conditions, reaching its maximum development in the Pacific coastlands of western Colombia, which is the wettest area in the Americas, receiving up to 7000 mm a year. The Caribbean margin of the Andean region, however, is one of sharp contrast between hot and humid climates supporting tropical forest in north-west Colombia and the surprisingly dry climates of the Guajira peninsula and parts of northern Venezuela, including the Coro peninsula and the region to the south of it.

Patterns of regional development imposed upon the complex mosaic of contrasting ecologies in the Andean region and its margins have increasingly depended both on the exploitation of resources and on the leadership of rapidly expanding metropolitan cities and regional capitals – seats of government and bureaucracy, preferred locations for industrial development, especially of import substitution industries, and magnets for the concentration of purchasing power and of population. In Peru, regional patterns of growth, with relatively high regional incomes and standards of welfare, have focused essentially on Greater Lima, the coastal zone and the hinterland of Lima in the central sierra of Peru. The geographical basis of the relative progress of the coastal zone rests on its irrigated agriculture and the exploitation of mineral and marine resources. Irrigation is made possible, in this naturally arid region, by the Pacific-flowing streams draining from the relatively well-watered Andes of central and northern Peru. Commercial agriculture has been facilitated since the sixteenth century by the ease of accessibility to coastal ports, and from the 1940s by the Pan-American Highway. It is a region dominated formerly by highly productive farming for export, particularly of sugar and cotton, and although these are still important exports, coastal agriculture is increasingly oriented to production for domestic urban markets, particularly that of Lima itself. Wine and brandy are specialities of long-standing in the Ica area, but production of fruit, vegetables, stall-fed dairy cattle, maize and potatoes is of increasing significance. Coastal ports, notably Callao and Chimbote, have generated industrial activity from the fishing industry, booming from the 1950s, but declining in the 1970s as a result of overfishing of the *anchoveta*, the raw material for exports of fishmeal to Western Europe and North America. The coast has benefited, too, from the exploitation of mineral resources on the Pacific slopes – oil in the far north-west, iron ore and low-grade copper ores to the south of Lima, near Arequipa and Matarani. Development of phosphates in the north at Bayovar is seen as the basis for further industrial growth. The hinterland of Lima in the Central Sierra is also the area in which much of Peru's copper, lead, zinc and silver have been exploited since the nineteenth century, and is well connected to Lima by road and rail. But the Lima market, and local mining activities have also encouraged the commercialization of agriculture in the Central Sierra for dairying, grains, potatoes and vegetables. Secondary urban centres have grown rapidly in recent years, and both Arequipa and Trujillo are important industrial centres, partly as a result of encouragement by government, but it is Greater Lima which has come to dominate Peruvian economic and social geography, with a population currently estimated at 4.5 million or about a quarter of Peru's total population, and over half of Peru's industrial activity.

Whereas the Spanish conquistadors rejected both Cuzco, heart of the Inca empire, and Jauja, briefly considered, in favour of Lima as a capital nearer to the coast and the life-line to Spain, Quito, in what was to become Ecuador, was retained from Inca times as capital for colonial government in spite of its distance from the coast. This fact has been of enormous importance in the regional development of Ecuador. Coastal Ecuador, like coastal Peru, was the location for export production from the late nineteenth century, but given its hot, humid equatorial climate, development focused on cacao, coffee, bananas and rice for the domestic market. Development has spread northwards to Esmeraldas, but Guayaquil, the major colonial port for Quito and the terminus of its railway link to the sea, was the main urban focus for external trade. Guayaquil, traditionally the commercial and banking centre, with a reputation for its liveliness and business enterprise, has continued to grow. Quito, always the seat of government and headquarters of the conservative landowning oligarchy of the sierra, has the metropolitan advantages which flow from the presence of government and an expanding bureaucracy and the concentration of purchasing power. It shares with Guayaquil the major part of industrial growth in Ecuador. By contrast functions dominated by Lima alone in Peru are in Ecuador shared between twin primate cities. The coastal zone of Ecuador remains the scene of new settlement and colonization, of highly commercialized agriculture and of immigration, but in the sierra Indian peasant farming, haciendas and the activities of regional urban centres, strung out like beads from Cuenca in the south to Loja in the north, are enlivened by the commercial possibilities inherent in Quito's expansion.

Bolivia, too, has its capital firmly located in the predominantly Indian highlands of the Altiplano, a region of dense Indian settlement near Lake Titicaca with a more humid and slightly more equable climate than the rest of the Altiplano, which becomes more arid, harsh and more sparsely settled towards the south-west. Since the agrarian reform began in 1952, Indian peasant farming has become significantly more prosperous and more commercially oriented towards the urban market presented by La Paz. But the spatial organization of Bolivia is more complex, aligned broadly on two axes: one of long standing from La Paz through Oruro to Potosí and associated with the exploitation of mineral resources; the second of more recent development from La Paz through Cochabamba to the boom city of Santa Cruz. The fabulous wealth in silver of Potosí, largest town in the Americas around 1600, and later at Oruro, was replaced in the late nineteenth century by tin-mining, still the major source of Bolivia's foreign-exchange earnings and the *raison d'être* of the western railway system linking La Paz with Arica and Antofagasta, Lake Titicaca and the Peruvian system. But the mining sector has been less dynamic than the eastern settlement round Santa Cruz and north of Cochabamba where production of tropical and subtropical products (notably sugar, rice, coffee, coca) and cattle have flourished in the context of oil and natural gas production. The centre of gravity of Bolivian development is shifting fairly rapidly from the Altiplano and the mining centres to the new east. Cochabamba, located in the centre of this axis, and in a zone of intermediate altitude, is well placed to benefit from industrial and commercial growth. But La Paz is still the primate city, and resource-based development elsewhere has by no means robbed it of economic leadership.

In the broadest sense, Colombia's make-up is similar to that of Ecuador and Peru – coastal margin, Andean ranges and eastern interior lowlands. In Colombia two structural troughs separating the three main ranges are lower in altitude than further south and more importantly are followed by partially navigable river systems – the Cauca and the Magdalena – draining directly into the Caribbean. Within the relatively open landscapes of the Colombian sierra there are larger areas appropriate for the production of temperate and tropical crops than further south, but the coastal regions tend to be hostile, swampy regions of forest or savanna. In spite of the early strategic importance of Cartagena, chief port until the rise of Barranquilla, the focus of government remained at Bogotá, always relatively difficult of access from the coast and from other parts of the country. Partly because of this, several urban centres of substantial regional importance developed. Medellín, focus of an early gold trade and then a centre from which agricultural colonization spread southwards, was the city to gain most from the expansion of coffee production; it then developed as an industrial city. Cali and Bucaramanga are the other urban poles which, with Bogotá, define a quadrilateral which contains over half the centre's population, its major cities and higher standards of income and welfare than the rest of the country.

Finally in Venezuela, the tripartite arrangement of coast, sierra and interior lowlands is repeated again, though the mountains are lower in altitude and less of a barrier except in the west, and the Guiana shield to the south of the Orinoco gives a fourth dimension. The coastal zone is complex with contrasting environments from the steaming rainforest south of Lake Maracaibo to the semi-aridity further east. Oil and its exploitation have elevated Maracaibo to be the second largest city, but it has always been the capital, Caracas, which has benefited most from the oil revenues, so that Venezuela, like Peru, offers one of the best South American examples of urban primacy, though industrial development is spreading southwards from Caracas and westwards to the older industrial area around Valencia, and even further west at Barquisimeto. There has been substantial progress, too, in the settlement of the inner flanks of the Andean range draining to the Orinoco and in the creation of a new urban–industrial complex at Ciudad Guyana, based on resources at the northern margin of the Guiana Highlands – iron ore, bauxite and hydroelectricity.

Chile is the exception among Andean countries, in that it is the coastal zone which is overwhelmingly dominant. Much of the Andean massif is uninhabitable, and the territory extends only to the crestlines of the Andean chain, except in the south. Chile's geographical differentiation is latitudinal and defined in terms of climate and vegetation. It is the Mediterranean climate of the Central Valley which was attractive for agricultural settlement from the early colonial period and which provided the bulk of its exports until the advent of mining. It is still the most densely populated zone of Chile, though expansion southwards towards Valdivia was accomplished from the nineteenth century with the assistance of a certain amount of immigration. The far south has few possibilities except for tourism, extensive sheep-raising and perhaps greater oil production. The north is desert, lacking the irrigation possibilities of coastal Peru, since the aridity of the high Andean ranges supplies few streams with adequate water for large-scale irrigation. Yet it is the desert which has produced the resources to sustain the Chilean economy: nitrates in the late nineteenth and early twentieth centuries; copper from Chuquicamata and El Salvador and elsewhere in the twentieth century, and iron ore from near Coquimbo. But the desert environment has precluded the generation of large and diverse settlements around the mining areas. Further south, Concepción has grown as a regional capital with coal and steel production nearby, but it is Santiago which, like Lima in Peru, or Caracas in Venezuela, has been the main beneficiary of urban and industrial growth. Efforts at regional development, such as the establishment of Arica as a free industrial zone, have failed to reduce significantly the primacy of Santiago.

The interior and Atlantic lowlands

Four well-defined lowland zones separate the Andean region from the ancient massifs of eastern South America: the Orinoco basin, the Amazon basin, the lowlands of the Paraná–Paraguay system, and the Atlantic-facing lowlands of the Argentine pampas and Patagonia. There is a corresponding differentiation in their ecology according to climate and vegetational patterns: the Orinoco basin has a highly seasonal rainfall regime which supports predominantly grassland vegetation of the savanna type with galería forest along the better-watered of its rivers; the Amazon lowlands are the largest area of surviving equatorial rainforest in the world, with rainfall all the year round, but with some marked features of seasonality in the incidence of rainfall, and with the highest totals tending to occur along the western margins of Amazonia; further south there is a gradual transition, with many areas of swamp vegetation, to savanna grassland and thorn scrub of the Gran Chaco, with a highly seasonal rainfall regime and a climate which, while the hottest part of South America in the southern summer, is liable in winter to occasional bursts of cold air drawn along the lowland corridor from the south. The natural grasslands of the pampas have a more equable temperate climate in which rainfall occurs throughout the year but with a summer maximum, but totals diminish westwards towards the semi-arid margins of the Andes. Soils are fertile, characterized by chernozems developed on the thick deposits of wind-blown loess derived from the Pleistocene glaciation of the Andes. But to the south, rainfall becomes scarce and summers cool in the arid desert of the Patagonian plateau, with its harsh landscapes of volcanic lavas and glacial moraine.

With the very important exception of the Argentine pampas, the interior lowlands are sparsely populated and relatively undeveloped – the empty heart of South America. Why this should be so is partly a result of its varied ecological character, but it is perhaps even more bound up with the cultural history of South America, not least of its pre-Columbian heritage. The indigenous cultures of the Amazonian rainforests were ethnically and linguistically highly fragmented. Their material cultures were based on shifting agriculture and the hunting and fishing of a wide variety of fauna. Population was sparse (though less so in the sixteenth century than later) and groups were probably separated by unoccupied forest. Intelligent use was made of the distinction between relatively fertile, regularly flooded soils of the *varzea* and the leached, mature and fragile soils of older terraces – the *terra firme*. But the indigenes were neither docile or numerous enough to provide a massive labour force for Spanish or Portuguese settlers, nor were there prospects of rich mineral wealth or raw materials to attract settlement. The forest and its inhabitants were ruthlessly exploited for rubber and cinchona in the nineteenth century, but it was not until recently that a serious attempt has been made by Brazil to exploit the potential resources of the area.

The building of the Transamazonian Highway and its feeder roads is in part strategic and military in conception, aiming at completing the occupation of national territory to its frontiers with the Andean states, and it is also, of course, economic. Large-scale clearing of forest and its replacement by more rapidly maturing, consolidated stands of timber or, more commonly, its replacement by grazing for cattle, together with plans for mineral exploitation of iron ore, tin, manganese and bauxite, have aroused grave apprehension of an ecological disaster. Equatorial soils are fragile – mineral nutrients are locked in the bio-mass rather than in the soil itself – and forest clearance has demonstrably resulted in rapid soil deterioration, apart from fears as to the effect of large-scale deforestation on the atmospheric oxygen balance, and on the future of the indigenous groups that have still survived, and other fears as to the social consequences of unbridled exploitation for peasant settlers and immigrant workers. Furthermore, the forest is subjected to a two-fold attack: from Brazil on the one hand, and from the Andean states on the other. Colombia, Ecuador, Peru and Bolivia are also concerned to validate their political boundaries by frontier settlement and see economic possibilities in the production of cattle as well as tropical crops from the eastern flanks of the Andes, where on the whole soils are richer than in the lowlands proper. Eastern colonization is more important to Bolivia than to other Andean states, lacking as it does a Pacific coast and alternative sources for such

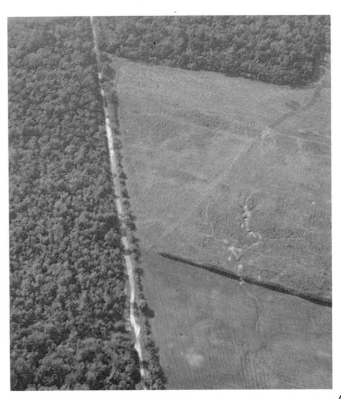

A section of the Amazon rainforest cleared for cultivation (original forest, left)

products; and it is here that eastern colonization has moved fastest in recent years. Everywhere there is potential conflict of interests between small-scale peasant farmers moving into the lowlands by a process of spontaneous colonization, and large-scale projects encouraged by governments or financed with abundant capital backing. Cacao, coffee, bananas, palm oil, sugar, rice and beef are among the potential products to supply domestic markets and even export revenues, but in the Andean states it is cocaine, derived from the leaves of the coca shrub, that has been the source of high and illegal profits in recent years, and it is also oil and the prospects of oil that have raised high hopes, partially realized in Ecuador, Peru and Bolivia.

To the north and south of the rainforest, the plains of the Orinoco and the basin of the River Paraguay seem to offer fewer possibilities of intensive development. Seasonal flooding of the Orinoco plains inhibits more intensive use of the natural savanna grasslands than the extensive stock-raising to which it is now devoted. Further south, seasonal flooding and vast areas of marshland alternating with thorn scrub on sandy soils discourage settlement in the Paraguay basin, shared among Brazil, Bolivia and Paraguay, though there is some development along the tenuous link from Brazil to

Corumbá and thence to Santa Cruz in Bolivia. Patagonia, with limited possibilities for extensive sheep grazing and arable crops where irrigation is possible, and with the descendants of its Welsh colonies still retaining an ethnic identity, is also an area of limited potential.

The empty heart of South America is thus, in one sense, a frontier of settlement, though one of hardship and of elusive possibilities, but it has also been a frontier zone in a political sense, in which rivalries between Spain and Portugal for control of the interior were worked out far away from the region itself. On the Spanish side, the religious missions to pacify and 'civilize' the Indian communities were one expression of a colonial strategy adopted to contain the Brazilian Portuguese – in the Orinoco basin in Venezuela, in eastern Peru, the Mojos region of north-east Bolivia, and also in the Jesuit 'state within a state' in the region of modern Paraguay. After independence, large slices of territory changed hands, with a greater significance, perhaps, on the maps than on the ground. Peru lost territory in the Amazon basin to Brazil, and gained from Ecuador (as late as 1941); Bolivia lost territory to Brazil in exchange for concessions, and the Bolivian border with Paraguay was only settled in 1937 after a long drawn-out and exhausting war.

In complete contrast to the lack of development in the interior plains the remaining lowland region – the Argentine pampas and its surrounding lowlands to the north in the lower Paraná – Paraguay and to the north-east into Uruguay – is intensively settled and constitutes the major productive areas of Paraguay, Uruguay and Argentina itself. Until the eighteenth century this, too, was a region as sparsely populated as the interior lowlands further north, its natural grasslands the habitat of a sparse Indian hunting population and of semi-wild cattle controlled by nomadic gauchos. The major exception was the sedentary agricultural Indian population, largely Tupi–Guaraní, of what is now Paraguay, organized into village life by the Jesuit missions (until their expulsion in 1767). Accessibility to the Atlantic by way of the River Plate estuary became of major significance from the late eighteenth century, and the economic revolution on the pampas which brought the railways, immigrant settlers from Europe, meat production for the European market and intensive arable farming only came after the mid-nineteenth century. Over a long time-scale, Argentina offers the best example of the movement down from the mountains, for in 1750 the major settled areas were still in the old north-west, in the irrigated, semi-arid intermontane basins from Salta and Jujuy southwards to Tucumán and beyond. By 1900, the pampas were effectively settled and were now the economic core of Argentina, linked to the old north-west by a chain of towns which still form the major economic axis of the country from Buenos Aires to Rosario and Córdoba. Settlement and agricultural development of the pampas is limited westwards by increasing aridity, but the northward expansion of

settlement for the production of livestock and a range of subtropical crops was still proceeding in recent years, particularly in the Argentine Mesopotamia between the Paraná and the River Uruguay. Eastern Paraguay is still an active area of new settlement, in which immigrant stock farmers play an important role. More obviously even than in the Andean countries, however, it is Buenos Aires which demonstrates the role of the metropolis as a major engine of growth, concentrating over 10 million people or over a third of the total population of Argentina, and its major industrial and commercial focus. On a smaller scale, Montevideo stands in an even more striking role in relation to Uruguay with over 40 per cent of the country's total population.

But in the rest of the interior lowlands there is no coherent urban network and only isolated urban centres acting as the focus of regional development: Belem, Manaus and Iquitos on the Amazon; Pucallpa in eastern Peru; Rondonia as a centre of new settlement in south-west Brazil; in Bolivia, Trinidad and especially Santa Cruz.

The ancient massifs and their Atlantic margins

Eastern South America is composed essentially of two unequally sized ancient massifs – the Guiana Highlands and the Brazilian Shield – divided by the lower Amazon basin. Although the geological structure is complex, the major physiographic features are those of an eroded plateau tilted towards the north-west with a relief of rolling country broken by residual ridges and escarpments of more resistant rocks and sinking imperceptibly towards the lowlands of the Amazon and the basin of the River Paraguay. To the east and south-east the plateau is at its highest, falling to the Atlantic by steep escarpments, such as the Serra do Mar between Rio and Santos or the Borborema in the north-east. With a rainfall that is increasingly seasonal in summer to the south of the Amazon basin, the interior of the plateau displays a transition from rainforest to tall grass savanna and to the *campos cerrados* of savanna with xerophytic trees and shrubs. But towards the Atlantic coast, rainfall amounts are higher, and more continuous throughout the year, supporting evergreen tropical forest under natural conditions and Araucarian pine forests or subtropical evergreen forests to the south. But in the interior of the north-east there is a sharp transition between the moist Atlantic coast and a dry, hot climate supporting the thorn scrub cactus and grassland vegetation known as the *caatinga*.

Compared with the Andean region, the interior plateau had little to offer to the initial Portuguese settlers. The relatively scattered Indian population, at a lower level of cultural development, lacked the homogeneity, docility and the skills which attracted the Spanish settler further west. Except in the south, soils are poor and easily eroded or exhausted, though extensive cattle-raising supported a sparse and scattered population and still does so. Above all, there were no obvious sources of precious metals until the discovery of gold and diamonds in the late seventeenth century brought settlement to Minas Gerais. Given its Atlantic orientation and colonial settlement from Portugal, it was almost inevitable that the east, with its humid climate, should be developed earliest. Indeed, although the distribution of population is changing, with a continued shift towards the interior, the general pattern is one in which most of the population and all of the large cities, with the exception of Brasília, Manaus and Belo Horizonte, lie within 160 km of the Atlantic coast.

Three major features, then, characterize the human geography of Brazil. One is the imbalance in its population distribution; the second is the scale and rapidity of the economic advance that has taken place in the south-east, and the third, stemming in part from the first two, is the inequality of regional development.

It was coffee which brought wealth, population and commerce, first to Rio and later to São Paulo (and its port at Santos) from the early nineteenth century. Rio de Janeiro, with its magnificent harbour, had grown with trade to the gold-mining areas of Minas Gerais, became the focus of the court and then capital of Brazil, and prospered with the coffee trade, later sharing pre-eminence with São Paulo as the coffee frontier moved south-west on to the fertile *terra roxa* soils on the interfluves of the upper Paraná system. It was coffee which ultimately financed the building of a railway system comparable in density and pattern to that of the pampas, and attracted European immigrants from the late nineteenth century. It was the commerce in coffee which financed early industrial development in São Paulo for a significant internal market. But industrial development, encouraged by the use of high-quality iron ore reserves to produce steel, first at Volta Redonda on any scale, has spread more widely in the industrial triangle of the south-east, defined roughly by Belo Horizonte, São Paulo and Rio de Janeiro. Brazil's industrial complex, backed by the largest internal market in Latin America, and contributing substantially to its export sector, is now wide-ranging in its variety of industrial activity, and is largely responsible for generating an average regional per-capita income which is far above the average for Brazil as a whole.

At the other extreme, the north-east, while densely populated, is the most economically depressed and impoverished region of Brazil, with an average per-capita income of only a fifth of that of the Rio de Janeiro area. Sugar plantations, worked by slave labour in the humid coastlands of the north-east, generated wealth for a few in the sixteenth and seventeenth centuries, but with impoverished soils and low yields in many areas it has never recovered prosperity, while retaining sharp inequalities in income distribution. The juxtaposition of large estates and smallholdings is one manifestation of inequalities of income, which persist in spite of attempts to bring industrial development to the cities of the north-east. Further inland, in the 'polygon of drought', irrigation schemes, as a response to the shortage and unreliability of rainfall, have failed to relieve rural poverty; nor have resettlement schemes in the Amazon basin had much effect.

Just as the Transamazonian Highway and its colonization schemes (Brazil's 'march to the west') attempt to settle the interior, so the foundation of Brasília as capital (inaugurated in April 1960) represents a bold, imaginative attempt to create an urban growth pole which will revitalize the interior plateau, still in general underpopulated and devoted to shifting cultivation and extensive cattle-raising. The elegant formal planned city has, in fact, generated a host of informal unplanned satellites which exemplify the social inequalities of the country as a whole.

Middle America and the Caribbean

Within this vast and complex region it is, broadly speaking, Mexico which conforms to a continental scale both in the characteristics of its physical environments and its economy. But in Central America proper and the Caribbean islands it is fragmentation which is the keynote in a physical, economic and political sense.

Mexico contains within its borders a rich variety of natural conditions. In the south, humid tropical and naturally forested lowlands on both Atlantic and Pacific coasts (with the exception of northern Yucatán) rise to the dissected highlands of the southern range, moderately well-watered and enclosing tectonic basins such as those of Oaxaca and Chiapas. The Volcanic Axis, crossing the country from east to west, includes snow-capped cones such as Orizaba (5750 m) and Popocatépetl (5452 m), but the important areas for settlement and agriculture are again the tectonic basins

Mexico City

enclosed within the ranges, including the Valley of Mexico at *c.* 2500 m above sea level. To the north, the coastal lowlands, widest near the US border, are better watered on the Caribbean shore than towards the Pacific, where there is a rapid transition towards the desert coasts of the north-west and the peninsula of Baja California. Inland the western branch of the Sierra Madre is more continuous, higher and more massive, and also more highly mineralized than the eastern branch, and they enclose within them the plateaus and range-and-basin country of northern Mexico, becoming increasingly more arid to the north and west. Irrigation has made possible more intensive and modernized agricultural settlement in some areas of the north, particularly near the US border and on the Pacific coast, but the north as a whole is relatively sparsely settled, and in many areas overgrazed and badly eroded.

Minerals have played a fundamental role in Mexico's development. Silver at Guanajuato, Zacatecas and San Luis de Potosí drew the Spaniards northwards to frontier regions beyond the Aztec empire, and silver has continuously played an important role in the external economy from the sixteenth century, though copper, lead, zinc, sulphur, and iron ore (combined with local coal for an expanding steel industry at Monterrey) have in this century supplemented silver, and all are now overshadowed by oil production from new Gulf offshore fields.

But it is Mexico City, once the capital city of the Aztec empire, which dominates the human geography of the country. Likely to be one of the world's largest cities in 2000 and with an estimated population of about 12 million people in 1980, it sprawls far beyond the lake margins where it originated as Tenochtitlán, creating vast problems of housing, traffic congestion, pollution, water supply and drainage, but containing a wide range of engineering and consumer goods industries. An industrial–urban axis has emerged parallel to the Volcanic Axis and extending from Puebla to Guadalajara, with Mexico City as its central focus. Although relatively poor areas exist near and within this prosperous industrialized zone, regional development in Mexico conforms to a pattern in which the northern border zone near the United States and the metropolitan region represent the highest levels of income and welfare, but the far south, with a high proportion of Indian population and relatively remote from urban or international markets, is the poorest region.

Fragmentation is the keynote of Central America and the Caribbean, though in rather different ways. Wet, forested lowlands and a confusion of dissected highlands with volcanic peaks and small-scale basins at varying altitudes define a region from Panama to Guatemala which has been accessible mainly by sea, though capital cities, except for Panama, are located in interior basins initially carrying a moderately dense Indian population. At independence, such unity as there was in Spanish colonial administration disappeared and the region fell apart into what are now seven independent states, each quite small, ranging from Belize (150,000 in 1979) to Guatemala (6.8 million in 1979), and with wide-ranging per-capita incomes, from that of Honduras, which shares with Bolivia the distinction of the lowest per-capita income in mainland Latin America, to Costa Rica and Panama, which rank in the top ten. Political profiles have ranged equally widely, from the harshest of personal and military dictatorships, like that of the Somozas of Nicaragua (up to 1979) to the relatively stable democratic structure of Costa Rica. The Central American Common Market (CACM) represents only the most recent, and now fading, attempt of many in the last 150 years to achieve a regional grouping of these small and economically vulnerable units.

The Caribbean islands present a distinctive pattern of fragmentation of a different kind. They comprise a series of island arcs ranging from the substantial highland massifs of the Greater Antilles to the low coral islands of the Bahamas or the volcanic peaks of Martinique, for example. Colonial rivalries of Spain, Holland, France, Britain and Denmark imposed very different political structures on the islands until their decolonization in the twentieth century, though Guadeloupe and Martinique are still departments of France and Puerto Rico a dominion of the United States. Indigenous Indian populations were replaced by slave labour to work the plantations which made fortunes for the planters and merchants of the colonial powers in the eighteenth century. Sugar above all, but also coffee, tobacco, cotton and bananas, and more recently tourists, and minerals such as bauxite from Jamaica, support the precarious and vulnerable external economies of political units too small to generate an internal market for much industrialization. As in Central America, political regimes range widely, from that of socialist Cuba to the harsh regime of Haiti, poorest of the Latin American countries. Attempts at co-operation and regional groupings tend to founder in the face of island particularisms, and while old colonial links are suspect, the basis for new groupings has not yet arisen. But for many of the islands, emigration overseas has provided something of a safety valve: from the islands to the neighbouring continental mainland, but, more commonly, from Puerto Rico to the United States; from Cuba of political dissidents to the United States; from the former British West Indies to Great Britain, Canada and the United States.

CTS

Further reading

H. Blakemore and C. T. Smith, eds., *Latin America: Geographical Perspectives*, 2nd edition (London, 1983)

A. Gilbert, *Latin American Development* (Harmondsworth, 1974)

P. E. James, *Latin America* (New York, 1969)

A. Morris, *Latin America* (London, 1981)

P. R. Odell and D. A. Preston, *Economies and Societies in Latin America* (London, 1978)

THE ECONOMY

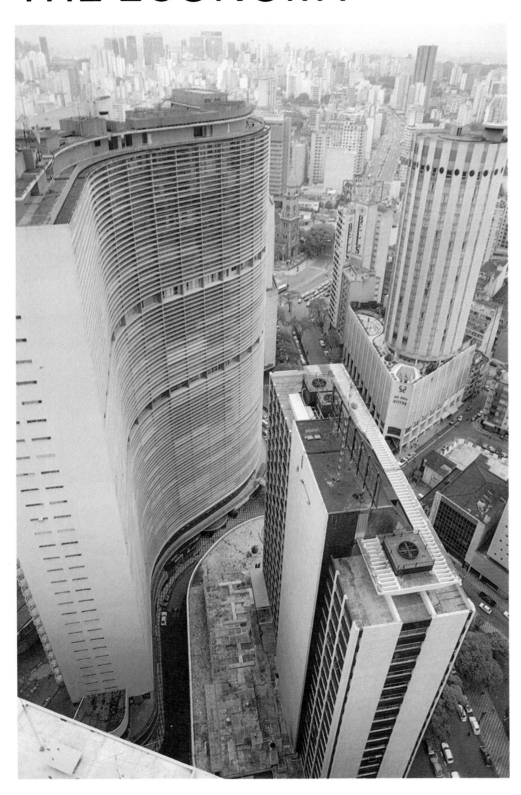

São Paulo, Brazil

Agriculture

Latin America and the Caribbean is distinctive among Third World regions in having a relatively small proportion of the population engaged in agriculture and fishing. This is largely because of the number of people who live in towns and cities. Although in Latin America farming only accounts for one in three employed people, compared with two in three in all developing countries, it is nonetheless the main livelihood of many families over vast areas of the continent and the Caribbean islands. Agriculture and fishing in Latin America can best be understood if it is recognized that both activities take place at two very different scales. On the one hand, large numbers of small-scale farmers produce in aggregate large quantities of foodstuffs largely for their own or local consumption, usually from very small farms which may not even provide work for all the family. On the other hand, large quantities of valuable foodstuffs are also grown on a small number of much larger farms, predominantly for export. This is illustrated by the fact that Brazil produces the largest quantity of bananas in Latin America; in 1979 Brazil produced 6.4 million tonnes, almost all of which were consumed in Brazil, while Ecuador, a much smaller country, is the leading Latin American and world exporter of bananas and yet only produced one-third of the quantity of bananas as did Brazil.

An agricultural geography of Latin America and the Caribbean

In Mexico and Central America the majority of the rural population is concentrated in the highland chain which forms the backbone of the continent, although the high and dry plateau of northern Mexico contains few people. The native Indian populations are found predominantly in these areas and they and the non-Indian populations are mainly small-scale farmers who produce maize, beans and pumpkins for their own use. In some highland areas there are middle-sized and large farms where excellent-quality coffee is grown, largely for export. Agricultural development of the lowlands, apart from colonization areas and the Yucatán peninsula in Mexico, Belize and Guatemala, is dominated by commercial farming, particularly by US corporations, which provides large quantities of bananas for export.

In the Caribbean, subsistence farming on the hilly islands has always occupied large areas but commercial farming is also important in the lowlands, producing fruit, especially bananas, for northern markets on plantations and middle-sized farms. In Cuba and parts of the Dominican Republic sugar is produced on large farms for export.

The farm population of western South America is densely concentrated in the highland zone which runs from eastern Venezuela to southern Chile and Argentina. Agriculture is carried on at all levels and as high as 3900 m in the Central Andes. Smallholdings predominate, although large farms are found in some areas (producing sheep and grains) and potatoes, maize and beans are the main food crops grown. The rearing of sheep, pigs, cattle and camelids (llamas and alpacas) is important for both small- and large-scale farmers. The lowlands to the east of the mountain are thinly populated although there are growing colonization areas on the fringes of the mountains. The number of Indians and non-Indian farmers in the lowlands east of the Andes form a very small proportion of the Andean countries' population. The coastal regions of Ecuador, Peru and Chile contain areas where commercially oriented farming is important. In Ecuador cacao and bananas are produced for export: in Peru, with the aid of irrigation, cotton and sugar are grown while in central Chile, between the coastal hills and the Andes, good farmland supports a large population.

To the east of the Andes, south of the Amazon basin, farming populations became established in the late nineteenth century after the demise of the Portuguese and Spanish colonial empires; much of the population is descended from nineteenth- and early-twentieth-century immigrants from Europe. The temperate farmlands of Argentina, Uruguay and southern Brazil produce grains, meat and, further north in Brazil, coffee, largely for sale to the big cities and for export. The frontier of farming in Brazil has been moving westwards during this century, and is increasingly associated with the spread of cattle farming. In central and north-eastern Brazil good farmland is concentrated, with the population, along the coast as far north as the mouth of the Amazon. While small-scale farming

An Aymara Indian ploughing in the Altiplano, Bolivia

CONCENTRATION OF AGRICULTURAL LAND

PROPORTION OF FARMS LESS THAN 5 HECTARES IN SIZE

	%	Year
Mexico	67	1960
Guatemala	75	1964
Honduras	47	1966
El Salvador	87	1971
Nicaragua	34	1963
Costa Rica	43	1973
Panama	45	1971
Venezuela	49	1961
Colombia	59	1970
Ecuador	66	1974
Peru	86	1961
Bolivia	(67)	est
Chile	66	1972
Argentina	16	1960
Uruguay	14	1970
Paraguay	46	1961
Brazil	37	1970

Source: FAO, *Land Reform, Land Settlement and Cooperatives,*
1979(1) p. 86

KEY

Category 4

Category 3

Category 2

Category 1

No data

This map shows the locations of
about 90% of non – agricultural
activites

Each square represents almost
0·5% of the total activities
shown

Agriculture

is widespread, cacao and sugar are among the major crops produced for shipment elsewhere. Fishing is practised by most coastal communities in tropical Latin America and on the major rivers and lakes, but few people live exclusively from fishing which is normally supplemented by farming. Fishing, often by simple methods, is geared largely to local needs or, at most, regional needs. In some countries commercial fishing is important and in Peru, Panama and Chile the export of fishery produce comprises between 7 and 17 per cent of the value of exports.

The declining importance of agriculture

Families in rural areas are seldom entirely dedicated to farming and it is commonplace, except in areas of large farms, for farm families also to be engaged in weaving, commerce or in working elsewhere for periods of each year. At a national level the proportion of the population that is recorded as working in agriculture varies markedly according to the relative importance of its urban centres and therefore of employment in industry and services. In table 1 it will be seen that the three southern states of Chile, Argentina and Uruguay, as well as Venezuela, have less than 20 per cent of their population working in agriculture and that a number of the more urbanized Caribbean islands also have a similarly low proportion of their population in agriculture. At the opposite end of the scale, the poorer countries have over half of their population in agriculture; Haiti, Honduras, the Dominican Republic and Guatemala all fall into this category. A second feature of table 1 is the universal decline in the proportion of the population in agriculture, although, in those countries with a high proportion of the population in agriculture, the *number* of people in agriculture is increasing.

Traditional farming systems

The majority of those farming in Latin America are not primarily concerned with producing a surplus for sale or with achieving the maximum yield from their land. They wish primarily to produce enough food to eat and possibly to exchange locally. The methods of production used by these small-scale peasant farmers are ever-changing but their basic system is based on long experience and is thus traditional. Such farmers have very little money and do not buy much factory-made chemical produce because of its cost and the uncertainty of the benefits that may result from its use. They are concerned with minimizing risks involved with farming since crop failure could mean hunger. A basic way of farming which ensures some success is to plant a wide variety of crops and often several crops in the same field. Therefore, if one field is hit by a hailstorm, only some of the harvest of a few of the crops is lost. Many crops were first used by prehistoric farmers in Latin America – potatoes and maize originated in the New World. Many different varieties of these and of other crops are used by farmers in any village and each

Field shelters at harvest time at Chinchero, Peru. The peasant farmers are making *chuño* (dehydrated potato) as they have since pre-Columbian times

Table 1. Decline of the farming population 1970–82 (percentage of the occupied labour force in agriculture)

Country	Per cent in agriculture, 1979	Per cent change since 1970
LATIN AMERICA	33	— 8
Mexico	34	—11
Guatemala	54	— 7
El Salvador	49	— 7
Honduras	62	— 5
Nicaragua	41	—10
Costa Rica	34	— 9
Panama	33	— 8
Colombia	26	— 2
Venezuela	17	— 9
Ecuador	43	— 8
Peru	36	— 9
Brazil	37	— 9
Uruguay	11	— 4
Paraguay	48	— 4
Chile	18	— 5
Bolivia	49	— 7
Argentina	12	— 4
Cuba	22	— 9
Puerto Rico	3	— 6
Jamaica	19	—10
Barbados	16	— 4
Dominican Republic	55	— 6
Guadeloupe	15	—11
Haiti	65	— 9
Martinique	14	—10
Trinidad & Tobago	16	— 3
Guyana	21	— 8
Surinam	17	— 6
Belize	27	— 7
United States	2	—1.7
Great Britain	1·9	—0.9

Source: FAO *Production Yearbook*, 1982.

variety has different attributes, perhaps being drought resistant, tolerant of cold, or able to withstand strong winds, so that each hazard does not affect all the maize or beans or potatoes in the same way.

Many of the areas where farming has been longest known in Latin America are hilly and animals were not used to till the ground before 1500. Thus, the means of cultivation involved simple tools – hoes, digging sticks or footploughs and human labour. Such systems are still commonplace in many parts of highland Latin America although cattle are now used to pull simple ploughs in some areas. Land is planted in crops usually for one to three years before being allowed to revert to scrub so that the soil may regain fertility; fallow periods can last from five to thirty years, depending on the land available and local practice. Livestock are corralled and brought food, or allowed to graze freely, frequently on land being fallowed where some edible plants have grown. Children frequently tend livestock, while planting is usually an adult male task. Women assist in all tasks and when men are absent do all save those which are physically impossible.

The system of cultivating different plots each year is often, especially in forest areas, referred to as shifting cultivation; it has been widely recognized as an effective and sensitive method of using land resources in such a way as to ensure that the soil can regain fertility and little erosion occurs. Fertility is assisted by use of animal dung but its collection is seldom meticulous and little use is made of human waste. Crops to which chemicals are applied are frequently those destined for sale; farmers may also be advised to apply fertilizer when using new crop varieties. Fishing and hunting are adjuncts to farming in many places and provide a further source of protein. Traditional diets based on a combination such as maize, beans and pumpkins (squash) can be well balanced without the consumption of meat. A range of plants is grown or collected for food flavouring and for medicinal use.

Commercial farming

Most farmers grow some crops and raise animals with a view to selling when the need arises. Livestock, in particular, are regarded as a valuable capital resource since a cow can be sold for cash more or less whenever the need arises. Fully commercial farmers sell a large part of what they grow or rear and buy the necessities of life with the cash received. Many such commercial farmers have small farms and are very poor but their farming system is cash-based and relies on few components. The major crops or products associated with specific Latin American countries such as coffee (Colombia, Brazil), bananas (Ecuador, Colombia), sugar (Cuba, Barbados) or cattle (Argentina, Uruguay) are produced on relatively large farms, employing workers who are paid in cash and using relatively modern methods of production. Some measure of the conditions

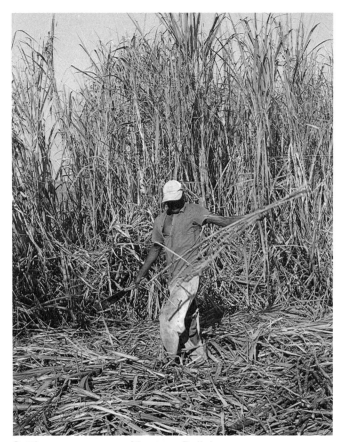

Cutting sugar cane at Montero, Bolivia

under which this other sort of farming takes place can be taken by surveying the systems of farming associated with a series of crops and livestock. Grains, especially wheat, are grown throughout Latin America but they are grown commercially in large quantities only in a few parts. Wheat, in particular, has long been a crop associated with large farms and it tends to be grown in areas where a degree of mechanization is possible, in large fields and using selected seed. New varieties of wheat developed in the past twenty years are resistant to disease and storm damage, and have proved responsive to the use of artificial fertilizers. However, it is mainly the larger-scale farmers who have benefited from these innovations and wheat production in general has not kept pace with the demand, inflated by a growing preference for white flours. Argentina is the only country producing sufficient wheat to export, although Mexico, Brazil and Chile also produce considerable quantities of wheat.

Major exports of agricultural produce from Latin America have always included fruit and sugar cane from the humid tropical areas, particularly from those areas with easy access to North America and Europe. *Sugar* production for sale has, since the colonial period, been associated with plantations for which slaves were imported from Africa until the early nineteenth century. Sugar production continues to be predominantly on large estates even where major social reforms have given control of the land to the people. Some mechanization is taking place but sugar production continues to be associated with large amounts of poorly paid manpower. Cuba remains the leading sugar exporter with the Dominican Republic, Brazil, Jamaica and Guyana also exporting large quantities. *Banana* growing for export has traditionally been associated with large estates wholly controlled by one of the few major US fruit companies, particularly in the Central American republics. In Ecuador since the 1950s, and subsequently in Colombia and elsewhere, banana-growing land has passed into the hands of middle-sized farmers – often city-based businessmen – who produce fruit under contract for the banana exporters, thus avoiding the odium of owning vast plantations but retaining full control over production and packaging. *Coffee* has long been associated with middle-sized farms in Colombia, Brazil, Guatemala and elsewhere but these are frequently run as small plantations with a lot of hired labour at harvest time and a sophisticated system of disease control and berry processing to maintain a high quality.

New agricultural exports from Latin America reflect not only changing world demand and prices but also Latin America's low labour cost and climatic advantages over many industrialized countries. Thus, avocado pears, tomatoes and strawberries are all grown intensively in Mexico, largely for export to North America, under conditions closely controlled by US companies; and the highly specialized production of flowers, including orchids, in parts of Central America, and specifically carnations in Colombia, can be expected to spread as air freight services improve their efficiency. Finally, soya beans have assumed major importance in the past decade in Argentina but especially in Brazil. In 1981 the export of soya beans and associated products (cake and oil) from Brazil was worth more than the export of coffee. Soya beans are grown largely on middle-sized and large farms and the processing of the beans is controlled by a small number of mainly foreign companies.

The organization of farming

As with so many aspects of Latin America and the Caribbean, it is the variety of levels of organization that is remarkable in any review of farming in the continent. At one end of the spectrum are large, highly-organized units producing tropical fruit for northern hemisphere markets and at the other are family units producing food crops in addition to hunting and fishing but with only occasional contact with the money economy. We shall identify the main characteristics of the land tenure, labour system and cropping arrangements for three very broad categories of Latin American farm.

Large-scale commercial farms

Certain crops in Latin America, such as sugar, cotton, wheat and bananas, and livestock, such as sheep and cattle, have customarily been produced on properties that have been so large as to need the labour of many people in order to function properly. Although some of these properties were originally created during the colonial period as Spanish families established their power in the New World, the majority were created during the past hundred years by the gradual piecemeal acquisition of land. In many countries such farms occupy 70 per cent of the farmland but employ only 15 per cent of the farm workforce. Such large farms are frequently owned by large corporations (often foreign-based), by the state, or by powerful families who do not live on the property. It is quite common too for the same family or company to own several such properties, maybe in different areas. Not necessarily all of the available land in these units is used for production. Some potentially fertile land may be held in reserve, particularly where the farm has been established where there are few people. Steep slopes and land that is in any way unsuitable for agricultural production are seldom farmed and frequently protected from grazing or tree felling; these measures help check soil erosion and increase the percolation of the soil by rainfall. Frequently, land in these large units is rented to a number of middle-sized farmers who contract their own labour, if necessary, and pay the landowner with a percentage of their crop or in cash. This was a practice much favoured in southern Brazil and Argentina as a means to get land cleared and/or ploughed for the first time and after an initial period tenants handed back the land ready ploughed or planted with coffee trees. In some areas it is customary to give permanent labourers on the estate a plot of land which they can cultivate for their own benefit. As much as half of the estate land may be given over to tiny plots and livestock flocks belonging to the workers. Where land is given as part of the remuneration for labour a range of other services is required besides working on the land and wages are frequently low.

Large-scale farmers produce livestock and crops for national and international markets, have access to credit from banks and from the government and have the ear of agricultural advisers. They thus have the opportunity to know of and to adopt agricultural innovations and are able to acquire funds to invest in improved techniques and to acquire the new equipment that is difficult for smaller farmers to acquire. Where such large farms are producing for an overseas market the quality of the end product must be high; this demands the greatest care with the preparation of the livestock, bananas or coffee, for instance, in order to meet the consumer standards of the northern industrial nations. Further, the packaging and transportation of the product needs care and organization which frequently means either that producer-organizations handle packaging, local and international transport, or that large international

A cattle *estancia* in Argentina

employ. Recent years have witnessed a tendency for the intensification of commercial farming and the establishment of highly capital-intensive farms, not always large in area, producing chickens, pigs, cattle and vegetables in large quantities.

Family farms

Family farms are simply defined as those units that give employment only to the nuclear farm family and where extra labour is only occasionally necessary. The essence of family farming is that it fully supports the family without need to have recourse to work elsewhere. Family farms occupy between a quarter and half of the farmland in Argentina, Colombia and Ecuador and employ a similar proportion of the agricultural force. In areas of Latin America isolated from markets and where it is difficult to buy manufactured goods, family farming is the way of life that can provide for most of a family's needs, with goods sold from the farm in order to buy only essential manufactured goods. Such farming systems may in fact produce specific staples such as wool or livestock but production is essentially for subsistence. These ways of farming presuppose adequate land resources to enable succeeding generations to farm there too. Because of the cost or difficulty of obtaining new seeds, chemical fertilizers etc., subsistence farms grow a range of traditional crops and use organic fertilizers. Where access to markets is easier, a wide range of goods is produced specifically for sale and the variety of items offered for sale in the course of a year helps to minimize the risk of economic crisis. For some cash crops many of the producers are small-scale farmers relying largely on family labour. Coffee, in particular, is often grown by family farmers as the principal means of earning cash, as is tobacco, and both crops benefit from the level of care that can be applied by family farmers. In pioneer areas in the Amazon basin, along the fringes of the Andes, in the new lands of Mexico's gulf coast and in newly settled areas of northern Argentina, family farms predominate in recently colonized areas; within a decade of initial settlement, however, more successful farmers – usually those with most capital resources – have acquired the land of colonists who have left or gone bankrupt and family farms do not always retain their importance in respect of agricultural production although they remain a large proportion of the farms.

Tenure in areas of family farms is varied. In some areas, such as parts of north-east Brazil, many family farms are rented from large, usually absentee, landowners; and the development of grain farming in the humid pampas and coffee in São Paulo was based on the preparation of the land by tenant farmers, most of whom were later displaced. Tenant farming has likewise become less common where some form of land tenure reform has taken place, since tenants are a liability to a large landowner if they cannot easily be replaced. Owner-occupiers predominate amongst family farms even though

companies handle the goods from farm to final market and themselves contract producers to grow what they wish.

In several countries large estates have been acquired by the state as part of a programme of *land reform*. This has happened to sugar estates in Cuba, to cotton and sugar plantations in Peru and to some estates in Mexico. The consequences of the change in ownership and the creation of a new political situation for the labour force have often been profound but production systems have not necessarily changed; the labour force has been better paid though not necessarily more productive. Periodic labour shortages, indeed, have often encouraged mechanization. Where the large estates produced temperate crops and livestock the large units of production have not usually been maintained after agrarian reform, although in Peru after 1968 large cooperative units replaced the big ranches of the highlands. The most dramatic effect of these changes in Cuba has been to increase the range of services available to rural people, in particular education and health care; this has happened to a lesser extent in other countries where effective land reforms have taken place, as in Bolivia and Peru.

For the most part, however, large estates remain important both for the large surpluses they produce, the modern technology that they use and for the relatively small number of people that they many may also farm some land that is rented, or sharecropped.

Although the labour force is basically all members of the family, which includes children of maybe eight years of age and over as well as the very old, at times when extra labour is needed others are employed. In many areas the payment of a daily wage and food is now usual, but exchange labour, where kinsfolk or neighbours help in return for the expectation that such work will be reciprocated, remains important in a number of areas and this serves to reinforce and establish links between members of a land-based community.

Land reforms of one sort or another have not affected family farms since they did not monopolize good land nor did they maintain 'feudal' relations with a clearly identified labour force. Indeed, some land reforms have specifically sought to give security of tenure to family farmers by issuing them with land titles, as in the case of Bolivia.

Smallholdings

Smallholders predominate in many Latin American rural areas. By smallholders is meant farm families whose land provides work for less than two people and some of whose household members are therefore forced to obtain work elsewhere or follow non-agricultural activity at home. In countries such as Guatemala, Ecuador, Peru, Haiti, Jamaica and El Salvador more than three-quarters of all farm families live on smallholdings, usually known as *minifundios*. They subsist on such small farm units because they have a variety of sources of income; farming, even on a small scale, provides a good deal of the food necessary for sustenance and it offers a minimum of security which is denied to landless people. Although smallholdings by our definition cannot provide enough produce to be sold to pay for all the family's basic needs, many different products grown or reared on smallholdings are sold according to the needs of the family and the price in the marketplace. The agricultural system of such farmers is closely geared to security of production for family consumption. Thus, traditional varieties of crops are more likely to be grown than new, potentially more productive ones and a wide range of crops is often grown. In mountain areas farmers may have small, widely separated plots at different ecological levels, producing maybe potatoes and other tubers, maize and beans and sweet potatoes, yucca and sugarcane at different altitudes. Livestock are kept for a variety of purposes so cows are also used to plough, and llamas are pack animals as well as wool producers. Many families have a few chickens, guineapigs, or pigs which can not only be eaten but may also be sold easily in a crisis whereas a ripening crop of bananas or coffee cannot be sold profitably prior to harvest.

Smallholders are reluctant to spend money on agricultural chemicals because it means use of scarce capital, because the chemicals may not prove effective (or even harm the crop) and because it could mean that part of a crop intended to feed the family would have to be sold to pay for the chemicals. By not buying seeds or chemicals or selling the harvest the farmer avoids the pitfalls of the marketplace where prices are determined by external and seemingly incomprehensible factors and where merchants conspire to minimize the return the farmer gets for his labour.

Although there is little need for outside labour on smallholdings, when some members of the family are working far away, labour may need to be hired. Likewise, many smallholdings are subdivided while the owners work and live elsewhere and other smallholders and family farmers rent or sharecrop these small parcels of land. Where the land is not productive it is not even worth renting and may be abandoned, as has happened to hillside land in some Caribbean islands.

Many smallholders in Latin America and the Caribbean are desperately poor but, where they have retained their independence, they are often poor largely in relation to improvements in levels of living elsewhere. The continual subdivision of land through inheritance frequently means a shrinking land base from one generation to another even where out-migration is common. The future of the extensive areas of smallholdings, especially in areas of hill-lands, is therefore uncertain. In some areas land continues to become concentrated in the hands of a few better-off farmers and merchants as a result of indebtedness and the manipulation of economic and social power; but in other areas such as the Guatemala highlands, the western Andes of Venezuela or the central Andes of Ecuador, Peru and Bolivia, the rate of social and economic change has not led to much change in the role of smallholders.

Fishing

For many coastal communities in Latin America fishing is an important activity alongside agriculture and it is engaged in both as a subsistence activity and to earn money. Frequently women and children tend the fields while men fish. Where there are good transport systems, fish and shellfish are sold to merchants who deliver them to the main urban markets. Where lobsters and crayfish are caught the price is such that alternative means of collection are devised to overcome the lack of roads, such as small aeroplanes which can land on the beach at low tide.

As with smallholders and family farmers, the level of technology is frequently low, associated with limited capital resources and the minimization of risk. The boats used are hollowed tree-trunks (canoes), and balsa log rafts powered with paddles or a single sail; such boats do not go far from land. Fishermen are frequently subject to domination by middlemen, especially because alternative means of marketing are difficult given the rapid deterioration of dead fish. They are thus as poor as smallholding farmers even though they derive a living from the land as well as the sea.

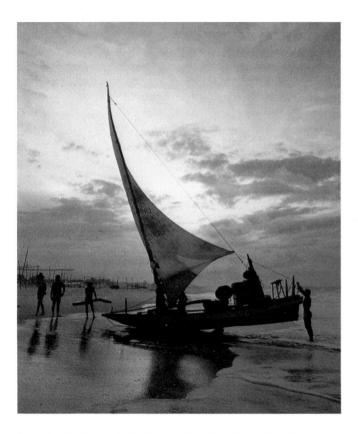

Bringing in *jangada* fishing craft at Fortaleza, Brazil

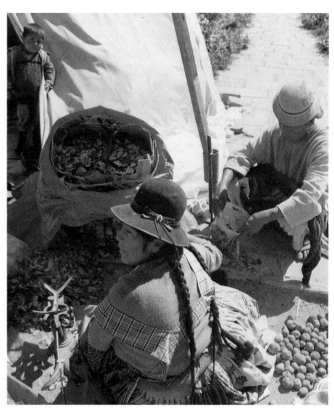

Quechua woman selling new potatoes and coca leaves at Ravelo, Bolivia

Industrial commercial fishing, except in Peru, is city-based and associated with considerable capital investment; it employs a labour force with which factory-style labour relations are maintained. In Peru, until overfishing depleted fish stocks in the 1970s, anchovy fishing for fishmeal caused dozens of small factories and harbours to be established along the coast, in part because of the nuisance caused by the smell and fumes from the processing plants. Fishing on this scale is concerned largely with the export of frozen and tinned fish as well as fishmeal, and northern hemisphere demand for certain seaproducts, such as lobsters and crayfish, encourages the construction of freezing plants near fishing grounds. Whaling and turtle fishing have declined over recent decades.

Marketing

Marketing is an important component of agriculture, even where subsistence farming predominates, for exchange of goods customarily takes place between farmers as well as between farmers and merchants or consumers. Marketplaces are an important part of the rural scene in Latin America, but particularly where the scale of farming is such that there is ample demand for intermediaries to collect small quantities of produce. Marketplaces, however, have a variety of functions and while they serve as centres for peasant exploitation through false weights, unfair prices and physical coercion, they are also important social and political meeting grounds. They have long been regarded by non-farmers, especially by local and regional oligarchies, as potentially dangerous and their foundation and development is frequently politically controlled.

The largest volume of agricultural produce in Latin American rural marketing systems is destined for export, but the marketing structures that are involved are frequently simple and bypass local markets; the bananas, coffee, or livestock are passed directly to national wholesalers who are part of or contracted by international marketing companies, and who grade and export the commodity to the northern industrialized countries. External demands for specific commodities articulated by marketing agencies not only stimulate production but also dictate the nature of the commodity produced.

Many rural Latin American areas have marketing systems that function through periodic markets where many small-scale producers sell goods and buy other items that they do not or cannot produce. The city- and town-based merchants not only collect quantities of farm produce for urban markets but they also sell manufactured goods. Such marketplaces are highly complex systems in which each actor may play several different roles.

A major drawback to rural marketing as far as small farmers are concerned is the extent to which the prices for farm produce rise more slowly than those of manufactured goods and also the large differences in prices at local markets and in cities. In part this is the result of government policy which seeks to minimize the cost of staple foods to the articulate urban proletariat, but it is also a reflection of a labyrinthine market system where multiple middlemen extract profit from dealing with farm produce. The numerous attempts to form cooperatives to overcome this have seldom been successful because of the hostility of merchants, the inadequate training of those who seek to encourage their formation and the deep suspicion with which farmers regard such externally inspired organizations.

Major contemporary trends in farming
Over many areas of Latin America large numbers of rural people are leaving for towns, cities, colonization areas and for other countries. This has led to an actual emptying of the countryside in areas as diverse as highland Colombia and lowland Argentina. Such a trend, which is part of the reduction in the proportion of Latin America's rural population, seems likely to continue and to accelerate. It is not only a consequence of the continuing impoverishment of rural Latin America but also a reflection of the penetration of rural areas by urban value systems which demean the rural farmer and exalt the town dweller. Schooling in rural areas, for example, prepares children for urban employment rather than for rural life.

A series of factors combine to decrease the production of a surplus of food crops and cause increased imports of the necessary goods. On the one hand, market systems do not stimulate commercial production of non-export crops, while, on the other, the middle-sized farmer seldom has access to credit and technical knowledge that is adequate to enccurage him to produce more of the crops that are needed in urban centres. Large-scale producers are increasingly encouraged to produce export crops for which prices are high. International market systems encourage vertical integration which provides the producer with the comfort of advice and security of a contract with an exporter but at the cost of the option to sell elsewhere. Major changes such as the dramatic recent increase in soya-bean production in Argentina, and especially Brazil, and in chickens and eggs, which may be regarded as by-products of maize and soya-bean production, have broadened the range of agricultural products exported from Latin America. Such changes are important because they signify the rise of a new form of agriculture, frequently known as 'agribusiness', in which either multinational or national metropolitan companies invest capital in high-technology farming

of export crops, making use of largely imported technology, cheap labour and often limited investment in land. Thus, Colombia has for a decade been a major exporter of carnations grown expressly for the North American and European market; Mexico exports large quantities of strawberries to the United States, largely during the period of highest prices when Californian fruit is not ready. Perhaps the largest-scale example of agribusiness has been the growth of large cattle ranches in Brazilian Amazonia during the early 1970s when Volkswagen, Armour-Swift and other major multinational companies were encouraged by the Brazilian government to obtain large blocks of land for the creation of cattle farms for the export of meat and meat products to the major population centres in eastern Brazil and to the northern hemisphere. To the overseas investor, Latin American agribusiness may be attractive because of the ready availability of cheap land, low wage rates and the consequent high return of capital invested, such that initial investment is often completely recovered within five years. Finally, the increasing involvement of multinational companies in food-processing industries in Latin America often provides a powerful stimulus to production. Thus, while soya beans in Brazil are grown largely by individual and co-operatives of Brazilian farmers, the milling of the beans is controlled by industrial corporations in which Anderson Clayton, Unilever, Cargill, and Bunge and Born predominate.

The importance of this trend in Latin America agriculture lies less in the land area that is devoted to producing export crops and industrial raw materials than in the priority that governments are thus encouraged to give to a form of farming that enriches very few rural people, usually at the expense of the vast mass of smallholders and family farmers who produce much of the basic food consumed by the working-class majority of urban people.

DAP

Further reading
R. Burbach and P. Flynn, *Agribusiness in the Americas* (New York, 1980)
A. de Janvry, *The Agrarian Question and Reformism in Latin America* (Baltimore, 1981)
A. Pearse, *The Latin American Peasant* (London, 1976)
D. A. Preston, ed., *Environment, Society and Rural Change in Latin America* (Chichester, 1980)

Mining

Mining and the development of Latin America

A Stone Age technology prevailed in Latin America before the arrival of the Europeans. The earliest mining was for non-metallic minerals which, because of their lithology or manner of fracturing, were particularly hard, easy to shape, or take and hold a cutting edge. Such mines were amongst the earliest industrial centres in Latin America. Archaeologists have established that tools fashioned from obsidian mined near the prehistoric metropolis of San Juan Teotihuacán, 40 km north of Mexico City, were traded over established routeways which reached hundreds of kilometres from the mines. An early trade in rock salt was practised in pre-Inca Peru, and continues between the Andes and the Amazonian lowlands of Bolivia today. The art of metallurgy arrived relatively late in the history of Latin America: not until about AD 800 in Mexico and Central America and the Central Andes. Placer gold and native copper were the main metals mined: they were generally cast and worked into ornaments, jewellery and objets d'art, and only in a few places were metals used for tools. Gold became one of the principal items of tribute, moving from the more distant parts of the Aztec and Inca empires to their centres in Tenochtitlán and Cuzco.

The search for precious metals and their sources was one of the main driving forces behind the Spanish and, to a lesser degree, the Portuguese exploration of the Americas. The gold ornaments on the Indians seen by Columbus on his voyage of discovery in 1492 meant that when he returned the following year he brought artisans and miners to work the alluvial gold fields of Hispaniola. The discovery of other gold fields in the Antilles quickly followed and slaving expeditions scoured the Caribbean to meet the new demand for labour. After 1513 attention shifted to the Spanish Main. In 1519 the treasury of the Aztecs fell to Cortés and, in 1533, that of the Incas to Pizarro: they disgorged the results of years of mining and provided the first of many huge shipments of precious metals from the New World to the Old. The conquistadors were quick to trace the gold to its sources, often enduring astonishing hardship in the process, and to marshall the local Indians to accelerate production. The sources were natural accumulations of alluvial gold and once one reach was exhausted the search for other new placers was resumed. Early colonial mining was thus a transient occupation which encouraged the rapid exploration of the continent but left a mark on the landscape which quickly faded. But in the middle of the sixteenth century the nature and locus of mining in colonial America changed. Silver ingots smelted from ores mined underground began to rival in value the gold bullion forged from native gold panned from the streams: many of the underground mines tapped sufficiently large reserves of ore to survive for centuries.

The great silver strikes began in Mexico with those at Zacatecas and Guanajuato in the 1540s, and were succeeded by others at Pachuca, San Luis Potosí and elsewhere. In 1545 the first silver vein threading the Cerro Rico de Potosí in Upper Peru (now Bolivia) was discovered: Potosí is close to the Inca mines at Porco. Fresh discoveries quickly followed and Potosí became for a time the richest and most populous city in the Americas. By 1560 exports of silver from Latin America outvalued those of gold and accounted for half of the value of goods leaving the continent. They continued to rise, and between 1570 and 1620 Potosí alone produced half of the world's silver. The perfection in 1571 of the amalgamation process, in which mercury was used to separate silver from its ore, gave value to the leaner deposits of silver and meant that the only major mercury mine in Latin America, at Huancavelica, 1200 km from Potosí, assumed enormous strategic importance. It became a state enterprise in an attempt to guarantee to the Spanish crown the royal fifth share of all precious metals mined in the empire. The mines of America underpinned Spain's new position as a world power. At a local level the demand for labour drew people to the mines – either Indians drafted under the *mita* (forced labour) system as in Upper Peru or free labour as in northern Mexico – and created systems of communication and administration which became fixtures in the fabric of the continent. The new towns became markets for the food and clothing consumed by the miners and the tools and draught animals needed for the mines. In Mexico oases of irrigated agriculture, employing hydraulic techniques not dissimilar to those employed in some mines, grew up around the mines; mining in Upper Peru stimulated suppliers as far away as the area now known as north-west Argentina. Such dependent economies have often outlived the mining economies they were born to serve.

During the seventeenth and eighteenth centuries Mexico overtook Upper Peru to become the pre-eminent mining area of the continent: the exhaustion of the Huancavelica mercury mine emphasized the costly remoteness of the silver mines of the High Andes and epidemics made mine labour scarce, whereas in Mexico production doubled in the eighteenth century. Meanwhile, the Portuguese in Brazil began to find the mineral riches they had searched for in vain for two centuries. In the 1690s Paulista *bandeirantes* found the first traces of the placer gold which quickly led to their discovery of the mother lode at Ouro Prêto (Black Gold) and the drilling of what was to become the biggest gold mine in South America. This stimulated the first of many gold rushes into the interior and a variety of mines were opened up in Minas Gerais (General Mines), Goias, Cuiaba and Mato Grosso. The supply routes to the mines helped to forge links between the north-east, the centre and the south of Brazil, links which withstood the strains of independence. It was profits earned from mining which helped finance the early coffee economy of the country. Indeed, the role of mining profits in the development of colonial Latin America can easily be underestimated: although in the early days most of the wealth generated by the mines was shipped across the Atlantic, by the eighteenth century it is probable that more of the profits were staying in Latin America than leaving it. Mining was the only important source of domestic capital and it was this that largely supported the import trade in consumer goods.

Spain, and to a lesser extent Portugal, tried to restrict the trade in mining products, as in other staples, to designated ports and routes. The weakening hold on the colonies in the eighteenth and early nineteenth centuries led to a relaxation of those restrictions to the benefit of the mineowners and the landed classes (and to the loss of the smugglers), and the trend was continued when the same classes came to political power with the independence of most of Latin America in the 1820s. The new countries committed themselves to more open trading policies. By this time mining was in relative decline – in Mexico silver accounted for only 15 per cent of the gross domestic product – and the plantations were supplying the more important export staples. But mining in Latin America was revitalized in the second half of the nineteenth century. Three circumstances contributed to this change: there was a growing industrial demand for non-ferrous minerals in Britain, Western Europe and the United States; the costs of transport were significantly reduced by the steamship and the railway, effectively creating a revaluation of Latin American mineral reserves; and the young Latin American countries welcomed capital and technology for mining from overseas as one way of both realigning political ties and of building a larger national economy. Mining was particularly encouraged in Mexico, Chile, Peru and Bolivia. Steam power and, later, electricity were harnessed to the new mine machinery and the experience of other mining fields around the world, for example, Cornwall and the western United States, was brought to bear upon the problems of exploiting Latin America's minerals. Roads and railways, ports and mining camps were built to expedite the flow of minerals and mining profits from Latin America to the industrialized world. In places the new mines lay beyond the frontiers of settlement and gave value to lands previously held in little regard. The northern Atacama Desert was one such barren area: here the nitrate industry was built up by British and German (as well as Chilean) capital particularly after the War of the Pacific in 1879–83 had established Chilean control. Elsewhere a distinctive geographical dualism was created with mines, railways and ports forming the long axis of an island of modernity in a sea of tradition, almost a foreign beachhead in an alien continent, with little exchange between the one and the other.

The laissez-faire attitude of Latin American governments to mining was jolted by the domestic consequences of the Great Depression of 1929: the shuddering fall in the prices and volume of exports of Latin American minerals in the 1930s devastated the modern sector of national economies dependent upon their share of the earnings from mineral exports. Chile was worst hit. The absence during the Second World War of a return flow of manufactured goods for minerals now in demand stimulated governments and individuals to promote local manufacturing and the diversion of domestic capital away from the mining industry. And even when peace returned, and brought with it an extremely high demand for minerals, Latin American countries felt that the controlled prices offered by the consuming countries (whose companies frequently owned the mines in Latin America) were debased by free-market standards and that Latin America was not getting a fair deal. Latin American governments began to adopt a more purposeful policy towards mining.

Since 1950 the state has begun to exercise more control over the mining industries of Latin America and today the continent is unusual in the degree of state involvement in mining. In some countries this has meant outright nationalization of all or significant parts of the industry. This occurred in Bolivia (1952), Cuba (1959–60), Chile (1971), Guyana (1971), Peru (1973) and Nicaragua (in 1979). Elsewhere the state or national private companies and individuals have negotiated majority holdings in existing mining enterprises: this has been the policy in, for example, Mexico, Brazil, Venezuela and Jamaica. The high degree of foreign involvement in the mining industries of Latin America gave such moves much popular support. By 1980 there was no country in Latin America where foreign capital effectively controlled output. In some countries these moves have deprived the mines of access to the capital, expertise and markets commanded by the erstwhile owners, frequently companies of international stature. And state ownership may have invested nationalized mining industries with some of the instability associated, rightly or wrongly, with the governments of Latin America. On the other hand, a growing accommodation between the interests of the international mining houses and those countries anxious to extract the maximum profit from the export of their mineral resources could be detected in the late 1970s and early 1980s. Joint development agreements have been particularly important in Brazil. The state has intervened in mining in another way, albeit an indirect one, in most Latin American countries since 1950. By deliberately fostering the growth of domestic manufacturing, through fiscal and other means, the relative attractiveness of overseas investment in the mining sector has been much reduced. It is true that in many countries this policy led to the establishment of a metallurgical industry as part of a politically inspired desire to provide forward linkages for the mining industry, and so integrate mining more closely with the national economy and to erode further the traditional and subservient role of Latin American countries as exporters of raw materials and importers of finished goods. But, whereas most manufacturing activity remains in private hands, most smelting, refining and metal-processing activities are state enterprises and effectively tie the mining industry more closely to the state.

Modern mining, like a modern metallurgical industry, is increasingly capital-intensive. Many of the developments in mining in Latin America during the second half of the twentieth century have been in the bulk-mining of low-value minerals using highly mechanized techniques: such projects usually require a heavy investment on development work and on infrastructure before they become productive and their economic feasibility is gauged upon a long-term view of operations. Success in floating new mining projects in Latin America is increasingly dependent upon the credit-worthiness of the state, for it is the state which is increasingly asked to act as guarantor by the international banking community: the inherent qualities of individual mineral deposits may be a factor of less importance. Oil-rich states with seemingly stable governments, such as Mexico and Venezuela, attracted significant new mining development in the early 1980s; the financial crisis which struck in 1982 deterred some new overseas investors but gave mineral production for export an enhanced attractiveness.

The situation in the 1980s

Latin America was responsible for about one-eighth of the value of all non-fuel minerals produced in the world in the early 1980s. Latin America's mines produced then about a quarter of the world's antimony and silver, one-sixth of its tin and copper, one-eighth of its iron ore, zinc, bauxite and molybdenum, and one-tenth of its tantalum, tungsten, and lead. The contribution of mining (excluding that of fuels) to the gross domestic product of the region has been declining. At the beginning of the 1980s it was a little below 2.5 per cent, in the 1970s it averaged about 3 per cent and in the 1960s about 4 per cent. Mining accounted for about 8 per cent of the continent's industrial activity in 1980 and gave direct employment to about half a million people or about 1 per cent of the total workforce.

Copper has been the most important mineral mined in Latin America during the twentieth century. In 1979 it accounted for approximately 40 per cent of the value of all metallic ores produced in Latin America. *Iron ore* accounted for about 27 per cent and was growing in relative importance. Together they represented two-thirds of the value of mine output. *Silver* (6 per cent) and *zinc* (6 per cent) were next in value, followed by *bauxite* (4 per cent) and *gold* (4 per cent) and *lead* (3 per cent) and *tin* (3 per cent). This pattern is likely to be maintained: a world survey published by the *Engineering and Mining Journal* in 1980 showed that half of the capital expected to be invested in metal mining in Central and South America during the following five years was for copper, half the remainder for aluminium and half of the residual quarter for iron ore – the three most widely used metals.

Most metals mined in Latin America are still destined for export, and metals make a larger contribution to the external trade of Latin America than they do to its internal economy. They represented

Table 2. Significant production of selected minerals and metals in Latin America, 1983
(thousand metric tons)

Selected countries	Bauxite	Aluminium	Copper	Lead	Zinc	Tin	Gold	Silver	Iron ore	Steel, crude
							(tonnes)			
Argentina	—	126	—	34	—	—	—	—	600	2 940
Bolivia	—	—	—	15	42	25	—	—	—	—
Brazil	4 200	402	—	31	73	13	51	—	92 000	14 660
Chile	—	—	1 257	—	—	—	20	—	5 100	609
Colombia	—	—	—	—	—	—	18	—	—	469
Cuba[e]	—	—	—	—	—	—	—	—	—	330[e]
Dominican Republic	—	—	—	—	—	—	11	—	—	—
Guyana	1 000	—	—	—	—	—	—	—	—	—
Jamaica	7 300	—	—	—	—	—	—	—	—	—
Mexico	—	43	193	172	241	—	—	1 770	8 200	6 969
Peru	—	—	317	207	560	—	—	1 720	4 500	291
Surinam	2 000	64	—	—	—	—	—	—	—	222
Venezuela	—	343	—	—	—	—	—	—	9 200	2 318
Total Latin America	14 500	942	1 809	468	998	38	134[e]	4000[e]	120 500	28 957
% of world	22	8	29	19	21	22	12	40	16	7

[e] Estimated.
Source: *Mining Annual Review* (1984).

about one-seventh of the non-petroleum trade of the region in 1980. Copper (3.4 per cent of the total trade in 1980) was the third export staple of the continent after petroleum (25.5 per cent) and coffee (8.2 per cent); iron ore (1.6 per cent) occupied sixth place and bauxite (0.6 per cent) eleventh place.

The mining industry of Latin America is based upon a relatively restricted portfolio of minerals and these are unevenly distributed over the continent. The major copper ore bodies are found on the western slopes of the Andes in central and northern Chile and southern and central Peru, and in north-western Mexico where they form an extension of those in Arizona and Utah. They are of the porphyry type – deposits in which the copper is disseminated widely and more or less uniformly, oxidized near the surface and the deeper deposits sulphides. Iron ore deposits are more widespread. They include ancient sedimentary 'iron formations', often several hundred metres thick, in which local enrichment to create high-grade (50–55 per cent Fe content) ores has taken place to produce residual ores which are earthy in texture: most of the iron ore mined in Brazil and Venezuela and some in Mexico is of this nature. Another set of deposits is of igneous origin: concentrations of magnetite which have replaced other rocks in the contact zones of metamorphic activity. Deposits of this type are typical of western South America and Mexico – the Marcona deposit in Peru is a good example. The bauxite ores resemble in origin the sedimentary iron ores with aluminium taking the place of iron: the Caribbean islands and the north-eastern quadrant of South America – Venezuela, the Guianas and Brazil – have the main reserves. Primary tin deposits of any size are restricted to veins which thread the high eastern Andes of Bolivia; alluvial and eluvial deposits occur in adjoining Brazil. Zinc, lead and silver are often associated either in veins or disseminated amongst limestone or similar deposits: Mexico and Peru are the leading producers.

This uneven distribution means that the mining industry is highly significant in the economic life of some countries and insignificant in others. The leading mining country is undoubtedly Chile. In 1980 it ranked sixth in the world table of major mineral producers. Peru (tenth place), Brazil (eleventh) and Mexico (twelfth) were very much on a par as were Venezuela (twenty-fourth) and Bolivia (twenty-fifth). The importance of mining in Chile is underlined when allowance is made for population and size. The per-capita income derived from mining of the average Chilean is comparable to that of the average South African or Australian: it is three times that of the average Peruvian or Bolivian, six times that of the average Venezuelan, twelve times that of the Mexican and twenty times that of the Brazilian. Amongst the smaller countries mining was worth about $130 to the average Jamaican in 1977, a figure only a little below the Chilean figure, and $90 to the Guyanese, more than to the average Peruvian or Bolivian. There is a

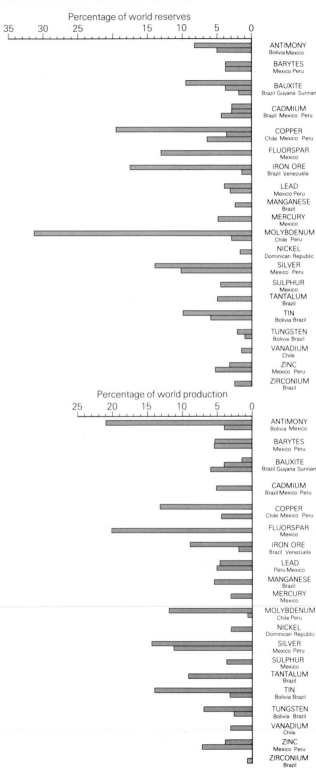

IMPORTANT NON–FUEL MINERALS (1980)

Percentage of world reserves

IMPORTANT PRODUCERS OF NON–FUEL MINERALS (1973)

Source: J. Sideri and S. Johns 1980

Mining

SHARE OF MINING AND QUARRYING IN THE GNP OF SELECTED COUNTRIES (1976)

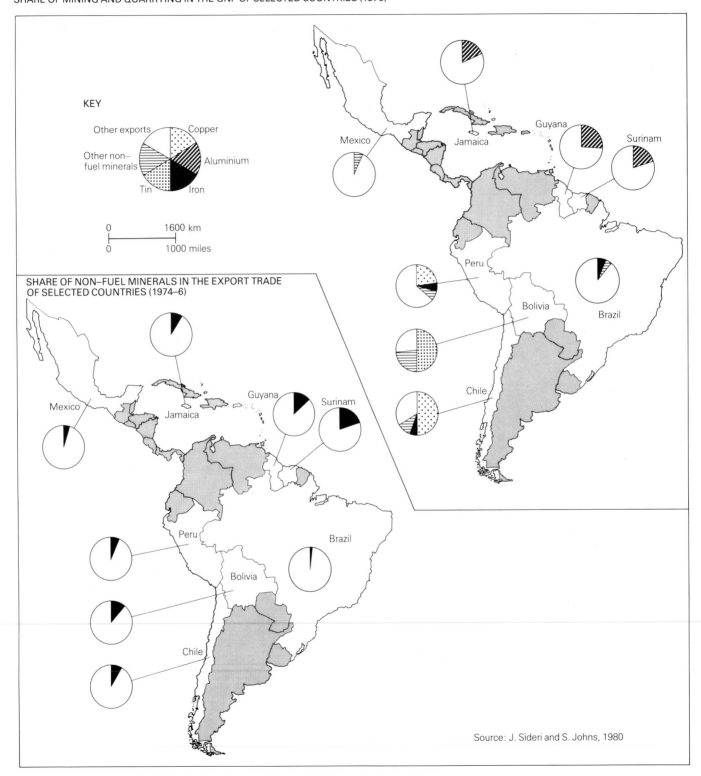

KEY

Other exports — Copper
Other non-fuel minerals — Aluminium
Tin — Iron

0   1600 km
0   1000 miles

SHARE OF NON–FUEL MINERALS IN THE EXPORT TRADE
OF SELECTED COUNTRIES (1974–6)

Source: J. Sideri and S. Johns, 1980

similar variation in the degree of dependency of the export trade upon the trade in minerals. Bolivia depends for two-thirds of its legitimate overseas earnings upon exports from mines and smelters. For Chile, without a drug trade, the fraction is half; for Guyana and Peru about one-sixth; and for Jamaica and Surinam about one-sixth. Nowhere else does the trade in non-fuel minerals remain a significant fraction of the national total, although in absolute terms and locally it may be highly important. For example, the value of Venezuela's mineral exports (excluding petroleum) is greater than that of Guyana and the Caribbean islands put together.

Mining in Chile

In 1983 Chile was the largest copper producer in the world, with an output of 1.26 million tonnes or 20 per cent of the non-Communist world's total. Production is rising: it first reached the million mark in 1976, having passed the half-million figure in the late 1950s and reached the quarter-million level in the late 1920s. There have been two phases to the copper industry in Chile. In the 1860s Chilean copper mines in the area known as Norte Chico on the western flanks of the Andes were meeting one-third of the rising world demand for copper: the mines were numerous and small; they worked veins of copper oxide and employed techniques of surface and underground mining inherited, like many of the miners, from the failing silver mines of Bolivia. Little capital, and that mainly local, was employed and mines were readily abandoned when the copper price fell or the boom in nitrates created more attractive opportunities elsewhere. Between 1890 and 1920 nitrates temporarily replaced copper as the export staple of the country and foreign capital displaced local capital in the Chilean mining industry. The new, twentieth-century Chilean copper industry is very different from the old. It relies on the bulk mining of relatively low-grade ores using techniques and capital originally derived from experience gained in the copper fields of the western United States. El Teniente, south-east of Santiago, was the first of the big mines to be developed (by the Kennecott Copper Company): the ore permeates a vitrified volcanic plug and the mine remains the largest underground copper mine in the world. In 1983, seventy years after entering regular production, it yielded 305,000 tonnes of copper, one-quarter of the national total, and had reserves of 20 million tonnes of copper in ore grading 1.54 per cent. In 1911 an even larger deposit was recognized at Chuquicamata, close to the Antofagasta and Bolivian railway on the edge of the Atacama Desert, and in 1916 the first excavations began of what was to become the world's largest open-pit copper mine. The pit is now over 350 m deep. It continues to be responsible for half Chile's copper output – Chuquicamata produced 559,000 tonnes in 1983 – and has enormous reserves left (1980: 25.4 million tonnes of copper in ore grading 2.13 per cent copper content). Anaconda, who opened up Chuquicamata, also

Chuquicamata open-cast copper mine, Chile

developed a third great mine at Potrerillos, 300 km to the south, extended in 1959 to the adjoining El Salvador ore body. El Salvador (1983: production 81,000 tonnes, reserves 8.6 million of 1.37 per cent ore) and not far from El Teniente a new mine, Andina (1983: 61,000 tonnes, 5 million tonnes of reserves of 1.25 per cent quality), account for half the remaining output of the country. The rest comes from about fifty medium-sized commercial mines, some with their own refineries, employing about 10,000 people and working more localized and richer deposits, and about 2000 small mines often worked intermittently. The ample reserves of the big four mines represent only 60 per cent of the 100 million tonnes that exist and give some credence to the Chilean regime's intention that, subject to demand, annual output could reach 2 million tonnes by 1990.

The scale of the Chilean copper industry has endowed it with particular political importance. Prior to 1955 the political arguments were mainly aimed at ensuring that Chile received a fair share of the return from a national resource which would clearly not last for ever. The share of the earnings from copper remaining in the country rose from about one-third in the late 1920s, to one-half a decade later, to over two-thirds in 1950 (a proportion high enough to damp down the flow of new overseas investment in Chile). From 1955 the policy changed to one of gaining more state control over the big mines: in the 1960s the big three mines accounted for over 80 per cent of Chile's copper production and consequently a very substantial part of the 8 per cent of the gross domestic product, 60 per cent of the value of exports and 80 per cent of government tax receipts contributed by copper to the national economy. In the late 1960s the state acquired a majority holding of the Chilean assets of Anaconda and Kennecott and an agreement, under threat of outright nationalization, of expanded investment and increased refining capacity. In 1971 the Popular Unity government of President Allende nationalized the three big mines and two others (Exótica near Chuquicamata, and Andina). After the overthrow of Allende in 1973, agreement was reached with the US copper companies indemnifying them against the results of nationalization, and they have returned to the country, but not to regain ownership of the big mines which since 1976 have been run by the state Corporación del Cobre de Chile (CODELCO). Similarly, all refining capacity in the country is in the hands of the state corporation ENAMI. Changes in the mining law in 1983–4 may, however, open the way to heightened foreign involvement in Chilean mining.

Other mining activity in Chile plays second fiddle to copper but is nonetheless significant. The continued extraction of evaporites – potassium and sodium nitrates, lithium and borax – from the Atacama region is, perhaps historically, the most interesting. As a by-product of copper mining Chile produced in 1983 15,264 tonnes or 33 per cent of the non-Communist world total of molybdenum, making Chuquicamata the world's single largest supplier. Chile is also an important producer of iron ore. Most of the mines are open-pit workings in the northern third of the country: El Romeral is currently responsible for half the national production, 80 per cent of which is exported.

Mining in Peru

Cerro de Pasco is the name most widely associated with mining in modern Peru. It housed one of the great silver mines of the continent until the end of the nineteenth century: since then the hill has been mined away and interest has shifted to the lead and zinc ores associated with the silver to the east and the copper associated with the silver mineralization to the south. Both underground and open-pit methods are used. The mixed ores are smelted at La Oroya with little concentration and at relatively low cost. Peru is the largest source of lead and zinc ores in Latin America and occupies fourth and third positions in the world in deposits of these minerals. Peru is lower down in the tables of metal production: only a little under one-third of both its lead and its zinc is smelted in Peru. Most of its lead, zinc and silver comes from mines in the Central Sierra, most of its copper, iron ore and gold comes from the south. The modern importance of copper in Peru begins in 1960 when the first shipments of ore began from the Toquepala deposits. Toquepala was

joined by Cuajone in the 1970s, and together these two open-pits produced 261,000 tonnes of copper concentrates (212,000 tonnes of blister copper) or two-thirds of the country's entire copper output (333,000 tonnes) in 1983. There are many other smaller copper deposits in the Andes, leaner (0.9–1.1 per cent copper content) than those of Chile, and national reserves were calculated at 27 million tonnes in 1977. Marcona, the major iron ore mine, is situated inland from San Juan and modern machinery excavates an enormous ore body with surface dimensions of 20 × 5 km. The development of the mine was coupled with the building of a small steelworks at Chimbote and financed by mainly American capital. Until the early 1970s three, all essentially American, companies – Southern Peru Corporation (in which ASARCO was a major shareholder), Cerro de Pasco Corporation and the Marcona Mining Corporation – controlled three-quarters of Peru's mining output, and a further 10 per cent came from medium mines which were foreign owned. In the 1970s the assets of the big three were nationalized and negotiated settlements reached. Today the state-owned Companía Minero del Centro (Centromín) runs the big mines and the Empresa Minera del Peru (Mineroperú) acts as the main purchasing and mining development agency.

Mining in Bolivia

Mining in Bolivia offers many contrasts with that elsewhere in Latin America. Tin is the most important mineral mined. It is found in veins associated with the granite batholiths which core the eastern Andes. Most tin mines are above the 4000 m contour line and some above the permanent snowline; the rarefied atmosphere affects the efficiency of men and machines. The mountains are arid and treeless; water and fuel for the mines are expensive and most mines are difficult of access. The veins are narrow, few exceed 10 cm, and even the selective underground mining methods employed yield ores averaging no more than 1 per cent tin. Half of the tin is lost in the concentration process and even then the concentrates shipped to the smelter at Oruro are of only moderate (40 per cent tin content) grade. In general the mines are poorly equipped and economically marginal. The mines are labour-intensive, wage rates are low and money for mining equipment and development scarce. Cataví, which for most of the twentieth century was the largest tin mine not only in Bolivia but in the world, mines less material in a year than Chile's Chuquicamata mine moves in a week; yet Cataví's labour force (4600 in 1980) is similar to that of Chuquicamata. Two-thirds of the tin produced by Bolivia and two-thirds of its mineral production comes from a dozen larger mines which were the property of the Patiño, Aramayo and Hochschild interests until nationalized in 1952 when they were amalgamated under the state mining corporation COMIBOL. The mines have suffered from lack of investment and expertise and were over their most productive

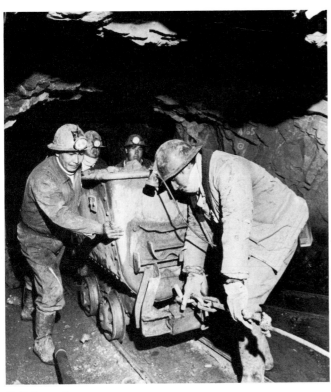

Bolivian miners

in 1983 or one-fifth of the total produced in the non-Communist world), and the famous colonial mining cities of Guanajuato and Fresnillo in Zacatecas remain foci for the industry today. Las Torres mine near Guanajuato was the largest silver mine in the world in 1982 but was challenged for that pre-eminent position when the Real de Angeles open-pit silver-lead-zinc mine came fully into production in 1983. Most of Mexico's silver is mined as a by-product of the older non-ferrous metals and it is these that have superseded silver in economic importance in Mexico during the twentieth century: copper was the most valuable until 1930, lead until 1950 and zinc since 1950. In 1983, Mexico occupied tenth place in world copper production, sixth in lead and sixth in zinc. But when the new La Caridad copper mine near Cananea comes into production it will be Mexico's largest copper mine and may raise Mexico to sixth place in the world copper stakes. Most of Mexico's copper comes from great open-pit workings in the north-west where two mines, Cananea (with 1700 million tonnes of copper reserves in ore grading 0.75 per cent Cu, or half those in Mexico) and Nacozari, are responsible for 40–45 per cent of the national copper output. Almost two-thirds of Mexico's lead and zinc comes from mines in Chihuahua where opencast working is increasing and underground mining in decline. Durango, Coahuila, Zacateças, Baja California Sur and San Luis Potosí are the other leading metallic mining states. Local iron ore reserves at Las Truchas and Peña Colorado in the Colima–Michoacán–Guerrero coastal regions have recently been developed to provide the core of the Lázaro Cárdenas iron-and-steel complex at the mouth of the Rio Balsas. Mexico also ranks second in world bismuth production, third in mercury and antimony, and fourth in arsenic.

Many of the older mines were developed by foreign – British and latterly US – capital. But since 1961 a policy of progressive Mexicanization has been pursued with the consequence that by 1980 48 per cent of the capital invested in the Mexican mining industry was drawn from private Mexican sources and 15 per cent from Mexican public funds; the remaining 37 per cent was from overseas sources. The nationalization of all private banks in 1982 meant that their shares in mining companies became state property; thus, Minera Real de Angeles, previously owned in equal portions by banking interest, the government and Frisco, came under majority government control. Several large Mexican mining houses have emerged and three – Peñoles, Industrial Minera Mexicana (IMMSA), and Minera Frisco – account for 60 per cent of the private domestic capital in Mexican mining. The state Mining Development Commission (CFM) is increasingly active in encouraging and initiating mining developments and the state has a majority share of the production of sulphur (100 per cent), silver (53 per cent), copper (65 per cent), manganese (88 per cent) and iron (58 per cent).

phases when nationalized. They include Huanuni and San José near Oruro; the Quechisla group in the south which produces lead, zinc, bismuth and silver, as well as tin; the Cerro Rico de Potosí, and others nearer La Paz. There is a second tier of small commercial mines under private ownership: these include significant wolfram workings, the Porco lead and zinc mines, and two tin dredges. The majority of miners (say 25,000) are peasant-miners, working individual concessions or on co-operative holdings as an adjunct to farming. Their methods are primitive and their lives appallingly deprived. They include those who pan the Tipuani River for gold.

Bolivia's dependence on tin (40 per cent of its export earnings 1976–83) is doubly unfortunate because the world market for tin is anticipated to grow at a lower annual rate (1.3 per cent) than that of any other major metal and Bolivia is a high-cost producer. It is compounded by Bolivia's decision, implemented in the 1970s, to spend scarce capital on smelting facilities. This was a political gesture as much as an economic investment. In the 1980s there is some doubt as to whether Bolivia will be able to produce enough feed for its smelters to keep them in operation.

Mining in Mexico

Mexico remains the world's leading producer of silver (1900 tonnes

Mining in Brazil

In 1983 Brazil (99 million tonnes) was second to the USSR (245 million tonnes) as a world producer of iron ore, and second to Australia (72 million tonnes) as a supplier to the world trade in iron ore. It was following the Second World War that Brazil, reversing an earlier policy of conserving its natural resources, adopted a policy of creating a domestic iron-and-steel industry on the back of an export trade in iron ore. Development was put in the hands of the government-owned Companhia Vale do Rio Doce (CVRD) and the deposits of the so-called Iron Quadrangle, south and east of Belo Horizonte in Minas Gerais, were attacked. Open-cast mines were dug and a railway built to the coast. The new port of Tubarão, near Vitoria, was opened in 1966: it is one of the few ports in the world capable of handling 250,000 tonne ore-carriers and in 1982 shipped 57 million tonnes of ore. During the 1970s work began on developing a second major iron ore deposit, at the Serra dos Carajás situated in Pará state to be linked by rail to a sea terminal at Ponta da Madeira near São Luiz in Maranhão; in 1977 US Steel withdrew from what was to have been a joint development, while the subsequent fall in demand for iron ore as a result of world recession and restriction on capital expenditure slowed the anticipated pace of development with production unlikely to begin until 1986. This is part of a more grandiose scheme – the Grand Carajás Project – in which mining is to underwrite the creation of a regional growth pole by constructing a basic infrastructure. In phase one, over $8 billion is to be spent developing not only iron ore mines but pig iron plants, bauxite mines and alumina and aluminium refineries, and exploiting local copper (1000 million tonnes of low-grade, 0.5–1.0 per cent, nickel-rich copper ores have been discovered), manganese, nickel, gold and tin deposits. Phase two will cost $19 billion. Agriculture, forestry and cattle raising will supplement mining. The railway from Carajás to Ponta da Madeira, the river ports of Barcarena and Itaqui (capable of taking ocean-going bulk carriers) and the hydro-electric resources of the Tocantin River are key elements in this development. An initial output of 10 million tonnes of iron ore is expected in 1986 and perhaps 35 million tonnes in 1990. Output of bauxite from the nearby Trombetas deposits, discovered by the Aluminum Company of Canada in 1966, began in 1979; in 1983 3.4 million tonnes were produced. The operating company Mineração Rio do Norte (in which CVRD has a 46 per cent interest and Alcan 24 per cent) has plans to expand output to 6.7 million tonnes. The mining of bauxite and the production of alumina are recent growth areas in the Brazilian economy: Amazonia alone has estimated reserves of 4000 million tonnes and cheap hydroelectric power potential. Manganese ore is another recent product of Amazonia with the major source to date being the mines inland from Santana in Amapá Territory; large reserves exist at Urucum near Corumbá in Mato Grosso. Brazil produces over 90 per cent of the world's niobium, used in alloy steels, from an open-pit mine at Araxa in Minas Gerais; a pilot plant began producing metal for market evaluation in 1983. Brazil has become a major, cheap producer of tin ore. Superficial deposits were discovered in Rondônia in the late 1960s and there was an invasion of prospectors, but emphasis recently has switched to Manaus and Goias state and to mechanical working. The national mining houses are also taking over from the individual *garimpeiro* (prospector) in the new gold fields of the Serra Pelada. Although Brazil is a significant producer of phosphates, it has not yet met its 1970 target of becoming self-sufficient in fertilizers.

Mining in Venezuela

Mining interest in Venezuela focuses on the iron mines of the middle Orinoco valley. In 1981 proven reserves of iron ore with an iron content of at least 55 per cent were 2116 million tonnes and production (12.2 million tonnes in 1982, 10.9 million tonnes in 1983) is expected to rise substantially in 1985 when the new San Isidro mine begins producing. The major mine is a huge open-cast working at Cerro Bolívar and a second is El Pao. The deposits were found in 1943–4 and developed by US steel companies to supplement declining supplies of domestic ore. Railways link the mines to Ciudad Guayana on the Orinoco, a new town (population 300,000 in 1980) built both to serve the mines and act as a regional growth centre. It now serves the newly built Matanzas iron-and-steel plant and is the site of an alumina plant, reducing bauxite mined 700 km upstream. Tributaries of the river have been harnessed for hydro-electric power and the main river dredged to take barges downstream to the bulk ore-carriers. Transshipment makes Venezuelan ore significantly more costly than Brazilian ore. The iron mines and processing plants are now, since 1975, in domestic ownership but many joint mining ventures with US steel firms are in hand. 1983 saw the first production of alumina from the new Interalumina refinery in Ciudad Guayana, a refinery financed almost entirely (88.75 per cent) by domestic funds. Initially the refinery is smelting imported ore, but following the development by the state-owned Venezuelan Investment Fund of the Los Pijiguaos bauxite deposits in the western part of Bolívar state it is expected that between one and three million tonnes will be produced from local ores by 1986.

Mining in Jamaica, Surinam and Guyana

Jamaica, Surinam and Guyana were the source of one-sixth of the western world's bauxite production of 65.2 million tonnes in 1983, a quarter (of 80.8 million) in 1980 and one-third (of 50.7 million) in 1970. The Caribbean bauxite industry has suffered recently because of the relatively high energy costs of the natural gas used by US Gulf Coast aluminium smelters, the main market for bauxite from the

Table 5. Population, total and manufacturing gross domestic product, level of industrialization, industrial weight within the region and per-capita manufacturing GDP, 1978

	Population thousands of inhabitants	GDP millions of 1970 dollars	Manufacturing GDP millions of 1970 dollars	Level of industrialization (manuf'g GDP as % of GDP)	Industrial weight within the region (%)	per-capita manufacturing GDP (1970 prices)
Large countries	*184 898*	*170 140*	*48 172*	*28*	*62.4*	*261*
Brazil	119 477	101 056	30 327	30	39.3	254
Mexico	65 421	69 084	17 845	26	23.1	273
Andean Pact (incl. Chile)	*83 394*	*66 662*	*13 132*	*20*	*17.0*	*158*
Bolivia	5 848	2 072	325	16	0.4	56
Chile	10 843	10 335	2 451	24	3.2	226
Colombia	28 424	19 162	3 384	18	4.4	119
Ecuador	7 798	4 434	905	20	1.2	116
Peru	17 148	10 323	2 554	25	3.3	149
Venezuela	13 333	20 336	3 513	17	4.5	264
CACM (incl. Panama)	*21 002*	*12 279*	*2 198*	*18*	*2.8*	*105*
Costa Rica	2 111	2 031	461	23	0.6	218
El Salvador	4 524	2 238	436	19	0.6	96
Guatemala	6 623	3 783	617	16	0.8	93
Honduras	3 362	1 166	185	16	0.2	55
Nicaragua	2 559	1 195	238	20	0.3	93
Panama	1 823	1 866	261	14	0.3	143
River Plate countries	*32 490*	*43 042*	*13 761*	*32*	*17.8*	*424*
Argentina	26 395	38 011	12 512	33	16.2	474
Paraguay	2 888	1 553	250	16	0.3	87
Uruguay	3 207	3 478	999	29	1.3	312
Total Latin America	*321 784*	*292 123*	*77 263*	*26*	*100.0*	*240*

Source: ECLA.

ment decline of 28 per cent between 1974 and 1978, and the food-processing and paper sectors recording employment increases of 6 per cent for the period. Less accentuated trends have been taking place in Peru and Colombia where 30 per cent tariff levels are favoured, and even Venezuela and Argentina have been making efforts at reducing levels of protection.

The record of Latin American industrialization in the predominantly import substituting period of 1950 to 1978 is summarized in tables 4 to 6. The association of manufacturing strength with the larger countries of Latin America has become considerably accentuated during the period. In 1950, Brazil and Mexico were responsible for only 42.1 per cent of manufacturing Gross Domestic Product on the continent. By 1978, however, with populations of 120 and 65 million respectively (55.4 per cent of the continental total), 62.4 per cent of Latin America's manufacturing GDP was generated by the two largest countries. Notwithstanding the formation of the Andean Pact, its member countries registered a relative decline in manufacturing GDP from 20 per cent of the Latin American total in 1950 to 17 per cent in 1978; only the two OPEC countries (Venezuela and Ecuador) managed to increase their industrial weight within the region. But the largest relative decline hit the River Plate countries whose industrial weighting within the

Table 6. Growth rates of the population and the manufacturing product, 1950–78

	Population 1950–78	Manufacturing product			
		1950–65	1965–73	1973–8	1950–78
Large countries					
Brazil	3.0	7.3	12.0	6.3	8.5
Mexico	3.3	7.2	8.1	6.3	7.3
Andean Pact (incl. Chile)					
Bolivia	2.4	2.0	5.6	8.3	4.2
Chile	2.1	5.5	3.4	−1.4	3.7
Colombia	3.2	6.2	7.7	5.4	6.5
Ecuador	3.2	5.3	7.1	11.9	7.0
Peru	2.8	7.8	6.6	1.8	6.4
Venezuela	3.5	9.5	5.0	7.6	7.9
CACM (incl. Panama)					
Costa Rica	3.2	7.9	9.4	8.1	8.3
El Salvador	3.1	7.2	5.8	5.2	6.4
Guatemala	2.8	5.4	7.7	6.2	6.2
Honduras	3.2	8.3	6.4	6.3	7.4
Nicaragua	3.0	9.5	6.9	3.6	7.6
Panama	2.9	10.1	8.1	0.2	7.7
River Plate countries					
Argentina	1.6	4.8	5.9	−1.0	4.1
Paraguay	2.7	3.3	6.0	7.2	4.8
Uruguay	1.4	2.7	0.9	5.9	2.7
Latin America	2.8	6.3	8.2	4.5	6.5

Source: ECLA.

continent fell from 35 per cent in 1950 to 18 per cent in 1978. The import substitution process was 'completed' earlier in these countries, but with the high costs of national industry preventing exports and further domestic expansion, such 'completion' brought industrial stagnation. As table 6 demonstrates, Argentine industry declined by 1 per cent per annum between 1973 and 1978, causing per-capita manufacturing GDP to fall from $531 dollars in 1973 to $474 in 1978. The limited success of the CACM is reflected in the slight rise from 2.5 per cent to 2.8 per cent in its contribution to Latin American manufacturing GDP.

Despite radical changes in the spatial distribution of manufacturing GDP between countries, industrial growth occurred in all countries and was generally substantial, as table 6 shows. The annual growth rate for Latin America between 1950 and 1978 was 6.5 per cent, which was above the world average of 5.9 per cent (1950–77). Even the more stagnant industrial economies of Argentina, Chile and Uruguay had average annual growth rates for the 1950–78 period of 4.1 per cent, 3.7 per cent and 2.7 per cent respectively. Thus, there were striking increases in the 'level of industrialization' (defined as the share of the manufacturing product in the total product) from 20 per cent in 1950 to 26 per cent in 1978, and, in per-capita manufacturing GDP, from $90 in 1950 to $240 in 1978 (both at 1970 prices). The regional variation of these two indices reflected the increasing relative strength of the two larger countries.

Present industrial structures

Import substitution industrialization has brought major structural changes in manufacturing. As would be expected, industries producing non-durable consumer goods have declined in relative importance as the industries producing intermediate goods, consumer durables and capital goods have developed. In 1950, non-durable consumer goods represented almost two-thirds of total manufacturing production, as opposed to 40 per cent today. In contrast, the relative importance of intermediate products in manufacturing output has risen from less than 25 per cent of the total to more than one-third at present. However, it is the consumer durables and investment goods sector where the relative change has been most striking. This sector represented 11 per cent of total manufactures in 1950 and now accounts for more than one-quarter of manufactures produced.

There are, however, great differences among Latin American countries according to size of country. Table 7 demonstrates that the process of import substitution has been much more 'complete' in the large countries than in the smaller countries. Intermediate manufactures and consumer durable/capital goods sectors accounted for 37 per cent and 28 per cent respectively of total value-added in the larger countries (including Argentina) by 1975, against 35 per

Renault's Santa Isabel plant in Córdoba, Argentina. Along with other French companies, Renault decided to locate its major Latin American plant in Argentina not Brazil. By the late 1970s, however, Brazilian plants were producing nearly seven times as many vehicles as the combined total of the three French companies in Argentina

cent and 17 per cent in medium-sized countries and only 26 per cent and 9 per cent in small countries. Indeed, in the period 1950–75 as much as 83 per cent and 87 per cent of Latin American growth in intermediate and capital goods respectively took place in the three larger countries of Brazil, Mexico and Argentina (see table 8). The production of non-durable consumer goods has, however, expanded considerably in medium-sized and small countries, where 48 per cent and 65 per cent of total value-added still corresponds to these sectors and where 17 per cent and 12 per cent of Latin American growth in these goods took place.

The production of intermediate goods has expanded significantly in medium-sized countries but less so in small countries, although average growth rates were registered in table 8's B classification of intermediate goods – paper, glass, wood and non-metallic mineral products (e.g. cement): for example, in the cement industry, 30 per cent of Latin American production corresponded to medium-sized and small countries in 1976. However, growth in the D classification of intermediate goods (basic metals such as steel and aluminium) is almost entirely restricted to the larger countries and the one medium-sized country, Venezuela, that benefits from considerable comparative advantages (in the form of cheap materials and power) in both steel and aluminium production at Ciudad Guayana. In 1976, 94 per cent and 100 per cent of Latin American steel and aluminium production respectively corresponded to Argentina, Brazil, Mexico and Venezuela.

Table 7. Structure of industrial production by size of country, 1950 and 1975 (percentage of value added in the manufacturing sector)

		Non-durable consumer manufactures A	B	Intermediate manufactures C	D	B+C+D	Consumer and capital manufactures E	Total manufactures
Large countries	1950	64	10	10	4	24	12	100
	1975	35	9	21	7	37	28	100
Medium-sized countries	1950	66	10	15	3	28	6	100
	1975	48	9	20	6	35	17	100
Small countries	1950	85	8	6	0	14	1	100
	1975	65	11	14	1	26	9	100

A. Food, beverages and tobacco (Division 31); textile, wearing apparel and leather industries (Division 32); furniture and fixtures, except primarily of metal (major group 332); printing, publishing and allied industries (major group 342); pottery, china and earthenware (major group 361), and other manufacturing industries (Division 39), according to ISIC (International Standard Industrial Classification).

B. Wood and cork products, except furniture (major group 331); paper and paper products (major group 341); glass and glass products (major group 362), and other non-metallic mineral products (major group 369), according to ISIC.

C. Chemicals and chemical, petroleum, coal, rubber and plastic products (Division 35 of ISIC).

D. Basical metal industries (Division 37 of ISIC).

E. Metal products, machinery and equipment (Division 38 of ISIC).

Source: ECLA.

Table 8. Estimation of the distribution of the growth of industrial output by branches of activity, 1950–75

	Total manufacturing industry %	Manufactures[a] Non-durable consumer goods A %	Intermediate goods B %	C %	D %	Consumer durables and capital goods E %
Large countries	80	71	80	83	86	87
Medium-sized countries	13	17	13	13	13	10
Small countries	7	12	7	1	1	3
Total Latin America	*100*	*100*	*100*	*100*	*100*	*100*

[a] Columns A, B, C, D and E represent the ISIC manufacturing branches and groups as indicated at the foot of table 7.
Source: ECLA.

The most pronounced concentration of industrial growth in the larger countries occurred in the consumer durable/capital goods sectors (87 per cent of continental growth). As table 3 demonstrates, 86 per cent of motor vehicle assembly took place in Brazil, Mexico and Argentina. Furthermore, the governments of these countries have demanded high integration levels, normally the equivalent of over 90 per cent of parts by value from national sources. The medium-sized countries, with the exception of Venezuela, have been much less ambitious, and accepted levels of 30 per cent or below. Meanwhile, the capital goods sector has 90 per cent of its production concentrated in the three largest countries, with Brazil having the technologically most advanced and broadest machinery sector; indeed, in certain areas, such as machinery and plant for sugar cane milling and alcohol production, Brazilian firms compete successfully on the world market. Increasingly, Brazil is attracting research and development functions; Volkswagen's 'Brasília' car was partly designed and developed by the Brazilian subsidiary for local conditions.

Post-war industrial expansion has not only brought changes in industrial structure but also changes in the productive agents of industrialization. In general, national private enterprises have been losing ground to both public enterprise and multinational corporations in terms of their relative contribution to the industrial product. There has also been a tendency towards a greater differentiation of roles.

The public enterprise, especially in the large and medium-sized countries, has focused on basic industries, such as iron and steel, oil refining and petrochemicals. In 1978, the steel production by state

The separating plant of Centromín at La Oroya, Peru

the production of basic petrochemical feedstock (ethylene, propylene, ammonia, urea) but sells them to either mixed (state/private) or private firms for further elaboration.

The national private firm is characterized by great diversity in terms of size, technological level and forms of organization. In most large and medium-sized countries, large national conglomerates have developed with a variety of manufacturing interests as well as important tertiary functions in banking, insurance, finance, tourism, commerce and often the media. At the other end of the size range, large numbers of small enterprises are at work, filling the demand gaps left by, or providing low-cost competition for the large state, national and international companies. Due to labour-intensive methods and low capital inputs, these enterprises generate a much higher proportion of employment than their production levels would indicate. The organization is simple, based around a single entrepreneur (or family), and most small firms are highly susceptible to changes in the macro-economy or the policy shifts of the large companies; as a result they have to be very adaptable and flexible in order to survive.

In terms of their relationship with multinational companies, it is often pointed out that the latter predominates in the technologically more dynamic sectors, leaving the national private firms to specialize in the more traditional industries. The 2700 largest private firms in Brazil, for example, account for 75 per cent of production in the non-durable consumer goods sector but only 33 per cent and 45 per cent in the intermediate and metal goods machinery sectors. However, such a distinction can be misleading. National private firms are active in some very dynamic sectors in Latin America. For example, in the motor vehicle industry, national private firms have specialized in components and parts production while leaving assembly and engine production to the multinationals. In Brazil, national firms figure prominently in the plastics, paper and machinery sectors. In Venezuela, the metal fabrication industry is dominated by such national firms as SIVENSA. Nevertheless, throughout Latin America, the majority of firms producing in the food, beverages, textiles, footwear, clothing, leather, cement, furniture and pottery sectors are of national private origin.

Direct foreign investment through multinational enterprises in manufacturing has become particularly significant in the latter stages of import substitution industrialization. Thus, while manufacturing activity accounted for only 20 per cent of total US direct investments in Latin America in the 1950s, this increased to approximately 65 per cent in the 1960s. Direct foreign investment has mainly been channelled into Brazil and Mexico where import substitution policies have been more successful. This trend became more accentuated between 1967 and 1976; 69 per cent of direct foreign investment in Latin American manufacturing was concentrated in these two countries in 1976, as opposed to 62 per cent in

iron and steel enterprises made up 69 per cent of total production in Argentina, 60 per cent in Mexico and Brazil and 80 per cent in Venezuela. The share of state enterprises in oil refining also stands out. In Brazil, Mexico, Chile, Colombia, Uruguay and Bolivia, 100 per cent of oil refining is carried out by the state enterprises. The contribution of such enterprises to the processing of chemical and petrochemical products is also substantial. In Argentina, Brazil and Mexico, there are large state enterprises which process basic products in these branches, while in Andean Pact countries such as Colombia, Peru and Venezuela all the enterprises which process basic petrochemical products are state-owned.

In the early stages of industrial development the state assumed the role of entrepreneur in basic industries in order to initiate locally the production of goods regarded as essential to accelerated industrial growth. More recently, state participation in basic industries has often been due to the conviction that such participation was a means of increasing national decision-making power in the industrial sector. In a number of countries, areas within certain industrial sectors have been defined for action by the public and private sectors, with the state reserving for itself the manufacture of basic products. In Venezuela, for example, PEQUIVEN controls

Table 9. Direct foreign investment (DFI) in the manufacturing sector of Latin American countries

	1967		
	DFI in the manufacturing sector millions of dollars	**Manufacturing DFI as % of total DFI**	**% distribution within region**
Large countries	*3 813*	*69.1*	*61.7*
Brazil	2 526	67.8	40.9
Mexico	1 287	72.0	20.8
Andean Group	*864*	*14.5*	*14.0*
Colombia	238	32.7	3.9
Chile	93	9.7	1.5
Peru	142	18.2	2.3
Venezuela	391	11.2	6.3
CACM	*114*	*19.0*	*1.8*
Argentina	*1 201*	*66.0*	*19.4*
*Others**	*189*	*14.1*	*3.1*
Total Latin America	*6 181*	*40.5*	*100.0*

	1976		
	DFI in the manufacturing sector millions of dollars	**Manufacturing DFI as % of total DFI**	**% distribution within region**
Large countries	*10 500*	*76.4*	*69.1*
Brazil	6 900	75.8	45.4
Mexico	3 600	77.4	23.7
Andean Group	*2 330*	*36.6*	*15.4*
Colombia	850	68.0	5.6
Chile	150	36.6	1.0
Peru	330	18.3	2.2
Venezuela	1 000	34.5	6.6
CACM	*350*	*36.1*	*2.3*
Argentina	*1 500*	*66.7*	*9.9*
*Others**	*503*	*13.3*	*3.3*
Total Latin America	*15 183*	*56.0*	*100.0*

* Bolivia, Ecuador, Panama, Paraguay, Uruguay, Haiti, Dominican Republic.
Source: ECLA.

Table 10. The role of private national, multinational, and state firms in the various sectors of the Brazilian economy, 1978

	Private national (%)	**Multinational (%)**	**State (%)**
Predominantly national			
Civil construction	100.0	—	—
Communications	100.0	—	—
Supermarkets	98.3	1.7	—
Furniture	97.4	2.6	—
Clothing, shoes	96.9	3.1	—
Retail business	90.0	10.0	—
Heavy construction	88.7	8.5	2.8
Printing and publishing	73.8	26.2	—
Food	66.6	33.4	—
Pulp and paper	59.9	32.9	7.2
Non-metallic minerals	58.0	42.0	—
Predominantly foreign			
Wholesale business	41.4	42.2	16.4
Machinery	41.5	48.8	9.7
Transportation equipment	37.7	53.6	8.7
Heavy vehicles	45.2	54.8	—
Petroleum distribution	11.0	60.8	28.2
Electronics	33.6	66.4	—
Textiles	31.8	68.2	—
Cleaning products	27.2	72.8	—
Plastics and rubber	21.5	76.1	2.4
Beverages and tobacco	23.6	76.4	—
Pharmaceuticals	15.6	84.4	—
Office equipment	13.8	86.2	—
Automobiles	0.6	99.4	—
Predominantly state			
Public services	—	—	100.0
Chemicals and petrochemicals	5.0	15.8	79.2
Steel	27.1	7.9	65.0
Minerals	29.5	12.0	58.5
Transportation	49.6	—	50.4

Source: S. A. Hewlett, *The Cruel Dilemmas of Development: Twentieth Century Brazil* (New York, 1980). These figures refer to the sales of the twenty largest firms in each sector.

1967. In 1976, another 22 per cent of investment was concentrated in Argentina, Venezuela and Colombia. Most of this investment is of US origin – 50 per cent in the large countries, 77 per cent in the medium-sized countries and 69 per cent in the smaller countries. However, both European and Japanese investments are increasing. Japanese investment is still most concentrated in the processing of raw materials (steel, aluminium) but European investment is shifting to high-technology sectors such as motor vehicles and chemicals. The impact of foreign investment on the pattern of Brazilian production is illustrated in table 10.

There is increasing evidence to show that the rapid growth of multinational investment in manufacturing in Latin America (an increase of 146 per cent between 1967 and 1976) has taken place in the more dynamic and technologically innovative sectors.

Conflicts of interest between multinational enterprise and the state have been frequent in Latin America. The state is basically interested in maximizing benefits for its own territory whereas multinational enterprise, in the words of a General Motors chief economist, attempts 'to find ways of achieving the economic efficiencies of world-wide specialization of production and development within the political constraints imposed by national policies'. While the state can control its own enterprises and strongly influence national private firms, it finds it difficult to exert influence over multinational enterprise. Again, there are major contrasts in the experiences of large and small countries with regard to multinational enterprise. The larger countries can often exert considerable power in bargaining with multinationals as their markets are valuable to obtain and rival companies will compete against each other for tenders. Smaller countries generally have substantially less bargaining power due to their small market size and the often low level of multinational interest.

However, in both large and small countries, governments are increasingly worried about the concentration of multinational corporations in those high-technology sectors that also enjoy the highest growth rates. This is mainly because governments see growth industries in their countries being dominated more and more by organizations over which they have little control. In the booming industrial economies of the larger countries, the vital technological component to industrial growth is already strongly associated with organizations that emanate from the more developed world. This leads Latin American governments to envisage their countries' future industrial growth as being highly dependent on forces and decisions external to their territory.

The concomitant concern of governments has led some to establish strict controls over the extent and nature of foreign investment. One of the more elaborate systems of control was that known as Decision 24 of the Andean Group in 1974. However, the major effect of this was to considerably reduce foreign investment and the scope of new industrial projects in the region. This was particularly the case in Venezuela which could have anticipated a significant expansion of foreign manufacturing investment in the 1974–7 period due to its large oil revenues and its policy of investing a large proportion of them in industrial development. However, foreign investment remained low during the period. In 1977, Venezuela introduced a much less restrictive foreign investment law, Decree 2442, allowing increased profit remittances, removing elaborate and often ambiguous financial controls and extending the time limits on transfer of technology contracts. As a result, foreign investment in Venezuelan manufacturing expanded more rapidly in subsequent years.

Controls, therefore, tend to restrict foreign investment and, because such investment tends to be in the more dynamic manufacturing sectors, industrial growth as well. Lack of controls can also have adverse effects, permitting excessive royalties and profit remittances, the financial juggling of costs across national boundaries and an over-reliance on locally generated capital. Lack of control can also affect the structure of industry, given that some world industries are now dominated by a small number of large corporations that can be described as forming an interacting oligopoly. In this context, a locational decision taken by one corporation can generate similar responses from other members of the world oligopoly. This can mean that once one member of the world

oligopoly has decided to locate a plant in a new market, other corporations will follow. In Latin America, such oligopolistic reaction has been noticeable in the motor vehicle and tyre industries. In large countries, such mass entry can lead to competition between firms utilizing most of their installed capacity. But in small countries the tendency has been for a large number of firms to produce at low capacity and high costs, thus considerably adding to problems of economies of scale. Despite this, few countries have attempted to control the number of multinational firms locating in their country – even within the framework of import substitution industrialization.

Within the context of the more recent government policies of export promotion in the manufacturing sector, multinational corporations have begun to play a particularly significant role in boosting exports. One impressive example is provided by the motor vehicle corporations in Brazil, in particular Volkswagen, General Motors and Ford. In 1980, Brazil exported 156,000 vehicles and in 1981 approached the 300,000 level – equivalent to the export levels of the United States. Most vehicle exports were to other less developed countries (Nigeria, Philippines, Chile), but significant exports of engines and transmissions were made by Volkswagen to its US and German plants. Such developments have contributed to a slight improvement in Latin America's highly asymmetrical trade structure in manufactures from a 1955 position in which exports of manufactures covered only 6 per cent of manufactured imports to a mid-1970s position where approximately 20 per cent of manufactured imports were covered by exports. Manufactured exports from Latin America mainly come from the traditional or semi-processed sectors of industry (leather, shoes, cellulose, timber, paper, fishmeal, refined oil products), while imports are mainly concentrated in machinery, intermediate and capital goods sectors. Most of the traditional and semi-processed exports (65 per cent) are destined for developed market-economy countries, while the major part of the increasingly sophisticated exports, such as motor vehicles and machinery, is exported within Latin American or to other less developed countries.

The location of industry

Industrialization has been a potent driving force in the rapid process of urbanization experienced in all Latin American countries. Although much of modern manufacturing is based on new technologies and is capital intensive, a significant proportion of the total workforce is either employed directly in manufacturing plants or in 'backstreet' workshops which depend on their orders from subcontracting agreements with modern plants. Furthermore, manufacturing growth should not be underestimated as a factor in the recent and rapid expansion of the tertiary employment sector due to manufacturing's increased demand for commercial and non-

THE INDUSTRIAL CORE OF BRAZIL

KEY

○ Towns with between 55,000 and 65,000 workers employed in manufacturing

■ Towns with between 20,000 and 30,000 workers employed in manufacturing

● Other important industrial centres

(M.V.) More than 40% industrial workers employed in motor vehicle industry

(S) More than 40% industrial workers employed in steel industry

(T) More than 40% industrial workers employed in textiles and clothing

— Major highways

Numbers in brackets after major cities refer to number of industrial workers

0 — 125 km
0 — 80 miles

THE VENEZUELAN INDUSTRIAL BELT

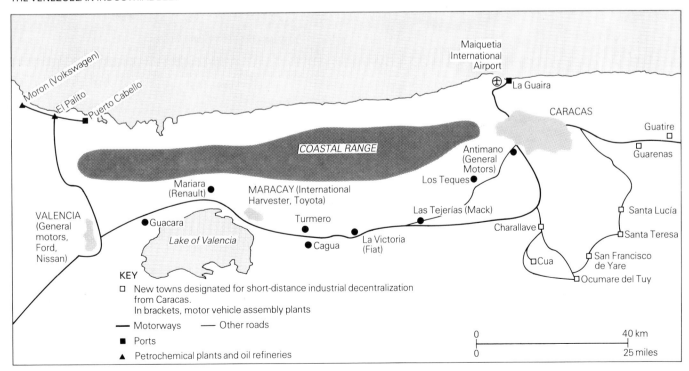

KEY

□ New towns designated for short-distance industrial decentralization from Caracas.
In brackets, motor vehicle assembly plants

— Motorways   — Other roads

■ Ports

▲ Petrochemical plants and oil refineries

0 — 40 km
0 — 25 miles

commercial services (lawyers, accountants, advertising, banks, financial services, insurance, medical services), and through the demand created by a relatively well-paid workforce.

Industrial growth has, however, been spatially very concentrated within most Latin American countries. In many countries, the primate city alone contains the great majority of manufacturing employment and value-added. In larger countries core areas or belts of activity have appeared – São Paulo–Paraíba valley–Rio de Janeiro–Belo Horizonte crescent (70 per cent Brazilian industrial activity), the Mexico City–Puebla core (50 per cent Mexican industrial activity), the Greater Buenos Aires metropolis (66 per cent Argentinian industrial activity), the Santiago–Valparaiso core (66 per cent Chilean activity), the Lima–Callao metropolis (70 per cent Peruvian industrial activity) and the Caracas–Maracay–Valencia axis (75 per cent Venezuelan industrial activity). Such concentration is observable at a continental scale, given that these six industrial belts or agglomerations contain 57 per cent of the continent's industrial activity.

Such spatial concentration of industry is likely to increase rather than decrease in the near future. This is because the core areas attract a disproportionate amount of dynamic, technologically innovative industry. In 1970 for example, Greater São Paulo, with 34 per cent of Brazil's industrial employment, contained 66 per cent, 64 per cent and 63 per cent of national employment in the electrical, vehicles and plastics sectors respectively. In 1967, Santiago, with 50 per cent of Chilean value-added in manufacturing, contained no less than 99 per cent, 98 per cent, 97 per cent and 97 per cent of national value-added in the pharmaceuticals, rubber, electrical and plastics sectors respectively; motor vehicles had been the target of a special decentralization policy since 1962.

Such concentration derives as much from the historical process of urbanization as from the advantages that large cities can offer industrialists in the form of external economies and a large market. After the early-nineteenth-century division of Spanish America into fifteen countries, each country adopted a highly centralized system of government in order to prevent further secession. The resulting

CHILE'S CENTRAL CORE

concentration of both government and population in one major city had a strong spatial effect on import substitution industrialization as the latter developed in the 1930–70 period. As such industrialization was both closely linked to government planning and orientated primarily towards the national market, a primate city location was advantageous on two very important counts. Not only did a capital city location offer the possibility of close interaction with members of the relevant government bureaucracies but it also gave proximity to the single largest and most affluent market in the country. Meanwhile, the historical development of transport systems, whether railways in the late nineteenth century or motorways in the last twenty years, in focusing on the major city or core area, meant that all other areas of the national market were easily served by plants located in the core area. Such transport advantages and market considerations have maintained the industrial supremacy of the Rio–São Paulo axis, despite government relocation to Brasília.

Industrial entrepreneurs perceive and probably receive a number of further benefits from a big-city location. In terms of basic costs, labour costs are no higher and sometimes lower than in smaller urban centres, while the cost of water and electricity is similar, and the supply often more reliable. The entrepreneur can rely on a wide range of external services which may act to reduce his costs, such as stockists, machine maintenance companies and high-order banking and financial services. He can find it easier to subcontract out parts of his operation to small, cheap workshops. Meanwhile, the executive of the multinational corporation is attracted by such facilities as the international airport, the cosmopolitan setting, varied cultural activities and private schools.

All Latin American countries have regarded industrial growth as a vital component of economic advance. However, the basic mode of industrialization since 1930, that of import substitution, has undoubtedly been more appropriate for the larger than for the smaller countries. Smaller countries have tried to counteract their market limitations by grouping together in schemes of economic integration. However, their success has been distinctly limited due to the unequal distribution of benefits that has resulted, the tension that this has created (CACM) and the elaborate bureaucracy and plans needed to ameliorate such inequality (Andean Group). Meanwhile, the larger countries, particularly Brazil, have come to form the industrial powerhouse of the continent and have led other countries into adopting industrial policies in which export promotion is stressed and tariff barriers are gradually reduced. These latter policies have already had some success in both Colombia and Chile, although in the latter country the exaggerated reduction of tariff barriers after the 1973 coup d'état has seriously affected some reasonably efficient industrial sectors. Most other non-oil countries are presently in the process of shifting their industrial policies from import substitution to export promotion.

The future of industrial growth linked to export promotion will, nevertheless, be difficult, not least in the adverse conditions created by the worldwide recession of the 1980s. In the context of the international division of labour, there are some industries in which Latin American wage rates are already too high for international competition to be viable – basic textiles, clothing and consumer electronic products. At the other end of the manufacturing spectrum, Latin American industry still has to import most of its technology in some form and will, therefore, find it difficult to progress, at least in the short term, in those high-technology sectors where rapid growth will occur – microchip technology, biotechnology, communications systems. Latin American industrialization linked to export promotion must concentrate on the middle ground – consumer products such as motor vehicles, intermediate products such as chemicals, steel and aluminium, and any other sector where comparative advantage may be attained; these can range from the bizarre (such as the recent boom in corn-fed frozen chicken exports from Brazil) to the innovative (such as the export of sugar cane and alcohol equipment from Brazil).

There are many problems even in these sectors with, in particular, intense competition being provided by Japan and the newly industrializing countries of Asia. A recent Ford estimate about the production costs of its first world car (known in Britain as the Ford Escort) is that, although the cost of its Brazilian model would be $800 less than the European, it would nevertheless be $1200 more than the Japanese. The economies of scale, level of robotization and flexible work practices of Japanese industry make their costs lower than those of Brazilian industry despite the latter's new plant and lower labour costs. The future of industrial growth based on export promotion will, therefore, be a difficult one, but the lesson of the fifty years from 1930 to 1980 has been that 'inward directed' industrialization can end in high-cost industry and eventual stagnation.

RNG

Further reading

W. Dean, *The Industrialisation of São Paulo, 1880–1945* (Austin, 1969)
J. P. Dickenson, *Brazil* (Folkestone, 1978)
R. N. Gwynne, 'The Motor-Vehicle Industry in Latin America', *Bank of London and South America Review*, 12, 9 (1978)
A. O. Hirschmann, 'The Political Economy of Import-Substituting Industrialization in Latin-American Countries', *Quarterly Journal of Economics*, 82 (1968), 1–32
R. O. Jenkins, *Dependent Industrialization in Latin America: The Automotive Industry in Argentina, Chile and Mexico* (New York, 1977)
R. Vernon, *Storm over the Multinationals: the Real Issues* (London, 1978)

Communications and transport

Evolution of the transport system

Provision of transport has been a crucial factor in the development process in Latin America, with profound influence on the nature and pattern of both society and the economy. Much of this impact has taken place in the past five hundred years for, prior to the discovery of Latin America by Columbus, native forms of transport were rudimentary.

Pre-Columbian transport. Early man moved into the Americas on foot or in small boats, and these remained the principal pre-Columbian modes of transport. Most overland travel used simple trails, but the Incas developed a more organized road system by which they controlled their empire and extracted tribute. Their roads took higher routes across the mountains and incorporated spectacular rope bridges, but did not have to bear wheeled traffic. They utilized the llama as a beast of burden, but such domestication was uncommon. Dignitaries in the more advanced civilizations travelled by litter. The Indians generally made limited use of water transport though dugout canoes and balsa rafts were constructed by some peoples.

The colonial period. The arrival of the Iberians was both effect and cause of a transport revolution. Advances in European shipbuilding and navigation facilitated the long voyages which resulted in the discovery of the Americas and the speedy exploration of the coasts of Latin America. The nature of the contact and the relationship which emerged between the Old World and the New shaped a pattern of settlement and economic activity which has largely survived up to the present day. The transport system which evolved was a major factor in these developments.

Contact was by sea; the points of contact were, therefore, ports, and these became major foci of settlement in the New World. From these places routes pushed inland, to the pre-existing settlements of the advanced Indian civilizations of Mexico and the Andes, to mineral resources and farmlands, or simply as a means of exploration. The Spaniards controlled trade with their new colonies closely, so that the fleets sailed to Veracruz for New Spain, to Nombre de Dios and later Porto Belo for Peru, and to small ports in the Caribbean. The arrival of the fleets was a time for trade fairs and a stimulus to town growth. Overland links remained limited, checked by the adverse terrain, vast distances and poor quality of such roads as did exist. Even on routes such as those from Veracruz to Mexico City and across the Isthmus of Panama, travel was slow, and the volume of trade low.

The Iberians did, however, introduce two profoundly important innovations in the land transport system: the mule and the wheel. These meant that pack trains and carts could move greater quanti-ties of goods. In some cases the routes followed were pre-Columbian, such as those from highland Mexico down to the tropical lowlands. Elsewhere (as in Peru) new routes were constructed, creating a land transport system linking the ports, other towns and the foci of economic activity.

During the eighteenth century trade expanded and diversified, internal trade increased, and the road system, in part at least, was improved. In Spanish America cart roads linked Buenos Aires and Tucumán, Lima and Paita, and Mexico City to Jalapa and Guadalajara. Elsewhere mule trains and llamas still provided the means of transport. In Brazil the discovery of gold in Minas Gerais prompted the building of roads over the difficult coastal escarpment, linking Rio de Janeiro to the gold fields and creating the first substantial settlement in the interior of Portuguese America.

The colonial period thus firmly established the pattern of settlement, the nature of the economy and the major lineaments of transport and communication. Trade linked Latin America with Iberia and later with the rest of Europe. Ships also provided a means of contact between the dispersed coastal settlements, isolated from each other by terrain and distance, with few, poor, slow and expensive overland connections. There were some interregional land links, but most trails and tracks penetrated inland to interior towns or sources of primary products. There was also some limited use of river transport.

The nineteenth and early twentieth centuries. Until well into the nineteenth century deep-sea and coastal shipping and generally poor overland links provided the basis for Latin America's transport and trade. Major transformation of the internal and external transport system came with the advent of steam power. The steamship permitted the movement of more cargo, and more rapidly. The use of refrigeration after the 1870s widened the range of products which could be transported. The steamship also assisted in the large-scale migration of Europeans to some parts of the continent.

The railway system developed particularly after 1850, improving the volume and speed of freight and passenger movement, reinforcing existing transport flows and opening up new ones. Though the continent was largely independent by this time, the rail network which evolved was in essence 'colonial' and served to facilitate trade between industrializing Europe and North America and the raw materials and markets of Latin America. Many of the railroads were built by foreign capital – British, French and North American – and in its interests. National control over the growth of the railway system was limited. There was relatively little coherent planning of railway construction as a device to integrate and develop the new republics. Instead, an often essentially penetrative system evolved, with lines running inland from the ports, linking them to interior capitals such as Quito and Santiago, and to sources of export commodities such as wool, meat, grain, coffee and minerals.

Most lines were those of exploitation, linking ports and producing areas; there were few links between existing coastal settlements, which tended to remain dependent on maritime contact. In difficult areas such as the Andes railroads were constructed essentially to exploit specific resources, such as the copper of Cerro de Pasco in Peru. Elsewhere the advance of the railway was a stimulus to development as new areas were made accessible and settlements were created or expanded. The advance of the railways across the São Paulo plateau, for example, is marked by beads of towns along their routes.

In most countries the railway system was skeletal; only in a few areas – Argentina, Uruguay, south-east Brazil, Chile and Cuba did closer rail networks develop. The terrain of the Argentine and Uruguayan pampas facilitated railway construction, so that a dense rail network quickly developed, to move grain, meat and wool towards European markets. The networks focused on Buenos Aires, Bahía Blanca, Rosario and Montevideo. In Argentina the network increased from 736 km in 1870 to 12,480 km in 1891. In Brazil, once the Santos–Jundiaí railway had crossed the severe

The Cuzco–Puno line. One of the last steam locomotives on the Southern railway

The Central railway, Peru: Infernillo bridge. The railway was previously owned by the Peruvian Corporation of Britain

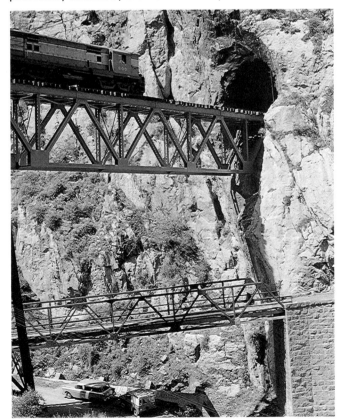

obstacle of the Serra da Mantiqueira in 1867, a dendritic rail net focusing on São Paulo spread across the *paulista* plateau, closely linked to the advance of the coffee frontier. Lesser nets evolved in the coffee lands of Minas Gerais and Rio de Janeiro, and in the sugar plantations of Cuba. In general, however, the importance of trade to Europe and North America meant there were few international or even interregional railways; trade flows were overseas not overland.

Much of the system thus constructed was single track, restricting capacity, and there was little control over gauges, so that most countries inherited mixed gauge systems, which have inhibited later integration of national railways. In the mid-1970s, though 87 per cent of Brazil's railways were metre gauge, the remainder were narrow gauge, or 1.44 or 1.60 m gauge. Difficult terrain, limited traffic and poor maintenance checked the long-term role of the railway. By the 1930s the railway 'boom' was over. The railways began to face competition from the automobile and improved roads, so that their share of freight and passengers has fallen, perhaps unduly, and, in response to their decline since 1945, much of the continent's railway system has passed into public ownership. The most striking feature of the railway pattern is its spatial concentration; of the 131,000 km built by 1945, three-quarters was in Argentina, Brazil and Mexico. Over large areas, in Amazonia, north-east Brazil and southern Argentina, there are few railways.

Governments began to take increasing interest in highway development from the 1920s onwards. The president of Brazil in 1927 noted that 'to govern is to populate, but it is not possible to populate without building roads of all types. To govern, then, is to build roads', and many countries embarked on road-building programmes during the inter-war years. The new highways often paralleled the railways, and served to hasten their decline. The road system offered greater flexibility in the movement of goods, with direct delivery between producer and consumer, rather than the multiple handling often involved in rail transport. In consequence, carriage of freight by road has grown markedly, to the extent of including long-distance, high-bulk, low-value goods, better suited to an efficient rail system. Road building requires less foreign exchange than railway construction and provides employment for large numbers of unskilled workers. Road transport has also made cheap, long-distance travel more accessible to low income groups. The liability of road transport has been its vulnerability to the increase in the world price of oil.

Most Latin American countries now have reasonable road networks and, in contrast to the railway era, some have been planned as concerted highway systems. In addition, in 1928 there was agreement to construct an inter-American highway, which would provide a road of longitudinal communication across the continent. By 1940 62 per cent of the Middle American and 87 per cent of the South American sections of this Pan-American Highway had been built as all-weather road. By no means all of the continent's roads are paved and all-weather. Away from federal and provincial highways, municipal roads may be dirt-surfaced, poorly maintained and seasonal.

In the post-colonial period transport by water remained signifi-

cant in the movement of people and goods in Latin America. Development of the railway, ports and shipping, and the export economy were closely related. Movement of agricultural and mineral produce by rail demanded increased shipping and improved ports. Many Latin American ports were small, ill-equipped and in some cases, including major ports such as Buenos Aires, Montevideo, Valparaiso and Veracruz, were little more than unprotected open roadsteads. As the amount of freight, particularly in commodities such as grain and coffee increased, port facilities were improved. The principal ports of Argentina – Buenos Aires, Rosario, Bahía Blanca and La Plata – were all improved between 1880 and 1900; Santos, Rio de Janeiro and Montevideo were improved in the first decade of the twentieth century. Much of the overseas trade was carried by foreign ships. As late as 1912 British ships were responsible for more than half of the foreign tonnage in the principal ports of Brazil and Argentina. This trade involved shipping lines such as the Pacific Steam Navigation Co., the Booth Steamship Co. and the Royal Mail Steam Co.

The inland waterways of Latin America have never lived up to their apparent potential. Although they provided means of travel for the Amerindians and lines of penetration for the Iberians, their role as arteries of commerce has been restricted. Superficially the continent appears to have a good inland waterway system, with the

COMMUNICATIONS IN URUGUAY

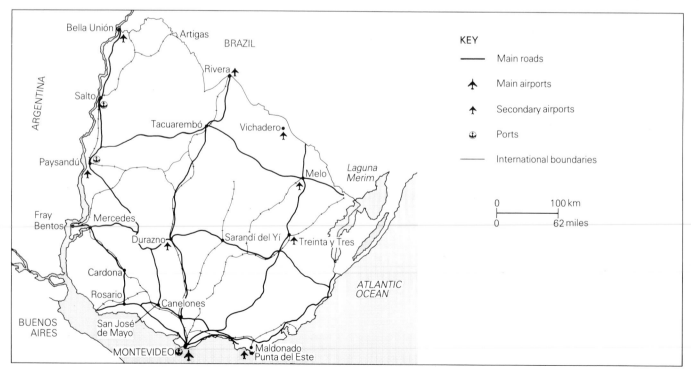

major systems of the Amazon, Paraná–Paraguay, Orinoco, Magdalena and São Francisco. Even these major rivers or their tributaries may not be navigable throughout their entirety, being broken by falls or rapids, so that as ship size and volume of cargo has increased, their utility has diminished. Most of the rivers of the east coast of Brazil and of the Andean republics are short, steep and broken by rapids, providing no access into the interior. Many rivers also have markedly seasonal regimes, with depth of water fluctuating in response to rainfall variations. Several of the major systems flow through areas which remain little settled or developed. The Orinoco, Amazon and São Francisco are, for example, remote from the settlement heartlands. Only the Magdalena and the lower Paraná–Paraguay system are close to foci of settlement, and played important roles in the evolving transport systems of their riparian states. In the late nineteenth century the Amazon provided the basic routeway which sustained the rubber boom, but declined in importance when the boom collapsed.

The Brazilian Alberto Santos Dumont was a pioneer aviator before the First World War, and air transport developed rapidly in Latin America after 1918. It provided both speed and the ability to overcome the barriers of distance and environment which restricted land and sea transport. Commercial air services began to operate in Colombia in 1919 – Colombia's airline AVIANCA claims to be the oldest in the western hemisphere – and in Mexico, Bolivia and Brazil by 1927. Foreign airlines such as Pan American began to operate in the area, and foreign interests, particularly French and German, also assisted domestic airlines. During the Second World War construction of air bases by the United States in the Caribbean and northern South America provided airports and infrastructure for later use by civilian air traffic. In the 1940s Latin American airlines increasingly passed to control by domestic interests. In addition to the development of scheduled links between major cities, aeroplanes gave access to interior areas previously isolated or poorly served by land transport, but which could be reached by small planes using simple landing strips.

The present-day transport systems

The railways. The railway system in Latin America has tended to decline from its former importance, relative in terms of the share of total passengers and goods carried, and in some cases absolutely as networks have been reduced. For example, railway passenger traffic in Argentina and Brazil, as measured by passenger-kilometres, fell

ANDEAN RAILWAYS, COLOMBIA TO CHILE

Table 11. Railway passenger traffic
(million passenger-kilometres)

	1940	1950	1970	1977
Argentina	4 404	13 326	12 828	12 011
Bolivia	125	—	271	395
Brazil	6 428	9 987	12 351	11 699
Chile	1 457	1 588	2 338	2 382
Colombia	457	790	249	—
Cuba	248	556	1 130	2 966
Ecuador	80	126	85	—
Mexico	1 862	—	4 534	5 040
Nicaragua	54	—	30	19
Peru	124	241	248	—
Uruguay	272	—	529	389

Railway freight traffic
(million net ton-kilometres)

	1940	1950	1970	1977
Argentina	13 028	17 117	13 357	11 567
Bolivia	219	—	326	579
Brazil	6 075	7 605	17 531	60 721
Chile	2 031	2 102	2 533	2 207
Colombia	309	615	1 173	1 215
Cuba	726	1 055	1 625	—
Ecuador	73	112	56	—
Mexico	5 764	—	22 863	36 232
Nicaragua	11	—	16	11
Peru	299	392	610	612
Uruguay	395	—	250	307

Source: UN, *Statistical Yearbook 1951* (New York, 1951), pp. 311–12, *1979*, pp. 541–2 and *1981*, p. 555.

by over 15 per cent between 1968 and 1977. The amount of freight carried generally stagnated or decreased over the same period, though with some exceptions. Brazil, with by far the largest amount of rail freight in the continent, experienced an increase from 22,000 million ton-km of freight to 60,000 million, largely due to expansion of the transport of iron ore and other minerals for domestic use and export.

The length of track has tended to decline. For eleven countries (which together contained over 90 per cent of the continent's railways) the system decreased from 125,701 km in 1950 to 112,900 in 1972, with major decreases in Argentina, Brazil and Mexico. Few new lines have been built in the post-war period, exceptions being the Chihuahua–Pacific line in Mexico, the Ferrocarril del Atlántico in Colombia, and an extension of Brazil's network to Brasília.

In addition to road competition, the high costs of maintenance of lines built in difficult terrain and dependence on foreign sources of locomotives, rolling stock and rails, have contributed to the decline of the railways. Physical decline and falling profits were partially responsible for the nationalization of most of the foreign-owned railways – for example in Mexico in the 1900s, Argentina in 1947 and Brazil in 1957. Few of the lines are now profitable, except the more specialized and efficient ones moving particular commodities such as those carrying coal – Río Turbio (Argentina) and Teresa Cristina (Brazil), iron ore – Vitória-Minas, and manganese – Amapá (both in Brazil). Movement of specialized bulky commodities is also a stimulus to current railway building, including, in Brazil, the so-called 'steel railway' from Belo Horizonte to São Paulo to carry minerals and metals, and the Carajás–São Luís iron ore railway, but it seems unlikely that the rail systems will otherwise be extended. Although a role exists for the movement of bulky freight, passenger traffic is likely to continue to diminish, other than on commuter services such as those of Buenos Aires and Rio de Janeiro.

Road transport. The automobile has been, in the present century, the principal agent of transport revolution, with great expansion of the highway system, a boom in car ownership, and the increasing role of the road in passenger and freight transport. By 1975 the continent had over 2.5 million km of road, although only about one-fifth of this was paved. In comparison the United States, only half the size of Latin America, had more than double this amount of road, almost half of it paved. In Latin America, although there are some spectacular multilane interurban and interregional highways, much of the system lacks a permanent surface, may not be all-weather, and may be little more than a rough track. As with other transport modes, Brazil, Mexico and Argentina have the largest share of the system, a total of 2 million km of road, though only 6, 18 and 13 per cent respectively of this is paved. Venezuela has possibly the best highway system in the continent with 41 per cent of its highways paved.

Table 12. Motor vehicles in use (thousands)

	1948	1970	1978
Argentina	508	2 194	—
Bolivia	11	48	67
Brazil	326	3 020	8 698
Chile	69	326	527
Colombia	55	322	—
Dominican Republic	6	59	136
Ecuador	7	63	175
Mexico	235	1 822	4 157
Panama	21	60	99
Paraguay	2	28	54
Peru	41	347	—
Uruguay	75	209	—
Venezuela	82	764	—

Source: UN, *Statistical Yearbook 1951,* pp. 317–18, *1979,* pp. 547–8, *1981,* pp. 561–3.

Length of roads, 1975

	thousand km	percentage paved
Argentina	309	13
Bolivia	37	3
Brazil	1 417	6
Chile	80	11
Costa Rica	24	8
Dominican Republic	10	54
El Salvador	11	13
Guatemala	13	19
Honduras	6	20
Mexico	324	18
Nicaragua	17	9
Panama	7	31
Paraguay	7	12
Peru	55	10
Venezuela	50	41

Source: J. W. Wilkie, *Statistical Abstract of Latin America,* Vol. 20 (Los Angeles, 1980), p. 252.

There has been an enormous growth in the road fleet of the area. The number of passenger cars in South America increased from 4 million to 13 million between 1968 and 1980. Expansion in some countries has been especially rapid. In Brazil there were about 100,000 passenger cars in use in 1928, by 1948 169,000; by 1968 1.7 million and in 1980 8.1 million! Such spectacular growth reflects the switch to road transport from other modes, some increase in prosperity, and the establishment of domestic car industries. Though vehicle assembly industries were established in some countries before 1939, manufacture using largely domestic components began after 1950. Most of the industry is controlled by multinational vehicle firms, with Volkswagen, Ford, General Motors and Chrysler accounting for three-quarters of total output. Brazil, Mexico and Argentina are the principal producers, Brazil ranking tenth in world output of cars and fifth in commercial vehicle

BRAZILIAN AMAZON HIGHWAY SYSTEM

output in 1979. The role of commercial vehicles in the expansion of freight movement and mass passenger transport is also very striking. The number of commercial vehicles in use in South America rose from 1.9 million in 1968 to 4.5 million in 1980. Over a longer time perspective, Argentina, Brazil and Mexico all had less than 65,000 commercial vehicles in use in 1928; by 1974 they each had over 700,000. Similar rates of expansion can be seen in the smaller countries – the number of commercial vehicles registered in the Dominican Republic rose from 6000 in 1960 to 46,000 in 1980; in Honduras the number of passenger vehicles registered rose over the same period from 5500 to over 20,500.

Cars, buses and trucks have become increasingly important in the transport structure of Latin America in private, mass transit and freight journeys, and have come to dominate intraurban and interurban transport. However, road transport provision is uneven; away from the major cities and principal highways, the quality of roads and the frequency and quality of vehicles decline. Much of the rural periphery remains poorly served.

Latin American road-building programmes have involved the construction of urban motorways and interurban highways to expand and speed up local and intranational passenger and cargo movement in existing areas of settlement; they have also been used to provide lines of penetration into frontier areas. The Amazon basin has been the major focus of such developments, with the penetration of roads into the region from the Andean countries, the proposal to build the *Carretera Marginal de la Selva* from Colombia to Paraguay, and the substantial Brazilian programme to open up and colonize its Amazon territories. The key to this latter programme is the 1200 km Transamazonia highway running from Brazil's north-east coast to Itaituba and ultimately to the Peruvian frontier. This is also to provide the spine for a system of other highways traversing the region.

A spectacular example of the potential impact of new highways on frontier development is provided by the Belém–Brasília highway, built along the eastern periphery of Amazonia in the late 1950s: it is claimed to have led to the influx of two million people, the growth of

The main city highway in Brasília

new towns and villages, and the opening up of new lands to farming and industry. More recently the completion of the highway from Cuiabá to Porto Velho has opened up the west Brazilian territory of Rondônia to both small-scale squatting and large-scale colonizing schemes. The territory's population rose from 113,000 in 1970 to over 500,000 in 1980, and between 1970 and 1975 the number of recorded landholdings increased from 7000 to 25,000 and the farm area from 1.6 million to 3 million hectares.

Such highway-settlement schemes have aroused controversy, because of their potential consequences for the environment, and have not always been successful in creating permanent settlements. Furthermore, the Brazilian experience points to one of the recent checks to the whole process of road transport development in Latin America. Part of the importance given to roads in transport programmes was based on the assumption of the continuing availability of cheap petroleum. The 'oil crisis' of the early 1970s and consequent rise in oil prices undermined this. While the impact on oil-rich countries such as Mexico and Venezuela was limited, the impact on those largely dependent on imported oil was substantial. It prompted a greater search for domestic oil and alternative fuel sources (in Brazil, the use of alcohol derived from sugar cane), greater emphasis on mass transit systems, reappraisal of other transport modes, and a slow-down in highway construction.

There is little doubt that the automobile has had the most profound impact on transport in Latin America in the twentieth century, increasing the speed, volume and flexibility of movement. It has facilitated greater accessibility within and between cities, and between core and periphery. Roads have provided most countries with a reasonably comprehensive net of communication, even if the

quality of that net varies. Yet international links are limited. The Pan-American Highway remains incomplete and uneven in quality. Such international highways could provide considerable stimulus to intraregional trade, and reduce dependence on long sea journeys. The completion, for example, of the Asunción–Paranaguá highway has had a substantial impact on the scale and pattern of Paraguayan–Brazilian trade.

Shipping. Shipping has always had a significant role in trade and transport in Latin America, linking parts of individual countries, and markets and supplies elsewhere. Only Bolivia and Paraguay are landlocked, and the countries of Latin America as well as the main clusters of settlement and economic activity tend to be separated by interior 'demographic deserts' so that water links around the periphery of the continent are substantial.

In the early post-war years shipping was handicapped by the age of the fleet, and inadequate ports. In addition, a good deal of the overseas trade was carried by foreign ships. In recent years both ports and ships have been modernized, and some Latin American countries now have substantial ship-building industries. The industry in Brazil and Argentina has grown rapidly; in 1969 they launched 105,000 and 23,000 tons of merchant shipping respectively; in 1981 the figures were 549,000 and 68,000 tons.

Shipping fleets have also grown rapidly. In 1969 the continent had a fleet of some 10 million gross registered tons; in 1981 this had increased to over 40 million tons, about 9 per cent of the world total. This high figure and growth rate is partly distorted by those countries which provide 'flags of convenience' for foreign ship-owners, and in fact the Panamanian registered fleet accounts for two-thirds of the Latin American total. Nevertheless, several other countries have doubled the size of their fleets over the period 1969–78, notably Brazil, Cuba, Ecuador and Venezuela. The fleets have become larger, newer and more specialized. In 1978 over 75 per cent of the Brazilian merchant fleet was less than ten years old, with 75 per cent of dry bulk carrier tonnage less than five years old. Fifty per

Table 13. Merchant shipping fleets (thousand gross registered tons)

	1939	1950	1970	1980
Argentina	291	914	1 266	2 546
Brazil	485	698	1 722	4 534
Chile	172	169	308	614
Cuba	26	—	333	881
Honduras	84	522	60	213
Mexico	30	144	381	1 006
Panama	718	3 361	5 646	24 191
Peru	34	86	378	741
Venezuela	75	157	393	848

Source: UN, *Statistical Yearbook 1951*, p. 320, *1979*, p. 552, *1981*, p. 567

cent of the Mexican fleet was under ten years old. Such improvements were not uniform, for almost 60 per cent of the Argentine and Venezuelan fleets were over fifteen years old.

There has been increasing use of specialized ships – oil tankers, bulk and ore carriers and the use of containerization. Much of the fleet is publicly owned, either directly by government shipping companies or as part of the operations of national petroleum or other commodity companies. In consequence major tanker fleets are operated by Pemex (Mexico), Petrobrás (Brazil) and Yacimientos Petrolíferos Fiscales (Argentina), and by the Brazilian mining company, Cia Vale do Rio Doce. In 1981 oil tankers and ore and bulk carriers provided over half the tonnage of the Argentine and Brazilian merchant fleets; oil tankers alone provided almost the same share of the Mexican, Ecuadorian and Venezuelan fleets.

The significance of petroleum is also indicated in the place that the commodity has in the trading pattern of some countries. In 1975 petroleum and petroleum products provided over 80 per cent of the maritime exports of Venezuela and Ecuador; for countries deficient in oil resources, import trade was dominated by these commodities. They provided over half the maritime imports of Cuba, Jamaica, Guatemala, Brazil, Chile, Peru and Uruguay for example.

Sea transport remains the dominant method of commodity movement between the countries of Latin America and, except in the case of Mexico, to other markets in Europe, North America and Japan. Although interregional trade accounts for only about one-tenth of their total trade, the countries of the Latin American Free Trade Association (LAFTA) have tried to ensure that an increasing proportion of their trade moves in national or LAFTA-member ships.

Modernization and specialization of the merchant fleets has been paralleled by onshore improvements in harbour facilities and cargo handling, movement and storage. Most of the principal ports now have facilities for handling containers and specialized cargoes. In addition specialist ports have been developed or expanded to handle particular cargoes. Examples include Tubarão (iron ore), Sepitiba (oil) and Paranaguá (cereals) in Brazil, the oil terminals of Aruba (Netherlands Indies) and Amuay (Venezuela) and the bauxite terminals of Jamaica.

Coastal and inland waterway traffic remain significant, particularly for bulk cargo, raw materials and petroleum, though there has been some loss of traffic in other goods to the highways. The potential of the navigable rivers, particularly those giving access to new frontiers of settlement, remains under-utilized. Improvements in the lower Orinoco gave better access to the iron ore deposits of Venezuelan Guyana, and the river and its tributaries offer some 10,000 km of navigable waterway in the east of the country. In Amazonia, Manaus is accessible to deep-sea vessels, and the river and its tributaries provide some 58,000 km of navigable waterways.

In the development of the Transamazonia highway it was envisaged that new resources discovered as a consequence of road penetration could be shipped out by these river routes.

Air transport. Air traffic has become increasingly important in Latin America, though in 1978 the continent generated less than 10 per cent of world air travel, as measured by kilometres flown by scheduled airlines. Despite this limited role on the world scene, air travel has expanded rapidly as a means of international and intranational travel in Latin America. Between 1970 and 1978 the distance flown by scheduled airlines increased by 54 per cent, the number of passengers and the amount of freight carried more than doubled. Predictably the three largest countries are the largest generators of traffic. Brazil has the most extensive flight network, with over 200 million km flown in 1980, followed by Mexico (157 million) and Argentina (93 million).

The major cities are the principal nodes for domestic and foreign flights, with Mexico City, Buenos Aires, Rio de Janeiro and São Paulo ranking among the most important. The most heavily used routes link these cities with other regional centres. Such routes are those from Buenos Aires to Córdoba and Mendoza, from Lima to Cuzco, from Caracas to Maracaibo, those linking Bogotá, Cali, Medellín and Barranquilla, and in Brazil the coastal system connecting São Paulo and Rio with Porto Alegre, Salvador, Recife, Fortaleza and Belém and the inland cities of Belo Horizonte, Brasília and Manaus. In Brazil heavy traffic in the south-eastern core of the country led to the pioneering of an 'air bridge' system of very frequent walk-on flights linking São Paulo, Rio de Janeiro, Brasília and Belo Horizonte. Over the past decade, internal airline systems have expanded and increased in usage, so that cities lower down the urban hierarchy have come to generate significant traffic. In most cases this has simply heightened the previous pattern, of a centripetal system focusing on the national capital. This for example, is the case in Argentina, Peru and Venezuela. The Brazilian

Table 14. Scheduled air services (million passenger-kilometres)

	1939	1950	1970	1977	1980
Argentina	—	—	2 395	4 874	8 037
Bolivia	4	19	109	558	944
Brazil	31	—	4 385	10 978	15 572
Chile	2	54	839	1 433	1 875
Colombia	—	—	2 063	3 376	4 198
Cuba	—	—	502	773	932
Mexico	34	626	2 939	8 520	13 870
Nicaragua	—	—	77	77	—
Peru	—	—	789	1 353	1 974
Venezuela	—	—	1 033	3 072	4 367

Source: UN, *Statistical Yearbook 1951*, pp. 335–6, *1979*, pp. 602–4, *1981*, p. 597, *1983*, pp. 1029–30.

system has, however, expanded into a more complex pattern, with a well-developed grid of services between the larger cities in the more settled eastern half of the country.

In addition to scheduled services, air charter facilities have become increasingly important in providing links to remote areas in the interior, otherwise accessible only by poor and slow means of communication. Air traffic has also become a significant element in intracontinental communications, providing a speedy means of transport which avoids the physical obstacles to land transport and the relative slowness of maritime links. The continent, or at least its major cities, are therefore interconnected by a net of scheduled airline services, with routes between Rio, São Paulo, Montevideo, Buenos Aires, Santiago and Lima among the most heavily used. It is also because of its role in providing rapid access over long distances that air freight, in the particular circumstances of the empty spaces which separate Latin American cities and countries, has shown especially spectacular growth; over the period 1970–80 global air freight doubled, while in South America it tripled.

The development of air transport has been accompanied by the expansion and modernization of aircraft fleets, the diffusion of small airports and landing strips to small towns and the rural backlands, and the modernization of old airports or the building of new ones in the principal cities to cater for international jet travel. As well as numerous domestic airlines and charter firms, most countries now operate, and subsidize, flag-carrier international airlines.

Urban transport. Development of rail and road transport has been of significance in the establishment and growth of Latin American towns. Recent improvements in transport have facilitated both movement to the city and mobility within it. In particular changing modes of urban transport have contributed to the sprawl of the metropolitan centres. The horse-drawn and later the motorized tram, the bus and most recently the private car have made it increasingly possible to separate workplace and home, giving rise to increasing functional differentiation in the city between office, factory and residential areas.

Increasing pressure from journey to work has generated growing problems of traffic congestion, and air and noise pollution in the major cities. Major urban highways have been constructed in an effort to ease the traffic congestion. In addition, in an effort to counter this problem and, in some cases, to reduce oil import bills, new mass transit systems have been developed, so that cities such as Mexico City, Rio de Janeiro, São Paulo, Santiago de Chile and (as from 1983) Caracas now have underground metro systems. By far the oldest such system in Latin America – and the only one for several decades – is that of Buenos Aires; the first of its five lines was constructed in 1911.

Conclusion. Transport provision is a crucial element in the development process, but Latin America's transport system is still

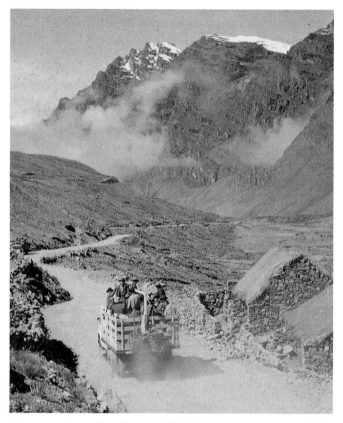

A mountain road to Yungas, Bolivia

imperfect. There is limited integration of networks within most of the republics and even less between them. There are few overland international links, and air transport provides the best articulated system of international connections.

Much of the system betrays its colonial and neo-colonial origins and even some recent developments serve primarily overseas demands rather than internal ones. The persisting pattern of peripheral settlement has deterred links between countries or deep into the interior, as have the obstacles of distance, terrain, vegetation and climate. The absence, except in the case of Mexico, Central America and Colombia, of countries with both Pacific and Atlantic coasts may have repressed the urge to build transcontinental routes such as those developed north of the Rio Grande. Transport by land, sea and air provides linkages between what are effectively economic and demographic 'islands' separated by considerable and empty spaces. Despite recent projects, Amazonia and the far south remains poorly served by land transport. Overall provision of transport remains low, whether in absolute terms or measured by density of road and railway per 1000 square kilometres or per capita, when compared with more developed areas.

Transport systems have been substantially extended and improved over recent decades, serving to integrate more fully established areas of settlement and to open up new ones. There have been particular improvements in the development of highways and air transport, at the expense of the railways, and, to a lesser extent, coastal shipping. Many of these projects have been carried out within the framework of plans to foster economic development, in which provision of a transport infrastructure is seen as an integral element. In addition to fostering this provision, Latin American governments have become increasingly involved in the ownership and operation of transport systems. Most of the railroads are nationalized, and about 60 per cent of merchant fleets and 40 per cent of airline services are publicly owned. There has also been considerable development of transport industries, in the manufacture or assembly of automobiles, the building of railway rolling stock and ships and, in the case of Brazil, the manufacture of small aircraft suited to local conditions.

Governments have thus had a major role in developing transport systems to serve national needs and, to some extent at least, to improve continental and intercontinental linkages. These developments have unquestionably brought considerable progress to Latin America, in improving mobility and accessibility. At the same time some projects have brought benefits only to relatively small segments of the population. Were investments in prestige projects such as international airlines, jumbo jets and new air terminals, in multilane intercity highways, or ultra-modern underground railways the best use of scarce resources? Do spectacular highways provide new opportunities and resources for a nation and all its people, or do they merely serve the interests of large landholders, big-city capitalists and multinational corporations, as against those of impoverished migrants, indigenous groups and the natural environment?

JD

Further reading

R. Bourne, *Assault on the Amazon* (London, 1978)
R. E. G. Davies, *Airlines of Latin America Since 1919* (London, 1984)
M. H. J. Finch, *South American Steam* (Truro, 1974)
C. J. Stokes, *Transportation and Economic Development in Latin America* (New York, 1970)

Trade and tourism

Attempts at economic integration

The outbreak of the First World War severed the traditional pattern of trade between Europe (manufactures) and Latin America and the Caribbean (raw materials), and the United States became the region's major trading partner. Following the Second World War, Latin America's non-involvement created strong demand for its exports, even of manufactures, but its favourable terms of trade were reversed as the United States and Western Europe rebuilt their industries. During the post-war period of shortages of manufactures throughout the world, their prices rose steeply, leading to a tendency in Latin America to turn to industrialization for import substitution. The industries thus created behind high tariff barriers proved inefficient in supplying domestic markets, and could not compete in world markets. However, they generated a higher level of capital imports in the 1950s to the late 1960s, which came increasingly not from the United States, but from Western Europe and Japan. At the same time, exports to these areas expanded, while trade with the United States grew at a slower rate.

As a consequence of Latin American trade adopting a more western-industrialized model in the mid-1950s (influenced greatly by the UN Economic Commission for Latin America – ECLA), intraregional trade fell by 25 per cent (exports between the Latin American countries constituted 12 per cent of total exports in 1953, 6 per cent in 1961), while imports from the rest of the world grew by 20 per cent between 1953 and 1961. To redress this imbalance (as a result of which raw materials could buy fewer manufactures in 1960), and to replace existing bilateral trade agreements in Latin America, free trade areas and customs unions were proposed.

The first of these was the Central American Common Market (CACM) formed under the General Treaty for Central American Economic Integration, Managua, 13 February 1960. The signatories were Costa Rica, El Salvador, Guatemala, Honduras and Nicaragua. In the 1960s, the CACM was regarded as an excellent example of a common market between low-income countries, but political and economic problems upset progress. Honduras and El Salvador broke all links in 1969 after the five-day 'Football War'; in 1970, Honduras, the least developed of the members, withdrew from the market claiming that it had nothing to gain from full membership. In 1973, Honduras made bilateral trade agreements with all but El Salvador, with whom diplomatic relations were not restored until 1980. But further limitations were imposed on the CACM's prospects by civil war in El Salvador (which began in 1979), external pressure on the Sandinista government of Nicaragua, and the severe debt crisis in Costa Rica. CACM rules have been contravened by various countries restricting imports and banning non-essential goods, and the overall effect on trade has been that intraregional imports, which grew from 7.5 per cent of total trade in 1961 to 25 per cent in 1980, fell back to 16 per cent in 1981. Meetings in 1983 and 1984 tried to formulate proposals to arrest the decline in CACM commercial activity (in 1982, CACM intra-regional exports declined by 16 per cent, and by a further 3 per cent in 1983). The main aims have been to provide preferential treatment among the Central American countries on debt payments, a common strategy on protecting the CACM countries' balance of payments and trade agreements with those members with a commercial deficit, and a review of regional tariff and exchange controls.

The Latin American Free Trade Association (LAFTA; Spanish acronym ALALC) came into being on 1 June 1961, after the Treaty of Montevideo (1960); its members were Argentina, Bolivia, Brazil, Chile, Colombia, Ecuador, Mexico, Paraguay, Peru, Uruguay and Venezuela. The intention of LAFTA was not only to renew intra-regional trade, but also to promote integration as a stimulus to industry. Trade concessions between members were drawn up without delay during the annual series of negotiations, but these were for products that either had been granted similar freedom before LAFTA was introduced, or were not important in intra-regional trade. Agreements for important items caused much more difficulty: by 1980, only 3 per cent of all existing concessions had been made since 1969. The fundamental problem facing LAFTA was that the differences, structure, and extent of industrialization between the individual members produced many pressures within the integration process. The long-term aims of LAFTA were submerged under the individual needs of its members. On 12 August 1980, a second Treaty of Montevideo replaced LAFTA with the Latin American Integration Association (LAIA; Spanish acronym ALADI), which has the same members, but a change of emphasis from economic growth to the defence of trade, principally through bilateral agreements, in the face of world economic recession.

The same problems of heterogeneity, and of integration not being a high national priority, still exist, but LAIA attempts to overcome these by 'partial agreements'. These agreements need not be signed by all members, but provide for new signatories later, leading ultimately to a Common Market; early progress has been made in replacing LAFTA accords with LAIA agreements, paving the way for the regional markets which will benefit the Association's least-developed members. Many bilateral agreements have been completed, one of the most notable being a complementary pact between Brazil and Mexico whereby the latter's petroleum is sold in exchange for soya, agricultural and oil-industry machinery. Against these advances must be set the number of outstanding issues on concessions and tariffs still to be ratified, and the threat posed by some countries' inability, owing to balance-of-payments problems,

to meet their commitments to the reciprocal payments agreement under which trade credit lines are set up between the central banks of participating countries (in 1981, 85 per cent of intra-LAIA trade – $93 billion – was paid for under this system).

Between 1960 and 1980, intraregional trade doubled, from 7 per cent of the total to 14 per cent, but this higher level is only 2 percentage points higher than the share in 1953. The largest growth area was in manufactured goods, which accounted for 43 per cent of intraregional exports in 1980 (12 per cent of exports to the world), compared with the early years of LAFTA when agriculture predominated. LAIA's total exports in 1982 were valued at $79.5 billion, of which $11.7 billion (14.7 per cent) were destined for the various markets in Latin America: $9.8 billion (12.3 per cent) were intra-LAIA exports, $0.8 billion were sales to CACM, and $1.1 billion to other Latin American countries. These results represented a 16.9 per cent decline in intraregional commerce over 1981. Four countries contributed more than 10 per cent of the Association's total exports in 1982: Brazil (28.9 per cent), Venezuela (16.4 per cent), Argentina (15.7 per cent) and Mexico (10.4 per cent), but in each the value of its contribution to LAIA exports was in decline. Although the principal reason for the intra-LAIA trade decline was a contraction in imports (due in the main to controls or restrictions by individual countries), imports from outside the region were reduced to an even greater degree.

The internal imbalance within LAFTA was highlighted in 1969 when Chile, Peru, Bolivia, Colombia and Ecuador signed the Andean Pact at Cartagena (26 May 1969); Venezuela joined in February 1973. Seeing that exports from Mexico, Brazil and Argentina represented nearly 50 per cent of total intraregional exports, but that their own contribution was not in the same proportion, the six Andean countries decided to coordinate their industrial development and trade liberalization ahead of LAFTA's stalled liberalization policies. Chile left in 1977 in disagreement over the treatment of foreign capital; Bolivia withdrew for four months in 1980/81, following the other members' condemnation of the coup led by General García Meza; a flurry of border fighting between Ecuador and Peru put further strain on the Pact in 1981. The individual members' support for the Andean Pact (Ancom) varies from Colombia strongly favouring the Pact, to Peru wanting a complete organizational overhaul, and a Common External Tariff, regularly set back since 1979, has still to be approved since agreement cannot be reached on the maximum to be set. In July 1983, a summit of Ancom presidents in Caracas aimed, among other things, to put an end to the import restrictions imposed, contrary to the Cartagena Agreement, by all but Peru in 1982 to protect members' foreign currency reserves. Despite these problems, there have been steps towards industrial coordination, diversification and trading. Between 1969 and 1979, non-traditional exports within the group grew at an annual average rate of 39.4 per cent from $35.1 million to $968.5 million, while overall exports grew by 33.7 per cent. Intraregional exports for Ancom countries in 1981 were worth $1.3 billion, representing 4.2 per cent of total exports; in 1982, intraregional exports fell to $1.2 billion although this was 4.7 per cent of total exports ($26.1 billion). The Group's exports to other LAIA countries increased from 11.5 per cent of total exports in 1980 to 11.7 per cent in 1981 and 12.8 per cent in 1982, but Ancom's imports from LAIA declined from 5.3 per cent in 1980 to 4.9 per cent in 1982 when total imports were $24.4 billion.

The fourth integration organization is the Caribbean Common Market (CARICOM) which was formed by Barbados, Guyana, Jamaica, and Trinidad and Tobago under the Treaty of Chaguaramas in 1973, to replace CARIFTA (the Caribbean Free Trade Association). In 1974, Belize and the seven members of the East Caribbean Common Market (Antigua, Dominica, Grenada, Mont-

serrat, St Kitts/Nevis/Anguilla, St Lucia and St Vincent) joined. The Bahamas were admitted in 1983. Since most rely on sugar and tropical fruits for foreign exchange, there is strong competition for markets. The similarity of economies makes complementation difficult; moreover, the need to import manufactures from outside the region has caused balance-of-payments deficits in all but Trinidad and Tobago which can offset import bills with earnings from petroleum products and natural gas. Relations within CARICOM have been strained by political divisions, by accusations that the four original members do not give enough support to their less-developed partners, and various individual actions that have threatened intraregional trade (Jamaica's import policy and two-tier exchange rate – introduced in January 1983 – provoked sharp criticism). Also threatening the integration process was Jamaica's and Guyana's inability to pay their debt to the CARICOM Multilateral Clearing Facility, which covers the group's trade credit. This last issue was resolved at a heads of government summit at Port of Spain in July 1983, which meeting (and an earlier one – the first for many years – at Ocho Rios in 1982) went a long way to improving relations and aiming towards a joint approach to the region's economic troubles. Proposed measures included the substitution of much of the huge imports of food and rationalizing energy supplies. Intraregional trade is only a small percentage of the total: exports were 8.1 per cent in 1975, rising to 9.5 per cent in 1978; imports in 1975 were 6.8 per cent, increasing to 8.4 per cent in 1978. The total value of intraregional trade was $235 million in 1973, rising to $525 million in 1979, and $900 million in 1982.

Table 15. Intraregional trade, CACM, 1978, 1982 (in millions US dollars)

Country	1978 Exports	1978 Imports	1978 Balance	1982 Exports	1982 Imports	1982 Balance
Guatemala	305.5	262.3	+43.2	322.3	222.4	+99.9
El Salvador	234.0	237.8	− 3.8	176.0	248.3	−72.3
Honduras	52.3	68.6	−16.3	48.0	130.2	−82.2
Nicaragua	147.2	139.9	+ 8.3	57.3	122.2	−64.9
Costa Rica	170.0	201.4	−31.4	172.9	104.6	+68.3

Source: Inter-American Development Bank (1978), *Central American Report,* 4.3.83 (pp. 68–9)–1982.

LAIA and Andean Pact intraregional trade, 1981 (in million US dollars)

Country	Exports	Imports	Balance
LAIA			
Argentina	1 695.4	1 879.5	− 184.1
Bolivia	423.4	457.8	− 34.4
Brazil	4 209.8	2 964.5	+1 245.3
Colombia	626.3	1 016.0	− 389.7
Chile	840.8	1 132.2	− 291.4
Ecuador	434.3	309.5	+ 124.8
Mexico	1 057.2	1 107.4	− 50.2
Paraguay	147.5	642.5	− 495.0
Peru	438.5	609.4	− 170.9
Uruguay	347.1	756.5	− 409.5
Venezuela	1 796.5	1 141.5	+ 655.0
Andean Pact			
Bolivia	41.6	46.5	− 4.9
Colombia	499.7	684.4	− 184.7
Ecuador	145.9	131.7	+ 14.2
Peru	224.5	125.9	+ 98.7
Venezuela	565.4	488.8	+ 76.6

Source: *El cronista comercial,* 21.10.82.

Patterns of trade

In general terms, except for CARICOM, intraregional trade has expanded in manufactures, while the region's world trade has been mostly in primary commodities. Sales of the latter are dependent upon the economic movements in industrialized countries, and in the case of the EEC these have not been favourable to Latin America. Restrictions on the import of tropical fruits and protectionist measures on meat by the EEC, plus Europe's preferential agreements with ex-colonies and dependencies under the Lomé Agreement, have caused a decline in trade between the two continents. The average percentage share of Latin American exports to the EEC between 1961 and 1963 was 29.4 per cent but by 1978–80 this had fallen to 20 per cent; imports were 28.1 per cent between 1961 and 1963, falling to 18.8 per cent between 1978 and 1980. Trade with the Middle East and Japan has increased (noticeably in the case of Middle Eastern oil imports), but until 1983 in both cases imports from these two areas grew faster than Latin American exports. Exports to Japan in 1975 were valued at $2.5 billion, in 1983 at $6.3 billion; imports from Japan in 1975 were worth $4.5 billion, and in 1983 $5.8 billion.

Table 16. Origin of Latin American and Caribbean imports, 1961–3, and 1979–81 (per cent)

Country	Average 1961–3							Average 1979–81						
	United States	EEC[a]	Japan	Canada	Middle East	Latin America[b]	Other countries	United States	EEC[a]	Japan	Canada	Middle East[c]	Latin America[b]	Other countries
Argentina	26.8	39.5	3.9	2.6	—	12.7	14.5	17.7	27.8	11.6	2.0	2.2	22.3	16.4
Bahamas	56.4	22.1	0.2	6.1	—	9.0	—	13.9	4.1	0.2	0.6	35.3	5.9	40.0
Barbados	14.7	44.5	1.8	10.5	—	10.4	18.1	19.9	31.1	2.0	9.6	0.1	26.9	10.4
Bolivia	43.6	27.6	7.3	0.3	—	15.1	6.1	24.8	16.7	14.2	1.4	—	33.0	9.9
Brazil	32.3	24.5	4.6	1.7	4.8	15.0	17.1	25.4	25.4	8.8	2.4	16.9	11.9	9.2
Chile	37.9	30.1	2.8	0.1	1.1	19.3	8.7	23.0	22.0	3.6	2.3	6.3	29.8	13.0
Colombia	51.8	26.2	3.2	2.0	—	5.6	11.2	41.5	22.5	8.5	2.8	0.9	12.7	11.1
Costa Rica	47.3	26.4	7.0	3.3	0.1	9.0	6.9	35.1	15.0	9.4	2.3	0.4	31.6	6.2
Dominican Rep.	47.4	28.0	6.8	6.0	0.1	2.7	9.0	51.6	11.2	6.7	3.5	—	17.4	9.6
Ecuador	43.8	33.5	3.5	3.5	0.1	7.4	8.2	37.0	23.4	14.2	1.5	0.1	14.3	9.5
El Salvador	36.5	29.9	6.9	2.1	0.1	21.4	3.2	30.8	18.7	8.0	1.5	—	36.2	4.8
Guatemala	47.8	24.9	5.2	2.0		11.2	8.8	32.8	18.1	9.2	1.3	—	32.7	5.9
Guyana	21.2	45.9	2.2	7.6	—	13.0	10.1	27.4	31.9	3.7	4.8	0.3	24.7	7.2
Haiti	57.9	23.2	0.2	2.6	—	2.5	13.6	48.6	21.6	7.0	6.4	0.1	3.6	12.7
Honduras	50.1	15.2	7.7	1.3	—	14.8	10.9	41.5	13.6	7.7	2.0	—	29.7	5.5
Jamaica	27.7	43.0	3.4	10.6	—	7.4	7.9	37.4	22.0	3.5	5.5	—	22.3	9.3
Mexico	69.1	18.1	1.8	3.2	—	1.3	6.5	61.9	17.0	4.3	2.3	0.2	6.1	8.2
Nicaragua	49.4	21.2	5.9	2.3	0.2	13.2	8.0	32.8	15.6	7.3	0.8	0.1	38.1	5.3
Panama	47.7	14.8	3.2	1.3		12.4	20.4	30.4	8.8	5.9	1.7	11.1	33.7	8.4
Paraguay	25.2	24.5	8.3	—		22.4	19.6	12.2	20.8	4.1	0.2	0.1	47.1	15.5
Peru	40.3	30.9	5.3	2.3	0.1	13.4	7.7	30.8	24.1	10.1	3.1	0.9	18.3	12.7
Surinam	n.a.	n.a.	n.a.	n.a.	n.a.	n.a.	n.a.	32.8	33.5	5.4	1.3	—	21.1	5.9
Trinidad & Tobago	13.3	27.0	1.1	4.8	20.4	26.6	6.8	16.0	11.4	2.6	2.7	36.3	9.9	21.1
Uruguay	19.0	37.8	1.5	1.5	5.3	21.6	13.3	9.0	19.1	1.7	1.7	19.7	34.1	14.7
Venezuela	53.5	28.1	4.1	4.4	0.1	2.6	7.2	46.6	26.1	8.6	3.5	0.8	6.9	7.5
Latin America	**41.8**	**21.1**	**3.7**	**3.0**	**1.8**	**10.7**	**10.9**	**33.4**	**21.4**	**7.3**	**2.5**	**8.6**	**13.7**	**13.1**

a, b, c See notes to table 17.

The expansion of extraregional exports in manufactures has met with mixed fortunes. The United States' Generalized System of Preferences (GSP) to developing countries gives manufactures duty-free status, except for articles that exceed $1 million, or 50 per cent of the total value of the item in a year. The administration of President Reagan reviewed the system in 1981, reducing the GSP's effectiveness as a stimulus to Latin American exports. However, the United States remains the region's largest market. Between 1961 and 1963 the United States' average share of total Latin American exports was 37.2 per cent; by 1978–80, this had fallen to 33.7 per cent – in the latter period eight countries depended on the United States purchasing over 40 per cent of their exports, compared with twelve between 1961 and 1963. Imports from the United States showed a greater decline, from an average share of 41.8 per cent in 1961–3 to 34.9 per cent in 1978–80, but the number of countries whose purchases from the United States were more than 40 per cent of the total fell from fourteen to five. A number of hindrances to prosperous trade have reduced the amount of commerce between the United States and Latin American trade groups, individually and collectively. First, of all the countries involved, only Brazil has a determined long-term trade policy – the USA has historically not required one; Latin American and Caribbean countries concentrate on the short term. Second, the United States is concerned about the possible price rises introduced by groupings such as the Union of Banana Exporting Countries, or the International Tin Agreement (of which Bolivia is a leading member), while Latin America wants US goods and technology on advantageous terms, with stable prices for its own commodities. Imports from the United States to the whole of Latin America were reduced in 1983 by 22.9 per cent, having fallen 21.6 per cent in 1982, by the foreign exchange shortage induced precisely because of the weakening of commodity prices caused by recession in industrialized countries between 1980 and 1983. The effect of this recession was reflected in the passage of President Reagan's Caribbean Basin Initiative (CBI) through the United States Congress; introduced in early 1982, its $350-million economic assistance provisions were passed in the same year, but its trade and investment sections were not approved until July 1983, having gathered numerous exceptions and safeguards to protect US industries and jobs against competition from most of the important exports of the twenty-eight countries it was designed to help.

Table 17. Destination of Latin American and Caribbean exports, 1961–3, and 1979–81 (per cent)

Country	Average 1961–3							Average 1979–81						
	United States	EEC[a]	Japan	Canada	Middle East	Latin America[a]	Other countries	United States	EEC[a]	Japan	Canada	Middle East[c]	Latin America[b]	Other countries
Argentina	9.1	60.1	3.5	0.4	0.4	13.1	13.4	7.9	35.2	4.4	0.4	2.5	24.9	24.7
Bahamas	91.7	5.5	—	1.8	—	1.0	—	84.2	4.4	0.3	3.0	0.3	3.5	4.3
Barbados	6.7	53.5	—	13.8	—	1.2	24.8	25.8	26.5	0.1	5.9	0.3	13.4	28.0
Bolivia	31.7	58.9	2.4	–	—	5.4	1.6	30.0	22.1	4.6	—	—	33.2	10.1
Brazil	39.3	31.0	2.6	1.6	0.7	6.4	18.4	18.4	31.6	7.3	1.3	4.2	16.7	20.5
Chile	35.7	42.1	6.3	0.1	0.1	8.9	6.8	10.3	42.3	15.4	2.0	0.3	18.1	11.6
Colombia	56.7	24.8	0.8	1.7	—	6.5	9.5	35.9	27.0	2.3	1.2	0.9	18.4	14.3
Costa Rica	57.4	32.1	0.6	0.6	—	5.4	3.9	36.4	23.8	1.4	0.3	0.3	28.3	9.5
Dominican Rep.	74.1	14.5	1.9	0.8	0.3	1.4	7.0	67.7	14.6	1.3	1.0	—	1.1	14.3
Ecuador	61.0	24.2	4.8	0.6	—	6.8	2.6	42.2	10.1	1.9	1.4	0.5	36.3	7.6
El Salvador	30.7	31.5	20.0	0.5	—	15.4	1.9	28.4	22.6	9.5	0.7	—	32.0	6.8
Guatemala	49.6	27.8	9.4	0.5	0.1	7.5	5.1	29.6	24.1	5.3	1.2	1.2	31.7	6.9
Guyana	18.7	27.5	0.5	28.8	—	13.6	10.9	22.9	33.1	2.5	3.9	—	16.7	20.9
Haiti	52.4	36.8	4.8	0.2	—	1.8	4.0	69.1	25.8	0.4	1.6	0.7	1.6	0.8
Honduras	60.7	13.1	0.8	2.9	—	19.2	3.3	51.5	18.8	3.9	—	0.3	20.9	4.6
Jamaica	36.0	29.7	0.2	21.3	—	1.7	11.1	42.0	20.8	0.8	4.6	2.1	6.0	23.7
Mexico	60.6	6.6	6.9	0.8	0.1	4.3	20.7	57.4	9.5	4.9	1.7	0.9	12.4	13.2
Nicaragua	42.6	25.1	20.3	3.3	—	5.3	3.4	27.1	23.1	11.8	1.2	—	26.1	10.7
Panama	75.1	6.0	0.5	5.1	—	5.0	8.3	53.5	19.8	0.3	1.2	0.4	8.3	16.5
Paraguay	22.5	26.0	0.1	—	—	30.3	21.1	11.1	40.8	1.5	0.4	—	29.4	16.8
Peru	35.4	40.1	7.3	0.5	0.3	9.3	7.1	31.5	21.4	13.3	0.3	0.2	12.3	21.0
Surinam	n.a.	n.a.	n.a.	n.a.	n.a.	n.a.	n.a.	37.1	28.7	2.3	2.9	2.0	2.7	24.3
Trinidad & Tobago	25.7	38.1	0.1	4.8	0.1	5.1	26.1	68.7	6.5	0.6	1.8	—	11.0	11.4
Uruguay	13.9	56.3	2.0	0.6	0.4	6.1	20.7	4.7	38.3	2.0	0.2	5.5	26.2	23.1
Venezuela	35.7	16.4	0.6	7.1	—	10.1	30.1	42.4	7.9	0.4	12.2	—	12.0	25.1
Latin America	**37.2**	**29.4**	**3.3**	**3.2**	**0.2**	**8.4**	**18.3**	**34.9**	**20.8**	**4.4**	**3.9**	**1.4**	**15.4**	**19.2**

[a] Belgium, Denmark, Federal Republic of Germany, France, Ireland, Italy, Netherlands, United Kingdom.   [b] Member countries of the IDB.
[c] Includes also the following petroleum countries: Iran, Iraq, Kuwait, Oman, Qatar, Saudi Arabia, United Arab Emirates.
n.a. Not available.
Source: International Monetary Fund, *Direction of Trade Tapes*, November 1982.

Traditional exports have not fared as well as non-traditional exports. In 1960, fifteen primary commodities represented 19.6 per cent of world trade, but in 1972 their share had declined to 16 per cent. Between 1970 and 1972, these fifteen commodities accounted for 56.3 per cent of Latin America's total exports, in the following proportions: crude petroleum (13.0 per cent), coffee (11.7 per cent), copper (6.3 per cent), sugar (4.2 per cent), beef (3.9 per cent), iron ore (3.2 per cent), cotton (2.7 per cent), bananas (2.4 per cent), maize (2.1 per cent), fishmeal (1.7 per cent), crustacea, cocoa and soya (all 1 per cent) and wool (0.8 per cent). During the 1970s exports of thirteen commodities (the above, excluding wool, crustacea and wheat, and including bauxite) declined in volume (their performance was static if crude oil is excluded), but their value increased by 6.8 per cent between 1975 and 1979. In contrast, non-traditional exports grew in value by 17.8 per cent in the same period, taking a share of 61 per cent of total Latin American trade in 1979.

Of the fifteen commodities mentioned above, two have declined in importance in relation to the region's trade since 1972: crustacea (exported by Mexico and Panama) and wool (from Uruguay and Argentina). But there are others whose importance to individual or a few countries is great, but whose proportion of the region's trade is not significantly large, for instance tin from Bolivia, zinc (from Peru, Mexico and Bolivia), nickel (from Cuba) and silver, of which Mexico is the world's largest producer.

Regarding the major agricultural commodities of the region, Brazil is the largest grower of coffee in the world (although it is that country's second export commodity). While new frost-free areas are being developed, the adverse effects of frost can sometimes have a marked effect on world supplies. As well as in Brazil and Colombia, the region's second largest producer, coffee is the main earner of foreign exchange in Costa Rica, El Salvador, Guatemala, Haiti and Nicaragua; it is the second commodity in Honduras. Latin American and Caribbean sugar producers account for about 60 per cent of world supplies. Cuba, the region's leading exporter, sells a large proportion of its crop to the USSR and the Socialist bloc; it also exports to Mexico, whose production is insufficient to meet domestic demand. In Brazil, where sugar counts for less than 3 per cent of total exports, production is increasing to furnish the country's gasohol and alcohol programme (for the substitution of petrol for cars – a programme also in operation in other countries). The Dominican Republic relies on sugar for 35 per cent of export earnings; other exporters are Guatemala, Colombia and Argentina. In the English-speaking Caribbean, only Barbados is in a strong position. Sugar is the dominant export in St Kitts/Nevis/Anguilla, but in Antigua, a once healthy sugar industry has almost vanished owing to inflation of wage demands when world sugar markets were depressed.

Owing to increased competition from cocoa substitutes and the popularity of cheaper non-chocolate sweets, world cocoa production has been reduced to levels which are nearer those of consumption. Latin America's chief exporters of cocoa are Ecuador and the Dominican Republic; other major producers and exporters are Brazil, Venezuela and Mexico. Production of cotton is not sufficient to meet world demand, but in most of Latin America crops have not been increased, principally because of the competition from man-made materials. Brazil is the exception, where export incentives operate, and its volume of exports to the EEC is greater than that of seven other major Latin American cotton exporters combined, Peru, Uruguay, Colombia, Mexico, Argentina, Guatemala and Haiti. Cotton is the chief foreign-exchange earner in Paraguay (representing over a third of its total), and is the second largest in El Salvador, Guatemala and Nicaragua.

The traditional markets for beef have been the USA, the EEC and Japan, exported mainly from Argentina, Uruguay, Costa Rica, and Nicaragua. By 1980, EEC subsidies and protectionist policies on beef, and the United States' prohibition of uncooked beef imports (as a precaution against foot and mouth disease), caused a fall in Argentine beef exports, but to some degree the USSR has replaced these markets. (Production and exports of beef in Brazil were boosted in the early 1980s as part of a trade expansion plan.) Argentina is the only Latin American exporter of wheat, and, following President Carter's wheat-export ban on US sales to Russia, one of its principal customers is again the USSR. Argentina is seeking to diversify its markets but farmers are also turning to other crops such as maize (another major Argentine export), soya and sorghum.

The chief Latin American growers of bananas are Brazil, Ecuador, Colombia, Costa Rica, Honduras, Mexico, Guatemala and Panama. In the Caribbean, bananas are the main crop in Dominica and St Lucia, and are important in Jamaica. Soya exports from Brazil have become the chief foreign exchange earner, replacing coffee; in 1970-2 soya exports were 4.9 per cent of the total, and coffee 28 per cent, but by 1979-81 soya was 12.1 per cent, coffee 10.1 per cent, and 1982 earnings were $1.9 billion (11.2 per cent)

and $1.5 billion (8.9 per cent) respectively. Paraguay and Argentina are also exporters of soya. The principal Latin American exporters of fishmeal are Chile and Peru. Overfishing and a change in the currents off the coast sent Peru's once-flourishing fishing industry into decline in the 1970s and 1980s, but Chile's fishmeal industry has expanded, overtaking Peru's level of exports.

Turning to minerals, production of copper increased throughout the 1970s in Peru and Chile (which has 23 per cent of total world-proved reserves and is the second largest provider of copper). In Chile this commodity is the largest export earner, in Peru it is the second largest. Mexico became an important producer with the opening of La Caridad mine in 1979. Latin America has one-fifth of the world's reserves of iron ore; the major exporters are Brazil, Chile, Peru and Venezuela. One of the world's main sources of bauxite is Jamaica. Guyana, for which bauxite is the major foreign-exchange earner, and Surinam are also large producers, as is Brazil whose output has grown to become the region's second largest after Jamaica. In Venezuela there are estimated reserves of bauxite of 500 million tonnes at Los Pijiguaos.

Two Latin American oil-producing countries are members of OPEC, Venezuela and Ecuador. Estimated Venezuelan exports in 1983 were 1.5 million barrels per day (bpd) with crude and refined petroleum providing 93 per cent of foreign exchange. Although Venezuela has historically been the region's leading exporter of petroleum; its OPEC quota is 1.7 million bpd, although it would like to increase this to 2.6 million. Mexico is now the region's largest producer (2.7 million bpd); exports averaged 1.5 million bpd in 1982 and 1983. Part of these exports, and part of those from Venezuela (160,000 bpd in all), are sold to eleven Central American and Caribbean countries at preferential rates under the terms of the 1980 San José Agreement (revised in August 1983). Principally, this agreement is designed to aid investment in exploration for, and diversification of, energy sources. In Ecuador, oil has replaced bananas as the major export commodity, but increasing domestic demand has curtailed exports. In Peru, as in Ecuador, oil comes from the Amazon jungle, on the eastern side of the Andes; in both cases, production and exports have been helped by the construction of a pipeline to the coast. Argentina has raised output of oil to cover 92 per cent of its needs, and has the potential to be self-sufficient in both oil and gas. The most recent oil-exporting country in the region is Guatemala. In the Caribbean, Trinidad and Tobago and the Bahamas (which imports the crude) earn over 90 per cent of their foreign exchange from petroleum products, but the former has shifted the emphasis of its energy policy to its national gas reserves after suffering severe losses of earnings from the collapse of the world oil market in the early 1980s.

Other Latin American countries with oil deposits have experienced lower output: Colombia, Chile and Bolivia (although exports of this country's natural gas have increased). Countries like Uruguay, which is 100 per cent dependent on imports, or Brazil, which imports 75 per cent of its crude oil requirement, were hard hit by rising oil costs, and have consequently pursued policies to diversify energy use away from oil in order to curtail imports.

For the oil-importing countries of the region, the import bill for fuels soared after the 'first oil-shock' of 1973, upsetting what until then had been a relatively stable structure of commodity imports. Increasing fuel costs and inflation in industrialized countries also adversely affected the price of capital and intermediate goods, and of raw materials for the region's manufacturing industries. However, the varying availability of foreign exchange, owing to fluctuating commodity export prices, meant that between 1970 and 1981 the growth of imports, although uninterrupted, was not at a steady rate. In 1982, both the volume and the value of imports to the region declined sharply, the former by 16 per cent, the latter by 19 per cent. The net effect of this slump was a trade surplus for the region of $8.8 billion, compared with 1981's deficit of $639 million, but the causes were devaluation, shortage of foreign exchange because of low commodity prices, and domestic economic stagnation (particularly in Argentina, Chile, Mexico and Bolivia). In 1983 imports were further restricted by the austerity measures adopted by a number of countries in order to confront foreign debt crises; their value fell by 29 per cent. This, plus a 7 per cent increase in the volume of exports, led to a trade surplus in 1983 of $31 billion. Imports of consumer durables are traditionally high, but intra-regional trade has absorbed some of the demand. Imports of capital goods depend to some degree upon direct investment for specific projects, but in general terms, those connected with the energy sector are destined for areas such as oil exploration, refining and petrochemicals, coal conversion, and hydroelectricity. Construction and infrastructure equipment rank highly in the composition of imports, particularly for road, airport and port facilities, and telecommunications. Although Latin America has the capacity to be self-sufficient in food production, there is much demand for imported agricultural technology, fertilizers and food-processing and packaging machinery. The volume of basic grain imports depends on harvests, but Brazil, Colombia and Chile are large importers of wheat.

With the rapid expansion of world commerce in 1972–3, Latin American trade with the world was invigorated. The convergence of economic expansion in industrialized countries and the cyclical rises in commodity prices led to a boom in the latter between 1971 and 1974. This allowed some countries to offset the concurrent massive rises in import costs which followed the first oil crisis. But in 1974, recession in the industrialized countries caused falling demand and a drop in all commodity prices except oil. For the oil exporters, oil-price rises were a constant source of exchange until the 1983

lowering of OPEC prices, but for those countries whose earnings are dependent upon one, or a few, basic non-oil commodities, revenue from exports has fluctuated after 1974 since their performance is tied to foreign markets. Depressed commodity prices owing to recession in the developed countries, coupled with high interest rates on foreign debt, were two of the main contributory factors to financial crisis in Latin America in the 1980s. But in a large number of countries, a small number of commodities contribute more than 40 per cent to export earnings: Argentina (cereals), Chile (copper), Colombia (coffee), Costa Rica (coffee and bananas), El Salvador (coffee and cotton), Haiti (coffee and bauxite), Honduras (coffee and bananas), Uruguay (wool and meat), Jamaica (alumina and bauxite), Dominican Republic (sugar, doré, coffee and ferronickel), Guyana (bauxite, sugar, rice), Surinam (alumina, bauxite, aluminium), Bolivia (tin, natural gas), Nicaragua (coffee, cotton, beef), and Paraguay (cotton, soya beans, timber).

The terms of trade for the region declined by 16.7 per cent in 1975 as primary commodity prices weakened and manufactured import prices rose. But in the four following years there was great variation, leading in 1979 to renewed export expansion (mainly in Mexican oil, Chilean and Peruvian copper, and diverse products from Argentina and Brazil), improving the terms of trade income. However, world recession was also reflected in terms of trade which fell by 7 per cent in 1981, 5 per cent in 1982, and 7 per cent a year later; in 1982, only seven countries increased their terms of trade (none by more than 4 per cent – Haiti; Colombia and Panama increased theirs by 3 per cent, El Salvador, Honduras, Trinidad and Tobago, and Venezuela by 1 per cent), in most cases helped by improved coffee and banana prices. Worst hit were the region's oil exporters, whose terms of trade in 1982 declined by 12 per cent and in 1983 by 7.5 per cent, in marked contrast to previous years. In addition to the fluctuation of commodity prices, the purchasing power of these prices did not increase in real terms in the years up to 1982; in constant dollar terms, the index prices for Latin America's major commodities fell between 1960 and 1979 by 7.4 per cent, and in 1982 alone by 6 per cent. In 1983, the non-oil-exporting countries' purchasing power increased by 6.5 per cent, owing to the increased volume of sales abroad, but this was insufficient to compensate for previous years' losses. The oil-exporting countries' purchasing power fell by 4 per cent in 1983. Not only has this instability affected earnings, but it has also limited the capacity to diversify the industrial base from which new exports can be generated, and the semiprocessing of commodities to increase earnings. According to UNCTAD (UN Conference on Trade and Development), if exports of copper, bauxite, cotton, cocoa and coffee could be brought up to semiprocessed stage, earnings could be increased substantially.

Unstable growth in world trade (an average of 8 per cent between 1960 and 1973, but only 4.8 per cent between 1975 and 1979)

Trade and tourism

Table 18. Total imports of crude and refined oil, by country, 1960, 1973, 1977–82
(thousand barrels)

Country	Crude							
	1960	1973	1977	1978	1979	1980	1981	1982*
Argentina	23 172	21 354	21 950	16 012	12 635	15 907	9 104	3 887
Bahamas	n.a.	n.a.	7	9	10	10	n.a.	n.a.
Barbados	n.a.	890	939	1 000	920	331	837	n.a.
Bolivia	—	—	—	—	—	—	—	—
Brazil	42 166	261 171	297 517	328 967	366 078	304 395	295 820	268 795
Chile	—	22 902	26 902	27 117	33 421	23 867	19 810	n.a.
Colombia	—	—	9 405	8 833	8 985	7 339	7 714	7 327
Costa Rica	—	3 195	2 377	2 927	3 483	3 483	n.a.	n.a.
Dominican Republic	—	8 912	12 056	11 582	12 563	10 914	11 828	9 944
Ecuador	1 566	5 813	5 175	178	b	—	—	n.a.
El Salvador	—	4 686	5 255	5 472	5 142	4 563	4 123	n.a.
Guatemala	—	6 297	5 291	5 829	5 723	5 443	5 324	4 341
Guyana	—	—	—	—	—	—	—	—
Haiti	—	—	—	—	—	—	—	—
Honduras	—	5 071	3 462	3 270	3 509	3 626	1 710	n.a.
Jamaica	n.a.	11 022	6 881	7 055	7 753	7 669[a]	n.a.	n.a.
Mexico	—	23 613	—	—	—	—	—	—
Nicaragua	—	4 110	5 413	3 928	3 124	4 457	n.a.	n.a.
Panama	—	26 894	20 111	16 161	16 940	13 841	10 685	11 752
Paraguay	—	1 537	1 860	2 334	2 198	2 030	1 839	1 741
Peru	—	11 157	14 659	—	—	—	—	—
Surinam	—	—	—	—	—	—	—	—
Trinidad & Tobago	38 016	43 434	62 376	56 651	41 984	49 796	n.a.	n.a.
Uruguay	9 147	12 045	13 500	15 063	11 716	13 389	12 300	n.a.
Venezuela	—	—	—	—	—	—	—	—
Latin America	**114 067**	**474 103**	**515 136**	**512 838**	**535 628**	**471 060**	**381 094**	**379 000[a]**

Country	Refined							
	1960	1973	1977	1978	1979	1980	1981	1982*
Argentina	12 469	6 397	3 855	1 390	1 266	2 450	3 887	736
Bahamas	—	—	—	—	—	—	—	—
Barbados	n.a.	1 220	1 233	1 390	526	1 282	1 225	n.a.
Bolivia	95	150	199	180	127	—	—	—
Brazil	31 857	12 900	10 064	7 088	8 560	13 244	8 043	7 300[a]
Chile	3 699	2 555	—	2 294	3 837	371	5 064	n.a.
Colombia	1 030	150	3 764	7 784	10 341	12 997	11 025	11 033
Costa Rica	1 530	755	2 493	3 117	2 821	3 460	3 486	n.a.
Dominican Republic	2 490	3 419	2 137	3 297	3 317	4 200	3 064	4 333
Ecuador	—	100	3 915	1 900	2 700	4 591	4 875	n.a.
El Salvador	1 590	—	—	—	—	—	—	—
Guatemala	2 930	599	4 356	4 522	5 679	5 369	4 054	3 932
Guyana	n.a.	3 677	4 290	4 590	4 100	4 387	4 452	n.a.
Haiti	620	942	1 493	1 643	1 704	1 625[a]	1 628	n.a.
Honduras	1 490	433	764	1 058	844	758	1 411	n.a.
Jamaica	n.a.	8 509	10 130	9 291	8 774	8 621	5 488	n.a
Mexico	3 804	24 156	3 807	1 138	1 264	1 719	2 146	4 516
Nicaragua	1 380	330	957	1 448	324	612	n.a.	n.a.
Panama	2 770	140	469	181	221	560	1 492	607
Paraguay	799	500	818	932	996	1 470	1 459	1 531
Peru	4 150	3 898	4 508	1 722	284	403	n.a.	n.a.
Surinam	n.a.	n.a.	n.a.	n.a.	n.a.	n.a.	n.a.	n.a.
Trinidad & Tobago	1 194	630	191	—	199	94	n.a.	n.a.
Uruguay	1 782	625	956	654	2 066	899	1 260	n.a.
Venezuela	—	—	—	—	—	—	—	—
Latin America	**72 679**	**72 083**	**60 399**	**55 619**	**59 950**	**69 112**	**64 059**	**60 000[a]**

* Preliminary estimate   [a] IDB estimate.   [b] Included in refined.   n.a. Not available.

Table 19. Total exports of crude and refined oil, by country, 1960, 1973, 1977–82
(thousand barrels)

	Crude							
Country	1960	1973	1977	1978	1979	1980	1981	1982*
Argentina	233	203	—	—	—	—	—	—
Bahamas	—	—	—	—	—	—	—	—
Barbados	—	—	—	—	—	—	—	—
Bolivia	1 093	11 845	4 480	2 863	165	—	—	—
Brazil	4 294	13 686	—	—	—	420	5 166	n.a.
Chile	—	435	—	—	—	—	—	—
Colombia	31 332	365	—	—	—	—	—	—
Costa Rica	—	—	—	—	—	—	—	—
Dominican Republic	—	—	—	—	—	—	—	—
Ecuador	—	71 126	50 453	42 000	46 000	39 636	46 449	n.a.
El Salvador	—	—	—	—	—	—	—	—
Guatemala	—	—	—	—	—	782	662	1 546
Guyana	—	—	—	—	—	—	—	—
Haiti	—	—	—	—	—	—	—	—
Honduras	—	—	—	—	—	—	—	—
Jamaica	—	—	—	—	—	—	—	—
Mexico	1 100	—	73 736	133 247	194 485	302 957	400 778	544 614
Nicaragua	—	—	—	—	—	—	—	—
Panama	—	—	—	—	—	—	—	—
Paraguay	—	—	—	—	—	—	—	—
Peru	2 931	123	586	1 225	11 521	17 744	20 586	n.a.
Surinam	—	—	—	—	—	—	—	—
Trinidad & Tobago	4 809	23 614	49 400	51 202	40 450	46 089	n.a.	n.a.
Uruguay	—	—	—	—	—	—	—	—
Venezuela	730 962	775 092	482 165	454 425	511 730	469 578	462 455	387 630
Latin America	**776 754**	**896 489**	**660 820**	**684 962**	**804 351**	**877 206**	**936 096**	**1 088 000**[a]

	Refined							
Country	1960	1973	1977	1978	1979	1980	1981	1982*
Argentina	220	905	1 184	2 428	2 078	9 430	19 881	15 713
Bahamas	n.a.	n.a.	n.a.	n.a.	n.a.	n.a.	n.a.	n.a.
Barbados	41	947	795	1 084	685	931	726	n.a.
Bolivia	—	1	—	102	1 181	727	312	592
Brazil	—	17 026	9 436	14 476	9 317	12 775	27 013	33 000[a]
Chile	112	525	371	—	—	—	—	—
Colombia	4 080	9 490	8 758	11 152	8 967	9 469	10 369	11 900
Costa Rica	—	—	—	—	—	—	—	—
Dominican Republic	—	—	—	—	—	—	—	—
Ecuador	—	823	1 037	7 900	7 400	7 957	5 846	n.a.
El Salvador	—	—	—	—	—	—	—	—
Guatemala	—	—	—	—	—	—	—	—
Guyana	—	—	—	—	—	—	—	—
Haiti	—	—	—	—	—	—	—	—
Honduras	—	1 586	119	490	383	48	28	n.a.
Jamaica	n.a.	560	428	308	1 042	n.a.	n.a.	n.a.
Mexico	6 447	8 669	1 652	673	3 701	17 062	23 645	14 704
Nicaragua	—	231	106	93	186	119	n.a.	n.a.
Panama	—	19 404	12 173	10 493	7 345	7 723	6 118	5 661
Paraguay	—	—	—	—	—	—	—	—
Peru	3 317	3 171	3 535	3 266	6 308	4 511	n.a.	n.a.
Surinam	—	—	—	—	—	—	—	—
Trinidad & Tobago	37 889	121 832	82 248	75 596	74 500	75 435	n.a.	n.a.
Uruguay	—	—	—	—	—	—	—	—
Venezuela	251 747	374 716	243 090	262 070	254 405	212 646	179 580	179 580
Latin America	**303 853**	**559 885**	**364 932**	**390 131**	**377 498**	**358 833**	**273 518**	**300 000**[a]

* Preliminary.   n.a. Not available.

Source: Inter-American Development Bank, based on official data.

Table 20. Contribution of major commodity exports to total value of merchandise exports, 1970–2 and 1980–2[a]
(per cent)

	First product			Second product			Third product		
	Commodity	1970–2	1980–2	Commodity	1970–2	1980–2	Commodity	1970–2	1980–2
Argentina	Beef	28.1	10.6	Corn	14.5	9.7	—	—	—
Bahamas	Petroleum products	70.6	95.3	—	—	—	—	—	—
Barbados	Sugar	56.6	17.4	—	—	—	—	—	—
Bolivia	Tin	33.9	37.3	Natural gas	4.9	35.0	Crude petroleum	12.0	—
Brazil	Soya beans	57.9	11.9	Coffee	28.0	9.2	—	—	—
Chile	Copper	4.9	45.2	—	—	—	—	—	—
Colombia	Coffee	70.0	54.1	—	—	—	—	—	—
Costa Rica	Coffee	28.5	26.0	Bananas	29.0	25.7	—	—	—
Dom. Rep.	Sugar	49.8	38.8	Doré	—	21.6	—	—	—
Ecuador	Crude petroleum	7.8	57.5	Bananas	47.7	9.2	Coffee	17.0	5.2
El Salvador	Coffee	46.1	57.5	Cotton	11.6	7.3	—	—	—
Guatemala	Coffee	33.2	28.2	Cotton	10.2	9.5	—	—	—
Guyana	Sugar	31.0	35.5	Bauxite	33.3	31.8	—	—	—
Haiti	Coffee	38.3	27.4	Bauxite	14.4	9.8	—	—	—
Honduras	Bananas	44.7	29.1	Coffee	12.9	23.4	—	—	—
Jamaica	Alumina	38.7	55.9	Bauxite	25.7	18.9	—	—	—
Mexico	Crude petroleum	2.0	70.4	—	—	—	—	—	—
Nicaragua	Coffee	15.3	31.2	Cotton	22.5	17.6	Beef	15.3	8.5
Panama	Petroleum products	19.5	19.8	Bananas	54.2	18.6	Shrimp	10.5	15.1
Paraguay	Cotton	4.0	38.3	Soya beans	2.2	19.5	Timber	15.1	15.5
Peru	Copper	21.8	16.6	Crude petroleum	—	15.9	Fishmeal	27.9	5.1
Surinam[b]	Alumina	45.2	55.1	Bauxite	27.6	13.8	Aluminium	16.2	11.2
Trin. & Tob.	Petroleum products	77.4	91.4	—	—	—	—	—	—
Uruguay	Wool	29.5	20.1	Beef	37.7	19.7	—	—	—
Venezuela	Crude petroleum	59.7	65.3	Petroleum products	29.2	29.6	—	—	—

[a] For each country, products listed are those representing 10 per cent or more of total exports in 1970–2 or 1980–2. Products are listed to their relative importance in 1980–2.
[b] Based on 1980–1 data.
Source: International Monetary Fund, *International Financial Statistics*, November 1983.

	Number of products	1970–2	1980–2
Argentina	2	42.6	20.3
Bahamas	1	7.6	95.3
Barbados	1	33.9	17.4
Bolivia	3	74.1	72.3
Brazil	2	32.9	21.1
Chile	1	70.0	45.2
Colombia	1	56.6	54.1
Costa Rica	2	57.5	51.7
Dom. Rep.	3	64.7	60.4
Ecuador	3	72.5	71.9
El Salvador	2	57.7	64.8
Guatemala	2	43.4	37.7
Guyana	3	71.7	67.3
Haiti	2	52.7	37.2
Honduras	2	57.6	52.5
Jamaica	2	64.4	74.8
Mexico	1	2.0	70.4
Nicaragua	3	53.1	57.3
Panama	3	84.2	51.5
Paraguay	3	21.3	73.3
Peru	2	49.7	37.6
Surinam[b]	3	89.0	80.1
Trin. & Tob.	1	77.4	91.4
Uruguay	2	67.2	39.8
Venezuela	2	88.9	94.9

restricted exports from Latin America and the Caribbean in general, and a further threat has been posed by the protectionist measures taken by the United States, Canada and the EEC, by agreements under the Tokyo Round of Multilateral Trade Negotiations (begun in September 1973), which favour the manufactured goods of industrialized, rather than developing, countries, and by the inability of subsequent international conferences (for example, General Agreement on Tariffs and Trade – GATT – in 1982, UNCTAD in 1983) to reach a compromise between the developed countries' view that only world recovery will revitalize international trade, and the developing nations' desire for more liberal trade policies, more aid, and less restrictive credit terms.

As in other regions of the developing world, Latin American and the Caribbean trade has suffered in that its interdependence with the international economy has meant that world recession has enforced regional recession. Declining trade was one of a number of negative factors which combined in 1982 and 1983 to produce a worse crisis than in 1974–6. With regard to trade in this climate, the report entitled *Bases for a Latin American Response to the International Economic Crisis*, produced by SELA and ECLA, suggests that Latin American trade with the industrialized West should be

Table 21. Exports, imports, trade balance, current account balance by country, 1970, 1975, 1979, 1982
(in millions US dollars)

Country	1970				1975			
	Exports	Imports	Trade balance	C/A balance	Exports	Imports	Trade balance	C/A balance
Argentina	1773.0	1449.0	274.0	−159.0	2961.4	3510.3	−548.9	−1287.1
Barbados	35.2	106.3	−71.1	−50.3	94.5	196.9	−102.4	−29.7
Bolivia	192.5	166.2	26.3	−21.5	462.7	514.9	−52.2	−157.3
Brazil	2739.0	2507.0	232.0	561.0	8501.8	12049.7	−3547.9	−7007.1
Chile	1135.0	848.0	287.0	−69.0	1570.0	1681.7	−111.7	−546.6
Colombia	782.0	802.0	−20.0	−293.0	1716.9	1424.3	292.6	−109.1
Costa Rica	231.0	286.8	−55.8	−74.1	493.1	627.3	−134.2	−217.7
Dominican Republic	213.2	278.0	−64.8	−125.2	893.9	772.7	121.2	−72.7
Ecuador	234.2	263.8	−29.5	−129.8	1012.9	1006.3	6.6	−220.0
El Salvador	236.1	194.1	42.0	8.7	533.0	550.8	−17.8	−92.8
Guatemala	297.1	266.6	30.5	−7.9	641.0	672.4	−31.4	−65.7
Haiti	39.0	47.7	−8.7	1.7	71.4	121.5	50.1	26.3
Honduras	178.1	203.4	−25.3	−68.3	309.7	372.4	−62.7	−112.5
Jamaica	342.1	449.0	−106.9	−152.9	808.7	969.7	−161.0	−282.8
Mexico	1429.0	2239.0	−810.0	−1068.0	3008.8	6292.0	−3283.2	−4054.3
Nicaragua	174.8	177.7	−2.9	−39.2	374.9	482.2	−107.3	−185.0
Panama	130.3	330.1	−199.8	−63.7	330.9	823.1	−492.2	−168.7
Paraguay	65.3	76.6	−11.3	−16.4	176.4	227.3	−50.9	−89.5
Peru	1034.0	699.0	335.0	202.0	1290.7	2389.5	−1098.8	−1540.9
Trinidad & Tobago	502.4	496.4	6.0	−70.6	987.4	676.6	310.8	273.2
Uruguay	224.1	203.1	21.0	−45.1	384.9	494.1	−109.2	−189.5
Venezuela	2756.0	1787.0	969.0	−136.0	8853.9	5461.5	3392.4	2169.7

Country	1979				1982[a]			
	Exports	Imports	Trade balance	C/A balance	Exports	Imports	Trade balance	C/A balance
Argentina	7816.6	6018.1	1798.5	−498.6	7600.0	4500.0	3100.0	−2000.0
Barbados	131.4	373.7	−247.3	−34.1	189.0	535.0	−346.0	−107.0
Bolivia	761.6	815.1	−53.5	−357.8	804.3	425.1	379.2	−131.3
Brazil	15235.3	17942.0	−2706.7	−10465.2	20200.0	19400.0	800.0	−14500.0
Chile	3835.9	4190.0	−354.1	−1189.9	3783.0	3565.0	218.0	−2382.0
Colombia	3506.5	2996.1	510.4	491.0	3830.0	5175.2	−1345.2	−2266.1
Costa Rica	941.4	1257.0	−315.6	−558.8	1010.0	819.0	191.0	−272.0
Dominican Republic	868.6	1093.9	−225.3	−340.8	784.1	1250.0	−465.9	−469.5
Ecuador	2171.5	2096.8	74.7	−616.9	2324.0	2220.0	104.0	−1178.0
El Salvador	1224.2	938.5	285.7	129.2	738.2	900.0	−161.8	−131.0
Guatemala	1221.8	1401.7	−179.9	−205.4	1161.0	1234.0	−73.0	−315.0
Haiti	138.1	234.1	−96.0	−58.6	157.1	283.8	−126.7	−115.0
Honduras	756.5	783.1	−26.6	−191.7	677.4	680.7	−3.3	−218.7
Jamaica	814.7	892.4	−77.7	−152.7	726.4	1202.7	−476.3	−426.4
Mexico	9295.9	12122.8	−2826.9	−5469.0	21391.0	14516.0	6875.0	−2685.0
Nicaragua	615.9	388.9	227.0	160.6	429.1	646.1	−217.0	−349.2
Panama	334.0	1104.9	−770.9	−302.2	345.0	1459.3	−1114.3	−453.9
Paraguay	384.4	577.1	−192.7	−206.0	362.8	750.0	−387.2	−515.3
Peru	2469.0	2087.9	1381.1	617.5	3212.0	3502.0	−290.0	−1401.0
Trinidad & Tobago	1649.1	1324.8	324.3	−39.4	2234.3	2455.5	−221.2	−223.3
Uruguay	788.1	1125.7	−337.6	−316.5	961.3	1123.5	−162.2	−594.2
Venezuela	14360.6	10004.0	4356.6	350.1	15952.0	13384.0	2568.0	−2218.0

[a] IDB estimates based on data furnished by member countries.

reduced in favour of trade with the Socialist bloc and the rest of the Third World, but principally with Latin America itself. The region should aim to reduce Western imports and substitute them with those of other Latin American countries to utilize more fully existing industrial capacity. A regional preference system and the strengthening of clearing mechanisms should also be adopted. This, basically, is the aim of LAIA and Ancom, and Brazil has been leading the field in paying for its oil needs with manufactures of commercial and domestic vehicles, steel products, paper, machine tools and aircraft. But the danger is that too rapid a shift would mean that the more developed regional economies (Brazil, Mexico) would replace the United States and Japan as chief suppliers, and continue to develop at the expense of the poorer countries which have little to offer. Furthermore, the intraregional trade groups have so far failed to implement plans to allocate specific industries to weaker partners, or to apply successful tariff agreements. It is unlikely that positive-enough steps towards integration will be taken in the short term to escape the region's reliance on trade with industrialized countries. But in the longer term, assuming the governments of the region can act jointly, as SELA and ECLA urge, it may be possible for Latin America and the Caribbean to build up sufficient commercial strength to respond to discriminatory restrictions placed on the region's exports.

Tourism

A continuing dependence on primary commodities has not permitted steady growth in the region. The result has been that the contribution of merchandise trade to the current account has varied. Import restrictions and export incentives have been applied to strengthen the countries' balance of payments, but deficits in the services accounts have been detrimental to current account balances. Even travel (tourists to and from a country), the one service sector in which a positive balance was regularly achieved in the 1970s, went into deficit in 1980 and 1981, principally owing to exchange rate policies which encouraged residents to travel abroad, while reducing the incentives to foreigners to visit the region.

Furthermore, political and economic factors have discouraged visitors: political instability in Central America has upset the area's tourist trade; the fear of terrorism and of street assaults exists in many countries; weak Eurocurrencies have tended to attract Americans away from Latin America. Many countries have a positive travel account (increasing particularly rapidly in Colombia since 1976): the Bahamas, Costa Rica, Haiti, Panama (mainly for Canal Zone free trade), Paraguay, Trinidad and Tobago, and Uruguay (the majority of tourists coming from Buenos Aires). Peru's tourist industry experienced strong growth until 1980 (133,500 visitors arrived in 1970, 256,200 in 1975, 390,200 in 1980), but since then numbers declined to 300,000 in 1982 owing to some factors common to most Latin American destinations (world recession, the high cost of air fares, domestic inflation, the repercussions of the Falklands/Malvinas War) and to other, local factors: publicity given to guerrilla activity and inadequate marketing of Peru's tourist potential.

In Venezuela and Brazil, the travel sector has been heavily in deficit. Venezuela has had to tighten controls on entry in an attempt to stop illegal immigration. In Brazil, where tourism is a government priority, the infrastructure – hotels, internal flights, roads – is being improved, not only to entice foreigners (especially to the

Table 22. Service transactions: travel, by country, 1975–82 (millions of US dollars)

Country	1976 Credit	1976 Debit	1978 Credit	1978 Debit	1980 Credit	1980 Debit	1982[a] Credit	1982[a] Debit
Argentina	180.1	115.5	280.4	587.2	343.6	1 792.2	n.a.	n.a.
Bahamas	362.7	43.6	489.8	60.7	584.3	70.7	664.6	119.2
Barbados	103.8	8.2	137.7	9.8	252.2	19.0	n.a.	n.a.
Bolivia	25.1	30.9	34.9	40.7	40.0	52.1	40.0	40.0
Brazil	56.6	360.2	67.6	254.2	126.2	367.0	n.a.	n.a.
Chile	87.7	109.7	108.9	130.2	174.4	200.4	200.0	210.0
Colombia[b]	188.2	174.3	283.0	229.1	402.4	223.0	420.0	274.8
Costa Rica	54.7	41.8	72.4	61.6	86.8	62.1	90.5	34.1
Dominican Republic	70.9	90.1	92.3	126.3	172.6	165.8	n.a.	n.a.
Ecuador	30.7	49.8	64.9	96.7	91.0	149.0	n.a.	n.a.
El Salvador	21.0	43.3	36.7	103.3	13.4	106.1	18.0	102.0
Guatemala	65.7	81.7	67.4	107.3	61.7	164.1	14.0	100.6
Guyana	3.0	6.3	3.4	5.1	3.9	8.5	2.6	12.0
Haiti	24.6	4.7	54.2	28.8	64.7	28.0	81.1	41.7
Honduras	11.5	16.0	16.8	23.2	24.5	31.0	25.0	22.9
Jamaica	105.8	58.9	146.9	10.4	241.7	11.7	357.0	29.0
Mexico	2 232.8	1 617.5	3 206.4	2 147.2	5 220.4	4 187.0	n.a.	n.a.
Nicaragua[b]	28.2	35.1	25.3	59.7	21.6	31.0	20.0	14.0
Panama	154.5	33.7	200.9	37.2	168.4	56.0	172.0	78.5
Paraguay	14.0	12.9	40.4	19.7	90.7	34.6	80.0	40.0
Peru	99.3	56.6	141.5	33.8	292.0	106.0	322.0	150.0
Surinam	11.0	16.3	17.8	22.9	18.7	33.4	n.a.	n.a.
Trinidad & Tobago[c]	75.9	37.2	111.1	66.2	151.1	139.5	137.6	176.3
Uruguay	68.0	60.0	137.2	108.7	298.0	202.6	106.0	304.0
Venezuela	108.5	616.5	205.3	1 545.0	243.4	1 980.6	n.a.	n.a.
Latin America*	**4 184.3**	**3 720.8**	**6 043.2**	**5 915.0**	**9 229.8**	**10 303.3**	**n.a.**	**n.a.**

* Total may not add because of rounding.
[a] IDB estimates based on data furnished by member countries.
[b] Provisional data for 1980–1.
[c] Provisional data for 1981.
n.a. Not available.
Source: Inter-American Development Bank.

Ipanema beach, Rio de Janeiro

Amazon), but also to stem the tide of Brazilians taking their holidays abroad.

Tourism can be the hub of investment for many economic sectors: the construction industry is an obvious beneficiary as are internal travel services. In the CACM, for example, tourism is a part of integrated development and is linked to trade through the improvement of roads and border crossings for more efficient road transport.

In the Caribbean, development is inextricably linked with tourism, which is a major foreign-exchange earner. In the Bahamas, tourism represents 70 per cent of GDP and provides 40 per cent of employment; it is 60 per cent of Bermuda's GDP, and 12 per cent in Barbados, providing 20,000 direct and indirect jobs. In the eastern Caribbean, where the islands compete with each other for visitors, poor internal air services have hampered tourism, but the Ocho Rios CARICOM summit made air services a priority. The Caribbean was also severely affected by the oil crises of the 1970s since all costs (not least of international air travel) rose sharply, with a consequent drop in the number of travellers. By the end of the decade tourism was returning to boom proportions, only to be hit again in 1981 and 1982 by world recession and weak Eurocurrencies. However, a large influx of foreigners can bring with it a rise in criminality (especially of theft and fraud), as seen in many Caribbean islands and the poorer countries of the continent, where crime is inspired by envy of the visitors' higher living standards.

'One of the most useful characteristics of the tourist industry,' Doreen E. Crompton de Calvo has written, 'is the permanence of its basic resources: no matter how intensive the exploitation of sun,

Top: Machu Picchu, Peru. Above: Iguassú falls on the border between Brazil and Argentina

snow, water, scenery or history, there is no danger of their eventual disappearance as with mineral resources, or need for their frequent replacement as with agricultural products.' Latin America and the Caribbean have an abundance of attractions to offer the tourist. In the Caribbean, beaches are the major draw, but generally there are few large resorts (such as Mar de Plata, Argentina; Punta del Este, Uruguay; Acapulco, and newer developments like Cancún, in Mexico). Commercial exploitation of this type of centre is often inhibited by difficult terrain. This is also true for some archaeological sites whose remoteness adds to the mystery of their undocumented history, for instance the jungle cities of the Central American Maya, or the Inca cities, such as Machu Picchu, in the Andes. This mountain chain also embraces Lake Titicaca, the highest navigable lake in the world, primeval temperate forests and an alluring lake district in Chile, glacial ranges in Patagonia, and snow-capped volcanoes near the Equator. Mountains, which also stretch through Central America and Mexico, do not provide the only natural beauty of the region; there are also great rivers such as the Amazon, with its surrounding jungle; waterfalls (the Angel Falls, Iguassú – although the flooding of the Guaíra/Sete Quedas Falls to make way for the Itaipú hydroelectric scheme contradicts Crompton's thesis), vestiges of cloud forests in Central America; lakes (in Argentina and Chile); wide open plains and the world's driest deserts. But the preponderance of high land, especially in the tropical zones, makes the climate more amenable than in similar regions throughout the world. Within the natural variety there are numerous social attractions for the traveller: Carnival in Brazil and Trinidad, Indian festivals (often overlaid with Christianity), and the countless crafts of every country, which link the present with the past.

BB

Further reading

Inter-American Development Bank, *Latin America in the World Economy, Recent Development and Trends* (Washington, DC., 1975)

J. D. Theberge, R. W. Fontaine, *Latin America: Struggle for Progress* (Critical Choices for Americans, Vol. XIV; Lexington, 1977)

D. W. Berensen, M. Carnoy, J. Grunwald, *Latin American Trade Patterns* (Washington, DC., 1975)

J. Brooks, ed., *The 1984 South American Handbook*, 60th annual edition (Bath: Trade and Travel Publications Ltd., 1984) is strongly recommended to all travellers to Latin America and the Caribbean as a quite incomparable guidebook. Published annually, it is a remarkable compendium of useful information, and has been eulogized by numerous well-known travellers, including the novelist Graham Greene, who once described it as 'the best guidebook in existence'.

Boston Bay, Portland, Jamaica

Energy

In 1983 Latin America produced 6.6 per cent (453 million tonnes of oil equivalent) and consumed 5.0 per cent (349 million tonnes of oil equivalent) of the world's commercial energy within an area which is approximately 17 per cent of the continental surface of the globe and by a population which is about 8 per cent of the world's total. Latin America has been a producer of surplus energy throughout most of the twentieth century and is likely to remain a net exporter into the twenty-first. It has been able to maintain this status in spite of rapidly increasing domestic demand: in 1950 each of Latin America's 158 million people consumed on average 0.43 tonnes of oil equivalent or a total of 68 million tonnes of oil equivalent of all types of energy, commercial and traditional; in 1983 the population of 365 million consumed 465 million tonnes or three times as much per capita. It is notable that although the role of traditional energy sources – firewood, sugar-cane bagasse and other vegetable and animal fuels – has declined from supplying 43 per cent (29 million tonnes of oil equivalent) of the continent's requirements in 1950 to only 20 per cent in 1982, the volume (93 million tonnes) of such energy consumed has risen significantly. In the same period the consumption of conventional commercial or primary energy – from oil, natural gas, coal, hydroelectricity, nuclear and geothermal power, and nowadays biomass – rose even more dramatically: from 39 to 362 million tonnes of oil equivalent or by a factor of almost ten.

Oil and natural gas dominate the commercial energy stage in Latin America: in 1983, as in 1950, these hydrocarbons accounted for 86 per cent of production and 80 per cent of energy consumed. In no other continent are they so important: for the world at large, oil

(41 per cent) and natural gas (19 per cent) supplied only 60 per cent of demand in 1982, coal a further 30 per cent (in Latin America 5 per cent), hydroelectricity 7 per cent (Latin America 15 per cent) and nuclear electricity (an almost negligible 0.17 per cent in Latin America) most of the rest.

Commercial energy sources – oil fields, natural gas reservoirs, coal deposits and suitable hydroelectricity generating sites – are scattered unevenly throughout Latin America: some regions are major producers while others are almost bereft of energy reserves. The economic effects – for good or ill – of such geographical disparities on the individual countries of Latin America have been greatly exaggerated by huge increases in the world price of oil since 1972. The beneficiaries have been the oil-producing countries with a surplus to export. Venezuela remains the largest exporter of energy whether measured in volume, in value, or in the contribution it makes to its overall trade; Venezuela also enjoys the highest per-capita income in the continent and has run up the second highest per-capita foreign debt. Mexico has grown in recent years to be the other major exporter of energy; it too, has used its oil as collateral for huge external loans. Both Ecuador and Trinidad and Tobago produce three times as much, and Bolivia over twice as much commercial energy as they consume; Peru produces almost half as much again (46 per cent in 1981) as it consumes, while Argentina and Colombia are more or less in commercial balance. Brazil is the major loser in the energy stakes and its net energy deficit (37.9 million tonnes of oil equivalent in 1981) accounts for almost all the energy imported by South American countries and half that by all Latin American countries. Brazil imports 60 per cent of its commercial energy requirements and this is a major drain on the country's finances: in 1984 Brazil's foreign debt ($93,000 million) was the largest in Latin America (though amongst the lowest when measured on a per-capita basis). Many Central American and Caribbean countries were in a worse position than Brazil with only traditional fuels locally available to supplement imported energy: Cuba (with a deficit of 9 million tonnes of oil equivalent in 1981) and Puerto Rico (7.3 million tonnes) suffer most although arrangements with Mexico, Venezuela, the USA and the USSR have reduced the price of imported oil below the prevailing world price for some countries.

To counter the need to purchase expensive energy from overseas, many deficit countries have spent heavily on developing domestic alternatives to imported petroleum. Brazil, for example, now draws upon a wider range of conventional and unconventional commercial energy sources than does any other country in Latin America. Remarkably, Brazil still meets over half its domestic energy requirements from firewood and sugar-cane waste (bagasse), energy sources largely ignored by most compilers of national energy balances. Colombia, too, draws on an almost equally broad spec-

trum of energy suppliers. But although there has been a notable expansion and diversification of energy sources used in Latin America, there is a limit to its ability to find economic substitutes for oil and natural gas. Fortunately, in 1984 the continent was blessed with 12.1 per cent of the world's proven oil reserves (that is more than those of North America and one-third of those of the western world if the Middle East is excluded) and 5.9 per cent of the world's reserves of natural gas. In contrast, no other area of the world is so poorly supplied with coal and lignite reserves: Latin America has less than 1 per cent of either.

Hydrocarbons

The petroleum industry has a double importance in Latin America. The first is its dominant role both in meeting the energy requirements of the continent and as a trading staple: since 1980 petroleum has accounted for over a quarter of the value of Latin America's export trade or more than the next dozen leading mineral and agricultural commodities in total. The second is its important political role. Latin America pioneered what has since become commonplace: the heavy involvement of the state in the oil industry. At the production end a precedent was set in 1938, subsequently followed worldwide, when Mexico nationalized the local assets of the international oil companies and created its own state oil company. At the marketing end it was Venezuela which promoted the establishment of OPEC in 1960 and has continued to play a leading role in what is now the most remarkable cartel in modern economic history.

Mexico and Venezuela dominate Latin America's petroleum economy. Together in 1983 they produced just over three-quarters of the continent's oil and natural gas, yet housed just under one-quarter of the population. Venezuela, on a cumulative basis, has produced almost two-thirds (5160 million tonnes) and Mexico one-seventh (1160 million tonnes) of the oil extracted from the continent's sub-soil. Figures released at the World Petroleum Congress in 1983 show that Mexico (3790 million tonnes) and Venezuela (3640 million tonnes) account for all but one-seventh (1240 million tonnes) of the region's demonstrated oil reserves and enjoy almost equal shares (12,000 million tonnes and 11,000 million tonnes) of all except one-sixth (5000 million tonnes) of the likely ultimately recoverable reserves of Latin America. Three of the world's thirty-five 'super-giant' oil fields are in Latin America: the Bolívar field in Venezuela was the first such field to be identified and has yielded more oil than any other worldwide; the other two in southern Mexico are the most recent to be discovered and have reserves larger than any except the largest Middle Eastern fields. Both countries have long-established oil industries: that of Mexico has been rejuvenated by the new discoveries whereas that of Venezuela is showing signs of middle age.

ENERGY PRODUCTION AND ENERGY BALANCE (1981)

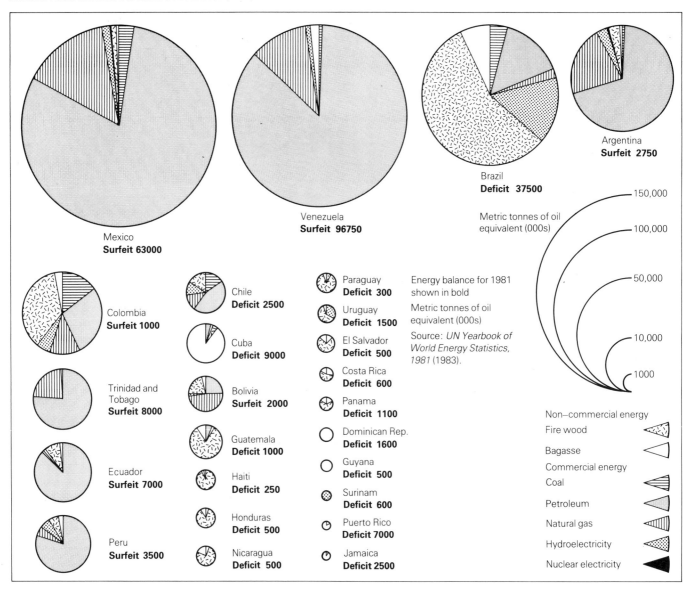

Mexico
Surfeit 63000

Venezuela
Surfeit 96750

Brazil
Deficit 37500

Argentina
Surfeit 2750

Metric tonnes of oil
equivalent (000s)

150,000

100,000

50,000

10,000

1000

Colombia
Surfeit 1000

Trinidad and
Tobago
Surfeit 8000

Ecuador
Surfeit 7000

Peru
Surfeit 3500

Chile
Deficit 2500

Cuba
Deficit 9000

Bolivia
Surfeit 2000

Guatemala
Deficit 1000

Haiti
Deficit 250

Honduras
Deficit 500

Nicaragua
Deficit 500

Paraguay
Deficit 300

Uruguay
Deficit 1500

El Salvador
Deficit 500

Costa Rica
Deficit 600

Panama
Deficit 1100

Dominican Rep.
Deficit 1600

Guyana
Deficit 500

Surinam
Deficit 600

Puerto Rico
Deficit 7000

Jamaica
Deficit 2500

Energy balance for 1981
shown in bold

Metric tonnes of oil
equivalent (000s)

Source: *UN Yearbook of
World Energy Statistics,
1981* (1983).

Non–commercial energy

Fire wood

Bagasse

Commercial energy

Coal

Petroleum

Natural gas

Hydroelectricity

Nuclear electricity

Mexico

The Mexican oil and natural gas industry has moved through several historical phases: the boom-and-bust of the first third of the twentieth century, a period of recovery and undramatic growth between 1940 and 1970 and, from 1972, a modern boom following the providential discovery of huge new reserves. Today Mexico is fourth in the world league of oil producers.

Mexico's first oil well was drilled in 1869 but it was not until 1904 that commercial oil first surfaced in what later proved to be the Panuco-Ebano field inland from the Gulf port of Tampico. The legal transfer of sub-soil mineral rights from the state to the owner of the surface rights in 1884, and the oil discoveries in Texas and Louisiana at the turn of the century paved the way for the Mexican strikes. By 1910 fresh discoveries inland from Tuxpan had begun to define the suite of fields which together form the Golden Lane (Faja de Oro). The unco-ordinated drilling of wildcatters was superseded as the large British and American oil companies were drawn into the country. The companies were able to co-ordinate their exploration efforts and to ensure that the oil fields were little touched by the civil war which swept the country between 1910 and 1917; rather, production and exports boomed to satisfy the huge demand for oil created by the Great War in Europe. From a little over 12 million barrels of crude oil in 1911, output soared to over 190 million barrels in 1921: for a brief period in the 1920s Mexico was second only to the USA as an oil producer and responsible for a quarter of the world's production. By the late 1920s a decline almost as spectacular as the original boom had set in: in 1931 output (33 million barrels) was only one-fifth of that a decade earlier. The World Depression, the lack of new finds to compensate for exhausted fields, the unsettling policies of the revolutionary governments, the increased taxes levied on oil exports, and the rise of Venezuela as an attractive alternative area in which to invest all contributed to the slump. Refineries closed, concessions lapsed and unemployment spread.

The decline in production was reversed in the 1930s, thanks to the discovery in 1932 of the Poza Rica field in the Gulf Plain behind Veracruz. The discovery was made by the British company El Aguila, managed by Royal Dutch Shell, which, in informal alliance with Jersey Standard, was responsible for well over half Mexico's oil production. Unfortunately for the oil companies, their technical success in finding fresh reserves was negated by their intransigence in dealings with the government and by the hostility of the oil workers' unions. In 1938 Mexico astounded the financial world by nationalizing its oil industry. British and American military intervention was contemplated, an international boycott was organized, and capital and skilled labour withdrew. But by then the home market was absorbing 60 per cent of Mexico's oil, the oil industry had ceased to be one primarily serving overseas markets and the effects of sanctions were thus limited. With the advent of the Second World War to divert British attention elsewhere, an agreement to pay compensation to the former owners, and with the political desire of the United States for hemispheric solidarity, Mexico was gradually drawn back into the international fold. Oil production, mainly from the Poza Rica field, increased (from 43 million barrels in 1941 to 78 million in 1951) but at a rate insufficient to satisfy the growing industrial and urban demands; in 1957 Mexico found itself a net importer of petroleum. Natural gas ceased to be a mere nuisance removed by flaring off and the Reynosa gas field close to the US border began commercial production. Exploration, including airborne seismic exploration, was increased in the 1960s and new fields in the swampy forests of Central and Eastern Tabasco, first discovered before 1938, were delineated and developed. By 1969 44 per cent of Mexico's oil and natural gas was being drawn from Tabasco and the Isthmus of Tehuantepec. In 1971 Mexico produced 177 million barrels of oil but the gap, bridged by imports, between domestic production and demand was widening.

In 1972 the Mexican oil industry entered a new phase. In May 1972 the first wells to draw on the Reforma fields in Chiapas and Tabasco were drilled. Since then a whole family of new fields has

Burning off gas at the Reforma oil field, Tabasco, Mexico

been discovered, extending north-eastwards below the Gulf of Campeche for 200 km in one direction and possibly into Guatemala in the other. Almost every well drilled has struck oil. The wells tap huge reservoirs of oil that are trapped in the Cretacious sediments which underly the Triassic sub-soil; the reservoirs are deeper than those tapped in earlier years but increased drilling costs have been easily covered by the rising value of oil.

The impact of these new discoveries has been dramatic. 1973 was the first year in which oil production surpassed the peak achieved fifty years earlier; by 1975 Mexico was once again producing oil surplus to its own requirements and the oil deficit of 1974 ($288 million) had been replaced by a surplus ($141 million) which was to multiply one hundred-fold in the next decade. In 1977 the true scale of the new reserves was first publicized and the new president, López Portillo (1976–82), took the decision to accelerate production. By 1977 the OPEC-induced rise in oil prices had greatly enhanced the value of these reserves and they underwrote the international loans necessary for their development. The new policy ran counter to one of the declared aims of nationalization in 1938: that Mexican natural resources should be used only to feed indigenous industries and when not required for current consumption should be conserved against future domestic demand. The export of large quantities of crude oil, incorporating very little value-added in manufacturing, would have been an anathema had it not been for the overriding needs of Mexico for development capital and for a restoration of financial stability.

Between 1977 and 1980, Pemex (Petróleos Mexicanos, the Mexican Petroleum Board) obtained loans of over $12,600 million; by the end of 1980 loans to Pemex accounted for 37 per cent of Mexico's foreign debts. Some of this money was used to hire foreign project managers to supervise the enormous new works undertaken in areas where Mexico's considerable technical expertise in petroleum matters was deficient: for example, the purchase, building and operation of offshore drilling platforms, the installation of gathering systems, and the building of onshore facilities adjoining the Gulf of Campeche. Additional money went into proving fresh reserves of oil and natural gas. These rose according to Pemex from 6338 million barrels of oil equivalent in 1975 to 45,800 in 1979 and to 72,000 in 1982; of these 80 per cent were of oil and 20 per cent (or 75×10^{12} million cubic feet) natural gas (see table 23). The United States Energy Information Administration took a slightly less optimistic view and gave 30,000 million barrels as the figure for proven reserves at the beginning of 1982 but also believes that there is a 90–95 per cent probability of between 70,000 and 120,000 million barrels of recoverable oil and natural gas in Mexico. The increase in reserves is largely accounted for by the discoveries in Chiapas, Tabasco and under the Gulf of Campeche. The Chicontepec field in northern Veracruz is in highly fractured strata which would need, on one estimate, 16,000 separate wells for its full potential to be exploited (in 1984 Pemex planned to drill only 350 wells nationwide).

A surge in production – from almost 400 million barrels in 1977 to almost 600 million in 1979 to almost 1100 million in 1982 – followed the new finds. In 1983 the old pre-1972 fields were responsible for only 10 per cent of Mexico's oil production; almost 60 per cent came from beneath the Gulf of Campeche, an area which only began to contribute to production in July 1979; and the rest from the Reforma fields of central Tabasco and northern Chiapas. The offshore oil platforms lie in a zone extending some 60 km from Ciudad del Carmen, the only part of Campeche directly affected by the oil boom; some of the wells are remarkable – Akal produced 42,000 barrels per day at its peak, a world record. Onshore, Villahermosa is the focus of the present oil boom: a small, provincial river town in 1970, it has grown in a distressingly disordered fashion to accommodate, perhaps, half a million people in 1983; it is notorious for its insalubrious housing, for a surfeit of immigrant labour, and for political chicanery. Villahermosa is also the new

centre of natural gas production: in 1982 the nearby gas field of Huimanguillo was responsible for one-third of Mexico's output and, together with the rest of the production from this, the Sureste, for 60 per cent. A further 20 per cent came from the offshore fields and only 20 per cent from the rest of the country. The Coatzacoalcos–Villahermosa–Ciudad del Carmen triangle and Mexico City axis has replaced the earlier Ciudad Madero–Poza Rica–Minatitlán triangle and Mexico City axis as the locus of Mexico's petroleum industry.

In 1982 Mexico was able to refine almost 40 per cent of the crude it produced as new refineries came on stream and old ones were expanded. New ports outside Tampico, near Coatzacoalcos, and at Salina Cruz were under construction to handle the increased flow of oil, and the existing gas, crude oil and product pipeline systems were being expanded. Another race to build new capacity was being run by the state petrochemical industry. The new Parajitos and La Cangrejera complexes are huge; their products supply the raw materials for a band of modern industries, manufacturing fertilizers, detergents, acrylic resins, polyester fibres, emulsifying agents and many of the other modern necessities of life. But the growth in crude oil production has been such that only the smaller part of Mexico's oil is capable of being absorbed by the domestic market. In 1981 Mexico regained the place it had lost to Venezuela in 1927 of being Latin America's leading producer and in that year, for the first time for over half a century, exported more oil than it consumed at home. Mexico's earnings from the export of oil (and, since 1980, natural gas) have risen from $1000 million in 1977 to $4000 million in 1979 and to $16,000 million in 1982. In 1970–4 petroleum accounted for only 1.6 per cent of Mexico's export trade; in 1975–9, 31.5 per cent; in 1980, 60 per cent and in 1982–3, 75 per cent. This heavy dependence on oil leaves Mexico's income very vulnerable in the short term to downward changes in the price of oil and in the longer term to the evaluation placed upon its oil reserves. Its public indebtedness rose from $7200 million in 1973 to $39,000 million in 1980, to $85,000 million in 1983; in 1983, 38 per cent of the value of exports of goods and services was expended in meeting interest payments partly incurred by too easy access to credit in the optimistic days of the late 1970s. But, whatever the external problems, Mexican consumers continued to benefit in 1983 from very cheap energy. Local petrol (gasoline) was half the US price and a quarter of that of Western Europe; natural gas, a quarter the consumer price in the United States; diesel, one-tenth of that in Western Europe. It can be calculated that one-third of the benefits of the policy of cheap domestic hydrocarbons accrued to the energy industry itself, 31 per cent to the transport sector and 21 per cent to industry; agriculturalists and the domestic consumer directly benefited little. In regional terms Mexico City (27 per cent), the three border states of the north-east (22 per cent) and Veracruz (15 per

Table 23. Proven hydrocarbon reserves in Mexico (million barrels of oil equivalent)

	Crude oil	Natural gas (liquids)	Natural gas
North	432	295	2 249
Central	1 416	195	756
South (incl. Gulf of Campeche)	35 312	7 101	6 659
Chicontepec	10 929	1 322	5 344
Total	48 083	8 914	15 009

Source: Pemex.

strung out in a north-to-south line running from the Colombian border south through Lake Agrio to Auca, account for three-quarters of Ecuador's reserves (2100 million barrels) and 93 per cent of its oil production (11.6 million tonnes in 1983). The state oil company (CEPE, the Corporación Estatal Petrolera Ecuatoriana), formed in 1972, holds a majority of the shares in the consortium (which includes Texaco) responsible for almost all Ecuador's oil and natural gas production and its refining capacity. Domestic prices are very low.

Trinidad was the most important oil producer in the British Commonwealth prior to the Second World War. Sir Walter Raleigh caulked his boats with tar from the Pitch Lake and the first commercial oil came from a reservoir immediately under the lake in 1908, forty-two years after the first oil well was drilled in the island. Since then many thousands of wells have been drilled in the south of the island and, since 1960, others offshore in both the quieter waters of the Gulf of Paria and the more exposed waters to the south-east. Production rose to a recent peak in 1978 but reserves have been depleted and output in 1983 (8.0 million tonnes) was the same as ten years earlier. Half Trinidad's crude and five-sixths of its refined petroleum are exported, providing 90 per cent of the country's export earnings.

Colombia shared with Venezuela the discovery in the 1920s of significant oil deposits and their exploration by foreign companies. Although a state oil corporation (Ecopetrol or Empresa Colombiana de Petróleo) was formed in 1951, the international oil giants have continued their involvement in the country. But production reached a peak of 10 million tonnes in the early 1970s and by 1983 had fallen to the same level as that a quarter of a century earlier; Colombia ceased to be a net exporter of oil in 1974. Hope of a recovery in the 1980s is focused upon new oil fields (Arauca and Cano Limón) discovered in the llanos close to the Venezuelan border and the offshore Guajira natural gas fields feeding into the Caribbean ports of Barranquilla and Cartagena. But petroleum is expected to supply a declining proportion (1980, 45 per cent; 1990, 32 per cent; 2000, 28 per cent) of Colombia's energy requirements and hydroelectricity (1979, 25 per cent; 1990, 37 per cent) and coal (1980, 17 per cent; 1990, 19 per cent; 2000, 30 per cent) increasing proportions.

Peru has some of the oldest oil fields of South America in the Talara fields off the north-west coast; they provided very large profits for their early developers. Production, which was five times local demand in the 1930s, rose more slowly than demand and by the early 1960s Peru had ceased to be self-sufficient. In 1968 the leading company (a subsidiary of Jersey Standard) was expropriated to form the core of the state petroleum corporation (Petroperú or Petróleos del Perú) already thirty-four years old. Drilling, by Petroperú and by other international oil companies, began in the Amazonian

lowlands and, after a false dawn, enough oil was found to triple output in the 1970s (to 9.5 million tonnes) and turn Peru into a net exporter. Today these new Selva fields of north-east Peru provide two-thirds of its oil, the Talara fields one-sixth, and offshore wells on the continental shelf most of the rest.

Bolivia's small oil industry around Camiri in the Oriente was nurtured by Standard Oil and continued under the state body (YPFB, Yacimientos Petrolíferos Fiscales Bolivianos) following nationalization in 1937. Gulf Oil expanded Bolivia's reserves in the 1950s and 1960s and provided a surplus for export; Gulf was nationalized in 1969. Although oil production declined in the 1970s and Bolivia ceased to be a net oil exporter in 1978, natural gas production expanded and major new gas finds were made in 1976 (Tila), 1978 (La Vertiente) and 1982 (Santa Rosa). Argentina imports Bolivian gas and Brazil is expected to be supplied by gasline from Santa Cruz.

Belize, where exploration work began as late as 1938 and the first well was not drilled until 1955, has been the scene of intense activity since 1981. Two areas have attracted most attention: offshore in the south where geological circumstances resemble those in Mexico's Bay of Campeche, and onshore in the north where geological conditions resemble promising areas in neighbouring Guatemala. Drilling is by the international oil giants who view Belize as a less risky political environment for investment than elsewhere in Central America.

Hydroelectricity

Latin America currently exploits only about 5 per cent of its huge but largely inaccessible hydroelectric potential. That potential stems partly from the enormous flow in some of its rivers (one-fifth of the world's river water is flowing in the Amazon system alone), partly from the height of its main watersheds (Aconcagua, the highest peak in the Andes, is almost 7000 m above sea level; Cittlalteptl in Central Mexico is 5700 m high), and partly from the abrupt changes of altitude where large volumes of water descend rapidly over short distances to provide natural power sites amenable to engineering. Unfortunately, many such sites, for example along the eastern flank of the Andes, are remote from demand for electricity, the generating process remains inefficient, and losses in transmission over long distances are large. Furthermore, harnessing potential requires time and heavy capital investment, both at the site and in transmission systems. Some attractive rivers, such as the Paraná, form political frontiers and their exploitation requires international agreement.

The earliest hydroelectricity stations in Latin America date from the late nineteenth century and were situated close to the towns they were designed to serve. Overseas companies usually built them destined later in life, like other foreign-owned public utility companies, to be nationalized; they now form part of a national electricity corporation. Later many Latin American countries, notably Mexico, followed the example of the Tennessee Valley Authority and began generating hydroelectricity as part of a co-ordinated programme of improving rural or regional infrastructure. Some sites drew to themselves large consuming industries, such as metal smelting at Ciudad Bolívar in Venezuela. These were state enterprises from the start and have been favoured investment targets for international agencies anxious to help local efforts towards self-sufficiency in energy: fully one-third of Latin America's installed hydroelectric power capacity has been built with the help of finance from the World Bank. In the past larger schemes have benefited more than smaller ones from such assistance but new technology has advanced the prospects of smaller-scale developments.

Hydroelectricity met 15.1 per cent of Latin America's demand for commercial energy in 1981: to have generated the same amount from oil-fired plants would have required 52.6 million tonnes of oil. The relative contribution of hydroelectricity is growing: between 1970 and 1983 hydroelectricity consumption grew almost three-fold while that of oil and natural gas grew by only a half. In 1981 Brazil was responsible for 56.9 per cent of the total hydroelectric power generated in Latin America as compared with 49.5 per cent in 1970; Mexico was in second place (10.7 per cent in 1981, 18.6 per cent in 1970): together they account for two-thirds of Latin America's primary electricity output. The Andean countries of Colombia (7.1 per cent, 7.7 per cent), Venezuela (6.6 per cent, 5.1 per cent), Argentina (6.4 per cent, 1.9 per cent), Peru (3.4 per cent, 4.7 per cent) and Chile (3.3 per cent, 5.3 per cent) were next in importance.

Brazil relies more on hydroelectricity as a source of commercial energy than does any other major country in Latin America. In 1981, hydro plants provided 92 per cent of Brazil's electricity and accounted for 83 per cent of its installed electricity-generating capacity; hydroelectricity accounted for 44 per cent of domestic production of commercial energy (compared with 20 per cent in 1970) and met 17.4 per cent (11.8 per cent) of its total commercial energy consumption. Brazil has an estimated 150 million kW of hydroelectric power potential – one-third in the basin of the Amazon, almost one-third in the Paraná, a tenth in the São Francisco, and most of the remaining quarter in the relatively short rivers draining the coastal ranges fronting the Atlantic; it had harnessed about one-fifth (31.3 million kW) of this potential in 1981. Half the installed capacity is on the Paraná. This includes the Jupiá (completed in 1970) and Ilha Solteira (1977) plants on the Mato Grosso border, both in their turn the largest hydroelectric power installations in the country and now with a combined capacity of 3.3 million kW, and others on left-bank tributaries closer to São Paulo. Construction is expected to be completed in

Itaipú dam under construction on the Paraná River on the border between Brazil and Paraguay

1988 of installations at Itaipú on the Paraná 15 km above its confluence with the Iguassú at the Argentine border. This plant will have the largest capacity (11.7 million kW) of any hydro-station in the world: although a joint project of Paraguay and Brazil, Brazil underwrote all construction costs and will purchase all the electricity generated. The nearby Iguassú Falls are indicative of the untapped potential remaining. On the São Francisco the major installations remain those of the Paulo Afonso where work began in 1945 and first provided power for the north-east in 1954; ultimately an installed capacity of 5 million kW can be expected. The Três Marias plant in the upper reaches of the river supplies power to São Paulo. Most of the new capacity has been built by a federal holding company (Electrobrás) created in 1961 to co-ordinate the work of individual states (especially São Paulo); today 98 per cent of Brazil's hydroelectric capacity is in public ownership.

Mexico, in contrast, has moved away from installing new hydroelectric capacity in recent years as cheap domestic oil has become more prolific. 1971 was the last year in which water generated more electricity than did oil; in 1981 twice as much thermal electricity as hydroelectricity entered the national grids. Mexico has harnessed about a quarter of the water power deemed exploitable and much of its capacity was created since 1950 as part of the multipurpose river basin developments associated with the Balsas, Fuerte, Papaloapan, Grijalva and other river valleys.

Colombia's abundant rainfall, high mountains and capacious valleys capable of storing great quantities of water give it an enormous potential of probably about 50 million kW but perhaps as large as 120 million kW. Only 3.5 million kW had been developed in

1981 but with plans for an installed capacity of 13 million kW in 1995. A national grid was established in 1970 linking the centre with the north coast.

Argentina increased its hydroelectricity output tenfold in the 1970s. The River Limay in northern Patagonia is being turned into a staircase of artificial lakes as first, in 1973, the 1.2 million kW El Chocón and then, 400 km up-river, the Alicurá (1 million kW) came on stream; the Piedra del Aguila plant (2.1 million kW) under construction on the Limay has benefited from the largest single loan ever made by the Inter-American Development Bank. Joint projects with Uruguay at Salto Grande (1.6 million kW) and with Paraguay on the Paraná at Yaciretá (2.7 million kW) are underway.

In both *Peru* and *Chile* hydroelectricity supplied two-thirds of national electricity in 1981 with resources best developed close to the capital cities. In Peru Lima consumed three-quarters of the electricity generated, much of it from the Mantaro Valley. In Chile any further development of the potential around Santiago will be expensive, and current development is focused southwards on Talca and the forested valleys of Puerto Montt.

Nuclear electricity

Nuclear-generated electricity makes a minor contribution to Latin America's indigenous energy production and is likely to remain of little significance. In 1984 the total generating capacity was only 0.9 million kW, hardly one-tenth of that of the United Kingdom or one-hundredth of that of the United States. *Argentina* has the longest experience of nuclear power: its 344-megawatt Atucha 1 heavy-water reactor has been operational since 1974. Argentina has had an active nuclear policy since 1950 and the generous support it has consistently received from governments of different hues and through difficult financial times makes it almost unique in recent Argentine history. With its nuclear power based upon local uranium (rather than imported enriched uranium) and carefully gathered expertise, Argentina enjoys near-autonomy in this area of high technology and exports advice and materials to, for example, Peru. However, in 1984 Atucha 1 was operating at only half-capacity because it was unable to compete with cheaper hydroelectricity; and work on Atucha 2, once scheduled for completion in 1987, had been delayed. Yet plans still exist to build an installed capacity of 4.5 million kW by the year 2000.

Brazil's first nuclear plant, situated at Angra dos Reis 100 km south-west of Rio de Janeiro, became operational in 1981. This is a 625-megawatt light-water reactor built with West German assistance (after Brazil was denied enriched uranium by the United States in 1974). Work on two additional neighbouring reactors, designed to add a further 2.6 million kW of capacity by 1990 has faltered. *Mexico* is constructing two 650-megawatt reactors supplied by the United States at Laguna Verde in Veracruz but engineering

difficulties, adverse public opinion and the oil bonanza have damped the enthusiasm for this programme. *Cuba* plans to add 1.7 million kW of nuclear electricity to the national supply in 1990 from plants at Huragua and Holguín built with Soviet assistance and *Chile* hopes to order a 600-megawatt plant to be operational in 1990. *Venezuela* has toyed with the idea of using a natural uranium, gas-cooled reactor to produce steam to be used in the extraction of oil from the Orinoco tar sands. But, in general, in the mid-1980s Latin America is having second thoughts about the usefulness of developing nuclear electricity capacity.

Geothermal power

Mexico and *El Salvador* generate a little electricity from geothermal heat and the World Bank is supporting the construction of new geothermal stations in Guatemala and Costa Rica. In general, the tectonically active parts of Mexico, Central America and the western rim of South America lend themselves to such exploitations. Once built, running costs are low and their necessarily small scale makes such stations well suited to meet rural needs.

Coal

Coal is, and has been, remarkably unimportant in Latin America. Coal production and coal reserves are only 2–3 per cent of those of North America, or Europe, or the USSR or China and one-tenth of those of, say, Australia. Under the stimulus of higher oil prices output doubled to 19.3 million tonnes (equivalent to 11.4 million tonnes of oil) in the ten years to 1982 and may redouble in the ten years following, but coal will still meet less than 10 per cent of Latin America's requirements of energy.

Colombia has the largest reserves of coal in Latin America (perhaps 16,000 million tonnes), is responsible for about one-third of the continent's current output, and is expanding production rapidly; coal met a quarter of Colombia's commercial energy demands in 1981, a larger fraction than in any other Latin American country. Coal is widely distributed in Andean Colombia, particularly in the Cauca Valley. The most active development is taking place at El Cerrejón in Guajira close to the Caribbean coast by the national coal company (Carbocol or Carbones de Colombia) and Intercor (a subsidiary of Exxon). Following an investment (by Intercor of $2000 million) shipments of coal from Bahía de Portete began in 1983 and will be significantly increased when the 150 km railway linking the new port with the mines is completed in 1985. Exports of 15 million tonnes from El Cerrejón Norte alone are anticipated in 1988 and of 60 million tonnes from Colombia at large by the end of the century.

Brazil is investing $10,000 million in an attempt to quadruple in a decade its coal production of 6 million tonnes in 1982. The bulk of its current output comes from Santa Catarina and is of coking quality; most of the new coal will come from ten mines, each capable of producing 1.7 million tonnes a year, being opened up with foreign expertise and a heavy expenditure on infrastructure in Rio Grande do Sul close to the Uruguayan border.

Mexican coal comes mainly from the Sabinas basin in Coahuila in the north-east of the country. Originally worked to supply the railways, its more recent outlets have been the iron and steel mills of Monterrey. *Chile* is reviving its small coal industry but shifting attention from the traditional underground mining region around Concepción to the strip mining of poorer quality coals in Magallanes province. *Argentina* has a small coal field at Río Turbio in the Andean foothills of southern Patagonia linked by rail to the coast at Río Gallegos; it is unlikely to expand production significantly. *Venezuela* is promoting open-cast coal mining at Guasare as part of a giant coal and steel complex in Zulia: it is a high-cost project in a country with surplus energy and much criticized on this score within Venezuela.

Traditional energy sources

Firewood is the most traditional of Latin America's primary energy sources. As recently as 1945 half the energy used in the region was of this home-grown type. In 1981 the energy equivalent of about 100 million tonnes of coal or 70 million tonnes of oil was provided by firewood – fully one-seventh of the total energy produced by Latin America or one-sixth of that used. In some countries the overall contribution of firewood to the total national energy output is crucial: in 1975 the proportion ranged downwards from poverty-stricken Haiti (90 per cent) through Paraguay (54 per cent), Guatemala (52 per cent), Honduras (48 per cent), the Dominican Republic (44 per cent), Bolivia (43 per cent), Grenada (43 per cent), El Salvador (42 per cent), Ecuador (38 per cent), Cuba (35 per cent), Nicaragua (34 per cent), Barbados (28 per cent) and Costa Rica (23 per cent) to Brazil (20 per cent). These are countries which still have a largely rural population, may be forested and where energy alternatives are expensive. Most firewood is used for domestic purposes but it is still possible (though rare) to see wood-burning locomotives in Brazil and some electricity is generated in small wood-burning power stations in Amazonia. Many of the simpler industrial processes – forming bricks, baking bread, making lime – use wood as a fuel and a substantial proportion of Brazil's pig iron (especially that produced in Minas Gerais) is smelted in charcoal-fed blast furnaces. Brazil has the world's second largest reserves of timber and the largest reserves of natural tropical forest. But, in the nature of things, firewood is a frontier resource distant from the main centres of energy demand. Like other frontier resources it is treated in a careless manner.

Sugar-cane waste or bagasse is another fuel which in sugar-growing areas is a highly significant domestic source of energy.

Following FAO estimates, bagasse provides Latin America with as much energy as would 25 million tonnes of coal or 16 million tonnes of oil. In Brazil, Cuba, Mexico and elsewhere, bagasse powers the sugar mills which produce not only sugar but more bagasse fuel.

Unconventional energy sources

Solar energy, clearly present in abundance in Latin America, remains largely unexploited except through vegetation. Solar panels drive some irrigation pumps, and the sun is used directly in crop and fish drying, heating and some distillation processes. The Dominican Republic has an international solar technology centre. Wind power is used to generate commercial electricity on some of the Caribbean islands, in Patagonia and at other windy, isolated places.

The ability to distil alcohol from plants seems one of man's oldest and almost universal skills. But it is only very recently that such alcohol has been used as a commercial fuel. In 1975 Brazil launched its Proálcool programme to distil ethanol from sugar cane in sufficient quantities to reduce its dependence upon imported oil. It had as its target for 1985 the building of about 400 distilleries consuming the cane from 2–3 million hectares, much of it growing in areas new to cane, and yielding 10,000 million litres of ethanol: the programme was costed at the equivalent in cruzeiros of about $5,000 million. By 1979 Brazil was half way to achieving its target; in 1985 it is expected that ethanol will have taken the place of 10 per cent of Brazil's total oil consumption. The higher cost of imported oil since 1980 has increased interest in the programme and raised expenditure. Although the programme does involve additional expenditure of hard currency on fertilizers it does create new jobs (perhaps over a million) and this adds to its political appeal. Initially the programme produced anhydrous ethanol which is used to dilute imported petrol in the proportion of one to four to produce 'gashol'; only slight modifications are needed to car engines to use gasohol. More recently a new market for hydrous ethanol has been created: although hydrous ethanol has only 60 per cent of the energy content by weight of petrol it can be used neat although only in cars with specially built alcohol engines. The programme has been able to establish a sufficiently wide network of alcohol pumps and has persuaded the domestic car companies to produce enough alcohol-driven vehicles (the millionth alcohol car to be manufactured in Brazil was sold in 1983) to ensure a significant measure of success. In 1982 alcohol supplied 25 per cent and petrol 75 per cent of the energy which went into the tanks of cars in Brazil and it is believed that the proportions will eventually settle down at 40 per cent and 60 per cent. The production costs in 1981 were probably about half as much again as that of imported oil when reduced to a common yardstick of dollar per barrel of oil equivalent. The programme has had a dramatic and, in some respects, disruptive effect on the agricultural economy of São Paulo where most of the new cane fields have appeared: the focus of new cane growing is now moving towards the centre-west and Maranhão as a more realistic assessment of the attributes required by the crop is reached. There is a parallel programme (Proóleo) to find a substitute for diesel: oil from soya beans, sage, sunflower seed, groundnuts and, in particular, the dende palm are targets for experiment. There is also interest in both Brazil and Colombia in developing new varieties of cassava from whose starchy roots substantial quantities of alcohol can be distilled.

Conclusions

The economies of the Latin American countries and the aspirations of their peoples were fashioned around cheap energy: the transition in the 1970s to high international oil prices had dramatic effects. For oil-rich, oil-exporting countries like Venezuela the new wealth has required fresh internal strategies to ensure that it is used to national advantage and that the benefits are distributed in a way that is seen to be equitable by the populace at large. In Mexico, as in most oil-producing countries, the new bonanza has meant that the state has become an even more dominant element in the life of the country. The search for, and development of, new reserves has led such countries to incur large debts, and the servicing and repayment of those debts has imposed a new version of dependent-client status upon countries which may have initially seen their new wealth in oil as liberating them from an old servitude.

For oil-importing countries increased energy costs have brought severe social and financial strains. A universal response to the new circumstances has been to adopt policies of substituting indigenous energy for imported oil. Brazil and Colombia, Guatemala, Belize and Barbados are countries which have found new oil. Further, the relatively unexplored nature of many of the geologically promising areas, particularly those offshore, favour a moderately optimistic view of the future. Heavy oil deposits, such as the Orinoco tar sands and the Brazilian oil shales are attracting fresh interest, and less natural gas is being flared-off and wasted. Brazil and Colombia are investing in large coal deposits and almost all countries in hydroelectric projects. But it is unrealistic to expect a significant contribution from unconventional energy sources: few seem to offer the prospect of energy which is cost-effective. A second response has been to promote a more conservative attitude to energy. Latin America has been slow in this area. Energy consumption rose at an annual rate of 4.8 per cent between 1972 and 1982, compared with 2 per cent in the world at large and negative rates in the United States and Great Britain. This is partly because Latin American countries were slow in raising domestic energy prices in tune with international prices. This meant a lessened incentive for domestic users to economize and energy consumed which might otherwise have earned an enhanced income as an export. There is clear scope for economizing energy consumption in Latin America. Forty per cent of commercial

energy is consumed by industry in plants, many of which could be modified to be more energy-saving. Thirty-five per cent is consumed in the transport field – seven-eighths by road vehicles – and a substitution of public transport for private cars and of bigger trucks for smaller lorries could reduce overall demand particularly for the lighter oils. The price of petrol – which varies by a factor of ten between the countries of Latin America and is still lower on average than in other parts of the world – is a delicate yet direct and effective instrument of government policy which has not been used to full extent to date. Fifteen per cent of the energy consumed is in the form of electricity and there are technical and distributional inefficiencies which could be modified to reduce wastage. Only 10 per cent is consumed in household activities, mainly in towns and by the more affluent.

Yet it is not the more affluent but the poor who have been worst hit by the new high cost of energy. In many parts of Latin America the real energy crisis is the growing shortage of traditional fuels. Thus many poor people have put into reverse the simple process of substituting bought-in kerosene for local firewood. Similar retrogressive moves by growing numbers of people have placed added pressure on the accessible woodlands of Latin America and added further impetus to the forces of ecological instability within the continent.

DJF

Further reading

British Petroleum Company, *B.P. Statistical Review of World Energy* (London, annual)

N. Choudri, *Energy and Development in Latin America* (Lexington, 1982)

Economic Commission for Latin America, 'Energy in Latin America', *ECLA Bulletin*, 1980

International Energy Agency (OECD), *World Energy Outlook* (Paris, 1982)

J. E. Katz and O. S. Marwah, *Nuclear Power in Developing Countries* (Toronto, 1982)

J. W. Mullin, *Energy in Latin America: the Historic Record* (ECLA, Santiago, 1978)

Petroleum Economist (London, monthly)

G. Philip, *Oil and Politics in Latin America: Nationalist Movements and State Companies* (Cambridge, 1982)

E. N. Tiratsoo, *Oilfields of the World*, 3rd edition (Beaconsfield, 1984)

United Nations, *Petroleum Exploration Strategies in Developing Countries: Proceedings of a U.N. meeting held in The Hague, 16–20 March 1981* (London, 1982)

United Nations, *Yearbook of World Energy Statistics 1981* (New York, 1983)

World Bank, *Renewable Energy Resources in Developing Countries* (Washington, 1981)

World Bank, *World Bank Country Studies* (Washington, irregular)

Banking

Introduction

The Latin American republics have generally well-developed banking and related financial services, especially in the larger countries. Commercial banking dates back well into the last century. Economic growth in the decades following the Second World War was paralleled by the rapid expansion of banking systems, the establishment of new and specialized institutions and the adoption in the more developed countries of innovations originating in North America and Europe.

In a region as diverse as Latin America there are considerable differences among the republics in the structure of their national banking systems, the variety of services they offer, the sophistication of their financial markets and the methods and scope of official control. Some general characteristics of present-day Latin American banking systems are: the importance of state-owned institutions in both commercial and development banking, the dominance within the private banking sector of a small number of commercial banks or banking groups, and the prevalence of nationwide branch banking on the European pattern, in the absence of restrictions on out-of-state banking that have been characteristic of the United States.

The development of commercial banking

The first bank so-called in Latin America was in fact an officially inspired enterprise, set up in Brazil on the initiative of the Regent in 1808 after the arrival of the Portuguese court, with the somewhat reluctant participation of Brazilian and Portuguese capitalists. This, the first Banco do Brasil, was liquidated in 1829. The first bank in Argentina, the Banco de Buenos Aires, was founded in 1822, largely on the initiative of Anglo-Argentine merchants, and dissolved by Rosas in 1836. More significant for the development of Latin American banking was the establishment of the second Banco do Brasil in 1851 by the industrialist and financier, the Barão de Mauá, which in 1853 merged with the Banco Comercial de Rio de Janeiro to form the first substantial institution for commercial credit, and the foundation in 1854 of the Banco de la Província de Buenos Aires.

Although these early banks were the result of local initiative, foreign banks were to play the dominant role in the development of banking in Latin America in the second half of the nineteenth century. Their functions were closely related to the growth of foreign trade and investment, the main instruments of the export-led economic development of that period. The foreign banks that were successful, provided stability and introduced European banking techniques.

British banks, following in the steps of British merchants and paving the way for British investors, led the way with the establishment of both the London Buenos Aires and River Plate Bank and the London and Brazilian Bank in 1862. Their example was to be followed by other British banks and by banks originating in Germany, France, Italy and other European countries linked to Latin America by trade or the flow of emigration. A name such as the Banco Chileno-Yugoeslavo (subsequently Banco Austral) indicates the origin of banks founded to serve a local immigrant clientele.

Many important locally owned commercial banks in Latin America were established in the last two decades of the nineteenth century. Argentina, by then the most developed country, had over forty banks by the end of the century. After the First World War, when the United States displaced Europe as the principal source of capital and became increasingly important in Latin American trade, US banks established an extensive branch representation in Latin America. Canadian banks became active, especially in the Caribbean area where there were long-established trading interests, and Japanese banks were set up in areas where Japanese immigration was significant. In the development of banking, as in so much else in Latin America, the depression years of the early 1930s marked a watershed.

Official banking

The mixed economy that is characteristic of most Latin American countries is reflected in their banking structures. The distinction between the privately and publicly owned institutions is by no means wholly functional. State-owned institutions are prominent in commercial banking as well as owning the more important institutions for the provision of long-term finance. Some of the early domestic, commercial and mortgage banking ventures were sometimes the result of state initiative or else fell under state control as a result of a financial crisis, and continued thereafter to consolidate their position in the banking structure. This process has continued up to the present, especially in those countries where the public sector has expanded more rapidly than the private. In Mexico, where the mixed economy subsists, all private and mixed-capital banks were taken over by the state in September 1982 by the outgoing administration of President José López Portillo after the onset of the external debt crisis.

Argentina has official commercial banks at the three levels of government – federal, provincial and municipal. The Banco de la Nación (founded in 1891) alone accounted for nearly 13 per cent of the total assets of all commercial banks in 1983 and is by far the largest bank in the country, followed by the Banco de la Provincia de Buenos Aires with 7 per cent; all official banks held about 34 per cent of total commercial bank deposits.

In Brazil, banks controlled by the federal government or the states also play an important role in commercial banking. The present Banco do Brasil, in which the government is the principal shareholder, is by far the largest commercial bank in the country; it is also the largest Latin American bank, and ranked nineteenth among banks of the world by size of its assets in 1982 (the equivalent of nearly $62 billion in that year). In Peru, the Banco de la Nación, in its own right and through the three commercial banks that it acquired in 1970, exercises a dominant influence. Such banks, as well as carrying out normal short-term commercial lending, generally have special functions – in the case of the Banco de la Nación Argentina, the financing of agricultural production and development. The Banco do Brasil and the Banco de la Nación in Peru act as agents of the treasury, and have other functions derived from government policy which they share with the central banks (see below).

During the depression years of the 1930s, governments became more actively involved in encouraging economic activity. In order to remedy the inability or unwillingness of commercial banks to provide medium-term finance for economic development and diversification these governments set up sectoral development banks. In Peru a Banco Agrícola (now Banco Agrario) was established in 1931, a Banco Industrial in 1936 and a Banco Minero in 1941. Similarly, in Venezuela a Banco Agrícola y Pecuario was set up in 1928, a Banco Industrial in 1937 and a Banco Obrero intended to finance low-cost housing in 1941. In Colombia a Caja de Crédito Agrario, Industrial y Minero was founded in 1931. In the larger republics the powerful state-owned commercial banks were directed towards providing larger amounts of medium-term finance for industrial and other development.

Wider in scope than the specialized official banks are development corporations such as the Chilean Corporación de Fomento (CORFO), set up originally to finance reconstruction after the Chillán earthquake of 1939. Other such corporations which have continued to play a central role in the provision of long-term finance for development are the Nacional Financiera in Mexico (1934), and the Banco Nacional do Desenvolvimento Econômico (BNDE) in Brazil (1952). These are funded in various proportions from budgetary allocations, the issue of domestic obligations, and borrowings from the international development agencies or on capital markets abroad. These institutions have in general played a vital role in mobilizing longer-term funds both domestically and abroad for financing electrification, communications and basic industrial development projects in the public sector, as well as for on-lending for private-sector industrial development.

Central banking and monetary control

In the nineteenth and early twentieth centuries banking was generally as little regulated as other forms of business enterprise. The establishment of an official monopoly of the note-issue, introduction of prudential controls and other general banking legislation, development of clearing systems, and the creation of central banks with the function of controlling the banking system and implementing monetary policy was a gradual process that continued right up to the 1960s.

In the 1920s and 1930s the first central banks were set up, usually accompanied by the first general banking laws. Professor E. W. Kemmerer of Princeton University was active in setting up central banks in the Pacific coast republics in the 1920s, as was Dr Herman Max of the central bank of Chile rather later in the Caribbean area; Argentina's central bank was established in 1935 with the advice of Sir Otto Niemeyer of the Bank of England. In some countries, notably Brazil and Uruguay, central banking functions were gradually assumed by one of the large official banks. The Banco do Brasil and the Banco de la República Oriental del Uruguay operated as both commercial and central banks until the two functions were formally separated with the creation of the Banco Central do Brasil in 1965 and the Banco Central del Uruguay in 1967. Only Panama is now without a central bank, reflecting the fact that the US dollar is the principal currency for transactions.

The limited powers of the early central banks were gradually amplified by amendment to their statutes. They, alone, or in conjunction with one or another of the official banks or an official body such as a Superintendency of Banks, now have far-reaching authority to impose credit controls in furtherance of monetary policy, regulate the activities of banks in other ways, administer special credit funds and operate exchange and trade control systems. General banking legislation has established prudential controls designed to ensure solvency and liquidity by prescribing minimum capital requirements, capital/deposit ratios, and other limits on credit creation.

The complexity of controls on bank lending, which has been characteristic of many republics in recent decades, is related not only to *dirigiste* traditions of government but also to the persistence of deficit financing of the public sector, high and variable rates of inflation and instability in the external accounts. Variable reserve requirements, prescription of interest rates for different types of operation and various forms of qualitative control designed to channel lending into particular sectors of the economy are common. The structure of interest rates is often complex; negative rates (i.e. less than the prevailing rate of inflation) have for long periods provided subsidies to certain classes of borrower. On the other hand, the destructive effect on savings and malfunctioning of financial markets caused by very high inflation led to the extensive application of indexation or 'monetary correction' to financial assets and liabilities, most notably in Brazil. Initially useful, indispensable even as a means of restoring long-term credit and capital markets, indexation tended, in the absence of appropriate fiscal and other measures and over a period of years, to institutionalize inflation rather than help to overcome it.

Central banks enjoy only a very limited autonomy. They generally respond to a monetary board or to the national treasury, and the presidency of the central bank is likely to be a political appointment. They are, nevertheless, by reason of the importance of their functions, the professionalism of their staff and the continuity that they provide, institutions of very considerable prestige both inside and outside their countries.

Foreign banks

The role of foreign banks in the nineteenth and early twentieth centuries was crucial. Their share of domestic banking business has, in general, much diminished over the past 40 years. In Brazil, for example, total deposits in foreign banks amounted to about one-third of those in domestic banks in 1929; a decade later the proportion was about one quarter, and by the early 1980s was probably not much over 5 per cent. The long-term decline in the relative importance of foreign-owned banks was due to several factors: the changing nature of economic development, which after 1930 was no longer so export-oriented; restrictions on their activities imposed in various countries; and, above all, the rapid growth of domestic banking after the Second World War.

The depression of the early 1930s naturally had serious effects on the business of foreign banks. The largest British bank in Latin America, the Anglo-South American Bank, was deeply involved in the Chilean nitrate industry and fatally weakened by its collapse. In 1936 the process of amalgamating all British banking interests into a single bank, the Bank of London and South America (now part of the Lloyds Bank Group) was completed. Some foreign banks passed into the hands of local shareholders and banks such as the Banco de Italia y Rio de la Plata and the Banco de Galicia y Rio de la Plata are now, despite their names, local Argentine banking institutions. From the Bank of London and Mexico ultimately evolved the present-day Banca Serfin, one of the largest of Mexican banking groups.

Current attitudes towards existing foreign banks and to new foreign investment in branches or locally-incorporated banks conform to no general pattern. In a few of the smaller countries foreign banks are still preponderant, notably in Panama (an important 'offshore' banking centre) and Paraguay. In Argentina, official policy towards foreign banks has varied considerably with changes in political regime, but has on the whole been fairly liberal in comparison with most of the other large republics; even so, foreign

Bank of London and South America, Buenos Aires

banks held in 1983 only about 15 per cent of total peso deposits of the commercial banking system. Elsewhere, conditions are often much more restrictive, though in only a few are foreign banks totally excluded. The latter include Cuba, where foreign banks as well as those domestically owned were nationalized in the early years of the Castro revolution; a similar process of nationalization took place in Chile under the Allende government of the early 1970s, though in this case the successor-regime reversed policy and offered the foreign banks the opportunity to re-acquire their former branches, so that by mid-1983 foreign banks held about 15 per cent of total local-currency deposits. The general trend towards reduction in the importance of foreign banks was also reversed in Uruguay where a consolidation of the banking system after the crisis of the mid-1960s led to the disappearance of many local banks and to the absorption of others by foreign institutions.

In Mexico the *de facto* ban on foreign investment in banking was made explicit in 1965 when any type of foreign participation in the capital of Mexican credit institutions was prohibited. Only one long-established branch of a foreign bank, Citibank of New York, continues to operate. Foreign banks may, however, set up representative offices in Mexico; these may not carry out any domestic banking transactions, but assist in the negotiation of foreign borrowings and support correspondent banking relations. By the early 1980s some 120 banks maintained such offices in Mexico City, reflecting the large scale of Mexican borrowings in the international markets.

In Brazil both the entry of new foreign banks and the expansion of existing ones are very strictly controlled, although many banks have, as in Mexico, opened representative offices. Among the Andean Pact countries, restrictions are most severe in Venezuela and Colombia. In the former, new investment from abroad in banks, finance companies and insurance companies was forbidden, and the maximum permitted holding for existing banks reduced to 20 per cent.

Many of the larger Latin American banks have themselves established branches abroad, reflecting their enhanced status within the world banking community, their countries' increased involvement in world financial markets and their own desire to participate in 'Eurocurrency' and other international business. Argentine, Brazilian, Mexican and other banks have set up in London, New York and other financial centres in the form of representative offices, branches or participations in consortium banks such as the European Latin American Bank (Eulabank) and European–Brazilian Bank in London. They have also set up branches in neighbouring countries, and banks from the larger Latin American countries are influential in the smaller republics such as Paraguay and Panama. All the republics except Cuba are members of the IMF, the World Bank group and the Inter-American Development Bank.

Recent evolution

The development of banking and related financial services after the Second World War paralleled general economic growth and diversification. In Mexico and Brazil particularly, these decades saw a sustained and substantial growth in the financial service industries, in the volume of transactions and in institutional development in both the public and private sectors. In some other countries, such as Argentina, Uruguay and Chile, political change and related economic instability led to a less ordered evolution of banking systems.

In the private sector the most notable post-war development was the proliferation of non-banking financial companies. Up to the Second World War private-sector financial institutions consisted almost entirely of commercial banks, mortgage and savings banks. Commercial banks were restricted in law or in practice to granting short-term credit. Economic diversification and controls on com-

mercial banking led to the development of other institutions, generally known as *financieras*. These differ widely in character, some carrying out a genuine development banking role by arranging longer-term finance, others specializing in consumer finance. In Mexico and Brazil they increased rapidly from the 1950s onwards, in the former to the point where their combined assets exceeded those of the commercial banks. As with the commercial banks, a small number of *financieras* generally conducted a large share of the total business and were often linked to one of the major banking groups. Other developments of recent years have been the formation of savings-and-loan associations in some countries, the introduction of leasing and the spread of credit card operations. Developments in the public sector have included the strengthening of official development banks, the creation of new specialized institutions, for example, for managing the investment of oil revenues in Venezuela, and the development of special financing facilities for exporters and others.

With the world economic recession of the early 1980s and the onset of the external debt crisis that affected so many of the republics, a period of general economic growth that had led to the expansion and deepening of Latin- American financial systems seemed to have come to an end. The magnitude of Latin American external borrowing had itself reflected not only these countries' need to supplement domestic savings but also the most serious deficiency of their financial systems – the inadequacies of their long-term capital markets, in turn related to the failure to control inflation. The events of these years also frustrated the experiments in 'liberal' economics in Argentina and Chile, where serious banking and related industrial failures occurred. The nationalization of banks in Mexico, mentioned above, was perhaps a political act rather than an economic necessity, but seemed unlikely to be reversed (except to the extent that a minor part of government-held shares might be offered to the public).

While full nationalization of banks has been exceptional, central banks have tried to shape the evolution of the banking system in various ways. In Uruguay and Brazil in the 1960s a determined effort was made to reduce the number of banks in the interest of the efficiency and stability of the system; in Brazil the number was reduced from 328 in 1969 to 108 in 1979. The functions of the various types of *financiera* were defined and their operations regulated. Commercial banks, with their wide deposit base, remain however at the centre of the private banking system, and some of the larger countries have accepted the inevitability that they should form the core of powerful financial groupings. In Mexico, where deposit or commercial banks, *financieras*, mortgage and other banks had been separately defined and licensed, the tendency to consolidate into powerful interlocking groups was recognized in 1975, and in 1978 they were allowed to function through a single banking corporation. This tendency seems likely to be reinforced after nationalization. In Brazil financial 'conglomerates' have emerged from the process of concentration, consisting of commercial bank, investment bank, finance company, leasing, brokerage and other subsidiaries. In both countries not more than half a dozen banking groups have a preponderant share of total business. In establishing the multi-purpose bank, Latin America again follows the European rather than the North American example.

HH

Further reading

A. Hendrie, ed., *Banking Structures and Sources of Finance in Latin America* (London, 1980)

D. Joslin, *A Century of Banking in Latin America* (London, 1963)

Current developments are best studied in *World Banking*, an annual survey, published by the *Investors Chronicle* (London), in the annual banking surveys of the *Financial Times* (London), and in specialized banking periodicals.

Inflation

The nature of inflation

Inflation is normally associated with rising prices, though where prices are held down by controls, inflationary pressures can surface in other ways, such as lengthening order books, queues, and a growing shortage of goods. This is referred to as 'suppressed' inflation.

The change in the price level can reflect an excess of aggregate demand in the economy over the supply of resources. Supply and demand have to be balanced at a new higher price level. Inflation can be viewed as a way of rationing scarce resources among competing claimants whose initial demand, expressed in money, exceeds the initial monetary value of resources available. An increased supply of money, however measured, is the means whereby the excessive demand works through into higher prices.

There is another type of inflation which is not obviously due to excessive money demand. 'Stagflation' is the occurrence of rising prices in the midst of recession, where excessive demand is not the prime cause. This has been common in the industrial countries in the late 1970s and early 1980s in the wake of successive oil price rises. It often results from cost increases due to rises in import prices (because of a devaluation, or changes in the terms of trade), wage increases which are insensitive to the state of demand or delayed adjustments to administered (or controlled) prices.

The term 'price level' is not unambiguous. Price changes can be monitored at the wholesale or retail level. Whatever prices are chosen have to be combined into an index to represent changes in

Inflation affects everything – even toll charges on public highways. This Chilean toll voucher, originally covering a payment of 7 escudos in the 1960s, was 'revalued' upwards to 3000 escudos in 1974, the year Chile's inflation reached its highest point

the price level as a whole. The compilation of the index is from a 'basket' of goods and services, and whatever basket is chosen may not reflect the spending pattern of particular social groups, hence separate indices are sometimes produced for different social groups. The most sophisticated measure of price changes is the GDP Deflator, a concept in national accounts devised to arrive at 'real' growth in national income, after allowing for price changes. Hereafter we shall use the consumer price index to measure inflation. This is the most easily understood and widely employed measure, and comparable data exist over the period concerned for the countries under discussion.

Twenty-five years of inflation

Over the last twenty-five years Latin America and the Caribbean have undergone greater inflation than the rest of the world. Tables 24 and 25 show that the rate of inflation in the western hemisphere (excluding the United States and Canada) has exceeded worldwide inflation by a substantial margin. The cumulative results, which show the power of compound interest, are startling: an item costing 1 unit (in the 'western hemisphere') in 1953 would cost 976 units in 1982.

Too much should not be read into the choice of the time periods. 1953 is a convenient date to start since the inflationary effects of the Korean War had largely worn off. In addition, some of the consumer price series reported in 'International Financial Statistics' (those used here) start in 1953 or soon after. There is no significance in the use of 1960 to close this period, except that it enables us to refer to the '1950s', a period of generally low inflation in which a number of our countries periodically reported *falling* price levels. On the other hand, there was an inflationary watershed around 1973 and 1974, and this is the reason for starting the third and final period in 1974, since when most countries have regularly experienced double-digit inflation. Data for 1981 and 1982 are shown separately.

Table 24 shows that most of the larger countries (grouped as South America plus Mexico) have seen growing rates of inflation in each successive period since 1953. (Paraguay is an exception, due to the decline from very high rates of inflation in the early 1950s.) Over the whole period the highest inflation has been in Argentina, Chile, Uruguay and Brazil, and Peru has recently joined their ranks. Venezuela has always had lower inflation than elsewhere. The averages conceal unusually violent inflationary episodes in particular countries, such as Argentina continuously since 1975, Brazil 1962–5 and since 1979, Chile 1973–7, Uruguay 1973–80, Peru since 1978, and Bolivia and Mexico in 1982.

Table 25 focuses on the Central American and Caribbean countries. It is apparent that inflation has been very much lower in Central American countries than in their larger South American neighbours. Indeed, in the 1950s inflation was frequently negative in some of these countries. The increase in the tempo of inflation from one period to another has certainly happened, but even in the 1970s Central America experienced relatively low inflation by regional standards. The only countries experiencing a sharp, violent inflationary episode were Nicaragua in 1979 (related to the fall of the Somoza dynasty) and Costa Rica in 1981–2.

A similar picture applies to the Caribbean countries in table 25. The table includes the larger islands (plus Guyana, which it is customary to include in the Caribbean rather than Latin America). Price data for these countries for the 1950s are weak and incomplete, but the patchy evidence suggests very little inflation in that period. Inflation in the 1960s was greater, though still modest by the standards of the hemisphere. It was only since 1973/4 that inflation rose into two digits for most of them, with the highest rates hitting Jamaica, Trinidad and Tobago, Barbados and Guyana.

It is not practical to include data for each of the smaller Caribbean islands. Many of them have only a few thousand inhabitants and price data are frequently weak and incomplete. Many are closely tied to metropolitan powers, and inflation mirrors that in the metropolis or the major trading partner (variously, Britain, France, Netherlands and the United States). Nor is Cuba discussed, since it is not a market economy and comparable price data do not exist.

A variety of circumstances

Before discussing the theoretical causes of inflation, it should be obvious that its incidence has varied widely in the region, even between apparently similar countries. This should already warn

Table 24. Inflation since 1953: South America and Mexico (average annual percentage changes in consumer prices)

	1953–60	1961–73	1974–80	1981	1982
Argentina	26.3	43.5	178.3	104.5	164.8
Bolivia	n.a.	7.5	19.6	32.1	123.5
Brazil	n.a.	38.5	45.7	105.6	98.0
Chile	n.a.	65.7*	184.1	19.7	9.9
Colombia	7.9	12.1	24.0	27.5	24.6
Ecuador	0.6	5.6	13.8	12.0	16.3
Mexico	6.1	3.7	21.2	27.9	58.9
Paraguay	22.0	4.7	15.3	13.0	5.1
Peru	7.7	9.0	42.5	75.4	64.5
Uruguay	18.1	52.1	60.1	34.1	19.0
Venezuela	1.3	1.6	10.7	16.2	10.0
Latin America†	15.1	22.1	43.6	63.8	80.1
World	2.6	5.1	12.2	14.1	12.0

n.a. Not available
* Incomplete series
† Excluding Venezuela
Source: International Monetary Fund, *International Financial Statistics* (Washington).

Table 25. Central America and the Caribbean (average annual percentage changes in consumer prices)

	1953–60	1961–73	1974–80	1981	1982
Central America					
Costa Rica	1.8	3.6	12.6	37.1	90.1
El Salvador	2.1	1.2	14.7	14.8	11.7
Guatemala	0.8	1.7	11.7	11.4	0.4
Honduras	0.7*	2.6	8.0	10.2	9.9
Nicaragua	n.a.	n.a.	16.7*	n.a.	n.a.
Panama	−0.3	2.1	8.2	7.3	4.3
Caribbean					
Bahamas	n.a.	5.9*	8.3	11.1	6.0
Barbados	n.a.	8.6*	15.7	14.6	10.3
Dominican Republic	−0.4	3.7	11.1	7.5	7.7
Guyana	1.4*	2.8	12.8	24.7	18.5
Haiti	0.3*	4.9	10.2	17.8	n.a.
Jamaica	2.4*	5.5	21.9	12.5	6.8
Trinidad & Tobago	2.4	4.5	14.8	14.3	11.6
Latin America	15.1	22.1	43.6	63.8	80.1
World	2.6	5.1	12.2	14.1	12.0

n.a. Not available
* Incomplete series
Source: International Monetary Fund, *International Financial Statistics* (Washington).

readers against accepting any single, or simple, explanation of inflation. For instance Argentina and Brazil have both undergone substantial industrial development during this period, for much of the time under military regimes, yet Argentina has had the higher inflation. Both countries have had much higher inflation than the other industrially developed country, Mexico. Inflation in Jamaica and Trinidad has been very similar, despite the latter's status as an oil producer. On the other hand, inflation in the major oil producer, Venezuela, has always been low.

Is inflation imported? Clearly, the enormous rises in petroleum prices after 1973 and 1979 hit virtually all our countries, save the oil producers. But the more 'open' economies, with a larger trading sector, had comparatively low inflation over the whole period (e.g. Bahamas, Barbados, Panama, El Salvador). For those inclining to the 'cost push' explanation of inflation, trade union pressure would be one of the major stimuli to rising prices. Certainly the political power of unions in Argentina, Jamaica and Uruguay has helped to sustain inflation (though whether it caused it is another matter), but inflation has recently reached high levels in Brazil too, where trade unions cover only a minority of workers.

Another mechanism for propagating inflation, indexing prices to the cost of living, has been extensively practised only in Brazil, and to a much lesser extent in Colombia. The impact of indexation on inflation is a matter of some dispute, and the bald statistical record is open to different interpretations. Brazil has had high inflation throughout the indexation period, and although the rate declined from the peak in 1964, it surged to high levels again in the late 1970s and early 1980s. Colombia, on the other hand, has never suffered the extremes of inflation.

It is also clear that the type of government is too simple an explanation of variations in inflation. Over this period most Latin American countries have had spells of government either directly by military regimes, or by civilian governments with the crucial support of the military. But authoritarian governments are not always or necessarily better than their civilian counterparts in controlling inflation. Mexico, Venezuela, and Colombia – ruled by civilian governments throughout this period – have relatively low rates of inflation, while Brazil and Argentina have persistently shown much higher rates. It could be argued, as in Chile and Brazil, that the intervention of the military to end a period of increasingly unstable civilian rule succeeds in getting inflation down over the ensuing few years, but thereafter it seems that deep-rooted factors supervene to determine long-term inflation (cf. Brazil since the early 1970s).

There is more reason to think that inflation should be understood against the background of a country's economic structure and its stage of development. As a preamble to discussing the causes of inflation, it might be helpful to distinguish a number of circumstances (some countries fall into more than one category):

1 *Oil exporters* (Venezuela, Trinidad and Tobago, and recently Mexico, Ecuador and Peru). These countries (except for Peru) seem to have suffered less inflation than the others. This could be due to their greater ability to control the pace at which the real increase in the value of oil percolates through to consumers. In addition, buoyant oil exports help to maintain exchange rates at a high level, which depresses the local price of imported goods. Of course, extravagant investment and consumption, based on

oil revenues, can be a massive inflationary force (as in Mexico since 1979), but this has not happened in the western hemisphere as much as elsewhere in the world.

2 *Large industrializing economies* (Argentina, Brazil, Mexico). These three countries are well diversified, each producing and exporting a range of primary and manufactured goods. Industrialization has been a primary aim of government policy throughout the period, (except for Argentine policy during the military government after 1976, when a neo-liberal experiment in reducing tariffs was attempted), and the main process has been through substituting local production for imports. Rigorous control over imports is an integral part of the process, as is the expansion of heavy industry, frequently under state ownership. Inflation commonly results from the forced growth of industry, free from internal or external competition, in an environment where public investment is also expanding rapidly. Inflation can be mitigated in the more open economies (e.g. Mexico), depending on the rate of inflation in the main trading partners.

3 *Small open non-industrial economies* (some Central American and most Caribbean countries). These countries show great variety in their economic structure, relying variously on the export of sugar and citrus (Belize), bananas and coffee (Honduras), tourism (Bahamas), workers' remittances (Dominica). However, all are too small to produce very many of the goods and services they need, hence they rely heavily on imports. At times of low world inflation, the high penetration of imports keeps domestic prices down. When world inflation quickens, as it did after 1973, inflation tends to be 'imported' into these open economies. A special case is the inflation triggered off by the rises in oil prices in and after 1973 and 1979, which was soon passed on to prices of imported manufactures too. Even so, inflation in this group has been moderate even in the most recent period. In many Caribbean countries, rudimentary monetary and fiscal arrangements limit the extent of deficit financing and expansion of the money supply.

4 *Dependencies of metropolitan powers* (Martinique, Curaçao, Montserrat, US and British Virgin Islands, Turks and Caicos Islands etc.). Although in recent years a number of Caribbean islands have achieved independence, some territories remain that are either dependencies of Britain, the Netherlands or the United States, or are constitutionally part of France (the last category including Guadeloupe, Guyane and Martinique). These countries tend to be governed by laws and institutions that help keep the cost of living in a close relation to that in the metropolitan power (through such mechanisms as minimum wages, social security payments, remittances from the mother country, price of imports, the level of government spending

etc.). The metropolitan currency may also be used as the unit of exchange (US dollars in the US Virgins, the French franc in Martinique), and this, plus ease of import, prevents prices getting greatly out of line with those in the metropolitan country of issue.

5 *Small open economies with some industry.* This is a clumsy but necessary way of describing those Central American and Caribbean countries that are small by South American standards and possess a relatively large trading sector, but are large enough to have established a range of – mainly light – industries. This group includes Jamaica, Barbados, Guatemala, El Salvador, Haiti, the Dominican Republic, Nicaragua, Costa Rica and Puerto Rico (the last-mentioned is constitutionally part of the United States, but in view of its size and industrial development it is convenient to group it here rather than with the micro-economies in category 4 above). The economic structure of these countries is intermediate between the industrializing countries (category 2 above and 6 below) and the open economies producing primary products or services. Table 22 shows that their levels of inflation are likewise intermediate. The presence of an industrial sector can be a source of pressure on prices where local products are being substituted for imports, where imported materials increase in price, and where the labour force successfully demands higher wages.

6 *Small/medium-sized industrializing countries* (Chile, Peru, Colombia, Uruguay). Several of these countries have witnessed explosive bouts of inflation at various times, while two of them (Chile and Uruguay) are identified with 'inflation' in popular history. Without wishing to overlook the differences between the countries mentioned above, we can draw attention to a few obvious similarities. All are sophisticated economies by regional standards, with middle to high living standards. They rely on a few primary products to provide the bulk of their export income (copper, coffee, livestock, gems, bauxite), which consequently fluctuate from year to year. The economies are large enough to support a range of consumer goods and services, but not much heavy industry, hence the pace and extent of industrialization runs into early limits. Government spending takes up a moderate to high proportion of national income. Organized labour has been or is strong. The consequence of such a structure seems to be that externally transmitted 'shocks', such as a sudden rise in import prices or a fall in exports, require painful adjustments to domestic living standards and economic growth which the various domestic socio-political groups are unwilling to bear. Inflation is the result of the struggle of the various groups to retain their former living standards and income shares.

Causes of inflation

As in other countries, there has been considerable debate in Latin America and the Caribbean about the causes of the inflation which has been such a prominent feature of their economic life. But whereas in other countries the debate has polarized between 'monetarists' and 'Keynesians', or in earlier, simpler days, between theories of 'demand pull' and 'cost push', in the western-hemisphere developing countries the division has traditionally been between monetarists and structuralists. It is worth outlining these latter two positions.

The monetarist explanation

Monetarism is more than a mere emphasis on the relation between the supply of money and the rate of price increase. This is, after all, a truism. It is not difficult to associate inflation with an increase in the quantity of money or the speed with which it changes hands (its 'velocity of circulation'). This can result from increased note issue by the Central Bank, increased credit from the commercial banks, and more government borrowing from the banking system (e.g. to cover a budget deficit). These, however, are the *means* by which inflation is transmitted to prices, and tell us nothing about how the inflation arose, or how it can be reduced.

Monetarists stress the importance of firm central-bank control over the liquid assets of the commercial banks in order to restrain credit expansion. They would abhor the government's printing money to finance budget deficits. They would, in fact, advocate fiscal restraint in order to prevent the emergence of budget deficits. If the latter were inevitable, they would advocate financing in non-inflationary ways, such as issuing public bonds (rather than borrowing from the banks).

More fundamentally, monetarists place greater faith in market mechanisms than in the use of direct administrative controls. Thus, they would advocate 'realistic' interest rates, reflecting the 'real' returns on capital and necessary to induce the required amount of savings. The foreign exchange rate should be determined by market forces, instead of being fixed for long periods at 'unrealistic' levels. Price control should, in general, be dropped, otherwise there is the risk of prices being fixed too low to induce sufficient supplies of the goods in question. Consumers should, as a general rule, pay the economic cost of their goods and services. The alternative is either the reduced supply of those goods and services, or the growth of consumer subsidies which enlarge the budget deficit. Monetarists claim that the strains and bottlenecks which accompany rapid growth and structural change would be greatly eased by allowing more scope for the operation of the price mechanism.

The structuralist view

Structuralists, on the contrary, view a degree of inflation as an inevitable concomitant of development in countries subject to the kind of structural changes seen in Latin America and the Caribbean. Attempts to eliminate inflation by firm monetary and fiscal policies bring on ills that are worse than the original malady, namely arrested growth, unemployment, and increased foreign dependence. They favour 'supply side' measures to control inflation, such as state investment, land reform, controls over private investment and foreign firms, etc.

Take food prices as an example. It is argued that agriculture is not able to respond to the rapidly increasing demand for food from a growing and urbanizing population. Landowners may lack motivation because of outmoded attitudes or tenurial forms. Complementary factors (machinery, seeds, fertilizer, and credit) may be lacking, together with know-how or enterprise. Hence food becomes increasingly scarce, causing price increases, consumer subsidies and/or imports.

Foreign exchange is another increasingly inevitable bottleneck, according to this view. The attempt to raise the growth rate, and push through industrial development, exacerbates a growing shortage of foreign exchange. Exports are sluggish, consisting as they do of primary products the demand for which is not responsive to income or price changes. The demand for imports by a growing population and expanding industrial sector rises rapidly. Neither exports nor imports are responsive to price changes such that movements in the exchange rate would bring about. Faced with a growing imbalance in foreign receipts and payments, the government is pressured into devaluation. This merely gives another twist to the inflationary spiral, since there is little effect in boosting exports or checking imports, the rise in the latter's price is passed on into wages and prices, and a further incentive is given to replace imports in a high-cost and inefficient manner.

It is argued that deficit financing is another 'structural' element feeding inflation. The choice of development strategy made by governments of developing countries often entails high public spending. On the other hand, the tax base is limited by the inequitable structure of incomes and wealth and by the smallness of the productive sector. At the same time, the poorer countries have limited recourse to such non-inflationary financial sources as overseas borrowing or the issue of domestic bonds. Hard-pressed governments start borrowing from the banks to cover the deficit in their budgets, and may even print money. Whatever the ultimate prime mover, the process normally shows in a budget deficit, which propagates further inflation.

A reconciliation

There is clearly a difference of view between these two schools about the ability of developing countries to cope with rapid growth and change without undergoing the tensions that show up in inflation.

But there is also an implicit difference in the priority that the two schools accord to controlling inflation as opposed to modifying growth policies.

Structuralists, faced with a 'trade-off' between inflation and growth, would prefer more of both, while monetarists would choose less of both. This is, of course, a gross simplification, since some structuralists would recommend 'supply side' measures to improve the economy's response to growth, and possibly devices like indexation to take the sting out of inflation. On the other hand, many monetarists would align themselves with 'gradualist' approaches to the control of inflation that did not jolt output and employment too severely, and would direct public and private investment into the more obvious bottlenecks. Indeed, monetarists tend to argue that in the long run there is no conflict between inflationary control and growth since a degree of price stability is essential for economic progress.

Reviewing the Latin American experience over two decades it is clear that prices and market forces have been neglected by policy makers, leading to an exacerbation of structural distortions and the loss of opportunities for output, employment and exports. When price signals – whether to farmers, banks or exports – are suppressed by price controls, legislation on interest rates, over-valued exchange rates etc., these sectors are discouraged and the myth of 'structural rigidities' arises. However, the greater play of market forces would lead to a different kind of economy and society, such as one with a larger farm sector, more open to the international economy, with more private investment, etc. The fundamental difference between the two schools may be traced to the kind of sociopolitical regime they wish to see in place.

Remedies?

If there were no cost involved in reducing inflation, in the sense of difficult policy trade-offs to be faced, then there would be little point in delaying anti-inflationary policy. But as the above discussions show, observers differ in the priority they place on reducing inflation, where this involves costs for output, employment, growth, and even social stability. All observers would, however, agree that the most outrageous inflationary episodes (Brazil 1963–4 and since 1979, Argentina since 1973 and especially 1976, Chile 1973–6, Uruguay 1972–6, etc.), where prices were virtually doubling every year (in some cases more), were simply not sustainable and drastic measures were called for.

There are, of course, ways of living with inflation. Individual people try to cope with inflation in various ways, such as resorting to the Black Market, taking on extra jobs, and smuggling. People differ in their opportunity to do this. Alternatively governments may try to link as many prices as possible to the index of inflation, so that suffering and distortion are mitigated. The most comprehensive attempt at 'indexation' has taken place in Brazil since 1964, although it was also tried in Chile and Argentina. Interest on government securities, tax obligations, deposits in investment banks, and housing finance have all formally been linked to the official cost of living index, and minimum wages have been indexed in a looser fashion.

Brazilian indexation, though widely applied to important sectors, has not been universal and, as applied to wages, has not maintained purchasing power for the lowest-paid workers. It certainly had an early and favourable impact on the growth of savings, which helped government finance and home ownership. More recently, though, it has been argued that indexation has helped to perpetuate inflation, not least because the government has only been able to finance its index-linked obligations by raising further finance in inflationary ways.

Since inflation is associated with price increases, it is tempting to think that price controls can form the cure. But, by making the supply of the goods and services in question increasingly unprofitable, price controls create scarcities or else they are simply evaded. Price controls can therefore only be effective for a limited period, as part of an attack on inflationary expectations.

The rapid growth of money supply 'causes' price rises in a proximate sense, just as petrol thrown on to a flame 'causes' a blaze, but we need to ask what makes people throw petrol on to flames if we are seeking a full explanation. The control of the money supply may be lax, and it may be irresponsible, but in many cases the creation of money results from the need to finance a budget deficit when all other, non-inflationary, means have been tried. In short, the excessive expansion in the money supply may contribute to inflation in its own right, but often it merely reflects the exigencies of public finance.

Unbalanced budgets are invariably a feature of inflation. Financing the gap between revenue and spending sometimes takes inflationary forms, namely borrowing from the banking system (which is then used to expand credit) or even printing new money to pay the government's bills. Balancing the budget has a pivotal part in any anti-inflationary measures. However, the budget is the result of pressures from different political, social and economic groups. A government that feels in peril will not have the will nor the power to take 'obvious' budgetary measures.

Thus ultimately the worst outbreaks of inflation in Latin America over the last twenty-five years have arisen from the lack of a political consensus about how the burdens and benefits of development should be distributed or how the costs of an exogenous 'shock' should be shared. Commonly, a series of events arises (e.g. a fall in export prices, leading to a decline in government revenues and a balance-of-payments deficit) which demands some remedial action by the government, but where none of the parties concerned is willing to bear the sacrifices (higher taxes, reduced government spending, higher food prices and utility tariffs, devaluation, higher interest rates, etc.). Each group tries to maintain its former share of the national cake, and in the process the aggregate pressure of demand on resources causes mounting inflation. Although sound 'technical' measures can go a long way towards preventing excessive inflation, the ultimate causes, and cures, for inflation often lie in the political domain.

Inflation, recession and debt

The early years of the 1980s were troubled by international recession and the emergence of debt crises in a number of industrializing countries. Argentina, Brazil and Mexico were especially prominent, though Peru and Venezuela shared their difficulties to a lesser extent. The common experience of these larger and wealthier countries was stagnation and recession, imbalances in the domestic budget and the external account, the re-emergence of serious inflation, and the impossibility of servicing the large volumes of foreign debt that had accumulated.

Mexico's problems came to a head in 1982, after several years of buoyant growth. The root of its problem was the rapid growth in public spending based on optimistic views about the growth of the petroleum economy after 1979. The public sector deficit was widening even before the fall in oil prices in 1981, and led to sizeable foreign borrowing. The deteriorating balance of payments led to a massive exodus of capital, and eventually to a large depreciation of the peso in 1982. This, with its attendant rises in wages and administered prices, caused the acceleration of inflation visible in table 21.

Argentina's crisis was more severe and intractable, and its causes more complex. National income fell in both 1981 and 1982, inflation remained in three figures and hit 165 per cent in 1982, and foreign debt reached $34 billion, half of it repayable within eighteen months. The anti-inflationary programme of 1978/9 was not sustained, partly because of the banking crisis of 1980. The stabilization programme that was renewed early in 1982 was interrupted by the South Atlantic War. Much of 1983 was spent with Argentina locked in talks with its creditors and the IMF, which continued after the restoration of democracy under President Alfonsín.

The trauma was probably greatest in Brazil. An economy accustomed to high rates of growth and structural change was well on the way to adjusting to high energy prices when the second major oil-price increase occurred in 1979. The economy had become very dependent on foreign export markets and sources of capital at a time when a recession hit the world economy and international interest rates rose.

The widespread indexation of prices and wages complicated the task of economic stabilization, and in the attempt to lower inflationary expectations the authorities interfered with adjustments in the exchange rate and the rate of monetary correction. This led, perversely, to an overvaluation of the cruzeiro, which compounded the problems of the balance of payments. A large previous uptake of foreign debt was the background to the protracted talks with the IMF and hundreds of creditor banks during 1983. Inflation settled at 100 per cent in both 1981 and 1982.

JTW

Further reading

W. Baer and I. Kerstenetzky, eds., *Inflation and Growth in Latin America* (Illinois, 1964)

A. Foxley and L. Whitehead, eds., *Economic Stabilization in Latin America: Political Dimensions* (A special edition of the journal *World Development*, November 1980)

K. Griffin, ed., *Financing and Development in Latin America* (London, 1971)

A. Hirschman, ed., *Latin American Issues: Essays and Comments* (New York, 1961)

R. Thorp and L. Whitehead, eds., *Inflation and Stabilization in Latin America* (London, 1979)

External debt

Scale of area

Latin America's land area is one-sixth of the world's total. It had a population of 215 million in 1960, 349 million in 1980 (66 per cent urban), and it is forecast at 570 million in 2000. Of its twenty countries, one, Brazil, with a population of 126 million, is larger than the continental United States. With regard to mineral resources, the region is so vast that its full extent has not been assessed. Its proven reserves of oil were 79 billion barrels at the end of 1982, 11 per cent of the world's total, of which Mexico accounted for 49 per cent. Latin America has the equivalent of 160,000 million barrels of oil in coal, 300,000 megawatts of hydroelectric potential and 90,000 megawatts of geothermal potential, as well as extensive uranium resources. The largest countries, Argentina, Brazil and Mexico, have in the 1980s well-developed industrial bases, and along with Colombia, are significant exporters of manufactured products. The region has the largest reserve of potentially productive cropland in the developing world.

Historical perspectives

In 1914, the total nominal value of foreign financial investment in Latin America was $8.5 billion, of which about one-third was in Argentina, about a fourth in Brazil, and a similar amount in Mexico. Up to that date the chief lending and investing country was the United Kingdom, but the USA gradually took over this position.

In the 1870s, some countries, such as Argentina and Uruguay, were at little or no economic disadvantage in relation to many countries which now comprise the industrialized world. The boom in world trade in the nineteenth and early twentieth centuries enabled the region (notably Brazil and Argentina), along with Canada and Australia, to begin to industrialize (in the later years of the last century a number of Latin American countries, including Brazil and Argentina, incurred substantial external debts to finance development, particularly the establishment of public utilities). In the 1930s, the level of development of Australia and Canada was comparable with Latin American countries such as Uruguay and Argentina. Immediately after 1945, Australia, Canada and Argentina had similar export earnings, but Canada and Australia were drawing rapidly ahead. At present, Canada's per-capita income is four times that of Argentina and Australia's per-capita income five times that of Mexico. Latin America is now classified as part of the developing world and is a debtor region on a substantial scale.

Considerable economic progress has taken place in the region since 1945. There have been moderately good growth rates, large improvements to infrastructure, periods of rising real wages, and a higher proportion of income has accrued to middle-income groups. Through improvements in productive capacity, many countries can now satisfy a large proportion of internal needs for basic goods. The region as a whole, however, has failed to generate autonomously the resources needed to fund development, especially to finance purchases of capital goods to implement industrial strategies of the larger countries.

The outstanding characteristic of Latin American international economic relations since the Second World War has been a consistently low proportion of total world trade; it increased from 13 per cent in 1963–70 to 15 per cent in 1976–80. At the end of the nineteenth century, Latin America's share of international trade was not substantially less than that of the United States. In the past forty years the international economy in general has increasingly been geared to acquiring technological skills and the achievement of high productivity rather than to the exploitation of natural resources. Despite growing industrialization in some countries, notably Brazil and Mexico, Latin America has not taken part fully in this; and many countries remain dependent on commodities for the bulk of export revenues. The total capital inflow to Latin America, in real terms, since 1950 has not been very much larger than financial resources received before the 1930s; but during the latter period exports were growing sufficiently to enable the region to meet its obligations. In recent years, and particularly since 1973, this has no longer been the case.

Because of economic diversification since 1945, the primary external concerns of Latin American countries are access to capital markets, trade, markets and technology. As a result of a political commitment to growth most countries have found it difficult to retrench, particularly in the face of successive oil-price explosions since 1973 and downturns in world economic activity at intervals in the past decade (the price per barrel of oil rose from $2 in 1971 to a peak of $35 in 1981). Most countries have been able to maintain a satisfactory rate of growth until 1981 or 1982, in large part by increasing external indebtedness. Brazil, Mexico, Argentina and Venezuela became leading borrowers in world capital markets.

World considerations and linkages

Latin America has now reached a level of development that places it in an intermediate position between industrialized countries and most of the rest of the developing world. According to the Inter-American Development Bank (IDB), the region's gross product per head (in 1980 US dollars) in 1982 was $1503; this included wide differences between countries, varying from $2538 in Venezuela to $266 in Haiti. However, the Latin American average, though all its countries are below the accepted developed/developing countries boundary of $2500, is three times that for all Africa and four times that of Asia (excluding Japan).

Latin American economies are linked with the world economy in four ways. Firstly, through commodity markets, in which not only demand variations associated with world business cycles are key determinants of price trends, but supply conditions (and disruptions) also play a major role. Secondly, world inflation, particularly in advanced industrial countries, heavily influences import costs of industrial raw materials, capital and consumer goods, and hence domestic price levels. Thirdly, a growing interdependence with world financial markets is shown by the appreciable increase in Latin American external indebtedness, foreign investment and credit availability in general, and this interdependence has grown appreciably in the past decade. Interest-rate fluctuations in the international capital market largely determine the region's cost of foreign funds, as well as the magnitude of interest payments on outstanding debt. Fourthly, there is a key link through a reliance on crude petroleum as an energy source: more than any other region except Western Europe, Latin America was dependent on imported oil when the 1973–4 oil crisis broke. In 1979, oil supplied 70 per cent of the area's total energy consumption, compared with 45 per cent for the world as a whole, and 50 per cent for developing countries in general. Its oil-import bill increased from $2 billion in 1973 to $18 billion in 1980. In some countries of the region, oil imports provide 90 per cent of total energy requirements.

In a world context, Latin America has experienced remarkable growth since 1960. The region has been expanding more rapidly than mature economies such as the USA and other OECD member-countries. In the period 1960–79, the annual average real GDP growth rate was 7.2 per cent against 3.4 per cent achieved by the United States, and 2.8 points higher than that attained by the other OECD countries in the same period. This rapid growth caused the economies of some countries of the region by 1979 to exceed in size various European economies. For instance, the economies of Brazil and Mexico, individually, were larger than those of Belgium, the Netherlands, Sweden and Spain; Brazil has the tenth biggest economy in the world, and the eighth largest free-market economy.

Recent economic development

However, since 1981 Latin America has entered a period of severe recession. Aggregate GDP rose by only 1.4 per cent in that year and fell, for the first time since reliable national accounts statistics were kept after the Second World War, by about 1.2 per cent in 1982. A second year of decline, with a 3 per cent GDP fall, followed in 1983.

In per-capita terms this decline was even more serious. For Latin America as a whole per-capita GDP fell by 1 per cent in 1981 and by more than 3 per cent in 1982 – with nine countries experiencing declines of over 5 per cent and three (Bolivia, Chile and Guyana) contracting by more than 10 per cent.

This regional setback took place for three basic reasons. First was the serious recession in the industrial countries which followed the second oil-price shock of 1979. This brought with it a decline in international trade and a precipitous fall in the prices of Latin America's commodity exports. World market prices of non-fuel mineral exports sank by 31 per cent between the beginning of 1980 and the end of 1982. The price of sugar (exported by most Latin American countries) dropped from $632 to $130 per tonne – below production costs in many cases. As a result, the unit value of Latin America's exports declined by 10 per cent in 1982, on top of which the volume of non-oil exports fell a further 3 per cent.

The second factor was unprecedentedly high real interest rates. In contrast to previous periods of recession, the 1980–3 period was characterized by a combination of restrictive monetary policies and expansionary fiscal policies in the OECD countries in general and the United States in particular. The major industrial countries had become convinced that the upward spiral of inflation had to be brought to an end. But, given the difficulties of cutting government spending, the burden of fighting inflation was borne almost entirely by restrictive monetary policies.

In consequence, average nominal interest rates (measured by three-month Libor – the London inter-bank offered rate) jumped from 12 per cent in 1979 to 14.1 per cent in 1980 and to nearly 17 per cent in 1981 (in real terms – deflated by the US GDP deflator – 3.2 per cent, 4.4 per cent and 6.9 per cent respectively). With the bulk of Latin America's debt geared to market interest rates following the explosion in commercial bank lending of the 1970s, this automatically increased debt-service charges. Each 1 per cent increase in interest rates, for example, raised Brazil's annual net debt-service bill by nearly $600 million.

The combination of high real interest rates and low commodity prices is sometimes referred to as the 'scissors effect'. It resulted in a rapid deterioration in the current account deficits of the major Latin American economies. The combined deficits of Argentina, Brazil, Chile, Colombia, Ecuador, Mexico, Peru and Venezuela widened from 21 per cent of export earnings in 1979 to 33 per cent in 1982.

The third factor was unsustainable domestic policies in the big Latin American debtor countries. Many relied on a strategy of import-substituting industrialization, with exports a secondary consideration. New industries often required heavy tariff protection to survive; easy foreign bank loans made it possible to undertake projects whose priorities were political rather than economic – Argentina's paper industry, Venezuela's steel mills, Peru's huge irrigation schemes and Brazil's nuclear power stations (to take just a few examples) were motivated primarily by prestige or employment considerations, neglecting the vital fact that the financial rate of return would not be sufficient to repay the capital cost.

Equally important has been the growth of the state sector. Latin American governments found it irresistible to hold down prices of the outputs of state-controlled utilities and public enterprises as an 'easy' way of combating inflation. The result has been ballooning public-sector deficits. Mexico's public-sector deficit, for example, grew from an average of 3.5 per cent of GDP in 1976–80 to 14.5 per cent in 1981 and a clearly unsustainable 18 per cent by 1982.

Furthermore, exchange-rate and interest-rate policies have been erratic and often counter-productive. In the name of anti-inflation policies, governments have kept exchange rates overvalued to make imports cheap. But, at the same time, this has encouraged domestic residents and local companies to borrow abroad, since the distorted exchange rate makes the cost of foreign borrowing seem artificially low. When the exchange rate has finally to be adjusted – usually following intense pressure on the reserves and large-scale capital flight – local industries find the burden of servicing the accumulated debts insupportable. The government is then obliged to take over those obligations to foreign creditors in order to avoid a wave of bankruptcies.

Finally, political prejudice continues against direct foreign investment. Many Latin American politicians appear to believe that loans create less 'dependency' than investment, which few countries in the region have encouraged. Direct investment dropped from 30 per cent of capital inflows in the 1960s to 20 per cent by the end of the 1970s. US investment in Latin America, which accounted for close to one-third of total US foreign direct investment in 1959, had dwindled to 19 per cent twenty years later. This trend was in part the result of a shift in direct investment, especially from the United States, away from Latin America to Canada and Western Europe. In practice, foreign investors have become far more flexible and accommodating than they were twenty-five years ago. Moreover, profit remittances – which require that profits be generated in the first place – may actually impose less of a financial burden than servicing external debt.

Evolution of indebtedness since 1960

Up to the early 1970s, international banks were little involved in the business of development finance in Latin America. In exceptional cases, some countries received bank loans for balance-of-payments support (often guaranteed by gold) or for projects guaranteed by third parties or by pledging of export contracts. But, overall, bank finance accounted for just 7 per cent of the annual capital inflows to Latin America in the 1960s; most of those inflows – 70 per cent – came from official credits and direct foreign investment.

By the end of the 1970s, that situation had been completely reversed. Banks accounted for some 70 per cent of net capital flows, and today (June 1984) around three-quarters of Latin America's total outstanding external debt of some $350 billion is owed to private banks. Moreover, nearly all the newly acquired bank debt was in the form of 'syndicates' – pooled-risk loans shared among many banks, all at floating rates of interest. This was the seed of the debt crisis of the early 1980s.

The surge in bank lending to Latin America, and to LDCs in general, began in 1974–5 after the first oil shock. Higher oil prices and the ensuing world recession quadrupled the current-account deficit of non-oil LDCs, while the oil-exporting countries piled up huge financial surpluses. Banks were the natural vehicle for re-cycling these surpluses. They were the recipients of OPEC's new-found wealth and were able to establish mechanisms for quick disbursement of loans to the deficit countries. The new lending was encouraged by the governments of the industrial countries which

DEBT STATISTICS
Table 26. Total external debt, public and private (billion US dollars)

	1971	1976	1977	1978	1979	1980	1981	1982	1983*
Argentina	2.2	5.6	6.1	7.9	19.7	27.1	32.3	38.7	43.6
Brazil	4.4	26.0	32.3	44.4	51.5	64.6	74.1	83.2	91.6
Chile	2.2	3.7	3.8	5.1	8.5	11.1	15.5	17.1	17.7
Mexico	3.5	21.4	25.6	30.5	40.8	52.7	75.5	82.5	86.5
Peru	1.0	3.7	5.1	6.1	7.1	8.8	8.8	10.4	11.6
Venezuela	1.3	4.8	5.7	9.7	23.7	27.5	29.3	31.9	32.8

* Preliminary.
Source: OECD and Inter-American Development Bank.

were concerned that the OPEC surplus (up from $7 billion in 1973 to $68 billion in 1974) would continue at very high levels because of what they saw as OPEC's limited capacity to absorb imports.

The American commercial banks have been the biggest source of bank lending to Latin America, in part because of geographic proximity and familiarity with the area, and because of their high liquidity. But, in the late 1970s, European and Japanese banks also became lenders on a significant scale.

By 1978 the combination of rapid growth in OPEC imports and a 20 per cent fall in the real price of oil led to the elimination of the OPEC surplus. Part of the benefit accrued to non-oil developing countries, whose current-account deficits narrowed. The LDC borrowers were helped by world inflation which continued to ratchet upward, cutting the real value of their external debts. And the expansionary policy reactions in the industrial countries kept interest rates low – often negative in real terms.

This successful adjustment to the first oil shock and rarity of losses on sovereign loans encouraged international banks to over-estimate the ability of LDCs to continue servicing their debts. They went on lending despite the fact that in many countries economic policies were clearly going to result in serious disequilibria and unsustainable balance-of-payments positions. The widespread attitude that 'companies may fail but countries do not' overlooked two important distinctions. First, although domestic loans often incorporate provisions which restrict a firm's overall indebtedness, such provisions are seldom, if ever, included in sovereign loans because they are difficult to enforce. And, second, while it is true that countries do not go out of business, they are not always able to pay their debts on time.

An important feature of the crisis has been the build-up of short-term debt. By itself, short-term debt need not be a cause for concern, since it is an integral part of international trade. For example, the production and processing of a crop for export is often financed by external bank loans which are automatically repaid some months later as the product is exported and payment received. A significant amount of short-term debt (perhaps the equivalent of three to six months of imports) is, therefore, quite acceptable. However, by early 1982 a number of Latin American countries (Brazil being the major exception) had borrowed short-term far beyond this level.

As market terms became stiffer for Latin American borrowers from early 1980, the countries found they were able to obtain lower interest rates and a larger volume of borrowings from the banks by 'temporarily' borrowing for short-terms of one year or less. The banks themselves were not unhappy with this shift to short-term funding, since they saw it as a crude way of cutting their risk without actually reducing credit to the borrower. Mexico alone increased its short-term debt from $3.2 billion in 1979 to $11.8 billion in 1980

Table 27. Debt service (interest and principal payments) as percentage of total export revenues

	1971	1976	1977	1978	1979	1980	1981	1982†	1983†
Argentina	26	26	20	42	23	43	53	113	150
Brazil	51	45	49	59	66	64	63	78	82
Chile	20	42	47	49	45	44	67	73	63
Mexico	34	50	62	66	75	40	45	66	59
Peru	23	34	35	40	30	40	58	50	66
Venezuela	6	11	14	22	26	26	28	32	27

† Portions of these payments have been rescheduled or are outstanding.
Source: OECD and Inter-American Development Bank.

and $22.7 billion in 1981. By mid-1982 Mexico's short-term debt was equivalent to fifteen months' imports, Argentina's to sixteen months', Venezuela's to twelve months' and Ecuador's to eleven months'. By the end of 1982, short-term debt accounted for nearly $70 billion of Latin America's total outstanding external debt of $315 billion – perhaps twice what it should have been under normal conditions. By the middle of 1982, it became clear to the banks that even more short-term lending would be required, just to offset maturing loans and keep the total outstanding debt constant. As a result, a major retraction of lending was already under way when the South Atlantic War broke out in April 1982. At that point the banks held back lending to Latin America altogether.

By August 1982 Mexico, once regarded by the banks as a 'blue chip' borrower on account of its oil reserves, was forced to admit it could not continue to service its debts. Argentina had already been forced into a similar position by the virtual embargo on new loans during the war with Britain. These liquidity problems accelerated the cutback in bank lending to other borrowers. Bankers demonstrated a 'block mentality', classifying virtually all Latin American countries as equally risky. Their reluctance to go on lending, even at a reduced level, in many cases precipitated the very debt-servicing problems they were (collectively) so anxious to avoid.

By early 1983 every Latin American country – with the exception of Colombia and Paraguay – had run into debt-servicing problems. Most were still managing to pay interest – but little more.

The rescue strategy

The approach of the international financial community was essentially one of 'fire-fighting' – seeking individual *ad hoc* solutions rather than a global initiative. The established pattern has been that countries go first to the IMF, negotiate an economic stabilization programme, and then agree on a rescheduling of their debts with both bank creditors and governments. For bank debt, the approach has normally been to transform debts maturing during the current year into new seven- or eight-year loans with a grace period (to provide time for economic recovery) of around three years. The question now is whether such arrangements will suffice to set the countries back on their feet.

It must be remembered that the prime objective is not to pay off the whole of the outstanding debt – that would require Latin American countries to become consistent net exporters of capital, a virtual impossibility. Rather the aim must be to reduce the required capital inflows (and the growth of external debt) to a level which equates the long-term willingness of lenders to carry on lending to Latin America with Latin America's capacity to borrow. In other words, capital inflows must be reduced to a level which is financially sustainable over the medium and longer term.

Some observers, both inside and outside the region, doubt that the present rescue strategy is either politically or financially viable. Some argue that the banks are merely deluding themselves that their loans to Latin America are still good; instead they should recognize their past mistakes (these critics argue) and write off the loans, whatever the short-term consequences might be for individual banks. Other critics (usually from within the region) maintain that the outstanding debt is so large that the banks are effectively the prisoners of the borrowers, who should extort favourable rescheduling terms by threatening to repudiate their debts.

Neither position seems entirely credible. On the one hand, while some of the bank lending did go to finance inappropriate investments or simply into capital flight, the evidence is that much of the money was put to productive use. Rates of domestic fixed capital formation rose sharply in Latin America in the 1970s. And, although the prospects for future economic growth are not as rosy as banks and governments both believed in the 1970s, once the world has made the painful adjustment to lower inflation, some growth will be resumed. Taking a longer-term view of Latin America, therefore, it would be premature (to say the least) to classify bank loans to the area as worthless.

Furthermore, banks as a whole have little incentive to declare a country in default, when it has difficulty servicing its debts, since the country's overseas assets (which the banks might seize after a successful default suit) are likely to be minimal in relation to the debt. True, the attraction of being first in the queue for those assets is an incentive for an individual bank to move first. But the legal mechanics of default are costly and uncertain, and so far pressure from the big banks has largely succeeded in keeping everyone in line.

From the bankers' side, unilateral debt repudiation is likely to be against a debtor country's own self-interest. A formal default would cut off the country's access both to new credits and to the use of the international banking system, which is vital for international trade. Adjusting to such an abrupt withdrawal of credit would be infinitely more painful than any economic medicine the International Monet-

ary Fund is likely to serve up. Of course, this does not rule out a domestic political upheaval which results in a perverse decision to default. But if the record is any guide such a possibility is remote.

Just how strong a bargaining counter is the threat of default? The American banks would clearly be most vulnerable. Nearly half the $200 billion they have loaned to all LDCs and to Eastern Europe is loaned to Latin America. A total write-off of all Latin American debts would pose grave threats to the banking system. Even limited write-offs would be hard for banks to digest. Setting aside 10 per cent of their loans to Latin America as reserves each year would wipe out virtually all of the pre-tax profits of the ten biggest American banks. A more pertinent question is, perhaps, whether interest will be paid. If Argentina, Brazil and Mexico paid no interest on their debts for a year, gross earnings of the three biggest American banks would decline by about 80 per cent – although the net (after-tax) effect would be considerably less.

However, the interests of the different debtor countries are sufficiently diverse to make the formation of even a limited 'debtors' cartel unlikely. So, present *ad hoc* stabilization-cum-rescheduling packages could work, provided that they result in a judicious mixture of adjustment and financing against the background of a sustained economic recovery in the industrialized countries. International institutions, developing countries, commercial banks and industrial countries all have a crucial role to play. Too much reliance on one could jeopardize the operation. If, for instance, too much reliance is placed on austerity programmes in the borrowing countries, then internal political and social repercussions could undermine any progress achieved.

Perhaps the biggest imponderable, and certainly the *sine qua non* of recovery in Latin America, is just how fast the industrial countries will pull out of recession. Real growth in the OECD area recovered to 2.4 per cent in 1983 propelled by strong growth in the United States. It was essential that this momentum be maintained in 1984 and 1985, an outcome which will require concerted efforts in Europe to shift the emphasis of economic policy away from the simple focus on inflation-fighting towards promoting steady and non-inflationary growth. This will not be easy, but it could be done.

Even on the best possible outlook, however, the debt problem will not disappear overnight. The big Latin American borrowers will have substantial debt-servicing burdens for the remainder of the decade. Both they and the banks are only just beginning to grope towards a solution to the difficulties. Meanwhile, both parties have learned some valuable lessons about just what kind of development is appropriate, and how it should be financed in the future.

RC and JH

THE PEOPLES

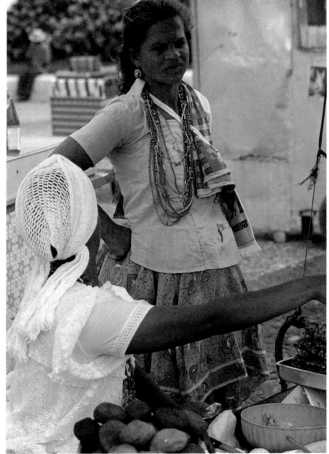

Top: A fiesta`crowd at Asunción, Paraguay.
Above: An Aymara Indian family from Bolivia.
Right: Mulatto women at market in Bahia, Brazil

Spanish Americans, like Spaniards, have *two* official surnames: their father's, which comes first, and then their mother's (maiden name), which comes second. For most everyday purposes (and on most occasions in this Encyclopedia) the first surname is used on its own, e.g. Fidel CASTRO, rather than Fidel CASTRO RUZ. When the first surname is very common, some people use both surnames all the time, e.g. the Chilean president (1956–52) Gabriel GONZALEZ VIDELA, who doubtless wanted to distinguish himself from all the other people in the world called González. In the old days, the conjunction 'y' ('and') was used to link the two surnames, e.g. José ORTEGA Y GASSET, but this has become less common in the Spanish-speaking world.

Marriage brings further complications. A Señor (Mr) Francisco AGUIRRE might marry a Señorita (Miss) María ROMERO. The bride will be known henceforth as Señora (Mrs) María ROMERO DE AGUIRRE. Their children, of course, will be called AGUIRRE ROMERO.

Brazilians who, of course, are Portuguese-speaking have a different system. The mother's maiden name comes first, the father's (or principal) surname second, e.g. the Brazilian statesman Getúlio DORNELLES VARGAS, nearly always referred to simply as Getúlio VARGAS. Senhor (Mr) VARGAS married a girl called Senhorita (Miss) Darcy SAMANHO. She became Senhora (Mrs) Darcy SAMANHO VARGAS. Their children (they had five) had the surnames SAMANHO VARGAS. (*Note:* the linking 'de' ('of') found in Spanish American married women's surnames – as in Romero *de* Aguirre, the example shown above – does not appear in Brazilian married women's surnames.)

It should not be forgotten that surnames in Latin America, as elsewhere, can sometimes be double-barrelled, e.g. Argentina's finance minister (1976–81) José Alfredo MARTINEZ DE HOZ (full name: MARTINEZ DE HOZ CARCANO), or Brazil's military president (1964–7) Humberto CASTELLO BRANCO (full name: DE ALENCAR CASTELLO BRANCO).

Don and *Doña* (or *Dom* and *Dona* in Brazil) are simply polite and nowadays slightly old-fashioned forms of address or reference, used (as with the title 'Sir' in Great Britain) before Christian names (never surnames), e.g. Don Francisco, Doña María, Dom Casmurro, etc. This use is still fairly common but is by no means universal any more, and conventions on this point differ from one Latin American country to the next.

Pre-Columbian settlement

Man entered America from Asia via the Bering Strait probably between 25,000 and 40,000 years ago, arriving in South America about 20,000 BC and reaching Tierra del Fuego by 9000 BC. The earliest areas of settlement were the uplands and upland slopes of the Mexican plateaus and the Andes, where man first hunted Pleistocene mammals, such as mammoths, mastodons, wild horses and ground sloths. As these mammals became extinct, as a result of climatic changes and over-exploitation, the Indians began to hunt deer and the wild ancestors of the llama and alpaca, and to collect wild berries, seeds and roots. From about 8000 BC they began to occupy the coasts and lowlands. On the coasts the Indians caught fish, shellfish and sea mammals and gathered wild plant products, but the lowland savanna and tropical rainforest areas offered little in the form of wild food resources so that their occupation occurred at a later date and was restricted to the river valleys and coasts, where a broad spectrum of wild plants and animals was to be found. Since these hunting and gathering bands were dependent on wild food resources they were forced to move in response to the seasonal availability of different sources of food; those bands which were more dependent on fishing, which generally provides more reliable sources of food, were less nomadic, often remaining in the same place for several months of the year. They lived in caves or erected temporary camps in the open. Because of the limited sources of food, the population was dispersed in small groups of under one hundred, but generally less than thirty people. When food resources were scarce the group would disperse and forage in smaller units composed of one or two families, whereas when resources were abundant they would come together in larger numbers and remain sedentary for longer periods. The population density that could be supported by hunting, gathering and fishing was probably only one person per 25 to 50 sq km. By the time of the Spanish conquest these bands were to be found mainly in areas which were either too cold, wet or arid for agriculture, for example, northern Mexico, southern Chile and Argentina, and eastern Brazil.

There is evidence of the beginnings of plant and animal domestication by about 7000 BC. At Tehuacán in south-central Mexico and at Tamaulipas in north-eastern Mexico there is evidence of seed-crop cultivation in semi-arid areas, whilst at Ayacucho in the central Peruvian Andes there is evidence of the cultivation of temperate seed crops and the domestication of the llama from about 5000 BC. By 4000 BC seed crops were being cultivated on the semi-arid coast of Peru and it has been suggested that the cultivation of root crops began in the Amazon basin about 5000 BC, although the first definite evidence of their cultivation comes from northern Venezuela and is dated at 2700 BC. Agriculture provided man with more productive and reliable sources of food; it enabled larger populations to be supported and thus laid the basis for the development of more complex societies and ultimately states. The growth in population associated with the development of agriculture was not only related directly to the increase in food supply, but also to the settled way of life which was made possible by more reliable sources of food. A sedentary mode of existence has the advantage of reducing both the dangers of miscarriages and the average number of years between child births; in a nomadic society children tend to be more widely spaced because of the difficulty of carrying more than one infant. Thus, the population did not expand dramatically with the beginnings of agriculture but with the establishment of permanent villages. This is demonstrated in the archaeological record of Tehuacán, where agriculture began about 5000 BC, but village life was not established until 3000 BC and the population did not increase dramatically until 500 BC.

Horticulture was probably the first type of agriculture practised, followed by a form of shifting cultivation of either seed or root crops. The latter form of cultivation requires that, after several years of cultivation, plots are abandoned to fallow in order that they may regain some of their lost fertility. This means that although

Agricultural terraces at Colca canyon in the western cordillera of the Andes

shifting cultivation supports larger populations than hunting, gathering and fishing, the density of the population is limited by the need for fallowing. Characteristically, populations associated with this type of cultivation formed permanent or semi-permanent hamlets and villages of several hundred, and occasionally up to 2000 people. Such communities were common in the Amazon and Orinoco basins at the time of the conquest; but in other areas, where agriculture was practised, more intensive forms of cultivation had been developed.

Amongst the techniques introduced to intensify and expand production were irrigation and the construction of *chinampas* (artificial islands constructed in shallow lakes), ridged fields and terraces. It has been estimated that whereas under shifting cultivation about 10 to 20 hectares of land are required to support a family, with irrigation and *chinampas* the amount is reduced to three-quarters and half a hectare respectively. Similarly, ridged fields, which were constructed to extend cultivation into seasonally flooded areas, could have supported about 1000 people per sq km, whilst terracing extended cultivation on steep slopes, particularly in the narrow valleys of the Andes. The increase in the size of the population that could be supported was accompanied by the beginnings of social stratification and political organization. Chiefdoms formed with populations of between 5000 and 20,000 people, or even more. For example, the five Chibcha chiefdoms (in what is now Colombia) each contained about 60,000 people. Minor ceremonial and civic centres emerged to serve outlying villages, thus indicating the beginnings of differentiation in the size, form and functions of

DISTRIBUTION OF CULTURAL TYPES

Bands

Tribes

Chiefdoms

States

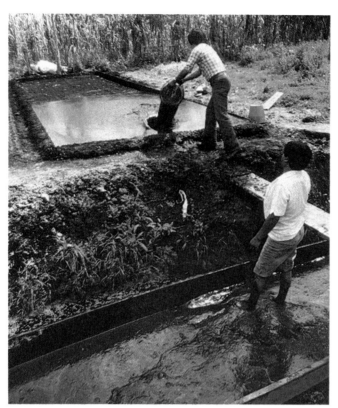

Chinampas in present-day Mexico

settlements. At the time of the Spanish conquest chiefdoms were to be found in Central America, Colombia, Ecuador, Bolivia and the Greater Antilles.

In Mesoamerica and the Andes chiefdoms were short-lived and were gradually transformed into states, which were characterized by the presence of a hierarchy of classes and a complex political organization, which wove populations of tens and even hundreds of thousands together into large social units. States were characterized by the presence of towns and cities. These may be distinguished from the earlier ceremonial centres by their larger size, the presence of a substantial residential population and the existence of distinct suburbs inhabited by different professions and social classes. These major towns and cities formed the apexes of extensive hierarchies of settlements ranging down to small villages and hamlets. The most notable of the early towns were Tiahuanaco in highland Bolivia, Tikal in the Guatemalan Petén and Teotihuacán in central Mexico, the latter with an estimated peak population of 50,000 to 100,000. At the time of the Spanish conquest the two major cities were Tenochtitlán, capital of the Aztec empire, and Cuzco, centre of the Inca empire, but they differed in size and form, as well as the functions they performed. Tenochtitlán had a highly concentrated

population of between 150,000 and 300,000, whereas Cuzco possessed about 100,000 to 200,000 people and consisted of a core area, where the nobles, bureaucrats and priests resided, with the rest of the inhabitants living in residential settlements around the city. Whilst both cities performed administrative and religious roles, Tenochtitlán was also a major manufacturing, trading and military centre, giving it a more metropolitan character than Cuzco.

From the entry of man into the New World the population increased, although there were short-term fluctuations caused by natural disasters, famines and warfare. Famines were not only caused by natural disasters but by population increase outstripping the ability of the land to support it given the available technology. Shortages of food were probably a contributory factor in the collapse of the Maya civilization after AD 900 whilst Sherburne F. Cook and Jeffrey R. Parsons have shown that in central Mexico there were fluctuations in the population in the immediate pre-conquest period. In the latter area evidence for soil erosion and famines at that time suggests that the population was reaching saturation point to the extent that even if the Spanish conquest had not occurred, there would probably have been a decline in the Indian population. Population pressure is seen by many as the cause of the incessant warfare and political instability that characterized Mesoamerica and the Andes for about five hundred years before the conquest. Similarly, the annual sacrifice of between 10,000 and 50,000 victims, mainly war captives, by the Aztecs, whilst ostensibly to honour the gods, also served to control population expansion. Disease, which became a major factor in the decline of the Indian population in the colonial period, does not appear to have caused major fluctuations in the population in pre-Columbian times. Although the Indians suffered from a number of gastro-intestinal and respiratory infections, as well as syphilis, they had built up a high resistance to them and they were relatively free from severe epidemics.

There is still considerable controversy over the size of the population of Latin America and the Caribbean on the eve of the Spanish conquest. Estimates vary from 7.5 million to between 80 and 100 million and the variations reflect not only the type of evidence used but also the methodology and basic philosophy of researchers. There is a wealth of documentary evidence available for making such estimates. It includes accounts of the early conquistadors, soldiers and explorers, later administrative reports, including counts made for the assessment of tribute and labour services, church and missionary records, as well as some native accounts and recorded traditions, the most notable of which are the Aztec codices. Despite the wealth of evidence there are considerable problems of interpretation which in part account for the divergence of estimates. For example, there are difficulties in estimating the total population from the numbers baptized or fighting in battle, or paying tribute. Archaeological, ecological and cultural evidence has also been used to reconstruct the nature of the resources and technology, settlement pattern and social structure of Indian groups, which by comparison with similar present-day cultures may be used to give general indications of the size of native populations. Estimates of the native population for small areas may be calculated using a wide variety of source materials, but such a task would be extremely time-consuming for the whole subcontinent and therefore a number of projection methods have been used. These generally involve the detailed examination of the demographic history of a small area, which is then taken to have been similar in areas with comparable cultures and environments. Often the rate of decline established is projected backwards from dates for which the demographic evidence is more reliable. The estimates of researchers have also been influenced by their interpretations of the nature of New World cultures and of history. Those who believe that the present is superior to the past and would emphasize the European contribution to Latin American culture are likely to underestimate the size of the native population and its decline as a result of European activities in the early colonial period, whilst those wishing

The Royal Valley of the Incas

to emphasize the native contribution and criticize the destruction brought about as the result of European domination are likely to exalt the native cultures and to come up with high population estimates. These views may strongly influence the interpretation of the evidence, for example, in judging whether the accounts of the early observers were exaggerated and in assessing the impact of disease.

Alfred L. Kroeber estimated that the aboriginal population of Latin America was a conservative 7.5 million, in the belief that the Indian population had grown at a regular rate since the time of the conquest and that the accounts of the early observers were exaggerated. Julian H. Steward accepted Kroeber's latter conclusion and, on the basis of evidence provided by the contributors to the *Handbook of South American Indians*, concluded that the aboriginal population of Latin America was 14.4 million. His estimate is not dissimilar to that of the Argentine scholar Angel Rosenblat, who on the basis of documentary evidence, has estimated that the population was 12.3 million. These three authors have provided the three lowest estimates of the native population which alternative approaches have suggested are too low. Karl Sapper, on the basis of the resources and available technology of the Indians, suggested that the population was between 35 and 45 million, whilst Henry F. Dobyns, reviewing the demographic history of the hemisphere concluded that insufficient account had been taken of the devastating impact of disease and suggested that the Indian population had been twenty to twenty-five times greater at the time of the conquest than at its nadir, which occurred at different times in different parts of Latin America. His estimate for Latin America was between 80 and 100 million and this high estimate is generally supported by Woodrow Borah, who has worked extensively on the demographic history of Mexico and the Caribbean.

Turning to estimates of the Indian population of specific areas there has been an equal diversity of opinion. For Mexico estimates range from Kroeber's 3.2 million to Dobyns's 30 to 37.5 million, whilst the most detailed study has been undertaken by Sherburne F. Cook and Woodrow Borah of central Mexico, which they estimate had a population of 25.2 million. This figure has been challenged on methodological grounds by William T. Sanders, who on the basis of archaeological, ecological and documentary evidence has estimated that the Aztec empire had between 5 and 6 million, and the whole of Mesoamerica only 12 to 15 million. Similar variations are to be found amongst estimates for the central Andes. They range from Kroeber's 3 million to Dobyns's 30 million, although the most frequently cited estimate is John H. Rowe's of 6 million. A recent review of the documentary evidence by Cook has led him to estimate 6 million for Peru alone, whilst a reworking of much of the evidence used by John H. Rowe has led C. T. Smith to suggest that the population of the central Andes was 12.1 million. Daniel E. Shea,

Pre-Columbian settlement

Table 28. Estimates of population in pre-Columbian America on the eve of the Spanish conquest

	Kroeber 1939	Rosenblat 1954	Steward 1949
Mexico	3 200 000[a]	4 500 000	4 500 000
Central America	100 000[b]	800 000	736 000
Caribbean	200 000	300 000	225 000
Andes	3 000 000	4 750 000	6 131 000
Lowland South America	1 000 000[c]	2 035 000	2 898 000
Total	7 500 000	12 385 000	14 490 000

	Sapper 1924	Denevan 1976	Dobyns 1966
Mexico	12–15 000 000	21 400 000	30 000 000– 37 500 000
Central America	5– 6 000 000	5 650 000	10 800 000– 13 500 000
Caribbean	3– 4 000 000	5 850 000	443 000– 553 750
Andes	12–15 000 000	11 500 000	30 000 000– 37 500 000
Lowland South America	3– 5 000 000	8 500 000	9 000 000– 11 250 000
Total	35–45 000 000	52 900 000	80 243 000–100 303 750

[a] Includes Guatemala and El Salvador.
[b] Honduras and Nicaragua only.
[c] Includes Costa Rica and Panama.
[d] Colombia, Ecuador, Peru, Bolivia, Chile.

on the other hand, believes that the decline in the population in the central Andes was less than in Mexico, partly due to the lesser impact of disease, and he has constructed a mathematical model to describe the demographic changes in the sixteenth century, coming up with a conservative estimate of 2.0 to 2.9 million. A number of other regional estimates have been made of parts of Central America, Colombia, Argentina, Brazil and Amazonia. Reviewing the conclusions reached in all these regional studies, William M. Denevan has estimated that the aboriginal population of Latin America was 52.9 million, which falls mid-way between the range of estimates.

Whilst Dobyns has suggested that the Indian population declined by a ratio of 20:1 to 25:1, that is by 95 to 96 per cent, between the time of contact and the population nadir, it is clear that there were regional and temporal variations in the rate of decline. Cook and Borah have calculated that in central Mexico between 1532 and 1608 the Indian population declined more rapidly on the coast, where the depopulation ratio was 26:1, than in the plateau area, where it was only 13:1. A similar difference in the decline of the Indian population on the coast and in the highlands has been identified by Smith in the central Andes, where the depopulation ratios between 1520–5 and 1570 were 58:1 and 3.4:1 respectively. Denevan also regards Dobyns's depopulation ratios for the highlands as too high, but maintains that they are not high enough for the tropical lowlands, which he suggests declined at a rate of 35:1. It is also clear that they are not high enough for the islands and fringing mainland of the Caribbean, where the Indian population became extinct within a

generation. Clearly the timing of the decline varied with the date of contact, although it is possible that diseases reached areas ahead of the Spaniards. Thus many Indian groups living in the remote tropical lowlands did not come into contact with Europeans until the seventeenth and eighteenth centuries, by which time the Indian population in other parts of Latin America had begun to recover. Unfortunately less research has been done on this aspect of Indian demographic history, but it would appear that the recovery began first in Mexico in the middle of the seventeenth century, while increases began to be registered in Central America in the last decades of the seventeenth century, but they did not occur in Peru until the second half of the eighteenth century.

Causes of the decline in the Indian population were manifold, complex and interwoven. Two major causes were identified by contemporary observers: disease and the systematic killing, over-work and ill treatment of the Indians, an interpretation often described as the 'Black Legend'. Epidemic diseases introduced from the Old World were undoubtedly a major factor in the decline of the Indian population, which had no immunity to them. The most notable killers were smallpox, measles, typhus, plague, yellow fever and malaria. There are numerous accounts of the populations of villages and whole areas being reduced by one-third or a half as a result of epidemics, including the Aztec capital of Tenochtitlán whose population was halved as a result of a smallpox epidemic in 1520. Many Indians were killed in military encounters with the Spanish, whilst under slavery, the *encomienda* and later the *repartimiento* Indians were forced to work in poor conditions for long hours, with little or no pay and under threat of punishment for shortcomings. Bartolomé de las Casas, one of the most outspoken critics of Spanish activities in the New World, estimated that by 1560 40 million had died from such causes. Although few contemporary observers attributed the decline in the Indian population to the cultural changes that occurred as a result of the Spanish conquest and colonization it is clear that they were considerable. Spanish demands on Indian lands, labour and production led to food shortages and famines, whilst the breakdown in social organization of Indian communities and the psychological impact of the conquest led to a decrease in the fertility rate, contributed to by an increase in birth control, abortion and infanticide. As the Indians became integrated into the socio-economic life of the empire, *mestizaje* or racial mixing became a more significant factor in the decline of the Indian population, particularly in the towns, haciendas and mining centres. The recovery of the Indian population in many parts of Latin America may be accounted for by the abolition of the worst excesses of exploitation in the early sixteenth century by the introduction of the New Laws in 1542; by the increased immunity of the Indian population to the newly introduced diseases; by improvements in the Indian diet brought about by the introduction of livestock, although they were by no means uniform; and by the Indians generally reaching a new cultural equilibrium by adapting to the realities of Spanish conquest and colonization.

LN

Further reading

S. F. Cook and W. Borah, *Essays in Population History*, 3 vols. (Berkeley and Los Angeles, 1971–4)

A. W. Crosby, *The Columbian Exchange: Biological and Cultural Consequences of 1492* (Westport, Conn., 1972)

W. M. Denevan, ed., *The Native Population of the Americas in 1492* (Madison, 1976)

N. Sánchez-Albornoz, *The Population of Latin America: A History* (Berkeley and Los Angeles, 1974)

Iberian colonial settlement

The study of Iberian migration to Latin America in the colonial period is for a variety of reasons of great importance to historians. First and foremost it is impossible to understand the origins and the nature of the societies which emerged in Spanish America and Brazil between the sixteenth and the early nineteenth centuries without detailed information on the motives, attitudes, and culture of the continual waves of Spaniards and Portuguese who crossed the Atlantic to the New World to form the apex of the sociopolitical pyramid created there in the colonial period. The investigation of the patterns of migration, the numbers of migrants, and their regional and class origins in the Old World is an essential part of the process of evaluating their behaviour in America. Consideration of these latter questions is also of significance for historians of peninsular Spain and Portugal, who desire to quantify and assess the impact on the mother countries of the drain of people to Latin America. The more that is known about the age, sex, occupational and regional distribution of emigrants, the easier it is, for example, to correlate emigration with other factors provoking economic decline in certain regions. This process, in its turn, throws light upon the more general question, relevant for all studies of migration, of whether the immigrant is pushed out by adverse conditions at home or pulled in by opportunities overseas. Finally a proper understanding of migration to Latin America in the colonial period provides a context and an antecedent within which historians of the nineteenth and twentieth centuries can study the massive trans-Atlantic migrations which occurred in the century before the Great Depression.

It is perhaps not surprising that more is known about the actual numbers involved in this latter period of migration than for the colonial period. Recent estimates suggest that some 11 million

Recruitment of Spaniards for the conquest of Peru (from Guamán Poma, *La nueva corónica*)

Europeans migrated to Latin America between 1824 and 1924 (compared with 48 million to North America), and that half of them went to Argentina, and one-third to Brazil. The majority – an estimated 38 per cent between 1854 and 1924 – came from Italy, although Spain and Portugal, which had enjoyed a virtual monopoly of colonial migration, remained in second and third places, with 28 per cent and 11 per cent respectively. An interesting feature, also present, as we shall see, in the colonial period, although to a lesser degree, was that 40–50 per cent of the immigrants to Latin America in the national period (the period since independence) eventually returned to their countries of origin. The data available on the numbers of migrants who left Spain and Portugal for Latin America in the colonial period is, by contrast, much less precise, particularly for the seventeenth and eighteenth centuries; for the sixteenth century, however, a reasonably clear picture has emerged, at least for Spanish migration, largely because of painstaking research into detailed passenger registers preserved in the Archive of the Indies in Seville.

As soon as the enormous economic and political potential of the discoveries made by Christopher Columbus and subsequent explorers impressed itself upon the Spanish crown it took steps to impose a rigid control upon migration to America, in the hopes of excluding heretics, Jews, foreigners, and other undesirables from contact with its new Indian subjects. The control was relaxed for a few years in the reign of Charles I, who experimented with the policy of admitting his non-Spanish subjects, but after 1538 non-Spaniards were strictly forbidden to settle in or even visit America. The policy could never be enforced with total rigidity, despite the fact that throughout the Habsburg period most shipping for the empire left from the single port of Seville: determined foreigners could bribe officials or obtain decrees of naturalization, while the very volume of trade which rapidly developed between Seville and America provided another loophole, for the ships engaged in it were often crewed by non-Spaniards – notably Portuguese and Italians – many of whom remained in the New World after voyaging there. But tens of thousands of *bona fide* Spanish emigrants faithfully went through the complex bureaucratic procedure required for obtaining licences of embarkation, and it is the surviving records of their applications, coupled with the lists of departing passengers prepared for the Council of the Indies by officials in Seville, which provide the best sources for researchers. The general consensus which has emerged from an examination of these records is that a maximum of 300,000 people migrated from Spain to America between 1492 and 1600; a similar result is obtained by the alternative method of multiplying the number of ships which sailed by the average number of passengers carried by a sample of them. From one standpoint the total may seem surprisingly small – by contrast up to 300,000 people were entering Argentina each year at the height of the migration boom of the national period. On the other hand it represents an average annual outflow from Spain of some 3000 people for over a century. Population in the mother country was probably rising in the sixteenth century, to reach about 8 million by 1600, but the majority of migrants were young, vigorous males, often with artisan skills, while an increasing percentage of those who populated the mother country were economically inactive. A detailed examination of no less than 55,000 individuals known to have sailed to America between 1492 and 1600 (undertaken by Peter Boyd-Bowman) also reveals that certain regions of Spain, notably Andalusia, Extremadura, and Castile, bore the brunt of the population outflow, whereas provinces in the north and the east were affected to a much smaller extent.

In the seventeenth century, as Spain itself declined and Spanish America grew richer, the pace of migration was accelerated, although not dramatically, and it also began to draw in an increasing number of northern Spaniards, traditionally thought of as more industrious and resourceful than their Andalusian counterparts. The estimate of 450,000 for the century as a whole, proposed by Antonio Domínguez Ortiz, is generally accepted, and is broadly confirmed by the ship-counting method, referred to above, which produces a figure of some 200,000 for the first half of the century. This relentless annual drain of 4000–5000 people was clearly a contributory factor of some significance in the economic and demographic recession which afflicted Spain in the seventeenth century, particularly as it removed men, and an increasing number of women, who were in the age group capable of producing children. But it has to be kept in perspective: great plagues in Castile in 1597–1602 and 1649–52 each cost half a million lives, the expulsion of the Moriscos from Valencia in 1609–14 accounted for the loss of at least 100,000 peasants, and between 1635 and 1659 the war in Flanders was costing an estimated 12,000 men a year. As the vicious cycle of depression was accelerated by these and other catastrophes the attractions of migration to America must have become increasingly evident to poor yet ambitious Spaniards who saw little prospect of bettering themselves in the mother country.

In attempting to assess the volume of migration in the eighteenth century from Spain to America, we have to rely upon fleeting glimpses and unsubstantiated suggestions, for virtually no primary research has been undertaken into the subject. It is recorded, for example, that in 1742 the viceroyalty of New Spain (modern Mexico and Central America) contained some 450,000 whites, of whom 29,000 were Europeans. Over 80 per cent of this immigrant group were male Spaniards, many of whom would marry into local families, thereby creating space for further waves of male migrants from the mother country. There is a substantial amount of literary evidence to suggest that the traditional influx of Basques and other northern Spaniards into the commercial sector accelerated in the last third of the eighteenth century: the number of peninsular Spaniards resident in Mexico City, 1182 in 1689, had doubled by 1792. In this period travellers in various parts of Spanish America commented upon the deep-seated hostility between creoles (whites born in America) and *peninsulares* or *gachupines*, as European Spaniards were described, caused primarily by the belief of the former that their native lands were being invaded by shiploads of parsimonious northern Spaniards, anxious to exploit the economic and commercial boom which characterized Spanish America as a whole in the second half of the eighteenth century. By the turn of the century the European-born constituted only 2 per cent of the population of Mexico City (2500 out of 137,000), according to the German traveller Alexander von Humboldt, whereas creoles accounted for 48 per cent (65,000); but the newcomers comprised the dominant entrepreneurial class, active in commerce and mining, whereas the creoles were represented primarily in landholding and

Spanish missionaries attempting to introduce Catholicism in Venezuela (from Theodore de Bry, *America*)

in the bureaucracy. The most senior positions in government, the army, and the Church were reserved for Europeans, however, particularly in this late colonial period, when the Bourbon kings of Spain made a determined effort to increase the actual authority of the crown in its far-flung American possessions. Spanish writers of the period confirm the impressions of visitors to America: the influential José del Campillo suggested in a work of 1742, for example, that some 14,000 people a year were emigrating, and that over the centuries about a million Spaniards must have gone to America, and Gerónimo de Uztáriz commented that most emigrants to America in his time were from Cantabria, Navarre, Asturias, Galicia, and Burgos. Andalusians continued to go in significant

numbers to certain parts of South America, and we also know of colonization schemes which took some 5000 Canary Islanders to Santo Domingo, Texas, and Florida between 1700 and 1764. No historian has yet hazarded a guess at total emigration to America in the eighteenth century, but it must have been at least as large as that of the seventeenth century, and was probably larger, particularly in the relatively peaceful and prosperous years between 1763 and 1796. The final great influx occurred, ironically, in the aftermath of the Napoleonic Wars, as Ferdinand VII despatched large contingents of European troops to America in an ultimately vain attempt to defeat the revolutions for independence which had begun in 1810: General Pablo Morillo, for example, took an expedition of 10,500 men to Venezuela in 1815, thereby almost doubling an immigrant population estimated to have numbered 12,000 in 1800.

The exact number of Europeans resident in Spanish America by the early nineteenth century is difficult to ascertain, partly because most population counts indiscriminately lumped creoles and *peninsulares* together as 'Spaniards' (*españoles*). Humboldt suggested 200,000–300,000, although this was probably an overestimate: his separate figure of up to 80,000 in New Spain compares with a modern estimate of a mere 15,000, which, in its turn, is perhaps too small. A figure of 150,000 for Spanish America as a whole is probably about right; in 1570, by contrast, there had been a mere 60,000. But at this earlier date the European Spaniards had outnumbered, albeit slightly, the creole element in a total white population of some 115,000, whereas by the end of the colonial period the 150,000 Europeans were swamped by a creole population of more than 3 million. By 1800 the creoles themselves formed a distinct minority of the total Spanish American population of 16.9 million, in which the largest racial groups were 7.5 million Indians and 5.3 million of mixed descent (mestizos). Many of them, moreover, were somewhat less white than the upstart immigrants whose social superiority they resented. But the creoles insisted on their 'Spanish' identity – in speech, dress, manners, and so on – in order to preserve their own supremacy over the Indian, mestizo, and black masses. When in 1810 there began the revolutions which brought independence to all the mainland of Spanish America by 1825, many creoles initially fought against the rebels, such was the strength of creole conservatism and allegiance to the crown; most (though not quite all) *peninsulares*, on the other hand, championed the cause of the mother country. The consequence was that the attainment of independence in most of the new states was swiftly followed by the forced expulsion of those European Spaniards who had not already left voluntarily: many went, with their capital and expertise, to the surviving Spanish colonies of Cuba and Puerto Rico, which were to enjoy unprecedented prosperity as sugar producers in the nineteenth century, whereas those who had been in government service, whether civilian or military, tended to return to the peninsula to join the scramble for office there.

If firm data on Spanish colonial migration to America is patchy, that relating to Portuguese migration to Brazil is almost non-existent, although general patterns can be identified. Systematic attempts to send settlers to Brazil did not begin until 1534 when, in an attempt to counteract a growing French presence there, John III established a dozen hereditary captaincies, and entrusted the *donatários*, or lord proprietors, to whom they were granted, with the responsibility for settling them and defending them against both Indians and European interlopers. At this time the population of peninsular Portugal was at most 1.4 million. Emigration was already a well-established feature, particularly from the northern provinces of Minho and Douro – one convincing estimate suggests that on average in the sixteenth century some 2400 people a year, mostly young, unmarried males, left for overseas. But the majority of them headed for the proven riches of the East, despite the high risk of shipwreck or disease during the eight-month voyage to India, rather than to dangerous Brazil where, in these early decades of colonization, the dangers of ending up in a Tupinambá cooking pot loomed large, at least in popular imagination. One consequence was that the Portuguese crown adopted a more liberal policy than its Spanish counterpart in relation to the admission of foreigners to America, allowing in all who professed to be Christian (i.e. Catholic) rather than attempting to restrict permission to Portuguese nationals. The latter predominated – although, paradoxically, many were Jews – but considerable numbers of Dutchmen and other non-Iberians were also to be found in Brazil in this early period. The union with Spain (1580–1640) ushered in the more restrictive policy already in force for Spanish America, but, by way of compensation, substantial numbers of Spaniards began to go to southern Brazil, particularly to the area around São Paulo. The old policy was reintroduced after 1640, with Dutch and English traders and adventurers being the principal beneficiaries, but major gold strikes in the 1690s ushered in a more mercantilist policy, which was to persist for the remainder of the colonial period, of restricting migration from Europe to Portuguese. The forced migration of black slaves from Africa to Brazil, which far exceeded white migration, was, of course, a separate issue, although one which was to have a profound effect on the nature and composition of colonial society in Brazil.

The introduction of both whites and blacks to Brazil is known to have increased substantially in the last quarter of the sixteenth century, primarily as a response to the boom in sugar cultivation in the area around Bahia. By 1600, it is usually suggested, there were about 100,000 non-Indians in Brazil, of whom 30,000 were whites and 70,000 blacks or of mixed descent. Migration continued at a moderate pace in the first half of the seventeenth century, when significant numbers of newcomers were deportees, but began to accelerate in the second half, when contraction in the East, caused by Dutch rivalry, coupled with recession in the metropolis, made Brazil a more attractive prospect. By 1700 the non-Indian population of Brazil had grown threefold to 300,000, of whom roughly 100,000 were nominally of Portuguese, and 200,000 of African origin. How many of these 100,000 were born in Portugal it is impossible even to guess, although it has been estimated that an average input of 500 immigrants a year from the mother country over the previous two centuries would have been sufficient to produce a white population of this size. Throughout this period the population of Portugal itself seems to have remained remarkably stable, despite the toll of migration, famine, epidemics and other disasters, at about 1.5 million. Migration to Brazil undoubtedly multiplied in the first two decades of the eighteenth century, reaching a peak of 5000–6000 a year, in response to rich gold strikes

THE PEOPLES

Iberian colonial settlement

in Minas Gerais. It remained substantial in the second half of the eighteenth century, too, as the mineral boom was followed by the revival of the sugar industry and rapid development of cotton and tobacco cultivation. The increasing attention which the mother country paid to Brazil saw the influx of substantial numbers of administrators and soldiers, particularly after 1750, and there was also a marked increase in the number of private emigrants anxious, as in Spanish America, to establish themselves in the commercial sector. The attitude of the crown fluctuated from an attempt in 1720 to limit the outflow by requiring all migrants to obtain government passports to ambitious schemes in the mid-century to send 4000 peasant families from the overpopulated Azores to the provinces of Santa Catarina and Rio Grande do Sul, in southern Brazil. Demographic growth in Portugal itself, where the population numbered 3 million by the end of the eighteenth century, more than compensated for the loss to Brazil. But by this period the population of the colony was also growing dramatically, reaching 3 million by 1798, of whom 1 million were of white descent (a tenfold increase since 1700), 1.5 million slaves, and the remainder Indians and free coloureds. By 1818, on the eve of the attainment of independence, total population had increased to almost 4 million, primarily because of a substantial increase in the black population.

The final decade or so of colonial rule in Brazil was a period of unprecedented prosperity, primarily because of the forced migration there in 1807–8 of the Portuguese royal family and thousands of its followers anxious to escape the Napoleonic invasion of Portugal. With the final defeat of Napoleon in 1815 the majority of these newcomers realized, as had generations of earlier immigrants, that they preferred to remain in Brazil rather than return to the mother country, thereby setting in train a complex series of political events which was to lead the heir to the Portuguese throne to declare Brazilian independence in 1822, with himself as the country's first emperor, Pedro I. The transition was much more peaceful than in Spanish America, primarily because most Portuguese residents in Brazil, like Brazilian whites generally, were willing to support a movement which preserved monarchical legitimacy and social stability. A small number of Portuguese returned to the peninsula immediately after 1822, and rather more in 1831, when Pedro was overthrown (to be replaced as emperor in due course by his son, Pedro II), but the majority recognized that slave-holding, patristic Brazil offered the safer haven for the relatively easy life to which they had grown accustomed.

The general phenomenon of re-emigration was one which certainly existed throughout the period of Iberian colonialism in America, although it is absolutely impossible to measure it. A detailed study of the 168 conquerors of Peru who were with Francisco Pizarro in 1532 shows that no less than 74 of them (44 per cent) eventually returned to Spain, and it may also be assumed that

some of the 36 (21 per cent) whose destiny cannot be ascertained also did so. A substantial proportion, probably a majority, of the senior administrators, soldiers, and churchmen sent out to the Americas over the next three centuries would have remained there for fixed terms rather than in perpetuity, while many merchants almost commuted across the Atlantic, particularly in the eighteenth century. On the other hand, the attitude of many ordinary migrants who financed their own journeys was probably similar to that of a tailor, Alonso Morales, who wrote in 1576 from Puebla (Mexico) to his cousin in Extremadura:

Your brother and I keep shop here and are doing well . . . So you would give me great pleasure in leaving that misery there and coming here, because it would be greatly to your advantage . . . Get my brother Pedro to come with you, and leave that wretched country, because it is only for people who have a lot of money, and here, no matter how poor a man may be, he never lacks a horse to ride and food to eat.

Men such as this, who probably constituted the vast majority of Iberian colonial migrants to Latin America, were never likely to return to Europe. Wealthy merchants, landowners, miners, and administrators frequently did return to Spain and Portugal to

Spanish lady in late colonial Peru (from Joseph Skinner, *The Present State of Peru*)

137

display their American-acquired wealth in somewhat vulgar ostentation until the very end of the eighteenth century. When they began to cease to do so in the first decade of the nineteenth century, because retirement to Rio de Janeiro or Mexico offered greater security and comfort than return to Lisbon or Madrid, the shift was symbolic of the fact that the American empires of Spain and Portugal had outgrown the mother countries. Independence was the inevitable outcome.

JRF

Further reading

P. Boyd-Bowman, *Patterns of Spanish Emigration to the New World (1493–1580)* (Buffalo, NY., 1973)

J. Lockhart, *The Men of Cajamarca* (Austin, 1972)

J. Lockhart and E. Otte, eds., *Letters and People of the Spanish Indies: the Sixteenth Century* (Cambridge, 1976)

M. Mörner, 'Spanish Migration to the New World Prior to 1810: a Report on the State of Research,' F. Chiapalli, ed., *First Images of America* (2 vols., Berkeley, 1976), vol. II, pp. 737–82

African slave migration

From small beginnings in the 1440s until its demise in the second half of the nineteenth century, the Atlantic slave trade carried one of the greatest forced migrations of history: that of African peoples taken into slavery in the Americas. Estimates of the volume of the slave trade vary widely, but there is no doubt that it uprooted millions of people and involved a significant depopulation of the African continent. Of the slaves taken in Africa, an unknown number perished before embarkation for the Americas and many more died in the harsh conditions of the trans-Atlantic crossing. Probably about 9.5 to 10 million survived to become slaves who, with their descendants, came to constitute an important, sometimes preponderant element of the American regions in which they were settled.

The Atlantic slave trade was first developed by Portuguese traders during the second half of the fifteenth century, taking black captives from sub-Saharan Africa as part of a trade in several commodities. Until the mid-sixteenth century the traffic in slaves – which soon came to dominate commerce with Africa – was primarily geared to meeting demands for unfree labour in the Old World. Between 1441 and 1550, more than half of the slaves extracted from the coasts of West Africa were destined for the labour market in Europe, particularly in the Iberian peninsula, or for use in the emergent plantation economies of the Atlantic islands. However, in

Table 29. Slave imports into the Americas, 1451–1870

Importing region	1451–1600	1601–1700	1701–1810	1811–70	Total per region
Old World (Europe, Atlantic Islands, São Tomé)	149 900	25 100	—	—	175 000
Spanish America	75 000	292 000	578 600	606 000	1 552 100
Brazil	50 000	560 000	1 891 400	1 145 400	3 646 800
British North America	—	—	348 000	51 000	399 000
British Caribbean	—	263 700	1 401 300	—	1 665 000
French Caribbean	—	155 800	1 348 400	96 000	1 600 200
Dutch Caribbean	—	40 000	460 000	—	500 000
Danish Caribbean	—	4 000	24 000	—	28 000
Total	274 900	1 341 100	6 051 700	1 898 400	9 566 100

Source: Philip D. Curtin, *The Atlantic Slave Trade: a Census*, p. 268.

quantitative terms, the slave trade to the Old World was to pale into insignificance compared to the formidable flows of human cargoes which swept across the Atlantic to the Americas after about 1550. Henceforth, the Atlantic slave trade assumed patterns of growth and distribution over time and space which responded to the rhythms of economic development in the areas of European settlement and dominion in the Americas. The principal patterns of temporal and spatial expansion in the African migrations generated by the slave trade may be traced in table 29.

In terms of distribution over time, the estimates given above suggest that slave immigration into the Americas passed through several distinct phases, in which changes in the scale of the slave trade were associated with variations in the distribution of slave imports between regions. The first broad phase of growth took place during the second half of the sixteenth century, when the number of slaves arriving in the Americas surpassed those who went to Old World destinations. At this stage, most of them went to the Spanish colonies which, between 1451 and 1600, took some 60 per cent of slaves landed in the Americas. Towards the end of the sixteenth century, the Portuguese settlements in Brazil gave a new impetus to African immigration and, by the early seventeenth century, Brazil emerged as the major market for black slaves. Over the century as a whole, Brazil absorbed about 42 per cent of all slaves brought to the Americas. In the latter half of the seventeenth century, the slave trade spread away from the Iberian powers' colonies into the possessions of North European nations in the Caribbean. The English West Indies, in particular, offered a new and important market in the latter half of the century when, in a burst of growth, they absorbed almost as many slaves as were taken into the Spanish colonies over the century as a whole. The emergence of new slave markets in the Caribbean presaged the great era of growth in the

SOURCES AND DESTINATIONS OF THE AFRICAN SLAVE TRADE TO THE AMERICAS

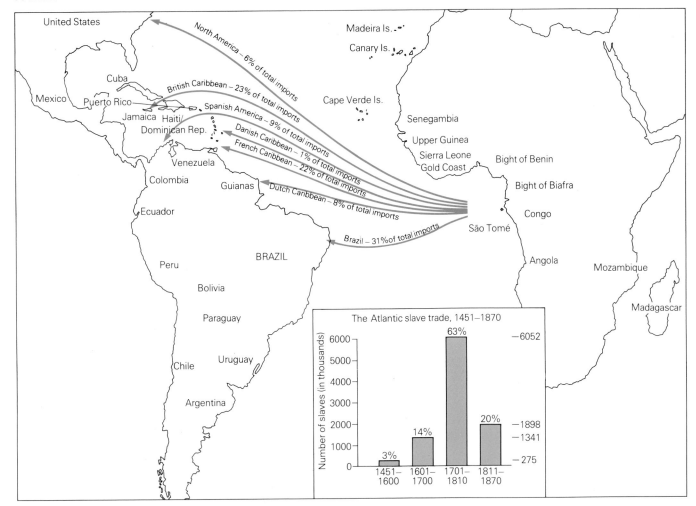

eighteenth century. Not only did Brazil continue to take in growing numbers of Africans, but demand in the Caribbean islands pushed the trade to unprecedented levels. The French and British islands alone accounted for about 45 per cent of total American slave imports during this period, while the additional demand of the Spanish, Dutch and Danish islands ensured that the Caribbean region received more than half of the six million slaves landed in the Americas during the period 1701–1810. Thus, the major phase of African slave migration (in which about 60 per cent of all slaves carried to the western hemisphere were landed) was closely bound up with developments in the Caribbean and in Brazil. Not surprisingly, these were the areas in which African immigration had greatest impact on social and economic development, for between them they had absorbed about 80 per cent of all African migrants to

the New World. Even when the trade entered into its final, declining phase in the nineteenth century, Brazil and the Spanish Caribbean islands continued to exert their baneful influence by keeping the institution of slavery and the currents of the slave trade alive long after they had been suppressed elsewhere.

These developments in the scale and spatial spread of African slave immigrants corresponded with changing requirements for manpower in the Americas. Already familiar with the use of African slaves, Spaniards took them as personal servants on their early expeditions of conquest and later extended the employment of slaves to meet a variety of special needs. By the end of the sixteenth century, African slaves and their half-caste offspring had become an important element in both Spanish and Portuguese colonial societies, and were almost as numerous as the white settlers themselves. The settlement and occupational patterns of nascent Afro-American society varied from region to region. African slaves were mainly located in areas where Amerindian labour was inadequate for the needs of white colonists. In the highlands of Mesoamerica and South America, where the Spaniards encountered dense Amerindian peasant populations whose labour could be used in agriculture and silver mining, black slaves were used chiefly as skilled artisans and domestic servants, and formed a relatively small part of the population. The main areas of African resettlement were in the tropical lowland regions of the Caribbean islands and the mainland coastal zones, where indigenous peoples were far fewer in number and where Africans provided a substitute labour force in both rural and urban areas. Here African slaves were used in a variety of occupations, including gold mining, but the main source of demand arose from the development of plantation agriculture, producing tropical crops for overseas markets.

The pre-eminent export crop was sugar, and the primary centre of its production was Brazil. By the late sixteenth century Brazil had become Europe's principal source of sugar, and the establishment of plantations on the rich alluvial soils of its north-eastern coastal centres greatly accelerated the transmission of African slaves to the Americas. Moreover, where Brazil had shown a way, others followed. When the Dutch were expelled from Brazil in the mid-seventeenth century, they transplanted the techniques of sugar cultivation on slave-based plantations to the Caribbean islands, where their rapid dissemination among the colonies of the new imperial powers soon undermined Brazil's lead in world sugar production. By the early eighteenth century, Jamaica had become the world's single largest sugar producer, foreshadowing the emergence of the English and French West Indies as the core of a transoceanic commercial system founded on sugar and slaves, a system which extended to include the Spanish islands, especially Cuba, in the latter half of the century. Thus most of the Africans who were forcibly resettled in the Americas were destined to work on the land, as labourers in plantations producing sugar and, on a lesser scale, tobacco, cacao, indigo, cotton and coffee.

As the slave trade expanded in response to these growing demands, so its organizers sought out new sources of supply on the African continent. When Portuguese traders initiated the trade in the later fifteenth century, slaves were mostly taken from the region of Senegambia on the West African coast immediately south of the Sahara. Gradually slaving expeditions extended the catchment area for slaves as the Portuguese established new bases farther south in the regions of modern Guinea and Sierra Leone. During the sixteenth century, this area – known as the 'Guinea of Cape Verde' – was to become one of two major zones for slaving; the other was much farther south, on the Central African coast, just beyond the mouth of the Congo River.

During the seventeenth century, Central African sources grew in importance, and Spanish America took an increasingly large proportion of its slave migrants from Angola. After the 1640s, Iberian control of the trade faced rising competition from Dutch, English, French and other northern European slavers and the pattern of African supply became more complex as the slavers of different nations concentrated on different regions in Africa. The vagaries of contemporary statistics preclude accurate identification of the ethnic origins of African slaves but, as the slave trade entered its phase of greatest expansion in the eighteenth century, a rough pattern of development may be discerned. The West African coastal regions from Senegambia to the Bight of Biafra continued to be exploited, but with greater intensity, mainly by English and French traders seeking slaves for their Caribbean colonies. However, while West Africa still supplied about 59 per cent of the eighteenth-century Atlantic slave trade, Central and East Africa opened new frontiers for growth. Over the century as a whole, the trade in these areas was dominated by the Portuguese and the majority of slaves entering Brazil came from the region of Angola. Slave migration from this region was further expanded in the 1780s, when British and French slavers stepped up their purchases of human cargoes drawn from among the Bantu-speaking peoples of the Central African hinterlands. In the late eighteenth century, growing numbers of slaves were also taken from East Africa, in a trade organized by the Portuguese from stations established in Mozambique, and were sent mainly to Brazil and southern South America. This shift towards

The living quarters of a slave ship (Rugendas, 1853)

Central and East African sources became more pronounced during the decline of the slave trade in the nineteenth century, when the great bulk of slave exports derived from the region just north of the Congo River, from Angola and, to a lesser extent, from southeastern Africa through Mozambique.

Drawn from such diverse regions, Africans sent to the Americas came from a wide range of economic and cultural backgrounds, including peoples from forests and savannas, from matrilineal and patrilineal societies, from simple tribal organizations and from stratified kingdoms, with many forms of religious life. Uprooted from their native habitats and thrust together in an alien environment dominated by whites, Africans were not able simply to reproduce their societies in the New World. Although imported slaves tended to be young, their introduction into new disease environments led to high rates of morbidity and mortality, while the generally high ratio of males to females discouraged a high rate of natural increase among African migrants. These factors, together with the breakup of African families and communities during and after shipment to slave markets, inhibited the physical and cultural reproduction of African social traditions. Instead, Africans were forced to submit to a system of social and economic stratification in which they, as slaves, were relegated to the lowest position, and excluded from full participation in the societies in which they were made to live.

As slaves, Africans were universally regarded as units of private property, disposable chattels who were subject to the ownership rights of their masters and deprived of the civil rights which the law bestowed on free persons. Although the laws of slave societies expressed the interests of slaveowners, slaves could not logically be regarded merely as inanimate objects devoid of recognized human needs for physical and spiritual sustenance. Consequently, the absolute power of slaveholders could be restrained, either by special legal codes laid down by governments, or by customs and conventions which emerged from local practices governing master–slave relations. In the Catholic cultures of Latin America, slaves were theoretically afforded rights to marriage, to protection from cruelty, and, under special circumstances, to manumission by self-purchase. In contrast, in the Protestant cultures of the West Indies and British North America slaves were supposedly denied such opportunities and treated with greater severity in more rigidly segregated societies. However, the recognition of the slave as a moral personality did not release him from a servile status, nor did it necessarily influence the treatment that he received. In practice, such differences in legal and cultural norms were less important in influencing the status and treatment of slaves than were more specific conditions, such as the type of economic activity in which the slave was engaged, the size of the productive unit in which he lived, and market conditions for the commodity which he pro-

duced. Thus, although slavery was not a homogeneous institution, differences in the character of slave regimes cannot be attributed solely to broad cultural differences between the host societies; strong regional and temporal variations were of equal, if not greater significance.

The importance of African slave migrants for the development of major regions in the Americas was not merely economic; Africans and their descendants also contributed to the formation of distinctively American cultures. Despite the deep trauma of capture, transportation and enslavement, with the consequent severance of family and community ties, slaves did not lose all contact with the cultures of their past. In Brazil and in the Caribbean islands, where the plantation was the central social and economic institution, where there was a constant influx of Africans, and where blacks and mulattos formed the largest element of the population, there appeared many of the most vigorous Afro-American cultural forms. African influences manifested themselves in music, language, work techniques, and, perhaps most importantly, in religious beliefs and practices. Little is known of the history of African cultural survivals before the eighteenth century; however, from that time at least there were distinctive religious cults in Brazil and the West Indies, fusing

A public slave market in Brazil (Rugendas, 1853)

with, and competing against the Christianity of dominant white society. Cults such as Obeah and Myalism in the Anglophone Caribbean, Vodùn in Haiti, and Candomblé, Xangô and Macumba in Brazil, all testified to the transmission of African patterns of worship.

The response of Africans and their offspring to slavery also took more tangible shape in various forms of open rejection of, and resistance to white society. Not only did individual slaves flee from servitude, but runaway slaves also formed their own communities, known as *maroons*, *palenques* and *quilombos*, which were *de facto* autonomous polities beyond the authority of white-controlled governments. Organized rebellions by plantation slaves, seeking the redress of grievances suffered at the hands of their masters, were also common throughout Latin America and the Caribbean, though they rarely resulted in concerted movements for emancipation. Only in Haiti did slave rebellion form the basis for a revolutionary movement which overthrew slave society and, in 1804, replaced colonial government with an independent republic headed by an ex-slave.

Elsewhere, an end to slavery came more gradually and was bound up with the decline and cessation of the slave trade. Although the slave trade had already passed its peak by the early nineteenth century, a crucial step towards abolition was taken in 1807, when Britain outlawed the slave trade in its colonial possessions and thereby inaugurated a movement to end the flow of slaves across the Atlantic. During the Spanish American wars of independence, creole independists followed this lead, with attempts to abolish the trade in Venezuela and Mexico in 1810, in Chile in 1811, and in Buenos Aires in 1812. Moreover, many slaves won their freedom through military service during the struggles for independence. But a definitive end to slave trading and slavery awaited the establishment of republican governments and increased British pressure to outlaw the trade. Chile, Central America and Mexico, where slavery was of marginal economic importance, were among the first Hispanic republics to emancipate their slaves, in 1823, 1824 and 1829 respectively. In the British Caribbean, abolition came in 1834, an example followed by the French in 1848, and the Dutch in 1863. In Venezuela, Ecuador, Colombia and Peru, where slaveholders were politically influential, complete abolition was delayed until the 1840s and early 1850s. In Brazil and the Spanish Caribbean islands of Puerto Rico and Cuba, slavery endured even longer. In Puerto Rico, abolition was finally decreed in 1878; in Cuba, it was not fully enacted until 1886, while Brazil remained the last area of slavery in Latin America until the 'Golden Law' of 1888 proclaimed unconditional emancipation for those who remained enslaved.

The termination of African slave migration to Latin America and the Caribbean was, then, a slow and uneven process. Even after provisions were made to free newborn slaves, and international agreements were made to end the slave traffic, an active clandestine commerce sustained trans-Atlantic and intra-American transfers of slaves until the 1870s. Their main destinations were the coffee zones of Brazil, where expanding coffee plantations sustained a market for slaves, and Cuba, where sugar plantations continued to draw on new, illicit supplies of slaves from Africa until the early 1870s. Thus, though greatly reduced by the mid-nineteenth century, the slave trade died hard. So long as the economic conditions which had created markets for African slaves persisted, then both the commerce in slaves and the institution of slavery endured. To exploit the resources of Latin American and Caribbean territories required supplies of manpower which, when not available locally, were brought from abroad. Thus, when the long waves of African slave migration finally subsided in the second half of the nineteenth century, new waves of free European migrants were gathering force, signalling the emergence of new configurations in the world economy and resulting in the next great era of trans-Atlantic migrations to the New World.

AMcF

Further reading

R. Bashole, *The African Religions of Brazil* (Baltimore, 1978)
P. D. Curtin, *The Atlantic Slave Trade: a Census* (Madison, 1969)
B. Davidson, *Black Mother: Africa and the Atlantic Slave Trade* (Harmondsworth, 1980)
P. E. Lovejoy, 'The Volume of the Atlantic Slave Trade: a Synthesis', *Journal of African History*, 23 (1982), 473–501
O. Patterson, *The Sociology of Slavery* (New York, 1967)
L. B. Rout, Jr, *The African Experience in Spanish America* (Cambridge, 1976)

Immigration since 1850

Immigrants are the unsung heroes of Latin American history. Although every Latin American country is, to a greater or lesser extent, a nation of immigrants, their contributions to society are only rarely acknowledged. There is nothing comparable in Latin America to the United States myth of immigrant pioneers conquering and taming an intractable wilderness.

In comparison with the 33 million Europeans who emigrated to the United States in the classic period of mass migration (1800–1930) only some 7 to 9 million went to Latin America, and these were concentrated in Argentina and Uruguay with their populations of predominantly European descent and in Brazil, Chile, Costa Rica, Cuba and Venezuela whose populations were more mixed. Elsewhere, the European strain stems from the earlier migrations of the colonial period and has since been diluted by miscegenation.

The uneven pattern of immigration settlement in the independence period was conditioned by labour needs, climate and politics. Where ownership of land was concentrated in the hands of a few families and where Indian or African slave labour was available, there was little incentive to attract land-hungry European peasants, for whom the United States offered clearer opportunities to own land, for social advancement and political and religious freedom. Nor were immigrants attracted to tropical regions with their risks of disease, or to countries racked by incessant political feuding.

Even in Argentina where, from the last quarter of the nineteenth century, economic development was in large part due to immigrants, attitudes towards immigration remained ambivalent, both on the part of immigrants themselves and governments. For many immigrants Latin America was an El Dorado where fortunes could be made quickly and then used to buy position and prestige in their country of origin. The low identification of many first-generation immigrants with their host country (by 1914 under 2 per cent of immigrants to Brazil had been naturalized and in Argentina only 3.2 per cent) was partly caused by the generous terms offered them by governments desperate for their labour. A foreigner could obtain most of the benefits of citizenship without becoming a national, at the same time keeping the protection of his consul. By contrast, in the United States naturalization was a prerequisite for voting and thus political parties had an interest in encouraging immigrants to become naturalized so that they could vote, whereas in Latin America restricted franchises or dictatorial governments removed this incentive and the majority of immigrants remained on the margin of politics. Even where governments were anxious to attract immigrants, official attitudes towards them were divided. Welcomed for racial reasons (northern Europeans were preferred) as a means of 'whitening' the racial stock, they were also sometimes distrusted as carriers of pernicious democratic, socialist or anarchist doctrines. This distrust can be explained by the prominent role played by immigrants in labour organizations. Germans founded the first Argentine socialist party, Spaniards introduced anarchist ideas into Buenos Aires, and Italians dominated the first labour unions in São Paulo. As the number of immigrants increased in the first decade of the twentieth century, so restrictive legislation (such as deportation for organizing strikes) was used to enforce social control. Immigrants, in short, were regarded as a source of docile, cheap labour rather than as positive contributors to the nation's social and political life. However, for the second and third generation there were few barriers to political ambition, as is attested by many presidents with non-Hispanic surnames – such as Carlos Pellegrini and Arturo Frondizi in Argentina, Arturo Alessandri and Eduardo Frei in Chile, and Juscelino Kubitschek and Ernesto

Geisel in Brazil, not forgetting General Alfredo Stroessner in Paraguay.

Economically, though, the immigrants' contribution was crucial – they were important not only as a source of cheap labour on the Argentine wheatfields or on the coffee plantations of São Paulo, but also as entrepreneurs. Lacking the social inhibitions of the creole elite, many made successful careers as businessmen and industrialists: families such as the di Tellas in Argentina, the Matarazzos in Brazil, the Gildemeisters in Peru and the Hochschilds in Bolivia could be mentioned as examples.

Although governments in the early nineteenth century attempted to foster immigration through colonization schemes, most of these proved impracticable. In Argentina, the interests of labour-intensive agriculture were sacrificed to those of the cattle barons. In Brazil and Cuba, colonization schemes failed in the face of opposition from the plantocracy and from the reluctance of Europeans to migrate to a slave society (similar to the situation in the southern United States). In Guatemala, an ambitious project to colonize jungle land in the New Liverpool experiment in the 1830s and 1840s collapsed. More successful were the German colonies of southern Chile, north-eastern Argentina and southern Brazil. In these cases, flourishing communities with a distinctive German culture were established in regions largely unsettled by creoles. The success of these colonies vindicated those who argued that northern Europeans made the best settlers in frontier regions. Numerically, though, northern Europeans were few, although the financial influences of the British and the cultural influence of the Germans and French were out of all proportion to their numbers. In Chile, Argentina and Brazil foreign merchants and entrepreneurs, especially British, contributed to these countries' economic growth, founding in the process dynasties of Anglo-Chilean, Anglo-Brazilian and Anglo-Argentine families who were reluctant to foresake their British connections and become completely assimilated. In other countries, too, there were smaller 'Anglo' communities with their own schools and clubs, as in Peru where their reluctance to become assimilated contrasts with the small Italian entrepreneurial elite whose influence in Peruvian economic growth has been insufficiently appreciated. The Italian contribution, however, was most apparent in Argentina and Brazil in the period of mass immigration during the thirty years before 1914.

Argentina was the immigrant country *par excellence*. In the 1840s future president Domingo F. Sarmiento, who had been greatly impressed by a visit to the United States, foreshadowed many later attitudes in favour of immigration, arguing that the 'barbaric' interior could only be tamed by the 'civilizing' influence of cosmopolitan, Europeanized cities, whilst his political rival Juan Alberdi coined the much repeated phrase *gobernar es poblar* (to govern is to populate). In Buenos Aires, which had grown from the *gran aldea*

An Argentine homestead in the 1880s

(the great village) of the 1860s to become the 'Paris of the southern hemisphere' by 1914, some three-quarters of its inhabitants were foreign-born.

Immigrants to Argentina – nearly half of them Italians, about one-third being Spaniards – were drawn into four main activities: shepherding, cattle pasturing, wheat growing and harvesting, and urban occupations. The gradual establishment of political stability after the fall of Juan Manuel de Rosas (1852) created better conditions for immigrants; the Constitution of 1853 guaranteed their legal position. An expanding sheep economy attracted Welsh, Irish and Basque shepherds, some of whom became founders of wealthy families. As sheep pushed cattle further westwards, so the need for pastures to fatten cattle before shipment attracted farmers, mostly Italians, who grew alfalfa as sharecroppers on limited tenancies. Wheat growing first developed in the 1860s in agricultural colonies of Swiss and Italian peasant farmers in the littoral

provinces but, when wheat moved south into the pampas, labour for the harvests was often provided by transitory *golondrinas* (swallows) from southern Europe who were able to work on the Argentine harvest during the European winter. One consequence of this type of seasonal migration was an imbalance between the sexes, which contributed towards Buenos Aires becoming one of the most notorious centres of the white slave trade.

Those migrants who stayed provided labour for the construction boom, meat-packing factories, flour mills, docks and urban services of the rapidly expanding coastal cities. By 1914, 41 per cent of the 2,358,000 foreigners living in Argentina were in Buenos Aires, 49 per cent were in the littoral and Córdoba provinces and the remaining 10 per cent were in the rest of the country. Immigration accelerated the division of the nation into a modern, cosmopolitan, urbanized and economically dynamic coastal region and a traditional economically retarded (and less populated) interior.

Italians, in particular, made their mark in Buenos Aires with their own districts, their contributions to the local argot (*lunfardo*) and the local cuisine, and even more so in the grain port of Rosario. The threat posed by an influx of poor non-Hispanic immigrants to traditional values generated nativist responses by the creole elite which took one form in the cult of the gaucho as the symbol of *argentinidad*. One way in which immigrants sought cultural identification with their newly adopted land was to form gaucho clubs and to enact rituals of gaucho life during weekend trips into the pampas.

As the number of Spaniards emigrating to Argentina increased, Spanish intellectuals attempted to strengthen cultural links through the ideology of *hispanismo* which emphasized the spiritual unity of all Hispanic peoples. But this was not regarded too seriously by most Argentines who continued to be bemused by British economic power, French culture, and German science and militarism.

Although Argentina's pre-1914 prosperity was largely due to the labour of immigrants, they were frequently regarded as money-grubbing materialists and were sometimes the butt of satirists. To escape the obloquy attached to commerce, second- and third-generation sons of immigrants sought prestige by entering the hitherto creole-dominated professions of law, medicine and politics. The army, too, was an important ladder of social mobility, as shown by the high proportion of generals with Italian antecedents.

In Brazil, efforts had been made during the imperial period (1822–89) to encourage immigration by subsidizing agricultural colonies, following the eighteenth-century precedent set by the

The British clocktower in Buenos Aires. Donated by the British immigrant community to Argentina to mark the anniversary of the May Revolution, 1810, it was damaged by a bomb in 1984

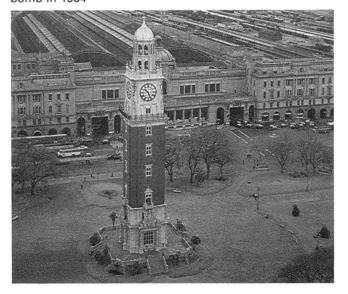

Portuguese crown of establishing colonies of Azoreans in Santa Caterina. However, few of the Swiss and German colonies founded in the 1830s and 1840s survived. It was not until after the Paraguayan War (1865–70) and the run-down of slavery that immigrants entered in any numbers and, once slavery had been abolished in 1889, the trickle became a flood. Between 50 and 60 per cent went to the state of São Paulo (in the 1890s the percentage rose to 80 in some years), where the coffee boom created a continuing demand for labour. Most of this was provided by Italians, at first mostly from northern Italy, from whence came many of the missionaries who were the earliest links. Transport costs were subsidized by the São Paulo state government under the *colono* system by which immigrants together with their families replaced slaves on the coffee plantations. By careful housekeeping *colonos* could save enough money to buy land on which to produce food for the growing towns or, alternatively, to move into the cities to become artisans or shopkeepers. Portuguese immigrants tended to prefer Rio de Janeiro and provincial towns where they dominated commerce and shopkeeping, often rousing nativist hostility during economic depressions, as in the 1890s. Between the 1880s and 1950s, 31 per cent of all immigrants were Italians and 30 per cent Portuguese, followed by Spaniards (13.8 per cent), Japanese (4.5 per cent), Germans (4 per cent) and thirty other nationalities with smaller percentages. The coffee boom, made possible by the *colonos*, provided the profits which fuelled the industrial development of São Paulo, turning it into a cosmopolitan financial centre.

The First World War and the early 1920s marked a change in the pattern of immigration. During the war many Italians returned to fight on the Italian front (many immigrants had come from the Veneto, the main war zone in Italy). After the war the establishment of immigration quotas by the United States diverted much of the migrant flow from war-torn central and eastern Europe to South America. Poles, Russians, Jews and central Europeans as well as Turks and Syrians swelled the small communities of these nationalities which pre-dated the war. In Brazil, one of the most important groups was the Japanese whose agricultural skills contributed to developing marginal land in São Paulo and frontier regions in Paraná and Amazonia. Japanese immigration was distinctive insofar as the Japanese government both encouraged and supervised the emigration process.

A major contrast between Latin America and the United States has been the reluctance of immigrants in the former to move into frontier regions. Apart from a few cases, such as Scottish sheep farmers in Patagonia, the Welsh colony in Chubut (dating from 1865), Germans in southern Chile, north-eastern Argentina and southern Brazil, the Japanese in Amazonia and religious groups like the Mennonites in Paraguay, most immigrants have settled in cities. Although in the 1880s Argentina passed legislation modelled on the

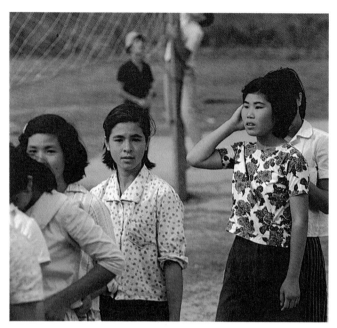

Japanese immigrants in a colony near Santa Cruz, Bolivia

United States Homestead Act of 1862 which granted settlers free land on condition it was cultivated, it proved ineffective due to the entrenched power of big landowners, land companies and political corruption. In Brazil, the Land Law of 1850 had been specifically designed to seal off the frontier to prospective settlers by making the price prohibitive and confining its distribution to the plantocracy. In this way immigrants would not be diverted away from the plantations where their labour was needed.

After Argentina and Brazil, Uruguay and Cuba were the countries most affected by large-scale immigration. In the former, Argentine experience was replicated. Montevideo became a city of immigrants – a high proportion of whom were Italians and French – with over one-third of the country's population. However, the experience of Cuba was distinctive, firstly because, as it was a Spanish colony until independence in 1898, Spaniards occupied a privileged position in society, monopolizing posts in the bureaucracy and commerce. The Cuban case also illustrates, in exaggerated form, the tendency for the regional attachments of the Iberian peninsula to be perpetuated in the Americas, exemplified by powerful regional clubs of Galicians, Catalans and Asturians. Few Spaniards except *isleños* (Canary Islanders) moved on to the land (Fidel Castro's father, a Galician, was one who did). Secondly, the early years of the nineteenth century created an inexhaustible demand for labour. This was met by rising imports of African slaves until the threat to the racial balance in the 1850s compelled the authorities to seek alternative sources of manpower. As Europeans

were reluctant to migrate to a slave society, over 100,000 Chinese coolies were imported between the 1840s and 1870s as semi-free contractual labourers, thus providing a bridge between slavery and a free-labour system. Some remained after their contracts expired and entered traditional Chinese occupations in restaurants, laundries and market gardens and were assimilated into Cuban society. A similar case occurred in Peru where Chinese coolies had been imported during the guano boom in the 1860s so as not to drain off Indian labour from highland haciendas, and where a small Chinese–Peruvian community took root.

With the abolition of Cuban slavery in 1879 the flow of Spanish immigrants increased and even after the fiercely fought war of independence (1895–8) Spaniards continued to enter until by 1930 some 16 per cent of Cuba's population were Spanish. This number dropped after the 'Cubanization' law of 1933 limited the number of foreign employees in any firm to under 50 per cent. Spaniards then either returned to Spain or became Cuban citizens. The absence of any large non-Hispanic immigration has meant that Cuban links with Spain are probably closer than those of any other Latin American country.

The Cubanization law was one expression of rising nationalism throughout Latin America in the aftermath of the Great Depression. This was reflected in restrictive immigration legislation and in nationalization policies designed to hasten the assimilation of groups who had hitherto been on the fringes of national life. Newspapers published in foreign languages perpetuated divided loyalties as did schools where teaching was conducted in a foreign language. In Brazil, the threat posed by self-contained German communities prompted an active policy of Brazilianization as well as the imposition of quotas restricting each nationality during any one year to 2 per cent of the number admitted between 1884 and 1933, and also stipulating that 80 per cent of each national group should be agriculturalists, reflecting Getúlio Vargas's ambition to settle the interior.

The restrictions of the 1930s changed the character of immigration. Previously the majority of immigrants were poor, whereas in the 1930s the political exiles who now became an important component were often intellectuals and professionals. The most important group were those from republican Spain. Every country in Latin America derived some benefit from this new type of migration and none more so than Mexico, which had previously attracted few Spanish immigrants. Spaniards now made substantial contributions to universities, publishing and the arts.

After the war the immigrant flow revived, especially to Venezuela to which Italians were drawn by the economic boom. Argentina continued to attract Spaniards of whom 60 per cent returned to Spain even though Franco was still in power.

With few exceptions immigration into Latin America has been

from southern Europe, thus perpetuating many of the values of a Catholic, family-oriented traditional culture. For those choosing to go to Latin America the term 'New World' did not have the connotations of a religious or political utopia associated with the United States. In Latin America the utopian dreams of sixteenth-century Franciscan missionaries and of patriot leaders such as Simon Bolívar evaporated in the confused anarchical early years of independence. Lacking the magnetic pull of free land, or of religious or political freedoms, Latin America tended to attract those who glimpsed possibilities of a future in economic activities despised by the creole elite. Opportunities may not have been as many or as varied as in the United States, but recognized success stories should not obscure the many failures, one of which has lately been documented in a classic immigrant autobiography edited by the late Juan Marsal.

Scholarly attention has so far focused on the statistics of migration and on immigrants' economic influence; little research has been done on social and cultural aspects such as the complex processes of assimilation, the incidence of intermarriage between creole and immigrant, on immigrants' racial attitudes, on the phenomenon of the returnee and on the wider questions of cultural influences. Is it possible to speak of a 'melting pot' in the case of Argentina as some historians have done? Or can Argentina's political difficulties be related to the early political marginalization of immigrants? These and many other questions need (and will surely receive) investigation by historians.

Compared with immigration studies in the United States, those in Latin America are in their infancy. Considering that the Americas share a common experience of immigration from Europe, this is a puzzling omission and one that needs to be rectified for a proper understanding of the continent's historical development.

AH

Further reading

N. Sánchez Albornoz, *The Population of Latin America* (Berkeley, 1974)

E. Fishburn, *The Portrayal of Immigration in Nineteenth-Century Argentine Fiction, 1845–1902* (Berlin, 1981; *Biblioteca Ibero-Americana* no. 29)

La emigración europea a la América Latina: fuentes y estado de investigación (Biblioteca Ibero-Americana no. 26)

J. Marsal, ed., *Hacer la América: una autobiografía de un inmigrante español* (Buenos Aires, 1969)

C. Solberg, *Immigration and Nationalism: Argentina and Chile, 1890–1914* (Austin, 1970)

Latin American migration (regional and abroad)

Immigration into Latin America from the Spanish and Portuguese conquests to the present day is, of course, a major feature of the continent's history. Interamerican migration has attracted less attention though it is both an historic and a contemporary factor of considerable significance.

Large-scale Mexican migration to the United States began in the 1880s with the expansion of the railroads. The Mexican Revolution of 1910 and the religious wars of the 1920s in central Mexico caused the flight of many Mexican workers to the United States. Puerto Rican migration to the United States became significant at this time, and reached major proportions after the Second World War, when the first massive 'air-borne' migrations in history took place. Puerto Rican migration dwindled after 1960, but already by 1950 there were over 225,000 Puerto Ricans living in the United States, as well as 75,000 others born there of Puerto Rican parents. Between 1915 and 1929, many Haitians and Dominicans migrated to Cuba to work in the sugar mills and plantations. Political upheavals in Paraguay and Bolivia were responsible for the flight of many persons to Argentina between 1915 and 1957. Since 1950, international migration to Latin America and the Caribbean from Europe has diminished. The total number of all persons entering from Europe between 1956 and 1970 was only 847,000. Most were highly skilled persons who went to Argentina, Venezuela and Brazil. There has been an expansion of intraregional migration in the area as a whole since 1950, primarily between contiguous nations or territories, but also among the Caribbean islands and other nations in the Caribbean basin.

Migrants can be of several types depending on their reasons for migrating, their length of stay, and their legal status in the host country. Many professionals, including doctors and engineers, migrate from Argentina, Chile, Colombia and Venezuela to the United States. From 1955 to 1968, for example, over 20,000 professionals from Colombia entered the United States; in 1967 alone almost 600 Latin American physicians, dentists, and nurses left their own countries. Argentina loses large numbers of physicians to the United States (over 1500 of them in the period 1950–70). Most professionals enter the receiving country with visas. Political refugees comprise a second category of migrants. Many Cubans were admitted legally to the United States between 1956 and 1972, particularly following Fidel Castro's revolution. In 1970, it was estimated that there were over 600,000 Cubans in the United States, half of them in the state of Florida. The third type of migrants are those who cross national borders seeking work. They are mainly unskilled or semi-skilled persons who enter illegally, that is, without a visa or work permit. Since 1960, undocumented migrant workers have constituted the bulk of migrants in Latin America and the Caribbean. Some remain only long enough to engage in seasonal work, then return to their own countries. They may make only a few trips during a lifetime, or migrate annually. Other persons remain in the receiving country for many years, returning home only to retire. Most such migrants are unaccompanied by their families.

There are a number of explanations for the intensive migration across borders which has occurred since 1950. The large-scale exodus of professionals, the so-called 'brain-drain', is caused by such conditions in the home country as low fees or salaries, insecure employment, lack of equipment and poor working conditions. Political refugees from Cuba initially comprised supporters of the previous (Batista) government, administrators within US-owned corporations, and persons with large land-holdings expropriated by Fidel Castro. It has been argued that the dramatic rise in wage-labour migration has occurred as a consequence of unequal development within the international economy. As industrial capital and technology from developed nations such as the United States and Canada is exported to Latin America, it creates displacement of unskilled workers, especially those in agriculture, who then flow to the more developed areas. Labour migration can also be seen as a response to both 'push' factors which expel workers in the sending country and 'pull' factors in the receiving country which attract workers from the unskilled sector. 'Push' factors include rapid population growth, the lack of opportunities in agriculture for absorbing workers, a disproportional number of small land plots relative to population (minifundismo), maldistribution of income, low or irregular wages, and rising consumption standards. 'Pull' factors include higher wages, more employment opportunities, a higher rate of monetary exchange for foreign currency, and a continuing need in the developing regions for a low-cost, manipulable workforce to fill the jobs in the lower rungs of the economy.

Estimation of the volume of international and interregional migration in Latin America and the Caribbean is difficult, insofar as much of it is covert and illegal. Since the 1950s, significant flows have occurred from Colombia, Panama, Ecuador and El Salvador to Mexico and Guatemala, from El Salvador to Honduras following the 'Football War' of 1967, from Brazil to the Paraguayan frontier, from Puerto Rico, Haiti and Cuba to the United States, and from former British colonies, the Virgin Islands and Haiti to Canada and the United States. The largest flows of undocumented migrant workers have been from Mexico to the United States, from Colombia to Venezuela, and from the other 'southern cone' countries of Chile, Bolivia, Paraguay and Uruguay to Argentina. There has also been a heavy outflow of political exiles from Chile after 1973 and Argentina after 1976.

Migration of Mexicans to the United States intensified from 1942 to 1964 when legal work contracts were issued to migrants under the Bracero programme designed originally to fill a gap in labour shortages resulting from mobilization during the Second World War in the United States. During the ten-year period, 1954–64, over 4 million Mexicans went as short-term agricultural workers. As many as 40,000 persons were admitted yearly during the peak years of the programme. Many other workers went illegally as well. The legal termination of the programme in 1964 under pressure from labour unions in the United States has not diminished the flow. Estimates of the number of undocumented Mexican workers in the United States vary greatly (from 2 to 12 million), but the likelihood is that there are about 4 million in any given year. Some have legal permits, most do not. Most migrants are found in California and the south-western states of the country and in Illinois. About half of them engage in seasonal agricultural work, the other half in urban occupations such as construction, petty industry, domestic service or the service sector generally. Most are temporary workers who return to Mexico after a stay of six to twelve months. Others remain longer and may eventually bring their families.

Venezuela has a small native population of only 14 million, yet it has been estimated that 2–4 million foreign workers, most of them illegal migrants, are now in Venezuela. About half of these are from Colombia, the rest from Cuba, the Dominican Republic, and Ecuador. Large-scale migrations to Venezuela began in the 1940s, when there was a shortage of labour due to Venezuela's rapidly expanding economy based on oil production. Intensive Colombian migration to Venezuela began in the 1960s as a consequence of an oil boom. Most Colombians are located in the border states where they work in the coffee and sugar plantations and in cattle raising. Others migrate to the city of Caracas to work in construction and in the service sector. Many women migrants from Colombia work as domestics. The need for foreign workers has risen since 1976 with the formulation of the Venezuelan Development Plan aimed at increasing industrial activity. Since 1950, international migration in South America's southern cone – Bolivia, Chile, Paraguay, Uruguay and Argentina – has been primarily from the other southern cone countries to Argentina, although that changed after the Argentine coup of 1976. As was the case in the United States, there was active recruitment of foreign workers until 1960; since that time, migrant flows have been voluntary. Migrants from Bolivia come mainly from the Altiplano and the Valles regions of the western highlands where 85 per cent of the population lives. The migrants are mainly owners of small plots of less than 10 hectares. It is estimated that in 1969 there were between 500,000 and 1 million Bolivians in Argentina. Many migrants work in the zafra or sugar harvest which annually employs 26,000 men. Many of them remain in Argentina after the zafra to seek work in the cities or in other agricultural regions to work in the tobacco and vegetable harvests.

Bolivian miner at work on the summit of Hucanquilcha Volcano, Chile (6000 m). Bolivians from the Altiplano are brought in because they are the only people capable of carrying out hard physical labour at these altitudes

Chile has an excess labour force to contribute to the migrant flow to Argentina due to its slow rate of industrial growth despite a relatively high level of development. Many rural Chileans travel to their own capital city of Santiago seeking work; others migrate to Argentine cities, including many women who work as domestics. Two-thirds of Chile's migrants work in fruit orchards, vineyards and in sheep farming.

Paraguay has a highly rural population and very few cities. Paraguayan migrants to Argentina work in the border cities and in the construction of hydroelectric plants in the border regions. Between 1950 and 1970, over 350,000 Paraguayans entered Argentina to seek work. Other Paraguayans go to the Matto Grosso area of Brazil or to southern Brazil to harvest maté leaves and twigs.

The Uruguayan exodus to Argentina intensified in the 1960s due to lack of employment opportunities in Uruguay for skilled workers. Between 1970 and 1974, 10 per cent of Uruguay's population, including many of these skilled workers, left Uruguay in search of jobs. Many men from Uruguay work in construction in Buenos Aires.

There are important effects of international and interregional migration in Latin America and the Caribbean for both sending and receiving countries. Receiving countries benefit from the 'brain-drain' by acquiring highly skilled and professional personnel without the need to bear expensive training costs. The cost of producing, maintaining and transporting large numbers of

unskilled temporary workers is also spared receiving countries. Such workers willingly work at menial, low-paying jobs which have no possibility of advancement and which are often shunned by the internal labour force. Those who oppose foreign workers argue that their presence contributes to the continuing existence of low-paying jobs, depresses wages, hinders unionization of workers, strains social services for which they do not pay, and contributes to hyperurbanization.

Benefits to sending countries include the reduction of under-employment, especially in agriculture; absorption of unemployable labour in productive activities which brings in foreign capital; use of foreign capital by migrants for investment and savings; reduced pressure on internal migration, especially to the cities; and the increased ability of individuals to move out of agriculture into more modern activities, either through investment of income in productive self-employment or because of new skills acquired abroad. Many believe that migration acts as a 'safety-valve' for stemming social and political unrest among the poorer segments of society. Those who do not favour outmigration as a solution to internal economic problems argue that it leads to the abandonment of important activities in the sending regions, such as land cultivation, perpetuates poor distribution of national income, and does not use foreign capital productively, inasmuch as most migrants invest in subsistence needs, improved housing, land or animals rather than new enterprises which create greater employment. They also argue that the safety-valve effect preserves ineffective governmental economic policies by dampening the demand for needed reforms.

Migration policies in Latin America reflect a desire to protect good wages for skilled workers and are, therefore, relatively restrictive. Despite this tendency, there is tacit agreement not to restrict freedom of egress, except in Cuba. Haiti charges exit and visa fees for legal migration as a way of acquiring foreign currency, and El Salvador includes emigration as part of a national migration policy. United States policy toward Mexican migration has been highly selective since the termination of the Bracero programme. There is a severe limit on the number of Mexican workers who can be issued work-permits. Most permanent legal migration from Mexico occurs under a 'family unification' clause in the immigration laws which enables a limited number of persons each year to join close relatives in the United States who are naturalized citizens or permanent resident aliens. During the administration of Presidents Carter and Reagan, reforms in the immigration laws as they affect Mexico have been sought but not yet enacted. These include the possibility of a pilot 'guest-worker' programme for 25,000 workers annually, employer sanctions for hiring illegal workers, and a national identity card for all workers, a proposal opposed by many civil-rights advocates and Mexican–American citizens. The Andean countries ratified a pact on labour migration in 1975, from which Chile later withdrew. The pact calls for the regulation of workers between Andean countries. Colombia is one of the few countries in Latin America (Cuba is another) with a labour migration policy. Created in 1975, it regulates the migration of Colombians to cities within the country and tries to minimize the impact of emigration by reducing and channelling the flow. Colombia tries to create contracts for workers in overseas countries such as Saudi Arabia, and to give assistance to migrants re-entering Colombia. It is the only country which uses income from labour contracts to build low-cost housing. Venezuela's migration policy has changed from a closed one before 1960 to one which is both open and selective. This change reflects the government's changing perceptions of its economic development needs. Long a major receiver of European migrants, Venezuela now has a migration policy for Latin American migrants which more closely resembles that of advanced industrial societies like the United States and Canada. Argentina's immigration policy underwent liberalization in 1973–5. Since then, due to a decline in the Argentine economy, it has become more restrictive as a means of reducing internal unemployment.

International migration in the area is likely to proceed steadily until at least the end of this century. Despite the recent discovery of large oil reserves in Mexico, it is unlikely that Mexico will be able to generate enough new jobs to absorb its growing and increasingly younger working population. High rates of migration to Venezuela are expected to continue, especially from Colombia, as economic development intensifies, based upon Venezuela's oil revenues. Migration to Argentina from Paraguay and Uruguay may taper off briefly due to the absorption of some workers in the construction of new hydroelectric plants there. A temporary decline in Argentina's economy may attract fewer migrants for a time, but its continuing need for unskilled workers and a shortage within the internal labour force are likely to offset the decline. Flows from Bolivia to Argentina may ebb as a consequence of successful efforts by the government to relocate Altiplano residents in new colonies in eastern Bolivia; thus far, however, the number of new colonies has not been significant. It is expected that there will be no major change in the trends which have characterized migration in the area since 1950.

IR-U

Contemporary size and distribution of population

The population of Latin America and the Caribbean, some 150 million at the end of the Second World War, more than doubled by 1980 when it reached 364 million, well above that of North America or Western Europe, as table 30 shows. In the last two decades of this century, its growth is projected to slow down so that the total will probably not exceed 570 million by the year 2000.

From the mid-1940s to the mid-1970s, Latin America's population growth was faster than Africa's or Asia's because birth rates in most Latin American countries had remained practically as high as in the rest of the Third World, while Latin America's death rates fell much more rapidly. Its current growth is at a rate of 2.4 per cent each year.

In the mid-1970s both tropical Latin America and Middle America (Central America, including Mexico), where the great bulk of the continent's population is concentrated, were exhibiting the first signs of the present downtrend of their birth rates. Although the already low death rates may be expected to fall a little more, there is no doubt that population growth will continue to slow down from the extraordinarily high rate of 2.9 per cent per year in the

CONTEMPORARY SIZE AND DISTRIBUTION OF THE POPULATION

KEY

Persons per square kilometre / Persons per square mile

Persons per square kilometre	Persons per square mile
0	0
0·4	1
2	5
10	25
40	100

■ Cities with population over 5 million
● Cities with population over 1 million

Table 30. Population of Latin America by regions, size and growth
(population in thousands)

Total	1950	Growth[a]	%[b]	1980	Growth[a]	%[b]	1990[c]	Growth[a]	%[b]	2000[c]	Growth[a]	%[b]
Latin America	164053	2.7	100.0	363704	2.4	100.0	459298	2.2	100.0	565747	1.9	100.0
Middle America	36101	3.0	22.0	92538	2.9	25.4	122382	2.5	26.6	155709	2.1	27.5
Caribbean	17476	1.8	10.7	31919	1.8	8.8	38215	1.7	8.3	45222	1.6	8.0
Tropical South America	85092	3.0	51.9	198181	2.5	54.5	252196	2.2	54.9	313210	2.0	55.4
Temperate South America	25437	1.9	15.5	41067	1.3	11.3	46505	1.1	10.1	51605	0.9	9.1

[a] Average annual percentage growth = birth rate minus death rate plus immigration minus emigration.
[b] Percent frequency distribution adding up to Latin America = 100%.
[c] United Nations projections based on 1980 data and recent trends.
Source: United Nations.

1960s to 2.3 per cent toward 1990 and perhaps as low as 1.8 per cent before the year 2000.

Well before the Second World War, temperate South America had modest growth as a consequence of its low, Western-European-style birth rates. Indeed, if it had not been for massive infusions of European immigrants and the very low death rates in Argentina, Chile and Uruguay, the population of these quite exceptional countries would not have grown even as gently as it had over the period 1920–60. Their maximum postwar growth rates, 1.9 per cent per year, occurred in the 1950s when immigration peaked, but this fell away to 1.3 per cent in the late 1970s. In sharp contrast, tropical Latin America's annual growth remained at 3 per cent until the 1960s and declined to 2.5 per cent only in the late 1970s. This drop of a half per cent is extremely important in itself because tropical South America now has more than 200 million people, and they are still multiplying at practically double the rate of the temperate countries.

Immigration from other continents has not been a weighty factor in South America since the 1950s when there had been large inflows to Brazil and Venezuela as well as to the temperate countries. Neither emigration from South America nor interregional migration among its countries have been large enough to make an appreciable difference over the last two decades (except in the relatively tiny populations of Guyane (French Guiana), Guyana and Surinam).

The strongest rate of population upsurge is in Middle America, where the total population is now almost 100 million. There, too, however, the pace of growth seems to be slackening very slightly. The considerable emigration from Mexico to the United States, including a large illegal movement which is uncounted, has not yet made much difference to Middle America's – nor indeed Mexico's – rapid population growth which still exceeds the fastest rates of all Asia's regions.

Postwar emigration has made a definite difference to the recent growth and present size of population only in the Caribbean and the smallest circum-Caribbean areas. In any case, Caribbean population growth was already lower than all but temperate South America's in the 1940s. In 1965–70, when Great Britain was fairly open to Commonwealth immigrants and the Netherlands was open to Surinam's people, the combined outflow from the Caribbean amounted to more than a quarter of natural increase. At that time, the Caribbean's birth rate had gone up and the death rate was down to European-style minimum levels. Without mass emigration, the resultant population upsurge would then have reached the continent's high average rate of growth. The American and French territories still have free access to their metropoles and their population growth is slowed down in consequence. But, even without such massive emigration, which is now impossible from Surinam and the British Commonwealth islands, the Caribbean's subsequent growth would not have stayed so high because family planning has become widespread through official programmes and commercial distribution in all of the region except Haiti.

Table 31 presents the population and its growth rates for all countries with more than a quarter of a million inhabitants, in the recent past, the present and at the end of the century. The smaller populations are discussed in the final note accompanying table 34.

Distribution among regions and among countries

Owing to the marked divergences among the various countries' rates of growth, the distribution of population across the continent is shifting quite dramatically in the second half of the twentieth century (as table 31 shows). Between the Second World War and the current decade, the demographic centre of gravity shifted northward as Middle America's population expanded. More than a quarter of the whole continent's population now lives along the isthmus, one-fifth in Mexico alone. It should not be forgotten that Brazil's 122 million and Colombia's 26 million together make up 40 per cent of the continent's total: Latin America's population as a whole still lives mainly near the Equator. Certainly for the rest of this century, the demographic trends of the continent will depend above all on what happens to the high birth rates of Brazil and Mexico which already hold more than half the inhabitants.

Contemporary size and distribution of population

Table 31. Population of countries: size and growth (population in thousands)

	1950	%	1980	%	1990[d]
Middle America[a]					
Costa Rica	858	3.5	2 213	2.3	2 776
El Salvador	1 940	2.7	4 797	2.9	6 484
Guatemala	2 962	2.9	7 262	2.9	9 676
Honduras	1 401	3.2	3 691	3.4	5 105
Mexico	26 886	3.1	69 752	2.9	91 976
Nicaragua	1 109	2.8	2 733	3.3	3 778
Panama[a]	825	2.8	1 896	2.2	2 346
Caribbean[a]					
Barbados	211	0.9	263	1.1	292
Cuba	5 858	1.9	9 732	0.6	10 540
Dominican Republic	2 361	3.0	5 947	2.4	7 534
Guadeloupe	210	2.3	329	0.3	339
Guyana	375	3.5	883	2.1	1 069
Haiti	3 097	1.7	5 809	2.5	7 509
Jamaica	1 403	1.9	2 188	1.5	2 535
Martinique	222	2.0	325	0.2	337
Puerto Rico	2 219	0.3	3 675	3.4	4 747
Surinam	215	3.0	388	2.7	527
Trinidad & Tobago	636	2.5	1 168	1.4	1 337
Windward Is.[b]	273	2.0	409	1.4	466
Other Caribbean[c]	396	1.7	805	2.1	984
Tropical South America					
Bolivia	2 766	2.1	5 570	2.7	7 314
Brazil	52 842	3.1	122 320	2.3	153 171
Colombia	11 597	2.9	25 794	2.2	31 820
Ecuador	3 307	2.8	8 021	3.1	10 949
Paraguay	1 371	2.7	3 168	3.0	4 231
Peru	7 988	2.3	17 625	2.8	23 355
Venezuela	5 139	3.8	15 620	3.3	21 284
Temperate South America					
Argentina	17 150	2.0	27 036	1.2	30 277
Chile	6 091	2.0	11 104	1.7	13 061
Uruguay	2 194	1.4	2 924	0.8	3 166

[a] The smaller populations of the Caribbean basin, including Belize and the Panama Canal Zone, are presented in table 34.
[b] Comprising Dominica, Grenada, St Lucia and St Vincent and the Grenadines. See table 34 for details.
[c] Comprising Antigua, Bahamas, British Virgin Islands, Cayman Islands, Montserrat, Netherlands Antilles, St Kitts, Nevis, Anguilla, Turks and Caicos, and the US Virgin Islands. See table 34.
[d] United Nations projections based on 1980 data and recent trends.
Source: United Nations.

The temperate countries made up only one-sixth of the continent's total population at the end of the Second World War. In the early 1980s these three countries stand at one ninth of the total. The Caribbean's share of the total has been falling too. Cuba, which held half of the archipelago's population, has been losing ground over the last three decades, although the dramatic upsurge of the Dominican Republic and Haiti has partly counterbalanced the shrinking of the Caribbean's percentage of the continent's total population.

While projections of future population have often proved inaccurate and certainly cannot tell us much about next century, current trends do point to further expansion of Middle America's population to possibly about 28 per cent of the total by the end of this century, with Mexico alone still accounting for 20 per cent. Tropical Latin America probably will not grow in the same proportion, going no further than 56 per cent of the total, with Brazil standing at one-third. The Caribbean population will continue to shrink in relation to the rest, down to less than one-tenth with Cuba's decelerating population growth setting the pace. Temperate South America is on the way to being only 9 per cent of the continent's total. Thus approximately four-fifths of the total population will be living in tropical Latin America and Middle America by the year 2000, according to current trends.

Density

In 1950, the Caribbean was the most thickly populated region of Latin America, as table 32 shows. Haiti had 112 people per sq km. Population pressure was even higher in some of the smaller countries, particularly Barbados with 490 per sq km and Puerto Rico with 249 per sq km.

The second most densely settled region was Middle America, particularly El Salvador. By 1980, the population density of El Salvador, 224, had far outdistanced any other Middle American country and is now denser than Haiti and indeed most of the Caribbean, apart from Martinique (295), Trinidad and Tobago (228), Barbados (609) and Puerto Rico (413) which will probably remain the most heavily populated until next century. Cuba is far more sparsely populated than any of the other larger islands. It was already in a demographic class of its own, with low birth rates and slow population growth, long before Fidel Castro took power.

Population densities in South America remain low, Colombia and Ecuador, the densest South American countries, have only 23 and 28 people per sq km, respectively. Ecuador will forge ahead but probably not go beyond about 50 per sq km by the end of the century. Colombia's population growth is slackening, however, and, like Venezuela, should not exceed 30–35 per sq km by the year 2000.

The low population densities of South America can be explained in part by the vast tracts of rainforest around the Amazon and Orinoco, the large stretches of the Andes which are not arable plateaux, the major fraction of the temperate countries in the wastelands of Patagonia, and the high percentage of land devoted to cattle grazing in Brazil, Venezuela and the temperate countries.

On the whole, it cannot be said that Latin America is overpopulated, relative to area and resources. El Salvador, Haiti and the Dominican Republic are the exceptions, because they lack emigration outlets and a good mineral resource base and because their birth rates continue to be high. Another exception is north-east Brazil, with its 35 million inhabitants living on inadequate resources. The Caribbean islands of the British Commonwealth do have the problem of no longer being able to siphon off population growth to Great Britain. Population growth in these islands is clearly falling, in any

Table. 32 Population densities: countries and regions (inhabitants per sq km)

	1950	1980	1990	2000
Latin America total	8	18	22	28
Middle America	14	37	49	62
Costa Rica	17	44	55	67
El Salvador	91	224	303	407
Guatemala	27	67	89	117
Honduras	13	33	46	62
Mexico	14	35	47	59
Nicaragua	9	21	29	40
Panama	11	25	31	37
Caribbean	71	129	154	182
Barbados	490	609	677	742
Cuba	51	85	92	102
Dominican Republic	48	122	155	191
Guadeloupe	118	185	190	199
Guyana	2	4	5	6
Haiti	112	209	271	355
Jamaica	128	200	231	262
Martinique	201	295	305	329
Puerto Rico	249	413	534	597
Surinam	1	2	3	4
Trinidad & Tobago	124	228	261	289
Windward Islands[a]	130	195	222	251
Other Caribbean[a]	23	47	58	68
Tropical South America	6	14	18	22
Bolivia	3	5	7	9
Brazil	6	14	18	22
Colombia	10	23	28	33
Ecuador	12	28	39	51
Paraguay	3	8	10	13
Peru	6	14	18	24
Venezuela	6	17	23	30
Temperate South America	7	11	13	14
Argentina	6	10	11	12
Chile	8	15	17	20
Uruguay	12	17	18	20

[a] See table 31, notes b and c, for details.
Source: United Nations.

Table 33. Rural–urban distribution of population: trends 1950–90

	1950 % Urban	1950–8 % Annual urban growth	1980 % Urban	1980–5 % Annual urban growth	1990[a] % Urban
Latin America total	41	4.6	65	3.3	71
Middle America[b]	40	4.7	61	3.9	67
Costa Rica	34	4.4	43	3.5	49
El Salvador	37	3.2	41	3.8	46
Guatemala	31	3.7	39	4.1	44
Honduras	18	5.8	36	5.4	44
Mexico	43	4.9	67	3.8	73
Nicaragua	36	4.3	53	4.4	60
Panama[b]	36	4.2	54	3.4	61
Caribbean[b]	34	3.0	51	3.0	56
Barbados	34	1.3	39	2.1	44
Cuba	49	2.9	65	1.4	71
Dominican Republic	24	5.5	51	4.2	60
Guadeloupe	42	1.6	44	1.3	49
Guyana	30	2.3	22	2.5	24
Haiti	12	4.2	25	4.9	32
Jamaica	30	2.9	41	2.8	47
Martinique	28	5.9	66	1.6	75
Puerto Rico	41	1.2	71	4.5	78
Surinam	47	3.1	45	3.1	48
Trinidad & Tobago	23	2.2	22	2.4	25
Tropical South America	36	5.5	65	3.5	72
Bolivia	20	3.8	33	4.4	39
Brazil	36	5.7	65	3.4	72
Colombia	37	5.6	70	3.2	77
Ecuador	28	4.9	45	4.4	51
Paraguay	35	3.0	39	4.0	44
Peru	36	5.1	67	3.9	75
Venezuela	53	6.2	83	3.8	88
Temperate South America	65	3.2	82	1.7	85
Argentina	65	3.2	82	1.6	86
Chile	58	3.6	81	2.2	85
Uruguay	78	1.7	84	1.0	86

[a] United Nations estimates based on trends up to 1980.
[b] Belize and the Panama Canal Zone are discussed separately, together with other small Caribbean populations. See table 34.
Source: United Nations.

event, as family planning has become widespread since the mid-1960s. Rapid mass urbanization has taken much of the direct population pressure off the land in almost all countries: Haiti is the glaring exception.

Rural–urban distribution

The concentration of rural–urban migrants in vast squatter settlements in and around the cities in recent decades has been one of the most conspicuous manifestations of modernization in all Latin American and Caribbean countries. They had been predominantly rural up to the 1950s, with the exception of Argentina, Chile, Uruguay and Venezuela which had already developed large primate cities which served simultaneously as capital and principal seaport.

While important rural majorities persist in several of the poorer countries, Latin America as a whole has shifted from a continent largely peopled by villagers to a continent with the majority concentrated in huge metropolitan centres. Certainly the rapidity of the post-war urbanization of Latin America and the size of its great cities make it more urban than Africa or Asia. Of the world's ten cities of 10 million or more inhabitants in 1980, four are in Latin America: Mexico City (15 million), São Paulo (13.5 million), Rio de Janeiro (10.7 million) and Greater Buenos Aires (10.1 million). Bogotá has already passed the 5 million mark, as will Lima–El Callao by the mid-1980s. Mexico City will probably exceed 20 million before 1990, followed closely by São Paulo.

Rural–rural movement has not been a major component of population redistribution. In particular parts of particular countries, these flows have been important where lowland areas

Contemporary size and distribution of population

were made attractive by the elimination of malaria, the construction of roads and the introduction of new agricultural techniques such as irrigation. Yet the larger highland–lowland migrations to newly opened-up agricultural areas in Bolivia, Ecuador and Mexico have been dwarfed by the master trend toward metropolitan agglomeration. The large movement from the arid lands of north-eastern Brazil to the factory farms of São Paulo's rural hinterland is unique.

The Caribbean has remained the least urbanized of the regions. While the temperate countries and Venezuela have stayed ahead of the other countries in the continuing rural–urban shift, the rest have rapidly followed suit over the last three or four decades as this profound transformation swept across the continent. By 1980, the rural population had shrunk to a minority of the inhabitants of several countries, notably Brazil and Mexico, the demographic giants of the continent, as well as Colombia, Cuba, the Dominican Republic, Martinique, Nicaragua, Panama, Peru and Puerto Rico. The continent is now two-thirds urban. Urbanization in the Caribbean does still lag behind the other regions, but half the archipelago's inhabitants now live in towns and cities.

This era of immense rural–urban population redistribution is drawing to a close: henceforth the great majority of Latin Americans will be urban born; indeed a large and growing fraction is being raised in large metropolitan areas.

The pace of urbanization is likely to slow down towards the end of the 1980s, mainly because the reservoir of potential rural migrants to the towns and cities will have shrunk. Moreover, the city-born population is itself now growing more slowly. Up to the 1970s, the birth rates in the towns and cities had been boosted by the continuing influx of countrywomen. Also, the natural increase of the city-born population had been rising in previous decades because the urban death rates were then still declining. At present very little improvement can be expected in urban death rates because they are close to the minimum possible under foreseeable public health conditions.

Thus, by 1990, probably some 71 per cent of the continent's people will be living in urban areas. In percentage terms Venezuela is well on the way to being the most urbanized country to the north of Argentina, Chile and Uruguay, where little more than one-tenth of the population will still be rural at the end of this decade.

In 1950, the countries which had been slowest to urbanize were Honduras in Middle America, Haiti, the Dominican Republic, Guyana, and Trinidad and Tobago in the Caribbean, and Bolivia and Ecuador in tropical South America. Costa Rica, Guatemala and El Salvador were also predominantly rural.

Half of the Caribbean population is still rural. Guyana and Trinidad and Tobago have become less urban so that Haiti, despite its gradual tempo of urbanization, has a larger fraction in its towns and cities. Neither Guyana nor Trinidad and Tobago can be

Table 34. Small populations of the Caribbean basin (1980 population and 1980–5 growth rates[a])

Areas with no more than a quarter of a million inhabitants	Population thousands	Annual growth rate[a]
Antigua	75	1.85
Bahamas	241	1.85
Belize	162	2.53
British Virgin Islands	14	1.85
Cayman Islands	17	1.85
Dominica	83	1.15
Guyane (French Guiana)	62	1.55
Grenada	111	0.88
Monserrat	11	1.85
Netherlands Antilles	256	1.84
Panama Canal Zone	31	0.66
St Kitts/Nevis/Anguilla	74	1.85
St Lucia	118	1.13
St Vincent and Grenadines	97	0.93
Turks and Caicos	6	1.84
US Virgin Islands	111	1.85

[a] Estimates for 1980–5 projected from last decade's rates, assuming that American, Dutch and French areas will continue to have unrestricted emigration to their metropoles and assuming severely restricted emigration to Britain.
Source: United Nations.

expected to urbanize much more rapidly during the present decade: the East Indian population in the villages continues to have relatively large families and there is little overflow to the cities; instead there is semi-urban ribbon development across these countries as the villages merge along the roadsides.

In tropical South America, Bolivia and Paraguay, the two poorest countries with no seaports to focus agglomeration, have the lowest urbanization.

Present trends imply that Costa Rica, Guatemala, Honduras and El Salvador will still have half or more of their people in rural areas in 1990. In the Caribbean, Guyana, Haiti and Trinidad and Tobago will retain two-thirds and more of their people in the villages. Bolivia and Paraguay are urbanizing more rapidly but will remain predominantly rural.

The smallest populations

Belize has the most rapid current growth, but, like Guyane, has a vast area which could be opened up to absorb double its population. Most of the other rapidly growing populations in table 34 have real problems of population pressure because they are ex-British-colonial and their emigration outlet in Great Britain is closed. However, these territories are already turning to intensive family planning programmes which have been very successful among their larger neighbours such as Barbados, Puerto Rico and Trinidad and Tobago since the 1960s. By the late 1970s the Windward Islands, from Dominica to Grenada, had quite slow growth rates due to a combination of continuing emigration (albeit reduced) and family planning. The slowest population growth is found in the Panama Canal Zone because, on the eve of its pending incorporation into Panama, a large fraction of its residents left for the United States.

JSMacD

Current ethnic profiles and Amerindian survivals

The survival of the original inhabitants of what has become Latin America can be gauged by assessing the vitality of their traditional cultures. Key features of Amerindian cultures are, of course, their languages of which more than 1650 different ones have been discovered. This multiplicity of languages makes it possible to assert with some confidence that the Spanish and Portuguese conquerors of the New World did not intrude upon a homogeneous culture but upon many different ways of life and, indeed, that they encountered many ethnic types within a Mongoloid race now popularly known as 'Indian'. Evidence of the persistence of this aboriginal American population has often been sought in the modern national censuses of the countries of Latin America and also in the detailed descriptions of tribal and peasant societies within these countries. National census takers have attempted to differentiate between members of the population by using as criteria their appearance and the languages they habitually speak. The problems in this approach are obvious: judgements as to the skin-colour of a respondent, for example, may be subjective, arbitrary or unrelated to the survival of his culture; on the other hand, whilst the speaking of an Indian language may be evidence of the persistence of other aspects of the related culture, a shift to Spanish or Portuguese speech by a full-blooded Amerindian does not necessarily denote a surrender of self to an Iberian way of life. The most useful linguistic evidence derives from national censuses which have been able to distinguish between those speakers of native languages who spoke no Spanish or Portuguese, i.e. what one might call the 'hard-core' of Amerindian survival, and those bilingual Amerindians who spoke both an American and Iberian language, i.e. those who had taken the first step away from a purely native culture.

Further attempts were made, by Mexico, Peru and Ecuador, to differentiate the population on the grounds of their material culture. All respondents to the census, for example, were asked if they customarily ate maize bread, an Amerindian characteristic, or wheaten bread, a European trait. The replies suggested that native cultural patterns have remained much more widespread than a purely linguistic count would lead one to suppose. Yet even this seemingly much more searching survey method remains open to question: for instance, peasant respondents to a census are quite as capable as the census taker of perceiving the status differences which may be made between, say, those who claim to wear sandals (Amerindians) and those who claim to wear shoes (Europeans) and are liable to present answers which will suit their own social aspirations. Thus even delicate soundings of the cultural depths of a population may be doomed to underestimate the values and norms it

really maintains. The fraternal mood of post-colonial Latin America, moreover, has tended to frown on status and ethnic distinctions despite the reality of frequent repression; increasingly, governments find it ideologically inconvenient to differentiate between their citizens, which does not help analysts assess the likely future fate of the continent's aboriginal populations. There are two propositions in the literature about them: some say that they will all slowly lose their identity under the weight of incoming migrants and of their alien cultures; others say that the Amerindians are the fastest-growing element in the fastest-growing population in the world. What is the reality?

Historical background

Any assessment of the current significance of the Amerindian element in Latin America must start with the native American populations before the Spanish and Portuguese discovery and colonization of the continent. They were not evenly spread, but concentrated in and around two agricultural empires in what now are Mexico and Peru, with thin dispersals in the central forests of the Amazon basin and on the savannas of what are now Argentina in the south and the Guianas in the north. The shock of military conquest was to reduce these figures very drastically, not so much due to deliberate slaughter but due to contact with the endemic diseases carried by the Europeans to which the Amerindians had not been able to develop any hereditary immunity. By the seventeenth century the aboriginal populations had begun to recover but they had, by now, to confront successive waves of migrants from two directions: Europeans, in search of lands upon which to settle, and Africans, brought in as slaves. Once again the demographic dispersal of these incomers was uneven: for three centuries the Africans were to take over the role of labourers in the islands, and in the coastal areas of the Caribbean and of north-eastern Brazil; whilst the Europeans sought landed property in the more favoured and accessible agricultural and herding valleys, extending and increasing their hold on arable and grazing land as the opportunity offered. The physical survival of the Amerindians in this period of colonization depended partly upon their ability to compete with African labour on the tropical coastlines and partly upon their determination to hold on to their traditional lands. Certainly a demographic catastrophe, which was immediate and almost complete, overtook the natives of the Antilles: before mainland Mexico was pacified, the large island which is now Cuba was virtually depopulated and today in the whole of the West Indies there are not thought to be more than 800 Amerindians. Similarly, on the plains of the River Plate region the Amerindians and their cowboy descendants fought the encroaching immigrant herdsmen until well into the nineteenth century, but were usually defeated or absorbed. Conversely, in the inhospitable northern deserts and mountain ranges of Mexico,

Current ethnic profiles and Amerindian survivals

peoples like the Yaqui and the Tarahumara and, in inaccessible recesses of the mountains and forests, peoples like the Araucanos were able to maintain their traditional ways of life. By far the most successful physical and cultural continuity with their Aztec and Inca forebears has been preserved by the populations of the great heartlands of Amerindian civilization, the mainly Nahuatl- and Maya-speakers of Mexico and Guatemala on the one hand, and the mainly Quechua- and Aymara-speakers of Peru, Bolivia and Ecuador on the other hand. The weight of sheer numbers has had much to do with the persistence over time of these two classic groupings, the one bestriding the isthmus of Central America and the other holding the mountain ranges of western South America. The early protection of the Indian afforded by the Roman Catholic Church may just have been enough to help the survivors through the aftermath of the conquest. Thereafter a paternalistic Spanish crown attempted to mitigate the effect of subjugation upon the indigenous populations by 'commending' their Indian souls to the care of the Spanish landholders and by appointing local governors with specific instructions to protect the natives and to promote their welfare. Unfortunately these Spanish *encomenderos* and *corregidores de indios* were more enthusiastic about enriching themselves than justifying their custodianship. However, they lived among the subject peoples and the descendants of the two groups have remained together ever since; from this close association over four centuries of Europeans

and Amerindians has arisen the classic Latin American of today. In more modern times the sympathy and encouragement of the agencies of some national governments have facilitated a revival of self-respect and pride in their distinctiveness of today's representatives of great cultural traditions. The populations of today's Latin America are growing apace and a correlation has been observed between low rates of growth, say between 1.5 per cent and 2.2 per cent, and small concentrations of Amerindians, as occurs for example in Argentina and Chile, whereas most Latin American countries have much higher growth rates, between 2.4 and 3.5 per cent, and many of these have large concentrations of Amerindians, for example Bolivia, Ecuador, Guatemala, Mexico and Peru. This reasoning has led some writers to suggest that the demographic explosion in the Latin American part of the whole continent is currently being led by the 'red man' whose home it was before it also became the home of the white man and the black man. Accepting this thesis of an Amerindian-led human increase, one can postulate a dynamic Indian population of over 23 million today for the Spanish-speaking part of the whole continent. The circular chart shows the proportions of Amerindians who live in each country; these segments are based on figures projected forward to 1980 by means of the most recently known rates of growth for each country. There are two significant omissions from this chart: the estimated 150,000 and 16,000 Amerindians in Brazil and the Guianas respectively. Native cohesion in these countries is reported to be decreasing, so the chart is restricted to Spanish-speaking countries.

Ethnic profiles

In Latin America, the powerful argument of 23 million recognized Amerindians serves to demonstrate indigenous survival; as relevant are four centuries of miscegenation. It is ethnocentric, or at least anachronistic, to believe that the offspring of unions between Europeans and other races will always identify with the former. Assuming for the moment that a child of mixed parentage has some sense of belonging to both, what is the magnitude of this factor in respect of Amerindians? What is the proportion of persons of mixed ethnic descent, generally known as mestizos, in the modern populations of Latin America? Is it significant anyway? At this juncture it is necessary to emphasize that the term 'mestizo' is an analytical one only: it is unusual for a person to so describe himself; it is, however, important for the debate about Indian survival to be able to gauge partial survival as well. In the history of the transmission of Indian culture, the mestizo is the muted witness. If one looks at each geographical area of Latin America in turn, the clear ethnic profiles of the continent can be discerned. Of the River Plate, out of a population of over 30 million today, Argentina counts a mere 175,000 as 'Indian', although it has been estimated that perhaps 20 per cent of the remainder are of mixed European and Amerindian

AMERINDIAN SURVIVAL

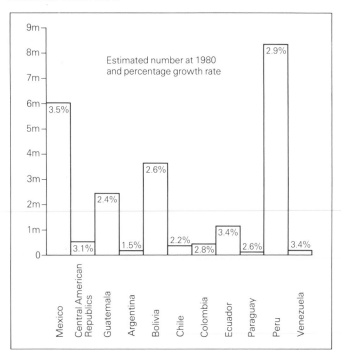

Estimated number at 1980 and percentage growth rate

CURRENT ETHNIC PROFILES

	Amerindians	Europeans	Africans/mulattoes	Mestizos
ARGENTINA	>1%	97%	—	2%
BOLIVIA	54%	14%	—	32%
BRAZIL	<1%	50%	50%	—
CHILE	5%	25%	—	70%
COLOMBIA	1%	20%	29%	50%
COSTA RICA	.5%	92%	—	7.5%
ECUADOR	40%	15%	5%	40%
EL SALVADOR	10%	1%	—	89%
GUATEMALA	54%	4%	—	42%
HONDURAS	5%	1%	2%	92%
MEXICO	10%	15%	—	75%
NICARAGUA	3%	10%	11%	76%
PANAMA	5%	14%	14%	67%
PARAGUAY	3%	20%	1%	76%
PERU	46%	12%	—	42%
URUGUAY	—	90%	2·5%	7·5%
VENEZUELA	2%	20%	8%	70%

descent; male immigrants heavily outnumbered female immigrants at first and the settlers who contested the pampas also dispossessed the Indians of their women, but between them they produced some of the cowboys of today's pampas. Out of 3 million Paraguayans, 113,000 are Amerindians and a large proportion of the remainder are adjudged mestizos. Indeed the people of Paraguay fulfil the prediction of some Latin American savants that a 'cosmic race' is emerging in their countries: a large part of the population makes use of the language of the Guaraní Indians and Spanish is spoken with a Guaraní accent. Uruguay, with a population of just over 3 million, is alleged to be 'the whitest country in Latin America' with only 5 per cent of mestizos; there are also 58,000 blacks and mulattos.

Of the Andean countries, the highest proportion of Amerindians live in Bolivia: 3,640,000 out of a total population of some 6 million; perhaps 32 per cent of the population are of mixed ethnic origin with only a vestige of African descent. Peru has a larger Amerindian element, 8,329,000 out of 18.5 million. In Andean countries citizens of mixed ethnic origin may be referred to as *cholos*, *cholitos*, or *montubios*, although these terms may occasionally also designate an urbanized Indian; they number perhaps 42 per cent of the total in Peru. In Ecuador census takers have not distinguished convincingly between Amerindians and mestizos, but there is general agreement that it is one of the most 'cosmic' nations with persons of direct European and African descent contributing at the most 20 per cent

to the total population of 8 million. Colombia has upward of 400,000 Amerindians in a total population of nearly 28 million, which otherwise is estimated to be half mestizo, with one-fifth of the population directly descended from Europeans and over a quarter descended from Africans. Chile has the smallest number of Amerindians in the Andean region, 370,000, and an insignificant number of citizens of African descent, but 70 per cent of the 12.3 million inhabitants are estimated to be of mixed European and Amerindian descent.

The giant of South America, in all senses, is Brazil. Some element of African descent is claimed for nearly half of its 123 million inhabitants. Official sources give vague and various reports of Amerindian numbers: from 45,000 to 1.2 million (with 150,000 the most popular estimate) and falling. The Amazonian coastal Tupi have been decimated, the riverine tribes in contact with Europeans driven away and Cintas Largas of the Mato Grosso ravaged by intrusive diseases. Paradoxically, ever since independence from Portugal, the offspring of unions between Portuguese and Amerindians, *caboclos*, have retained an honoured place in the romantic imagination of some Brazilians who take pride in tracing their Amerindian descent.

Venezuela lies on the north coast of South America and its population is the result of a three-way fusion of its indigenous tribes with Spanish adventurers and with African slaves, to which has

Current ethnic profiles and Amerindian survivals

Top left: Guaraní–Spanish girl from Paraguay. Above: Mulatto woman at Rio carnival. Top right: Girl of mixed black–Indian origin from Manaus, Brazil. Right: Man from north-east Brazil been added in this century a large influx of Europeans attracted by the discovery of oil. In consequence, out of a total of 15 million, one in six persons is foreign-born, so that 20 per cent of the inhabitants count as white, 8 per cent count as black, 70 per cent are 'mixed' and a mere 2 per cent are Amerindians. The three former Guianas (now including Guyana and Surinam) have comparatively small populations whose Amerindian elements are being absorbed culturally by the ethnic groups of Asian and African descent which surround them, so that these countries have most in common ethnically with the islands of the Antilles like Jamaica (2 million) and Trinidad (1.3 million), both of which have significant Asian elements. Apart from Cuba, with a total population of 10 million, three-quarters of whom are of European descent having long ago absorbed the indigenous survivors of the Spanish conquest, and Bermuda with a 40 per cent European element, the mode for the islands is to have small, predominantly black populations counted in tens or hundreds of thousands: thus 82 per cent of the English-speaking Bahamians are of African descent; as are 84 per cent of the Spanish-speaking Dominican Republic; 90 per cent and 92 per cent in Barbados and Jamaica; and virtually 100 per cent of French-speaking Haitians. In the islands, then, Amerindian language and culture were long ago extinguished.

Belize, on the Central American mainland, has often been associated with the Antilles because of the large African and small European elements among its 140,000 inhabitants, yet important indigenous groups persist there, perhaps 8000 black Caribs and 23,000 Mayas with their separate languages. Of the seven remaining countries of Central America, four face the Caribbean and these coastal lowlands have supported many people of African descent in the past who have worked on the banana plantations; hence their significant numbers in Honduras, Nicaragua and Panama, although those in Costa Rica have been absorbed into the general population: apart from some 14,000 Amerindians, the Costa Rican population is designated as entirely white. Honduras, Nicaragua and Panama have larger Amerindian nuclei, 202,000, 71,000 and 114,000 respectively, surrounded by a mestizo population which totals barely 9 million over all three nations.

The remaining Latin American countries either face away from the Caribbean, or have massive aboriginal populations, or both. In consequence, in these countries the Amerindian presence remains dominant. El Salvador has 190,000 Indians surrounded by nearly 5 million mestizos; Guatemala has 2.5 million Amerindians; and Mexico over 6 million.

Amerindian survivals

For the whole of Latin America, then, one can arrive at a figure for inhabitants positively identified as Amerindians which approximates the credible total calculated by some historical demographers

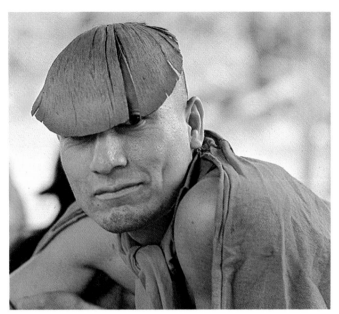

Colorado Indian from Ecuador (the name is derived from the red paint used on their bodies)

as being alive at the time of the Spanish conquest. It is not sufficient, however, to say that an Amerindian physical presence is almost back to where it was despite four centuries of attrition and depredation. Through miscegenation there have arisen many millions of Latin Americans with memories of, and potential attraction towards, a way of life which belonged to their own forebears and of which they are constantly reminded by their purely Amerindian cousins. These mestizos, numbering perhaps 120 million, often uphold the values of their Amerindian heritage, even if they do so subconsciously. Although they may have become acculturated to the life-style of the Spanish side of their ancestry in terms of dress, language, technological skill and even in terms of religion, there are aspects of their social organization which disclose the conservation of an indigenous tradition which is uniquely theirs. This tradition is, in the main, the inheritance bequeathed to them by the great agricultural civilizations of the Incas, the Mayas and the Aztecs, which often includes: the collective exploitation of land, which seems to reflect European anarchist thinking but which has developed quite separately; the ritual accumulation of life-long personal bonds, which has taken on the outward appearance of Iberian godparenthood but whose purpose often relates to purely Latin American needs; the devotion to a whole series of supernatural beings, who have Christian names but who are better understood in terms of a non-western past; the ritualized remembrance of, and hospitality towards, deceased relatives, which has more in common with Oriental ancestor-worship than with All-Souls' Day; the reverence for, and cultivation of,

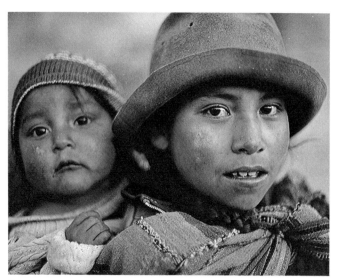

Quechua girl and child

transitory political leaders, which harks back to the pre-conquest treatment of an Inca or of a Montezuma rather than reflecting the respect due to the holder of an elective office; and so on.

We must recognize that the great nations with an organized past and with an Amerindian and mestizo present have a continental culture which is qualitatively different from that of the conquistadors who briefly impinged upon them. This culture appears hybrid only insofar as it displays an alien form and has an alien terminology; the important thing is that at its heart is an Amerindian content which is as different from any other major cultural pattern as it is ingenious. But Europeanized Mexicans and Peruvians also must recognize their own roots: there is a Brazilian saying that 'O gato que nasceu num armazém não é biscoito' ('The cat born in a store is not a biscuit'); the time has perhaps come for the biscuit to stand up and proclaim that he is not a cat either.

So, by reason of the strong inference that in many countries the Indians are not only participating in population growth but are actually leading it, and by reason of the recognition of the genetic and cultural inheritance from past Amerindians which is represented by a putative 120 million current mestizos, it is possible to claim that the survival of the Amerindians, at least in some form, is secure. That, however, should not cause one to be complacent about what is still happening to some small tribal societies, particularly in central South America, which are threatened by misguided 'emancipation', economic development and unpremeditated contact with other human beings. Paradoxically, the onrush of civilization brings more ills to non-immunized and hitherto isolated societies than it cures. The choice for governments with primitive humans in their care is a stark one: integration or reservation. If secluded and vulnerable

communities are not integrated officially and with safe deliberation, they may become integrated unofficially to their cultural and physical cost, as has already happened to the Eskimo (Inuit) and to the Australian Aborigine. If their lands are not reserved to them, these may be encroached upon and indigenous peoples may become vagrants, derelicts and dispossessed. Perhaps the most promising road being followed is in Mexico, where the Indigenist Institute brings the benefits of western civilization to the Tarahumara, to the Tzeltal, to the Mixtecs and to many others; it brings education and modern medicine and offers only gradual and voluntary integration into the wider nation. Precipitate incorporation of hunter–gatherer peoples into a state society, on the other hand, is the threatened fate of many dwellers of the Amazon region. This option, presented in the guise of emancipation, has long been recognized by the great Brazilian Indianists as a recipe for the exploitation, degradation and destruction of the very people whom government has a duty to protect.

PEBC

Further reading

D. C. Chaplin, *Population Policies and Growth in Latin America* (Lexington, 1971)

R. Darcy, *The Americas and Civilization* (London, 1971)

S. H. Davis, *Victims of the Miracle: Development of the Indians of Brazil* (Cambridge, 1977)

C. McEvedy and R. Jones, *Atlas of World Population History* (London, 1978)

M. Mörner, *Race Mixture in the History of Latin America* (Boston, Mass., 1967)

N. Sánchez-Albornoz, *The Population of Latin America* (Berkeley, 1974)

HISTORY

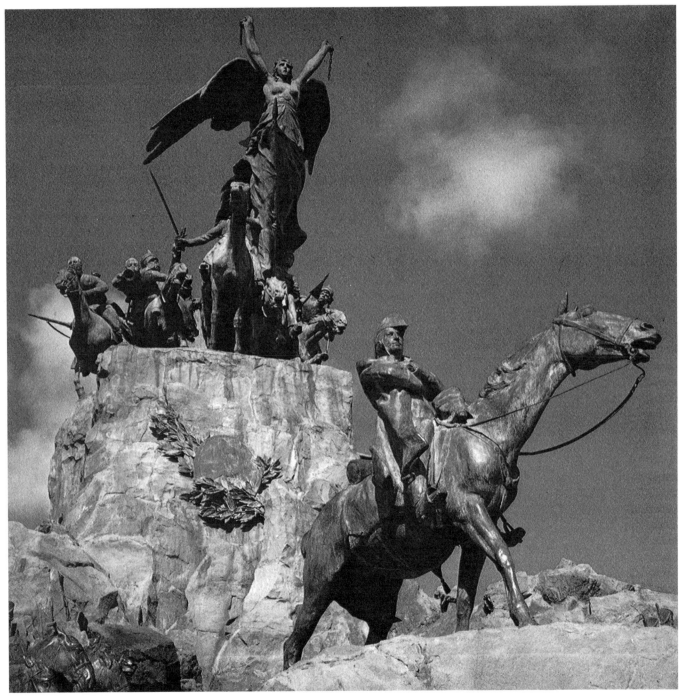

La Gloria monument to General José de San Martín in Mendoza,
Argentina

The first human cultures

Origins

In physical appearance, blood grouping, and the form and arrangement of the teeth, the American Indians demonstrate their origin in eastern Asia. The initial colonization of America took place during the final glaciation, at a time when much of the earth's precipitation remained on land in the form of ice sheets, causing a fall in sea level which converted the Bering Strait into a temporary land bridge between Siberia and Alaska.

The precise date of man's arrival in America is still uncertain. The first immigrants were few in number, mobile in their habits, and have left little trace of their presence. The oldest archaeological sites so far discovered in Latin America are in Mexico, at El Cedral (San Luis Potosí) where stone tools and extinct animals are at least 30,000 years old, and at Tlapacoya (Puebla) with lakeshore camp sites of around 20,000 BC. In South America a handful of dubious artifacts from the deepest strata at Pikimachay (Flea Cave) in the Peruvian Andes are dated *c.* 18,000 BC, but there is no reliable evidence until the Late Pleistocene (13,000–9000 BC) when sites suddenly become abundant.

To this period belongs Taima Taima (Venezuela) with a dismembered mastodon skeleton and a date of at least 11,000 BC. Further south, the more recent deposits at Pikimachay are dated around 12,000 BC, and Guitarrero Cave, in the Peruvian Andes, falls somewhere within the eleventh millennium BC. By 10,000 BC, at latest, man had reached south-east Brazil (the Arroio dos Fósseis and Alice Boër sites) and had penetrated as far south as Los Toldos in Patagonia.

During the closing millennia of the Pleistocene Ice Age, all of Latin America, except perhaps the Amazon basin, was populated by small bands of foragers who lived by hunting game and collecting wild plant foods. This is the era of the spectacular mammoth-kill sites in the Basin of Mexico, though evidence from cave shelters indicates that the bulk of the meat supply came from smaller animals, including rodents and birds. At the kill site of Tagua Tagua, Chile, charcoal fragments in the archaeological stratum suggest the use of fire-drives.

Occupation was not exclusively in caves and rock shelters. Open-air camp sites are documented by scatters of stone tools, while chipping debris indicates the localities where the raw material was quarried. Usually all evidence of structures has disappeared, but at Monteverde (south-central Chile) a habitation zone of some 3000 sq m became covered by a layer of peat which has preserved organic materials of 12,000–10,000 BC, or even older. This site gives an idea of what has been lost under less favourable conditions. Archaeologists have unearthed implements of bone, wood and stone, as well as a structure with wooden posts and several hearths. Nearby were five butchered mastodon skeletons and evidence of fresh-water shellfish and plant foods.

By the late Pleistocene, distinct regional traditions of stone working had emerged, each with its characteristic technology and range of forms. Ignoring the variability in the shape of the tools, and concentrating more on their function, we can identify spear and dart points, knives and cutting tools, scrapers for whittling wood or cleaning hides, and a range of artifacts used for engraving, chopping, mashing, pounding and hammering. Guitarrero Cave has also yielded fragments of basketry and netting, but the archaeological record of this early period remains biased and incomplete.

The beginnings of agriculture and village life

Between 8000 and 7000 BC the Pleistocene Ice Age came to an end. Mammoth, mastodon, horse, ground sloth and several other large mammals became extinct. Ice caps and glaciers retreated. Sea levels rose to approximately their present heights, drowning the old Pleistocene coastlands and encroaching as much as 70–100 km in parts of Peru, with consequent loss of all archaeological sites in this area. These climatic changes brought with them changes in vegetation, until gradually the modern landscape began to emerge. In these new conditions, techniques of food procurement had to be modified and the first experiments with farming took place.

Between 8500 and 2000 BC American Indians brought into cultivation a wide range of crops. Of these, maize, potatoes and manioc/cassava became worldwide staples after the European conquest of America in the sixteenth century, and many others (beans, pumpkins and squashes, sweet potatoes, peanuts, chili peppers, pineapples, tomatoes, avocados, tobacco and cacao, or chocolate) are widespread in the Old World today.

By comparison, animal resources were scanty. Mexico has contributed the turkey to international gastronomy, but it was only in the Andes, where the ancestors of the domestic llama and alpaca were native, that stock raising became important with the development of herding and pastoral economies on the high *puna* grasslands. This process of domestication began as early as 4500–4000 BC. At much the same time, in Peru and Colombia, the domestic guinea pig became a cheap, and easy to rear, source of meat.

The figure below, which is typical of the general pattern in all regions, demonstrates that agriculture was adopted only slowly. There was no single centre of origin. The people of each region experimented with the plants and animals that were locally available, and which they had already collected or hunted for thousands of years. At first the cultivated crops were no more than a supplement in a diet based on game and wild plants. Gradually, however, in response to new selective pressures and to genetic manipulation by man, improved races of plants were developed

MAIN ARCHAEOLOGICAL SITES

Tamaulipas
El Cedral
Santa Luisa
Zohapilco
Tehuacán
Oaxaca
Cuello
Angí
Lake Gatún
Cueva de los Ladrones
Taima Taima

Vegas

Huaricoto
La Galgada
Kotosh
Guitarrero Cave
Rio Seco
Aspero
El Paraiso
Piedra Parada
Asia
Pikimachay (Ayacucho)

Alice Boër

Arroio dos
Fósseis

Tagua Tagua

Los Toldos

A note on the dates

For the prehistoric period, before the earliest written inscriptions, dates are based on radiocarbon measurements of organic materials from archaeological deposits. All such dates are quoted in 'radiocarbon years', which are not precisely equivalent to 'calendar' years. For the period under discussion, the radiocarbon technique consistently gives figures that are too recent. At 1500 BC (in 'true' or 'historical' terms) the discrepancy is only some 300 years, but by 5000 BC the radiocarbon dates are about one thousand years too young. All figures quoted are based on radiocarbon measurements, but detailed conversion charts can be found in the journals *Antiquity* (vol. 49, no. 196, pp. 251–66, Dec. 1975) and *Radiocarbon* (vol. 24, pt 2, pp. 103–50, 1982).

PLANT AND ANIMAL DOMESTICATION IN THE TEHUACAN VALLEY, CENTRAL MEXICO, 10,000 BC TO THE SPANISH CONQUEST, BASED IN EVIDENCE FROM ARCHAEOLOGICAL EXAMINATION

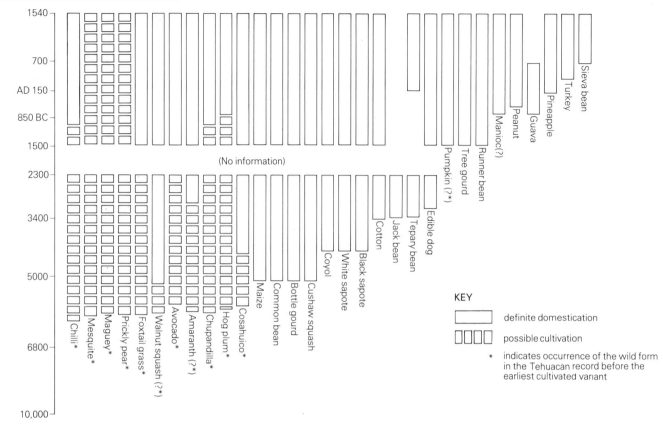

from the less productive wild forms. Useful species were transferred from one region to another, and more and more effort was devoted to gardening at the expense of foraging. New food-processing techniques were discovered (e.g. freeze-drying the bitter Andean potato to convert it into storable *chuño*, or the washing of certain seeds to leach out toxins), and irrigation increased productivity still further, until eventually the balance changed, and farming came to provide the bulk of the diet.

It seems that the 'agricultural revolution' was not a sudden revolution at all, and can be explained without recourse to population pressure, environmental change, or any other 'prime movers'. Instead, the change from foraging to farming can be seen not as a matter of conscious planning for thousands of years ahead, but rather as the cumulative outcome of a series of short-term decisions whose long-term consequences could not have been appreciated at the time. This process of agricultural development took place in many different environments and, within the general pattern, each region has its own individual history.

Some of the most detailed evidence comes from highland areas with dry caves in which foodstuffs are preserved. These have been investigated in the Ayacucho basin of Peru and in the Mexican states of Tamaulipas, Puebla and Oaxaca. In these regions the early post-Pleistocene inhabitants were omnivorous foragers who organized their lives around the seasonal harvests of wild plants and the movements of animals. Desiccated human faeces contain grass seeds, roasted maguey cactus, roots, chili seeds, and fragments of worms, grubs, snails and grasshoppers. For much of the year the community was split into small bands of only a few families, and the corresponding archaeological sites include winter hunting camps and caves occupied seasonally in localities where collection of wild plants could be combined with small-scale cultivation. During the months of abundance, camp sites are bigger and the scattered bands came together in larger groups. In arid zones of this kind, settled village life was impossible without effective agriculture, and it was not until 2500–1500 BC that villages of pottery-using farmers made their first appearance.

In the moist tropics of America preservation is poor, and the evidence suggests a greater emphasis on root crops and on forest products such as palm nuts. From Amazonia we have no information before 2000 BC, but studies of pollen grains and phytoliths (silica skeletons of plant cells) from deep cores at Lake Gatún (Panama) show what sort of thing must have been happening in the rainforests during these critical millennia. Human intervention first appears at Lake Gatún around 2800 BC, with small-scale forest clearance and shifting cultivation which included maize. By the time of Christ, manioc was also grown.

A major controversy surrounds the origin of cultivated maize. Some botanists believe that its ancestor is a wild form of maize which is now extinct. Others maintain that maize derives from its closest living wild relative, a weedy grass (with edible seeds) called teosinte. Teosinte does not grow south of Honduras and, if this plant gave rise to all known races of maize, the implication must be that Mesoamerica is the region where maize cultivation began. If, on the other hand, the ancestral form is a wild maize, South America comes into contention as a possible source of origin.

Leaving aside the problem of origins, there is agreement that maize is a highland plant, not initially adapted to tropical lowlands. Finds of maize cobs, or maize phytoliths, at lowland sites show surprising antiquity: 2000 BC at Cuello (Belize), the fifth millennium BC at Cueva de los Ladrones (Panama), and around 6000 BC at the sites of the Vegas culture in coastal Ecuador. These dates indicate a long period of genetic adaptation, which in turn pushes back the age of the first experimental cultivation in the highland centres of origin.

The consequences of the changeover to agricultural life were not the same everywhere. In dry inland areas settled life had to await the development of high-yield crops and efficient farming technology; elsewhere, and especially in coastal, riverine or lake-shore environments providing food throughout the year, sedentary life preceded effective farming. Zohapilco, beside the lake that once filled the Basin of Mexico, had year-round occupation as early as 5500 BC, and Santa Luisa (Veracruz) was probably a riverine village by 3000 BC. The huge shell mound at Angí (Nicaragua) is dated 5650–3650 BC and may represent an early sedentary occupation of the Caribbean coast.

The most precocious development of settled life during the pre-ceramic period was in coastal Peru. This desert coast has virtually no rainfall and no indigenous crop plants, but the waters of the Humboldt current are rich in fish, birds, sea mammals and shellfish. These wild resources, supplemented by a little cultivation of introduced crop plants, allowed permanent villages to develop soon after 3000 BC.

By 2500, canal irrigation made farming more productive, and maize was introduced from the Andes to the littoral. Farming villages have been discovered all along the coast, and a few sites were already developing into regional centres of government. El Paraíso covered more than 50 hectares, with 3000–4000 inhabitants living in complexes of masonry rooms whose construction required some 100,000 tons of rock. Sites like Aspero and Piedra Parada had massive public buildings on terraced platforms, dominating the dwellings of the ordinary people. Some cemeteries of this period were large (2500 graves at Rio Seco), and at Asia, on the south coast, there was a clear distinction between rich and poor burials. Late pre-ceramic society was neither homogeneous nor egalitarian, and was controlled by some form of organized government, religious or secular, with the power to call out labour for public works. Andean Peru was also participating in these developments, with temple sites at La Galgada on the Pacific slope, Huaricoto in the high Andes, and Kotosh on the eastern side of the watershed.

These three Andean sites, and several of the coastal ones, continued in occupation after 2000–1800 BC, when pottery was introduced – and the future pattern of Peruvian civilization now becomes clearly recognizable.

WB

Pre-Columbian Mesoamerica

When he entered the city of Tenochtitlán with Hernán Cortés on 8 November 1519, Bernal Díaz del Castillo, the conquistador and chronicler, was astonished by the opulence and beauty of the Aztec capital. In fact he was witnessing the end of an extraordinary episode in human development which, in a mere four millennia, had transformed man's conditions of life from primitive village agriculturism to a degree of urban concentration and sophistication unsurpassed by societies of comparable technology elsewhere in the world. The area where this occurred is known as Mesoamerica, a term with both geographical and cultural connotations. It covers central and southern Mexico, Guatemala, Belize and the northern parts of El Salvador and Honduras. Here man has found the conditions and resources favourable for the creation of cultures which, despite regional and evolutionary variations, display common characteristics ranging from diet and domestic architecture to mythology and religion. Here, at the end of the archaic period man formed small settled communities by the edge of lake, river and sea and began the experiment in sedentary living that led to Tenochtitlán.

The history of that experiment is conventionally divided into three phases which, borrowing from Old World archaeology, are called Pre-classic (or Formative), Classic and the Post-classic. Recently an alternative terminology, free of analogies with the

Recently excavated remains of the Templo Mayor in the Aztec city of Tenochtitlán, near the colonial cathedral in Mexico City

small hamlets of one-roomed houses built of poles and thatch, with daub-and-wattle walls and compressed-earth floors, often on a low earth platform. Their inhabitants cultivated maize and other crops domesticated in the archaic period and they supplemented their diet by hunting and fishing. Their tools were of stone or of perishable materials. Burials with offerings occurred and structures with stucco floors may have constituted a simple form of public architecture. Social organization was simple, but elites and site ranking appear early in the archaeological record as does regional diversity, most clearly expressed by pottery variability; ecological conditions must also have produced wide variations in subsistence patterns.

About 1400 BC a striking change occurred throughout much of Mesoamerica when the Olmec (whose early type site, San Lorenzo, was located in the tropical lowlands of south-eastern Veracruz) imposed its distinctive style of pottery and decorative motifs. The evidence of Olmec influence stretching from the highlands of central Mexico to the Pacific coastal plain of El Salvador persists for some 500 years but has not yet been fully explained. Military conquest, proselytism and trade exploitation may all have played a part, but the location of Olmec settlements at key intersections of trade routes suggests that the security of an Olmec trade network

Gigantic Olmec head carved in basalt

eastern Mediterranean and more suggestive of the complex ebb and flow of Mesoamerican cultural development, has been devised. In this usage three 'horizon' periods, in each of which the influence of one dominant culture – Olmec, Teotihuacán or Aztec – extended over the whole of Mesoamerica, are alternated with 'intermediate' periods of greater diversity when regional influences prevailed.

Our knowledge of the early stages of this process is derived entirely from archaeology and the physical sciences, and is predictably sketchy. As written records in the form of stone inscriptions become a significant source of information during the first millennium AD, detail can be filled in up to the time when native manuscripts and Spanish chroniclers provide a full, if occasionally garbled and conflicting, history of the last centuries before the conquest.

As a starting point, it is convenient to take the introduction of pottery (although some sedentary settlements in Mesoamerica date back to the pre-ceramic period). The first primitive fired-clay figurine, found in a hearth at Zohapilco, a lacustrine site in the Valley of Mexico, has been carbon-dated to about 2300 BC, but it is only some centuries later that domestic pottery emerges. It is simple and undecorated but the lack of a truly primitive antecedent has led to doubts whether pottery-making was of local invention or was imported from South America. It is safe to say, however, that early in the second millennium BC several different wares came into use in the central highlands and in the semi-tropical lowlands of the Pacific and Atlantic coasts.

Archaeological evidence suggests that population density at that time was very low and that seasonal nomadism was only gradually transformed into a sedentary life. The earliest settlements were

PRE–COLUMBIAN MESOAMERICA

Gulf of Mexico

KEY
▲ Ancient site
● Modern city

0   320 km
0   200 miles

secular arts are manifested in well-made pottery figurines, notably the 'baby face', whose puffy childlike features and downturned mouth have been dubiously identified as the product of the union of human and jaguar.

The 'First Intermediate' period, which coincides roughly with the first millennium BC, was introduced by a waning of Olmec influence outside the heartland. It was accompanied by a renewal of local traditions in the arts and, it may be assumed, local political autonomy. Processes which were to lead to the great classic cultures asserted themselves in highland Mexico, the Valley of Oaxaca and the Maya area. Population growth was persistent if erratic and was accompanied by the occupation of previously uninhabited lands and the emergence of a more complex hierarchy of urban settlements. The move into marginal lands was accompanied, perhaps made possible, by improvements in technology, with the introduction of irrigation and terracing to what had previously been subsistence ground-water agriculture.

The differentiation of human settlements which had already begun continued with a proliferation of small urban communities and the rapid expansion of some villages into regional centres with stone-built public architecture. By the middle of the first millennium BC Monte Albán in the Valley of Oaxaca had an estimated population of 10,000–20,000 with an immense plaza surrounded by impressive buildings decorated with stone sculpture. A similar population is attributed to Cuicuilco, a contemporaneous site in the Valley of Mexico, with a circular pyramid some 80 m in diameter.

handling such materials as obsidian and jade was a major factor.

Within its lowland heartland Olmec culture is most conspicuously manifested in colossal monolithic heads, altars and stelae of basalt and in ceremonial architecture on a grand scale. At San Lorenzo, large mounds, courts and pyramids built of earth bear witness to the importance of state and religion. A slightly later site, La Venta, has similar architecture with an earth-built pyramid of unprecedented height (110 m). The absence of household refuse and remains suggests that La Venta may have functioned as a ceremonial centre rather than an urban settlement, but its satellite population has been estimated as 18,000. The human effort required to construct the public works and to import stone from a distance of 80 km for the many large sculptures indicate a degree of population concentration, social organization and discipline unprecedented in Mesoamerica to that time. We can only guess how the society functioned but its sanctions were, in part, religious. The motifs on pottery and bas-relief sculpture reflect an intricate system of belief, some of which appears to anticipate the themes that were elaborated into the complex of later Mesoamerican religion. The jaguar and the serpent are central to Olmec iconography and their stylized traits are incorporated in images which recur repeatedly in modified form and are well known to us in their Aztec versions. The

Aerial view of Teotihuacán

Elsewhere in Mesoamerica urban development on a substantial scale continued in the south-west at sites such as Kaminaljuyu and Izapa and began in the Maya lowlands at Tikal and El Mirador.

These trends were accompanied by the crystallization of a cultural pattern which was to persist to the end of the pre-Columbian period. Social structure responded to the need for leadership and control with the consolidation of ruling elites whose existence is confirmed archaeologically by wide differences in housing standards and grave offerings. Religion, already a pervasive force in the Olmec culture, came to dominate society quite literally in the temples that formed the ceremonial centres of any sizeable community and was more generally expressed by a ubiquitous religious symbolism. Increasing wealth brought craft specialization which in turn nourished a long-distance trading system of ancient origin that assured the exchange of the specialized products of the different ecological zones of Mesoamerica. Material progress was accompanied by intellectual achievement: the earliest certain evidence of hieroglyphic writing and calendrics, both intimately related to the religious system, comes at this time from the Valley of Oaxaca.

Together with these elements of cultural similarity a note of diversity is struck by the regional art styles that developed during the First Intermediate period. Distinctive pottery originated in the Valley of Mexico, at Chipicuaro and in western Mexico. At Monte Albán the Zapotec styles of pottery, sculpture and architecture took form. The stone sculpture of Izapa and the south-west Pacific coast

exploited a rich tradition of religious and ritual iconography while, further south, Usulután lent its name to a decorative technique for pottery that spread through the Maya area. However, none of these styles imposed itself on all of Mesoamerica; the threshold between this period and the Middle Horizon is marked by the emergence of a culture which succeeded in doing so.

Teotihuacán was, in many ways, an unlikely candidate for primacy in Mesoamerica. It lies 48 km north of Mexico City in an area that was marginal to human settlement until about 500 BC. Even when, in the next two or three centuries, small communities formed around its fresh-water springs, they were dwarfed by the well-established town of Cuicuilco. It is said that the site is a holy one, a shrine built over a sacred spring, which may explain its rapid growth and, more miraculously, the obliteration of Cuicuilco by eruption of the volcano Xitle near the turn of our era. Be that as it may, at about that time Cuicuilco fades from the scene and the population of Teotihuacán is estimated at an astonishing 50,000. The main axis of the city was laid out and the two great pyramids of the Sun and Moon were largely built. Simultaneously a population decline occurred in the rural areas of the Valley, suggesting that the growth of the city was the result of a policy of enforced urban concentration. The expansion continued, although at a slower pace, for 500 years and by about AD 650 some 125,000 or more persons were living in an area of 20 sq km of ceremonial centre, residential compound and craft workshop, making Teotihuacán the largest city of Mesoamerica and the most populous until the latter days of Tenochtitlán. This extraordinary trajectory, the meticulous urban planning of the city with its astronomically-oriented grid and modular structures, the monumental public works and the organization needed merely to sustain a population of this size all indicate incontestable political control backed by powerful sanction. Yet there is little evidence in the material remains or early iconography of Teotihuacán to suggest military compulsion, and the site is remarkable for its lack of the commemorative monuments with which authoritarian rulers celebrate their achievements. One possible explanation, reverting to the city's holy origins, is that the leadership was essentially theocratic; the combination of religious and political function is an old tradition in Mesoamerica that persisted up to the time of the conquest.

Teotihuacán's growth was fuelled by the successful exploitation of economic resources on a huge scale. The immediate stimulus was the development in the swampy area around its many springs of intensive raised-field agriculture, the antecedent of the productive *chinampa* system of the Aztecs. Its location astride important trade routes and in the immediate vicinity of the richest Mesoamerican deposits of fine obsidian was decisive for its subsequent expansion and prosperity. This obsidian, a volcanic glass used to produce tools of razor sharpness, was traded in exchange for the staple commodities required by the city's increasing population and for the necessities and luxuries which were not available in the Valley. There is early evidence of obsidian workshops in Teotihuacán and its typical products are found in archaeological deposits throughout Mesoamerica.

Teotihuacán remains along the main Mesoamerican trade routes and evidence of more permanent contact and even settlement as far afield as Kaminaljuyu, in highland Guatemala, suggest that by the fifth century AD at latest the city had become the hub of a vast trading network that stretched from Chalchihuites in the north to El Salvador in the south. The Teotihuacán presence is often associated with the symbolism of their most prominent deity, the rain god later known as Tlaloc, giving that presence a religious dimension. There are also more tenuous grounds for thinking that Teotihuacanos were assimilated into the early ruling lineages of several Mayan centres.

Coinciding roughly with the Teotihuacán florescence, other societies of more regional compass developed vigorous and brilliant cultures. The most noteworthy were the Maya, who occupied the south-east of Mesoamerica. Their art and architecture, notably finely-carved stone stelae, polychrome pottery and the corbel arch, challenge comparison with those of Teotihuacán while their intellectual achievement in elaborating hieroglyphic writing and one of the world's most complex and accurate calendrical systems surpasses that of the metropolis. However, they did not approach Teotihuacán's genius for organization and control. Their political system is best described as that of the city-state, no one of which seems ever to have succeeded in dominating the Maya area. Their settlement pattern was much more dispersed than that of the central highlands and their cities were relatively smaller. Tikal, for example, had an estimated 45,000 inhabitants at the height of its power. They, nevertheless, created a civilization considered by many to represent the highest achievement of the Americas.

The other main focus of regional culture in the Middle Horizon period continued, as in the preceding period, to be the Valley of Oaxaca where Monte Albán, with a peak population estimated at 30,000, became the leading city in the southern highlands. Its pre-eminence rested in part on conquest but it entertained peaceful relations with its more distant neighbours. Monochrome grey pottery and urns in the form of deity effigies, local variants of familiar Mesoamerican creator and fertility gods, are characteristic of its distinctive art style which also shows some traces of Teotihuacán influence in the two centuries after AD 300.

Early in the second half of the first millennium a waning of Teotihuacán influence is apparent throughout Mesoamerica. The metropolis itself continued to flourish for another two centuries or so, renewing itself with major architectural projects and innovations in pottery and painting, but its artifacts are less traded and its iconographic motifs fall into disuse outside its near frontiers. The

Mayan hieroglyphic inscriptions on a stone stela at Copán

reason for these changes remains to be clarified but they seem to reflect inroads into the Teotihuacán monopoly of long-distance trading by rising centres such as Xochicalco and the outpost states.

Even before the grip of the centre was seriously weakened, new cultural vigour was displayed at the periphery. On the Gulf coast, El Tajín, and on the Pacific coast of Guatemala, the Cotzumalhuapa area, exemplify a reassertion of regional differentiation. Although widely separated, both are notable for their depictions in stone sculpture of a form of the Mesoamerican ballgame involving human sacrifice. This may be a symptom of a wider Mesoamerican deviation from a simple theocratic tradition to the callous exploitation of credulity that characterized the militaristic states that closed the last chapter of pre-Columbian history.

The ultimate decline and depopulation of Teotihuacán occurred about AD 750 against the background of these many regional readjustments. Much the same fate attended the other great cities of the Middle Horizon period shortly thereafter. By the end of the ninth century Tikal, Palenque and Copán had been abandoned as was Monte Albán. For El Tajín the end was delayed until about AD 1100. The reasons for this widespread collapse of advanced and long-lived urban cultures remain obscure. Both ecological and social factors may be cited without any certainty as to their relative importance: among them the depletion of local resources, economic imbalance, disintegration of the regional trading system, rigidity of the social structure, internal disaffection and external aggression.

The Second Intermediate period, following the fall of Teotihuacán, was a time of complex ebb and flow in the movement of peoples and balances of power throughout Mesoamerica which have not yet been fully documented but of which an outstanding feature was successive waves of 'barbarian' invasion from the nomadic tribal areas to the north. The first of these may have contributed to the ending of the Middle Horizon period; the last, that of the Aztecs, ushered in the Late Horizon, the concluding phase of pre-Columbian history.

The immediate consequence in the Valley of Mexico was a redistribution of population towards north and south. The growth of Tula, later the Toltec capital, dates from this period. To the south, Xochicalco and Cholula also probably attracted Valley inhabitants. Cholula, while long influenced by Teotihuacán, had a somewhat cosmopolitan culture with ties to the Mixteca in the south and the Maya area to the east. It was to become the centre of the Mixteca–Puebla style, the last brilliant florescence of polychrome pottery decoration and codex illustration, which left its mark on the arts of the Toltec and Aztec and the mural paintings of the Maya. At this time, however, it seems to have suffered a partial eclipse possibly following invasion by the Mexicanized Maya of Tabasco, the Olmeca–Xicalanca or Putun. Their aggression within the Maya area has been blamed for hastening the collapse of the classic sites and for paving the way for the Toltec conquest of Yucatán. In the central highlands to the west they have been identified in the last centuries of the first millennium at Cholula and the nearby fortress

The Castillo at Chichén Itzá

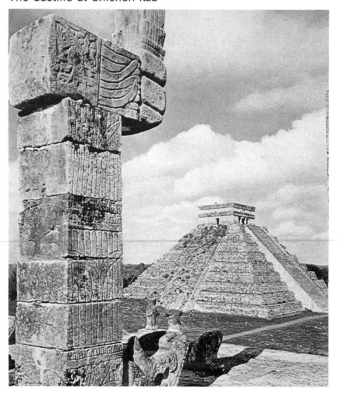

sites around Cacaxtla. If their role was as mischievous as history suggests, their enjoyment of their spoils was shortlived for, in the gradual realignment of power that ensued, they were displaced by the Toltecs.

Although they are not always consistent and on occasion confuse myth with reality, the native codices and early Spanish chronicles, in which the history of the last five centuries of pre-Columbian Mesoamerica is recorded, give a vivid picture of the rise and fall of the two peoples that successively dominate that history: Toltecs and Aztecs. They speak of the Toltecs as composed of two main ethnic groups, which accords well with our knowledge of the northward drift of Valley population and of nomadic invasion at the beginning of the Second Intermediate period, and record the deeds of their pre-eminent leader Quetzalcoatl. Enlightened rule and the spread of Toltec power are credited to him as are more mythical deeds of which the most dramatic involve his exile from the Toltec capital at Tula, followed by wanderings which take him to Cholula and then further east to found a new kingdom. Archaeology has confirmed much of this story. Toltec rule was consolidated over most of central Mexico in the period AD 900–1150 and its collapse seems to have been precipitated by internal schism. The most spectacular Toltec remains lie 1500 km to the south-east at Chichén Itzá which bears a remarkable resemblance to the ceremonial centre at Tula and whence people of presumed Toltec affiliation dominated northern Yucatán for perhaps a century after the fall of Tula.

The terminal phase of pre-Columbian history centres once again on the Valley of Mexico. The Toltec collapse left the way open for further waves of northern incursion which were chiefly remarkable for the speed with which the primitive nomads assimilated the culture of those they displaced in the Valley. Seven Chichimec tribes had thus established small kingdoms when their tardy kinsfolk, the Aztecs, made an unwelcome appearance on the scene after a long migration. Despite many hardships and efforts to expel them, the Aztecs persisted in the Valley and finally in AD 1325 established themselves at Tenochtitlán in the unpromising swampy reaches of Lake Texcoco.

Even in their humble beginnings, the Aztecs considered themselves a chosen people destined to military greatness under the tutelage of their god Huitzilopochtli. A naturally combative disposition was reinforced by a religion based on the concept of a universe whose very existence depended on a continuous supply of sacrificial blood which only wars could satisfy. Conquest became a condition for human survival and a spiritual duty as well as a source of wealth through the tribute exacted from the subject peoples. The result was the expansion of the lacustrine hamlet in less than 200 years into an empire created and maintained by military power. By the time Tenochtitlán fell to the Spaniards on 13 August 1521, its empire extended over most of central Mexico between the Tarascans to the north-west and the Maya to the south-east. The city itself had by that time some 250,000 inhabitants and was laid out on a grid of canals, streets and causeways, with elaborate hydraulic works, ceremonial centres, palaces and markets. It was described by Cortés as being as large as Seville or Córdoba and was in fact more populous, and possibly more memorable, than any city of the Americas or Europe. We can only guess what might have followed had Europe failed to discover the New World.

JCL

Further reading

N. Davies, *The Ancient Kingdoms of Mexico* (London, 1982)
N. Hammond, *Ancient Maya Civilization* (Cambridge, 1982)
W. Sanders and B. J. Price, *Mesoamerica: the Evolution of a Civilization* (New York, 1968)
M. P. Weaver, *The Aztecs, Maya and their Predecessors*, 2nd edition (New York, 1981)

Pre-Columbian South America

Culture areas of South America

By the second millennium BC in South America different areas had begun to develop distinctive cultural characteristics. The major distinction was between the Andean cultures, especially the central Andean ones, and those of the Amazon basin. The archaeological record for the central Andes is much more comprehensive, especially for the coastal desert where much inorganic material is preserved, than for the Amazon. By the time of the European conquests the area of highest cultural development was Tawantinsuyu (often spelt 'Tahuantinsuyo' in Spanish texts), the name that the Incas gave to their empire.

The central Andes

This area comprises both highland and coastal Peru along with the Lake Titicaca basin. Here developed the cultures that culminated in Tawantinsuyu.

During the period between about 2300 and 1500 BC the earliest permanent villages were founded in the Peruvian highlands. On the coast settlements moved inland and the earliest irrigation systems were built. Towards the end of this period pottery appears in local styles throughout much of Peru except the far south. The actual techniques of pottery making probably came from further north, since the earliest South American ceramics have been found in Ecuador and Colombia. The oldest Peruvian pottery has been excavated in the eastern highlands and on the central coast. At Kotosh, a temple near the headwaters of the Huallaga River, the earliest pottery has been dated by radiocarbon to about 1800 BC. The

PRE–COLUMBIAN SOUTH AMERICA

NA Northern Andes
CA Central Andes
SA Southern Andes
TA Tropical forest of lowland South America
— Boundaries of culture areas

KEY
● Modern town
▲ Archaelogical site

0 ——— 320 km
0 ——— 200 miles

most common shapes are open vessels resembling cups and vases. Stirrup-spout bottles, consisting of a chamber with a stirrup-shaped handle set on top, appear for the first time in the central Andes. This form continued to be made in north Peru right up to the Spanish conquest. Decoration consisted of bands of fine incised lines filled with white, red or yellow pigment. This early Kotosh pottery is too elaborate to be considered an initial stage.

During the second and first millennia BC a tradition of erecting large public buildings, often regarded as ceremonial centres, also continued developing. These are thought to have been built by 'corporate labour' which consisted of construction gangs drawn from extended families or communities. The work would have been directed by a higher authority. Sometimes actual sections built by different groups of workers can be seen in these structures. This system of construction for large buildings was to continue right up to the Spanish conquest. The central coast was the main area where many early ceremonial centres were built by this method. Most of them, like Garagay near Lima, were artificial hills built of clay and irregularly shaped stones in the shape of an animal, possibly a feline. The 'head' faces west, the tail east and the abdomen north. The abdomen is the most important part, having stairways and terraces at the end of a large plaza bounded by elongated platforms which may represent the legs.

Between about 1200 and 1000 BC the first monumental stone sculpture in Peru was erected at the ceremonial centre of Cerro Sechín on the north-central coast. The large stones depict entire human beings, possibly warriors, while the smaller ones show trophy heads, human heads or parts of human bodies. These

CHRONOLOGICAL TABLE

DATES	CENTRAL ANDES	NORTHERN ANDES	SOUTHERN ANDES	TROPICAL FOREST
Spanish conquest	Spanish conquest	Spanish conquest	Spanish conquest	European conquest
1500	Inca empire	Inca empire	Inca empire	
	Chimú	Chibcha		
1000			Fortified towns	
	Huari Pacheco		Tiahuanaco influence	
500	Conchopata			
	Tiahuanaco			
AD	Moche culture Nazca culture			
BC				
500	Chavín influence		Pottery–making cultures	
1000	Chavín de Huantar			
		Machalilla Phase		
1500	Garagay			
	Huaca de los Reyes			
	Cerro Sechín			
	Kotosh – pottery			
2000				
2500				
3000		Pottery (coastal Ecuador and Caribbean lowlands)		

carvings all seem to concentrate on various aspects of warfare or rituals involving the dismemberment of human beings. These themes reappear in later Peruvian art.

Central Andean pottery, especially that from tombs, has been used by North American archaeologists to construct a chronological scheme. This begins with an Initial period about 1800 BC followed by three 'horizons', termed Early, Middle and Late, characterized by varying degrees of cultural and political unification. In between came periods of regional cultures termed the Early and Late Intermediate periods.

Early Horizon. The Early Horizon is marked by an elaborate art style whose principal motifs involved felines, people with feline attributes, serpents, birds of prey and other animals. Elements of this style spread through most of Peru except the far south and have been found on murals, pottery, goldwork, textiles and shells. The most elaborate forms were on stone sculpture at the temple of Chavín de Huantar in the northern highlands. Until a few years ago it was thought that this art style emanated from Chavín itself and spread throughout much of Peru as a religious cult.

The most widespread of the Chavín deities is the 'staff god'. He is shown as a standing feline in human form with outstretched arms, snakes for hair and an elaborate staff in each hand. He could have been a sky god associated with the cyclical movements of the stars and planets.

Recent archaeological fieldwork and analysis have shown that there were significant local variations in this art style. The 'mythical beings' varied from place to place. According to radiocarbon dates, the Early Horizon began about 1500 BC on the central and north coast at ceremonial centres like Garagay and Huaca de Los Reyes near Trujillo. Chavín itself did not become established until about five hundred years later and only reached its height between 600 and 300 BC when it influenced both the highlands and south coast.

Therefore the Early Horizon was really a religious phenomonon which arose in several centres in different areas. There seem to have been regular contacts between these centres, producing a shared body of ideas.

Early Intermediate period. Towards the end of the Early Horizontal regional cultures with their own art styles began to emerge throughout the central Andes. In particular the Nazca culture, typified by its distinctive pottery style, emerged towards the beginning of the Christian era on the south coast of Peru. Most is known about these people through their polychrome pots which depicted everything from mythical beings with trophy heads to farmers with their crops. The trophy heads suggest that ritual decapitation was practised.

A Nazca stirrup pot depicting a mythical being with trophy heads

A tenoned head depicting one of the forms of fanged being at the temple of Chavin de Huantar

At the beginning of the first millennium AD another distinctive regional culture variously called Mochica or Moche (the latter after the name of the village on the north coast where it was first identified) emerged. Like Nazca it was distinguished by its fine pottery, but the emphasis was on sculptured form and fine line drawing rather than polychrome painting. Although Moche pottery has been found from the valley of Lambayeque in the north to that of Nepeña in the south, its style is not exactly the same in each valley. Pottery scenes show similarly dressed Moche warriors fighting each other using wooden clubs with stone heads and metal spikes. Other features are trophy heads and dismembered human limbs. Boundary walls have been found along the northern edges of the Santa and Moche valleys. There may have been a loose alliance of chiefdoms with one in each valley. Evidence from tombs shows that some people were more wealthy than others since they had more and better quality possessions deposited in their graves.

Both the Moche and Nazca employed irrigation to grow crops like maize and beans. In addition the Moche erected substantial mud-brick structures using corporate labour. An example is the Huaca del Sol which may have functioned as a sacred burial mound where occasional religious ceremonies were performed.

Middle Horizon: Tiahuanaco and Huari. While the Moche and Nazca cultures flourished, Tiahuanaco, on the eastern side of Lake Titicaca, began developing as a large ceremonial centre. Excavations have shown that most of the temples there were built between AD 200 and 500. The main stone carving set up was a gateway on the lintel of which was carved a figure with a radiating headdress of puma heads and a staff held vertically in each hand. The figure has been said to represent Viracocha, the creator god of Peruvian mythology.

A locally modified version of this Tiahuanaco god has been found about 600 km to the north on smashed oversize urns at Conchopata near Ayacucho. This version seems to have been adopted by the people of Huari, an ancient city of walled compounds about 25 km north-east of Ayacucho, between about AD 550 and 700. Another important religious centre was at Pacheco on the south coast. Here oversize urns of a religious or ceremonial type have been found painted with polychrome representations of a male and female version of the god depicted on the Conchopata urns. Maize ears feature prominently as appendages on both these variations of the Pacheco god.

It has been argued that during the eighth century AD the political and religious influence of Huari spread in the form of an empire through much of highland and coastal Peru in what is termed the Middle Horizon. However, there is little concrete evidence for such an 'empire' outside southern Peru since there were no administrative centres beyond the immediate vicinity of Huari. Also outside the southern highland Huari pottery is relatively rare and hardly ever occurs in domestic refuse. Almost all the evidence for Huari–Tiahuanaco influence has come from the style of offerings, especially pottery in tombs. In fact the cultural unity of the Middle Horizon seems to have been exaggerated. The reality appears to have been a series of regional states or spheres of influence like Tiahuanaco and Huari. What unifying forces there were in the Middle Horizon seem to have ended about AD 800, with Huari itself being abandoned by AD 900.

Late Intermediate period. With the disappearance of Huari and Tiahuanaco influence after about AD 1000 regional cultures developed, especially along the coast. These are known archaeologically through their artifacts and architectural remains together with some Spanish documentary records. Powerful states arose along the coast and these were encountered by the Incas when they were establishing their empire in the sixteenth century. In particular we know most about the north coast.

The Chimú became established in the Trujillo area about AD 1200. By the time of their conquest by the Incas in the 1460s the Chimú had established an empire that stretched from the frontier with Ecuador to the Rimac valley on the central coast, a distance of over 1000 km. The capital, Chan Chan, situated at the mouth of the Moche valley, covers an area of over 6 sq km. The site is dominated by ten large enclosures or *cuidadelas*, rectangular or rectilinear in

The Huaca del Sol at Moche. A large mud-brick pyramid built by the Moche people during the first half of the first millennium AD shape, with exterior walls between 200 and 600 m long and up to 10 m high. They were almost certainly the residences of various Chimú rulers.

The Chimú were ruled by a line of dynastic kings of which the first is supposed to have come from the Lambayeque area. Like the Incas, they maintained that before their appearance Peru had been ruled over by a series of hereditary chiefs. The Chimú governed through a system of hereditary local nobility. There was a strict division between nobility and commoners as well as a distinct hierarchy. Women were granted nearly equal rights with men. The marriage ceremony stressed the equality of both parties. Chimú society seems to have been organized along the lines of the *ayllu* (described by the Spaniards as a related group of kinsmen or a lineage descended from a common ancestor). These Chimú *ayllu* had particular names that were handed down in the male line from father to son.

The Chimú legal system was very strict. The punishment for disrespect to shrines consisted of burying the prisoner alive with the bones of other offenders and of unclean animals. Adulterers were thrown from cliffs. Stealing was regarded as very serious and the punishment of thieves was not just a civil but also a religious matter. This gives the impression that property may have been regarded by the nobles as being owned by divine right.

The Spaniards recorded ten different stages of life in the Chimú kingdom from childhood through the adult span to old age. The stages of childhood and youth continued until the twenty-fifth year when an individual was considered to be a full citizen and a warrior with rights to his own home and community fields. From fifty to sixty he was regarded as 'half old', having only to do light work. After sixty he had to pay no tribute and could not be called on for war service.

When a Chimú died there was a five-day period of mourning. Then the body was washed and buried with the knees drawn up. It was wrapped in cloth to form a bundle on top of which a stuffed false head covered with a face mask was placed. The location and type of burial depended on one's status. The ordinary people of Chan Chan were buried in unlined graves in a cemetery just south of the city. The rulers were interred in specially built platforms, one of which is usually found inside each *ciudadela*. At one of the smaller burial platforms in Chan Chan large numbers of skeletons of young women have been found recently. They were probably the wives and other ladies of a Chimú ruler who were sacrificed to accompany him.

The Late Horizon: the Incas. The Incas, according to archaeological evidence and legends, were originally one of a number of small tribes in the Cuzco area. They appear to have settled in Cuzco about AD 1200 under the leadership of their legendary founder Manco Capac. However, it was not until about AD 1438 that they gained ascendancy in the Cuzco area and started expanding. First under Pachacuti, then under his son Topa Inga, and finally under Guayna Capac, their empire eventually stretched from the present-day border of Colombia with Ecuador to the Maule River in central Chile by about AD 1520.

The Inca emperors ruled by divine right as representatives of the Sun on earth. They claimed direct descent from the Sun through Manco Capac. The Inca emperor or Sapa Inca had absolute power and in theory considered all the men in his empire his sons and all the women his wives. He governed through an elite class of nobles some of whom were of royal blood while others were 'Incas by privilege'. Both groups belonged to the Inca class and could wear the types of headband and earplugs worn by the Inca himself. The nobles of royal blood formed lineage groups called *panaca* which consisted of all the descendants of a ruler in the male line. 'Incas by privilege' were not Incas by birth although some were related through alliances and political marriages to Inca rulers before Pachacuti came to power in 1438. These Incas by privilege spoke Quechua, the official language of Tawantinsuyu. Many of them were sent to different parts of the empire to set an example and to indoctrinate the local people with Inca culture.

The Inca Temple of the Sun or Coricancha in Cuzco. The Spaniards built a church on the original masonry

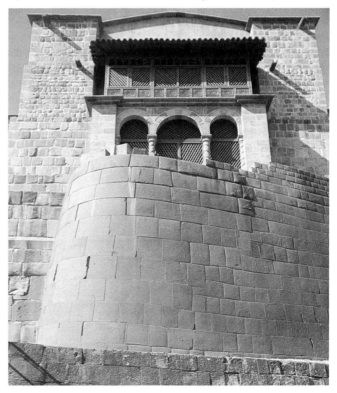

Inca society was stratified, with the commoners at the bottom and the Inca royal family at the top. Within the empire the social structure was essentially one of small local groups, each with its own ancestor cult. In addition, groups of colonists or *mitimas* were established in certain areas but some seem to have remained under the control of local rulers (*curacas*) of the districts whence they came.

Inca society was also divided by age groups. Twelve standard age divisions were made for the purposes of census and tax assessment. The transition from one age grade to another did not occur at a certain time since the Indians kept no exact record of their age. More important were obvious changes in physical condition such as puberty. The most significant age grade was that of adulthood which was entered at marriage and lasted as long as both parties could do a full day's work.

Most commoners were agriculturalists who paid their taxes in labour or *mita*. Archaeological evidence suggests that they were rewarded with a maize beer called *chicha*. The *mita* was used to build and maintain roads, erect public buildings and provide food and cloth for imperial storehouses. Specialist craftsmen paid their *mita* by working at their trade. Transport for goods was on the backs of men and llamas since there were no wheeled vehicles in pre-Columbian South America.

Inca laws were recorded on *quipus*, a system of knot records also used to keep accounts, since there was no writing in pre-Columbian South America. There was a wide range of laws extending from Municipal Law, concerning tribal rights, to *Mitachanacuy*, which regulated the distribution of work so that everyone did their fair share. Punishments for individuals were physical and there were neither fines nor imprisonment. The type of punishment received depended on the rank of the individual. Women in Inca society had a lower legal status than men: husbands were justified in killing their wives for adultery while wives who killed adulterous husbands were hanged by the feet until dead.

Tawantinsuyu represented a degree of organization and sophistication which was not matched elsewhere in pre-Columbian South America. It included many pre-Inca elements which were inherited or taken over from conquered peoples like the Chimú. For example, many of the gold ornaments that Pizarro and his companions had melted down when they kidnapped Atahualpa were very likely made by metal workers brought from Chan Chan. Tawantinsuyu had been in existence for just over sixty years before it fell to the Spaniards. In fact it had already shown signs of considerable strain and was only just recovering from a civil war. If the Spaniards had not conquered it, then sooner or later it could well have disintegrated into regional cultures.

Northern and southern Andes

In the southern Andes, comprising southern Bolivia, Chile and highland Argentina, farming and pottery-making cultures became established by the middle of the first millennium BC. During the first millennium AD there were signs of influence from the high plateau of Bolivia and more complex societies developed. In the latter half of the first millennium AD the northern parts of this area came under the influence of Tiahuanaco. However, most of the south Andean region appears to have remained culturally, and probably politically, autonomous. At this time pottery and other crafts flourished.

After about AD 1000 settlements were concentrated in fortified towns and villages and there was some aesthetic decline. These fortifications were particularly apparent in the northern part of the area, suggesting warfare between towns or small regional states. The Incas made their presence felt in this area by armed force between 1450 and 1490.

The northern Andes comprise the highland and coastal areas of what is now Ecuador and Colombia. The earliest pottery in South America, dating to about 3000 BC, has come from coastal sites in Ecuador and the Caribbean lowlands. There are also similarities between some of the decorated bowls of the Machalilla phase (*c.* 1500–1000 BC) of Ecuador and those of the Pre-classic cultures of Mesoamerica. This Mesoamerican influence continued right up to the conquest of Ecuador by the Incas in the sixteenth century. Seaborne trade, using large rafts, seems to have been the most likely explanation for this phenomenon.

A quipu: the knotted-string recording device of the Incas

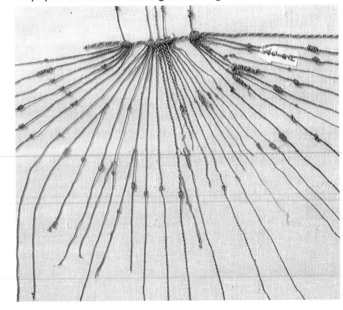

As is the case in the southern Andes, the pre-Columbian peoples of the northern Andes never developed an empire on the scale of Tawantinsuyu. The political organization of the northern Andeans, like the Chibcha of Colombia, encountered by the Spaniards, was based on chiefdoms. The Zipa, one of the Chibcha chiefs, had his capital at Bogotá. When the Spaniards saw the Chibcha in 1537 they were impressed at the size of their population and their numerous palisaded towns and villages. In addition they not only had palaces and temples but also a prosperous agriculture and thriving internal trade.

Tropical forest of lowland South America

This area includes the tropical forests of Venezuela, the Guianas and the Amazon basin. The archaeology of this region still has considerable gaps in it although much research is currently being carried out. Pottery appears early and was in use in the Upper Amazon by 1800 BC. The first European explorers reported substantial Indian settlements, particularly along the banks of the Amazon and its tributaries. The main food was manioc, supplemented by game and fish. The level of cultural and political sophistication reached here did not match that of the central Andes. However, Inca armies made no significant headway into the Upper Amazon and did, in fact, recruit bowmen from that area to serve in their own forces.

GHAB

Further reading

G. Bawden and G. W. Conrad, *The Andean Heritage* (Cambridge, Mass., 1982)
D. W. Lathrap, *The Upper Amazon* (London, 1970)
B. J. Meggers, *Ecuador* (London, 1966)
G. Reichel-Dolmatoff, *Colombia* (London, 1965)

The Spanish conquests, 1492–1580

America in the 'age of discovery'

The hundred years from 1450 to 1550 were an 'age of discovery' without precedent in world history. This was the dramatic moment when European civilization began, in J. H. Parry's words, 'to think of the world as a whole and of all seas as one'. In principle, other civilizations might have initiated this decisive historical shift. In several far-ranging expeditions between 1405 and 1433, the great Chinese admiral Cheng Ho conducted imposing fleets of large junks – the world's biggest and best ships at the time – on voyages of reconnaissance to places as far from China as Aden and the Persian Gulf. These impressive Chinese forays were abruptly halted by the

reigning Ming dynasty. Had they continued, modern history might well have looked very different. As it was, the initiative thus abandoned in the East was taken up in the West – by the rising states of the Atlantic coast of Europe, especially Portugal (the true pioneer-nation in this respect) and Spain. These two countries were the first to take advantage of the vital late-medieval innovations in ship-design and navigation that made long-range oceanic seafaring feasible. Their quest for new trades, for new territories, and for new converts to Christianity opened the way to an astonishing period of maritime exploration and (on the heels of exploration) imperialism. It was, by any standard, one of the great turning points in history. The world is still living with the consequences.

Three supreme maritime feats stood out in this age of discovery. In 1492–3, the Genoese seafarer Christopher Columbus (1451–1506), backed by the Spanish crown, led an expedition of three ships across the Atlantic to the outlying islands of the then unknown American continent. In 1497–99, the Portuguese commander Vasco da Gama (*c.* 1460–1524), in a technically more audacious voyage, sailed to and from India by way of the southern tip of Africa – the culmination of a Portuguese national effort reaching back over eighty years and associated in its earlier phases with Prince Henry 'the Navigator' (1394–1460); an impressive monument to him now stands on the Lisbon waterfront. Just over two decades later, the globe itself was circumnavigated for the first time by a ship from Ferdinand Magellan's notable expedition of 1519–22. Magellan (1480–1521), a Portuguese subject working for Spain, did not

A model of Columbus's flagship the *Santa Maria*

The colonial period

	SPAIN		PORTUGAL
1492–3	COLUMBUS'S FIRST VOYAGE to the Caribbean.		
	1493	The Papal Bull *Inter Caetera* divides the world into Spanish and Portuguese zones of conquest, settlement and trade.	
	1494	TREATY OF TORDESILLAS. Spain and Portugal adjust the Papal line of demarcation to a longitude 370 leagues west of the Azores.	
1493–6	COLUMBUS'S SECOND VOYAGE. Establishment of a Spanish colony on island of Hispaniola. Foundation of **Santo Domingo**, oldest Spanish-speaking city in western hemisphere (1496).		
		1500	Pedro Alvares Cabral discovers Brazil while on his way to India.
1508–9	Conquest of Puerto Rico by Juan Ponce de León.		
1509–13	Small mainland colonies established.		
1511	Conquest of Cuba by Diego Velásquez.	1500–30	Brazilwood (dyewood) trade established along the coast of *terra do brasil*, 'brazilwood land'.
1513	Vasco Núñez de Balboa crosses Panama isthmus and becomes first European to see the Pacific.		
1519–21	CONQUEST OF MEXICO by Hernán Cortés. Fall of Aztec confederacy. Destruction of Tenochtitlán and foundation of **Mexico City** (1521).		
1522	Pascual de Andagoya reconnoitres Peruvian coast and learns of existence of Inca empire.		
1523–40	Various expeditions conquer Yucatán and Central America.		
1529	The Welsers (Augsburg bankers) undertake colonization in Venezuela under licence from Emperor Charles V (King Charles I of Spain).		
1531–5	CONQUEST OF PERU by Francisco Pizarro. Fall of Inca empire (1533). Foundation of **Lima** (1535).	1532	Portuguese colony at São Vicente.
		1534	Captaincy system introduced.
1535	First viceroy of New Spain (Mexico) assumes office.		
1535–7	Expedition to River Plate by Pedro de Mendoza. Foundation of **Buenos Aires** (1536) and of the upriver colony at **Asunción**, Paraguay (1537). Buenos Aires later abandoned (1541).		
1536–8	Conquest of Chibcha kingdoms of New Granada (modern Colombia) by Gonzalo Jiménez de Quesada. Foundation of **Bogotá** (1538).		
1540–2	Francisco Vásquez de Coronado leads an expedition (the most notable of several in this direction) to parts of what is now the United States, reaching as far as the modern Kansas.		
1540–1	Pedro de Valdivia undertakes the conquest of Chile. Foundation of **Santiago de Chile** (1541).		
1542	The New Laws of the Indies. Peru designated as a viceroyalty.	1549	First governor-general of Brazil appointed, with his capital at **Bahia**.
1544–8	Rebellion against Spanish authorities by Spanish settlers in Peru.		
1550–1	The Valladolid Debates.		
1567	Foundation of **Caracas**, Venezuela, by Diego de Losada.	1554	Foundation of **São Paulo**.
1580	Re-establishment ('second foundation') of Buenos Aires by Juan de Garay and colonists from Asunción, Paraguay.	1567	Foundation of **Rio de Janeiro**.
		1580–1640	Portugal under the Spanish crown.

THE SPANISH CONQUESTS

Mexico

Cortés 1519

Columbus
1492

1493

Aztecs

1511

1493

1508

TORDESILLAS LINE
agreed by Spain and
Portugal (1494)

Jiménez de
Quesada 1536

Pizarro 1531

Chibchas

Cabral 1500*

Brazil

Peru

Incas

→ main expeditions

Incas main native American states

Valdivia 1540

Garay 1580

Mendoza 1535

Magellan 1519

survive this altogether spectacular journey; he was killed in the Philippines en route. The honour of becoming the first navigator to sail round the world thus fell to the Basque sea-captain Juan Sebastián del Cano (c. 1486–1526), who guided the remnants of Magellan's party back to Spain.

Columbus was not the first European to set foot in the western hemisphere – the intrepid Norse sailors of AD 1000 can claim certain priority – yet he was in a real sense the true discoverer (from the European standpoint) of America. The Norse voyages had no after-effects in history; the Norsemen lacked the numbers and the resources to found lasting settlements. They had been forgotten by the fifteenth century, except perhaps in Scandinavia. By contrast, immense and long-lasting consequences flowed from Columbus's first journey of 1492–3. Columbus himself – 'Admiral of the Ocean Sea', as Spaniards called him – made four voyages in all. On the third and fourth of these (1498–1500, 1502–4), he reconnoitred part of the South and Central American coastlines. Other navigators, including the Florentine, Amerigo Vespucci (1454–1512) – whose Christian name was later to be given to the new-found landmass in the west – established that a huge western continent, undreamed of by Europe, lay on the map of the world. Columbus's purpose had been to prove the existence of a direct, westward ocean route from Europe to Asia – had his geographical opinions been correct, Japan would have been roughly where Mexico is – and he never fully grasped that what had been disclosed as a result of his efforts was truly a 'new world'. 'Our world,' wrote the sixteenth-century French essayist Montaigne (quoted here in Florio's contemporary translation), 'hath of late discovered another, . . . no lesse-large, fully peopled, all-things-yeelding, and mighty in strength than ours.' Europeans' mental horizons were ultimately to be greatly stretched as a consequence of the discovery of America. So too, and rather sooner, were their political and economic horizons. For discovery was to be followed immediately by conquest.

The Spanish conquests

For Spain, recently united under its 'Catholic Monarchs', King Ferdinand of Aragon and Queen Isabella of Castile, the New World offered an alluring field for territorial expansion. Columbus's second expedition, to the island he named Hispaniola (now shared by two countries, the Dominican Republic and Haiti), consisted of seventeen ships carrying around 1400 men (no women), horses, cattle, pigs, farm implements and seeds. It was probably the biggest colonizing venture yet mounted by a European nation. Spain's intentions in America were thus clear from the outset. The Spanish urge to conquer territory was deep-rooted. It came in large part from the turbulent medieval history of the Iberian peninsula, and in particular the long struggle of the Christian kingdoms (with Castile always to the fore) to expel the Muslim invaders who had over-whelmed the Visigothic kingdom of Spain after AD 711 – the *Reconquista*, 'reconquest', as Spaniards called this struggle. The last Muslim redoubt in Spain, the Moorish kingdom of Granada, was subdued by the Catholic Monarchs only a few months before Columbus's first voyage. The cult of honour and the martial virtues – so movingly expressed in the final stanzas of Spain's finest fifteenth-century poem, the *Coplas* of Jorge Manrique; so immortally satirized later on in the most famous of all Spanish books, *Don Quixote* – was well-developed in late-medieval Spain. It provided strong psychological reinforcement to the Spanish con-quistadors who marched and fought their way across the vast, alien landscapes of America in the sixteenth century.

Spanish colonization was at first confined to the main Caribbean islands, starting with Hispaniola (1494), and spreading from there to Puerto Rico (1508) and Cuba (1511). This was merely the prelude to an astonishing sequence of conquests. Of the scores of expeditions, large and small (generally fairly small) that penetrated the American mainland over the next few decades, two were particularly momentous, for they brought about the downfall of the two most populous and sophisticated native American states. In 1519 Hernán Cortés (1485–1547) and some 600 followers landed in Mexico. Two years later, the once-powerful Aztec confederacy was in ruins, its ruler, Montezuma II, dead, its beautiful capital, Tenochtitlán, reduced to providing the foundations for a new Spanish city. A similar catastrophe befell the Inca empire of Peru, overwhelmed in the early 1530s by Francisco Pizarro (c. 1470–1541) and, at the outset, around 150 men. The Inca emperor, Atahualpa, was garrotted. Thus, in the course of fifteen years, two great Amerindian societies were devastatingly assaulted by a handful of Spanish adventurers. These appalling events were the most incredible of the sixteenth century – among the most incredible, surely, in world history.

From newly-conquered Mexico (New Spain, as it became known to the Spaniards) and Peru, subsidiary expeditions of conquest spread out across adjacent territories – into northern Mexico, Yucatán, Central America, Quito (the Incas' 'northern kingdom'), Chile, and what are now Bolivia and north-west Argentina. Meanwhile, separate expeditions incorporated other areas of America into the now fast-expanding empire. Gonzalo Jiménez de Quesada (c. 1510–79), in the mid-1530s, advanced from the Caribbean coast into the highlands of what we now call Colombia (New Granada was its colonial name) and there subdued the Chibcha kingdoms. Ironically, perhaps, the single most powerful expedition mounted from Spain itself in these years of far-flung conquest – the one led by Pedro de Mendoza (1487–1537) to the River Plate in 1535 (one of its members was St Teresa of Avila's brother) – yielded little in the way of immediate territory. Here the nomadic Indians of the Argentine pampa held back the advance of the would-be conquistadors, and colonization had to focus for the moment on Asunción, in Paraguay, hundreds of miles upriver from the sea. It was from this modest Paraguayan base, in 1580, that a party of settlers sailed downriver to re-establish an abandoned Spanish outpost called Buenos Aires – later to become perhaps the grandest of all Spanish-speaking cities. By 1580, all the main segments of Spain's new American empire were in place.

The rapidity and sheer scale of the Spanish conquests never fails to impress those who read about them. Yet the Spanish crown, eager enough to accept the fruits of conquest, played a relatively small part in its organization. After Columbus's voyages, the expansion of Spain's overseas empire was largely the work of small private bands of armed adventurers operating spontaneously. These bands were invariably licensed by the crown (or later the crown's agents in America) but they were organized, recruited and financed (often on borrowed money) by individual conquistadors or partnerships. At a time when Spanish troops were heavily engaged in European wars, virtually no regular soldiers were used, even if expeditions often contained their share of veterans. At sea, likewise, few if any recognizable warships took part; expeditions used any vessel they could find. The essential element in all the expeditions (there were at least fifty, many of them fruitless) was one of leadership and motivation. Most of the leaders came from the lower fringe of the aristocracy: they were *hidalgos*, to use the Spanish term. One or two, Pizarro for instance, came from lower down the social scale. Often they were impecunious *hidalgos*, eager to acquire the seigneurial style of life to which they felt themselves entitled. A disproportionate number of the most prominent conquistadors came from Extremadura, the hard, arid region to the west of Castile. Their followers, the majority in any expedition, consisted of a great variety of lower-class Spaniards, including ex-soldiers and a whole gallery of craftsmen, many of them from Andalusia – which was to have consequences for the American variants of the Spanish language. They were sometimes turbulent and unruly; more than one conquistador faced (and some did not survive) mutiny in the course of an expedition.

For leaders and led alike, motivation was all-important. The late-medieval cult of honour was here combined – in what proportions it is hard to say – with crusading zeal on behalf of Christendom, and in most cases with sheer greed. Bernal Díaz del Castillo, the doughty footsoldier who later (in old age) wrote a classic eye-witness account of Cortés's expedition, tells us crisply and without irony that he and his companions went to Mexico 'to serve God and His Majesty the King, to give light to those who were in darkness, and also to get rich – which all of us came looking for'. Here it is worth remembering that the late-medieval cult of honour included the notion that the noblest method of securing wealth was to *win* it, preferably through deeds of valour – deeds of a kind then being extensively chronicled

Hernán Cortés

in 'books of chivalry', a type of literature achieving its greatest popularity at the time of the conquest of America. Thus the lure of material gain *and* honour drove the conquistadors to accept extra-ordinary odds and to submit themselves to heroic feats of endurance.

The speed with which the great native American civilizations were conquered is certainly astonishing. The technological superiority of the Spaniards should not be exaggerated as a reason: firearms undoubtedly gave them an edge at times, while the horse (unknown in America) allowed them a vital degree of mobility. Yet they were always vastly outnumbered by their Indian opponents. The Spaniards were certainly able to take advantage of divisions among Indian peoples: Cortés, for instance, found a small Indian state, Tlaxcala, which was hostile to the Aztecs and had resisted inclusion in their confederacy, and his alliance with the Tlaxcalans was a key factor in his success. Similarly, the Inca empire at the time the Spaniards arrived had recently gone through a civil war; Pizarro was able to play on this to a certain extent in subjugating Peru. In the end, however, it seems to have been the sheer determination (not to say ruthlessness) of the conquistadors that decided the outcome. Indian resistance to the conquests was sometimes fierce enough – the great Inca rising in Peru in 1536 was a moderately close-run thing for the Spaniards – but it was patchy, and only in a few cases did it last very long. A conspicuous example of where it *did* was the remote southern 'frontier' of Chile, where Araucanian Indians maintained their resistance to European domination right into the nineteenth century. But the Araucanians lived on the fringe of an

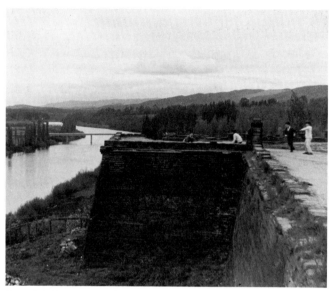

Spanish fortress at Nacimiento, Chile

unimportant colony. In the imperial heartlands, as in most other areas, the Indian population was rapidly subordinated to the will of its new European overlords. Sporadic Indian rebellions, however, continued throughout colonial times.

Patterns of colonization

Spanish colonization in America was based on (and subsequently focused on) cities. Whenever an expedition conquered a territory, its leader's first action was (with prescribed ceremonial) to found a township – formally a 'city', with a municipal council (cabildo) chosen from among the conquerors, a street-plan carefully traced out (nearly always on the simple grid-iron pattern), and urban properties distributed among the colony's founders. Spanish settlers aspired to an upper-class style of life; for most, that could best be achieved within an urban setting. The 'urban nucleus' thus became fundamental to the pattern of Spanish imperialism. Nearly all the modern Spanish American republics have capital cities that can trace their history back for well over four hundred years and to a 'foundation' by a particular conquistador. In Mexico, the victorious Spaniards built their capital on the ruins of Aztec Tenochtitlán. In Peru, by contrast, they spurned the old Inca capital at Cuzco, in the mountains, and founded a new one of their own – for ease of communication – on the coast, at Lima. At the outset, these colonial capitals were very modest settlements, but given the Spaniards' desire for a decent urban setting, some of the capitals quickly grew into important centres of wealth and power. By 1580, the year the struggling settlement at Buenos Aires was re-founded, Mexico City and Lima were already very respectable cities.

The colonial cities did not, of course, grow up in an economic vacuum. The Spaniards, as already mentioned, arrived in America with very definite ideas of gaining wealth. The conquistadors were particularly attracted by the lure of precious metals. When offered an estate by the governor of Cuba, Hernán Cortés retorted: 'I came to get gold, not till the soil like a peasant.' In any case, the colonists needed something to export to Spain. In the early stages of colonization, gold was washed from rivers on the Caribbean islands. On the mainland, silver was the precious metal found in greatest abundance. Spectacular silver-strikes occurred around the mid-point of the sixteenth century: in 1545 at Potosí in Upper Peru (now Bolivia), in 1548 and 1558 at Zacatecas and Guanajuato in Mexico. From this time onwards, silver-mining became an important factor in consolidating settlement patterns in the Spanish American empire. Mining centres such as Potosí became significant markets, with large populations, while the need for safe and regular transport of silver to Spain helped determine major trade-routes and the shape of the commercial system in general.

Mines needed labourers. The growing Spanish colonial cities needed to be fed. Spaniards took their tastes in food with them to America; these could not be satisfied by traditional Indian agriculture, so Spaniards established their own farms and ranches. The large native American populations that surrounded the Spanish settlements were viewed as a convenient source of labour for both mining and agriculture. The basic pattern of relations between conquerors and conquered was sadly apparent from the first years of Caribbean colonization. The Spaniards mobilized Indian labour by means of what they termed the *encomienda*. Under this system, groups of Indians – though not (in theory anyway) their lands – were 'distributed' among the leading settlers, who were supposed on paper to Christianize them and 'civilize' them (on Hispanic lines), while in return using their labour or receiving their tribute. (Indians not included in *encomiendas* were required to pay tribute direct to the crown.) As a labour institution, the *encomienda* was of significance chiefly during the first century or so of Spain's colonial rule, but during this period the system was widely abused by colonists. The coercion and exploitation (sometimes very cruel) of the native Americans undoubtedly contributed to the steep demographic decline that now occurred in the New World.

While most settlers (especially, no doubt, the *encomenderos*, the holders of *encomiendas*) regarded their exploitative position as acceptable, some did not. Many conscience-stricken Spaniards (particularly in the religious orders) reacted strongly to the abuses they saw around them, and called on the crown to remedy the evil. The great Dominican, Fray Bartolomé de las Casas (1474–1566), himself a former *encomendero*, spent the latter part of a long life agitating relentlessly on behalf of Amerindian rights. But by the time the crown took steps to reduce the scope of the *encomienda*, in its New Laws of the Indies (1542), it was already too late. The crown's attitude – at least in the short term – had to be tempered by colonial resistance to the legislation. Agitation by ecclesiastics and others did, however, have the effect of bringing the whole question of conquest and its effects on the native population under official scrutiny. In 1550 a ban was actually placed on further conquests while a group of distinguished lawyers and theologians sat down, at Valladolid in Spain, to hear a debate on the rights and wrongs of Spain's imperial activities – one of the more remarkable episodes in the history of imperialism. The debate, in which Las Casas took a prominent part (at one point making a five-day speech), was inconclusive. In any case the conquest was by then largely over.

In the long run, however well-intentioned or otherwise the crown may have been, there was little that could lessen the traumatic impact of the conquest on the native population. The Indian, in W. H. Prescott's deservedly famous phrase, became 'an alien in the land of his fathers'. Indian culture certainly survived, at the level of the local community, but it was now exposed to unprecedented pressures and strains. Not only were Indians now liable to have to supply labour for their overlords, either under the *encomienda* or through other forced-labour systems presently introduced; their lands, too, were steadily encroached on by the newcomers, although it was not until the seventeenth century that the great estate began to assume its place as the dominating feature of the Spanish American rural scene – and even then, much land remained in the hands of the Indian communities. Sometimes the Indian communities adapted to the new circumstances, with a degree of success only now beginning to be recognized by historians. Sometimes they did not. Occasionally, too, humanitarian clerics such as Vasco de Quiroga (*c.* 1470–1565), an admirer of Sir Thomas More's *Utopia*, tried to set up model Indian communities – something the Jesuit order accomplished in its province of Paraguay in the seventeenth and eighteenth centuries. These experiments, however, did little to diminish the overall impact of the conquest.

It must also be remembered that from the start the simple dividing-line between conquerors and conquered was blurred by fraternization and the natural concomitant of miscegenation – racial mixing – that continued throughout colonial times. The conquest, by its nature, was largely a masculine adventure; unions between Spaniards and Indian women were very common; in consequence, mestizos (half-Spanish, half-Indian) made their appearance at an early date. One of their outstanding early representatives was the Peruvian chronicler Inca Garcilaso de la Vega (1539–1616), son of a Spanish conquistador and an Inca princess. Some conquistadors fathered literally scores of mestizo children. One of the conquerors of Chile, Francisco de Aguirre (1508–81), actually recognized at least fifty, and boldly declared (to the displeasure of the Church) that 'the service rendered to God in engendering mestizos is greater

Spanish doorway of the house of the marqueses de San Juan de Buenavista built on the foundations of the palace of Inca Roca

than the sin incurred in so doing'. Miscegenation was one of the deepest legacies of the period of conquest, since it did not stop, and led directly to the multiracial societies of today.

An empire established

The age of the conquistadors was fairly brief. The Spanish crown had no intention of allowing these vigorous, ambitious men to rule the colonies unchecked. (For much the same reason, later on, it limited the extent of *encomienda*-grants, fearing that *encomenderos* might become a powerful colonial nobility, difficult to control.) The conquerors fell victim to the centralizing absolutism Spanish monarchs were trying to consolidate, at home as well as across the ocean. A framework of settled colonial institutions was speedily imposed on all the newly conquered territories. In Spain itself, in the aftermath of the conquest of Mexico, a separate royal council (the Council of the Indies) was set up to supervise the government of the new empire. In America, political and administrative jurisdictions were soon defined: both Mexico (New Spain) and Peru were designated as 'viceroyalties' within a decade of their respective conquests. Spanish governors, bureaucrats and (not least) treasury officials took up their places in the emerging structure of imperial government. Surviving conquistadors were edged aside, sometimes paid off with titles or lands. Thus Cortés, who had personally governed Mexico in the years immediately after his triumph, was gradually deprived of his power (though not his wealth), as was Jiménez de Quesada, the conqueror of New Granada, passed over in favour of another governor almost as soon as he completed his conquest. (In Peru, the conquistadors indulged in civil war amongst themselves – Pizarro was assassinated – and briefly rebelled against the incoming Spanish authorities.) Columbus himself, earlier on,

The colonial period

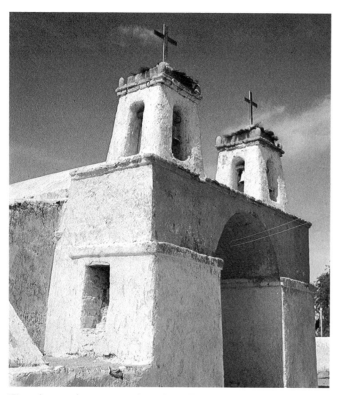

The sixteenth-century church at Chiu-chiu, Chile

had been treated in a similar fashion: the pattern was unmistakable from the outset. Spain's empire was to be an empire, not a patchwork of unruly territories governed by powerful warlords. (That was to come later, after independence.)

The Catholic Church, too, assumed its place – a fundamental place – in the new framework of empire. Generous concessions by the Papacy allowed the Spanish crown a high degree of control over the Church in America. It soon built up an appropriate diocesan and parochial structure. In 1545, with the creation of the archdioceses of Mexico, Lima and Santo Domingo, the colonial hierarchy became separate from that of Spain. The various religious orders (including the Jesuits after their papal recognition in 1540) were present in force in the colonies, extremely active over the next decades (in fact, centuries) in what has been called the *conquista espiritual*, the 'spiritual conquest' of the native populations – an extraordinarily tenacious effort, however it may be judged by a more secular (and relativist) culture. The Spanish Inquisition set up branches in the two viceregal capitals in 1570–1. It was never quite as active in America as in Spain: it sponsored about a hundred burnings in colonial times.

The commercial system, as it developed, reflected the Spanish desire for control and regulation. The *Casa de Contratación* (Trade

House) at Seville was the very earliest specifically imperial institution to be created, opening in 1503. It closely supervised trade between America and Spain. With the great silver-strikes of the mid-sixteenth century – production expanded massively after 1550 – trans-Atlantic trade assumed the shape it was to retain for two hundred years. From now onwards it was based on regular annual sailings of 'fleets' – convoys – to and from a small number of approved ports. Two fleets left Spain each year, one bound for Mexico, the other for the Panama isthmus and northern South America. A single convoy, carrying silver to Spain, completed the round-trip. A subsidiary system operated up and down the Pacific coast of South America. From the 1570s, also, regular sailings between Acapulco in Mexico and Manila in Spain's newly conquered Asian colony, the Philippines, enabled Mexican silver to be traded for Chinese silks. (Year after year the 'Manila galleon' plied its lonely course across the north Pacific, never once sighting the Hawaiian islands, which were discovered only in 1778, by Captain Cook.)

By 1580 Spain's huge American empire was well into its period of consolidation. It had already become legendary. The Spaniards who ruled the empire regarded it, in the manner of successful imperialists throughout the ages, with pride and satisfaction. Other Europeans, it is fair to say, were awed by the magnitude of Spanish acquisitions in the New World, and this awe long outlasted the sixteenth century. Intelligent foreigners were sometimes to reflect on the stability of the empire, with its large mixed population. 'I have marvelled sometimes at Spain,' wrote Francis Bacon, 'how they clasp and contain so large dominions with so few natural Spaniards.' But it was the sheer geographical span of Spain's empire that impressed most Europeans, so that Dr Samuel Johnson, in the eighteenth century, could still ask, with only a light touch of irony:

> Has heaven reserved, in pity to the poor,
> No pathless waste or undiscovered shore,
> No secret island in the boundless main,
> No peaceful desert yet unclaimed by Spain?

SC

Further reading

B. Díaz del Castillo, *True History of the Conquest of New Spain*, trans. A. P. Maudslay (New York, 1956)

J. Hemming, *The Conquest of the Incas* (London, 1970)

F. A. Kirkpatrick, *The Spanish Conquistadores* (London, 1934)

M. León-Portilla, *The Broken Spears: the Aztec Account of the Conquest of Mexico* (Boston, Mass., 1962)

J. Lockhart and E. Otte, eds., *Letters and People of the Spanish Indies, Sixteenth Century* (Cambridge, 1976)

J. H. Parry, *The Discovery of the Sea* (London, 1974)

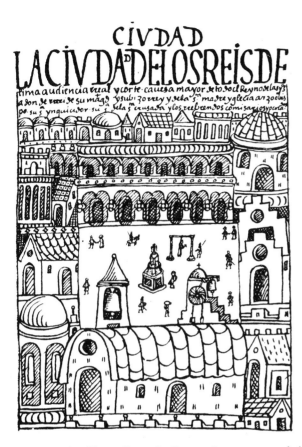

The city of Lima (from Guamán Poma, *La nueva corónica*)

The very prosperity of Peru by the end of Toledo's viceregency was the material factor which turned Francis Drake's circumnavigation of 1577–80 into such a profitable enterprise, for the four months which the *Golden Hind* spent off the coast of Peru in 1579 culminated in the seizure of a shipment of silver on its way to Panama. That Drake was able to behave with such impunity drew attention to the fact that the defences of Peru had depended hitherto upon inaccessibility rather than naval or military resources. But attempts at settlement rather than piracy by Spain's potential colonizing rivals in northern Europe had not yet begun. England's first faltering attempts at colonization in America, the abortive Roanoke voyages of 1584 and 1587, were still to come, and the successful settlement of Virginia was to wait until 1607. Portugal, Spain's one serious challenger as a colonial power in the sixteenth century, had confined its American activities to Brazil, a land of vast potential, but one which did not attract Spaniards because of its apparent scarcity of precious metals and its certain shortage of sedentary natives. In any case the union of the Spanish and Portuguese crowns in 1580 in the person of Philip II of Spain, while not guaranteeing peace on the frontier between Spanish Paraguay and Brazil, at least provided the Habsburg monarchy with theoretical control of the vast Portuguese overseas empire.

By 1580, the initial phase of exploration and settlement which had characterized Spanish expansion on the mainland of America for more than sixty years had given way to one of consolidation and stability. Spain had emerged from the process with an enormous empire stretching, nominally at least, from California, Texas and Florida in the north, through Central America, the major islands of the Caribbean, and all of South America except Brazil as far as Cape Horn. There remained within these boundaries extensive expanses of territory which Spain claimed but did not or could not subdue, in some cases because of physical barriers, in others because of fierce indigenous resistance. The latter was particularly important in southern Chile, Patagonia, and northern Mexico; the former in the almost impenetrable forests east of the Andes from modern Colombia down to Bolivia. Although frontiers were gradually pushed forward into these inhospitable areas throughout the colonial period, the majority were not effectively incorporated into the republics which replaced the Spanish empire until the latter part of the nineteenth century. Nevertheless, by 1580, and sooner in some areas, what might be defined as the heartland of the Spanish empire in America was secure, settled, and subdued, and men like Toledo, who had made such an important personal contribution to the imposition of the authority of the Spanish crown in these distant lands, were able to take pride in their creation of a colonial structure which would endure for a further two centuries and more.

Colonial government

The twin hubs of the Spanish empire in America after 1580 were the viceregal capitals of Mexico and Lima. The viceroyalty of New Spain, which was governed from the former, extended over all Spanish territory on the mainland north of the isthmus of Panama; the viceroyalty of Peru covered all of Spanish South America except for the coast of Venezuela (which was governed from Santo Domingo) until the eighteenth century when two further viceroyalties – New Granada and the River Plate – were created from its northern and southern kingdoms, leaving a rump viceroyalty confined roughly to the territory of modern Peru. Each viceroyalty was further divided into a number of separate areas technically described as kingdoms, each with its own political governor and a tribunal known as an *audiencia* which exercised a mixture of judicial and administrative authority. In the Habsburg period there were four such kingdoms in the viceroyalty of New Spain (Mexico, Guatemala, New Galicia, and Santo Domingo), and six in the viceroyalty of Peru (Peru, Chile, Charcas, Quito, New Granada, and Panama); in the eighteenth century three new *audiencias* were established in South America, with their capitals in

The city of Mexico (Antonio de Solis)

Cuzco, Caracas, and Buenos Aires. These colonial divisions were to prove to be of enormous significance for the construction of the independent republics of the nineteenth century, for in most cases national boundaries were drawn along the lines of the old kingdoms: Charcas, for example, became Bolivia; New Granada became Colombia; the kingdom of Quito became Ecuador.

Within the central kingdom of each viceroyalty the viceroy himself acted as political head; within the subordinate kingdoms of his jurisdiction his actual authority varied according to whether they were classified as presidencies or captaincies-general. In the former routine administration was delegated to the president of the *audiencia*, but matters of policy and military affairs were reserved to the viceroy. This, at least, was the theory, but, in practice the president of a remote capital such as Quito usually enjoyed considerable freedom from the control of the viceroy in distant Lima, except in times of crisis or unless the viceroy was particularly vigilant. In kingdoms which enjoyed the elevated status of captaincies-general, usually those considered by the crown to be particularly vulnerable to foreign intervention – Guatemala, Santo Domingo, New

Granada, and in the eighteenth century Chile and Caracas – the viceroy's authority was almost entirely nominal, with the captains-general acting like mini-viceroys, directly responsible to the Council of the Indies and the king in Madrid. The viceroys and captains-general who governed Spanish America in the name of the crown were almost exclusively rich, powerful Spaniards sent out to the empire for fixed terms with the prospects of returning to high office and rich rewards in the peninsula. In the Habsburg period, when a common pattern was for a successful viceroy of New Spain to be promoted to Peru, they sometimes held noble titles before appointment, while many others were ascetic churchmen or conciliar lawyers; in the eighteenth century the more pragmatic Bourbons tended to look with great favour upon men with military or naval experience, often on the American frontiers. Several viceroys of Peru in this period were former captains-general of Chile. The viceroyalty of Peru lost its primacy to New Spain as the silver production of the latter multiplied in the eighteenth century, but the salaries attached to both – 60,000 pesos or £16,000 in this period – were the same; those attached to the newer viceroyalties of New Granada and Buenos Aires were somewhat lower – 40,000 pesos – but still very generous.

The provision of good salaries for high officials – senior judges were also well-paid – reflected a somewhat naive hope in Madrid that corruption might thus be prevented in distant overseas territories. It was commonly accepted in the Americas, in fact, that a viceroy could live well on the fees and presents which his extensive powers generated, saving his salary for his retirement. As the king's representative, a status confirmed by his title, he was head of both civil and military establishments, he supervised the work of treasury officials, and he exercised important powers of vice-patronage (a point stressed by Toledo in his 1582 memorial) in relation to Church appointments; his own patronage covered many minor posts in the colonial bureaucracy, posts for which status-seeking colonists were often willing to pay, and he also appointed to senior posts during vacancies, which were often extensive; in the legislative field he had power on the one hand to issue ordinances for municipalities and for the regulation of certain activities, subject to ultimate royal approval, and on the other to formally suspend the implementation of crown instructions which he deemed to be inappropriate; he presided over the *audiencia* of his central kingdom, and over the municipal council, or *cabildo*, of his capital city. Conscious of the need to provide checks upon the possible abuse of such extensive powers, the crown itself made some provision of deterrents against maladministration. The council of the Indies, established in 1524 as part of the general conciliar system of the Habsburgs to administer the empire for the crown, had the power to send out a general inspector, or *visitador general*, to investigate the conduct of a viceroy, captain-general, or president who was suspected of serious maladministration. Although effective when applied, this device was used sparingly; much more common, although ultimately less useful in practice than in theory, was the judicial review of conduct, or *residencia*, imposed upon a senior official at the end of his term of office; the Spanish name derives from the requirement that a retiring official remained in residence for a fixed term while a commissioner called for and investigated complaints against him. The files of such cases provide historians with invaluable information about individual abuses, or alleged abuses, which, in the more extreme cases, the crown punished severely. But bribery and influence often rendered the device ineffective, particularly as, on grounds of economy and convenience, the policy was adopted for second-rank administrators of entrusting the inquests to officials arriving to replace those whose conduct was being investigated. According to popular legend, when a provincial governor took up office in the interior of Peru he was usually handed by his predecessor as a bribe a bag of silver which he kept, unopened, to hand on to his own successor in five years' time.

A more effective check upon executive authority in the American capitals, although one which inhibited progressive reforms as well as maladministration, was the complexity of the colonial bureaucracy and of the legislative framework within which it functioned. Treasury ministers, ecclesiastical dignitaries, city councillors, military commanders, and members of closed corporations – of merchants, priests, lawyers, and miners, for example – jealously guarded their prerogatives and privileges, enshrined in a bewildering maze of ordinances and decrees, and could be relied upon to report unfavourably to Madrid upon administrators who attempted to encroach on them. The most powerful and influential watchdogs of all were the judges, or *oidores*, of the *audiencias*. These tribunals not only acted as the superior judicial bodies in their respective kingdoms – appeals to the Council of the Indies were allowed in civil but not criminal cases – but also enjoyed the right to be consulted by the relevant political head in administrative matters. Ultimately the authority of the latter was paramount, but it was generally recognized that the crown would regard with disfavour an administrator who could not work in harmony with his *audiencia*. The sizes of the tribunals varied, but by the eighteenth century they ranged from fourteen ministers in the viceregal capitals to five or six in other cities. In the early Habsburg period strict regulations prohibited the judges from marrying or acquiring property while holding office, but the extension of sale of office in the seventeenth century gradually made it possible for these rules to be evaded and also for rich colonists to obtain appointment as judges in their native cities, where ties of family and influence militated against their impartial administration of justice. Recent research into appointments shows that this state of affairs was at its worst in the first half of the eighteenth century, when colonists attained majorities over

peninsular judges in many of the tribunals, usually by purchase. An incoming viceroy found himself confronted upon taking office in what was usually a strange city with a body of entrenched and powerful officials, often allied by family or business ties to other established groups. The consequence was that inertia, corruption, bribery, and easy social relationships became commoner features of the administrative system than did enterprise, integrity, and honesty. It was in an attempt to reverse this state of affairs that the reforming ministers of the Bourbons began after 1750 to implement a determined policy of appointing peninsular Spaniards to these and other important posts in the empire. They did so, however, at the cost of making the colonists feel that their local interests were being subordinated to those of an increasingly oppressive, centralizing monarchy.

The administration of justice at a local level was delegated to provincial governors known as *corregidores*, who also exercised military and administrative authority within their jurisdictions. Gradually introduced in the second half of the sixteenth century to

A *corregidor* maltreating Indians (from Guamán Poma, *La nueva corónica*)

replace the overmighty *encomenderos*, these officials, who were appointed by the crown, were seen as essential guardians of royal authority. But, although nominally subject to supervision from their superiors in the capital of each kingdom, the *corregidores* themselves often enjoyed virtually unrestricted authority, particularly in remote areas inhabited mainly by Indians. The abuse which provoked most comment from contemporary observers was that known as the *repartimiento*, under which the *corregidor* distributed merchandise to the Indian communities in his province, with the sanction of judicial authority to punish those who were reluctant or unable to pay for the goods which he forced upon them. The practice was defended as a device for incorporating the Indians into the market economy, but its economic benefits were outweighed, particularly in the eighteenth century, by the fierce resistance which it provoked. After legalizing and attempting to control it in the 1750s, the crown went to the opposite extreme in the 1780s by totally prohibiting the *repartimiento* system as part of a general reform of local government, centred on the introduction of a new class of administrators known as intendants. The latter were usually peninsular Spaniards, committed to efficiency, particularly in the collection of taxes, and to the actual rather than nominal recognition of royal authority. But it was only after a major Indian rebellion, led by a descendant of the Incas who called himself Túpac Amaru, which spread through the Andean area in 1780–3, that the ministers of the reforming Charles III (1759–88) introduced this new system first in Peru (1784) and then in New Spain (1786). In the first decade or so after their introduction the intendants did succeed in reducing forced trade with the Indians. They also multiplied the yield of tribute, the head tax paid annually to the crown by adult male Indians, by eradicating fraud in its collection. But they were hampered by increasing confusion in metropolitan government after about 1800, which meant that their reports and suggestions were often not answered, and by the fact that their own subordinates, known as subdelegates, tended to co-operate with the creoles (those of Spanish descent born in the Americas) from whose ranks they were recruited, rather than with their more idealistic superiors.

Indians, mixed castes and whites

The *repartimiento* system and the Indian tribute were two devices which, besides generating revenue for the crown and its officials, forced the indigenous communities to participate in the money economy introduced by the Spaniards. In order to earn the money to meet these burdens Indians had to produce and sell a surplus – usually of agricultural goods or textiles – or they had to hire themselves out to landowners and mineowners. An even cruder institution was that known as the *mita* (or, confusingly, in New Spain as the *repartimiento*), whereby Indian communities were required to provide fixed quotas of men on a rotation basis to work

for either the public authorities or private employers. Rates of payment, maximum distances to be travelled, and similar details were laid down in legislation, but were often ignored. The worst abuses were associated with forced work in the mines. In southern Peru and Bolivia, for example, where Toledo established a rigorous system for the recruitment of 12,000 men a year to work in Potosí, and for a smaller number to work in the mercury mine of Huancavelica, the consequence was a continuous decline in the native population of the contributing provinces throughout the seventeenth century.

The debate among historical demographers about the extent of native depopulation in colonial Spanish America is never likely to be settled satisfactorily, because of uncertainty about the numbers already there when the Spaniards arrived. What is clear is that there was extensive demographic decline in the sixteenth and early seventeenth centuries, followed by stabilization, and then gradual recovery in the eighteenth century. However many Indians lived in New Spain in 1519, we do know that there were only about 1.25 million by 1625, but 2.5 million in 1800; in Peru the initial decline may have been somewhat less catastrophic – to 500,000 at the end of the sixteenth century, rising to about 700,000 in 1800. Extensive and casual cruelty, faithfully chronicled by critical Spanish observers, contributed to this disaster, but it was less significant than the impact of European diseases – measles, influenza, smallpox – against which the natives had no natural resistance. The forcible resettlement of hundreds of thousands of families in *reducciones* or *doctrinas*, new communities where they were accessible to missionaries and crown officials, also disrupted traditional life in New Spain and the Andean area, weakening the will to survive of peoples whose world had been turned upside down within a very short space of time. In Peru these dramatic changes in native settlement and the introduction of the *mita* system are associated with the viceregency of Toledo, who imposed a pattern which was to endure for the rest of the colonial period; in New Spain they were introduced over a longer period, but with consequences for native society which were no less catastrophic. It is important to note however, that, as his 1582 memorial indicates, Toledo regarded his policies for the native population as improvements upon the almost unregulated system of exploitation which he had found in Peru in the 1560s. He at least succeeded in erecting a framework of legislation to protect the Indians from the formal enslavement which many of the conquistadors sought to impose upon them. It is also the case that throughout Spanish America they enjoyed much greater protection from economic exploitation in the colonial period than in the nineteenth century, when republican governments representing the heirs of the conquerors sought to transform them into a mere rural proletariat.

Black slaves working on a sugar plantation (Antonio de Solis)

By the end of the colonial period Indians comprised about 7 million of an estimated Spanish American population of 17 million. They formed the base of the social pyramid, despite the fact that Indian society was itself stratified – theoretically the 'republic' of Indians functioned alongside that of Spaniards – with the consequence that individual native leaders, or caciques, could often be men of considerable wealth and status. Technically inferior to the free Indians were the black slaves, numbering perhaps half a million, who were concentrated in the Caribbean islands, other areas of plantation agricultures, such as the coast of Peru, and in the cities of the empire, where they functioned as artisans and domestics. Historians have debated intensively the proposition that Spanish American (and Brazilian) slavery was milder than that of Anglo-Saxon America. The consensus is that where plantation agriculture was organized on uncompromising capitalistic lines – as it was in Cuba from the late eighteenth century for the production of sugar – there was little difference in practice between the two systems, despite the greater benevolence of Spanish legislation and the role of the Church in keeping slave families together. But the urban slave, ubiquitous in Spanish America, probably did enjoy more benevolent treatment, which often compared favourably with that meted out to Indians by whites. The manumission of slaves, moreover, was a common practice in colonial Spanish America, and accounted for the presence of large numbers of free blacks in those areas where slavery itself was important. It is difficult to give a

precise figure, but by 1800 freemen of African descent probably numbered about another half million.

The intermediate layer of the social pyramid consisted of a broad band of people of mixed blood, predominantly mestizo (Indian and white), but with pockets of mulattoes (black and white) in tropical areas where slavery was important. The emergence and continuous growth of this mixed population was a product less of the Iberian racial democracy, which historians have often emphasized, than of the irresistible fusion which occurred as relatively small numbers of European immigrants settled amongst large numbers of Indians whom they wished to assimilate for a variety of social, economic and cultural reasons. The leading conquerors of Peru formally married Inca princesses; later generations of Europeans were often less scrupulous about the sacrament of matrimony, but as the white population increased and the recruitment of Indian labour was regulated, so, too, the mixed race population expanded, particularly in the cities, to which Indians flocked from rural areas to avoid conscription for the mines. The definition of a mestizo was often imprecise, reflecting social rather than strictly racial classification: those of mixed descent who lived in Indian communities and wore native dress were 'Indian', whereas those who lived in towns and wore Spanish dress were 'mestizo', unless they became very rich, in which case they would be considered 'Spanish'. In the economically more dynamic parts of the empire, or in areas where centuries of attrition had gradually worn down the resistance of nomadic Indians – central Chile is a good example of the latter – there were by 1800 few surviving pockets of genuine Indian culture; in the Andean area, in Central America, and in southern Mexico, however, large numbers of native communities survived the colonial period to await the onslaught of nineteenth-century liberalism.

The upper class in colonial Spanish America consisted of a minority of whites, estimated to number 3.2 million by 1800. They were officially designated *españoles*, Spaniards, although only 150,000 of them – the so-called *peninsulares* – were born in peninsular Spain; the remaining 95 per cent were American Spaniards, or creoles, many of them second- or third-generation colonists whose fathers or grandfathers had gone out to the empire as bureaucrats, soldiers, or private settlers, while others could claim descent from the first conquistadors. It was this white minority, comprising less than 20 per cent of the total Spanish American population, which dominated society, economic life, and government. Its members owned the great haciendas, many of which each employed hundreds of peasants in debt-peonage, the textile factories, and the mines, the ten largest of which were each employing up to 1000 men in New Spain by the late eighteenth century; they staffed the colonial Church, itself a great owner of urban and rural property, sustained by the tithes of the rural population; they filled the honourable professions of soldier, lawyer and university teacher, and were present in tens of thousands in the less prestigious but often more profitable commercial sector. The top echelon could aspire to serve the crown as judges, treasury ministers, and bishops, or could purchase noble titles, while many more obtained employment in government offices as intermediate bureaucrats. Traditionally the most important posts in the administrative hierarchy – viceroy, archbishop, *audiencia* minister, and so on – were reserved for peninsular Spaniards, although the increasing demand of creoles for at least a share of high office in the late colonial period represented not just a remote aspiration but also a desire to return to the situation which had begun to prevail by the early eighteenth century. It would be misleading to suggest that creoles and peninsular Spaniards saw their interests as divergent. In New Spain and Peru, the last of Spain's American colonies to secure independence, they tended to form a cohesive group against the Indian majorities; in Venezuela and the River Plate, where increasing prosperity in the eighteenth century bred a brash self-confidence, the creoles tended to be more ambitious to consolidate their socio-economic status with at least participation in government. Not all European Spaniards in America disagreed with them: first generation migrants who had left the poorer parts of Spain to make new lives in the empire could be more hostile to the mother country than, for example, creole aristocrats whose families had served the crown for generations. It

A mestizo professor and pupil (Joseph Skinner, 1805)

remains true, nevertheless, that by the early nineteenth century a significant minority of whites in Spanish America was beginning to question the validity of Spain's imperial title. In part this situation was a result of the changes which had occurred in the empire in the second half of the eighteenth century as a result of the application there of the Bourbon reforms.

Habsburg decline, Bourbon recovery

The traditional chronology of abject decline in seventeenth-century Spain and glorious recovery under a new monarchy in the eighteenth century is increasingly being questioned by historians, who now suggest that the reign of the last Habsburg, Charles II (1665–1700), was less disastrous, and those of his Bourbon successors less dynamic than has usually been asserted. There is still a massive amount of evidence, nevertheless, to confirm that from the standpoint of the metropolitan government the system devised in the sixteenth century to control, defend, and obtain profit from Spanish America had lost much of its efficiency by the end of the seventeenth century. This was not because Spanish America had 'declined', but rather because more of its wealth was being retained in America or diverted into clandestine trade with other nations. By the late seventeenth century Spain still possessed Cuba, Puerto Rico, and the eastern half of Hispaniola (now the Dominican Republic), but most of the other significant islands in the Caribbean had been seized by its northern European rivals: England had Jamaica, Barbados, and St Kitts; the Dutch had Curaçao; the French had Martinique, Guadeloupe, and Saint-Domingue (modern Haiti). Their presence there posed no permanent threat to the security of the mainland of Spanish America, but it virtually destroyed the integrity of the imperial commercial system, devised in the sixteenth century to secure the safe remission of silver from America to Spain and to preserve Spanish America as a closed market for producers of manufactured and agricultural goods in the peninsula.

The hallmark of the Habsburg commercial system was control by restriction. In Spain only Seville (later Cádiz) was licensed to trade with America; in America only Vera Cruz (serving New Spain), Santo Domingo, and Portobello (serving Peru via the Pacific port of Panama) were licensed to receive the fleets from Andalusia, which were supposed to arrive annually to supply the American market and to take back silver to Spain. The system worked well for the merchant guilds of Seville, Lima, and Mexico, whose members controlled the distribution of merchandise, but it lost its vitality as the colonists turned increasingly to contraband traders to satisfy their demands, often at lower prices than the official channels, and relieve them of their raw materials, including not only silver but also agricultural products. The first Bourbon kings tinkered with the system, replacing convoyed fleets with individual licensed vessels, some of which entered the Pacific, in the early eighteenth century, but it was not until the reign of Charles III that a comprehensive reform of the commercial structure occurred. Alarmed by the British capture of Havana in 1762, during the Seven Years' War, and impressed by its captors, Charles III's ministers gradually extended *comercio libre* (unrestricted trade) within the Spanish empire. Although it was not completely available to New Spain and Venezuela until 1789, the major reform came in 1778 when the principal ports of the empire obtained permission to trade freely with each other and with the thirteen leading ports of Spain.

Seen against the backcloth of the unreformed system, the commercial boom unleashed by the 1778 legislation was a brilliant success: between 1782 and 1796 exports from Spain to America were worth on average four times their 1778 value, and for the first time for many years goods produced in Spain became more important than re-exports; at the American end mining production doubled in Peru and quadrupled in New Spain in the last quarter of the century. Although silver remained the most important commodity exported to Spain, agriculture, which had always been more important than mining in the American domestic economy, also began to

A colonial hacienda near Potosí

SPANISH AMERICA IN 1808

contribute to trans-Atlantic trade, as sugar from Cuba and New Spain, cochineal from Central America, cocoa beans and tobacco from Venezuela, and hides from the River Plate region began to be exported to Europe in ever-increasing quantities. The export of hides through Buenos Aires, to take but one example, rose from 150,000 a year before 1778 to some 1.4 million after 1783, as the capital of the new viceroyalty of the River Plate, created in 1776, entered an era of unprecedented prosperity. Here, as in Venezuela, Chile, and other parts of the empire which had been economic and political backwaters until the ministers of Charles III recognized their potential, the more oppressive fiscal and administrative regime associated with the intendant system was acceptable as long as the mother country was capable of supplying the commercial stimulus which revolutionized economic life after 1778. For two decades it seemed that Spain could, indeed, fulfil this function, despite the fact that the modest industrial growth which it experienced in the second half of the century was overshadowed by that of England. But Spain's entry in 1796 into the French war against Britain – a war which was to persist in different stages until 1815 – threw its trans-Atlantic trade into turmoil, as the British navy blockaded Spanish ports. In a desperate attempt to maintain the flow of commerce with Spanish America, and the revenues which it generated, Spain opened trade to neutral vessels in 1797, but refused steadfastly to accede to the growing clamour from its American subjects for the right to trade freely with the world at large.

The first decade of the nineteenth century was one of growing estrangement between Spain and Spanish America, as the financial demands of the metropolis intensified and the prosperity of the late eighteenth century began to fade. An increasing number of articulate creoles began to apply the same process of rational enquiry which had underpinned the Bourbon reforms to the very relationship between the Spanish crown and its American possessions, and to wonder whether the latter had attained sufficient maturity to follow the precedent set by the United States and establish their independence. The abortive attempt of Francisco de Miranda to mount an emancipating invasion of Venezuela in 1806 demonstrated that only a very small minority sympathized openly with this point of view; the British invasions of Buenos Aires and Montevideo in 1806–7, also dismal failures, emphasized that even fewer creoles were willing to exchange Spanish rule for that of Britain, notwithstanding their readiness to trade with the invader. Both episodes coupled with the increasing weakness of Spain in Europe, did draw attention, however, to the fact that Spanish America was relying increasingly upon its own military resources for its defence. When, in 1808, Napoleon Bonaparte invaded Spain, deposed Ferdinand VII, and installed Joseph Bonaparte as king in Madrid, the instinctive response of Spanish Americans was to rally to the mother country and support the improvised resistance movement there which held the French at bay in 1808–9. But as news began to arrive in 1810 of the collapse of the anti-French forces, small groups of determined revolutionaries seized the opportunity to depose the peninsular authorities, thus initiating the bloody wars which finally brought independence to the whole mainland of Spanish America by 1825.

A majority of creoles did not aspire to independence in 1808, despite an awareness that the Spanish Bourbons had turned their American possessions for the first time in their history into real colonies, rigorously exploited for the benefit of the metropolis. By 1810 more were becoming aware of the feasibility of securing it, perhaps even the necessity to do so, if Spanish America was not to

fall under French control. But when the revolutions for independence began, the immediate reaction of most Spanish Americans was to fight not for independence but to preserve the ties which bound them to Spain. That they did so was a reflection of both their innate conservatism and the strength of the imperial tradition which had persisted for over three centuries.

JRF

Further reading

C. Gibson, *Spain in America* (New York, 1966)
C. H. Haring, *The Spanish Empire in America* (New York, rev. edn, 1952)
J. Lockhart and S. B. Schwartz, *Early Latin America: a History of Colonial Spanish America and Brazil* (Cambridge, 1983)
J. Lynch, *The Spanish American Revolutions 1808–1826* (London, 1973)
M. Mörner, *Race Mixture in the History of Latin America* (Boston, Mass., 1967)
J. H. Parry, *The Spanish Seaborne Empire* (London, 1966)

Colonial Brazil, 1600–1808

Portuguese monarchs	
[Aviz Dynasty]	
1481–95	John (João) II
1495–1521	Manoel I 'the Fortunate'
1521–57	John III 'the Pious'
1557–78	Sebastian
1578–80	Cardinal Henry
1580–1640	*Portugal under the Spanish crown*
[Braganza Dynasty]	
1640–56	John IV
1656–67	Afonso VI
1667–1706	Pedro II
1706–50	John V
1750–77	José I [Pombal ministry]
1777–1816	María I
1816–26	John VI

The growth of a sugar colony

By 1600 the essential economic, social, and political patterns of Portugal's Brazilian colony had been firmly established. A population of about 100,000 including some 30,000 whites, 15,000 black slaves, and a remainder of Indians and people of mixed origin lived in and around the twenty or so settlements along the coast. The few cities like Salvador (Bahia) and Olinda were on the coast, serving as administrative control points and as commercial centres for the growing sugar industry. The social and cultural patterns of Portugal were transferred to the colony, but like the European population, tended to concentrate in the larger coastal towns. Salvador, as the capital, also became an episcopal see in 1552 (later raised to archiepiscopal status in 1674) and by the end of the century Franciscans, Carmelites and Benedictines had joined the Jesuits in developing the colony's religious life. Administration and the judicial structure were strengthened in 1609 with the creation of a high court of appeals (*Relação*) staffed by royal judges. Increasingly, however, social and political forms in Brazil were determined by the colony's economic *raison d'être*, the sugar industry.

Sugar cane, introduced from Madeira and São Tomé, grew well in Brazil and by 1585 some 120 sugar mills (*engenhos*) were scattered along the coast, although two-thirds of them were found in the north-eastern captaincies of Pernambuco and Bahia. By 1600 Brazilian production was probably about 8–9000 tons, and in the next thirty years, aided by the introduction of a new milling system, the number of mills and total production increased rapidly. Brazil became in this period the largest producer of sugar in the Atlantic world, and the colony experienced a vigorous expansion. By 1630 there were 350 mills in operation, and during the next decades sugar constituted over 90 per cent of the colony's export value.

The structure and needs of the sugar industry set the context of Brazilian society. The *engenhos* combined industrial operations with the growing and harvesting of sugar cane because of the need to process the cane immediately after cutting it. Thus each *engenho* was a factory in the field, demanding the investment of large amounts of capital for land, buildings, machinery, oxen, and labour. Those who lacked sufficient capital to set up their own mill often grew cane and supplied it to an *engenho* under a variety of sharecropping or other contractual arrangements. These *lavradores de cana* or cane farmers usually owned their own slaves and sometimes their own land and they hoped eventually to establish mills of their own. Above all, the *engenhos* needed large amounts of skilled and unskilled labour. Technicians and artisans were essential for sugar production. In addition, from the beginnings of the industry in Brazil, the plantations depended on coerced or enslaved labour. Estates with over 200 slaves were not unknown but were exceptional, and an average *engenho* might have ten or twenty free labourers and sixty to a hundred slaves in addition to three or four dependent cane farmers each with their own group of six to ten slaves.

From well before 1600, the Portuguese had turned increasingly to Africa for their supply of labour. In the seventeenth century about 4–5000 slaves a year were imported from West Africa and Angola. Slavery and the Brazilian economy became inextricably linked. 'Without Angola no slaves, without slaves no sugar, without sugar no Brazil,' was a common expression in that century. Brazil remained continually dependent on the slave trade. During the eighteenth century over 1 million slaves were imported from Africa to Brazil. African-born slaves always outnumbered those born in Brazil and the cultural impact of Africa was very strong in the plantation regions.

Slavery and the plantation regime imposed a social hierarchy that eventually characterized even non-plantation regions. The mill-owning families became an aristocracy controlling the social and political life at the local level. Invariably white, this aristocracy was always open to merchants or recent immigrants who by purchase or marriage took on the role of *senhor de engenho*. The planters, and to a lesser extent the merchants, controlled local politics through the municipal councils and they shared authority with the thin layer of royal bureaucrats sent out from Portugal who themselves often became linked by personal or business ties to the local aristocracy. Cane farmers were often in effect proto-planters, drawn from the same origins but lacking sufficient funds to set themselves up independently. At the bottom of the social scale was the mass of the population distinguished primarily by its colour and legal status, black and slave. In this sense, the social structure resembled the plantation's organization. A significant portion of the colonial population, however, was composed of people of mixed origin, the result of miscegenation between European, Indians, and Africans, as well as some poorer whites, manumitted blacks and their descendants, and free Indians. These people often performed artisan occupations in the towns or lived as peasants, herdsmen, and free labourers in rural areas. While miners, ranchers or merchants formed the upper class in non-plantation regions, the principles of stratification remained the same.

Foreign attack and internal expansion

The rise of Brazil from an imperial backwater to a wealthy plantation colony was not without its costs. The union of Spain and Portugal under the Spanish Habsburgs (1580–1640) made the Portuguese empire a prime target for Spain's enemies. The Dutch seized Salvador for a year in 1624–5 before they were dislodged by a joint Luso-Spanish fleet, but they soon returned, taking Olinda in 1630 and then expanding their control over much of north-eastern Brazil. The Dutch West India Company tried to stimulate the sugar industry in Netherlands Brazil by extending credit to Portuguese planters and by regularizing the slave trade, to which end they seized Luanda in 1641. These policies, along with religious toleration extended to Catholics and even to the Portuguese crypto-Jewish population, worked relatively well under the enlightened rule of

Governor Johan Maurits of Nassau, but his departure and the recall of loans by the Dutch West India Company combined with nationalistic sentiments to bring about a rebellion against the Dutch in 1645. This movement received the unofficial support of Portugal which by this time was supposedly at peace with Holland and at war with Spain. In 1654, after suffering a major defeat at Guararapes (1649), the Dutch were forced to abandon their last strongholds.

Although the colony was unified once again under Portuguese control, the economic situation at mid-century was gloomy. The revolt and ten years of warfare had destroyed many plantations and disrupted the sugar economy. Matters were made worse by competition from places like Barbados and other West Indian islands, which not only drove down the price of sugar, but also drove up the price of slaves. Despite some recovery in the last decade of the century and the development of another staple, tobacco, the agricultural prospects of Brazil were dim. The second half of the seventeenth century was thus marked by increasing efforts to find new sources of wealth in the colony. Leading the way in this were the frontiersmen from the southern town of São Paulo which, located inland, had turned its fortunes towards the interior. Beginning in the late sixteenth century, bands of these *paulistas*, many of whom were in fact *mamelucos* of mixed European-Indian back-

A mulatto soldier (Albert Eckhout)

ground, moved into the interior in search of minerals and Indians who (under loopholes in the legislation) could be enslaved. By the 1620s these expeditions or *bandeiras* were raiding Jesuit missions in Spanish-controlled Paraguay and were moving southward onto the plains of Uruguay and northward into the centre of the continent, pushing well beyond the line of Tordesillas that divided the Spanish and Portuguese possessions in America. While the *paulistas* were noted for their independence and arrogance, the crown could not ignore their skills as explorers and backwoodsmen. The great *bandeira* of Antonio Raposo Tavares (1648–52) that traversed the continent had governmental support. The combination of private initiative and governmental sponsorship led eventually to the establishment of a Portuguese outpost at Colonia do Sacramento on the banks of the River Plate in 1680 and the subsequent settlement of the lands that lay between it and São Paulo. Government-sponsored expeditions also searched for silver and emeralds in the 1670s, with little success, but by 1695 news filtered out to the coast that the *paulistas* had found gold in the interior.

As news of the gold strikes spread, a great 'rush' quickly ensued. Swarms of men left the coastal towns and plantations and poured into the areas of the gold washings in the region that was soon to be known as Minas Gerais. They were joined by a wave of immigration of some 4–5000 a year who came out from Portugal and the Azores. Since labour in Brazil was associated with slavery, voluntary immigration was matched by an active slave trade fuelled by demand for labour and facilitated by the ability of the prospectors to pay in gold. By 1720 Minas Gerais had some 35,000 slaves. In fact, the discovery of gold in the south-central interior of Brazil caused a decided population shift away from the coast. In 1775 half the 300,000 inhabitants of Minas Gerais were slaves. At this time Minas Gerais had about 20 per cent of the colony's people, making it the most populous captaincy of Brazil.

It took a decade and a civil war to control the wild and raucous miners. The *paulistas* considered the gold strikes to be theirs and hostilities between them and the 'tenderfeet' (*emboabas*) erupted in a civil war (1708–9) in which the *paulistas* lost to their opponents, who were backed by the crown. Rough mining camps eventually evolved into a network of towns around the administrative centre of Vila Rica de Ouro Preto, and an active bureaucracy designed especially to collect taxes and control smuggling was firmly in place by 1730. New gold strikes and finds of diamonds between 1715 and 1735 led to a further movement of population and extension of governmental control. Production of gold rose steadily, reaching a high of over 15 tons of gold between 1750 and 1755. After this point, production began to fall, so that by the 1770s Brazil was once again faced by the problem of declining exports. Even so, the Brazil fleets carried great quantities of gold back to Portugal and much governmental activity in Brazil was devoted to methods of taxation,

GOLD PRODUCTION IN BRAZIL

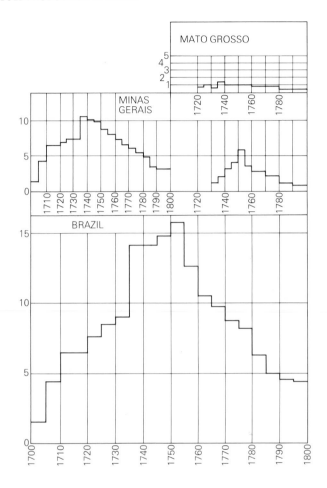

new importance, which along with its proximity to the southern borderlands on the River Plate, made it a more attractive administrative centre than Salvador. In 1763 the colonial capital was moved to Rio de Janeiro. In Minas Gerais itself a distinctive society developed in the gold-mining towns in which the miners' wealth was used to sponsor the buildings of churches which stimulated a whole range of artisan activities. Like the coast, however, the hierarchy of colour and legal status applied in Minas Gerais as well, where so large a proportion of the population was composed of slaves or free persons of colour.

The Pombaline reforms

The effects of Brazilian mineral wealth on Portugal were in the long run unfavourable. Militarily and commercially closely aligned with England, especially after the Methuen Treaty of 1703, Portugal paid its balance of trade deficit with Brazilian gold which flowed in large quantities into the hands of English merchants who increasingly penetrated the lines of Portuguese colonial commerce.

The loosening of Portuguese dependence on England, the increase of central authority in Lisbon, and the resuscitation of the colonial empire, especially Brazil, became the primary goals of Sebastião José de Carvalho e Melo, later Marquis of Pombal, who from 1755 to 1777 was prime minister and virtual dictator of the Portuguese empire. He frontally attacked groups whose position or power were in conflict with his regalist sentiments. Thus, the nobility was persecuted and the Jesuits were expelled from all Portuguese lands in 1759. A series of administrative changes and fiscal reforms were instituted by Pombal, designed to increase the flow of wealth into the royal coffers and to weaken the grip of foreign merchants on Portuguese commerce. Realizing that the key to Portugal's prosperity lay in Brazil, he instituted a series of reforms in the colony, appointing vigorous administrators to carry them out. Both diplomacy and warfare were used in the 1760s and 1770s in an attempt to define the extent of Brazil's boundaries with neighbouring Spanish American colonies. His measures like the creation of Boards of Inspection and the use of monopoly companies like the Company of Pernambuco and Paraíba (1750) were designed to increase agricultural exports. Fiscal policies and tax collection in the mining areas were tightened. In all this, however, he did not exclude the colonials. While many Brazilians objected to the constraints of more effective government, elite Brazilian families were not displaced from their traditional positions of authority or prevented from gaining new ones. Brazil had neither a university nor a printing press prior to 1808 and while it did develop a small intelligentsia among the elite, their intellectual, professional, and political life was always tightly linked to Portugal. Pombal did nothing to change that pattern.

Certain regions especially benefited from governmental reforms

the creation of colonial mints, and contraband control in order to assure the continued flow of this golden stream to the metropolis.

Gold proved to be a mixed blessing to Brazil and Portugal. At first, it seemed that the movement of population away from the coast and the new demand for slaves with resulting higher prices would spell the death knell for staple export agriculture, but limitations placed on the slave trade to Minas Gerais and other measures eventually softened the impact of the gold rush. Commercial agriculture survived and, in fact, even at the height of gold production, the value of sugar exports exceeded that of gold. Mining not only opened new regions to settlement but created new demands as well. The new markets in the mining zones caused an expansion of ranching in the north-east, and created a whole new ranching area on the plains of Rio Grande do Sul in southern Brazil. The shift of population into south-central Brazil and the importance of gold in the economy gave Rio de Janeiro, the port closest to the mines, a

The colonial town of Ouro Preto

and the conditions created by them. Rio de Janeiro's new importance as the colonial capital was matched by an expansion of its agricultural exports. The vast, previously undeveloped region of northern Brazil became a major target for Pombal's reforms. Created as a separate state of Maranhão (1621), its two principal captaincies of Pará and Maranhão with their respective cities of Belém and São Luiz were for much of their previous history colonial backwaters. The European population was small, efforts to set up a plantation economy had failed (and thus there were few black slaves), and there was little in the region to attract settlement. Despite laws to the contrary, Indian slavery in various forms persisted in the Amazon basin, where the colonists competed with Jesuit missionaries for control of the population.

Pombal's policies were designed to make northern Brazil an integral and valuable part of the empire. A Company of Grao Pará and Maranhão was created in 1755 to promote development of exports. It stimulated the export of cacao from Pará, but its greatest success was in Maranhão where it supplied slaves to a now rapidly expanding cotton economy. Like its sister company of Pernambuco it distributed European goods to the colony and provided a regularized trade, but it was sorely disliked by some merchants in

Lisbon and by many colonials. Both companies were abolished shortly after Pombal's fall from power in 1777. In other areas, too, Pombal's reforms were confused or misguided. The system of missions in the far north was replaced in 1757 by the directorate system in which Indians were placed under lay administrators in an attempt to integrate them into the wage labour force and to stimulate their contact with the Portuguese. The directorate system was a disaster for the Indians and failed to produce the desired results. Even in 1800 the Amazonian region remained an area of extractive economy dependent on Indian labour with a predominantly mixed-blood population. Maranhão by that date, however, had developed an active staple economy based on slavery and to that extent resembled more closely the rest of Brazil.

Whatever the deficiencies of Pombal's policies, the decline of gold production and weak prices for Brazilian products created a context in which any reforms were doomed to limited success. Despite the Pombaline measures, the value of Brazilian exports in 1776 was only 40 per cent of their value in 1760. Nevertheless, his policies set the stage for an economic renaissance at the end of the eighteenth century. New staples like cotton, rice, and indigo from regions such as Rio de Janeiro and Maranhão joined more traditional exports of sugar, hides, and tobacco, stimulated by growing demand abroad. In the 1790s with the elimination of Saint-Domingue (Haiti) as a sugar producer, Brazilian production soared, expanding into new regions like São Paulo and intensifying in traditional sugar areas like Bahia and Pernambuco. This economic growth was paralleled by an expansion of the population, growing from about 1.5 million in 1776 to over 2 million by 1800. Much of this population was of African or Afro-American origin, a result of miscegenation and of a slave trade expanding rapidly at the end of the century in response to the agricultural revival. Import levels for slaves in the last decade of the eighteenth century and first decade of the nineteenth were over 20,000 a year. Around 1800 about one-third of the Brazilian population was slave, two-thirds of the remainder were black or mulatto, and one-third was European. There was considerable regional variation in this pattern.

By 1808 the role of Brazil within the colonial empire of Portugal had changed considerably. In the 1770s almost 75 per cent of the crown's colonial income was generated by Brazil and by 1807 over 60 per cent of all the goods Portugal exported were of Brazilian origin. Brazilian products allowed Portugal to establish a positive balance of trade with the rest of Europe, but this situation in turn caused the metropolis to have a deficit with its own colony which increasingly, if illegally, purchased goods directly from England. With this inversion of the colonial relationship, Brazilians became restive under Portuguese restrictive policies such as the limitation on local textile industries (1785). Agitation grew for free trade and open ports.

The signs of strain in the colonial relationship were showing. Earlier manifestations of nativism like the War of the Emboabas or the War of the Mascates (1710–11) in Pernambuco had not aimed at deep political or social change, but in the spirit of the times such ideas began to emerge in the late eighteenth century. Nevertheless, as several episodes showed, the dissatisfaction of Brazilian planters and merchants over economic policy was always muted by the fear of social unrest in this essentially slave-based society. When, however, in 1807 the prince regent of Portugal and the whole court were forced to flee Napoleon's army by sailing under English protection for Brazil, the economic and political basis of the colonial relation between Portugal and Brazil was already in question. Dom João VI, as prince regent and later as king, was faced with the problem of reconciling the aspirations and power of the Brazilian colony with the needs and interests of Portugal. As the period from 1808 to the declaration of Brazilian independence in 1822 demonstrates, it was perhaps an impossible task.

SBS

Further reading

D. Alden, *Royal Government in Colonial Brazil* (Berkeley, 1968)

C. R. Boxer, *The Golden Age of Brazil, 1695–1750* (Berkeley, 1962)

G. Freyre, *The Masters and the Slaves: a Study in the Development of Brazilian Civilization* (New York, 1964)

J. Lockhart and S. B. Schwartz, *Early Latin America: a History of Colonial Spanish America and Brazil* (Cambridge, 1983)

C. Prado, Jr, *The Colonial Background of Modern Brazil* (Berkeley, 1967)

S. B. Schwartz, *Sovereignty and Society in Colonial Brazil: the High Court of Bahia and Its Judges, 1609–1751* (Berkeley, 1973)

The non-Spanish Caribbean islands to 1815

New island colonies

When the tide of Spanish conquest engulfed the American mainland in the 1520s and 1530s, the Caribbean island colonies (Hispaniola, Puerto Rico, Cuba) set up after Columbus's voyages lost much of their importance. Even so, the Caribbean sea was part of the vital maritime link between America and Spain; in any case, it lay on the western (Spanish) side of the Tordesillas Line, the line separating Spanish and Portuguese zones of dominance. Spain therefore claimed a monopoly on all trade and navigation throughout the West Indies, and sought to enforce it.

The Tordesillas principle was never taken very seriously in other European countries. 'The sun shines for me as for others,' said King François I of France, 'and I should very much like to see the clause in Adam's will that excludes *me* from a share of the world.' Assertive nation-states such as France, England and (a bit later) the newly independent Netherlands were eager to grasp the commercial opportunities they saw in the Caribbean – to grasp them, of course, at Spain's expense. From the 1530s, French privateers were a serious menace to Spanish shipping. In the mid-1550s they even sacked Havana, in Cuba, then virtually undefended – the impressive fortifications visible there today show that Spain quickly took the hint. From the 1560s the English too conducted aggressive trading and raiding forays into the supposedly 'closed' sea, with John Hawkins (1532–95) and, especially, Francis Drake (c. 1543–96), legendary as 'El Draque', inspiring terror in Spain's colonies. After 1600 it was the Dutch who were the most forceful in their assaults on the Spanish monopoly.

The obvious need was for local bases – bases from which to trade and, if necessary, maraud. With little prospect of wresting major territories from Spain, the European interlopers focused their gaze on the small Windward and Leeward Islands – the beautiful chain of the Lesser Antilles. These were islands the Spaniards had generally left alone, in some cases deterred by the fierce native Carib populations, which, indeed, continued to deter and harass later colonists. In fact, the islands of Dominica, St Vincent and St Lucia were to remain Carib redoubts till the eighteenth century, though increasingly infiltrated by European (especially French) squatters. (As late as the Treaty of Aix-la-Chapelle in 1748 these islands were still declared 'neutral' by the European powers. All eventually became British.) When a French party took possession of Grenada in the 1650s – the first of several invasions of that beautiful island – the local Caribs eventually leapt to their death from a cliff rather than surrender. The village at that spot is still called Sauteurs, 'Jumpers'. (A handful of Caribs survives today on the island of Dominica.)

In the two decades after 1620, England, France and Holland all gained permanent colonies in the West Indies. The English settled on St Kitts (1623–5), Barbados (1625), Nevis (1628), Antigua (1632) and Montserrat (1632). The most important of these was Barbados. France also colonized St Kitts (1625) – the island was long shared by French and English – and in 1635 the French Compagnie des Iles d'Amérique began settling Martinique and Guadeloupe. In the 1630s also, the Dutch secured the trading bases they needed on the small islands of the Curaçao group, off the Venezuelan coast, and on the even smaller islands of St Eustatius, St Martin (shared with France after 1648) and Saba, in the Leewards. Denmark, too, became a Caribbean power by colonizing St Thomas

Colonial fortifications at St Kitts

Table 35. Sugar production (in tons) and slave populations in four Caribbean island colonies

BARBADOS			JAMAICA		
Year	Sugar	Slaves	Year	Sugar	Slaves
1680	—	38 400	1703	4 782	45 000
1712	6 343	42 000	1730	15 972	74 500
1757	7 068	63 600	1775	47 690	190 000
1792	9 025	64 300	1789	59 400	250 000
1809	6 062	69 400	1808	77 800	324 000
GUADELOUPE			SAINT-DOMINGUE		
Year	Sugar	Slaves	Year	Sugar	Slaves
1674	2 106[a]	4 300	1739	—	117 411
1730	6 230	26 800	1764	60 000	206 000
1767	7 898	71 800	1791	78 696	452 000
1790	8 725	85 500	[Haitian revolution]		
1820	22 300	88 400	1836	8	none

[a] metric tons

Source: Franklin W. Knight, *The Caribbean: the Genesis of a Fragmented Nationalism* (New York, 1978), p. 237.

and St John in the Virgin Islands in the 1670s. Other European states marginally involved in this story are Brandenburg–Prussia, which held minuscule St Peter (Virgin Islands) for a quarter-century after 1689, and Sweden. Sweden's hopes were long frustrated. Only in 1784 did it gain a base, the island of St Barthélemy, ceded by France in exchange for a concession in Europe. (The island reverted to France after a referendum in 1878. Its capital still bears the Swedish name Gustavia.)

Attacks on the well-established Spanish possessions in the Greater Antilles were not very successful. In the vigorous period of the Commonwealth, England sent a force to conquer Hispaniola – Oliver Cromwell's 'Western Design' – but the attack was a fiasco. The expedition did, however, capture the poorly defended island of Jamaica (1655), English possession of which was recognized by Spain in the Treaty of Madrid (1670). At around the same period, French settlers – ranchers and planters – began infiltrating the depopulated western side of Hispaniola, eventually forming the colony of Saint-Domingue. Spain accepted this *fait accompli* in the Treaty of Ryswick (1697).

Sugar and slaves

In the earliest phase of island colonization the English and French intention was to foster settlement colonies in which (among other things) tropical crops were produced by predominantly European labour. Tobacco was such a crop in many of the islands, often bought up and marketed by the ever-obliging Dutch, who were much more interested in trade than in settlement. (As the English governor of Jamaica reported in 1673, 'The Dutch have a proverb: "Jesus Christ is good, but trade is better!" ') Without the Dutch

commercial network (and naval actions against Spain at the critical period) the island colonies might well have perished at birth. History allows no place for gratitude: Dutch predominance offended against the restrictive, monopolistic ideas of 'mercantilism' shared by all early modern empires, and both England (in its Navigation Acts) and France (with Colbert's 'Exclusive') acted later in the seventeenth century to shut the Dutch out from their respective colonial trades.

The heyday of the European settlement colonies was brief. Indentured labour (in the French case *engagé* labour) was unable, in the end, to sustain a successful pattern of colonial life. Nor were transported convict labourers satisfactory. Would-be English settlers eventually found the new mainland colonies of North America more attractive than the tropics. The West Indian islands did, however, lend themselves admirably to sugar cultivation. Once again the indispensable Dutch were on hand to get things going, having gained much experience and expertise during their occupation of north-east Brazil. After 1650 there was a general shift in this new direction. It was a change whose importance for the history of the Caribbean can scarcely be overstated: sugar cultivation brought about a profound transformation of the islands' social structure and, not least, their ethnic make-up. The equation of sugar with slavery is a constant in western-hemisphere history. In the seventeenth and eighteenth centuries, more than half the slaves transported from Africa went to the Caribbean. Europe's sweet tooth (particularly England's) exacted a hideous price in human suffering.

The first important slave-based sugar-producing colony was Barbados – the 'brightest jewel in the crown' for the English long before India took over that description. Barbados was later eclipsed by Jamaica, and Jamaica, in its turn, was surpassed by Saint-Domingue, where there were getting on for half a million slaves by the 1780s. Nearly all the islands went over to sugar monoculture. The commercial importance of the sugar colonies was considerable. In 1773, for instance, Great Britain took a quarter of all its imports from the West Indies – double the imports from the thirteen colonies of North America. At roughly the same period, shipments to and from the West Indies accounted for about one-third of all France's external trade. The Caribbean islands were highly prized by the European powers.

The spread of sugar plantations across the islands soon gave rise to a society that was rigidly divided along lines of colour and legal status. The white minority consisted of a small, powerful elite of planters, along with merchants and professional men, and a miscellaneous group of poorer whites: smallholders, artisans, storekeepers, drifters. All of these, whatever their social status, were free. The overwhelming majority of blacks, by contrast, were slaves – working the plantations, engaged in specialized tasks, employed in domestic service. (Plantation slavery had its own subtle social distinctions.) Alongside the slaves there emerged a class of free mulattoes and blacks – *gens de couleur*, in French colonial parlance – who were sometimes able to acquire property and become prosperous. This group distanced itself from the slave population, but it was usually denied entry to white circles, and its relative success was often resented by the poor whites.

Social tensions of various kinds were thus always latent on the islands, and there were occasional explosions. Slaves themselves periodically rose in desperate revolt. On the Danish island of St John in 1733, for instance, nearly all the local whites were killed. Planters were continuously nervous of such episodes. Another form of black resistance was escape. Where suitably inaccessible terrain was to hand (as in the Cockpit Country and Blue Mountains of Jamaica, or the rugged highlands of Saint-Domingue) runaway slaves – Maroons – were able to live in stable, independent communities that often lasted over several generations. The nucleus of Jamaica's 'Maroon towns' was provided by slaves who ran off when the English arrived: these particular communities held together far longer than similar settlements on other islands, or even in Brazil, where this phenomenon (known locally as the *quilombo*) was familiar in the era of slavery.

Buccaneers and admirals

The Caribbean, from the outset, was an arena of intense international competition. Spain made fitful attempts to dislodge its European rivals, ultimately to no avail, and the new colonial powers frequently fought amongst themselves to win territorial or commercial advantages. Islands were often captured and recaptured: Dutch-held St Eustatius – until devastated by Admiral Rodney in 1781, the most flourishing free port in the Caribbean – once changed hands ten times in as many years (1664–74). This extremely fluid political situation allowed ample scope for unofficial enterprise, and in particular for that notorious seventeenth-century activity, buccaneering.

The buccaneers (known by the Dutch as *zee-roovers*, by the French as *flibustiers*) overshadow a whole phase of Caribbean history. These communities of ruthless cut-throats roamed the West Indies, raiding Spanish settlements (regarded as fair game by all), terrorizing local populations, preying on shipping, and sometimes acting as mercenaries in inter-colonial warfare. Like many such fraternities, the buccaneering bands evolved a distinctive subculture, with rules and conventions – the Custom of the Coast. Despite their reprehensible depredations, they were often regarded as useful allies by colonial governors. In practice, they were only really dependable when it came to attacking Spanish colonies.

Buccaneering was at its height between the 1640s and the 1680s. Its most prominent centres were the French-held island of Tortuga (Tortue), off Hispaniola – headquarters of the notorious Jean-David Nau (d. 1668), better known as L'Olonnais – and the township of Port Royal in Jamaica, which long enjoyed a possibly exaggerated reputation as 'the wickedest town in the world'. Port Royal was the base for the famous (or infamous) Henry Morgan (c. 1635–88) – originally an indentured servant on Barbados – who repeatedly raided Spanish settlements around the Caribbean. His final foray was an audacious and brutal assault on Panama City (1670–1). Morgan survived to win respectability, a knighthood, and the lieutenant-governorship of Jamaica. With the inclusion of the West Indies in standard diplomatic negotiations, and with the introduction of more formalized warfare, buccaneering gradually lost its impetus. In a neatly symbolic way, Port Royal was destroyed by an earthquake in 1692. Morgan's tomb slid beneath the sea. Buccaneers were last hired as mercenaries in a successful French attack on Cartagena in 1697. After that, little more was heard of them.

Their place was taken, in the eighteenth century, by well-organized navies and the distinguished admirals whose names – Vernon, Ogle, Keppel, Rodney, Hood on the British side; de Bouillé, de Grasse, d'Estaing among others on the French – loom so large in the naval annals of the period. The pattern of events in the West Indies was now largely determined by the long struggle for global mastery between France and Great Britain. There were also smaller flurries of Anglo-Spanish warfare. The island colonies once again became pawns in a wider political game – pawns to be seized in war and (as often as not) returned at the ensuing peace conference, when gains and losses were sorted out on a global scale. In the long cycle of Anglo-French wars that started in 1744, to end only in 1815, Great Britain clearly had the edge, and made most of the gains. In the Seven Years' War (1756–63), for instance, the British made a clean sweep of all French possessions (except Saint-Domingue) in the Caribbean, also capturing Havana. Most of these gains, however, were returned under the Treaty of Paris (1763), even though British opinion seriously debated whether to retain Guadeloupe in preference to Canada, which had also been taken from France during the war and was, so to speak, on offer. This was a reflection of the esteem in which the island colonies were held in Europe. There were many in London who thought sugar-rich Guadeloupe a far greater prize than the territory Voltaire had dismissed as *quelques arpents de neige*, 'a few acres of snow'. In the end, broader political considerations prevailed. Canada was taken instead of Guadeloupe.

One reason for the general British superiority in the West Indies was intelligent naval strategy. From the 1740s – in part at the behest of the planters' lobby, influential in British politics – the Admiralty stationed squadrons of warships in the area, with naval dockyards at Jamaica (Port Royal) and Antigua (English Harbour); the latter, now restored, has become a notable yachting centre. (Minor facets of modern Jamaican and Antiguan culture are said to be traceable to this long presence of that most British of British institutions, the Royal Navy.) France did not station a squadron in the West Indies until 1784. Despite short-term reverses in the War of American Independence (1778–83 in its Anglo-French dimension), British pre-eminence in the area was both confirmed and reinforced during the final great struggle with France (1792–1815), at the end of which Trinidad, Tobago, and St Lucia were added to Great Britain's already extensive colonial holdings in the Caribbean.

The Haitian revolution

In the prosperous colony of Saint-Domingue, France's 'Pearl of the Antilles', plantation slavery produced its own drastic denouement before the end of the eighteenth century. Here the French Revolution of 1789 sparked off one of the great explosions of Caribbean history.

Some of Saint-Domingue's rich planters (*grands blancs*) reacted to the upheaval in France by demanding colonial autonomy. But, true to form, they strongly resisted the French National Assembly's decision (May 1791) to enfranchise the *gens de couleur*, the colony's mulattoes and free blacks, who were now pressing their claims to equality with some vehemence. While these dissensions were in progress, the ignored slaves of the plantation-rich Plaine du Nord area – perhaps as many as 100,000 of them – rose in sudden, massive revolt, burning cane-fields and killing whites (August 1791). It was the start of more than a decade of confused, often very savage conflict. A small army sent from France – accompanied by Jacobin commissioners, hostile to the planters and sympathetic to mulattoes and slaves – merely added to the chaos. Only one thing seemed clear by 1793–4: white supremacy in Saint-Domingue was doomed. Planters all round the West Indies were terrified. Nervous feelings

Toussaint
Louverture

were expressed in the southern states of the newly-independent United States.

Encouraged by some of the *grands blancs*, British (and also Spanish) troops invaded Saint-Domingue to restore the status quo. The increasingly shadowy French authorities were obliged to accept the insurgent ex-slaves as their allies. In this situation the numerical strength of Saint-Domingue's blacks was bound to tell. Amidst the bloody turmoil of the 1790s, the initiative passed by stages to a truly remarkable black leader, François-Dominique Toussaint Louverture (1743–1803), himself a former slave from Plaine du Nord. By the end of the decade, having forced the withdrawal of the British (1798) with his now formidable army, Toussaint was supreme in Saint-Domingue, recognized as its governor-general by France, but acting to all intents and purposes as the ruler of an independent country.

By now Saint-Domingue had been devastated by the years of cruel conflict. The plantations lay desolate; the country's 'infrastructure' – not least the superb colonial irrigation systems of the Artibonite Valley and the Plaine du Cul de Sac, important agricultural areas – was destroyed beyond repair. Toussaint did what he could to revive economic activity. His policy on racial matters was conciliatory. He hoped that Saint-Domingue would become if not independent then at least 'a colony forming part of the French empire but subject to special laws' – the 'special laws' including, of course, the abolition of slavery. This posture was not acceptable to France's new ruler, Napoleon Bonaparte. A powerful armament descended on Saint-Domingue, covertly aiming to restore slavery. Toussaint eventually surrendered. He was kidnapped and taken to France, where he soon died in prison (April 1803), though not before William Wordsworth had eulogized him in a famous sonnet.

> There's not a breathing of the common wind
> That will forget thee; thou hast great allies;
> Thy friends are exultations, agonies,
> And love, and man's unconquerable mind.

Toussaint's people, too, proved unconquerable. The French army in Saint-Domingue was checkmated by yellow-fever and by renewed black resistance – resistance stiffened by French atrocities and by the news that slavery, briefly abolished on Guadeloupe, had now been forcibly restored there. The cleverest (and also most ruthless) of Toussaint's lieutenants, Jean-Jacques Dessalines (1758–1806), brought the revolution to its triumphant conclusion. At the start of 1804 he declared Saint-Domingue an independent nation, under the old Indian name of Haiti. He also embarked on a policy of killing the remaining whites.

Within a few months of independence, Dessalines had himself crowned as emperor – Jacques I – of the new nation. He was murdered two years later, after which Haiti became divided for a while into two states: the black-led north, under the remarkable Henry Christophe (1767–1820), a Grenada-born leader who later proclaimed himself King Henri I, strictly regimented his subjects, and built monumental palaces and fortifications, the ruins of which are among the most impressive sights in the Caribbean; and the mulatto-led south, under President Alexandre Pétion (1770–1818), whose easy-going policy (if it can be called that) set the pattern for the rural Haiti of the future, with its struggling peasantry and eroded landscapes. After the deaths of Pétion and Henri I, the country was reunited under the mulatto leader Jean-Pierre Boyer (1776–1850; president 1818–43).

SC

Further reading

C. L. R. James, *The Black Jacobins*, 2nd edition (New York, 1963)

F. W. Knight, *The Caribbean: the Genesis of a Fragmented Nationalism* (New York, 1978)

T. O. Ott, *The Haitian Revolution* (Knoxville, Tennessee, 1973)

J. H. Parry and P. M. Sherlock, *A Short History of the West Indies*, 3rd edition (London, 1971)

E. Williams, *From Columbus to Castro. The History of the Caribbean, 1492–1969* (London, 1970)

Spanish American independence, 1808–26

The independence of Spanish America was precipitated in 1808 by Napoleon's invasion of Spain, a blow which severed the metropolis from its colonies and created a crisis of authority among its subjects. Demands were made for political autonomy and economic emancipation, and as these were rejected so Spanish Americans took to arms. The forces of liberation advanced across the subcontinent in two movements: the southern revolution crossed the pampas from Buenos Aires and was carried by General José San Martín's Army of the Andes to Chile and beyond; the northern revolution, more closely shadowed by Spain, was led by Simón Bolívar from Venezuela to New Granada, back to its birthplace, and on to Quito and Guayaquil. Both converged on Peru, the fortress of Spain in America, where the last great battle of emancipation was fought at Ayacucho in 1824. In the north, Mexican insurgency followed a course of its own – violent social rebellion, prolonged royalist reaction, and ultimate conservative revolution. By 1826 Spain had lost everything except the two islands of Cuba and Puerto Rico, and three hundred years of empire were at an end.

Preconditions and precursors

The Napoleonic onslaught of 1808 was the occasion rather than the cause of independence. Spanish Americans had already begun to possess a pride in their homelands, a consciousness of their own interests and identity, a conviction that they were Americans, not Spaniards. The new Americanism was a more powerful influence on men's minds than the Enlightenment. This inspired in its disciples not so much a philosophy of liberation as an independent attitude towards received values and institutions, a preference for reason over authority, experiment over tradition, ideas which were agents of reform, not destruction, and did not necessarily conflict with loyalism. A number of Americans, however, looked beyond reform. Francisco de Miranda (1750–1816), who had read the works of the French philosophers during his army service in Spain, transformed ideology into revolution. So did Simón Bolívar (1783–1830) whose liberal education, wide reading, and extensive travels in Europe opened his mind to new horizons, in particular to French thought and to English political practice. Men of this kind were true precursors of independence, though they were a small minority and probably ahead of public opinion.

Most of the independence movements began as the revolt of one minority against a smaller minority, of creoles (Spaniards born in America) against *peninsulares* (Spaniards born in Spain). Around 1800, in a total population of 16.9 million in Spanish America, there were 3.2 million whites, of whom only some 30,000 were

Main events in the struggle for independence

1807   Napoleon invades Portugal: Portuguese royal family and court move to Brazil.

1808   Napoleon invades Spain, dethroning King Ferdinand VII. Crisis of authority in the Spanish empire.

1810   Autonomous governments (juntas) established by creole patriots in Venezuela, New Granada, Argentina and Chile. Fr Miguel Hidalgo leads anti-Spanish revolt in Mexico.

1811   Defeat and execution of Fr Hidalgo. Venezuela declares independence from Spain.

1812   Royalist forces defeat First Venezuelan Republic.

1813   Venezuela liberated by Simón Bolívar (1783–1830). Royalists return to the attack under José Tomás Boves.

1814   Ferdinand VII restored to the Spanish throne, determined to crush rebellious colonists. Montevideo captured by patriots. Chilean patriot government defeated by an expedition from the viceroyalty of Peru, focus of loyalty to Spain in South America.

1815   Spanish expedition under General Pablo Morillo 'pacifies' Venezuela and New Granada. Bolívar goes into exile in Jamaica and Haiti. Fr José María Morelos, successor to Fr Hidalgo in Mexico, captured and executed. The whole of Spanish America except for the River Plate is now restored to colonial rule.

1816   João VI becomes King of Portugal and Brazil.
United Provinces of South America (Argentina) declare independence. Bolívar lands with a small force in Venezuela.

1817   General José de San Martín (1778–1850) and the Army of the Andes invade Chile from Argentina. Battle of Chacabuco (12 February).
An army from Brazil invades the Banda Oriental (Uruguay).

1818   Battle of Maipó (5 April) confirms the independence of Chile. Bolívar liberates part of Venezuela.

1819   Bolívar liberates New Granada at the battle of Boyacá (7 August) and proclaims the formation of the vast Republic of Colombia (Grancolombia) embracing Venezuela, New Granada and Quito.

1820   Liberal revolution in Spain. Six-month truce in Venezuela. San Martín executes a seaborne invasion of the viceroyalty of Peru from Chile, the navy commanded by Admiral Lord Cochrane.

1821   The battle of Carabobo (24 June) confirms the final liberation of Venezuela. San Martín proclaims the independence of Peru but fails to defeat the royalist armies in the Peruvian highlands. Independence of Mexico proclaimed by General Agustín Iturbide.

1822   General Antonio José de Sucre (1795–1830) liberates Quito at the battle of Pichincha (24 May). Bolívar and San Martín confer at Guayaquil: San Martín retires. Independence of Brazil proclaimed by Prince Pedro of Braganza, son and heir of João VI: he becomes Emperor Pedro I of Brazil.

1824   Campaigns of Bolívar and Sucre in the Peruvian highlands. Battles of Junín (August) and Ayacucho (December) conclude the wars of independence.

1826   Last Spanish garrisons in South America capitulate to the patriots.

1830   Dissolution of the Republic of Colombia into the three states of Venezuela, New Granada (later renamed Colombia) and Ecuador (the former Quito). Death of Bolívar (December).

peninsulares. But these distinctions were not clear-cut. The function of colonial elites as economic entrepreneurs investing in agriculture, mining and trade, tended to fuse the peninsular and creole groups into a white ruling class, which preferred to co-opt the imperial bureaucracy by marriage and interest rather than confront it. In Mexico the creoles were frustrated to find that there was a limit to their influence, but this did not necessarily make them supporters of independence. In Peru the creole elite, with all its grievances, was slow to be convinced that independence would serve its interests. Everywhere the wars of independence were civil wars between defenders and opponents of Spain, and the creoles were to be found on both sides. Nevertheless, rivalry between creoles and *peninsulares* was a definite part of the social tension of the time.

The creole aristocracy was a powerful group of landowners, office holders and town councillors, who profited from trade expansion between Spain and America in the second half of the eighteenth century to increase their exports. But economic growth menaced as well as favoured them. Spanish monopoly merchants tightened was explosive, and the whites were always aware of the simmering indignation of the Indians and castes. The pent-up anger of the Mexican masses exploded in 1810 in a violent social revolution, which proved to the creoles what they had long suspected, that in the final analysis they themselves were the guardians of social order and the colonial heritage.

When the Spanish monarchy collapsed in 1808, the creoles could not allow the political vacuum to remain unfilled, their lives and property unprotected. They had to move quickly to anticipate popular rebellion, convinced that if they did not seize the opportunity, more dangerous forces would do so. The creoles did not necessarily begin by espousing the cause of absolute independence. Many of the elite wanted no more than autonomy within the Spanish imperial system. They were prepared to bargain with Spain, but the metropolis would not respond, and the elite soon found that Spanish liberals were no less imperialist than Spanish absolutists. The lesson was learnt quickly in the River Plate; in Chile it was reinforced by the experience of a harsh counter-revolution. And when counter-revolution prevailed, in Venezuela and New Granada as well as in Chile, the property of creole dissidents was at risk and the whole economy plundered for the royalist war effort. Creole moderates thus joined creole revolutionaries because Spain offered no alternative to imperialism and this was proving to be too expensive.

The armies of independence

The wars of independence were cruel and the battles heroic. But not all Americans fought for political ideals. The creoles had to mobilize blacks, Indians and castes; they did this without relinquishing the instruments of power or allowing any of these classes to wage an autonomous revolution. In general the masses had to be forcibly conscripted into the armies, if they could be caught before fleeing to the hills or forests. The royalists, too, found it difficult to recruit, both in Spain and in America, and their ultimate defeat was due in part to the impossibility of receiving continued reinforcements from home.

Recruits were sought among black slaves, and manumission was offered in return for service in the revolutionary armies. This was a qualified freedom. Even Bolívar, a true humanitarian, tied emancipation to conscription, though without much success. The slaves were not interested in fighting the creoles' war, while it was also clear that they had little to gain from the royalists. San Martín declared that 'the best infantry soldier we have is the black and mulatto'. Former slaves formed a substantial part of the Army of the Andes which liberated Chile – 1500 out of 5000 – and of General Sucre's army which completed the liberation of Peru at Ayacucho. There was a price to be paid for freedom of this kind; blacks, being in the infantry, suffered the heaviest casualties.

The Indians fought on both sides as a matter of opportunism or

Simón Bolívar

tried to avoid fighting at all. The Araucanians of southern Chile simply changed their resistance to the imperial power into hostility to the new rulers. The Indians of Peru were plundered by forces of both sides: they were pushed into battle by those who dominated a particular region, to be subsequently punished if the enemy took over. Both sides treated the Indians as serfs, transforming the personal services demanded of them in peace time into military services in time of war. Basically the white minority in Peru feared the blacks and Indians. The people of Lima were panic-stricken when the Spanish viceroy decided to abandon the capital in July 1821; they feared that the slave population might rise against the whites, and that the Indians and guerrillas in the surrounding districts might invade the city, once the Spanish troops had gone. The leading citizens invited San Martín to enter and occupy Lima, and in effect they sought protection rather than liberation. In Upper Peru, too, the creoles feared the emancipation of the Indians. The local elite of mine owners, landed proprietors and office holders turned against the liberating armies from Buenos Aires and then supported the security forces against the patriot guerrillas. They remained openly royalist until, in 1825, they were forcibly liberated by the Colombian army of General Sucre, thus inheriting an independence which they did not make. Wherever the creoles' fear of the American masses caused them to prefer the protection of the Spanish army, independence could not make progress without external stimulus. Some countries like the United Provinces of the River Plate (Argentina) were in a position to provide this; others like Peru depended on receiving it.

A conservative revolution

Independence was a political movement, in which a national ruling class took power from the imperial rulers, with only marginal change in economic organization and social structure. Spanish America rejected monarchy but then searched for a powerful substitute. Bolívar, republican though he was, really favoured a form of enlightened absolutism. Appalled by his compatriots' lack of experience in self-government and by the anarchy and social conflict which the wars unleashed, he sought to contain the forces of disorder by imposing a series of authoritarian constitutions. In his superbly analytical Jamaica Letter of 1815 he wrote, 'Events in Tierra Firme [northern South America] have proved that wholly representative institutions are not suited to our character, customs, and present knowledge.' Four years later, in his famous Angostura Address, he proclaimed, 'Complete liberty and absolute democracy are but reefs upon which all republican hopes have foundered . . . Let the legislature relinquish the powers which rightly belong to the executive.' On more then one occasion, in Venezuela, Peru, Ecuador and Colombia, he was himself persuaded to assume dictatorial powers, in order to resolve anarchy or defeat the Spanish enemy. Bolívar's search for a strong executive outlasted the war. His final constitutional views were enshrined in the Constitution which he wrote for Bolivia in 1826. This document provided for a president with not only life-long tenure but also authority to choose his successor. 'This supreme authority should be perpetual', he wrote, thus avoiding 'the changing administration caused by party government and the excitement which too frequent elections produce.' This was the realistic Bolívar, his democratic ideals tempered by anarchy and dissent, though it has to be added that he saw strong government as an instrument of reform as well as of authority.

The pioneers of independence, the intellectuals, bureaucrats and professional politicians, soon gave way to the caudillos, the chieftains whose rule was based on personal power. While he was originally a war leader, the caudillo also fulfilled other roles. He represented powerful economic interests, often of a regional kind. He was a distributor of patronage, of office and of land, the apex of a patron–client network. The decades following independence were the classic years of primitive caudillism, when Juan Manuel de Rosas in Argentina, José Antonio Páez in Venezuela, and Antonio López de Santa Anna in Mexico ruled whole nations as extended haciendas. Caudillos were created and ultimately controlled by the new ruling class. But even when they were subject to lawful challenge or replaced by constitutional models, these were highly restricted. The franchise was often limited to those who were literate and possessed property, the legislature was weak, and the executive consisted of extremely strong presidents, as in Chile. But whatever the system of government, it reflected and did not change the prevailing economy and society.

Independence destroyed the colonial monopoly and opened the ports of Spanish America to the trade of the world. This was an inevitable though not unmixed blessing. The wars were destructive of life and property; terror and insecurity caused a flight of labour and capital, which made it difficult to diversify the economy. The principal owners of capital – Church and merchants – had little inducement to invest in industry in the absence of a strong and protected market. It was easier to allow British manufactures to supply national needs. And in the wake of British manufactures came British merchants, shippers and later bankers, who filled the entrepreneurial vacuum left by Spain. Foreign interests, of course, could not completely control national economies. Policy was made by the new rulers and interest groups. These sought to build their particular centre into a new metropolis and to reduce other regions to a continuing dependence upon themselves. The subregions protected their economies by insisting on various degrees of autonomy: Uruguay and Paraguay opted for complete independence of Buenos Aires; the interior provinces of Argentina chose the way of federalism. Elsewhere, as in Mexico, artisan industries were exposed to foreign competition and while they usually continued production they failed to gain the protection which they demanded. The national economies, therefore, were divided originally by internal rivalry, by conflict between agriculturalists seeking export outlets and those who favoured industry or mining. In the end the promoters of exports and cheap imports won the argument, and the British traders were waiting to take advantage.

The basic economic institution, therefore, was the hacienda, a relatively inefficient organization, absorbing too much land and too little capital, and carried ultimately on the back of cheap labour, seasonal or servile. But the hacienda was also a social and political organization, a means of control, a base of the new rulers. The elite of independence relied on their haciendas for economic support. Landowners took over from the colonial urban sectors of mining, trade and bureaucracy, and displaced too the first republican rulers, those professional politicians and military who had made a career out of the revolution and whose liberal tendencies had to give way to more conservative regimes.

The new rulers

The polarization of society between an elite of landed proprietors and their associates on the one hand and the rural masses on the other was the characteristic feature of independent Spanish America. Haciendas and their owners were not always financially strong or able to exercise automatic social control. But land was the ultimate asset and on the whole land remained in the hands of a relatively small group of creoles, often bound together by ties of family and kinship, which enabled them to dominate offices, resources and labour. In the course of the wars the composition of the creole elite was modified, as soldiers, merchants and others who profited from the hostilities managed to turn themselves into landed proprietors. In Venezuela, where revolution and counter-revolution decimated the ranks of the colonial aristocracy, the great estates passed into the possession of a new oligarchy, the victorious caudillos of independence, who in fact frustrated Bolívar's plan to distribute land to the troops. The republican governments promoted private property rights in the llanos, deprived the nomadic plainsmen of their traditional communal usages, and reduced them to the status of rural labourers. In the pampas of Argentina a similar process could be observed. The merchants of Buenos Aires began to invest commercial capital in land, acquired vast territorial concessions from a compliant state, and added to them territory won during wars against the Indians. The *estancieros* then inexorably tamed the gauchos and reduced them to the status of hired ranch hands, tied to the *estancias* by anti-vagrancy laws and the threat of military conscription.

After independence, control over labour was greater than before. The slave trade, it is true, was abolished almost immediately throughout Spanish America, but abolition of slavery itself was a slow and difficult process, except in those countries where slavery was already obsolete. In general, the chronology of abolition was determined by the number of slaves in a country and their importance to its economy. Chile abolished slavery in 1823, Bolivia in 1826, Mexico in 1829. Elsewhere it took almost half a century: 1851 in Colombia, 1853 in Argentina, 1854 in Venezuela and Peru. Bolívar regarded it as 'madness that a revolution for liberty should try to maintain slavery', and he urged the Venezuelan and Colombian legislators to decree abolition. But freedom for Venezuela's 40,000 slaves had to await the time when landowners appreciated that slaves were expensive and uneconomical workers, and that a cheaper labour force could be obtained by turning them into 'free' peons tied to the estates by anti-vagrancy laws or by a coercive agrarian regime.

The Indians in a sense *were* emancipated, for they were now free citizens and released from the payment of tribute and the obligation of forced labour. The liberals of post-independence, however, regarded the Indians as an obstacle to national development, and believed that the autonomy which they had inherited from the colonial regime should be ended by integrating them into the nation. In Peru, Colombia and Mexico the new legislators sought to destroy corporate entities in order to mobilize Indian lands and release Indian labour. The policy involved the division of communal lands among individual owners, theoretically among the Indians themselves, in practice among their more powerful neighbours.

While the prospects of Indians and blacks were little improved by independence, those of the mixed races, the mestizos and *pardos*, were hardly better. The *pardos* struggled for equality with the creoles. They were already free men, ready to use existing avenues of advancement and to acquire property and status. They now sought access to education, office and political rights, from which they had been debarred by colonial law. Their claims could not be ignored, for in numbers alone they were indispensable to the whites in the wars of independence. Their presence in the army opened the way to promotion up to officer of middle rank. Finally they obtained legal equality. The new republican constitutions abolished all outward signs of racial discrimination and made all classes and castes equal before the law. In effect the new rulers sought to release tension from the colonial social order by abolishing the caste system, which defined social status in law, and substituting a class society, divided by economic criteria. Inequality came to be based not on law but on wealth; for the franchise confined voting rights and therefore full citizenship to property owners. In a few cases the mixed races moved successfully upwards, but the majority were less fortunate.

'Independence', lamented Bolívar, 'is the only benefit we have gained, at the cost of everything else.' Stability, growth, welfare – these had to await the achievement of later generations. Yet victory was not hollow. Spanish Americans had won a hard war, a new freedom, and a place among the nations of the world. The gains were historic and irreversible.

JL

Further reading

T. E. Anna, *The Fall of the Royal Government in Mexico City* (Lincoln, Nebraska, 1978)
The Fall of the Royal Government in Peru (Lincoln, Nebraska, 1979)
S. Collier, *Ideas and Politics of Chilean Independence 1808–1833* (Cambridge, 1967)
J. I. Domínguez, *Insurrection or Loyalty. The Breakdown of the Spanish American Empire* (Cambridge, Mass., 1980)
T. Halperin Donghi, *Politics, Economics, and Society in Argentina in the Revolutionary Period* (Cambridge, 1975)
J. Lynch, *The Spanish American Revolutions 1808–1826* (London, 1973)

Brazilian independence

Though Brazilian independence was proclaimed by Prince Pedro of Braganza on the bank of the Ipiranga River near São Paulo on 7 September 1822, the struggle for independence had begun in 1789, and in a sense was not to end until 1834. By 1834 the idea of a Luso-Brazilian or 'Atlantic Monarchy' was dead, and a powerful group of planters and merchants had begun to rally behind the figurehead of the emperor Pedro II, constitutional ruler of one of the world's great slave-holding nations.

That Brazil emerged as a centralized unitary monarchy was due to four major factors: an overall shift of economic and political power within the Portuguese empire towards Rio de Janeiro, accomplished by 1815; the growth of regional sentiment and political revolt in reaction to rule from either Lisbon or Rio de Janeiro; the destruction of royal absolutism, between 1820 and 1831; and the emergence of plantation oligarchy, affirmed by 1841.

The shift of economic power from Portugal to Brazil had long occurred when Sebastião José de Carvalho e Melo, Marquis de Pombal (1712–82), attempted to forge an Atlantic mercantile empire firmly centred on Lisbon. Though his vigorous actions certainly reinforced mercantile oligarchy in Lisbon, they also created powerful groups of merchants and planters in many parts of the country. The expulsion of the Jesuit Order in 1759 destroyed a countervailing force; the expansion of the administration and creation of local militia units provided the means by which local men could become a powerful opposition to Lisbon's rule. Common interests cemented the empire together after Pombal's fall from power in 1777; a boom in sugar and cotton production in the northeast of the country brought intensive imports of slaves to Brazil. Loyalty to the Metropolis would, so planters and merchants believed, prevent the spread of slave revolution from Haiti. A prominent younger generation of Portuguese leaders, led by Pombal's godson, Rodrigo de Souza Coutinho, sought to make the royal government, led by the regent, João, aware that the economic change brought about by Pombaline reform must lead to the establishment of an Atlantic empire, based perhaps on the administrative centre of the colony, Rio de Janeiro.

Souza Coutinho's strategy represented the only alternative left to João when Napoleon ordered his armies into Portugal in late 1807, provoking the flight of the royal family to Brazil.

The transfer of the court across the Atlantic, to Rio de Janeiro, was naturally followed by the opening of all Brazilian ports to international commerce (28 January 1808). Brazilian ports now traded directly with Britain and the United States, while the pre-eminence of the colony was formally recognized by a measure of December 1815 which created a monarchy consisting of two king-

'Proclamation of the independence of Brazil' by Affonso Taunay

doms, Brazil and Portugal. Such concessions to Brazilian interests antagonized merchants in Lisbon and Oporto, who had been deprived of valuable markets and were incited by officers of the Royal Army, chafing under the rule of the English Marshal Beresford. In October 1820 a military rising broke out in Oporto, and won support in Lisbon. The new government in Portugal demanded the return of King João VI, and the convocation of a Cortes (parliament).

Though João returned to Lisbon, and a provisional constitution was accepted by the government in Brazil, it quickly became apparent that the majority in the Cortes were determined to destroy the autonomy ceded since 1808. The Brazilian reaction was not unexpected; the heir to the throne Prince Pedro, who had stayed in Brazil, immediately became the focus of local opposition to the Cortes. In January 1822 he announced that he would not return to Lisbon, making his famous declaration, 'I remain!', and refused to dismantle the administrative machinery in Rio. The Cortes replied by ordering that provincial governors report directly to Lisbon, abolishing the general treasury in Rio, the prince's State Council, and the Court of Appeals. Pedro's refusal to depart for Lisbon and his subsequent declaration of Brazilian independence were the inevitable reply to such measures. Though the Cortes sent troops to Rio de Janeiro and Bahia they were eventually dislodged by local forces, while Pedro managed to improvise a fleet with which to seize the northernmost provinces of Maranhão and Pará, which had always remained loyal to Lisbon and held out against Rio de Janeiro.

Independence was achieved in military terms by the end of 1823.

The shape of the new regime was to be tempered by regional forces. Attempts to coerce the powerful oligarchies established under Pombaline rule had already led to a republican conspiracy in Ouro Prêto, Minas Gerais, in 1789, while others had threatened in Rio de Janeiro in 1794, Bahia in 1797, and Recife in 1801. Pedro's new government was to be mindful of the necessity to cater to provincial demands for constitutional government, emanating from Pernambuco and Ceará in the north-east, and Minas Gerais and São Paulo in the centre of the country. Appropriately enough he was crowned 'Constitutional Emperor and Perpetual Defender of Brazil' on 1 December 1822.

By inclination a liberal, in practice an autocrat, Pedro I faced severe difficulties from the outset. In order to consolidate Brazil's independence he had to come to terms with Britain and the Portuguese government before he could obtain recognition from other European powers. In practice this meant assuming the responsibility for debts contracted by Portugal in order to retain its colony, the acceptance of a powerful and privileged British commercial presence, and the abolition of the African slave trade by 1830. None of these measures was popular with local groups, many of whom were actively interested in commerce and beneficiaries of the slave trade. Many resented the assumption of substantial obligations by the fledgling government, and were concerned when the country entered into a war with Argentina in 1825. Anti-Portuguese feelings among the Constituent Assembly were inflamed when Pedro closed it on 12 November 1823; the monarch's desire to preserve the royal prerogative was confused with his Portuguese origin by a suspicious and determined assembly.

As Portugal was once again under absolutist control after 1823, and Pedro was suspected of dynastic ambitions, so his conduct became more and more suspect to local liberals. Meanwhile the new Constitution, promulgated unilaterally by the emperor in March 1824, was viewed as 'despotic in practice'. The emperor's refusal to consult with the Chamber of Deputies, his appointments to high office were all construed as autocratic and pro-Portuguese by a hostile group with powerful regional interests. They were assisted in their campaign by the evident unpopularity of a government defeated in the River Plate by 1828, in deep financial trouble, and at odds with the richer provinces of the north-east and Minas Gerais. The destruction of royal absolutism was complete when the army deserted Pedro on 7 April 1831, forcing him to abdicate in favour of his six-year-old son, Pedro II. A regency was set up to govern the country until the young monarch could assume the throne. Five provincial revolutions occurred between 1832 and 1838, but each was contained, thereby insuring the new empire's unity. Pedro I had died in 1834, thus removing any lingering possibility of a reunion of Brazil and Portugal. In 1840 Pedro II assumed the throne and began a reign that lasted until the republican coup of 1889.

The most important legacy of independence was ideological and political. The Brazilian elite, composed mostly of planters and merchants, split over the nature of Brazil's ties to Portugal. The pro-Portuguese faction eventually became the Conservative Party, and fought for a strong centralized monarchy in Brazil. The anti-Portuguese faction formed the Liberal Party and argued for a limited monarchy, subject to elected authorities within a federal structure. These two parties came to dominate imperial politics, with conservatism becoming the more influential ideology.

FC

Further reading
E. Bradford Burns, *A History of Brazil* (New York, 1980)
K. R. Maxwell, *Conflicts and Conspiracies: Brazil and Portugal, 1750–1808,* (Cambridge, 1973)
A. J. R. Russell-Wood, *From Colony to Nation. Essays on the Independence of Brazil* (Baltimore, 1975)

'Public servant', a satirical study by Jean-Baptiste Debret

PRESENT-DAY LATIN AMERICA AND THE CARIBBEAN

Modern Latin America: general historical trends

Following the wars of independence, Latin America fragmented into a mosaic of separate nation-states. By 1903, with newly-created Panama and an independent Cuba, the number reached twenty. Portuguese America held together, first as an empire and then as a republic. But the former Spanish colonies split up into separate nations, which frequently followed the jurisdictional boundaries of the former colonial administrative sub-units. Today's Latin American republics have thus been on the world political map longer than almost any others in the developing world. This section of the Encyclopedia covers the history of the individual countries (or regions). There are, however, some common themes worth bearing in mind when trying to understand Latin America's historical development as a particular region of the world.

The 'national period', i.e. the period since independence, is best divided into three phases: 1820s–70s, 1870s–1930, 1930 onwards.

1820s–70s

The first decades after independence were marked by power-struggles, often violent, with 'strong men' (caudillos) assuming a prominent role in many countries. Brazil and Chile were the exceptions, both consolidating stable political systems fairly soon after independence. Some republics (e.g. Argentina, Mexico, Colombia, Venezuela) went through recurrent spasms of civil war. With the old commercial restrictions of colonial times now eliminated, Latin America participated more widely in international trade, the main trading partners being Western Europe and (for the countries around the Caribbean in particular) the United States. Several countries (e.g. Argentina, Chile, Brazil) experienced a spurt in their overseas trade during this phase. Other nations (e.g. Mexico, Colombia, the states of Central America) tended to stagnate economically. In general, these early decades of nationhood saw little dynamic growth. Latin America's population remained predominantly rural, illiterate and poor.

The chief foreign influences after independence came from Great Britain, whose ships and traders were now everywhere, and France, whose cultural and intellectual achievements Latin America's elites greatly admired. Despite the evident weakness of the new nations, outside powers generally respected their sovereignty and territorial integrity. Exceptions were the British occupation of the Falkland Islands (Islas Malvinas) in 1833, the US invasion of Mexico in 1846–7 (which resulted in the transfer of vast Mexican territories to the rapidly expanding United States), and the French intervention in Mexico in the 1860s. Spain had retained Cuba and Puerto Rico – and these remained Spanish colonies until the end of the nineteenth century – but made no serious attempt to recapture its former mainland territories elsewhere in Latin America, though in the mid-1860s a Spanish naval squadron in the Pacific attacked both Chile and Peru.

1870s–1930

From around 1870 a second phase of modern Latin America's development began, as the international capitalist economy (centred chiefly, at that period, on Great Britain) expanded and strengthened new global networks of international trade and exchange – a 'world economy' made possible by the steamship, the railway and the electric telegraph. Latin America's exports – foodstuffs and raw materials – now met increasing demand in the European industrial countries (and soon the United States), and many Latin American nations experienced export booms, thereby financing the import of a full range of manufactured goods to 'modernize' transport and urban life. Argentina's growth in this period was spectacular. In other countries, national leaders saw export-led growth and inputs of foreign capital as the key to progress. This seemed a rational calculation at the time. (More recently there has been speculation about the costs, as well as the benefits, of the dependence on the outside world such policies implied.)

As national wealth increased (especially in the larger countries), the traditional social structure underwent change. Cities expanded; more people became literate. Embryonic 'middle classes' emerged, as did small urban working classes (and labour movements) in countries where the export booms had created a sizeable market for locally-produced consumer goods, which encouraged the beginnings of manufacturing industry. These economic and social changes – the 'social diversification' of the period – inevitably affected political life. The state itself became more organized. Some countries experienced greater political stability as older forms of caudillo rule began to recede. The newly-emerging social groups challenged traditional elites for a place in the sun. This was especially noticeable between 1900 and 1930 in political changes in the Southern Cone of South America (Argentina, Chile, Uruguay), but also, in a very different manner, in Mexico, where ruthless 'modernization' during the lengthy regime of Porfirio Díaz opened the way to violent upheaval and a major social revolution after 1910.

While many Latin American nations retained close commercial and cultural links with Western Europe (Imperial Germany now included) during this phase, the rise of the United States as a great power after 1890 created new patterns of influence in the region. This was demonstrated decisively when the United States pre-empted the key role in Cuba's war of independence (1898), when the United States stage-managed Panama's separation from Colombia (1903), and in numerous military interventions in the Caribbean and Central America. (US military interventionism was halted by President Franklin D. Roosevelt in the 1930s.) The First World War – in which twelve out of the twenty republics remained neutral – marked a significant shift. Latin America's external trade was now redirected towards the United States. By the end of the 1920s, also, the United States had supplanted Great Britain as the leading source of foreign capital for the region.

1930 onwards

The world depression, followed by the six years of the Second World War, saw the international economy seriously disrupted. With the contraction of trade, Latin America's opportunities for further export-led growth abruptly dwindled. Furthermore, every country except Argentina and Haiti had to default on its foreign debt. Latin America was therefore cut off from foreign finance. Governments were at first bewildered by the harsher economic climate of the 1930s, but gradually adopted new policies, such as increased government intervention in their economies. Domestic industrialization – 'import-substituting industrialization' (ISI) – was now pushed, although hindered by the inability to import needed capital goods. The war brought an export bonanza which helped finance industrial growth, so that by 1960 Brazil, Argentina and Mexico had become the most industrialized countries in the developing world. Several middle-sized countries (e.g. Chile, Colombia) were also advancing fast along the same track. (Smaller nations, such as those of Central America, remained dependent on their agricultural or other primary product output.) A particular feature of this process was the role of the state, which created new state enterprises and marketing boards, as well as new financial and monetary structures.

The social diversification of the earlier period was accelerated in the era of import-substituting industrialization. The middle classes continued to grow. Organized labour, too, became more important in politics – sometimes on its own, sometimes as one element in a multi-class 'populist' coalition of the type set up by Getúlio Vargas in Brazil or Juan Perón in Argentina. A genuinely pluralistic political party system, on the Western European model, was most evident in Chile. Argentina came to be dominated by the Peronists, who never lost a free presidential election from 1946 to 1983. Brazil's pragmatic party politicians ruled by coalition until the military seized the initiative in 1964, holding it over the next two decades. In Mexico, one-party (PRI) hegemony has survived every challenge. Latin America from the 1930s to the 1960s, as in the past, displayed a diversity of regimes: electoral democracies (with women given the franchise everywhere by 1961), dictatorships, and Mexico's unique political system, consolidated in the 1930s by President Lázaro Cárdenas.

The Latin American panorama after 1930 was overshadowed by the unchallenged supremacy of the United States, which by 1945 accounted for half the world's manufacturing output. Every Latin American country had joined the Allied cause before the end of the Second World War, even Argentina, whose military were openly pro-Axis. Already by 1946–7 the United States was pushing Latin America to enlist in the Cold War against the USSR. The intervention of the CIA to help remove a left-wing regime in Guatemala in 1954 was a striking example. The US omnipresence in the western hemisphere prompted new stirrings of nationalism in Latin America, where the desire for autonomous development was increasingly voiced.

US economic hegemony, in fact, was diluted after 1960 or so by the re-emergence of Western Europe as an important trading bloc and investor, by the rise of Japan, and also by more nationalist policies on the part of some of the Latin American governments – as shown in the nationalization of foreign mining and oil companies in Peru, Chile and Brazil. The Cuban revolution of 1959 – expressing the aspiration to autonomy – profoundly influenced Latin America. But if Cuba's example (in the early phase of the revolution) inspired hope in some, it also frightened others into revamping and strengthening their military. That, in turn, led at least indirectly to the new military regimes of the 1960s, as in Brazil and Peru.

In the 1960s – which opened the 'contemporary' era in Latin America – the earlier hopes of progress through industrialization became more muted. Industry failed to produce the many jobs needed by the country-people who migrated to the cities in ever-increasing numbers. Large-scale poverty persisted in nearly all countries (Argentina being the great exception), usually combined with chronic unemployment or underemployment. In addition, the population was rising at an alarming rate, notably in tropical Latin America and Mexico. In consequence there was an increase in social and political tensions (sometimes reflecting class conflicts) with which political systems often could not cope.

While some countries (e.g. Mexico, Colombia, Venezuela, Costa Rica) avoided institutional breakdown or upheaval, others (including supposedly well-established democracies like Chile and Uruguay) did not. The new 'institutional military' regimes (sometimes called 'bureaucratic–authoritarian' regimes) of the 1960s and 1970s – Brazil initiated the trend in 1964 – attempted to control or contain social pressures (by repression) in the interests of renewed economic expansion based on an economic policy geared to a market-orientated strategy which would rely on exports. These 'neo-liberal' experiments reached their most extreme form in Argentina (1976–83) and Chile (after 1973). When recession struck, in the early 1980s, this strategy, too, seemed to be discredited. The Peruvian military regime of 1968–80 tried an alternative course, involving social reform. Meanwhile, civil war in Nicaragua resulted in 1979 in the triumph of a new revolutionary regime, while El Salvador (small and very overcrowded) staggered into a bloody civil conflict, much exacerbated by outside meddling.

The tide of military rule receded in the early 1980s, with several countries experiencing a rebirth of electoral democracy. Are other revolutions of the Nicaraguan type likely to occur? Whatever the outcome of Latin America's unfolding modern dramas, our age has certainly presented Latin Americans with large (and mostly unresolved) dilemmas in their quest for political viability, economic progress, and greater social justice.

TES/SC

Further reading

B. Albert, *South America and the World Economy from Independence to 1930* (London, 1983)
C. Furtado, *Economic Development of Latin America*, 2nd edition (Cambridge, 1976)
W. P. Glade, *The Latin American Economies* (New York, 1969), parts 3 and 4
T. E. Skidmore and P. H. Smith, *Modern Latin America* (New York, 1984), chs. 1 and 2, and Epilogue
C. Véliz, *The Centralist Tradition of Latin America* (Princeton, 1980), chs. 7–13

Mexico

Stagnation and political chaos

In 1821 the last viceroy of New Spain signed the Treaty of Córdoba which, in defiance of the Madrid government, recognized the independent state of Mexico. It had been a difficult birth. The country had been ravaged by ten years of intermittent civil war: agricultural production had fallen by a half, mining – the export staple of New Spain – by two-thirds. Once flourishing cities like Guanajuato now lay devastated and depopulated. Yet this sacrifice had purchased an imperfect independence. Spanish colonial rule had been overthrown; a feeble attempt at reconquest in 1829 was easily parried and the old metropolis formally recognized the Mexican Republic in 1836, some ten years after the United States and the major European powers. Thus, a ponderous but stable bureaucracy gave way to a shifting, semi-praetorian regime, in which national administrations came and went at rapid intervals (fifty in as many years after 1821), usually at the behest of the army, and according to scant political principle. But, in the absence of any profound social revolution, the basic contours of colonial society remained intact: independent Mexico, like colonial New Spain, was predominantly rural, illiterate and – compared with the nascent industrial societies of Europe and the United States – economically backward; its citizens were rigidly divided by barriers of class,

geography and ethnicity, many of which stayed firm until the twentieth century.

After a brief imperial episode – the regime of Agustín Iturbide, 'Emperor Agustín I' (1822–3) – Mexico assumed a form of representative government, under the federalist Constitution of 1824. But, like most subsequent constitutions, it was chiefly honoured in the breach. Elections were meaningless, and the great majority of the population remained marginal to national politics; the presidential chair lay in the gift of the army which, alone in a fragmented polity, was capable of concerted political action. As for formal political labels, these were only somewhat less fanciful than the Constitution itself. In theory – and to a limited extent in practice – Liberals confronted Conservatives. The Liberals believed in representative government, federalism, and a moderate curtailment of the power and wealth of the Church. Strongly wedded to the vague notion of progress, and to the more concrete reality of property, they looked to the democracies of Europe and the United States for their inspiration; they espoused free trade and repudiated – on paper, if not always in practice – the paternalism, protection and concern for caste and status which had permeated colonial society. They garnered their support among the small urban middle class, in the traditionally Liberal port of Veracruz, and in the outlying provinces, north and south, where federalism fed on resentment against Mexico City.

The Conservatives favoured centralist (sometimes authoritarian) rule and were more sympathetic to the privileges of Church and

General Santa Anna

MEXICO

MEXICO	
Area	1,967,183 sq km
Population	70 million
GDP per capita (1980)	$1534
Capital	Mexico City
Currency	Peso

KEY

+—+—+ Railways

——— Roads

———— International boundaries

| 0 | | 320 km |
| 0 | | 200 miles |

army (where, among the creole officers, they enjoyed ample support, just as the Liberals could usually count on a phalanx of provincial caudillos). If, like the sophisticated Conservative intellectual, *político* and historian Lucas Alamán, they entertained economic ideas, the Conservatives leaned towards protection, *dirigisme*, and industrialization, which harmonized with their 'colonial' mentality; and they won support in the populous and devout heartland of Mexico, the Mesa Central. But this ideological polarity was vague and shifting: it offered inspiration to some – like Alamán, or his Liberal counterpart, José Luis Mora – mere alibis to others. Individuals shuttled between the rival camps, impelled by considerations of place and patronage, rather than principle: hence Antonio Lopez de Santa Anna, the hardy perennial of this period, could serve in both Liberal and Conservative administrations; and military opportunists like Mariano Arista could achieve meteoric promotion. Political parties were unknown, the closest approximations being the rival Masonic lodges, whose York and Scottish rites were aligned with Liberal and Conservative factions respectively.

By the 1830s the hopes born of independence were dissipated. Self-government had produced neither stability nor prosperity. Initial British loans had done little more than inflate the national debt, and chronic insolvency now partnered and aggravated chronic political instability. Some Liberals concluded that they must go beyond the mere provision of constitutional norms and demolish those still strong pillars of the colonial regime which blocked the path of progress – in particular the Church (as a political and economic actor) and the army. Yet when, in 1833–4, reformist policies were attempted, the Conservatives rose in rebellion, imposed a new, centralist Constitution (1836), and established an outright Santanista dictatorship (1841–4). For the time being, the reformist thrust had been parried.

Mexico's foreign relations in these early years were overshadowed by the emerging power of the United States. Brief, *opéra bouffe* wars were fought with Spain (1829) and France (1838: the 'Pastry War'), but the chief threat to Mexico's flimsy territorial integrity came from the north where, with the initial encouragement of the Mexican government, North American immigrants braved the Comanche and flocked into the open expanses of Texas. Remote from Mexico City and resistant to Mexican political control, the Texan colonists went their own way until, in the early 1830s, the government belatedly sought to impose its authority, thereby provoking open rebellion. Defeated by superior Mexican forces at the legendary Alamo, the Texans won their independence after defeating Santa Anna's army at San Jacinto (1836). Nine years later, when the US Congress agreed to Texas's admission to the Union, Mexico contested the decision by force of arms. To many in the United States – including the eagerly expansionist President Polk – this was a fine opportunity to assert the Manifest Destiny of the United States of America, and to stake American claims not only to Texas but also to California and the vast tract of intervening territory. Polk launched a two-pronged invasion of Mexico: by land across the Rio Grande to Monterrey and Saltillo, by sea to Veracruz and thence to Mexico City. Its forces outgunned, if not outnumbered, its treasury empty, its citizens distracted by governmental disputes and a major Indian rebellion in Yucatán, Mexico was compelled to sue for peace. By the Treaty of Guadalupe Hidalgo (1848), Texas, California and the entire present-day American south-west – over half the area of Mexico – were ceded to the United States in return for a cash settlement of $15 million.

The 'Reforma'

The trauma of military defeat and territorial mutilation did not unify the country; on the contrary, it radicalized domestic politics and deepened existing divisions. A new generation of Liberals now came to prominence: men like the idealistic intellectual Melchor Ocampo, and the stern, honest Benito Juárez; they sought more radical solutions than those of their Liberal predecessors of the 1820s and 1830s and, in particular, they set out to punish what they saw as an unpatriotic and reactionary Church by the wholesale confiscation of ecclesiastical property. The Conservatives, in turn, resisted and began to flirt with the idea of a Mexican monarchy, which alone could act as a dyke against internal dissolution and external pressure.

In 1854 the old Liberal caudillo of Guerrero, Juan Alvarez, initiated a rebellion which toppled Santa Anna's last administration. This, the Revolution of Ayutla, proved to be more than just another political reshuffle of the kind so common in the previous generation. In the wake of the Liberal triumph – though not without the usual internal squabbles – the government embarked on major reforms: the Ley Juárez (Juárez Law) of 1855 which stripped the Church and the military of their judicial privileges and established equality before the law, and the Ley Lerdo (Lerdo Law) of 1856, named after the Finance Minister, Miguel Lerdo de Tejada, which abolished corporate property-owning, thereby converting both Church and village communal lands into freehold, and throwing them onto the real estate market. These measures were further incorporated into the new Constitution of 1857, which went considerably beyond that of 1824 (though not as far as some radical anti-clericals wanted) and which, with its commitment to freedom of education, worship, and the movement of men and property, represented an attempt to curtail military and ecclesiastical power and to push Mexico along the path of liberal, capitalist

Benito Juárez

development.

On the other side, the Conservative response was no less vigorous or doctrinaire. The Church excommunicated those who took the oath to the Constitution, and there was an immediate spate of rebellions in the name of 'Religion and rights'. For three years (the War of the Reform, 1857–60) the country was racked by a civil war more sustained and serious than any since the upheaval of independence. Juárez, now elevated to the presidency, led the Liberals as their forces were defeated and driven from the Conservative heartland of central Mexico; thereby he became a symbol of popular, Liberal resistance, which manifested itself in constant guerrilla harassment of the Conservatives' regular armies. Gradually, the Conservatives were worn down; the Liberal stronghold of Veracruz held out, aided by American naval support and the steamy, malarial climate; by 1860 the assorted Liberal commanders were strong enough to defeat their enemies in pitched battles and install Juárez in the National Palace.

It was something of a Pyrrhic victory. Radicalized by the conflict, the Liberals had decreed the confiscation and sale of all Church property, save the church buildings themselves: while this measure further alienated the devout, it benefited the large *hacendado* rather than the aspiring yeoman farmer, as the Liberals had hoped. Furthermore, the treasury was empty, and the prosecution of the

MEXICAN LOSSES OF TERRITORY, 1836–53

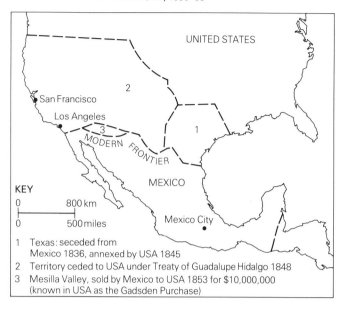

KEY

0   800 km
0   500 miles

1   Texas: seceded from
     Mexico 1836, annexed by USA 1845
2   Territory ceded to USA under Treaty of Guadalupe Hidalgo 1848
3   Mesilla Valley, sold by Mexico to USA 1853 for $10,000,000
     (known in USA as the Gadsden Purchase)

war had involved the seizure of foreign assets, for which reparations were now demanded. With Juárez barely ensconced in the presidency – and the United States coincidentally immersed in the Civil War – Britain, Spain and France mounted an expedition to seize Veracruz and thereby to compel payment. What for Britain and Spain was an exercise in international debt-collection, not unusual for the times, was for France and Napoleon III a *démarche* in global geopolitics. For the Mexican Conservatives' hankering after monarchy now meshed with Napoleon's quixotic desire to boost French influence – and offset that of the United States – in the New World; and the unfortunate Maximilian of Habsburg, the younger brother of the emperor of Austria, was chosen as the standard-bearer and victim of their grand designs.

Reluctant to connive at such plans, the British and Spanish withdrew, leaving the French to march – not without reverses – on Mexico City (1862). Juárez resumed his travels in the north; the Liberals fell back before the Franco-Mexican forces; and Maximilian, installed as emperor (1864), made a valiant attempt to woo his sullen subjects, affecting Mexican manners and – to the chagrin of his Conservative backers – enacting a series of liberal laws covering labour, education, the press and Church–state relations, none of which had much impact. Increasingly dependent on foreign advisers, and on the 30,000 bayonets of Marshal Bazaine, Maximilian's regime was fundamentally precarious, despite its initial successes. By 1865 Napoleon wearied of his Mexican adventure and, with the conclusion of the American Civil War, US influence was brought to bear in favour of the Juaristas. The Liberal forces

waxed; Bazaine retreated and was finally ordered to withdraw altogether; in May 1867 the remaining imperialist forces, gathered for a last stand at Querétaro, were obliged to surrender, and the emperor was executed.

But, once again, the patriot hero Juárez faced a sour post-war fate. Liberal hopes of progress and prosperity were disappointed or, at best, deferred: the country's economy was gravely weakened, government finances were in a parlous state (the foreign debt defaulted, the internal debt standing at 300 million pesos), and, now that the forces of Conservatism had been decisively defeated (the one definitive result of thirteen years of fighting), the victorious Liberals fell out among themselves, with radicals wrangling with moderates, demobilized Liberal forces rising in rebellion, and rival presidential aspirants, like Sebastián Lerdo de Tejada and Porfirio Díaz, manoeuvring for ascendancy. In 1872, a year after his fourth re-election to the presidency, Juárez died. Lerdo, the epitome of the smooth creole intellectual, succeeded and, four years later, he attempted his own re-election; this provoked Díaz, a tough, *parvenu* mestizo caudillo from Oaxaca, to rebel, denouncing the re-election and demanding 'effective suffrage'. Díaz's swift triumph was one of caudillo over intellectual, the sword over the pen.

Porfirio Díaz

But if Díaz's seizure of power bore all the hallmarks of the traditional *coup de main*, it in fact inaugurated a new phase in Mexico's political and economic development. Save for a four-year period (1880–4) when his loyal compadre Manuel González occupied the presidency, Díaz went on to govern Mexico for the following thirty-five years. Potential presidential rivals, initially prolific, were eliminated or won over; local caudillos learned the wisdom of collaborating with the new national caudillo; and Díaz's regular, easily rigged re-elections demonstrated the artificiality of Porfirian 'democracy', even though the façade of the 1857 Constitution remained. Díaz, who never relinquished personal power throughout this period, proved to be a deft, pragmatic *político*. He employed the educated elite – the old liberal cadres, the *licenciados* and intellectuals – and, in particular, he drew upon the expertise of a new generation of technocrats, the so-called *científicos* (literally 'scientists'), who preached a positivist philosophy of economic development and strong government, while they themselves acquired large private fortunes in law and business. Meanwhile – as the *científicos* rationalized – individual rights and the finer points of democracy would have to be compromised for the sake of economic development; and the old Church–state conflict was gradually muted in the interests of social and political stability. Thus, a new, positivistic Liberalism, stressing 'Order and Progress' (or, according to the Porfirian slogan, 'plenty of administration and no politics'), supplanted the old, idealistic Liberalism of Mora and

Juárez. Over time, Díaz slimmed and tamed the army (by 1910 it stood at a mere 15,000, compared with over 90,000 in 1867) and he tightened his grip on the provinces, relying on the new railways and telegraph to garner information, transmit orders and, where necessary, suppress opposition. State governorships were in the gift of the president while, lower down, free municipal government wilted in the long shadow of the *jefe político*, the political boss, appointed by the executive, whose job it was to fix elections, silence dissent, and generally keep order to the president's satisfaction.

Above all, the Pax Porfiriana depended upon – and in turn encouraged – Mexico's accelerating economic development. If the old Liberals' political ideals went by the board, their economic hopes now seemed to approach fruition. The legislation of the 1850s, designed to dissolve corporate property and to release individual initiative, now began to have a dramatic, belated effect; and it was supplemented by fresh legislation framed to attact foreign investment and immigration, to colonize virgin territory, and to develop mining, railways and commercial agriculture. The immigrants never came; but the investment flowed in, with the United States providing the lion's share – 1.2 billion pesos of the total 2.9 billion pesos of direct foreign investment accumulated by 1911. Meanwhile (and as the necessary corollary of this investment),

Porfirio Díaz

Mexico responded to mounting European and American demand for raw materials: the old staples of gold and silver, now supplemented by copper, lead and zinc, and cash crops including coffee, sugar, henequén, rubber and tropical fruits. At the same time, the secular depreciation of the silver-based Mexican peso stimulated exports further. Hence the long economic doldrums of 1820–70 (which had seen only a modest recovery in mining and agriculture, and no major, qualitative change in economic production) now gave way to the brisk breezes of the Porfiriato, and to a new climate which invigorated some, but chilled many.

The government was a major beneficiary. Tax receipts, chiefly derived from customs, rose, enabling the treasury to achieve a genuine budget surplus by 1895. Mexico's international credit was restored. The new wealth also gave the government greater opportunities for patronage, as well as a greater capacity for repression: Díaz wielded a bigger stick as well as a bigger carrot than any of his predecessors. Thus, in compelling order and obedience from the most distant provinces and stiff-necked provincials, Díaz outdid even the prestigious Bourbon viceroys.

As economic life quickened, towns expanded and a relatively prosperous middle class developed, for the time being content to follow the positivist injunction to work and invest, without too much regard for constitutional niceties. Industrial production also rose, and a genuine factory proletariat appeared, chiefly in the textile centres of Puebla, Veracruz and the Federal District. Despite bad conditions, the infant working class was far from militant: it sought practical solutions to concrete problems, notably through mutualist (self-help) societies, and early trade unions whose objectives were essentially 'economist' i.e. for bread-and-butter gains. Though anarcho-syndicalism exercised a limited appeal, those workers who participated in politics – such politics as there were – were as likely to listen to enlightened Porfiristas, like the *científico* mayor of Mexico City, Landa y Escandón, or to spokesmen of a revived liberalism. Meanwhile, rising industrial production hit the large artisan sector, which found its oldest and surest defence – Mexico's poor internal communications – crumbling before the onslaught of the railways, which knitted local into national and international markets.

The pressures of change were even greater in the countryside. Landlords (talk of 'feudalism' notwithstanding) had always shown an eye for profits: astute operators like the Sánchez Navarro of Coahuila had amassed considerable fortunes during the nineteenth century. But the limitations of the market – the result of poor communications, lack of capital, and weak demand – imposed severe constraints on production. Now the railways opened up new markets, foreign and domestic capital was more plentiful, and rising demand, home and abroad, created new incentives. The sugar planters of Morelos, the cotton growers of the Laguna, the henequén producers of Yucatán, entered upon a phase of expansion which incurred all the risks and benefits of large-scale production for the market. To secure land and water they dispossessed villages and smallholders (usually quite legally), converting subsistence farmers into sharecroppers, peons or rural proletarians; and, where the local labour supply was inadequate, they relied on *enganchados* ('hooked' debt-peons) and other forms of semi-servile labour. Some haciendas – especially the producers of Mexico's staple, maize – preserved more 'traditional' ways, exercising a paternalist control over their resident workers, and eliciting deference and loyalty in return; but as these tended to decline, the price of food rose, outstripping wages. The prevailing trends – market production, rising land values, and entrepreneurial initiative – penetrated lower in the rural hierarchy too, where go-ahead *rancheros* expanded and prospered, often at the expense of communal village lands, and of the corporate solidarity these had underwritten. Mexico was becoming a more fluid and, in many regions, a more socially polarized society.

Change of this kind could not but generate social protest, particularly as real wages declined. Local protests – against agrarian dispossession, or the rule of unpopular *jefes políticos* – were endemic throughout the Porfiriato; but the regime had sufficient resources to isolate and suffocate such movements. Some rebellions – like those of the Yaqui Indians of Sonora, or the Maya of Yucatán – smouldered for decades, but alone they could not threaten Díaz's position, or the march of Porfirian progress. By the 1900s, however, a new brand of respectable, urban, middle-class protest became evident, in Mexico as elsewhere in Latin America. Such protest had political rather than economic roots. The urban middle class – a burgeoning, literate and prospering class – resented the apparent immutability of Díaz's personal dictatorship, and of the rule of his local minions; they feared for the future when Díaz died; and they compared Mexico's sad political condition with that of 'advanced' countries in Europe or North America, and with the good old days of Juarista Liberalism (days that acquired a roseate hue as they receded in time). Die-hard Liberals pointed critically to the revival of clerical influence and, lamenting Mexico's lack of civic spirit, they reversed the Porfirian motto and called for 'plenty of politics and good administration'.

In the course of the 1900s, this protest gelled into an organized national opposition, the first of the Porfiriato. The Mexican Liberal Party, founded in 1901, initiated the process; but internal splits and government repression soon drove its leaders into exile and pushed the party towards a militant anarcho-syndicalism which had only limited appeal. Subsequently, as Díaz's seventh re-election loomed up (1910), as the Mexican economy was hit by the American recession (1907–10), and as the dictator was quoted as welcoming a democratization of political life (1908), so new parties assembled

under the leadership of General Bernardo Reyes, strong man of Nuevo León, and Francisco Madero, scion of a wealthy northern family, who espoused an idealistic brand of socially conscious liberalism. Reyes flattered only to deceive, but Madero and his anti-re-electionists marshalled support in the major cities, even among sections of the working class, and posed a serious challenge to the regime which the regime finally met in the way it knew best: Madero was arrested and Díaz's re-election was rigged.

While most of his respectable followers were now prepared to throw in the towel, Madero escaped to the United States and issued a call to arms (November 1910). Where so many previous local revolts had failed, Madero's revolution succeeded and did so by mobilizing disaffected groups in the countryside, where agrarian tensions and resentment against government abuses were strongest. Emiliano Zapata captained the campesinos of Morelos, where the regime of the sugar planters weighed heavily; Pancho Villa, bandit turned revolutionary bushwhacker, was among the many leaders who sprang up in the rebellious north. Neither Díaz's modest army, nor his vaunted rural police, could meet the challenge, and control of the countryside slipped from their grasp. In May 1911 the president was forced to resign and, after an unusually free election, Madero was voted into the National Palace. It was the start of a great revolutionary upheaval.

Emiliano Zapata

Zapata's entry into Mexico City, 1914

The revolution (1911–40)

Madero and his liberal experiment lasted only fifteen months. Conservative groups attacked Madero's supposed weakness and his halting steps towards political and fiscal reform; the press took advantage of unprecedented freedom to snipe without mercy or scruple; and the Federal Army which Madero both retained and favoured proved ungrateful and restless. The president's erstwhile revolutionary supporters, looking for quick results by way of agrarian reform, municipal freedom, and changes in the personnel of government, were swiftly disillusioned. Revolutionary leaders like Zapata in Morelos and Pascual Orozco in Chihuahua rebelled anew, now bitterly opposed to the regime they had helped establish. Caught in this political crossfire, Madero found his position increasingly precarious, his popularity ebbing away. His own middle-class constituency, meanwhile, drifted to the right, losing faith in the liberal experiment, fearing social upheaval, and yearning for a strong man who could dominate the situation.

Many thought they had found such a man in General Victoriano Huerta, a career soldier whose minor laurels were augmented and refurbished by a successful campaign against Orozco in 1912. When the predictable military coup occurred in Mexico City in February 1913, subjecting the capital to the 'Ten Tragic Days' of bombardment, Huerta switched to the rebel side, had Madero arrested and shot, and proclaimed himself president. The liberal experiment gave way to the militarist solution. Madero's supporters were purged; civilian politics were phased out; the Federal Army, expanded some fourfold, became the supreme arbiter of the nation's life. But the militarist solution – a crude attempt to recreate the stability of the Porfiriato by means which canny old Porfirio would not have countenanced – was bound to fail. In death, Madero became a martyr, his failings and equivocations forgotten or pardoned. President Woodrow Wilson refused to recognize the regime of Madero's assassin. Popular rebels like Zapata fought on, well aware that Huerta's regime, for all its occasional, verbal reformism, offered them nothing, and their numbers rapidly grew. In the north, Venustiano Carranza, a liberal landlord and Maderista state governor, assumed the leadership of a conglomerate revolutionary movement which, in the name of 'Constitutionalism', united rebels of different regions and classes in a common front against Huerta. Thanks in particular to the prowess of Pancho Villa and his Division of the North, and to the more prosaic achievements of the Sonoran state forces, the Constitutionalists reduced the cities of the north and began to march on Mexico City. By summer of 1914, with the country's economy and currency now seriously affected by the revolutionary troubles, and his regime politically and financially bankrupt, Huerta was forced into exile.

The victorious Constitutionalists, eschewing Madero's naive tolerance, at once purged supporters of the old regime, silenced press criticism, and sequestered property (including Church property: it was alleged, with some justification, that the Church had favoured Huerta). But they could not agree among themselves. The Constitutionalist Revolution therefore bifurcated, with Carranza and Villa leading hostile factions, each deriving more from expedience and patronage than any clear class divisions. Though the Villistas – allied to Zapata's forces – were more numerous, Carranza

223

enjoyed the services of the revolution's best general, the shrewd Sonoran, Alvaro Obregón. Once a rancher, now a scientific strategist and a smart *político* who won support among the labour unions, Obregón decisively defeated Villa in a series of bloody battles (1915). The last major bout of civil war was over; Carranza's faction ruled, at least in the capital and the major cities.

But they ruled a sad country, ravaged by disease, malnutrition, rampant military graft, and continuing rural revolt and banditry. Zapata fought on until his treacherous assassination in 1919; Villa survived to be amnestied in 1920. Meanwhile, the victorious faction sought to bring order out of chaos. A new Constitution was promulgated (1917), in which the liberal political framework of 1857 was supplemented by 'social' provisions: state education, strict curtailment of clerical education and political involvement, protection of the rights of labour, and a declaration of the nation's ownership of land and subsoil deposits, which would afford the constitutional basis for both agrarian reform and the confiscation or regulation of foreign assets. Like previous constitutions, however, this was basically an ideological document – a statement of intent rather than a manual for the practical government of the country.

Aided by providential oil revenue (oil production, beginning in the 1900s, peaked in 1921, when Mexico provided a quarter of the

The revolutionary song 'Adelita' celebrates this *soldadera*, one of the many women who actively served the revolutionary cause

world's supply) Carranza almost lasted out his presidential term. In 1920, however, an inept attempt to foist his chosen civilian successor on the country led to his overthrow and assassination. Obregón, for some time the heir-apparent, became president (1920–4). His successor was a fellow Sonoran, Plutarco Elías Calles, who ruled first as president (1924–8), then as *jefe máximo* ('big boss'), twitching the strings of successive presidents until 1934. Hence, during the fifteen years of post-revolutionary reconstruction and consolidation, the 'Sonoran Dynasty' governed, bringing to bear ideas and policies which clearly betrayed their origin in that prosperous, progressive, Americanized part of the country.

The Sonorans slimmed the army and cut the military budget from almost two-thirds to about a quarter of government expenditure. In the process, they faced serious, recurrent revolts (1923, 1927, 1929), all successfully put down. By way of a counterweight to the troublesome military, the Sonorans angled for support among the urban workers and, to a lesser extent, among the peasantry. The Regional Confederation of Mexican Workers (CROM), established in 1918, became the first national labour confederation: its leader, Morones, held ministerial rank, collaborated closely with government, and amassed great personal wealth; some benefits filtered down to the rank-and-file. The Sonorans approached the question of agrarian reform in a calculating and pragmatic fashion. Obregón distributed a million hectares to landless claimants, Calles over three million; in a few regions, like Morelos, the power of the old landlords was broken. More commonly, however, landlords survived, trimming their sails to the new wind, seeking the shelter of accommodating generals and *políticos*, who were not hard to find. Those agrarian veterans who continued to campaign on behalf of the villages denounced the slow pace of reform, and the impedimenta of corruption and conservatism which stalled its advance.

Not that the Sonorans could altogether be blamed for this. Their commitment to agrarian reform was lukewarm: they saw Mexican agriculture through Sonoran eyes, favouring the dynamic capitalistic entrepreneur over the subsistence peasant. By 1929, Calles declared, the reform had run its course, and it was pronounced a failure. Calles's chosen priorities were different: his objective – his vision – was a strong state, a thriving capitalist economy, and a literate, hard-working, patriotic and obedient people. To this end, the Sonorans expanded rural education, built roads, created a central bank and incurred a bitter civil war (1926–9) in an attempt to curtail the spiritual and educational role of the Catholic Church. Where the nineteenth-century liberals – most of them Catholics – had sought to eliminate the Church's economic and political power, some twentieth-century dogmatists, Calles included, looked to the virtual extirpation of Catholicism. When the Church resisted implementation of the anti-clerical provisions of the 1917 Constitution, war broke out, most virulently in west-central Mexico, where

Lázaro Cárdenas

revolt), the shockwaves of the depression now began to affect the Mexican economy. Export earnings and foreign investment slumped; the very model of development espoused by the Sonorans was called into question. Thus, even while Calles still ruled (and Calles had grown more conservative with age), new economic initiatives were attempted: a Five-Year Plan, provision for greater state intervention, a revival of agrarian reform. But these initiatives were greatly expanded under the presidency of Lázaro Cárdenas (1934–40). Cárdenas, though an ally and protégé of Calles, disappointed his mentor; he would not play the puppet, and he favoured more radical policies. In 1934–5 Mexican politics were dominated by a bitter struggle between Calles and Cárdenas, a struggle fought out in the cabinet, in the statehouses, in the labour and peasant unions, and in the streets. Finally, Cárdenas's presidential weight told: Calles and his die-hard supporters were ousted, and the *jefe máximo* was sent into exile. Cárdenas now had a free hand, and he had aroused expectations which had to be met.

Unlike his presidential predecessors, Cárdenas was a firm believer in the agrarian reform, and he favoured the creation of *ejidos*, in which land was vested in the community, though it might be farmed either individually or collectively. Over 17 million hectares of land were distributed and, by 1940, ejidal production accounted for nearly half the country's agricultural output. Peasant land-hunger was assuaged, if not eradicated, and the peasantry was firmly incorporated into the governmental system, with revolutionary *políticos* and bureaucrats replacing the old caciques and landlords. At the same time, the era of the sprawling, 'feudal' hacienda was finally ended, although landlords who invested, irrigated and produced efficiently were not only guaranteed against expropriation, but also given state assistance in the shape of roads, grants, and technical advice.

If Cárdenas's agrarian policies were original within Latin America in the 1930s, his support for organized labour was more typical. In his battle against Calles, Cárdenas won the backing of Vincente Lombardo Toledano and labour elements hostile to the CROM. In 1936 Lombardo organized a new, dominant labour confederation, the CTM, which, a year later, became an integral component (along with the peasant CNC) of a newly constituted official party, the PRM. Labour also received more tangible benefits by way of arbitrated wage settlements and, in the case of the railways, nationalization and a brief experiment in workers' control. More spectacularly, when the foreign oil companies rejected an arbitrated wage settlement, Cárdenas ordered their expropriation (1938): an act which, while it elicited fierce foreign protests, also met with widespread and emotional acclaim among Mexicans of all political persuasions, including Catholic and conservative enemies of the regime. But the oil expropriation was not altogether typical: in other sectors of the economy, such as electricity generating,

Cristero rebels (so called because of their war-cry 'Viva Cristo Rey!' – 'Long live Christ the King!') fought the Federal Army tenaciously until a compromise settlement – approved by the Vatican and the bishops, to the disgust of many of the rebels – ended the conflict. Compromise also proved necessary in Calles's squabble with the foreign oil companies, who resisted the constitutional conversion of their freehold rights to leasehold. As this example showed, the economic nationalism of the Sonorans implied greater regulation and taxation of foreign interest, but it in no sense required expropriation or outright rejection; on the contrary, foreign investment increased during the 1920s, and had an important role to play in the Sonoran model of development.

1928–9 were years of political and economic crisis. In 1928 Obregón was assassinated by a Catholic fanatic, just as he prepared to assume the presidency for the second time. Debarred from immediate re-election, Calles instead convened a revolutionary convention at which a loosely unified 'official' party was, for the first time, created: the National Revolutionary Party (PNR). Its lineal descendants have governed Mexico to the present day. But if the successful institutionalization and demilitarization of the revolution appeared well under way (1929 also saw the last serious military

Cárdenas welcomed increased foreign investment. In foreign policy, too, Cárdenas tempered principle with pragmatism: he proved to be one of the stoutest friends of the Spanish Republican cause, yet he beat the Allies' oil boycott by selling to the Axis powers. Far from being a doctrinaire socialist – as he was sometimes depicted – Cárdenas was essentially a radical nationalist who, by his agrarian reform, his alliance with labour, his consolidation of the party, and his pragmatic economic nationalism, sustained the broad strategy of the revolutionary victors in the changed circumstances of the depression. In doing so, he greatly strengthened the revolutionary state, and laid the groundwork for the post-1940 'economic miracle'.

Post-revolutionary Mexico

Economic growth has been the *leitmotiv* of recent Mexican history. Cárdenas's successors, Manuel Avila Camacho (1940–6) and Miguel Alemán (1946–52), stressed industrialization over agrarian reform, and political stability over radical new departures. Close collaboration with the American war effort stimulated growth and in subsequent decades industrial production continued to boom, affording healthy (and lightly taxed) profits to both foreign and Mexican businesses, and enabling the manufacturing sector to usurp the leading role once held by mining. But while GDP grew fivefold in the twenty-five years after 1940 (and population doubled), agriculture boosted its output fourfold, thus benefiting the balance of payments and keeping industry's labour costs low. By the 1970s, however, as population continued to grow at 3–4 per cent per year, and migrants streamed from the countryside to the city (especially to the massive, polluted metropolis of Mexico City), so Mexico's agricultural self-sufficiency came to an end, and governments were forced to consider methods to augment production, while restraining population growth. Fortunately, new oil reserves came on tap at the same time and briefly seemed to offer a way out, until a worldwide recession and oil glut plunged Mexico into its most severe economic crisis since the Great Depression. By 1982 Mexico had succumbed to a 600 per cent devaluation of the peso and a de facto moratorium on its foreign debt, then the largest in the developing world. Application of an IMF-endorsed stabilization plan sharply improved the balance of payments by early 1984, at the cost of reduced real wages and industrial stagnation. Mexico was able to bring off this economic adjustment thanks to its unique political system.

That system had earlier produced the political stability needed to sustain economic growth. The official party (named since 1946 the Institutional Revolutionary Party, or PRI) has retained a virtual monopoly of political office, conceding only token representation to opposition parties of right and left. Successive presidents, emerging from the mysterious PRI selection procedures, have all triumphed by large pluralities; some observers have detected a pendulum effect, whereby reformist administrations (Adolfo López Mateos, 1958–64; Luis Echeverría, 1970–6) alternate with conservative (Gustavo Díaz Ordaz, 1964–70; José López Portillo, 1976–82 and Miguel de la Madrid, 1982–8). Only at a local level, in specific regions, have genuine opposition candidates seriously challenged the PRI – and then not for long. Hence, pressure groups – and aspiring politicians – see the advantages of working within rather than outside the official framework. This has been the case with many peasant groups, less so with organized labour, where there is a long tradition for some unions to operate independently of the suffocating embrace of the CTM. The late 1970s also saw a modest but potentially significant revival of the independent left, including the hitherto weak Mexican Communist Party.

The PRI, meanwhile, acts as a broad church, encompassing diverse groups, from right-wing businessmen to left-wing intellectuals. Some see its role as that of legitimating decisions previously reached within a small coterie of top *políticos*, bureaucrats, businessmen and labour leaders. There have been constant demands – and an occasional promise – that the party's internal workings be democratized, that candidates subsequently assured of election be chosen by open selection, not covert brokerage. But the PRI has remained doggedly unreformed. Meanwhile, protests which the government will not tolerate receive tough treatment, as the student movement of 1968 found. Then and subsequently predictions of breakdown and revolution have erred. The army has remained apolitical; political offices, from the presidency downwards, have changed hands regularly and peacefully; most – though not all – of the population have benefited from the 'economic miracle'. Seventy years after the outbreak of the revolution which gave it birth, and whose myths and symbols it still constantly invokes, the regime retains power and legitimacy: a phenomenon unique not only in Latin America but perhaps in the world as a whole.   *AK*

Further reading

D. Brading, ed., *Caudillo and Peasant in the Mexican Revolution* (Cambridge, 1980)

C. C. Cumberland, *Mexico: the Struggle for Modernity* (New York, 1968)

R. Hansen, *The Politics of Mexican Development* (Baltimore, 1971)

M. C. Meyer and W. L. Sherman, *The Course of Mexican History*, 2nd edition (New York, 1983)

J. Womack, Jr, *Zapata and the Mexican Revolution* (New York, 1970)

The Central American republics

The failure of union

Central America achieved independence as the result of a general reaction to the Liberal revolution of 1820 in Spain. No unified independence movement developed in the captaincy-general itself, and there was no fighting there. Instead, beginning with the declaration of independence in the regional capital, Guatemala City, on 15 September 1821 the various cities of the isthmian region made their own decisions over a period of months. The short-lived empire of Agustín de Iturbide in Mexico (1822–3) sent an army to recapture the isthmus, but with its collapse the disunited provinces were left to work out their own destiny. One, Chiapas, opted to remain with Mexico (1823). The district of Soconuzco, claimed by Guatemala, was occupied by Mexico and in 1825 a plebiscite of its inhabitants ratified its transfer.

Five provinces remained, reaffirming their independence in a second declaration on 1 July 1823. They were Guatemala, El Salvador, Honduras, Nicaragua and Costa Rica, collectively known as the Provincias Unidas del Centro de América. The course of independence had left their leaders strongly polarized between Liberals and Conservatives (locally termed *Serviles*), and while a Constituent Assembly met between June 1823 and January 1825 to draw up the new Constitution of the Federation as a whole, the factions struggled for control of the new state governments that were simultaneously being created. The Constitution of 1824 for the Central American Federation, written under strong Liberal influence, established a federal government reminiscent of that of the United States, limited clerical influence, and among other libertarian provisions, abolished slavery. Under it, elections for president of the Federation in 1825 gave one vote short of an absolute majority to José Cecilio del Valle, author of the Declaration of Independence of 1821, and a distinguished scholar. The Congress, however, as the result of a political deal, chose instead his Liberal opponent, Manuel José Arce.

Arce's government (1825–9) was rapidly recognized by the United States, Mexico, Colombia and other Latin American states, and in 1826 was one of only four to attend Bolívar's abortive Congress of Panama. But it was nearly bankrupt, lacked federal military or police forces, and was constantly embroiled in disputes between the state governments. Guatemala, whose capital was seat of the Federation until 1834, with a population three times that of any other state, focused the hostility of the others. Between 1827

CENTRAL AMERICAN REPUBLICS

COSTA RICA		EL SALVADOR	
Area	50,900 sq km	Area	20,935 sq km
Population	2.2 million	Population	4.8 million
GDP per capita (1980)	$1527	GDP per capita (1980)	$680
Capital	San José	Capital	San Salvador
Currency	Colon	Currency	Colon
GUATEMALA		HONDURAS	
Area	108,889 sq km	Area	112,068 sq km
Population	7.0 million	Population	3.7 million
GDP per capita (1980)	$1198	GDP per capita (1980)	$639
Capital	Guatemala City	Capital	Tegucigalpa
Currency	Quetzal	Currency	Lempira
NICARAGUA		PANAMA	
Area	139,000 sq km	Area	77,082 sq km
Population	2.4 million	Population	1.8 million
GDP per capita (1980)	$897	GDP per capita (1980)	$1197
Capital	Managua	Capital	Panama City
Currency	Cordoba	Currency	Balboa

and 1829 the Honduran caudillo Francisco Morazán was able to build on this to wage a successful war against the Federation. Having installed the Guatemalan José Francisco Barrundia as president (1829–30), Morazán then directed a Liberal purge of the Conservatives and their clerical supporters, as the prelude to his own Liberal government (1831–9). It was Morazán who gave Central America the only brief period of unity it has ever known, but its very success fostered the unity of its conservative opponents. After the Federation capital had been moved to San Salvador, a cholera epidemic in 1837 aroused mob violence in Guatemala which, skilfully channelled by the Indian Rafael Carrera, destroyed the flimsy unity of the Federation. In April 1838 both Costa Rica and Nicaragua stated that the Federation had already ceased to exist. It ceased formally to do so when fresh elections were not held to renew Morazán's term in 1839, but the fallen leader tried several times to recover his position until he was executed in Costa Rica in 1842.

Between 1839 and 1898 the five separate states (a sixth, Los Altos, formed in 1838, was reabsorbed by Guatemala in 1840) pursued very similar courses. Each underwent longer or shorter periods of dictatorship punctuated by periods of weak, shifting governments, and even civil war. In turn, major political leaders, once in power, succumbed, as often as not, to the dream of recreating Morazán's republic by force, diplomacy or both. In the early 1840s, with the Conservatives in power generally, this seemed quite possible, but localism reasserted itself, and Guatemala under Rafael Carrera (president 1844–65) formally declared its independence in 1847. The following year Costa Rica followed suit, and with, in the main, Liberal governments in power in the three middle states, a brief period followed in which external influences assumed prime importance. Great Britain, entrenched in Belize and claiming a protectorate over the Mosquito Coast of Honduras, disputed control of the trans-isthmian route with the United States. Settled for a generation by the Clayton-Bulwer Treaty of 1850, the dispute led to local concerted action against the activities of the filibustering American, William Walker, to install himself as president of Nicaragua and leader of a new Federation. By 1863 some eight formal meetings had been held to reconstruct the Federation, but all succumbed to opposition or indifference, and the United States in turn had withdrawn from Central American affairs for a generation.

Following revolts which brought Liberal governments to power in Guatemala and El Salvador in 1871, Justo Rufino Barrios, president of Guatemala (1873–85), carried through an astonishing modernization of his country on Liberal lines, and built up his army. On 28 February 1885 he proclaimed the reunification of Central America under his command, but his ally President Zaldívar of El Salvador refused to accept his lead, and Barrios was killed in battle at Chalchuapa on 2 April. Further attempts to

Francisco Morazán

confederate all five states in 1887, and to join the central three in an association in 1896, were destroyed by military coups in each case within a period of months. As the more restricted aims of these attempts showed, by this time the traditional independence of Costa Rica and the assertiveness of Guatemala had been recognized as major obstacles. The fact was that in the two generations since independence, the Central American countries had grown not together but apart. Guatemala's conservative and dictatorial regime had consistently been at odds with its Liberal neighbours, but the fact that still more effectively divided it from its neighbours was that before the time of Barrios it lacked so much as a single all-weather cart track. El Salvador's leaders aspired to leadership of the confederation, but this was ruled out by the small size of their state. Honduras lacked unity. In Nicaragua the internal conflict between the Liberals of León and the Conservatives of Granada, which led in 1852 to the choice of Managua as a compromise capital, lasted until the arrival of American adventurers in the 1850s, which forced the consolidation of an oligarchic republican regime. Costa Rica held aloof from the squabbles of its northern neighbour, divided from it the more effectively by the perennial boundary dispute over the Guanacaste territory, and insulated from the long-running dispute over federation.

At the beginning of the independence period Costa Rica was already an exporter of coffee, while the main export crops of El Salvador and Guatemala were indigo and cochineal respectively. Costa Rica's exports continued to expand, therefore, while the introduction of aniline dyes finally destroyed the already moribund trade of its neighbours in the 1870s.

Justo Rufino Barrios was responsible for the introduction of coffee growing in Guatemala, which had already begun in El Salvador under his namesake Gerardo Barrios (president 1859–63). By the end of the century coffee had become the major export of both countries, and in El Salvador the basis for a new coffee growers' oligarchy, which was able to regulate peacefully the succession to office among its members. The Vaccaro brothers of New Orleans founded (1899) the company that was to make bananas the major export crop of Honduras, and which ultimately grew into the Standard Fruit Company. Alone among the five countries, Nicaragua failed to develop a major export crop in the nineteenth century. It was therefore keenly interested in the alternative possibilities of wealth offered by the use of its territory for an interoceanic canal. When, after 1898, reasons of strategy and commerce alike made the United States interested in such a canal, Nicaragua, then under the rule of the Liberal José Santos Zelaya (president 1893–1909), offered one of the two best possible routes.

A steam shovel at work on the Panama Canal, *c.* 1910

American domination

United States sponsorship of the revolution for Panamanian independence from Colombia (1903) not only destroyed Nicaraguan hopes, but created a new, sixth state, which, although historically part of South rather than Central America, focused American influence in the area. While work on the canal went on from 1904 to 1914, the United States came rapidly to exercise a hegemony which European powers could no longer challenge. The United States, in fact, came to sponsor a new departure in the long-running debate over unification. In 1902 President Zelaya had acted as host at Corinto to a conference of heads of state on the resolution of differences between the republics. A tribunal was set up to arbitrate disputes (though not boundary disputes) and Guatemala failed to accede to the treaty. In 1906, when an attempt by exiles to overthrow the dictator of Guatemala, Manuel Estrada Cabrera (president 1898–1920), escalated into a full-scale war between Guatemala and El Salvador, President Theodore Roosevelt, urging an immediate settlement, sent the US warship *Marblehead* to the coast of El Salvador. The ceasefire signed on board between the two states was followed in September 1906 by a conference at San José, Costa Rica, which reaffirmed the Corinto Pact, and created a Central American Bureau. Zelaya, who had refused to attend the conference, took advantage of a boundary clash with Honduran forces to overthrow the president of that country early in 1907; and

was on the point of war with El Salvador when the United States again intervened. Together with the president of Mexico, Roosevelt invited all five presidents to a peace conference in Washington, at which a ten-year peace programme for the region was agreed and subsequently ratified. At its core was the creation of a Central American Court of Justice (1908) with its seat in Costa Rica, the first permanent international court in the world. Annual meetings of ministers were held from 1909 to 1914.

Neither the 1907 treaty nor the Court of Justice had any practical effect, however, for after 1910 the United States under President Taft ceased to encourage unification. In that year, Taft's administration actively aided the overthrow of Zelaya and his successor José Madriz. Nicaragua became a virtual protectorate of the United States; and in 1912 its new president, Adolfo Díaz, who had requested and received the support of a detachment of United States marines, agreed to the Bryan–Chamorro Treaty by which the United States gained the right to build a canal in Nicaragua. This treaty was not regarded with favour by the other republics. Nicaragua now withdrew from the Central American Court, which ceased to function at the end of its ten-year life (1918).

Throughout his long rule, which became harsh and vindictive after an attempt on his life in 1907, the Guatemalan president Estrada Cabrera pursued a similar policy of friendship with the United States, which reinforced the effect of the American presence in Panama and Nicaragua. Honduras, freed for the moment from intervention, enjoyed political stability until 1920, while El Salvador, under the rule of the Meléndez–Quiñónez families, was, except for the assassination of Arturo Araújo in 1913, to enjoy an orderly presidential succession from 1898 to 1931. Ironically it was Costa Rica, where a well-established pattern of smallholding, rich soil, and an educated population had helped to facilitate the emergence of genuine democracy, which incurred the disapproval of President Woodrow Wilson when the Minister of War, Federico Tinoco Granados, seized power in 1917 in a near-bloodless coup. Within two years he was forced to resign by American non-recognition and political opposition at home, and the 1871 Costa Rican Constitution was restored. This blatant external pressure, in turn, brought about the last serious attempt to federate Central America once more, appropriately enough on the occasion of the centenary of Central American independence.

In increasing hostility to the domination of the United States, a Union Party had been growing up in the five republics. When the Guatemalan Congress declared Estrada Cabrera insane in 1920, the Unionists seized their opportunity. A conference at San José drew up a new pact for unification. Nicaragua, however, refused to accede to it while the other states did not accept the Bryan–Chamorro Treaty. Costa Rica, fearful of United States influence, also refused to ratify the pact. The three northern states, still not deterred, formally created their new common Constitution on the appointed date. Within weeks it was destroyed by the overthrow in a military coup of President Carlos Herrera of Guatemala. His successor withdrew from the Federation in January 1922 and was speedily recognized by the Harding administration in the United States. That administration then proceeded to sponsor a new Treaty of Peace and Amity between the five republics, but this served only to preserve the dominant position of the United States.

By now that position was effectively ensured by sheer economic power. The First World War had ended the likelihood of an effective European challenge to the growth of United States interests, though German investment, encouraged by Estrada Cabrera, remained strong in Guatemalan coffee until 1944. The new force in the region, however, was that of the US businessman Minor Cooper Keith, who had first become interested in bananas while building a railway in Costa Rica in the 1880s. In 1912 he welded together the two northern states with his International Railways of Central America (IRCA), while serving as vice president of the United Fruit Company of Boston (founded 1899) which grew the bananas that provided the freight. In 1929 United Fruit effected a merger with the Cuyamel Fruit Company of Samuel Zemurray, who controlled the largest fruit interests in Honduras. United Fruit (UFCo), known familiarly as 'El Pulpo' (The Octopus), thus emerged as a formidable foreign political influence in the region. Its influence,

moreover, continued to be felt after 1933, when the United States ceased direct intervention in Central America.

Nicaragua still lacked a major export crop. Its railway system was confined to the west of the country; it connected with that of Honduras only by sea, and had no link with that of Costa Rica. It was under United States control until 1924, as was the management of the national finances, while the presence of United States marines guaranteed the continued tenure of the Conservatives. When in 1925 the Coolidge administration withdrew the marines, factional fighting among the Conservatives offered the Liberals, led by Juan Bautista Sacasa, the chance to seize power. In 1926 the United States again intervened to ensure the second term of President Adolfo Díaz (1926–9). This second intervention was challenged by a guerrilla movement led by the dissident General Augusto César Sandino, whose name was later to be given to a more successful movement than his own. The marines, who proved unable to capture Sandino, were withdrawn finally in January 1933 in the first and most decisive evidence of Franklin Roosevelt's 'Good Neighbour' Policy. Sandino, however, remained an independent force under Sacasa (president 1933–6) until he was murdered while leaving the presidential palace after dinner (1934), at the orders of the commander of the American-trained National Guard, Anastasio Somoza García. In 1936 Somoza pressured Sacasa himself into resignation and assumed a direct control of Nicaraguan affairs which ended only with his assassination in 1956.

Democracy, dictatorship, revolution

The Great Depression of 1929, the indirect cause of United States withdrawal, caused great hardship in the export-orientated economies of the region. Political repercussions were immediate. Guatemala ended nine years of democratic government early in 1931. Jorge Ubico's (1931–44) stern and unimaginative rule systematized the exploitation of the rural Indians under local officials who lived in fear of his sudden visits on a powerful motor cycle. In El Salvador, General Maximiliano Hernández Martínez (1931–44) shot down thousands of peasants early in 1932 in a confrontation with trade unions, and (despite a constitutional succession) established a rigorous dictatorship. In Honduras, Tiburcio Carías Andino, fairly elected in 1932, ended elections for sixteen years till his voluntary withdrawal in 1949. Only Costa Rica continued to maintain a democratic system of government throughout the Second World War, though all five countries leapt to the side of the Allies in 1941 at the news of Pearl Harbor.

Stimulated by Allied propaganda, the citizens of Guatemala and El Salvador deposed their presidents by massive general strikes and demonstrations in 1944. Guatemalans chose ex-university professor Juan José Arévalo (1945–50), a proponent of 'spiritual socialism', who survived numerous attempted coups in the course

Nicaraguan militia members celebrating the fourth anniversary of the revolution of 1979

of introducing social security programmes, legalizing trade unions and sweeping away the restrictive bonds on the Indians. His successor, Colonel Jacobo Arbenz, relying increasingly on the aid of a small group of Communist activists, incurred the direct hostility of the United States when he attempted to expropriate the unused banana lands of the United Fruit Company for redistribution. He was finally overthrown by the army when he attempted to distribute arms to workers to resist an invasion of exiles aided by the United States. Since that time, with the exception of the four-year term of Mario Méndez Montenegro (1966–70) the presidency has remained in military hands, and elections since 1970 have been between military candidates only. At the same time, confronted by a number of guerrilla movements inspired by the Cuban revolution of 1959, the army has fought back with help (since the mid-1960s) from a number of right-wing paramilitary 'death squads' whose activities have effectively eradicated all possible bases for a democratic system.

In El Salvador no civilian leader emerged on the fall of Hernández Martínez and a series of coups merely consolidated the power of the army as an institution. The reforms of Major Oscar Osorio (1949–56) and his successor José María Lemus (1956–60), though considerable, represented moves by the country's oligarchy to forestall trouble by keeping up with the 'New Deal'-inspired moves then taking place in neighbouring countries. When Lemus was deposed by younger officers and students in 1960, a second coup quickly restored the control of Conservative officers. A series of coups in Honduras after the retirement of Carías similarly led after 1963 to an army nervous of a Cuban-style revolution arrogating power to itself. It was therefore two military regimes that found themselves drawn in 1969 into the bizarre episode of the 'Football War' (Guerra de Fútbol), also called the 'Soccer War'. It took its title from its origin in a disputed decision in the third qualifying round of the World Cup, but its root cause was the social tension aroused by the migration of workers from overcrowded El Salvador into Honduras, and in a brief thirteen days it killed some 2000 before being ended by a cease-fire arranged by the Organization of American States (OAS).

The Football War arrested at a critical point the growth of a new sort of regional organization for unity, the Central American Common Market (CACM), created in 1960 under the auspices of an earlier regional organization, the Organization of Central American States (ODECA) set up by the Treaty of San Salvador of 1951. Honduras withdrew from CACM in pique, and for twelve years (until late 1980) the two governments, largely because of internal instability, were unable to sign a peace treaty. When it came, it was only because by that time El Salvador had become the scene of a virtual civil war between left- and right-wing forces, both emulating events in neighbouring Nicaragua the previous year.

There, the assassination of the elder Somoza had given way to a dynastic succession unparalleled in the Americas. His elder son, Luis Somoza Debayle (1956–63), under United States pressure, allowed the election of a trusted supporter, René Schick, but the family retained the all-essential control of the National Guard, and when Schick died in office in 1966, Anastasio Somoza Debayle took over the presidency. Under him, cotton became a major export, coffee plantations were created and Nicaragua was run as a family business, until, after the devastating Managua earthquake of 1973, the family's blatant speculation and the brutality of the Guard earned it universal unpopularity. Eventually the Somoza regime was overthrown in 1979 by the forces of the Sandinista National Liberation Front (FSLN), an alliance of radical and left-wing groups taking its name from General Sandino. The provisional government installed by the revolution has striven to implement a programme of 'socialist transformation' and re-education in Nicaragua along lines somewhat reminiscent of those of Cuba. US apprehensions led to a policy of 'containment' of the revolution and support of its enemies, though elections in 1984 (adjudged honest by observers) confirmed that the revolution was backed by the majority of the people.

The success of the Nicaraguan revolution inspired a similar (but initially much less universally popular) revolt in El Salvador whose American-backed governments proved only just able to stem the

US troops land for manoeuvres in Honduras in 1983

resulting civil war (1982). It also eventually forced the government of Guatemala, which had since 1938 claimed possession of the territory of Belize (formerly known as British Honduras), to reconsider its position and to tolerate Belizean independence.

In Costa Rica a somewhat different kind of revolution had come earlier, in 1948, when the belief that the freedom of elections was being infringed by the Teodoro Picado administration led to a popular revolt led by José Figueres (president 1953–8). In a dramatic move Figueres ended militarism in Costa Rica by disbanding the army; Costa Rica relied upon the Inter-American Treaty of Guarantees of 1948 to repel invasions by Somozan Nicaragua in 1949 and 1955, and did so successfully. It later aided the FSLN revolt against the Somozas, also successfully. Internally, however, democratic tradition seems to have been strengthened rather than weakened by the events of 1948.

In the years since 1944, therefore, the five countries have further developed their very different personalities. In 1971, at the 150th anniversary of independence, federation was hardly mentioned and even the CACM was in limbo. The events of the past decade do not suggest that this pattern is likely to alter much. Central America remains proof that language, historical, geographical and cultural ties do not in themselves imply unity.

PARC

José Figueres

Further reading

R. H. Immerman, *The CIA in Guatemala* (Austin, Texas, 1982)

T. L. Karnes, *The Failure of Union: Central America, 1824–1960* (Chapel Hill, 1961)

J. Pearce, *Under the Eagle* (London, 1981)

R. L. Woodward, *Central America: a Nation Divided* (New York, 1976)

Colombia, Venezuela and Ecuador

Birth of three republics

Gran Colombia,* whose coasts stretched from the Orinoco delta on the Atlantic to the north of Peru on the Pacific, was the successor state to the old Spanish imperial divisions of the viceroyalty of New Granada, the captaincy-general of Caracas, the *audiencia* of Quito and the province of Panama. Formally established by the congress that met in Cúcuta, in present-day Colombia, in 1821, it was an imposing diplomatic façade, but as the old administrative divisions hinted, not a whole that would be easily governed from one place. The façade served its purpose in securing men, resources and diplomatic support for the final stages of the War of Independence both within its territories and in the viceroyalty of Peru to the south, but the hold of its government in Santa Fé de Bogotá over the lands and peoples outside the old viceroyalty of New Granada was precarious. Vice-President Francisco de Paula Santander (1792–1840), who was the head of the government while Bolívar was on campaign (1821–7), found his authority frequently challenged. Bolívar himself on his return from Peru made concessions, particularly to feelings in Caracas, and finally removed Santander from office. However, he could not maintain Gran Colombia against the feelings and interests which sought to divide it once its military necessity and diplomatic convenience were past. It was well on the way to dissolution by the time his death in December 1830 removed the last obstacle to the emergence of not one but three new states. These were now more firmly based on the demarcations that three centuries of experience had found to be practical, and which, with the exception of the separation of Panama from Colombia, were to persist to the present day. Like many subsequent crises, the break-up of Bolívar's political creation coincided with depression and financial crisis, and default on the substantial loans that in the mid-1820s Gran Colombia had raised on the London market.

Economic development from independence

Colombia, Venezuela and Ecuador in 1830 possessed certain common characteristics. They had scant and scattered populations: the conventional estimates gave Colombia 1,500,000, Venezuela 900,000 and Ecuador 500,000. These populations were heavily rural: Bogotá, Caracas and Quito all numbered somewhere around thirty thousand inhabitants at this time. Communications were everywhere poor, particularly in Colombia and Ecuador, two of the most mountainous countries in the world. Local wealth and

*Gran Colombia is the name used by most historians, in order to distinguish the larger state from the modern Colombia, which covers only the old New Granada.

economic potential disappointed the expectations of the early 1820s. All three populations were racially mixed, though distinctively so. All three republics inherited from Spain three cardinal institutions, the Church, the judiciary and the army, again in distinct degrees: as Bolívar had pessimistically predicted, 'Venezuela a barracks, Colombia a law-court, Ecuador a convent'.

The largest share of Gran Colombia's population lay in Colombia. It was then settled mostly in the colder highlands of the interior, and it did not represent a large capacity in international trade. Colombia's per-capita exports were to remain among the lowest in Latin America throughout the nineteenth century: in 1830 its main export was gold from the mines of the provinces of Antioquia, El Choco and Cauca. Colombia was one of the world's leading gold producers before the discoveries in California and Australia, but it had little else to offer and its annual export of specie was less than a peso a head. Mining, like so much else, did not respond to foreign hopes at the time of independence. Expansion of exports came in the late 1840s first with tobacco, particularly from the district of Ambalema on the upper Magdalena River, which also brought with it the establishment of regular steam traffic on the river. To tobacco was added cinchona bark, the source of quinine, which grew wild in certain parts of the country and for which an always erratic demand collapsed entirely in the early 1880s when plantations were established in Ceylon and the Dutch East Indies. Coffee began to be exported from Colombia in visible quantities in the 1860s and by the end of the century was the leading export, tobacco having collapsed with quinine in the early 1880s. But as a coffee exporter Colombia did not overtake Venezuela as South America's second producer after Brazil until well into the twentieth century. The 1920s were the first decade of relative optimism and prosperity since the short-lived buoyancy of the 1860s and 1870s, coffee being supported by bananas from Santa Marta and petroleum. Those supports were also to fall away, and coffee has obstinately remained the mainstay of Colombian international trade. Coal and other mineral resources are more likely to rival or replace coffee in the future than the more publicized marijuana and cocaine.

The slow development of exports was reflected in small state revenues, slow improvement of communications (Colombia had less than 1000 km of railroad by 1900), tardy development of banking and finance and little foreign investment. It also kept Colombian trade in native hands to a degree not common in Latin America. Colombia received little immigration and the few immigrants who did settle in the country were absorbed into native social, commercial, religious and political practices. The largest single group of immigrants has been the Lebanese, who began to arrive in the last years of the nineteenth century. Foreign cultural influences up until the 1920s were predominantly French and British, though Bogotá's isolation and clerical–legal tradition ensured the persistence of

COLOMBIA, VENEZUELA AND ECUADOR

VENEZUELA	
Area	898,805 sq km
Population	15.0 million
GDP per capita (1980)	$2457
Capital	Caracas
Currency	Bolívar

COLOMBIA	
Area	1,138,338 sq km
Population	26.1 million
GDP per capita (1980)	$921
Capital	Bogotá
Currency	Peso

ECUADOR	
Area	270,670 sq km
Population	7.8 million
GDP per capita (1980)	$789
Capital	Quito
Currency	Sucre

KEY
+++++ Railways
——— Roads
——— International boundaries

0   640 km
0   400 miles

creole–Hispanic elements, again to an unusual degree. Great Britain maintained a predominant position as Colombia's leading trading partner until the First World War. The beginnings of native industry can be traced to the end of the last century, though they have no continuity with the artisan weaving and hat-making of Boyacá and Socorro. Modern textile factories came to be concentrated around Medellín, where capital and market expertise derived from the coffee trade of the Antioquia frontier, and before that from the control of foreign trade Antioqueño merchants exercised through the gold production of the province.

At the time of independence Venezuela and Ecuador were the world's leading producers of cacao. The crop's dominance was supplanted in Venezuela by coffee, first grown in the centre of the country around Caracas and then in the western Andean states. Coffee remained Venezuela's leading export until it was overtaken by petroleum after the First World War. Foreign trading houses were more prominent than in Colombia, particularly those of north German origin, but these merchants were well integrated with the local community and in most respects can be considered to be native. The country also exported hides, some cattle and a certain amount of gold from the Guayana region and the llanos. The presence of asphalt and petroleum had always been known, and the earliest commercial production of petroleum dates from over a hundred years ago. The First World War and troubles in Mexico brought Venezuela's potential into prominence, and development by British and United States companies was then rapid. President Juan Vicente Gómez (1908–35) was more successful than he has usually been given credit for in balancing foreign interests against each other and in imposing terms on the companies, but much of what was gained was absorbed in corruption, and the effect on the rest of the economy was to make Venezuela entirely dependent on petroleum; its agriculture was weak and what little industry existed was stifled by its strong propensity to import. These patterns have persisted. General Gómez for reasons of political security did not encourage immigration, but his successors reversed this policy and since the 1940s Venezuela has attracted large numbers of immigrants from Spain, Portugal and Italy, and from other South American and Caribbean states, particularly from Colombia. Venezuela may be said to have originated the idea of OPEC (Organization of Petroleum Exporting Countries), and aspires to greater influence as a result in hemispheric, and particularly in Caribbean affairs. Venezuela also possesses in the Cerro Bolívar in Guayana immense reserves of iron ore.

The development of cacao exports from coastal Ecuador provided the country with a relatively continuous expansion of its foreign trade in the nineteenth century, though this expansion starts from a small base and for long had little effect on the upland sierra. The sierra provinces possessed a textile industry based on the semiservile system of the *obraje*, but this was already in decline in the eighteenth century in the face of increased imports and imperial readjustments such as the decrees of *comercio libre*. It declined further in the nineteenth century. Hat making in the coastal region of Montecristi and in Azuay expanded, and gave the world the Panama hat. Despite the eventual completion of the Quito–Guayaquil railway in 1908, twentieth-century development was undramatic until the advent of, first, bananas and then petroleum after the Second World War.

COLOMBIA

Slow economic growth in the nineteenth century was in all three republics reflected in politics. Colombia emerged as an independent nation under the liberal guidance of Francisco de Paula Santander (president 1832–6). Despite his prestige and political industry, he was succeeded by an opponent, José Ignacio de Márquez, a 'moderate' of more conservative stamp. Márquez himself was faced by a series of populist–federalist revolts, the most important being that of the clerical south around Pasto led, in self-defence against the revived charge of having murdered Bolívar's faithful lieutenant Marshal Sucre in 1830, by General José Maria Obando. These were eventually defeated and Generals Pedro Alcántara Herrán (1841–5) and Tomás Cipriano de Mosquera (1845–9) governed under a more conservative, centralist and authoritarian constitution. The Conservatives were defeated by a revived Liberalism in the elections of 1849, and a period of conflicting radicalisms and Conservative resistance followed under the presidencies of José Hilario López (1849–53) and José Maria Obando, returned from exile and briefly president (1853–4). Under his faltering direction, conflict between the artisans, allied with the small military element, and free-trade radicals produced a short-lived coup d'état by General José María Melo. A united reaction of Liberals and Conservatives against this restored civilian rule, first all-party under President Manuel María Mallarino (1854–7), then Conservative under President Mariano Ospina Rodríguez (1857–61). Ospina's administration planned to consolidate Conservative rule by relying on a clergy reinforced by the return of the Jesuits, but it was frustrated by the rising in the Cauca of former President Mosquera, protesting against Ospina's allegedly unconstitutional interference in provincial affairs. Mosquera's victory – apart from the removal of Melo, the one example of a successful advance on Bogotá by a provincial army that the history of Colombian civil wars can show – reinforced federalist currents that had been active for two decades, and which reflected

Coffee pickers in Colombia, 1900

the country's geographical and cultural diversity as well as the fiscal weakness of central government and the current fashions of democratic philosophy. Both Liberals and Conservatives had been federalists in competition with each other. The Constitution of Rionegro, which, with modifications, lasted from 1863 to 1885, divided the country into nine 'sovereign' states which did, indeed, exercise wide autonomy. The Church was disestablished and lost its properties. The powers of the presidency were much reduced, and the presidential term reduced to two years. The local governments produced by this system reflected in their competence the wealth or poverty of the state concerned, and defenders of the system argued that it produced governments suited to local conditions and reduced the scope of conflict. It could not however produce order or guarantee prosperity, and it broke up with the economic down-turn of the early 1880s. Free-trade radicalism, whose leading figures were Manuel Murillo Toro (president 1864–6), Santiago Pérez (president 1874–6) and Aquileo Parra (president 1876–8), had failed to keep its promises.

The Constitution of 1886, which with important changes is still the basis of Colombian political life, was the product of the 'independent' Liberal positivist Rafael Núñez (president 1882–4 and 1885–94) and the Conservative Miguel Antonio Caro, first Núñez's vice-president and then president himself from 1894 to 1898. Rafael Núñez's 'Regeneration' promised to bring peace and progress through centralization, a restricted suffrage (the Constitution of Rionegro had laid down manhood suffrage, which its Liberal manipulators consistently and necessarily rigged through fraud and the federal army), a Church restored to recognition and influence, a larger army, and a less doctrinaire economic policy, which would include recourse to paper money. It also promised guarantees and participation to the opposition, promises which it failed to make good, and looked forward to an economic revival, which failed to occur. Its too exclusive composition can account for the short Liberal rising of 1895, and the same fault combined with a pronounced slump in coffee prices led to the 'War of a Thousand Days' (1899–1901), with its heavy price in destruction and the indirect consequence of the loss of Panama, which aided and abetted by the United States declared its independence from an impotent Colombia in 1904. President José Manuel Marroquín, the harmless Conservative *littérateur*, whom Theodore Roosevelt in the heat of that separation referred to as a well-known South American bandit, was followed in the same year as president by General Rafael Reyes, who extended his term of office until hostile opinion drove him abroad in 1910. Reyes admired Porfirio Díaz of Mexico; Colombia's lack of resources on the whole frustrated his attempt to bring progress through 'plenty of administration and no politics', but he achieved some success in cleaning up the financial chaos left behind by the last civil war. He also gave the Liberal Party some participation in government, an essential element in national peace which was continued under his 'Republican' or coalition successor Carlos E. Restrepo (1911–14), and under the Conservatives José Vicente Concha, Marco Fidel Suárez, Pedro Nel Ospina and Miguel Abadía Méndez, the successive presidents before party division and the Depression brought the Liberals to power in 1930.

This was the first peaceful change of party in power in the history of the republic. The Liberals had maintained in opposition, in the civil wars and after, a certain popular appeal, a tradition emphasized by leaders such as General Rafael Uribe Uribe (assassinated 1914) and General Benjamín Herrera (died 1924). This tradition was muted under the prudent coalition government of Enrique Olaya Herrera (1930–4), but was fully exploited by Alfonso López Pumarejo (1934–8), in the 'Revolución en Marcha' ('Revolution on the March'). The Liberal Party introduced modern social legislation and encouraged the labour movement. The pace was not maintained by the following government of Eduardo Santos (1938–42), and could not in wartime conditions be revived by Alfonso López Pumarejo in his second term. This ended in scandal, disillusion and resignation in 1945. In 1946 the Conservative candidate Mariano Ospina Pérez was elected president against a Liberal vote that was divided between Gabriel Turbay and Jorge Eliecer Gaitán. On 9 April 1948 the assassination of Gaitán, a complex demagogue who by then had captured the leadership of the Liberal Party, intensified

what was already an atmosphere of violent antagonism. The 'Bogotazo' riot the assassination caused was perhaps the most destructive in Latin America's history. Sectarian violence broke out in wide areas of the countryside, and 'la violencia' (as it became known) could not be contained by Ospina Pérez or by his successor, the party's main force and ideologue Laureano Gómez. His increasingly authoritarian rule was ended on 13 June 1953 by a military coup carried out under strong civilian pressure by General Gustavo Rojas Pinilla. His government lasted until 1957; though it at first had some success in pacifying Liberal guerrillas, the army had neither the numbers, the training nor the political understanding needed to govern effectively. It was forced to give way to a Liberal–Conservative coalition, formed by a pact which laid down that the two parties should alternate in the presidency and share public office evenly for four terms – sixteen years. This arrangement effectively ended sectarian violence, though it failed to end rural guerrilla activity under other forms and allegiances. The 'National Front' coalition presidents Alberto Lleras Camargo (Liberal), Guillermo León Valencia (Conservative), Carlos Lleras Restrepo (Liberal) and Misael Pastrana Borrero (Conservative) were opposed by various dissident groups from the two traditional parties, and by the Alianza Nacional Popular movement of General Rojas Pinilla. Since the return of controlled competition in 1974 the presidency has been held by Alfonso López Michelsen (1974–8), son of Alfonso López Pumarejo, by Julio Cesar Turbay Ayala (1978–82), and by Belisario Betancur (1982–).

The Colombian political tradition can be characterized as follows: by the persistence and dominance of civilian liberalism and conservatism, to a degree unknown elsewhere in Latin America; by the presence of the Church as a powerful component of conservatism until the 1960s; by constant electoral activity, though rates of abstention remain high; by widespread and early politicization of a population without strong racial or cultural barriers against some sort of participation; by the ability of both parties to co-opt emerging leaders, and of the Liberal Party not to be outflanked on the left; by the lack of a single dominant city or region, which has enforced collaboration between cities and regions; by a strong journalistic tradition.

VENEZUELA

The contrast with Venezuela was not at first so apparent. General José Antonio Páez was as opposed to the presence of Simón Bolívar and the Gran Colombian army of liberation in Venezuela as Santander was to its presence in Colombia. Though a military rising soon ended the presidential career of his successor, the medical doctor José Maria Vargas (1834–6), Páez was careful of appearances under the administration of Carlos Soublette (1843–7). The 'Conservative Republic' allowed wide liberties at first to the Liberal opposition, and the 1840s were a fertile time for the Venezuelan press: the polemical level of the Liberals Antonio Leocadio Guzmán and Tomás Lander and of the Conservative Juan Vicente González was higher than could be attained under the successive authoritarian regimes that followed. The Liberal opposition to Páez exploited the economic claims of *hacendados* and artisans against merchants and monopolists, and did so with an intensity and efficiency not matched elsewhere in the successor states of Gran Colombia. Páez was strong enough to suppress Antonio Leocadio Guzmán, but had to compromise in the 1847 presidential elections by adopting the candidacy of the neutral and independent General José Tadeo Monagas, strongly entrenched in the east and, as it turned out, not disposed to be a puppet. Páez's attempts to control Monagas through Congress were frustrated by a popular riot on 19 January 1848 (the first revolution of that year) which Monagas is wrongly credited with instigating; he did take advantage of it. In the ensuing civil war Páez was defeated and went into exile. The Liberal domination of José Tadeo Monagas and his brother José Gregorio did not survive exhaustion of reputation – there was much familial corruption – and worsening economic conditions at the end of the 1850s. Páez's attempt to return to power led to the widespread but desultory *Guerra Federal* (Federal War), in which Venezuelan Conservatism met its definitive defeat at the hands of the Liberals led by Marshal Juan Crisóstomo Falcón, General Ezequiel Zamora and General Antonio Guzmán Blanco. The Liberals declared that the cause of federalism was that of democracy and equality against the *godos*, the Conservative oligarchs, and Zamora in particular gave the war a certain populist élan until killed in battle. Guzmán Blanco became president in 1873, and with short interruptions he ruled either in Caracas or from Paris, until 1888. In theory Guzmán was a Liberal, and he was so more than just in theory in that he believed in systematic material progress, in education and in secular control of the Church – the never powerful Venezuelan Church was further reduced and humiliated by his government. He ruled as an autocrat, and his grand titles and bombastic self-adulation were part of the scheme that set him above his rivals, just as his buildings in Caracas set his capital above other cities. His powerful political intelligence can be seen in the length of his rule and the degree to which his successors have imitated him. He can also claim a measure of administrative and material progress. His share of the latter made him the first noticeably rich South American in Paris.

Guzmán Blanco's ascendancy was followed by the more transient administrations of Juan Pablo Rojas Paúl (1888–90), Raimundo Andueza Palacio (1890–2), and Joaquín Crespo (1892–8). The last might have been less transient had Crespo not been killed in battle, but none of these figures, all Liberals of no strong definition or imagination, has the significance of Guzmán Blanco or of the leader to emerge in 1899. General Cipriano Castro. Castro invaded from

General Juan
Vicente Gómez

the Colombian border with only sixty men, but his small band of *andinos* (from the western Andean region) succeeded in installing their leader in the presidency through a combination of fighting and diplomacy. Castro was debauched and corrupt, but his radicalism and nationalism were not entirely faked, and he was a feared and inspiring leader. He survived a number of risings and an Anglo-German debt-collecting blockade, and only yielded office to his vice-president, General Juan Vicente Gómez, to go to Europe for an operation. Gómez's thoroughgoing tyranny lasted from 1908 to his death in 1935: had it not lasted so long, his genuine contributions to national order and progress would be less overshadowed by his implacable treatment of political opposition, his cultural sterility and his own, his family's and his entourage's greed. Military power was exclusively entrusted to *andinos*. In public finance, in oil matters, in building a modern army and in the ideological defence of his regime he was served by able men (in oil by Gumersindo Torres, in the army by General Eleazar López Contreras, in intellectual argument by Laureano Vallenilla Lanz), but their efforts were offset by a high price in isolation and stultification. Gómez's death was followed by two increasingly liberal military governments under first General López Contreras, 1935–40, then General Isaias Medina Angarita, 1940–5. General Medina was overthrown by a military coup which installed the first short-lived Democratic Action (AD) governments of Rómulo Betancourt and Rómulo Gallegos, the last overthrown by another coup which evolved into the revived *andino* military regime of Marcos Pérez Jiménez (1948–58). Representative democracy, with an enviable record of civil liberty, has since survived under Rómulo Betancourt (1959–64), Raúl Leoni (AD)

(1964–9), Rafael Caldera of the Christian Democrat COPEI, (1969–74), Carlos Andrés Pérez (AD) (1974–9) and Luis Herrera Campíns (COPEI) (1978–84). Herrera Campíns was succeeded in 1984 by Jaime Lusinchi (AD). The challenge to the constitutional regime mounted by guerrilla movements in the early 1960s was resolutely surmounted.

Venezuelan democratic policies have their origins in the opposition to Gómez and to Pérez Jiménez. Venezuelan parties are elaborately organized and lavishly financed, and their internal structure preserves something of the authoritarianism of the country's tradition. Government patronage, derived from oil revenues, is far more persuasive than in Colombia or Ecuador. The army has been carefully integrated into the country's political structure. The social and commercial elite are less openly politicized than is common in the region. The spirit of Venezuelan society is markedly egalitarian, which is not incompatible with rampant consumerism.

ECUADOR

Ecuador began its independent existence under a Venezuelan General, Juan José Flores, who contrived to command the greater share of influence with the Guayaquil Liberal Vicente Rocafuerte until the mid-1840s. Ecuadorean governments thereafter were unstable constructs of different local influences, the sierra predominating, until the era of Gabriel García Moreno, a progressive theocrat–Conservative of Guayaquil origins whose sway lasted from 1861 until his assassination in 1875. García Moreno believed in public works, in education and in discipline, whose principal

Eloy Alfaro

support would be a reformed ultramontane clergy. Some of his most persistent enemies were therefore Ecuadorean clerics, but the most famous was the Liberal polemicist Juan Montalvo. The twenty years after his death were occupied partly by General Ignacio Veintemilla, a military opportunist, and partly by governments which sought a compromise between the interests of upland landowners and the exporting groups of Guayaquil. In 1895 these frail arrangements collapsed in the face of the assault of radical coastal Liberalism led by General Eloy Alfaro, a tenacious and warlike idealist for whom the closest model is Giuseppe Garibaldi. Alfaro's coastal forces won the sierra, and his government and that of his successor General Leónidas Plaza carried through extensive anticlerical reforms – the Ecuadorean Church had not suffered the earlier Liberal attacks of Colombia and Venezuela. Alfaro, with the American entrepreneur–idealist Archer Harman, also succeeded in completing the Quito–Guayaquil railroad. Unwilling to compromise or retire from politics, Alfaro was murdered by the Quito mob in 1912, and General Plaza emerged as the architect of the coast-sierra compromise that, despite appearances, was to be the persistent note of twentieth-century Ecuadorean politics. The Church had to recognize its reduced position.

General Plaza's compromise was not a guarantee of political tranquility. In 1922 a Guayaquil strike was suppressed by troops with many deaths, and in 1925 the short-lived July Revolution, a reformist military affair, was seen as the beginning of a new era of social preoccupation. In the 1930s José Maria Velasco Ibarra began a political career that was to last four decades: he could appeal to coast and sierra; his combination of ruthless opportunism and disinterestedness gained him the presidency five times (1934–5, 1944–7, 1952–6, 1960–1, 1968–72). But to concentrate too much on this figure is to exaggerate the instability of Ecuadorian politics. The country has known periods of sober civilian government even under Velasco Ibarra, and with particular success under Leónidas Plaza's son, Galo Plaza Lasso, between 1948 and 1952. Recent military governments have not departed from a political tradition that can now be characterized as peaceful, unrepressive and remarkably decentralized: there is more genuine provincial autonomy in Ecuador than in either Colombia or Venezuela. A measure of agrarian reform has lately removed the worst features of exploitation from the countryside.

MD

Further reading

G. Carl, *First among Equals: Great Britain and Venezuela, 1810–1910* (Ann Arbor, 1980)
J. Lombardi, *Venezuela: the Search for Order, the Dream of Progress* (New York, 1982)
M. Palacios, *Coffee in Colombia, 1850–1970: an Economic, Social and Political History* (Cambridge, 1980)

Peru and Bolivia

Peru's independence from Spain was confirmed in 1824, Bolivia's in 1825, but for several years after that it remained uncertain whether Peru and Bolivia would survive as two separate countries or be combined into one. At independence, Peru's population was about 1,200,000, more than half of them Indians, with an additional 50,000 black slaves; Bolivia's population was estimated at 1,100,000, nearly three-quarters of them Indian.

As Lower and Upper Peru, these two major administrative areas in the central Andes had long formed the political and economic heart of Spain's South American empire. Both had retained strong regional identities, and in the final stages of the wars of liberation, small but determined groups of Upper Peruvians demanded independence from Lima as well as from Spain. They succeeded in establishing the new state of Bolivia despite Bolívar's own misgivings about the future prospects of such an isolated state, and the many reminders from Upper Peruvians living in the western city of La Paz that union with Lower Peru would make greater commercial sense.

Restless beginnings

The early years of independence brought no peace to either state. Peru, deeply conscious of former imperial glory, was anxious to extend its authority into the new neighbouring states of Bolivia and Ecuador. In 1828, Peru's General Gamarra invaded Bolivia to begin a thirteen-year period of intermittent but extremely bitter fighting between rival national armies facing each other across the high, broad Andean plateau surrounding Lake Titicaca, known as the

PERU AND BOLIVIA

PERU	
Area	1,280,219 sq km
Population	17.6 million
GDP per capita (1980)	$1137
Capital	Lima
Currency	Sol

BOLIVIA	
Area	1,098,581 sq km
Population	5.6 million
GDP per capita (1980)	$566
Capital	La Paz
Currency	Peso

KEY

Pan–American Highway	
Other main roads	
Marginal Forest Highway	
Railways in operation	+++
Oil pipeline	− − −
International boundaries	

0   480 km

0   300 miles

Altiplano. No lasting gains were made by either side: Peru failed to capitalize on the pro-Peruvian breakaway movements in and around La Paz; Bolivia failed to win the Pacific port of Arica. This rare desert oasis on the world's most arid coastline had been the traditional port for Upper Peru in colonial times, but as it was located within the boundaries of *Lower* Peru, Arica did not become part of Bolivia at independence. Peru was adamant in its refusal to part with Arica and noted with grim satisfaction, as the fighting continued, that Bolivia was too weak to beg, borrow or steal it.

Ambitious, quarrelling generals and rootless guerrillas in both countries found civilian life little to their liking. Violence, political intrigue, and the chaotic conditions in the mines plunged much of Peru and Bolivia into turmoil during the critical early decades of independence. The successful attempt by Andrés Santa Cruz in 1836 to form a Peru–Bolivian Confederation lasted only three years. Santa Cruz had held power briefly in Peru before being installed as president of Bolivia in 1828, but the Confederation never inspired the confidence internally that Britain and the United States displayed towards this larger unit. If Chile had not in any case put an end to the union in 1839 at the battle of Yungay, the Peru–Bolivian

Confederation would almost certainly have collapsed from within. At that time, overland transport and methods of communication throughout a region virtually the size of Europe were poor or non-existent. The more remote areas of northern Peru, and of central and eastern Bolivia remained hostile to the idea, and to everyone connected with it.

1840s–1880s: guano, nitrates, and the War of the Pacific

The 1840s began an important new phase in the fortunes of Peru and Bolivia with the economic exploitation of their coastal guano deposits. It was a phase which was also to reveal their weakness under the growing pressure of Chilean expansion. The thick beds of dried dung produced by the millions of sea birds feeding and nesting along the desert coast were soon in great demand as a rich source of natural fertilizer for Western European agriculture. Guano, which was state-owned, rapidly became the mainstay of Peru's economy. Most Chilean settlement lay well to the south, avoiding the desert, but the Atacama's new wealth was located right by the ocean, on the coastal cliffs and islands, and thus within easy reach of Chilean ships.

MODERN SETTING AND ORIGINAL CLAIMS OF PERU

MODERN SETTING AND ORIGINAL CLAIMS OF BOLIVIA

An hacienda owner and workers in the Chumbivilcas region
of Peru, *c.* 1945

Bolivia became the first to experience the effects of vigorous
Chilean exploitation of the guano deposits. Bolivia had inherited
about 560 km of the Pacific coast but managed to maintain only the
one small port of Cobija along this barren shoreline, separated by
hundreds of kilometres of desert and mountain trail from the main
Andean centres of population. As a result, Bolivia was powerless to
prevent Chilean, or any other foreign exploitation of its guano
deposits – in fact such exploitation was periodically encouraged by
Bolivia's caudillos as the only way of obtaining a share of the profits.

Until the 1870s, Bolivia's buffer location tended to insulate Peru
from the more immediate effects of Chilean expansion. Indeed, in
1866, differences between them were temporarily forgotten when
Ecuador, Peru, Bolivia and Chile formed a defensive alliance against
Spain during the latter's ill-judged attempt (1865–6) to reassert its
authority in the region by seizing Peru's guano-rich Chincha
Islands, and (before withdrawing its squadron) by bombarding
Valparaíso. Fears of Spain were short-lived, however, and Chileans
were soon exploring the Atacama Desert for new sources of wealth.
As the thickest and purest guano deposits became exhausted,
exploitation of the desert's nitrate beds intensified. These lay well

preserved just below the surface in the desert interior. Chilean
prospectors had made important discoveries of sodium nitrate and
silver in the Bolivian section of Atacama in the late 1860s, and with
the backing of British capital, Chilean development of the region,
and its new port of Antofagasta, proceeded without interruption.
British and Chilean interests, working under concession, were now
increasingly active in Peruvian territory. The Atacama Desert was
fast becoming the focus of a new world-trading monopoly in natural
nitrate. Commercial uses included dynamite as well as fertilizer
production, and the huge potential in profits from nitrate was
eagerly pursued as the guano revenues began to decline.

Chile seized control of the main Bolivian centres in the Atacama
by armed occupation in 1879 and then proceeded for the first time
openly to challenge the authority of Peru. The ensuing War of the
Pacific (1879–82) was to demonstrate Chile's skilful use of sea power
in its bid for the leadership of Pacific South America. The 'Nitrate
War' was a fight for possession of the land's economic wealth but it
was a victory for sea transport, and for the greater flexibility of
attack and co-ordination possessed by the state which controlled it.
Lima itself, far beyond the nitrate region, was occupied by Chilean
forces in 1881, and remained so until 1884, when the Ancón peace
treaty (1883) was finally ratified. As a result, Bolivia lost its entire

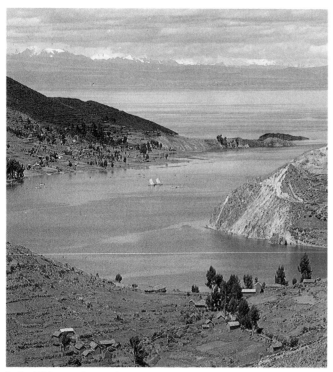

Lake Titicaca from the west

coastline, Peru its nitrate province of Tarapacá, and the port of Arica. Peru's Tacna province was not retrieved from Chilean occupation until an arbitration award by the United States in 1929 resolved what had become a wearying fifty-year dispute between Chile and Peru over the ownership of Tacna and Arica.

Defeat in the War of the Pacific, therefore, marked a humiliating end to the distinctive second phase in Peruvian and Bolivian history. Peru's President Ramón Castilla had provided nearly twenty years of skilful administration and political stability until his retirement in 1862, but after that, internal rivalries and incompetence had seriously weakened the state at a critical stage of its development. Increasing corruption in the handling of the 'windfall' guano and nitrate revenues, and in the manipulation of foreign loans, rocked successive governments. Sales of guano had financed an ambitious and costly programme of railway construction in the Andes between 1868 and 1874, masterminded by the irrepressible North American engineer, Henry Meiggs. Peru's first civilian president, Manuel Pardo, was elected in 1872 but deteriorating conditions permitted only a few of his important economic and public works policies to be implemented.

Bolivia's problems at the end of the Pacific War more than matched those of Peru, as the country looked back on thirty years of almost continuous violence and disorder, particularly under the inept, often vicious rule of Presidents Manuel Belzú (1848–55), Mariano Melgarejo (1864–71) and Hilarión Daza (1876–79) – the 'barbarous caudillos' as they were later called by Bolivian writer Alcídes Arguedas. The loss of the littoral to Chile, together with territorial concessions to Brazil in 1867, emphasized Bolivia's internal weakness, and its failure since independence to cut a reputable figure on the international stage.

1880s–1930s: the effects of increased foreign investment and the beginnings of modernization

Under the firm control of General Andrés Cáceres (1885–90), Peru negotiated the transfer of its external debts to a newly-formed London-based company known as the Peruvian Corporation (1890). In return, the Corporation took over the operation of Peru's railways (and the linking steamship line on Lake Titicaca), acquired free use of seven ports, and received additional cash payments and guano revenues. In the era after the Pacific War, political parties, including Civilist, Constitutionalist, Liberal, and Democratic, became more important in Peru, though all were still dominated by the oligarchy, including the so-called 'forty families of Peru' – mainly landowners and mineowners. Bankers, lawyers, industrialists, and military officers were also prominent.

Peru's economic and trading prospects slowly improved, and in the early decades of the twentieth century, United States business interests began to challenge Britain's hitherto dominant role. Many American bankers by now regarded South America as a fruitful field for investment, and offered loans for new railway and port construction, and for much-needed urban reconstruction and development. New public buildings, parks, public utilities, streetcars, lighting, water supply, sewerage, and a host of other improvements were much in demand in order to make life in the city centres (especially Lima) smarter, safer and more efficient. At the same time, Peru's President Leguía was actively encouraging North American companies such as W. R. Grace (shipping, sugar estates and sugar-refining, textiles), Standard Oil (later its subsidiary the International Petroleum Company), and the Cerro de Pasco Copper Corporation to expand their operations. Augusto Leguía was in power for most of the period between 1908 and 1930, but as his determined handling of economic policies became increasingly dictatorial, the emerging middle class began to complain that a civilian caudillo was no more acceptable than a military one. There were growing demands for greater freedom of the press and for civil rights; growing dissatisfaction with the traditional concentration of power in the hands of a few wealthy landowners, and with the total failure to improve the lot of most of the Indian population.

In 1924, Víctor Raúl Haya de la Torre founded a new political party while in exile in Mexico; this was APRA (American Popular Revolutionary Alliance). Conceived originally as an international moderate 66-year-old constitutional lawyer.

The elections of 30 October 1983 produced a historic result as Raúl Alfonsín and his resurgent Radical Party convincingly defeated the Peronist opposition by winning the presidency, outright control of the Chamber of Deputies and a respectable number of provincial governorships. For the first time in forty years the Peronist movement was defeated in a free election. Dr Alfonsín was inaugurated as president in December 1983, amidst hopes that – despite considerable economic difficulties; and the bitter legacy of the recent past – Argentina was now at one of the great turning points of its history, and on the way to better times at last.

PARAGUAY
Dictatorships and wars
In contrast to many of the Spanish American nations, Paraguay achieved independence from Spain without great bloodshed or prolonged conflict. Initially, the people of the territory refused to heed the call of the Argentine revolutionaries to join the struggle against Spanish authority, and they actually repulsed an army of liberation sent from Buenos Aires in December 1810. Nonetheless, Paraguayan patriots eventually took action on their own, in May and

June 1811, deposing the Spanish governor, severing the links with Spain and appointing a junta to rule the new republic.

From the junta emerged a leader by 1814 with the will to build a Paraguayan nation, Dr José Gaspar Rodríguez de Francia, known as El Supremo. Dr Francia took on the character of a populist dictator and sealed off Paraguay from the outside world by prohibiting movement in and out of the country. With foreign trade allowed to stagnate, El Supremo channelled the energies of the nation into the development of domestic activities, particularly cattle raising and agriculture for internal consumption.

The death of Francia in 1840 without an obvious successor created political uncertainty; however, a new leader, Carlos Antonio López, came to the fore in 1844 to become Paraguay's first constitutionally designated president. While less stern than his predecessor, López ruled autocratically and used his office to become the foremost landowner and cattle owner. The new president ended the country's self-imposed isolation and opened up Paraguay to external influences such as trade, immigration and foreign technicians. Paraguay's more outward-looking policies ran afoul of the designs of the Rosas government in Argentina, which had closed the River Plate to Paraguayan commerce, and thus López from 1845 sided

PARAGUAY

José Rodríguez de Francia

with the enemies of the Buenos Aires strong man. The eventual fall of Rosas had important implications for Paraguay, as the new leader of the Argentine Confederation, Justo José de Urquiza, renounced in effect any Argentine claim to sovereignty over the nation by recognizing its independence in 1852.

Upon the death of Carlos Antonio López in 1862, the leader's son and vice-president, Francisco Solano López, became president. López, an admirer of Napoleon, came to power determined to make his country's weight felt in the River Plate region. When Brazilian forces intervened in Uruguay in 1864, the decision of the Paraguayan leader to attack Brazil by crossing through Argentine soil only succeeded in uniting the governments of Argentina, Brazil and Uruguay against him, triggering off the War of the Triple Alliance, which lasted from 1865 to 1870. Paraguay was quickly forced back upon the defensive in 1865 and had to mobilize ultimately the entire male population from adolescents to the elderly. Gradually, the allied forces broke through the tenacious Paraguayan defensive redoubts and captured the capital city of

Asunción by January 1869. The war ended in March 1870 with the defeat and death of López at Cerro Corá.

The War of the Triple Alliance left Paraguay with a bitter legacy. Not only was the economy in ruins, but the male population had been reduced by nine-tenths, making the country (for a generation) a land of women and small children. Paraguay remained under foreign occupation until 1876, with some of its territory annexed.

From 1870 onward, in theory, Paraguay operated under a new constitution, but in practice it entered a new era of chronic political instability as few governments were immune to the threat of uprising or overthrow. Two important political parties were founded in 1887, the conservative Colorado Party and the Liberal Party which first tasted the fruits of power in 1904, becoming the strongest political force. In the decades after 1870, both the economy and population recovered from the catastrophe of war, and a small inflow of immigrants from Spain, Italy, Germany and Argentina made considerable impact on the nation's agrarian and forestry industries.

But national attention could not remain focused merely upon internal matters, as the territorial dispute with Bolivia over the sparsely populated Chaco region now took on growing importance. During the first decade of the twentieth century both Paraguay and Bolivia began to increase their military garrisons in the area. Small army units of the two countries clashed in 1928, and a full-scale war erupted in the Chaco in 1932. Under the able command of General José Félix Estigarribia, the Paraguayan army drove the Bolivians from much of the disputed territory, but the belligerents were thoroughly exhausted and agreed to a cease-fire in 1935. The eventual peace treaty of 1938, signed at the Buenos Aires peace conference, awarded Paraguay about three-quarters of the area in contention in the Chaco.

The new strong men

While a rallying point for the nation, the Chaco War did unleash new forces in the political life of Paraguay. Thirty-two years of Liberal Party rule ended on 17 February 1936 when a group of disgruntled army officers and anti-Liberal politicians overthrew President Eusebio Ayala and appointed Colonel Rafael Franco head of the government. The new president, who was imbued with nationalist and reformist ideas, was in turn deposed by a military revolt in 1937; nevertheless, Franco and his followers, later to be called Febreristas, constituted a reform-minded movement attracting support from student and labour groups, such as they were. The Liberal Party regained control of the government once more when the war hero Estigarribia stood under its banner and won the presidency in 1939. Estigarribia, worried about the social and political climate, assumed temporary dictatorial power in 1940 and obtained the electorate's approval for a new constitution which concentrated all authority in the hands of the executive branch. But the life of the hero of the Chaco was tragically cut short by an aeroplane crash in 1940, and General Higinio Morínigo was designated interim president.

Morínigo, to the surprise of the army officers and Liberals who had installed him as head of state, took on dictatorial powers and restricted political activity for most of his years in office from 1940 to 1948. He experimented briefly with a coalition government in 1946 with Febrerista and Colorado elements, but in the following year he had to put down a bloody civil war initiated by Liberals and Febreristas which left the economy in shambles.

Morínigo gave way to Juan Natalicio González who triumphed in the presidential election of 1948. Neither González nor his immediate successors remained in office very long, but in 1949 the leader of the Colorado Party, Dr Federico Chávez, became a provisional president. Chávez contested and won the presidential election of 1953; however, he was removed from his post by the military coup of 1954 which brought to power the then army commander-in-chief, General Alfredo Stroessner.

Relying on a power base of the army and the Colorado Party, General Stroessner fashioned the longest and most durable regime in the country's history. Initially, he imposed tight restrictions on political activity and found it necessary to repel a series of raids in 1959 and 1960 by exile groups operating from Argentina. But from the 1960s on, the Stroessner government has permitted a limited degree of opposition while managing the nation's political scene so that the traditional parties have not been able to challenge (in any realistic sense) the dominant position of the Colorado Party. President Stroessner himself, re-elected without trouble at regular intervals, was already Latin America's longest-serving ruler by the 1970s.

During Stroessner's three decades in power, Paraguay has devoted considerable attention to developing an economy largely oriented towards the production and processing of farm, ranch and forestry products. The state, utilizing foreign loans and aid, has engaged in an extensive programme of road building, the expansion of the national merchant marine, the improvement of air facilities and, more recently, the construction of hydroelectric power plants. Following orthodox and conservative economic policies aimed at maintaining a strong and stable national currency, the Stroessner government in the 1960s and early 1970s opted for moderate economic growth and the gradual industrialization of activities processing domestic raw materials.

In the 1970s, however, the economic circumstances of Paraguay underwent a change thanks to the decision of President Stroessner to undertake, at Brazil's urging, the binational development of the Itaipú hydroelectric project on the Paraná River, one of the largest civil engineering works of this century. The project, which started in 1973, stimulated throughout the rest of the 1970s and the first two years of the 1980s an unprecedented economic boom, expanding the domestic construction industry, providing much employment and producing a massive inflow of foreign currency into the nation's small financial market. From 1976 to 1981, the Paraguayan economy registered one of the highest growth rates in the world, more than 10 per cent per annum, but it became exposed for the first time since the 1950s to a taste of moderately strong inflation. Industrial growth accelerated as did unionization in a trade union movement which the Stroessner government had always sought to control.

The winding down of the Itaipú dam construction project, the delays in the start-up of the similar but smaller Yacyretá hydroelectric project with Argentina and the political and economic troubles in the important Argentine market all cast shadows on national economic activity as Paraguay's economic growth plunged to an estimated 1.6 per cent in 1982. Also contributing was the worldwide recession which struck in 1981.

With a more sobering economic panorama from 1982 onward, the Stroessner government was confronted with a more restive political scene. Exporters were strongly critical of the overvalued guaraní and importers complained of the crippling shortage of foreign exchange. There was even some uncertainty as to whether General Stroessner would step down or would seek to contest the presidential elections to be held in February 1983. The president, however, put an end to the conjectures about his political intentions by campaigning and winning his seventh term. In the elections of February 1983, Stroessner obtained 91 per cent of the vote in the usual way; opposition parties boycotted the elections. By the mid-1980s, new political and economic challenges were very much on the horizon for Paraguay.

URUGUAY

Uruguay achieved nationhood in 1828 in part through the diplomatic efforts of the British government, whose mediation brought to an end the conflict between Brazil and Argentina over the territory. For many decades thereafter, the new republic had the character of a buffer state which was neither politically stable nor free of outside interference. It was a sparsely populated land with a rudimentary economy geared to stockraising and with only about a quarter of its 60,000 or so inhabitants living in the port and capital city of Montevideo.

The lawless nineteenth century

Under the constitution adopted in 1830, Fructuoso Rivera became the first president. He relinquished power in 1835 to his elected successor Manuel Oribe, but later organized a revolt against the incumbent. This civil war between the partisans of Rivera and

URUGUAY

URUGUAY	
Area	186,926 sq km
Population	2·9 million
GDP per capita (1980)	$2164
Capital	Montevideo
Currency	Peso

'Los tres chiripaes': rural characters depicted by Juan Manuel Blanes

With Rosas's fall from power in Argentina in 1852, the siege of Montevideo was lifted, leaving the Colorados in full control of the country. Their hold remained precarious as a result of the opposition of the Blancos as well as frequent divisions within their own ranks. At the same time, external forces continued to be the arbiters of national destiny. The Colorado leader General Venancio Flores requested Brazil's assistance in the 1850s to protect his presidency and again in 1865 when his forces combined with Brazilian troops to enter Montevideo and topple the government of President Atanasio Aguirre. This latter action so angered the ruler of Paraguay, Francisco Solano López, that it provided the catalyst for the War of the Triple Alliance, pitting Argentina, Brazil and Uruguay against Paraguay.

Flores's assumption of power in 1865 marked the beginning of uninterrupted Colorado political control of the government extending well into the twentieth century. Even so, political turmoil continued to be the rule, with numerous presidents ousted in revolutions occurring in the last three decades of the nineteenth century.

While very prone to political instability and civil insurrections, Uruguay after 1870 was no longer just a lawless frontier society. In that year, barbed wire was first introduced to fence off livestock ranges. During the 1870s, the social and educational reformer José Varela was instrumental in convincing the government of Lorenzo Latorre to modernize the nation's educational system and introduce universal education. Immigrants had begun to flow into Uruguay in increasing numbers, so that by 1872 one-quarter of the population was foreign born. Economic changes of importance were soon under way as a railway system under the direction of British interests took shape.

Even in the political sphere the warring Colorados and Blancos

Oribe had historic significance as it laid the basis for the eventual formation of the two political parties destined to dominate national politics in the nineteenth and twentieth centuries, the Colorados and the Blancos. Rivera's Colorado forces, with the aid of Argentine Unitarios, obliged Oribe and fellow Blancos to take refuge in Argentina under the protection of the dictator Juan Manuel de Rosas.

The fierce Colorado–Blanco rivalry had international ramifications. Oribe's followers, strongly backed by troops of Rosas, besieged the Colorado-controlled city of Montevideo from 1843 to 1852. Even outside maritime powers such as Britain and France found themselves drawn into the conflict occurring in the River Plate waterway. During the nine-year siege of Uruguay's most important commercial centre, pastoral and general economic activity stagnated.

were beginning to move towards an accommodation of their differences. After the civil war of 1896, the two factions struck a compromise whereby the Blancos gained control of six of the nation's departments while the Colorados were entitled to control the remaining twelve departments. At the turn of the century, therefore, Uruguay was on the threshold of political and economic stability. Large-scale foreign investment went into infrastructure and productive activities, and the construction of the first refrigerated meat-packing plant in 1904 heralded the demise of the salted beef industry and the onset of modern operations processing frozen, chilled and tinned meats for the external market.

Uruguayan democracy

Uruguay's transition in the early twentieth century from a strife-ridden society to a stable, prosperous nation owed much to a far-sighted Colorado politician, José Batlle y Ordóñez. His influence as president (1903–7 and 1911–15), as well as the force of his ideas on his contemporaries, laid the foundations for a modern, democratic society and for Latin America's first welfare state. Batlle's reforms extended across a wide range of political, social and economic matters. Impressed with the Swiss form of government, he persuaded the Colorado and Blanco parties in 1919 to modify the constitution and to create a plural executive system whereby the president shared his power with a National Council of Administration composed of nine councillors, six from the majority party and three from the opposition party. Extensive social and labour legislation was put on the statute books, including better and shorter work conditions as well as generous medical and pension benefits. State intervention in the economy grew, often at the expense of foreign capital, and public monopolies were authorized to run the electric power network, the telephone system, domestic insurance opera-

José Batlle y
Ordóñez

tions, mortgage banking, the port administration and other diverse activities. The ideas and reforms of Batlle transformed most aspects of national life. Furthermore, Uruguay now enjoyed a good standard of living, with much of the country's prosperity deriving from an export-oriented economy devoted principally to the production of meat and wool products.

The nation faced considerable economic hardship in the Great Depression of the 1930s. In addition, President Gabriel Terra in 1933 circumvented the constitution by taking on special executive powers and ruled as a virtual dictator until he was succeeded by his brother-in-law, General Alfredo Baldomir, the winner of the presidential elections of 1938. Baldomir showed contradictory constitutional tendencies by first postponing the national elections scheduled for February 1942, but then allowing the elections of November 1942 which restored the country to a democratic footing. Later on, in 1951, the electorate voted to abolish the presidency altogether and create a plural executive office known as the National Council of Government, which was composed of nine members, six belonging to the party receiving the most votes and three to the party polling the second largest number of votes. This, for Latin America, was a unique experiment.

The eclipse of democracy

In the 1950s the nation's revamped system of government faced formidable economic challenges. High rates of inflation, poor economic growth, stagnant exports of meat and wool products, a less than dynamic manufacturing industry and the problems of funding public expenditures all put great strains upon the operation of Uruguay's welfare state. General dissatisfaction among the electorate culminated in 1958 with the victory of the Blancos, now known as the National Party, who ended ninety-three years of rule by the Colorado Party. Nevertheless, the Blancos, with their conservative and rural bias, were themselves defeated in the 1966 elections when the Colorados staged a comeback. In that election, also, the voters sanctioned a return to the presidential system and put into office General Oscar Gestido, who became president in 1967, but he died in the same year and was succeeded by Jorge Pacheco Areco.

Progressively in the 1960s, the attention of the country was directed to the emergence of what was to become Latin America's best-known urban guerrilla organization, the Movement of National Liberation, more popularly known as the Tupamaros. This movement, which attracted students, professional people, bureaucrats and others, taunted the government and the police with a series of bank robberies, bombings, temporary seizures of business properties and kidnappings of influential citizens and foreigners, including the British ambassador, Mr (later Sir) Geoffrey Jackson (1971).

With civil authorities making little headway in the fight against the Tupamaros, President Pacheco turned to the military in 1971 in a desperate attempt to smash the guerrilla organization. His presidential successor, Juan M. Bordaberry, who won office as the leading Colorado candidate in the 1971 elections, declared a state of 'internal war' in April 1972. During 1972, the armed forces in a relentless counter-insurgency campaign broke the back of the guerrilla movement, with members or sympathizers imprisoned or forced to flee the country. Many innocent citizens also fell foul of one of Latin America's most brutally repressive security operations.

Although decisively crippling the Tupamaros, the armed forces showed no disposition to recede into the background. On the contrary, they exerted pressure on President Bordaberry in February 1973 to create a National Council of Security composed of both civilian and military members to deal with matters of security and economic development. In particular, the military wanted the executive branch to embark upon a programme of economic reforms, to root out corruption in government and to monitor the operations of the public administration. With a confrontation looming with the national legislature, President Bordaberry dissolved Congress in June 1973 in a move that soon led to restrictions on political, student and trade union activities. Over a period of time members of different left-wing organizations were arrested. Furthermore, a Council of State was created to assume the legislative function and to rule the country by decree.

While the head of state remained a civilian, a junta of generals and admirals became the real wielders of power. The security forces continued to have free rein for their arbitrary and unchecked repressive activities. In 1976, the military obliged Bordaberry to resign; Alberto Demichelli was appointed as interim president, but he was replaced in the same year by Aparicio Méndez who was to serve as president until 1981. In December 1980, Uruguay held a plebiscite to decide upon a constitutional reform guaranteeing the armed forces a role in national decision making; however, the electorate defiantly rejected the proposal. In August 1981, the Council of State appointed General Gregorio Alvarez president for a three-and-a-half-year term beginning in September 1981.

General Alvarez's government had to grapple with a deteriorating economy in 1981 and 1982 caused to a large extent by the world recession and also the economic downturn in neighbouring Argentina. It was also confronted with the question of charting a return to constitutional rule, an issue which the new president acknowledged in his first speech on taking office.

On 3 June 1982 the Council of State approved a law providing for internal party elections for the following November designed, among other things, to select party officials who would then be in a position to choose presidential and congressional candidates in national elections scheduled for November 1984.

These internal elections furnished once more a rebuff to the government's political aims as candidates critical of military rule gained more votes than the pro-administration politicians. Undeterred by the result, in May 1983, the nation's military rulers began a dialogue with the two main political parties in an effort to work out the details of the elections to be held in the following year.

The negotiations between military authorities and politicians reached an impasse and, when the government began to initiate a wave of arrests of different political leaders and student activists, the political parties broke off their discussions in July 1983. Relations between the government and the politicians worsened the following month when the military banned all political activity and clamped tighter censorship controls over the press. The military crackdown only intensified political tensions and, for the first time in ten years of armed forces rule, the nation's main political parties and the trade unions organized co-ordinated protest actions in August and September 1983. These continued, growing in intensity in 1984, and the military finally made a number of important concessions, such as releasing some political prisoners – though not all – in preparation for the elections of November that year. At the moment of writing, the restoration of democratic government in Uruguay in 1985 seems much more than a pious hope, how certainly remains to be seen.

EFE

Further reading

Argentina
N. Fraser and M. Navarro, *Eva Perón* (London, 1980)
J. Lynch, *Argentine Dictator: Juan Manuel de Rosas 1829–1852* (Oxford, 1981)
J. A. Page, *Perón: a Biography* (New York, 1983)
Y. F. Rennie, *The Argentine Republic* (New York, 1945)
D. Rock, *Politics in Argentina 1890–1930: the Rise and Fall of Radicalism* (Cambridge, 1975)
J. R. Scobie, *Argentina: a City and a Nation*, 2nd edition (New York and London, 1971)

Paraguay
P. H. Lewis, *Paraguay under Stroessner* (Chapel Hill, 1980)
H. G. Warren, *Paraguay: an Informal History* (Norman, Okla., 1949)
J. H. Williams, *The Rise and Fall of the Paraguayan Republic, 1800–1870* (Austin, Texas, 1979)

Uruguay
S. G. Hanson, *Utopia in Uruguay: Chapters in the Economic History of Uruguay* (Westport, Conn., 1981; reprint of 1938 edition)
E. Kaufman, *Uruguay in Transition: From Civilian to Military Rule* (New Brunswick, NJ, 1979)
M. I. Vanger, *José Batlle y Ordóñez of Uruguay, the Creator of His Times, 1902–1907* (Cambridge, Mass., 1963)
M. I. Vanger, *The Model Country: José Batlle y Ordóñez of Uruguay 1907–1915* (Hanover, NH, 1980)

The Falkland Islands/Islas Malvinas

Lying some 640 km east of southern Argentina, and on that country's continental shelf, the Falklands consist of about 200 bleak and treeless islands, which have been governed by Great Britain since 1833. The vast majority of their tiny population of some 1800 lives on the two largest, East and West Falkland. The islands suddenly gained international prominence in 1982, when the Argentine military government of General Leopoldo Galtieri sought through armed invasion to realize Argentina's long-standing national claim to them. The ensuing war with Great Britain resulted in a complete military victory for the latter but left a difficult legacy of territorial, diplomatic and international controversy.

The complex history of the dispute between Argentina and Great Britain is critical for understanding the current situation. Mariners from many nations have been credited with the discovery of the archipelago. The British name derives from the designation given to the strait between the two main islands by Captain Strong of HMS *Welfare* in 1690 to honour Viscount Falkland, a high official of the Admiralty. The Argentine name, Las Malvinas, derives from the customary French designation, Les Malouines, after sailors from St Malo, seal-hunters in the South Atlantic in colonial times. But nomenclature and discovery are less relevant to the islands' history than effective possession and asserted rights of sovereignty.

The first real settlement was Port Louis, on East Falkland, established by the French explorer, Antoine Louis de Bougainville,

West Falkland

in 1764. Spain, which claimed a historic right to the area, soon protested and the French withdrew in return for compensation in cash. Spain then appointed a governor, and Port Louis became Puerto de la Soledad.

During this protracted process, Commodore John Byron – grandfather of the poet – on HMS *Wager* landed on the uninhabited West Falkland, claiming it and adjacent islands for Britain. He established a settlement called Port Egmont. Byron's successor discovered Port Louis, and in total ignorance of the Franco-Spanish accord, ordered its residents to leave.

The critical years were 1770 and 1771. In June 1770, a heavily-manned Spanish frigate entered Port Egmont and expelled the British, bringing Britain and Spain to the brink of war. Spain agreed to negotiate and, in January 1771, agreed to return Port Egmont; however, according to the Spanish ambassador in London, Prince Masserano, this was only after British ministers had made a 'secret promise' to withdraw completely from the islands once the issue had died down in Parliament and public opinion. No positive written evidence of any such promise has ever come to light. In 1774, Britain abandoned Egmont for reasons of economy: a plaque and a flag were left at the site, asserting sovereignty. Yet, whatever the truth of the obscure diplomacy of 1770–1, Puerto de la Soledad remained in Spanish hands, administered from 1776 by Buenos Aires, seat of the new viceroyalty of the River Plate. Only in 1806 was the site abandoned, its inhabitants returning to Buenos Aires on news of the British invasion of that year. Argentine independence from Spain – effectively achieved in 1810 but not proclaimed until 1816 – resulted in the assertion by the successor-state of sovereignty over the islands, whose complex history now took an even more

THE FALKLAND ISLANDS/ISLAS MALVINAS

WEST FALKLAND

EAST FALKLAND

Port Stanley (Puerto Argentino)

complicated turn.

In 1820, the independent government at Buenos Aires sent Captain Daniel Jewitt, a North American in its service, to raise the national flag at Puerto de la Soledad: this he did, but nothing else. Then, in 1824, a Frenchman, Louis Vernet, long resident in Hamburg and regarded by Argentines as a German, secured from the Argentine government permission to establish a colony on East Falkland, obtaining additionally, in 1828, the title of governor and, in 1829, usufruct of all the islands. Britain protested, but events there moved faster than its government seemed disposed to do. In July 1831, Vernet, annoyed by the actions of North American seamen in waters he thought were his alone, seized three ships flying the US flag, and proceeded in one of them to Buenos Aires to prosecute charges of illegal fishing. Unfortunately for him, the US consul at Buenos Aires, George W. Slocum, was not only an ardent patriot; he also had at hand the USS *Lexington*, whose captain, Silas Duncan, was immediately despatched to the islands to throw off the Argentines, destroy military batteries and declare the territory *res nullius* (free of government), all this with the backing of the US government. Argentina responded in September 1832 with the appointment of Juan Estivier as governor, to which Britain protested; and Estivier's establishment of a penal colony at San Carlos proved abortive when its inhabitants mutinied and murdered him. Argentine attempts to restore order were interrupted by the arrival of HMS *Clio* under Captain Onslow in January 1833. He reasserted British control; in 1834 a British governor was appointed: and the process of British settlement proceeded. The Argentine government protested vigorously at the time, though maintaining relations, and successive Argentine administrations since have persistently regarded the British action of 1833 as illegal, arbitrary, and imperialist.

The British claim to the islands is based on uninterrupted possession for over 150 years and on the avowed intention of the present-day islanders to remain British. That desire, based on principles of self-determination enshrined in the UN Charter, is difficult to refute; on the other hand, the islands' geographical remoteness from Britain and their proximity to Argentina, their sparse population, and neglect by Britain seem to many as powerful arguments for a transfer of sovereignty. Argentine irritation, at what its government and people see as a colonial anachronism, has surfaced from time to time; it was particularly strong during the period of Juan Domingo Perón's first presidency (1946–55) and in the 1960s, and it has always been present in Anglo-Argentine relations. The United Nations after 1960 sought to reach accommodation between the parties, which, for their part, agreed on specific measures of economic co-operation. Thus, a runway at Port Stanley was built by Argentines; postal, medical and oil facilities were extended to the inhabitants in the early 1970s by the Argentine

Goose Green settlement

authorities. In the latter part of the decade, both Labour and Conservative governments in Britain looked to resolve the dispute through dialogue with the islanders and Argentina. They failed; the total incompatibility of British insistence on self-determination and Argentine stress on their sovereign rights was finally exposed by the Argentine invasion of April 1982. The war which followed, costing more than 1000 lives, entrenched each country's historic position. What had been a peripheral issue for British foreign policy throughout that period became a central concern and a major event in domestic affairs; the 'Falklands factor' undoubtedly helped the previously unpopular Thatcher government to win re-election in June 1983. For Argentina, the war hastened the demoralization and subsequent demise of an already unpopular military government, but did not affect in any way the national aspiration to recover the islands. A solution of the conflict is more elusive in the mid-1980s than in 1771 or in 1833, since the South Atlantic as a whole – including numerous national claims to parts of Antarctica – has now been thrust to the forefront of international attention.

HB

Further reading

P. Beck, 'Co-operative Confrontation in the Falklands Islands Dispute: the Anglo-Argentine Search for a Way Forward, 1968–1981', *Journal of Inter-American Studies & World Affairs*, vol. 24, no. 1 (Feb., 1982) pp. 37–58

J. Goebel, *The Struggle for the Falkland Islands*, with a preface and an introduction by J. C. J. Metford (New Haven, 1982)

M. Hastings and S. Jenkins, *The Battle for the Falklands* (London, 1982)

Latin America Bureau, *Falklands. Whose Crisis?* (London, 1982)

Brazil

The empire, 1822–89

Nineteenth-century Brazil was unlike other Latin American countries. It broke its connections with the mother country, Portugal, by a simple declaration of independence, which preserved the monarchy and the existing social structure and left the economy untouched by the kind of war that occurred in many parts of Spanish America. Prince Pedro, heir to the Portuguese throne, placed himself at the head of the Brazilian independence movement, such as it was, and was immediately acclaimed as emperor of the new state (1822). Thus independence was attained with very little fighting, with the social structure intact, and under an already existing monarchy and centralized government – all factors which gave Brazil a tendency to order and compromise lacking almost everywhere else in Latin America.

Prince Pedro (emperor 1822–31) was intelligent enough to realize that the monarchy would be strengthened by the grant of a constitution, but he was too autocratic to accept any restraints on his power. As he was faced by politicians who were determined to rule by themselves his reign was stormy. He dissolved the first constituent assembly and himself drew up the 1824 Constitution which gave the emperor preponderant influence; he appointed ministers and prov-incial officials and was given the 'moderating power' to arbitrate disputes between the other branches of government. Parliament's refusal to accept Pedro's choice of ministers led to a deadlock in government, and the emperor's position was weakened by the loss of a short war against Argentina and his insistence on retaining Portuguese advisers. In 1831 he took the pretext of an army mutiny to return to Portugal, leaving his six-year-old son as emperor.

The abdication was followed by an extremely unstable period – four regencies in nine years. Brazil was saved from breaking up by the Additional Act of 1834, which gave power at municipal level to the local political bosses (coroneis), but there was a series of provincial revolts against the central government. Two political parties appeared, the Conservatives, who supported the central government and the rule of the bureaucracy, and the Liberals, who stood for devolving power to the provinces and the extension of civic rights; they then alternated in power amidst armed risings and threats of force. Padre Feijó (1835–7) attempted to enforce firm government but was overthrown by the Conservatives; in revenge the Liberals ousted the Conservative regent and proclaimed the fourteen-year-old emperor to be of age in 1840.

Under Pedro II a constitutional monarchy evolved, combining order, progress, and freedom. This came about slowly as the landowners, the main political class, realized that political disorder might lead to social revolution. At first the Conservative and Liberal

BRAZIL

KEY	
Completed roads	
Projected roads	
International boundaries	

0	1600 km
0	1000 miles

Brazil: population	
1810	3 000 000
1850	7 200 000
1900	17 300 000
1930	33 600 000
1960	70 000 000
1970	93 200 000
1980	121 500 000

BRAZIL	
Area	8,511,965 sq km
Population	120 million
GDP per capita (1980)	$1664
Capital	Brasília
Currency	Cruzeiro

parties were manipulated by Aureliano Coutinho, the young emperor's mentor, and the Liberals rose in revolt when turned out of office in 1842 and 1848. But gradually the system began to evolve peacefully; the creation of the post of prime minister in 1847 ended Aureliano's influence, and the rigid division between Liberals and Conservatives ended with a coalition government in 1853. After that the emperor used his 'moderating power' to appoint prime ministers and remove them; this was obviously undemocratic but provided for peaceful changes of government, and Pedro II also insisted on freedom of the press and of debates.

1850 also marked the beginning of Brazil's development. Britain forced Brazil to abolish the slave trade in 1850, and thus released capital which went into economic development. Coffee overtook sugar and tobacco as the main export crop; steamers began to improve communications; the formation of limited liability companies made it possible for Brazilians to make other investments than in land. In the 1850s the first railways appeared; the telegraph began to bind the country together, and linked Brazil directly to Europe in 1874. As a result several native entrepreneurs began to develop the country, notably the Visconde de Mauá, who built up a business network extending to Buenos Aires and Paris. Immigration also began to grow, although this was hampered by the continued dependence of the big estates on slave labour. The 'frontier' also moved inland, particularly in São Paulo.

Brazil's position as a stable monarchy made it a major power in Latin America. Its alliance with Britain was severely strained by the persistence of the clandestine slave trade, and the nation moved into an alliance with the United States which has lasted ever since. Brazil's influence was felt particularly in the River Plate, where its interventions on behalf of the Argentine Liberals led to the defeat of the Argentine dictator Rosas and a similar attempt to isolate the Paraguayan dictator López led to the War of the Triple Alliance (1864–70). The emperor obstinately prolonged the war until Paraguay was completely destroyed, and his management of the struggle began the disillusionment with the monarchy among the officer corps which was to be one of the reasons for the fall of the empire.

In the end, the monarchy collapsed because it could not adapt itself in time to new social and political forces, although its actual fall was largely accidental. In politics the emperor's use of the 'moderating power' was called into question after 1868, when Pedro II broke the tradition of bi-partisan governments and appointed a Conservative prime minister. The Liberal Party reacted by attacking the emperor's position and demanding the abolition of the 'moderating power'; some of its extremists formed a Republican Party in 1870. Although this crisis can be exaggerated (the Liberals returned to power in 1878 and the emperor continued to choose prime ministers) it did bring the monarchy into political controversy. The situation was worsened by the unpopularity of the Emperor's only

daughter, Princess Isabel, and her French husband, the Comte d'Eu.

Other factors weakened the monarchy. In the early 1870s the crown clashed with the Church; young bishops brought up in the spirit of the first Vatican Council opposed the emperor's eighteenth-century latitudinarianism. The army became increasingly opposed to the government, as the emperor refused to increase military expenditure and his son-in-law, the Comte d'Eu, had made himself unpopular in Paraguay. The abolition of slavery also weakened the traditional landed classes, although the old theory that the empire collapsed when the former slaveowners withdrew their support is too simplistic. Brazilian slavery ended in stages; it began to decline after the abolition of the slave trade in 1850, and became obsolete in the north-east and the south. By the 1870s the remaining slaves were concentrated in Rio de Janeiro State and the east of São Paulo. Slavery was, therefore, associated with declining parts of the country, while in the United States it flourished until the outbreak of the Civil War; this is why Brazil abolished slavery peacefully in 1888.

By the 1880s it had become apparent that changes were on the way. The emperor was dying of diabetes, and his daughter Isabel was unpopular (rather unfairly; she had already acted very capably as regent in her father's absence). In June 1889 the last prime minister of the empire proposed the creation of a federal system 'which would make the republic unnecessary'. It was never introduced. On 15 November 1889 the commanders of the army demanded the dismissal of the prime minister. This was agreed, but the civilian Republicans went on to proclaim the fall of the monarchy. The emperor had come into Rio de Janeiro to deal with the situation; he was easily captured, forced to abdicate, and sent into exile. Thus the empire fell owing to a series of coincidences, but only because its main sources of support had withered away.

The first republic, 1889–1930

The Republicans came to power by accident and were divided amongst themselves. Some were army officers who wanted to introduce a 'Republican dictatorship', under which technocrats would develop Brazil in accordance with the ideas of the positivist Auguste Comte, which were influential in late-nineteenth-century Latin America. Other Republicans were Liberals, notably Ruy Barbosa; they wanted to federalize Brazil and encourage free elections. Many became Republicans out of opportunism after the fall of the monarchy. As a result the new government was an uneasy coalition presided over by Marshal Deodoro da Fonseca, who had joined the revolution at the last moment for personal reasons. It is not surprising that the new republic was unstable.

For the first two years Ruy Barbosa was the main figure in the government. He drew up the Constitution of 1891, which gave

Ruy Barbosa

Brazil a government similar to that of the United States; the states were allowed very wide powers, including permission to form private armies, raise foreign loans, and collect their own customs. He also attempted to develop Brazil (and pay government debts) by printing money, which led to serious inflation. Meanwhile, the removal of strong central government led to a return to the chaos of the 1830s in the different states. There were three main groups involved – the supporters of a radical military dictatorship (Jacobins); the civilian Republicans like Barbosa (Historicals); and the mass of ex-monarchist politicians (Adesistas). In 1891 Deodoro was overthrown by a coalition of Historicals and Jacobins, alienated by his autocratic manner and preference for ex-monarchist ministers. He was succeeded by Floriano Peixoto, 'the Iron Marshal', who tried to impose a Jacobin dictatorship, overthrowing state governments and jailing his opponents. The Jacobins combined anti-monarchism and xenophobia with a confused desire to develop the country under an elite of reforming army officers; but they had too little support to do anything, and their harsh methods united both Historicals and Adesistas against them. In 1893 a series of risings, notably in the navy and the southern state of Rio Grande do Sul, put Floriano under pressure. His successor was an elected civilian president representing São Paulo, the most important state

in the federation, and by now the main focus of Brazil's increasingly huge export of coffee.

After 1894 the early political parties disappeared, and the struggle for control of the national government was fought out between the oligarchies controlling the different states. These oligarchies varied widely; São Paulo was developed enough to have an opposition party, and Minas Gerais tried to bring in all groups, while Rio Grande do Sul was in the grip of two Jacobin strong men. But they had two features in common; the local bosses (*coroneis*) used the powers of government to keep themselves in power, and they could only be removed by an internal civil war or by the intervention of the central government. As a result there were frequent bloody struggles between local clans for control of the state governments and their resources.

At national level peace was precariously maintained; a candidate for president was selected by a meeting of the state governments, who then used their control of the electoral machinery to elect him by 80–90 per cent of the vote. Obviously the states were not equally important; many, especially in the north-east and the interior, were too weak to defy the central government. São Paulo was the wealthiest state; its coffee revenue allowed it to raise larger loans and maintain an effective army; Minas Gerais had the largest population, but was less economically developed; and these two could control the federation if they acted together. Bahia was their most consistent opponent; it had been important under the empire, but had shared in the decay of the north-east. Of the other states only Rio Grande do Sul could play an independent role, but it remained isolated under two dictatorial governors, the last important Jacobins.

After the fall of the military government in 1894 São Paulo provided three civilian presidents. This was the most successful period of the first republic. Prudente de Morais (1894–8) restored order and broke the power of the remaining Jacobins; Manoel Campos Salles (1898–1902) restored business confidence by stabilizing the currency; and Francisco de Paula Rodrigues Alves (1902–6) carried out a building programme in Rio de Janeiro and eliminated yellow fever. But this stability was always precarious. The collapse of coffee prices weakened São Paulo's economic supremacy, and in 1906 the state oligarchy had to agree to alternate the presidency with Minas Gerais in return for state subsidies to keep up the price of coffee. In 1910 the states quarrelled over the presidency for the first time; the convention chose a military candidate, Hermes da Fonseca (nephew of Deodoro), and Ruy Barbosa stood against him with the support of São Paulo and Bahia. Hermes won, but Ruy got 40 per cent of the vote – a sign that the state political machines were divided.

The alliance after 1906 between Minas Gerais and São Paulo (irreverently known as 'coffee with cream', after their main products) was always uneasy, though it lasted to 1930. There was a series of risings in the north-east in 1911, in which several state oligarchies were overthrown, and the rotation between the two states never worked smoothly. New groups began to enter politics; the working class began to agitate, although unions were very small and handicapped by the foreign origin of their leaders, and general strikes failed. Intellectuals also protested; the Modern Art week in São Paulo in 1922 introduced Brazilians to post-Impressionist work and stimulated a new interest in national music and folklore. Even the oligarchs realized the need for change; the presidency increased its power and began to provide social aid by undertaking drought relief in the north-east.

In the 1920s the regime was again under attack from radical army officers. In 1922 young *tenentes* (lieutenants) seized a fort at Copacabana; in 1924 another group seized São Paulo for a month and then went on a 'Long March' through the interior of Brazil in an attempt to rouse the masses. (Their chief, Luis Carlos Prestes, later led the Brazilian Communist Party.) But the first republic did not collapse under attack from revolutionary groups; the struggle among the state oligarchies for the presidency got out of control. The Great Depression hit Brazil extremely hard, and in 1930 the São Paulo elite was divided over the proper policy towards coffee export prices and the exchange rate. The official presidential nominee, from São Paulo, was opposed in the presidential election by an alliance of Minas Gerais, Rio Grande do Sul, and Paraiba, who put up Getúlio Vargas, the governor of Rio Grande do Sul, for President. Vargas lost, but gained 800,000 votes against the official candidate's 1 million, a sign of the degree of polarization. When São Paulo tried to take reprisals against the opposition states a revolutionary plot was formed; it was put into effect when the opposition vice-presidential candidate, the governor of Paraiba, was assassinated (though this was the result of an internal state feud). The central government collapsed and Vargas became provisional president. Thus the 1930 revolution came about as the result of a quarrel within the elite, though tensions were building up within society. As the governor of Minas Gerais said, 'We must make a revolution before the people make it for us.'

Getúlio Vargas, 1930–45

1930 resembled 1889; the revolutionaries came to power unexpectedly and without a common programme. Most of them were old-guard politicians, whose main aim was to end São Paulo's domination, but there were two more extreme groups. The 'democrats', who were concentrated in São Paulo, wanted free elections and an end to the power of the political bosses; the *tenentes*, the radical army officers, wanted to regenerate Brazil under the leadership of the army. Vargas as president played the various groups off against each other, using his gift of pragmatism to climb gradually to supreme power. At first he handed power over to the *tenentes*, and abolished the state governments. They introduced a mass of social reforms such as compulsory education, labour laws, and attempts at moral improvement, but failed for the same reasons as the Jacobins; they were too few, they were divided, and they had no organized popular support. In the end they became members of the political elite or returned to the army.

But the *tenentes* achieved one negative result; they provoked and angered the older politicians. This was especially true in São Paulo, which lost in 1930 and where Vargas had placed an outsider in temporary power. In 1932 the state seceded from the federation; this caused a serious crisis for Vargas, who was forced to promise a return to constitutional government in order to prevent other states joining in. The bargain worked, the rising was suppressed, Vargas treated São Paulo with great leniency, and a constituent assembly was duly elected in 1933. Most of its members were traditional oligarchs, but it carried out several reforms to satisfy the democrats, such as votes for women and proportional representation. Vargas was elected president for four years; the whole episode was a good example of his ability to be all things to all men.

Getúlio Vargas

270

The return to constitutional government satisfied the oligarchs and the democrats, while the *tenentes* had shot their bolt. But this did not bring peace to Brazil. The revolution and the world depression had shaken the power of the landowners; the mass of the people were still largely outside politics, but the middle and lower middle classes, previously employed in professional occupations, were seriously affected. As a result they joined mass political movements, the first to appear in Brazil. The National Liberation Alliance (ANL) was a 'popular front' controlled by the Brazilian Communist Party, but appealing to many progressives and lower-middle-class people; Brazilian Integralist Action (AIB) was a radical nationalist movement which borrowed many trappings from European fascism and was strongly backed by the German minority, but which appealed to middle-class people who wanted to regenerate Brazil. By 1935 these movements had about half a million members (out of an electorate of 2 million), and their demonstrations and street fighting frightened the elite, who were not used to mass political mobilization.

Vargas, as usual, exploited the situation for his own ends; he frightened the old politicians into giving him more and more power. The ANL was first to fall into his trap; it attempted an unsuccessful coup in November 1935, spearheaded by non-commissioned officers in the army. Many officers were killed and the rebels were very harshly treated; this illustrates the elite's shock at radical mass movements and also Vargas's determination to prevent anyone but himself from organizing mass support. In 1937-8 it was the Integralistas' turn to be crushed by Vargas's political cunning; first he forestalled an Integralista victory in the presidential elections by abolishing the constitution, then he dissolved the movement when it staged an unsuccessful coup (May 1938). After eight years of dividing in order to rule, Vargas was supreme.

From 1937 to 1945 Vargas ran a mild dictatorship, called the New State (*Estado Nôvo*) after Salazar's regime in Portugal. It was not fascist, although several fascists (or at least fascist-leaning men) sat in Vargas's cabinet and a corporatist constitution was drawn up and partially implemented. Vargas never formed a totalitarian political movement and never seriously attempted to be a charismatic dictator; his regime was more like that of an eighteenth-century despot – personal government through an administrative regime of hand-picked experts. He successfully created the image of a paternal estate owner, 'O Paizinho do Povo' ('the daddy of the people'), while quietly transforming Brazil.

Vargas's chief problems were centralization, industrialization and nationalism. Centralization came first; the president now controlled the whole of Brazil to a degree unequalled since 1889. The states' powers were greatly reduced, an event symbolized by the burning of their flags – from now on Brazil was to have only one flag. The machine of government had been greatly expanded since 1930

with the creation of labour and industry ministries; now it was brought under the control of the Public Service Administrative Department (DASP), a body of specially chosen advisers to ministers intended to be the equivalent of the British administrative class. As with much of Vargas's work, the experiment was not entirely successful, but it did unite Brazil more than ever before.

Another major feature of the *Estado Nôvo* was the state's role in laying the foundations for industrial growth. The government attempted to improve the railways and began the creation of a road network, while the coming of the aeroplane made it possible to link Brazil up effectively for the first time. The regime's great showplace was the Volta Redonda steel mill, which opened in 1941 and was intended to mark Brazil's coming of age in manufacturing. Again, these efforts were partially successful; industry did begin to develop, but the country remained dependent on agriculture for its major exports. The government tried to rescue staples like coffee and sugar by organizing state marketing systems, but they remained largely at the mercy of the international market.

The *Estado Nôvo* also tried to create an atmosphere of popular mobilization and national pride by propaganda and encouragement of sport and folklore. Every radio station spread government information by means of a compulsory 'Brazilian hour', although this inevitably aroused counter-productive ribaldry. The government was more successful in its search for prestige through football, which was rapidly becoming the national obsession, and attempts were made to organize Carnival and to use popular music and art to create a favourable image. Again this effort was largely nullified by the Brazilian talent for ridicule, but Brazilians did take more pride in themselves as a result.

The end of the *Estado Nôvo* was brought about by external events – notably the entry of the United States into the Second World War. Brazil, as usual, followed the North American lead, and benefited from large amounts of aid; in return Brazil patrolled the South Atlantic and sent an expeditionary force to Italy. But it was obviously incongruous for an authoritarian regime to be fighting for democracy, and Vargas began (with his usual pragmatism) to propose a return to constitutional government. From 1942 he began to encourage the organization of the new skilled working class into government-run trade unions, which provided benefits for their members and some degree of protection (although independent workers' action was deterred). This was supplemented by more traditional patronage in the form of gifts to the unorganized poor and the promotion of a cult of Vargas among the unsophisticated. In 1945 the president announced elections for a constituent assembly, and began to build a new political machine. This consisted of two political parties appealing to different bases of support. The Social Democrat Party (PSD) belied its name; it was a conservative coalition of pro-Vargas landowners, who still controlled the rural vote, and businessmen who had benefited from the expansion of the *Estado Nôvo*. The electorate now included a large block of skilled urban workers; Vargas appealed to them through the Brazilian Labour Party (PTB), based on his trade unions. There were also opposition parties, the most important being the National Democratic Union (UDN), a 'liberal' coalition of anti-Vargas landowners and middle-class people who believed in human rights and honest government and saw Vargas as a dictatorial demagogue.

The PSD/PTB coalition won the 1945 elections but, ironically, it did not help Vargas; he was at this point overthrown by the army, whose commanders suspected that he intended to keep himself in power yet again; they also feared his appeal to the masses. Nonetheless the election showed the huge changes which had occurred in Brazil since 1930. Then the electorate had been 2 million; now it was 7.5 million. Then most of the electors had voted at the command of the landowners; now there were national political parties (at least in name), and the opposition got 40 per cent of the vote. Large areas of the interior remained politically and economically backward, but leadership had passed to the cities, with their European-style middle and working classes. Like Peter the Great of Russia, Vargas had not totally modernized his country, but he had given it a decisive push forward.

The democratic republic, 1946–64

Brazil's experiment with modern democracy lasted eighteen years, and was stormy as well as short. Only two presidents, Dutra (1946–51) and Kubitschek (1956–61) completed their terms at the appointed time: Vargas (1951–4) ended his second term by committing suicide, Café Filho (1954–5) and Quadros (1961) resigned, and Goulart (1961–4) was deposed. The reason for this, apart from the incompetence of the incumbents, was that the Brazilian political system had become less controllable. In the first republic the quarrels of the state elites had brought about the revolution of 1930; the landowners were still a powerful force, and they had been joined by the middle classes and the skilled urban working classes. By the 1960s the unskilled urban workers and the peasants, hitherto voiceless, were also making demands on the system. In a society that ran on patronage the presidency could only hope to satisfy so many demands when the economy was booming; when resources were scarce the flimsy façade of constitutional government was torn to pieces by the conflicting demands of the different interest groups.

The presidency of Eurico Gaspar Dutra, a conservative general (1946–51), was relatively quiet; the political system had not fully developed and Brazil was prosperous as the result of the Second World War. The two main developments were the banning of the Communist Party, which had shown surprising strength by gaining 9 per cent of the votes in 1946, and the consequent growth of the PTB under Vargas, who began to campaign for a second term in office in 1948. Vargas appealed to the electorate on the social achievements of his last years in office, and won the 1950 presidential elections by effective use of public relations for the first time in Brazil. He got over 5 million votes, a record in presidential elections, but under half the total vote – another sign that the electorate were voting freely and that the oligarchs no longer controlled the system.

Vargas's second presidency was a failure. The complexity of political life had vastly increased since 1945; the post-war boom was over; the president himself was nearly seventy and his political grip was weakening. Vargas made two major mistakes; he alienated everyone by his mismanagement of the economy (inflationary wage increases followed by a stabilization plan), and he angered his political supporters by his promotion of his *protégé* João Goulart, who he made Labour Minister and put in charge of the trade unions with all their opportunities for patronage. But Vargas's final downfall was due to his resentment of opposition. In August 1954 an assassination attempt was made on a muckraking journalist, Carlos Lacerda; violence at national level broke the unwritten rules of Brazilian politics, and the armed forces were also angered, since an Air Force major had been killed trying to protect Lacerda. Investigations showed that the killing had been ordered by the president's chief bodyguard; senior officers demanded the president's resignation, and Vargas responded by committing suicide. His death, and the wills issued in his name, created a 'Vargas legend'; he was supposed to have died as a 'sacrifice' protecting the 'poor and humble'. At any rate he had taken vital steps towards modernization and created both a middle class and a skilled proletariat.

But Vargas's suicide had shown up the strains within the political system, and these got worse after his death. The president was elected separately from the vice-president, with the result that Vice-President João Café Filho, who succeeded Vargas, belonged to the opposition UDN, and throughout his term there was trouble with Congress. Vargas's political machine showed its durability by winning the 1955 elections, with Juscelino Kubitschek of the PSD gaining the presidency and Goulart of the PTB the vicepresidency, but the armed forces had to intervene again to prevent anti-Vargas factions from staging a coup. The running of Brazil was becoming increasingly dependent on the military.

Kubitschek represented two new forces in Brazilian life; he was the first president of immigrant stock and the first to represent the business community. He had the dynamism and charisma of a super-salesman determined to give Brazil 'Fifty years' progress in five'; and he largely succeeded. Industrial production rose by 80 per cent, the growth rate by 7 per cent a year. Brazil developed a self-sufficient motor industry; structural bottlenecks were ironed out; the nation acquired an international airline and an expanded merchant navy. All this was accomplished with an infectious drive and

Juscelino Kubitschek

enthusiasm, aided by the achievements of the national soccer side and the popularity of Brazilian music, dancing, and folk culture. The symbol of the Kubitschek era was the new capital, Brasília, empty scrubland in 1956 and already a masterpiece of modern architecture by 1961. Brazil had finally come of age; it was no longer a string of trading posts along the sea, but a potential world power developing its interior from its own resources.

There was a price, however, to be paid for all this. Kubitschek's boom was built on massive foreign investment and short-term loans, and his waste and prodigality horrified conservative international financiers. Brazil rapidly got into arrears over repayments, and the government worsened the position by inflationary policies. As a result Brazil began to achieve 'Fifty years' inflation in five', with a great increase in corruption and mismanagement. Revulsion at this, combined with the influence of ideas about development planned by the state, led to a surprise in the 1960 elections. The PSD/PTB coalition still controlled Congress and Goulart was again elected vice-president, but the presidency was won by Jânio Quadros, an independent candidate backed by the UDN.

Quadros was a new phenomenon in Brazilian politics; he owed his election to public opinion without the backing of a landowner or a political machine. He came to power by championing the ordinary person against the 'establishment' and as councillor, deputy, and governor for São Paulo he had established a reputation for honesty and efficiency. As presidential candidate he offered an end to corruption and politicking, economical and effective government and properly planned development; many middle-class people, particularly intellectuals and civil servants, believed in him and worked hard for his election. His failure dealt Brazilian democracy a disastrous blow.

Quadros's presidency began well, with stabilization of the economy, cuts in expenditure and negotiations with foreign creditors; the only mildly controversial policy was a tendency to friendship with newly independent Third World nations. His award of an honour to Che Guevara was questioned. After eight months in office he suddenly resigned (August 1961), alleging that 'terrible forces' were hindering him from governing. The reasons for this have never adequately been explained; was Quadros under attack from the United States, was he suffering a breakdown, or was he trying to shock Congress into giving him more power? In any case his departure caused a further crisis. The next president was João Goulart; but Goulart was unpopular with the military. A civil war was averted; Goulart became president, but most of his executive powers were given to a prime minister responsible to Congress.

Goulart's coming to power showed the increasing strain being suffered by constitutional government in Brazil. His presidency destroyed it. Goulart was a totally incompetent politician who could not control the nation or even his own supporters; his only claim to prominence was the patronage of Vargas; under his government the economy collapsed and the demands of different sectors of society tore the political system apart. Goulart's ambitions were satisfied when he got the full powers of the presidency restored in 1963, but

Brasília

his supporters included abler men who wanted to carry out radical social change. Leonel Brizola, governor of Rio Grande do Sul, wanted to turn the PTB into a party with a socialist, even a Marxist, programme, while Miguel Arrais, governor of Pernambuco, brought the peasants into political life and used them to break the landowners' stranglehold on local power. Elsewhere Peasant Leagues began to rouse people whom all politicians had previously ignored. Meanwhile inflation rose to 100 per cent and economic growth sank to 2 per cent (against 4 per cent population growth). Brazil seemed headed for disaster.

The final crisis came in 1964, amid a political polarization not seen since the 1930s. Goulart was opposed by most of the governors of the large states, and demonstrations of women organized by the right-wing Catholic organization, 'Tradition, Family, and Liberty', attracted large numbers of supporters. Goulart responded by making a demagogic appeal to the poorer urban workers; at a public demonstration in March 1964, he signed decrees nationalizing oil refineries and some land and promised tax changes and votes for illiterates. It was a challenge to the privileged, and their response showed the hollowness of the president's support. Preparation for a coup began, and were put into action when Goulart committed what in the eyes of the military was a mortal sin by conniving at the formation of left-wing cells in the navy. The rising of 31 March–2 April met little resistance. Goulart's presidency collapsed with the undignified flight of its leaders; few realized immediately that it was the end of democracy in Brazil for twenty years.

Military government in Brazil from 1964

The military leaders who came to power in 1964 had negative rather than positive aims; they wanted to 'clean up politics', and only gradually developed ambitions to govern for themselves. But the purge they conducted was so drastic as to make their final takeover inevitable. Humberto Castello Branco, chief of the army staff, took over as president; Congress continued to sit, but most leading politicians were banned from politics for ten years on charges of 'corruption', 'demagoguery', and 'communism' (which were wide enough to cover almost anything). Meanwhile the economy was taken in hand; inflation was gradually reduced to tolerable levels, and growth began to revive, helped by North American official aid and unofficial investment.

At this stage the military still did not want a dictatorship; they thought that the 1965 elections (for some governors and state assemblies) could still be won by 'respectable' politicians, mainly of the UDN, the party many of the military favoured. A UDN politician who hoped to benefit from military support was Carlos Lacerda, governor of Guanabara, the journalist whose attacks had caused the fall of Vargas and who had developed into a political gadfly with a following among the lower middle classes of Rio de Janeiro; but his hopes were shattered when the PSD/PTB coalition won the two most important states, Guanabara and Minas Gerais. The military responded by transferring the election of the president and state governors from the direct vote of the electorate to the indirect vote of Congress and the state assemblies, which could be manipulated more easily. They also dissolved the existing political parties and forced all elected representatives to join one of two new parties, either the pro-government ARENA (National Renovation Alliance), mainly UDN and PSD, or the opposition MDB, (Brazilian Democratic Movement), the remnants of the PTB after most of its leaders had been banned from politics.

The new political system survived uneasily for four years. The 1966 congressional elections were held, and ARENA beat MDB two to one; but both parties were largely meaningless, and the military only kept the political game going out of a residual shame at setting up an outright dictatorship, which was against the official Brazilian tradition of conciliation and compromise. Castello Branco retired in 1967; his successor, Artur Costa e Silva, was selected by the chiefs of the armed forces and then submitted to a compliant Congress for rubber-stamp approval. Costa e Silva was more easy going (and also more corrupt), but he could do little to increase the regime's popularity. The political situation continued to polarize. The military became more and more touchy at the slightest sign of opposition; they insisted on the imprisonment of a newspaper editor who published an insulting article on Castello Branco's death in a plane crash. On the left the opposition began a guerrilla offensive, stimulated by Cuba's encouragement of such movements.

1968 marked the crisis point at which the military definitely turned to authoritarianism. Government mishandling of student grievances led to a series of massive anti-government demonstrations, supported by the clergy and many middle-class people, which demanded a return to democracy and which were backed by most of the prominent civilians still left in political life. At the same time urban and rural guerrilla groups, particularly National Liberation Action under Carlos Marighela, went into action against the government, which replied with widespread use of torture and the 'death squads' (groups of off-duty soldiers and policemen allowed to kill members of the opposition). The climax came when an MDB deputy called on the people to refuse to celebrate Armed Forces Day because the army had become 'a gang of torturers'. When Congress refused to censure him the military struck back; Congress was closed, ninety-four opposition figures, including Kubitschek and Lacerda, the last civilian politicians of presidential quality, were arrested, and the government took dictatorial powers. The military had wanted to collaborate with the civilians, but they were not prepared to tolerate any dissent.

After 1969 the military ruled without much consultation of the civilian politicians; the press was severely censored and the guerrilla movements ruthlessly crushed. Costa e Silva, paralysed by a stroke, was removed from power in September 1969; the generals, irreverently known as 'the college of cardinals', replaced him with Emilio Garrastazu Médici, who had little power of his own. His government was an alliance between right-wing army officers and civilian technocrats; the Brazilian military, unlike many others, has always worked closely with outside experts and made good use of their talents. The most prominent of the technocrats was the Finance Minister, Antônio Delfim Neto, who created an 'economic miracle' in the early 1970s by raising new loans, paying off old debts, and encouraging foreign investment. These policies were successful for a time. The growth rate went up to 10 per cent a year, the inflation rate went down to 15–25 per cent, and Brazil finally reached 'take off' point by exporting manufactured goods. Coffee ceased to be the largest single export for the first time since 1850. Prosperity partially reconciled the middle classes to the lack of freedom, and the sense of wellbeing was heightened by the achievements of the national football team (success in soccer is as important to Brazil as athletic prowess to the Soviet Union); the celebrations of 150 years of independence in 1972 passed amidst a feeling of euphoria – at least for the elite.

Luis da Silva (Lula) addressing crowd at a trade union gathering in São Paulo, 1980

'Decompression', 1974–

This euphoria did not last. The oil crisis of 1973 brutally revealed the fact that Brazil depended on cheap foreign petroleum and that its exports were vulnerable in a world recession. It also became apparent that social progress had lagged behind economic prosperity and that the price of the 'miracle' had been paid by the poor. Devastating epidemics revealed the low priority given to health and sanitation; even the football team did badly, while inflation rose to 50 per cent and growth fell to 5 per cent. In the 1974 elections the opposition MDB won two senate seats, the only serious political posts open to direct election, and nearly won the Chamber of Deputies; it was obvious that the developed part of the nation had rejected the government.

The military bowed (to some extent) to the national mood by electing Ernesto Geisel for the 1974–9 presidential term. Geisel was of German immigrant stock (he was the first non-Catholic president), and favoured a more rationalist and frugal approach to government. The economic crisis continued, but did not become intolerable, while Geisel sought a policy which would reconcile the electorate to the regime. 'Decompression', as this was known, involved the gradual relaxation of political repression while a return to democracy was promised – but only for the future. This policy worked reasonably well; the political leaders of the democratic republic returned from exile (in most cases only to die) and the MDB failed to win the 1978 election. But this degree of relaxation could only be a temporary palliative.

Geisel angered both right and left among the military by imposing João Baptista Figueiredo as his presidential successor in 1979 without any discussion. But the storm passed, and Figueiredo attempted to continue and develop Geisel's policies. These included an increase in social expenditure and populist gestures such as the president arguing over prices in supermarkets, combined with political sops like the promise of direct elections and an end to the two-party system. (The PSD and the UDN reappeared under other names, while the PTB split into small, largely personalistic factions.) In 1980–1 the most interesting phenomenon was the appearance of an independent trade union movement in opposition to the government controlled syndicates. The new unionism and its charismatic leader Luis da Silva (Lula) in São Paulo were based on the most modern factories, which perhaps indicated the appearance of something new in Brazilian life – a political movement rising from 'the people' themselves.

But the military government went on with its cautious programme of liberalization. The elections held in November 1982 were the first since 1965 in which more than two parties could stand and state governors were directly elected, although the opposition was handicapped in various ways. As it turned out, this made surprisingly little difference. The pro-government PDS (the PSD

Political rally preceding political elections in 1982

under another name) gained the largest number of votes through its control of the more backward states, while the PMDB (Brazilian Democratic Movement Party, uniting the old UN and PTB) swept the developed areas of the centre-south. Leonel Brizola, almost the last survivor of the old-guard politicians of before 1964, was successful in Rio de Janeiro, but a new party under the independent trade unionist Lula did poorly in São Paulo, and the opposition failed to win Rio Grande do Sul owing to an internal split. The army remained firmly in control; however, a political opening has been indicated by the decision of the military to allow indirect presidential elections in 1985; both candidates, Tancredo Neves and Paulo Maluf, were civilians.

Brazil, unlike many other parts of Latin America, has generally been successful in avoiding revolution. There has been little political violence at the centre, though more at local level; debate has usually been possible; politicians have generally tolerated each other. This stability has achieved a great deal – economic growth, respect abroad, and a flourishing intellectual and cultural life at all levels. But a price has been paid for this: the persistence of social stagnation and a society whose benefits are all too often confined to the elite. The Brazilian elite has already accommodated a middle class and a skilled proletariat; it must now bring the unskilled workers and peasants fully into the national society, or all its other achievements will be at risk.

FL

Further reading

R. Bourne, *Getúlio Vargas of Brazil* (London, 1974)
E. Bradford Burns, *A History of Brazil*, 2nd edition (New York, 1980)
P. Flynn, *Brazil: a Political Analysis* (London, 1979)
C. H. Haring, *Empire in Brazil* (Cambridge, Mass., 1958)
T. E. Skidmore, *Politics in Brazil, 1930–1964* (New York, 1967)

Cuba and Puerto Rico

Cuba

The independence of Spain's mainland colonies left Cuba and Puerto Rico as the last vestiges of Spain's American empire. Spain was determined to preserve them at all costs. Both islands were placed under the strict autocratic rule of military governors sent out from Spain, and revolutionary conspiracies, not uncommon in Cuba during the nineteenth century, were ruthlessly suppressed. Spain turned down lucrative offers from the United States to purchase Cuba and warded off US-based filibustering expeditions in the early 1850s designed to detach Cuba from Spain and make it an American slave state.

In the latter part of the eighteenth century Cuba had begun its transformation into a slave plantation society, a process completed in the nineteenth century. Under absolute military rule the island was dominated by a colonial elite and harnessed to a sugar monoculture economy. By the 1860s, Cuba was producing more than 30 per cent of the world's cane sugar. Most of the work was done by African slaves, supplemented by indentured Chinese labourers brought to the island during the 1850s and 1860s. Slavery itself was fed by the Atlantic slave trade, under which an estimated 600,000 African slaves were brought to Cuba in the nineteenth century prior to 1867 when it ended. Puerto Rico received perhaps 10 per cent of the number of slaves brought to Cuba. Spain yielded to British pressure to sign treaties outlawing the Atlantic slave trade in 1817 and 1835, but colonial officials openly connived at continued importations. The largest concentration of Cuba's slave population was located on the island's sugar plantations. These had increased in size by 1860 to the point where many were becoming latifundios and by the latter half of the century were increasingly mechanized.

With the outbreak of a ten-year civil war in the eastern part of Cuba in 1868, Spain at last embarked on some modest political concessions designed to maintain its hold on its Caribbean possessions. The Spanish legislature passed the Moret Law in 1870, freeing all children of slaves born after 1868 and any slave over sixty. This first step towards the abolition of slavery was followed by complete abolition in Puerto Rico in 1873, but in Cuba abolition became a prolonged social process not finally completed until 1886.

Puerto Ricans were permitted to elect delegates to the Spanish legislature beginning in 1869, but as long as Cubans were in arms against Spanish rule the privilege was withheld from Cuba. The Convention of Zanjón in 1878 ended the civil war, enabling Cubans to elect representatives to the Spanish Cortes in 1879, but it did not bury Cuban dreams of independence. These resurfaced under the extraordinary leadership of José Martí (1853–95), poet, intellectual and revolutionary, who worked from an exile base in the United

José Martí

States in the early 1890s to unite the diverse factions of a Cuban independence movement. His 'Cuba Libre' campaign culminated in an invasion of Cuba in 1895, beginning Cuba's second war of independence. Martí personally led the invasion, but tragically he was one of the first casualties, dying in an ambush in May 1895. For three years fighting raged across the island. Spain was unable to suppress the nationalists and they, in turn, were unable to expel the Spanish. It was the United States declaration of war against Spain which decided the fate of Spanish Caribbean colonies.

American entry into Cuba's war of independence with Spain in 1898 thwarted Spanish hopes of retaining its most valuable colony, but it also deflected Cuban aspirations for independence from Spain. With Spain's defeat, Cubans found themselves first under American military occupation for four years and then with limited independence granted to them by the United States. The Republic of Cuba, proclaimed in 1902, was constrained by the Platt Amendment passed by the United States Congress. By it the United States claimed the right to naval bases on Cuba, including Guantanamo which the Americans continue to hold. But the provision of the Amendment which clearly made Cuba a protectorate of the United States stated:

> Cuba consents that the United States may exercise the right to intervene for the preservation of Cuban independence, the maintenance of a government adequate for the protection of life, property, and individual liberty.

The amendment was not repealed until 1934 and its psychological effect lingered on until 1959 (and beyond) as a powerful stimulus to the anti-American nationalism of Castro's revolution. American political and military intervention occurred with some regularity before the repeal and paralleled the growth of United States economic influence in the island.

CUBA

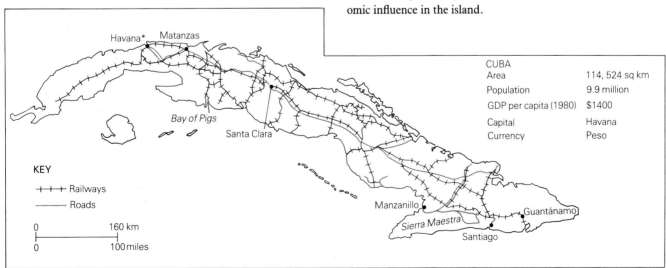

KEY

+++ Railways

— Roads

| 0 | 160 km |
| 0 | 100 miles |

CUBA	
Area	114, 524 sq km
Population	9.9 million
GDP per capita (1980)	$1400
Capital	Havana
Currency	Peso

American investment in Cuba expanded rapidly in the twentieth century, exceeding one billion dollars by 1929. Even in the late 1950s approximately two-thirds of Cuba's sugar exports went to the United States at prices fixed in Washington under a quota system. In most years these prices exceeded world-market prices, but the arrangement virtually made Cuba an economic client of the United States even after the repeal of the Platt Amendment. Cuba purchased nearly three-quarters of its imports from the United States during the 1950s. American investment in the island, after declining during the 1930s, rose again in the 1940s and early 1950s. Cuba's economy remained closely integrated with that of the United States until Castro's revolution. In politics, the island oscillated between authoritarian rule – from 1934 to 1944 the effective 'strong man' being Fulgencio Batista (1901–73), originally an army sergeant – and a somewhat corrupt form of democracy.

Cuba by the 1950s was a society of contrasts. The largest of the Caribbean islands, it had a population of over 6 million people, of whom a million lived in or around Havana. Measured by material standards, it was one of the most advanced states of the Latin American world. More Cadillacs reputedly were sold in Havana in 1954 than in any other city in the world. Cubans in the 1950s, no doubt because of their proximity to the United States, enjoyed the highest number of TV sets per capita of all Latin American countries. Through radio and television Cubans absorbed American culture, and in turn the media perhaps stimulated the forces for change within Cuba; certainly television was a medium which Fidel Castro was soon to exploit very effectively. Yet Cuba suffered from grinding rural poverty, high unemployment, illiteracy and inadequate health care, especially in rural areas. The glitter of Havana's gambling casinos could not hide the glaring social and economic inequalities in the country.

General Batista seized power once again in his coup d'état of 1952, bringing to an end eight years of democratic government under Presidents Ramón Grau San Martín (1944–8) and Carlos Prío Socorras (1948–52). Batista's restoration of dictatorship had profound effects. Of all his opponents none proved more effective in the end than a young Cuban lawyer, the son of a Spanish immigrant. Fidel Castro (b. 1926; prime minister 1959–76; president 1976–) was twenty-six when he launched his first, unsuccessful attempt to topple Batista. Castro had absorbed the nineteenth-century revolutionary tradition of Cuba. He saw himself as the logical successor to José Martí, the man to complete the revolution Martí had begun. In 1953, the 100th anniversary of Martí's birth, Castro engineered a bold attempt to seize the Moncada military barracks in Santiago de Cuba. It failed; Castro was captured and put on trial, but the date of the assault, July 26, provided the name for Castro's revolutionary movement, and the event bequeathed a legacy of martyrs to add to those of the nineteenth century.

Castro's overall programme in 1953 was revolutionary, but in no recognizable sense Marxist–Leninist. It called for radical social and economic reforms and a return to the democracy of Cuba's 1940 Constitution. Castro used his trial to publicize the evils of Batista's regime and his own revolutionary programme. He received a prison sentence, but was soon pardoned under an amnesty. In 1955 Castro went to Mexico in preparation for a new attempt to overthrow Batista. Here he teamed up with an Argentine doctor Ernesto 'Che' Guevara. Castro's revolutionary band sailed to Cuba in the autumn of 1956 to begin a successful three-year struggle against Batista from the Sierra Maestra mountains in eastern Cuba. On 1 January 1959 the remains of the Batista regime dissolved, and Fidel Castro, to universal popular acclaim, assumed control of the island.

Over the next eighteen months, he revealed to his own countrymen and to the rest of the world just how radical he intended the transformation of Cuba to be. Gone was any thought of restoring the 1940 Cuban Constitution and the western-style democracy it symbolized. Instead, the leadership of Castro and the 'revolutionary family' of his guerrilla comrades-in-arms governed Cuba without any formal constitution until 1976. On 1 December 1961, Castro publicly proclaimed his allegiance to Marxism–Leninism. The economic policies of the early revolutionary years reflected this philosophy, especially in the movement towards the collectivization of the means of production. Most important was agriculture and, in particular, the sugar industry. Successive agrarian reform laws steadily trimmed the private sector until it was (by 1977) only 20 per cent of the acreage, although representing much more in terms of production. Co-operatives and state farms replaced private holdings. Where foreign-owned estates or industries existed, they were nationalized, mostly without compensation.

Economic policy during the 1960s was markedly experimental. Che Guevara, Minister of Industry in the early years of the revolution, headed a crash programme to industrialize Cuba, with help from Eastern Europe. Industrialization was part of the larger goal of diversifying the Cuban economy to emancipate it from sugar's historic domination. The strategy of accelerated industrialization was, however, a failure, and it had to be abandoned. Sugar soon controlled the Cuban economy once again. After dramatic declines in sugar harvests during 1963 and 1964, the government targeted a 10-million-ton crop by 1970. This was not achieved, but the frenetic attempt to reach the target aggravated the distortions in the island's economy, causing serious repercussions throughout Cuba. The revolution *has* had some modest success in diversifying the economy, most notably in the expansion of the fishing industry. Nevertheless, the inability of Cuba's socialist economic system to break out of the bonds of a monoculture economy has increased the island's economic dependence on the Soviet Union.

The Soviet link has been of fundamental importance. Once in

Fidel Castro

power, Castro was determined to establish Cuba's independence from the United States. Nationalization of American holdings and Castro's campaign to export his revolution soon put Cuban–American relations on a collision course. Fearing American retaliation, Castro looked for and found support from the Soviet Union. Relations between Cuba and the United States steadily worsened until diplomatic ties were broken on 3 January 1961. They have never been restored although a small step was taken in 1977 with the establishment of 'interest' sections in both countries. The United States imposed a trade embargo in 1962 which is still in effect.

Meanwhile, American plans to dislodge Castro by force had been set in motion. In April 1961, an invasion of the island by anti-Castro Cuban exiles collapsed on the beaches of Cuba's Bay of Pigs. Castro now requested more military assistance from the Soviet Union to repel any further American attacks. The Soviet Union readily complied and the arms supplied included missiles sent to the island in the autumn of 1962. When he discovered the existence of the missiles, President Kennedy insisted on their withdrawal. The crisis which ensued in October 1962 brought the United States and the Soviet Union to the brink of nuclear war, but it was resolved by a Soviet agreement to withdraw the missiles in exchange for a United States promise not to invade Cuba. Cuban independence was thus assured – though at the cost of a high degree of dependence on the Soviet Union.

United States diplomacy concentrated on securing the support of the Organization of American States for sanctions against Cuba, thus insulating the rest of the Caribbean and the Americas from the spread of Castro's revolution. Under American pressure all but two western-hemisphere countries, Mexico and Canada, broke trade and diplomatic relations with Cuba in the early 1960s. Castro was equally determined to export his revolution and his 1963 claim that 'the Andes would become the Sierra Maestra of Latin America' shows how far he thought the potential market for revolution extended. The most vivid sign of the failure of this policy was the capture and death of Guevara in Bolivia in 1967. Guevara's death marked the beginning of a retreat from the idea of exporting the revolution and a belated realization within Cuba that the Cuban revolutionary model might not be universally applicable.

The second decade of the revolution saw Cuba under Castro become more firmly entrenched as a member of the Soviet bloc. Castro publicly supported the Soviet invasion of Czechoslovakia in 1968, a portent of the more docile semi-satellite role Cuba would play in the 1970s. Internally the Sovietization of the island became more pronounced. The Communist Party grew in strength and size. More Soviet and eastern-bloc technicians came to Cuba while growing numbers of Cubans received training in Russia. Central controls were clamped more tightly on education and culture. The Cuban economy has been subsumed into the Soviet economic sphere with Cuba now a formal member of COMECON and tied to the Soviet Union through numerous technical agreements. Soviet techniques of central planning have been introduced and Cuba has adopted five-year economic plans. Cuba's financial debt to the USSR, measured in billions of dollars, has steadily mounted as has the island's overall dependence on the Soviet Union for economic assistance and as a trading partner. The Soviet Union has continued to supply military assistance to the Cuban armed forces including sophisticated weaponry such as the MIG-23. Virtually all of Cuba's oil is supplied by the Soviet Union at prices well below OPEC price levels.

Almost certainly at the suggestion of the Soviet Union, Cuba's leaders focused on the institutionalization of the revolution during the 1970s, using the Soviet model. The post-revolutionary Communist Party had been formally created in 1965 and its first, long delayed, Congress finally occurred, ten years later, at the end of 1975. A new socialist Cuban Constitution was approved in 1976. The Cuban judiciary was reorganized in 1973, the same year that the executive-legislative power in Cuba altered with the creation of a new body, the Executive Committee of the Council of Ministers.

The apparatus and power of the state and its attendant bureaucracies have grown, but Fidel Castro continues to place his own unique personal stamp on the direction his revolution takes. In spite of the institutionalization which has occurred, the Cuban revolution is still highly personalized and dominated by Castro.

Cuba's close ideological identification with the Soviet Union has been mirrored by developments in its foreign policy. From active assistance to Latin American guerrilla movements in the 1960s, Cuba lined up with the Soviet policy of detente in the 1970s, which for Cuba had the advantage of a greatly reduced threat to the revolution from the United States. Cuba concentrated less on trying to export revolution to Latin America and more on improving relations with key Latin American countries in an effort to reduce its isolation. In 1975 the OAS sanctions on Cuba were lifted and during the decade diplomatic relations were established with a number of Latin American countries. Castro paid special attention to helping left-wing governments, especially the Allende government in Chile.

Fidel Castro's foreign policy also concentrated on the Third World in general in the 1970s, and most notably on Africa. Castro and the Cuban revolutionaries had shown considerable sympathy to African liberation movements during the 1960s. In the next decade this sympathy extended to military intervention in support of these movements. The Cuban decision to intervene on a large scale in Angola in 1975 was, from all available evidence, made by the Cubans acting on their own. Approximately 20,000 Cuban troops aided the MPLA forces in their successful struggle to defeat rival movements and claim victory in an independent Angola. Cuban technicians were then sent to Angola to help build the socialist revolution while Cuban army units were gradually withdrawn.

Subsequent to the Cuban military success in Angola, Castro offered military assistance to Ethiopia in its conflict with Somalia and by 1978 thousands of Cuban troops were in the Horn of Africa. Smaller numbers of Cuban military and technical advisers were to be found in a variety of other African countries from Mozambique in the south to Libya in the north. Castro's stress on the Afro-Cuban heritage led to a new and contemporary Afro-Cuban revolutionary connection and has helped to propel Fidel Castro into prominence among Third World countries in spite of his ideological alignment with Moscow. A summit conference of world non-aligned nations was held in Havana in September 1979 under Castro's leadership, an event which marked a high point of Fidel's personal influence with the leaders of the non-aligned countries. Cuban actions in Africa also helped to strengthen relations with the Soviet Union for whom Cuba had become an invaluable ally.

Cuban links with neighbouring Latin American countries entered a more difficult period in the early 1980s. Colombia broke off diplomatic relations in the spring of 1981. Revolution in Nicaragua and civil war in El Salvador have focused world attention on Central America. Cuba has supported the revolutionary government in Nicaragua but tensions with neighbouring Latin American countries and with the Reagan administration have mounted.

After more than twenty years of Cuba's revolutionary experience and in spite of the current problems faced by the Cubans, the revolution engineered by Castro appears more solidly entrenched than ever, as does Fidel himself. In some areas the successes are marked. Life expectancy is greater now for the average Cuban than it was in 1959. Birth rates and infant mortality rates have declined, signs that Cuba has overcome the problems of rapid population growth confronting many Third World countries. Education and health services have been made available to all sections of the population and illiteracy has been eradicated. These particular achievements continue to impress many Latin Americans.

Yet the Cuban economy remains fragile and to a high degree dependent on the Soviet Union. In addition, natural disasters have added recent complications. Blue mould almost destroyed the 1980 tobacco crop, rust adversely affected sugar production and African swine fever devastated the island's pig population. Protests by discontented Cubans escalated in 1980 to the point that the Cuban government permitted those who wanted to escape the revolution to do so. Up to 125,000 Cubans migrated – most of them to the United States. Several hundred thousand Cubans had left the island in the early stages of the revolution – not least the professional classes.

The Cuban revolution has thus created two Cubas: one contained in the island itself where the revolution permeates all aspects of life, and another among the expatriate Cubans most of whom live in the United States. For the latter, exile has become a permanent condition, necessitating either accommodation with American culture or assimilation. For the Cuban revolution and for Fidel Castro, the United States is the chief enemy, the personification of the counter-revolution which must be resisted at all costs. In contrast, the Soviet Union remains Cuba's protector and the model to be followed whether in ideology or foreign policy.

Puerto Rico

Puerto Rico has experienced the colonialism of two imperial powers. Madrid was the real capital of the island until 1898 when a defeated Spain ceded Puerto Rico to the United States and the centre of government shifted to Washington. Since then Puerto Rico's colonial status has gradually evolved to the present Commonwealth association with the United States. The name 'Commonwealth' came with a new internal constitution in 1952. While the term itself suggests similarities with the British Commonwealth, the reality is very different. Ultimate legislative power resides now, as it has since 1898, in the United States Congress, although internally the island enjoys democratic self-government. The American conquest imposed the boundaries of the debate on the

PUERTO RICO

PUERTO RICO

Area	8800 sq km
Population	3.2 million
GDP per capita (1980)	$3000
Capital	San Juan
Currency	US dollar

Main roads
Major urban centres

0   32 km
0   20 miles

American economic control of the island was another consequence of the shift in imperial masters. Sugar, coffee and tobacco had been major export crops in the nineteenth century. Coffee and tobacco production declined after the American takeover, but sugar cultivation, carried out mainly by large American-owned companies, expanded as did exports to the United States under free-trade and American tariff protection. The Depression, however, caused sugar prices to fall drastically with a corresponding blow to the island's economy. Following the Second World War, with the political leadership of Luis Muñoz Marín (b. 1898; governor 1948–64), Puerto Rico rapidly industrialized under 'Operation Bootstrap'. The industrialization experiment, heavily subsidized from the mainland, had many successes, but by the 1970s serious economic and social problems re-emerged. One was a serious neglect of agriculture, which turned Puerto Rico into a net food importer. Another problem was the capital-intensive nature of the industries, which never generated jobs in the number that Puerto Rico needed. As a result, many Puerto Ricans left the island and tried their luck on the mainland, usually in greater New York City.

Puerto Rico today is still divided between its Caribbean tradition and its American connection. The division has widened appreciably as the other Caribbean islands have become independent and developed new relationships with each other and with the outside world. Puerto Rico shares with them many of the problems of underdevelopment in spite of 'Operation Bootstrap'. A majority of the population are either government employees or dependent on American social security. Unemployment rose during the 1970s as did poverty, and with them has come the environmental fallout of heavy industrialization. The two issues of political status and economic development seem inseparable, but few would prophesy an imminent separation of Puerto Rico from the United States.

DRM

island's status that have continued to the present; on the one extreme, full United States statehood and on the other, independence. Adherents of both these causes have flourished during the eighty years of American control, although neither has triumphed. A referendum held in 1967 revealed that 60 per cent of the population were satisfied with Commonwealth status, while 39 per cent wanted full statehood and less than 1 per cent desired independence.

The evolution of Puerto Rico's relationship with the United States took a major step in 1917 when Puerto Ricans were granted collective United States citizenship which they continue to hold. With citizenship came other American imports, and, curiously for this rum-producing island, the first was prohibition. By the same Jones Act granting American citizenship, the islanders were required to hold a referendum on prohibition. It passed; and Puerto Rico became 'dry' even before the United States. As United States citizens, male Puerto Ricans became eligible from 1917 for the draft and entry into what was then a racially segregated army. Many of the more than 17,000 who were inducted volunteered. None saw any fighting, but over 4000 guarded the Panama Canal for the United States during the remainder of the First World War. Not until 1948 was the governor of the island a Puerto Rican. Until that time the governors were Americans, political appointments of the United States president and responsible to him through the American Bureau of Insular Affairs, but not accountable to the people they governed.

Further reading

Cuba
J. I. Dominguez, *Cuba: Order and Revolution* (Cambridge, Mass., 1978)
R. Guerra y Sanchez, *Sugar and Society in the Caribbean* (New Haven, Conn., 1964)
C. Mesa-Lago, *The Economy of Socialist Cuba: a Two-Decade Appraisal* (Albuquerque, NM, 1981)
R. F. Smith, *The United States and Cuba: Business and Diplomacy, 1917–1960* (New Haven, Conn., 1960)
H. Thomas, *Cuba: the Pursuit of Freedom* (New York, 1971)

Puerto Rico
R. Carr, *Puerto Rico: a Colonial Experiment* (New York, 1984)
T. R. Clark, *Puerto Rico and the United States 1917–1933* (Pittsburgh, Penn., 1975)
G. K. Lewis, *Puerto Rico* (New York, 1968)

Haiti and the Dominican Republic

Haiti

In the island of Hispaniola, divided between the new state of Haiti and the old Spanish colony of Santo Domingo, the early nineteenth century was overshadowed by the legacy of the Haitian revolution. With the assassination of Dessalines in 1806, newly-independent Haiti split into two parts; a military oligarchy under Alexandre Pétion (1807–18) ruled the south and west while Henry Christophe (1806–20) ruled the northern state. The country was reunited at the death of Christophe in 1820 and two years later the Spanish colony in the eastern part of the island was incorporated into the republic of Haiti. These early years of independence saw a struggle for land between the former free coloureds, who formed a new elite, and the liberated slaves. Pétion and later Christophe made grants of land to army officers; also some of the large estates were broken up and given to ordinary soldiers or sold to civilians. Many former slaves deserted the plantations and squatted on vacant land. Despite efforts by Jean-Pierre Boyer (1818–43) the plantation economy was never to revive and agricultural production throughout the nineteenth century consisted largely of coffee for export and food crops for local consumption.

Internal conflicts led to the fall of Boyer, and in 1844 the Dominicans took the opportunity to declare the independence of the Spanish-speaking part of the island. In Haiti the blacks, who had systematically been excluded from power under Boyer, reasserted themselves and after some years of unstable and short-lived governments, Faustin Souloque (1847–59) became president and later emperor. In the sixty-three years which followed, different elites struggled for control of the state. One party tended to be composed predominantly of mulattoes engaged in commerce, though also owning considerable estates. Their strength was in the capital and in the cities of the south; they were generally francophile and in favour of the *Concordat* reached with the Vatican in 1860. The other party was usually controlled by black generals and landowners; their strength was in Cap Haïtien and in the rural areas. They sometimes sought support from the United States and were frequently anti-clerical, being freemasons or Protestants. Although the leadership of each party was predominantly of one colour (black or mulatto) the parties were never monochrome. Black presidential candidates were often put forward by mulatto politicians who hoped to exercise effective power behind the façade of a black president, while disaffected mulattoes frequently associated themselves with the predominantly black party. Though the colour issue was rarely absent from Haitian conflicts it was never the sole factor determining alliances. The mass of the population who were poor, black and illiterate, engaged in sporadic revolts against unpopular regimes but were rarely able to exert constructive pressure upon the succeeding government.

Haitian independence was founded upon the idea of race. The first constitution (1805) proclaimed that Haitians of all shades were to be known as '*noir*' and that no whites could own property in the country. Throughout the nineteenth century Haiti produced a number of important and articulate writers and poets who defended the black race against European racialists. Nevertheless, among the elite groups, European culture predominated and this was reinforced by the Roman Catholic Church's role in the field of education, following the *Concordat*. Among the masses, however, African customs and in particular the Voodoo religion prevailed; the popular language was and remains *créole*, a French patois.

In 1825 France had recognized Haitian independence after a huge indemnity to the dispossessed planters had been agreed to by Boyer. Foreign intervention in the affairs of the black republic increased throughout the century and was both facilitated by and contributed towards the bitter rivalry between contending elites. After the fall of Antoine Simon in 1910, a period of acute governmental instability culminated in the United States invasion of the country in 1915; this was part of a general plan for the strategic and economic control of the Caribbean region. A puppet president was installed and the policy of the US administration was principally concerned to make Haiti a safe and attractive field for US private investors by ensuring strict debt repayments, improving the infrastructure and strengthening the middle class (a step which it was believed would lead to stable and democratic government). In the early years the occupation met with miliary resistance from peasant irregulars (*cacos*) under Charlemagne Péralte; later a growing nationalist movement, encompassing Haitians of different colours and ideological commitments, demanded the withdrawal of US troops which was agreed to in 1934.

One effect of the US occupation was the re-establishment of the mulatto elite in political power. President Sténio Vincent (1930–41) managed by skilful tactics to deflect the challenge of the growing black middle class, but his successor was less astute and in 1946, after a military coup, a black school teacher, Dumarsais Estimé (1946–50) became president, with strong support from the countryside. The presidency of Paul Magloire (1950–6) represented a return of the old elite and his demise led to a bitter struggle culminating in the election in September 1957 of François Duvalier who had support from the more radical black groups (*noiristes*). Inspired partly by a *négritude* ('blackness') ideology, deriving from his involvement in the ethnological movement of the occupation period, Duvalier dealt ruthless blows to opposition groups and drastically reduced the political power of the army, the Church, the trade unions, the business community and the US embassy. From 1966 onwards, however, he came to terms with each of these groups

The body of Charlemagne Péralte, resistance leader during the US occupation of Haiti, nailed to the door of Cap Haïtien town hall, 1919

and his son, Jean-Claude, who succeeded him as president for life in 1971, has continued this policy of accommodation.

Although there has been some urban growth in Haiti, associated in recent years with the arrival of a large number of US-owned light manufacturing industries and assembly plants, the economy is still centred on agriculture, with about 90 per cent of the population of over 5 million living in rural areas. Contending with serious soil erosion, frequent droughts, occasional earthquakes and hurricanes, the Haitian peasant ekes out a meagre existence; the country has the lowest annual per-capita income in the hemisphere, estimated by the World Bank to be $300 for 1981.

The Dominican Republic

Haiti had taken over the Spanish eastern part of the island in 1822. Nationalist sentiment soon gathered momentum; and in 1838 a secret society known as La Trinitaria was founded by Juan Pablo Duarte and others to work for independence. Encouraged by Britain and France, the Dominicans proclaimed independence from Haiti in 1844. The leaders of the movement, Duarte, Sánchez and Mella were, however, forced into exile by Pedro Santana who became the first president of the republic. The early years were marked by war with Haiti and the consequent search for foreign protection which ended in 1861 with the re-establishment of Spanish colonial rule. Soon a new independence struggle led by a mulatto general, Gregorio Luperón, broke out and after two years the Spanish forces withdrew (1865).

The political history of the sixty years which followed was marked by a struggle for power between rival generals, often in league with

HAITI AND THE DOMINICAN REPUBLIC

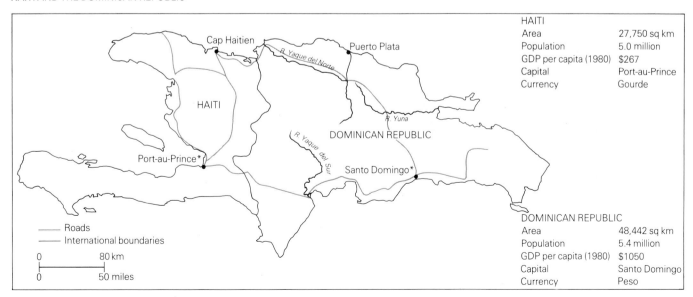

HAITI	
Area	27,750 sq km
Population	5.0 million
GDP per capita (1980)	$267
Capital	Port-au-Prince
Currency	Gourde

DOMINICAN REPUBLIC	
Area	48,442 sq km
Population	5.4 million
GDP per capita (1980)	$1050
Capital	Santo Domingo
Currency	Peso

Roads
International boundaries

0   80 km
0   50 miles

Haitian leaders. Foreign loans were contracted, leaving the country with enormous foreign debts; the non-payment of which provided an excuse for foreign intervention in the affairs of the republic. An additional reason for such intervention was the desire by foreign governments, particularly that of the United States, for a naval base at Samaná, on the north coast. From 1882 the fortunes of the country were in the hands of a black general, Ulises Heureaux, whose dictatorial regime achieved some improvement in communications and a growth in coffee production, though at the cost of increased foreign involvement. His assassination in 1899 inaugurated sixteen years of governmental instability broken only by the regime of Ramón Cáceres (1905–11).

The eastern part of the island of Hispaniola was, compared with its neighbour, relatively undeveloped during the nineteenth century. The economy was dominated by cattle ranching and tobacco growing, together with crops for local consumption grown particularly in the fertile Cibao valley. The rapid growth of the sugar industry which took place in the 1870s was partly due to the arrival of many thousands of Cubans who left their country during the first war of independence. Plantations of coffee and cocoa for export were also developed, while Lebanese and other immigrant groups started small manufacturing industries. Towards the end of the century US financial involvement in the Dominican economy became a major factor in determining the future of the country, and in 1905 a customs receivership was set up by the United States to ensure the repayment of foreign debts.

Throughout its history the Dominican Republic has looked with unease upon its more densely populated neighbour. The 1844 independence movement stressed the European, Catholic, 'civilized' culture of the Dominicans over against the African and 'barbarous' Haitians, and on these grounds appealed for sympathy and support to the United States and to European nations. Racialism has, in fact, played a significant part in relations between the two countries, as many Dominican historians today acknowledge. The literary heritage of the country has naturally developed from its Spanish roots, but it was not until the present century that literary figures of international significance emerged. Despite possessing the oldest university in Latin America, the education system was primitive though it was reorganized and improved in 1880 by Eugenio María de Hostos, the Puerto Rican educationalist.

The US occupation of the republic lasted from 1916 to 1924 and affairs were administered directly by the US military government. A programme of public works was undertaken but the economic crisis of 1921 led the country into debt. It was during this period that Rafael Leónidas Trujillo Molina began his rise to power through the ranks of the national police force. In 1927 he became commander of the Dominican army and three years later was elected president of the republic. Thus began thirty-one years of ruthless personal

dictatorship ending only with the assassination of 'the Benefactor' on the evening of 30 May 1961. The Trujillo era saw a significant expansion of the Dominican economy which became inextricably interwoven with his personal and family fortunes. The population increased from 1.5 million in 1935 to 3 million in 1960. Enormous public works schemes were undertaken and a large number of manufacturing industries sprang up. In the early years he posed as the defender of 'European' and 'Catholic' civilization and his policy of 'de-Africanizing' the border involved the massacre of many thousands of Haitians in 1937. During the 1950s there was increasing disaffection on the part of the Dominican population and even the Church became critical of the regime. Trujillo's attempted assassination of President Betancourt of Venezuela in 1960 and the sanctuary given to such former dictators as Juan Perón, Pérez Jiménez and Batista led to opposition from most Latin American countries and eventually the United States decided it was time he went.

The years following the fall of Trujillo were characterized by a series of short-lived governments culminating in the crisis of 1965 when the United States, fearing a 'second Cuba', invaded the country. A presidential contest the following year between two former heads of state, Juan Bosch and Joaquín Balaguer, resulted in victory for the latter who was supported by the United States and the remaining US troops were withdrawn. Balaguer's conservative

Generalissimo Rafael Trujillo

Movements for Latin American unity

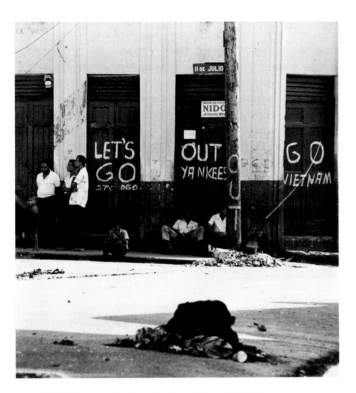

Anti-US slogans during the invasion of 1965

regime lasted effectively until 1978 when he was defeated by Antonio Guzmán, a rich agriculturalist with a radical reputation, which subsequently proved to be undeserved. In 1982 (after a short interregnum following the suicide of Guzmán) Salvador Jorge Blanco – also of the Partido Revolucionario Dominicano – was elected president. Significant economic developments of the post-Trujillo era have been in the field of mining, particularly of ferronickel, silver and gold. Despite problems of poverty and unemployment, the population of about 5 million generally enjoys a standard of living considerably higher than that of its western neighbour with the 1981 per-capita income estimated at $1260 by the World Bank.

DN

Further reading

I. Bell, *The Dominican Republic* (Boulder, Colorado, 1981)

J. Leyburn, *The Haitian People* (New Haven, Conn., 1966)

R. W. Logan, *Haiti and the Dominican Republic* (London, 1968)

D. Nicholls, *From Dessalines to Duvalier* (Cambridge, 1979)

B. Weinstein and A. Segal, *Haiti: Political Failures, Cultural Successes* (New York, 1984)

S. Welles, *Naboth's Vineyard: the Dominican Republic 1824–1924* (New York, 1928)

The very term 'Latin America' suggests a degree of unity which masks the very considerable differences – in such important respects as size, natural resources, racial composition and the degree of political and economic maturity each has achieved – among the twenty republics (eighteen Spanish-speaking, one Portuguese-speaking, one French-speaking) it embraces. (Twenty-five republics are members of the Inter-American Development Bank, but some of these are not strictly speaking part of *Latin* America as such.) Latin America has never, of course, been united, and both geography and history have encouraged disunity. Relations among the eighteen Spanish American countries often have been bedevilled by territorial disputes, some of them unresolved today. Brazil's power and ambitions have aroused fear and suspicion among the other republics, especially on the part of Argentina, its rival for leadership in South America.

Nevertheless, the ideal of Latin American – or, at least, Spanish American – unity has persisted virtually from the time of independence to the present day. It has been associated, above all, with Simón Bolívar, the most revered of Latin American historical figures, whose bicentenary in 1983 was very extensively celebrated in the region. Bolívar inspired the congress held at Panama in 1826, which attempted to form a Latin American confederation. Although it was attended by only a few Spanish American countries, and failed to achieve its objective, the Panama Congress is regarded as the precursor of all later attempts to bring about Latin American unity. During the nineteenth century there were further Spanish American congresses, again with limited attendance and no significant achievement. All of these congresses, including the one held at Panama, were concerned with security against possible aggression from outside the region.

Then, towards the end of the century, the United States promoted 'Pan Americanism', based, not upon Latin American unity, but rather the concept of a special relationship between the countries of Latin America and itself. Yet those promoting and supporting it claimed that Pan Americanism expressed the ideals of Simón Bolívar. The International Union of American Republics was established in 1890, with a permanent agency in Washington later to be called the Pan American Union. Thus began the inter-American system, which, since 1948, has centred upon the Organization of American States (OAS). The inter-American system has basically been an instrument of United States policy towards Latin America. Yet it has been within the inter-American system and, more recently, *in reaction to it*, that movements for Latin American unity have very largely developed.

Statue of Simón
Bolívar

The inter-American system has played a significant role in bringing the countries of Latin America together, and encouraging the emergence of a Latin American 'identity' – though this is not to say that they often have been united in dealing with the United States. It was reaction to the latter's unwillingness to give them the substantial economic aid to which they felt their membership of the inter-American system entitled them that led the Latin American countries in 1948 to insist upon the establishment of the United Nations Economic Commission for Latin America (ECLA). ECLA stimulated Latin American economic integration: the first of two major, interrelated movements for Latin American unity which have taken place in the last two decades.

Two agreements for economic integration were signed in 1960: a treaty establishing a Free Trade Area and instituting the Latin American Free Trade Association (LAFTA – its Spanish acronym being ALALC), of which eventually all ten South American republics and Mexico were signatories, and the General Treaty for Central American Economic Integration (CACM). However, progress in LAFTA towards liberalizing trade among its members soon slowed down, and the divergence of interests between the largest of them (Argentina, Brazil and Mexico) and the others became more marked. Nor, after greater initial success, did CACM fare very much better. A subgroup, formed in 1969 by the Andean countries (Bolivia, Chile, Colombia, Ecuador, Peru and – subsequently – Venezuela), had more ambitious objectives than LAFTA, including planned industrialization and a common policy on foreign investment. But, as with the earlier agreements, progress under the

Andean Pact was greatly limited by conflicting national interests and some serious disputes between members. Meanwhile, Latin American economic integration had been included in the programme of the 'Alliance for Progress', initiated by the United States in 1961, and its achievement became an objective of the inter-American system.

Dissatisfaction with the Alliance for Progress – and with United States aid and trade policies generally – combined with a significant global development to stimulate the second major movement for Latin American unity: attempts to establish a 'Latin American position' in the international economic order. In 1964 the first United Nations Conference on Trade and Development (UNCTAD) was held in Geneva. Prior to the UNCTAD, the Latin American countries met to draw up a common position to be taken there, and subsequently set up a Special Latin American Co-ordinating Commission (CECLA). CECLA affirmed 'the distinctive personality of Latin America' in its international relations. The Latin Americans helped to form 'The group of seventy-seven' developing countries (now well over a hundred) with the aim of persuading the developed countries to make concessions in matters of aid and trade (the 'North–South Dialogue').

In 1975 a new Latin American forum for economic co-operation and consultation was established: the Latin American Economic System (SELA). The new organization had two broad objectives: to promote regional co-operation for economic development, principally through the creation of Latin American multinational enterprises; and to establish a system of consultation for the adoption of common economic positions in relation to other countries and international organizations. In the furtherance of the second objective SELA was to replace CECLA, and this to date has

The Pan-American Union Building, Washington DC

been its main role. Only modest progress has so far been made towards creating Latin American multinational enterprises.

Prospects for Latin American unity in the foreseeable future do not seem to be good. Such factors as divergent national interests, serious disputes between individual republics, and the very small share of Latin America's international trade that takes place within the region itself, greatly curtail the progress of economic integration. The growing economic strength of the larger countries – especially Brazil and Mexico – and the division between the main oil producers and the rest, prejudice the adoption of a common position within the North–South Dialogue. Yet in 1980 a new attempt was made towards economic integration: LAFTA was to be superseded by a Latin American Integration Association. Two years later the Falklands crisis provided a new rallying point for Latin American unity: support for Argentina's claim to the islands was virtually unanimous. But the rhetoric of solidarity was not matched by tangible assistance and, ironically, the Falklands issue revived concern with other territorial disputes within the region, which themselves have been such a serious obstacle to Latin American unity. Nevertheless, in spite of the very limited success so far attained in giving it practical effect, the goal of Latin American unity and movements to achieve it will persist.

GC-S

Further reading

R. D. Bond, 'Regionalism in Latin America: Prospects for the Latin American Economic System (SELA)', *International Organization*, vol. 32 (1978)

G. Connell-Smith, *The Inter-American System* (Oxford, 1966)

R. Hilton, ed., *The Movement Toward Latin American Unity* (New York, 1969)

E. S. Milenky, 'Latin America's Multilateral Diplomacy: Integration, Disintegration and Interdependence', *International Affairs*, vol. 53 (1977)

The Bolivarian Declaration of Caracas (1983)

In the final week of June 1983, several hundred Latin American politicians (including ten former presidents) and intellectuals gathered in Caracas, Venezuela, at the invitation of the Venezuelan Congress, to discuss the contemporary position and future prospects of Latin America and the Caribbean. This Congress on Latin American Political Thought, convened as one of the major events in the commemoration of Simón Bolívar's bicentenary, conducted an impressive series of meetings and seminars, lasting one week, designed to see whether something like a common Latin American political consensus could be established. The Bolivarian Declaration of Caracas, produced at the end of the conference, was approved by all participants. It contains a resonant reaffirmation of Simón Bolívar's old dreams of continental unity.

Gathered together in Caracas on the happy initiative of the Congress of the Republic of Venezuela, and on the occasion of the Bicentenary of the birth of the Liberator Simón Bolívar, we address ourselves to our peoples with a message of encouragement and hope. We are citizens who adhere to various ideological tendencies, and we come from all the countries of the Great Latin American Nation. Over the past week we have reflected on the destiny of our people and on the historic commitment demanded by the times in which we live.

We have reverently evoked the glorious memory of the Liberator – not the inert effigy of traditional commemorations, but rather his living presence and his meaning for our time. We have evoked the Bolívar who still has work to do in Latin America, and who devoted his life to its freedom, independence and unity. Bolívar's project for Latin America – which he himself called 'a Nation of Republics' – now assumes its historic role as the only possible guarantee for development, for economic emancipation, for authentic political independence, and for the attainment of an irrenounceable cultural identity derived from many contributions from around the world.

We urge the governments and peoples of Latin America and the Caribbean to realize their economic, social, political and cultural integration – to overcome the limitations of petty and anti-historical outlooks, and the divisive snares laid by foreign interests. In a world characterized by the overwhelming presence of great powers, we should not persist in displaying the lamentable spectacle of our disunity. It is time for bold, firm and resolute action. Everything that can be said in favour of integration – the contemporary name for the Bolivarian ideal of unity – has already been said. It is our task to bring it about. As part of this unifying process, we exhort the peoples of Latin America to undertake the peaceful resolution of their territorial differences and controversies – among these, the landlocked situation of Bolivia. We call upon governments, as the best possible act of homage to the Liberator, to carry out his essential proposal by founding a Latin American Community of Nations, endowed with the institutions and powers necessary to achieve the aim of integration.

We aspire to see Latin America united, under the sign of liberty and justice. We condemn those regimes which, in Latin America and the Caribbean alike, perpetuate oppression, fraud and economic and social injustice as instruments of government. We affirm that there can be no national sovereignty that is not based on, and justified by, the sovereignty of the people. We hear the clamour of thousands and thousands of political prisoners, of those who are persecuted, tortured and exiled – not forgetting the accusatory silence of those who have disappeared – and we insist on an accounting for so much American suffering. We demand the rule of democracy, unhampered respect for human rights, the practice of political pluralism, self-determination for the peoples, and freedom of information without restraints. The unification of Latin America cannot become authentic or enduring if the governments concerned do not share a minimum of ethical values, political ideals and democratic practices.

Only the affirmation of Latin American unity will permit historic fulfilment for our peoples and confront the aggressions, threats and pressures of imperialism in all its forms. This position entails for us a rejection of all foreign intervention in the problems of the continent – we particularly emphasize here the critical situation in Central America, which should be resolved by its respective peoples and by them alone . . . We condemn imperial aggression in the Islas Malvinas – historically and legally part of Argentina – and the presence of foreign military bases in our America. Colonial and neo-colonial forms should not be tolerated either in the Caribbean or anywhere in the Latin American continent. We therefore demand for the people of Puerto Rico – whose liberation Bolívar signalled as the final phase of the emancipation of our America – their inalienable right . . .

We who approve this manifesto, by virtue of our position and in exercise of our political and intellectual responsibilities, commit ourselves irrevocably to carry out this common wish.

Caracas, 2 July 1983

Wars in Latin America

Wars between Latin American nations have been relatively uncommon in the period since independence. Internal warfare, as articles on individual countries in this Encyclopedia show, is another matter. War scares have occurred from time to time – as, for instance, between Argentina and Chile in the years 1895–1901 and again in 1978 – but war itself has not usually resulted. The principal international conflicts have been:

The Argentine–Brazilian War, 1825–8
This was the first war between newly independent states in the region. It was started by the invasion (in April 1825) of the Spanish-speaking Banda Oriental (now Uruguay) by the 'Heroic Thirty-Three Orientales', rebels who wished to free their homeland from Brazil, which had occupied the area in 1817, subsequently annexing it and calling it the Cisplatine Province. Argentina proclaimed the incorporation of the Banda Oriental into its own territory, and Brazil retaliated by declaring war. Fighting was intermittent, but February 1827 saw two significant Argentine victories: the naval action of Juncal and the battle of Ituzaingó. The war ended soon afterwards through British pressure and mediation, which resulted in the creation (1828) of a 'buffer country', the new Republic of Uruguay, in the disputed territory.

The war between Chile and the Peru–Bolivian Confederation, 1836–9
The establishment (1836) of the Peru–Bolivian Confederation by General Andrés Santa Cruz (1792–1865) aroused immediate hostility from the government of Chile, which declared war on the new state. Two Chilean expeditionary forces were sent to Peru. The first of these was trapped by Santa Cruz into withdrawing (Treaty of Paucarpata, 1837). A second and stronger expedition, commanded by General Manuel Bulnes (1799–1866; president of Chile 1841–51), occupied the Peruvian capital, Lima, and went on to win the decisive battle of the war at Yungay, in the Andes (January 1839). The Peru–Bolivian Confederation rapidly dissolved.

The War of the Triple Alliance (or Paraguayan War), 1864–70
The background to this war was complex, one of the key issues being control of the upper Paraná River basin, which formed a vital transport line into south-west Brazil. Combat started with a Paraguayan invasion of Rio Grande do Sul, Brazil – an effort by the Paraguayan dictator Francisco Solano López to counteract Brazilian influence in Uruguay. In order to reach Brazil, Paraguayan troops had to cross Argentine territory, which drew Argentina into the conflict. In May 1865, Argentina, Brazil and Uruguay signed a Triple Alliance to defeat López. The empire of Brazil supplied the largest contingents of troops. The Allied army was commanded first by the Argentine president Bartolomé Mitre, and then, from 1867 to 1869, by the distinguished Brazilian general Luis Alves de Lima e Silva, Marquis (later Duke) of Caxias (1803–80). Obstructed by the impressive fortress-complex at Humaitá, just inside Paraguayan territory, the Allies' advance up the line of the River Paraguay was slow and extremely costly. The Paraguayan capital, Asunción, fell to the Allied army only in January 1869. López himself was hunted down and killed (1 March 1870). 'I die with my homeland!' he is supposed to have said. Approximately 100,000 Allied soldiers died in the war, which is also believed to have reduced the male population of Paraguay by nine-tenths, making this the most devastating war in modern Latin American history.

WARS IN LATIN AMERICA

The War of the Pacific, 1879–83

This war arose out of Bolivia's threat to confiscate a Chilean nitrate concern operating in the Atacama Desert, then a coastal province of Bolivia. To forestall this move, Chilean forces occupied the port of Antofagasta (February 1879) and the Bolivian littoral. Peru was drawn into the conflict by virtue of a secret treaty of alliance with Bolivia (1873). After several months of naval warfare – the chief battles being those of Iquique (May 1879), a Peruvian victory, and Cape Angamos (October 1879), a Chilean victory – Chile gained command of the sea, and was thus enabled to dispatch large armies to the northern deserts. Two major campaigns gave Chile possession of the Peruvian territories of Tarapacá and Tacna-Arica, after which Bolivia played no further part in the war. A third Chilean expedi-tionary force, under General Manuel Baquedano (1826–97), was sent to capture Lima, which it did following the bloody battles of Chorrillos and Miraflores (January 1881). If the wars of independence are included, this was the third occasion in the nineteenth century when Chilean soldiers occupied the Peruvian capital. Peruvian guerrilla bands continued the war for two years, but to no avail. Peru finally bowed to the victors' demands in the Treaty of Ancón (October 1883), ceding Tarapacá to Chile in perpetuity and Tacna-Arica for a limited period. (The Tacna-Arica territory became the focus of a lengthy diplomatic wrangle, settled only in 1929.) Bolivia also eventually accepted the cession of Atacama to Chile, and thus became a landlocked nation. The war left bitter feelings of defeat in Peru and Bolivia alike.

The Chaco War, 1932–5

The only major international conflict in twentieth-century Latin America, the Chaco War was a struggle for territory between Bolivia and Paraguay. A number of armed clashes had taken place in the Northern Chaco (an area whose ownership had long been disputed by the two states) prior to the outbreak of war in mid-1932. Although outnumbered by their Bolivian opponents (who were commanded for a time by a German general, Hans Kundt), the Paraguayans, led by the brilliant Colonel José Felix Estigarribia (1888–1940; president of Paraguay 1939–40) – noted for his *corralito* ('encirclement') tactic – succeeded in winning most of the area in contention. International pressure finally brought about a cease-fire (June 1935). Paraguay's victories on the battlefield bore fruit in the eventual peace treaty (July 1938). Some 50,000 Bolivians (the total is sometimes put at 70,000) and some 35,000 Paraguayans died in the Chaco War. Bolivia's loss of territory led to a traumatic soul-searching among the country's elite, especially the officer-corps.

The Ecuador–Peru Conflict, 1941

Peru had long laid claim to large sections of Ecuador's *Oriente* (Amazon territory), much of which had already been transferred by treaty to Brazil and Colombia. In July 1941 Peruvian forces invaded the Ecuadorian coastal province of El Oro, bombing several defenceless villages and speedily capturing the provincial capital. Fighting continued until October 1941. At the western hemisphere foreign ministers' conference at Rio de Janeiro in January 1942 – with the Second World War uppermost in ministers' minds – Ecuador was persuaded to part reluctantly with a large tract of disputed territory. (There were further border clashes in 1981.)

The Football (or Soccer) War, 1969

Honduran actions against the large Salvadorean community established in Honduras (driven there by overcrowding in El Salvador) led in 1969 to much ill-feeling between the two Central American states. These recriminations came to a head when the two national soccer teams were playing each other in qualifying games for the 1970 World Cup. On 14 July 1969 the Salvadorean army launched an attack over the border into Honduras, expecting an easy victory. Fighting lasted for several days, some 2000 men being killed, until proposals from the Organization of American States brought this lightning war to a close.

SC

The non-Latin Caribbean islands since 1815

The peace settlement of 1815 at the end of the Napoleonic Wars was a watershed in the island-juggling game of the European powers. Britain emerged supreme once again in the Caribbean, gaining St Lucia, Tobago, Trinidad, Demerara, Essequibo and Berbice; France retained Martinique and Guadeloupe; and Spain kept Puerto Rico and Cuba. By then, the French had been driven from Hispaniola (Haiti/Dominican Republic) not by European rivals or indigenous tribes, but by the very slaves they had earlier imported. Since 1791, the French-held western part of the island of Hispaniola had passed through the hands of Toussaint Louverture, the triumphant leader of the Haitian revolution, and in 1821, the eastern part of Hispaniola declared its independence from Spain as the Dominican Republic. The struggle against European colonialism had thus begun. The liberation of Spanish and Portuguese colonies in South America and the US Monroe Doctrine of 1823 sounded a warning to the colonial powers.

Colonial rule, slavery and the struggle for independence all overlapped from place to place. There was never a static colonial pattern in the development of the West Indian societies. Many bear the imprint of a succession of European masters. The nationality of the colonial settlements was not the line of most significant divide in the region. Except for the administrative elite, the plantation structure provided the most powerful force in the formation of Caribbean 'creole' societies.

Before emancipation

The economies of the West Indies waxed and waned, but everywhere they were characterized by two common features – monoculture and absentee ownership. Cotton was a principal crop until the early nineteenth century, and tobacco until that century's end. However, the crop which determined the economic value of the region and governed social structure from the mid-seventeenth century was sugar.

Sugar was big business, requiring large inputs of capital for land and machinery, together with vast supplies of labour for harvesting the cane. The plantations, and even entire West Indian territories, became part of a wider international system whose rules were determined elsewhere. Production was geared to the needs of the metropolis and the profits went to the planters, who were often absentee.

The number of African slaves imported into the West Indies corresponded directly to plantation expansion. Their continued arrival from Africa was both cause and consequence of the successes of sugar production. Millions of slaves had been imported into the

THE LESSER ANTILLES

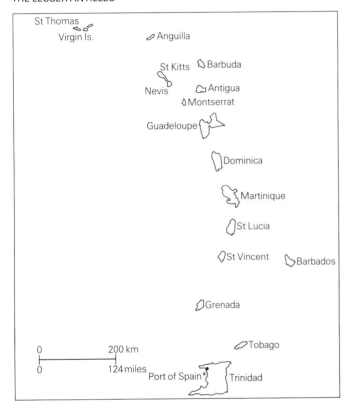

region between the seventeenth and eighteenth centuries and by the end of the eighteenth century, Barbados and Hispaniola had the highest proportion of slaves to free men that the world has ever known. In those territories where sugar production was not dominant until later in the nineteenth century – Trinidad and British Guiana, for example – slave imports were relatively low.

All blacks were not slaves, though the majority certainly were, for manumission was impossible for most. Yet there were groups of runaway slaves (Maroons) and urban slaves, too, were sometimes able to purchase freedom with savings from their craft income. The most significant group of non-white free persons was the coloureds, many of whom, through their part-white parentage, had escaped the ranks of the slaves. Miscegenation between Europeans and Africans, then between Europeans and mulattoes, occurred at first by an illegal, but at all times an informally accepted, pattern of concubinage. Despite miscegenation, however, the brown groups formed a relatively small proportion of most West Indian populations and the early ratios of black to brown and white at the time of emancipation of slaves have been generally maintained to the present day.

After emancipation

The plantation was shaken though not shattered by the emancipation of slaves in the nineteenth century. Emancipation did not occur simultaneously throughout the region: in 1834, slaves in the British colonies were freed, but not until 1848 and 1863 did this happen for French and Dutch slaves respectively. With the acts of emancipation affecting various parts of the Caribbean at different times over half a century, the impact necessarily varied.

After emancipation, the former slaves sought to leave the plantations. Many established themselves as independent cultivators forming the origins of the black West Indian free peasantry. Some left their island altogether, even repeatedly, to take advantage of the new circumstances of the labour market abroad and with the objective that on their return, armed with their saving, they would be independent of planters and all other local employers.

Meanwhile, Caribbean cane sugar was facing stiff competition from European beet sugar. The problems of the planters were greatly exacerbated by their loss of labour, although the illegal importation of new slaves from Africa continued long after the British abolished the trade in 1807. In Trinidad, British Guiana and Surinam, where slaves were no longer available by the time the sugar industry was expanded in the mid-nineteenth century, a labour supply had to be sought elsewhere. India was the principal, though not the sole source of contract labour brought in during the nineteenth century. Portuguese from Madeira went chiefly to British Guiana, Chinese were imported to British Guiana, Trinidad, Martinique, and in even larger numbers to Cuba.

The Asian immigration was significant, not only because of the numbers involved, but also because of its social implications. Only four Caribbean territories – Haiti, the Dominican Republic, Puerto Rico and Barbados – were not included in the new demographic revolution of the nineteenth century. In virtually all other territories, the demographic composition by the end of the nineteenth century comprised a small minority of whites, some mulattoes, a majority of blacks and another segment made up of Indians,

Chinese, Javanese or Portuguese in various combinations and degrees of miscegenation. The only other ethnic groups in the West Indian societal mix were Jews (especially in Jamaica and Curaçao), Syrians, Palestinians and Lebanese. Ethnic antagonisms developed in the late nineteenth century which have been carried on to the present day, particularly between the Indian and black communities in Trinidad (and also in Guyana).

The contemporary era

Later social influences in the West Indies were not principally from Europe, Africa or Asia, but from North America, especially the United States. As with the former colonial influences from Europe, so those from the United States affected the entire Caribbean, though the extent of Americanization has varied from place to place. The strategic and economic significance of the West Indies to the United States was greatly enhanced towards the end of the nineteenth century, when European and US interests focused upon the need to build a canal across the Central American isthmus. It was to be a vital military and economic link between the Atlantic and the Pacific. The United States was quick to grasp the opportunity of seizing Cuba and Puerto Rico in 1898, following the Spanish–American war, and later became heavily involved in the internal affairs of Haiti and the Dominican Republic. The entire region was further brought under US influence by the establishment of military bases at Guantánamo in Cuba and Chaguaramas in Trinidad. Finally, in 1917, to forestall the possibility of Germany

An oil rig at Pointe-à-Pierre, Trinidad

constructing a naval base on the Virgin Island of St John, the United States purchased the island from Denmark, along with St Croix, part of St Martin and St Thomas.

Throughout the early decades of the twentieth century the entire Caribbean region became enveloped by American 'dollar diplomacy'. Sugar interests were consolidated in Cuba, the Dominican Republic and Puerto Rico, and the United Fruit Company expanded to form a vast empire in Central America. A similar pattern developed in oil in Trinidad and bauxite in Jamaica and Guyana, as well as manufacturing and tourism in many territories of the region. Many West Indian lands, and especially those under direct US control, became re-shaped by the process of Americanization.

Caribbean peoples faced problems of identity, which related chiefly to colour and ethnicity, a sense of place and nationality. Modern Caribbean societies have responded to the inherited lack of a meaningful racial identity. *Négritude* as a literary movement emerged in the French island of Martinique in the 1930s in the writings of Aimé Césaire. This movement stemmed chiefly from Cuban literature while the philosophy behind it, glorifying Africa and rejecting Europe, derived from Haitian folklore. Only in Haiti was an African cultural element as fundamental as Voodoo given official support at the expense of European forms. The Black Power movement of the 1970s throughout most of the region was the culmination of the search for an identity through the dramatic transformation of the image of the black man. In Jamaica, the eastern Caribbean and Guyana, the result has been a major reversal of racial attitudes which, contrasting with the former situation, has had the effect of alienating the white, light brown, Indian and Chinese groups in society. Exceptions to this reversal of racial attitudes have been the countries of the Spanish Caribbean – Cuba, Puerto Rico and the Dominican Republic.

The West Indian's sense of uncertain racial identity is compounded by an ambivalence about his belonging to the West Indies. All West Indians are relative newcomers and they have tended to lack many of the deep-rooted emotional ties to their country found among indigenous societies. Even peasantries in the West Indies are not closely attached to the land. The 1910s and 1920s saw the rise of Garveyism which pointed towards Africa as holding the only promise for the black man. Marcus Garvey's call for repatriation to Africa did not meet with an immediate response, but later became the rallying cry for the Rastafari cult. Despite all the difficulties surrounding the question of identity in the West Indies, however, nationalism has continued to grow.

Island loyalties can best be seen in terms of autonomy vis-à-vis the rest of the Caribbean. The failure of the West Indies Federation (1958–62) underscored the lack of a regional sense of identity. Anguilla's stand against constitutional inclusion with St Kitts and

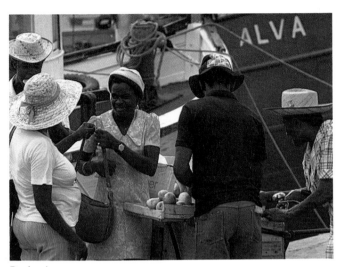

Barbados

Nevis, the cause of a minor crisis in 1969, emanated from the same type of separatist sentiment. Aruba objected to independence proposals from the Netherlands because of fears of being subjected to Curaçao.

Post-emancipation diversifications in West Indian agriculture and the twentieth-century development of industry were generally unaccompanied by any significant structural change. Each new crop or industry has occurred within a framework strikingly reminiscent of the original plantation. Control, and in many cases ownership, have been absentee, production has been primarily geared to export needs and the bulk of the profits have been realized outside the region. Despite many changes in welfare for the workers and national government participation, the islands have remained primary-product producers.

Where industrial development included the manufacture of finished goods, only the local provision of assembly plants and cheap labour have been involved. In some territories, ownership has been localized, as in the case of Guyana's bauxite since the 1960s. In Jamaica, the state increased its ownership of shares in bauxite production to 51 per cent in 1977. Even sugar production has been nationalized in most West Indian territories since the 1960s and 1970s. Despite these changes, however, the main issues for West Indian self-determination relate to economic viability.

Economic growth is frequently, though mistakenly, taken to imply development. It does not imply, nor in the Caribbean does it necessarily include, social development. The bauxite boom years of the 1950s and 1960s in Jamaica were accompanied by a widening of the gap in the distribution of real earnings. Furthermore, unsustained economic growth can coexist with high unemployment rates.

The increasing West Indian populations are inevitably regarded as a problem of over-population in the context of inadequate local resources, accompanied by inadequate re-investment of profits. Between 1960 and 1970 growth rates were approximately 4 per cent throughout the British Commonwealth Caribbean while the population increase was 2 per cent or more. The rate of per-capita growth in the Commonwealth Caribbean, as elsewhere in the region, was therefore limited. In describing 'the problem', many observers have disproportionately blamed the population increases rather than the discrepancies in the growth of different sectors of the economy. Likewise, heavy migration to the towns and cities has been regarded more as a cause than a symptom of national problems. Population increases and the concentration of the poor in the cities merely bring to a head many of the issues inherent in West Indian societies.

Constitutionally the West Indies includes republics, colonies, associated and Commonwealth states, protectorates and departments (in the case of the French possessions). In general, however, independence has been the main political goal since the 1960s. Jamaica and Trinidad and Tobago achieved independence in 1962, and Guyana and Barbados in 1966. Other territories became independent later, such as the Bahamas in 1973 and Grenada in

Michael Manley

1974. Like emancipation, independence is, in a constitutional sense, merely a redefinition of the legal status of the society in relation to the metropolis. Neither brought about an instant metamorphosis of society. Even the earlier example of Haitian independence was a hollow victory in real terms. French colonial masters were replaced by tyrannical mulatto regimes and Haiti's people have never been truly liberated.

West Indian societies have not yet rid themselves of their age-old and recurring sense of defeatism. Virtually every generation has been intimidated by threats of impending doom. This absence of national confidence, so typical throughout the region, reflects the precariousness of West Indian fortunes which have traditionally balanced between the internal struggles of the societies on the one hand, and on the other hand, the economic and political pressures of the world outside. Such constant flirtation with defeat and the destruction of national morale place limitations on the development of national independence. Nevertheless, the internal cleavages inherent in West Indian social structure have not yet been resolved and it is also the case that external pressures stemming from the relationships of dependence exacerbate the internal problems. The reconstruction of the social order and social relations in the West Indies is a necessary accompaniment to the wider national struggle against the conditions of dependence. These are likely to remain the outstanding issues for the future.

EMT-H

Further reading

E. de Kadt, ed., *Patterns of Foreign Influence in the Caribbean* (London, 1974)

F. W. Knight, *The Caribbean: the Genesis of a Fragmented Nationalism* (New York, 1978)

G. K. Lewis, *The Growth of the Modern West Indies* (New York, 1968)

D. Lowenthal, *West Indian Societies* (London, 1972)

S. Mintz, *Caribbean Transformations* (Chicago, 1974)

H. O'Shaughnessy, *Grenada: Revolution, Invasion and Aftermath* (London, 1984)

E. M. Thomas-Hope, ed., *Perspectives on Caribbean Regional Identity* (Liverpool, 1983)

E. Williams, *From Columbus to Castro: the History of the Caribbean, 1492–1969* (London, 1970)

Political changes in the Caribbean

The Commonwealth Caribbean

Jamaica became independent in August 1962. The Jamaica Labour Party (JLP) won the elections of 1962 and 1967, but lost in 1972 to the island's other main political movement, the People's National Party (PNP) under Mr Michael Manley, an eloquent advocate of democratic socialist ideas. The PNP won office again in 1976, but was defeated, in a bitterly-fought election, in 1980, when Mr Edward Seaga (JLP) became prime minister on a platform of private enterprise.

Trinidad and Tobago (administratively associated in 1888) also became independent in August 1962, and a republic within the Commonwealth in 1976. Its political life was shaken in 1970 with 'Black Power' disturbances and the mutiny of part of the army, but the ruling People's National Movement (PNM) was confirmed in power by a handsome majority in 1971. The country's long-serving first prime minister, Dr Eric Williams, a noted historian of the Caribbean, died in 1981. He was succeeded by Mr George Chambers.

Bardados became independent in 1966. The Democratic Labour Party (DLP) was ousted in the elections of 1976 by Mr Tom Adams's Barbados Labour Party (BLP), which was re-elected in 1981.

The Bahamas became independent in 1973 under the Progressive Liberal Party (PLP) and prime minister Mr (later Sir) Lynden Pindling. The PLP was returned to office in the elections of 1977 and 1982.

Grenada became independent in 1974. Its first prime minister, Sir Eric Gairy, leader of the Grenada United Labour Party (GULP), adopted an increasingly authoritarian style, and was overthrown in a revolution (March 1979) by the New Jewel Movement (NJM) – 'Jewel' being an acronym for Joint Endeavour in Welfare, Education and Liberation – under the popular Mr Maurice Bishop. Grenada's radical stance and links with Cuba aroused the hostility of the Reagan administration in the United States. Dissensions within the NJM leadership led to Mr Bishop's murder by hard-liners (October 1983). A few days later a US invasion force (without consulting Grenada's head of state, Queen Elizabeth II) took control of the island. An interim administration under the governor-general, Sir Paul Scoon, led to elections in December 1984 which were won by Herbert Blaize and the New National Party (NNP) coalition.

Dominica became independent, as a republic within the Commonwealth, in 1978. Its first prime minister, Mr Patrick John, was ousted during a political crisis the following year. The elections of 1982 were won by the Dominica Freedom Party (DFP) under Miss Eugenia Charles, who became prime minister.

St Vincent became independent in 1979, its first prime minister being Mr Milton Cato of the St Vincent Labour Party (SVLP). The elections of 1984 brought victory to Mr James Mitchell and his New Democratic Party (NDP).

St Lucia became independent in 1979, prime minister Mr John Compton of the United Workers Party (UWP) then being in office. Later that year the St Lucia Labour Party was elected to power, but Mr Compton and his party returned to government after the elections of 1983.

Antigua became independent in 1981, under the prime ministership of Mr Vere Bird of the Antigua Labour Party (ALP).

St Kitts–Nevis became independent in 1983 under the prime ministership of Dr Kennedy Simmonds (People's Action Movement).

Montserrat remains a self-governing British colony.

Anguilla seceded from St Kitts–Nevis in 1967, and its 'unilateral declaration of independence' in 1969 provoked a slightly comic crisis. It is a British colony administered under the Anguilla Constitution Order (1982).

The British Virgin Islands, the Cayman Islands, and the Turks and Caicos Islands, three small island-groups with very small populations, are British Crown Colonies with varying degrees of internal self-government.

The Netherlands Antilles

Under a Charter issued in 1954 by Queen Juliana, the islands of the so-called 'ABC' group, off Venezuela, Curaçao, Bonaire and Aruba, and the Leeward Islands of St Eustatius, St Martin (Dutch part) and Saba were constituted politically as an autonomous part of the Kingdom of the Netherlands. They have a Governor appointed by the Dutch Crown, and an elected (22-member) legislature, the *Staten*. Full independence for the islands has been mooted, and it is expected that referenda on this subject will be held on all the islands by 1988.

The French Antilles

In 1946 the islands of Martinique, Guadeloupe, St Barthélemy and St Martin (French part) ceased to be colonies and became two Overseas Departments (*Départements d'Outre-Mer*) of the French Republic, enjoying the same status as the Departments of metropolitan France. In addition to sending senators and deputies to the National Assembly in Paris, each of the two Departments – (1) Martinique, (2) Guadeloupe and the other islands – has a locally-elected General Council. Separatist feelings have often been voiced in the French-speaking islands, but have not attracted widespread support.

The US Virgin Islands

The former Danish Caribbean islands of St Thomas, St John and St Croix were sold by Denmark to the United States in 1917 for $25,000,000. They are (and seem likely to remain) a self-governing American colony (technically an Unincorporated Territory subject to the Department of the Interior) with a locally-elected Governor and legislature.

SC

Belize

Though geographically part of Central America, Belize is culturally quite distinctive, as a former British possession, the foundations of which derive from the activities of buccaneers and log-cutters in the early seventeenth century. Britain rejected the claims of both Mexico and Guatemala when they achieved independence from Spain, and in 1871 declared Belize a crown colony. Mexico renounced its claim in 1893 but Guatemala has persisted in its claims, with practically no international support in doing so. Racially, about 10 per cent of the population of Belize is of European stock, 50 per cent creole (of mixed origin), 20 per cent Mayan Indian and 15 per cent Black Caribs. The economy is based on timber products, sugar (the main export), citrus fruits and bananas.

From 1964, the colony exercised self-government through an elected bi-cameral legislature, with the People's United Party (social democrat) and the United Democratic Party (conservative) as the main contenders. The PUP led by George Price has been in power since then, and it was he who led the country to independence in 1981. Guatemala has consistently refused to recognize this, and Britain retains a substantial military force in Belize and off-shore against Guatemalan pretensions. With a population of only 145,000, and an economy dependent on primary products, Belize must remain dependent on Great Britain for some time to come, particularly so long as the uncertainty regarding Guatemala persists. But independence for the infant state, as a separate entity with its own cultural identity, is a matter of profound belief for the majority of its people. In the general elections of December 1984, Manuel Esquivel, leader of the UDP, won a landslide victory over George Price's PUP which had dominated the politics of Belize for more than thirty years. His successor stressed that there would be no dramatic change in his country's policies.

HB

The Guianas

This area, stretching between the Amazon and the Orinoco rivers in northern South America, was once a magnet to European travellers. The Guiana coast was originally discovered by Christopher Columbus on his third voyage to the West Indies. In 1593 Antonio Berrio, governor of Trinidad, sent the first proper description of the region to the king of Spain; Sir Walter Ralegh's famous description was published two years later. During the seventeenth century, the British, Dutch and French made attempts to trade and settle in the Guiana territory, despite clashes with the Spaniards along the coast and in the Orinoco. The common denominators in the Guianas were European imperialism and slavery. Although Spain claimed all the territory, the British, Dutch and French were the first to open it up to commerce. Trading posts and small settlements were established by these nations. Later on European settlers began to concentrate on the production of commercial crops, sugar, cotton, coffee, and cocoa, on plantations worked by slaves brought in from the west coast of Africa. This resulted in a society of masters and slaves and, later, indentured immigrants. Though the population in Guyana and Surinam in particular became ethnically mostly African and Indian, the cultural influence was mainly European – whether British, Dutch or French.

In the early centuries the langour and lushness of tropical life, the romantic vision of a land paved with gold, all meant adventure. The march towards the discovery of its identity and common goals still spell adventure to the complex society of the peoples of the Guianas.

GUYANA

When in 1598 the Dutch began to investigate the 'Wild Coast', as the Guiana territory was called, and to establish trading depots or posts, they relied on the Amerindian tribes, especially the Arawaks, Caribs, Warraus, and Akawaios for the trade goods of annatto, dyewoods and tobacco for which they exchanged their axes, knives,

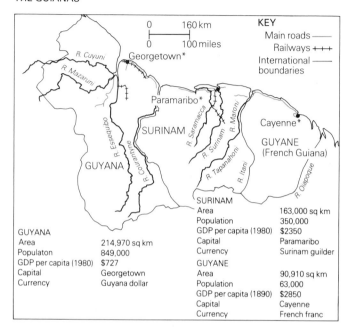

THE GUIANAS

KEY
Main roads ——
Railways +++
International —— boundaries

GUYANA
Area   214,970 sq km
Populaton   849,000
GDP per capita (1980) $727
Capital   Georgetown
Currency   Guyana dollar

SURINAM
Area   163,000 sq km
Population   350,000
GDP per capita (1980) $2350
Capital   Paramaribo
Currency   Surinam guilder

GUYANE
Area   90,910 sq km
Population   63,000
GDP per capita (1890) $2850
Capital   Cayenne
Currency   French franc

cloth, beads, and scissors. Meanwhile the British, Spanish and French were all laying claim to the whole region from the Amazon to the Orinoco. In 1604 the English under Captain Charles Leigh and in 1609 under Robert Harcourt made unsuccessful attempts to settle small colonies. The Dutch finally established a fort, Kyk-over-al (See-over-all) at the junction of the Essequibo, Cuyuni and Mazaruni rivers and at Nova Zeelandia on the Pomeroon. No formal government was set up until 1621, when the Dutch West India Company was formed. By the 1750s sugar cultivation was on the increase. The Dutch hold on Guiana was greatly enhanced by the administration of the director-general of Essequibo and Demerara, Laurens Storm van's Gravesande (1743–72). By 1775 there were over 300 plantations of sugar, coffee, and cotton, worked by over 100,000 slaves. Van's Gravesande introduced the College of Kiezers (Electors) – a body which was not abolished until 1891.

During the 1781 war with Holland the British captured the settlements in Essequibo, Demerara and Berbice. Between 1781 and 1803 the colonies were tossed back and forth between the British, French and Dutch, falling in 1803 to Great Britain. Finally, at the end of the Napoleonic Wars, Demerara, Essequibo and Berbice were ceded by the Netherlands to Great Britain in the Treaty of London (1814) which ratified the Articles of Capitulation of 1803. By the terms of that Capitulation the former rights and privileges of the people, including the Dutch constitution and Roman–Dutch law, were upheld. The legislature consisted of a Court of Policy and a Combined Court – the latter under its

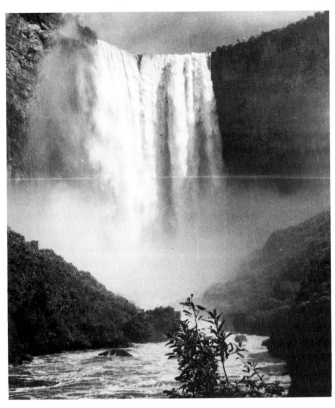

Kaieteur Falls

imperial preference to sugar in the British colonies, severely affected the planters. The 1856 Portuguese riots in which Portuguese property was destroyed by the Africans did not augur well for future race relations. The discovery of gold in the 1860s gave a small boost to the economy, while the 1870 discovery of the Kaieteur Falls by Charles Barrington Brown brought fame. Two significant events marked the last decade of the nineteenth century: the new Constitution of 1891, which did not really oust the plantocracy from politico-economic control, and the border dispute with Venezuela. The 1899 settlement awarded the Orinoco to Venezuela but in the 1960s Venezuela revived her claim to 138,000 sq km. The 1970 Protocol of Port of Spain proclaimed a twelve-year moratorium on this dispute but it has been revived in the aftermath of the Falklands conflict.

In 1917, through pressure from the government of India, East Indian immigration was stopped. The East Indians, numbering almost 127,000, became the rice farmers on the coastal areas and later the businessmen and professionals in the city. Agitation for political reform led to crown colony status in 1928 in which the Court of Policy and Combined Court were replaced by a Legislative

Forbes Burnham

Financial Representatives controlling finance and taxation. This Dutch-style constitution lasted until 1891. In 1831 the three colonies were united as British Guiana. The Dutch town of Stabroek was renamed Georgetown and served as the capital.

The nineteenth century saw the rise and fall of the sugar industry in the colony, though sugar thereafter remained the key factor in its development. The abolition of the slave trade in 1807 and the later abolition of slavery in 1834 in the British colonies ruined many planters. The loss of their labour force of slaves led to the importation of indentured labourers first from Germany, England, Ireland and Malta, as well as Portuguese from Madeira. The largest number, however, came from India. From 1838 to 1917, 340,962 Indian immigrants arrived in British Guiana. From 1853 a number of Chinese also came in. Yet from 1838 to 1846 over 100 plantations had to be sold to satisfy debts. At the end of the apprenticeship system in 1838, freed African slaves bought abandoned estates and established villages. By the end of 1848 over 400 estates had been purchased by ex-slaves. The 1850 Commission noted that 47,000 workers had left the estates, which were being run mainly by the East Indian immigrants, the Portuguese having by now branched out into trade. The Sugar Duties Act of 1846, which withdrew the

Statue of Queen Victoria knocked over during independence celebrations in Guyana

and Executive Council. The franchise was also extended to women. Throughout 1928–36 there were series of strikes on the plantations. The recommendations of the 1939 Royal West Indian Commission were not put into effect until after the Second World War in 1945 when the colony received economic aid under the Colonial Development and Welfare Fund. The 1949 general elections brought the East Indian dentist Dr Cheddi Jagan into the government as spokesman for labour. Later he and his wife formed the People's Progressive Party (PPP) together with Forbes Burnham, a black barrister, as leader. When in 1953 the avowedly Communist PPP won the general elections there were strikes and fear of Communist leanings. Great Britain declared a state of emergency and suspended the Constitution. These events led to a split in the PPP Burnham left the party and later founded the People's National Congress (PNC). Though in 1957 the PPP again won the elections financial problems as well as racial and ideological issues kept the country in a state of unrest. Despite the opposition of Forbes Burnham and Peter D'Aguiar, leaders of the PNC and United Force (UF) respectively, the conference for independence opened in October 1962. The 1963 and 1964 strikes in the city and on the sugar estates crippled the economy and further exacerbated political and racial tensions. In a tense atmosphere general elections were held and won by the PPP with twenty-four seats; the PNC gained twenty-two and the UF seven. A coalition government was formed under the PNC leader Forbes Burnham and under this government independence was granted on 26 May 1966. The new nation took the name Guyana ('Land of Many Waters'). On 23 February 1970 Guyana was proclaimed a Co-operative Republic within the Commonwealth. That year also marked the opening of the new University of Guyana (established since 1963) which now offers degrees in arts, social

sciences, natural sciences, education, and technology and agriculture.

The 1980s opened depressingly. Prices for and productivity of sugar, rice and bauxite had fallen while oil prices rose. There was a sharp decline in living standards while thousands of Guyanese emigrated to the United States, Great Britain and Canada. The government has been heavily financed by massive loans from the IMF and the World Bank for hydroelectric and irrigation projects. In the general elections in December 1980 the PNC gained forty-one out of the fifty-three seats in the National Assembly, claiming 'an overwhelming mandate'. Under the new Constitution Prime Minister Burnham was inaugurated president with greatly increased powers. The society is split by political and racial tensions, aggravated by violence. In 1982 exports in the major industries of bauxite, rice and sugar fell by 33 per cent, 14 per cent and 50 per cent respectively causing severe depletion in foreign currency reserves. Shortages of basic food items, raw materials and drugs among other items have truncated health, education, and social services. Despite government action, the parallel economy of the huckster trade functions as the vital supply channel. There is strong government control of the media together with increasing violation of human rights.

SURINAM

The history of Surinam, Guyana's neighbour to the east, was one of early trade, settlement and establishment of plantations, influenced by European rivalries in the seventeenth and eighteenth centuries. In the early seventeenth century several attempts were made to colonize the territory. In 1650 a more permanent settlement was made when Lord Willoughby took possession of the area which is now Surinam, and claimed it for England. Willoughby brought in British and French colonizers as well as African slaves, making Surinam a plantation colony. Between 1651 and 1667 about 500 plantations were established under the British. In 1664 wealthy Portuguese Jews fleeing the Inquisition came to Surinam after being unsuccessful in Brazil and Cayenne. The 1665 war which broke out between the Netherlands and England had the usual repercussions in the colonies. In 1667 Abraham Crijnssen with a Zealand fleet captured Surinam. At the Treaty of Breda which marked the end of the Second Dutch War in 1667 England exchanged Surinam for New Amsterdam (New York). However, claiming ignorance of the treaty, an English fleet recaptured the country and sent Crijnssen to Barbados as a prisoner of war. Later in May 1668 Crijnssen was returned to Surinam. With the exception of two British interregnums (1795–1802 and 1804–16), Surinam remained a Dutch possession until independence in 1975. Like their counterparts in Guyana, the Dutch maintained friendly relations with the Arawak and Carib-speaking Amerindians who lived along the rivers and in the hinterland. Many of these Amerindians today live in Christianized villages while others uphold their traditional customs in their jungle habitat.

Throughout the eighteenth and nineteenth centuries Surinam was a typical plantation colony with its two classes: planters and slaves/manual labourers. The plantation economy depended on sugar and slave labour. Imports of slaves into Surinam had been the monopoly of the Dutch West India Company, along with the city of Amsterdam, which supplied over 2500 slaves annually. Although the slave trade was abolished in Dutch territories in 1814, over 1000 slaves were still brought in clandestinely to Surinam every year. These slaves worked the sugar, cotton, and coffee plantations and greatly outnumbered the white population in a 1:25 ratio. The colonists, paralysed by fear of this numerical superiority, were especially cruel. Slaves retaliated by not only murdering their masters but running away into the deep jungle surrounding the plantations. These fugitives, known as Bush Negroes or Maroons, remained a threatening force on the edges of the plantations. In 1770 the number of Bush Negroes was estimated to be between 5000 and 6000. Today, this is the largest of Bush Negro populations (six tribes numbering 39,500), now called Bushland Negroes. They play an important role in Surinam's lumber industry yet, like the indigenous Amerindians, live mostly in the interior and exist on hunting, fishing and shifting agriculture.

The causes for the decline of the plantation system in Surinam in the nineteenth century were somewhat similar to those in other plantation regions: abolition of slavery and the development of beet sugar in Europe and the United States, and cotton in the United States. After the abolition of slavery in the Dutch colonies in 1863, when it became obvious that liberated slaves would not remain on the plantations, over 5400 labourers – Portuguese, Javanese, and West Indians, mostly from Barbados – were brought into the colony. Others were imported from China and Hong Kong until 1870 when their emigration was prohibited by the Chinese government. This restriction led to the Dutch concluding a treaty with the British entitling them to recruit labourers from India. The first batch of 'East Indians' arrived from Calcutta in 1873. Between 1873 and 1916 more than 34,000 East Indian immigrants came to Surinam. Immigration ended in 1918, when Great Britain prohibited indentured labour in all its territories and terminated the immigration contract with the Netherlands. The Moslems and Hindus later became independent farmers, educated their children in the Netherlands and became the professional class of teachers, doctors, and lawyers. With the stoppage of East Indian immigration, labourers were recruited from Java. Between 1891 and 1939 over 32,000 Javanese entered Surinam and now form 15 per cent of the population.

After 1800 the government changed its form several times.

Between 1828 and 1845 Surinam shared a Governor-general with the Netherlands Antilles. The European revolutions of 1848 influenced the adoption of more liberal policies and caused more attention to be given to the colonies and native populations. In 1865 the government was administered by a *Koloniale Staten* (Colonial Assembly) of thirteen members, nine elected and four nominated by the governor from among the planters and merchants. In 1876, as in British Guiana, compulsory education for children from seven to twelve was introduced. The 1886 *Koloniale Staten* allowed an increase of elected members from the high-income, educated group. The policy of the *Koloniale Staten* was to establish Surinam as an overseas province similar to the Netherlands in language, culture and religion.

At the turn of the century there was an increasing political awareness among a rising middle class of creoles and Hindustanis. The 1922 Netherlands Constitution Act changed Surinam from a colony to an integrated territory of the Kingdom of the Netherlands. The *Koloniale Staten* became the *Staten van Suriname*. Yet political discontent increased, especially during the Second World War when connections between Surinam and the Netherlands were temporarily suspended. Insistent political demands won universal suffrage in 1949. In 1950 Surinam attained internal autonomy with a governor-appointee and representative of the Queen, a ministerial council, an advisory council and a legislative branch – the *Staten*. On 29 December 1954 Surinam gained an equal partnership in the Tripartite Kingdom of the Netherlands.

With universal suffrage in 1949 racially-orientated political parties mushroomed. The Indians, both Moslem and Hindu, formed one party; the Indonesians, mostly Moslems, formed two others. The National Party of Surinam (NPS) composed mainly of creoles, became the leading party. Its charismatic leader, Johan Pengel, dominated the country's politics from 1958 until his fall in 1969. Though the Hindustani party won the 1969 elections, the president, Jules Sedney, was chosen from the creole NPS as the Hindustanis did not want to emphasize the victory of the Hindu community. The government tried to build up a strong national consciousness over and above racial and ethnic groups. Yet, after Surinam gained independence on 25 November 1975, many Surinamese emigrated to the Netherlands fearing racial upheavals.

Prior to 1937 Surinam was a relatively poor country but after the Second World War the expansion of the bauxite industry boosted the economy. Its main revenue is derived from bauxite and lumber which are exported mainly to the United States and the Netherlands. Its affiliation with the EEC through membership in the Kingdom of the Netherlands brought with it millions of dollars in Development Fund grants. Surinam is also backed financially by loans and grants from the Netherlands. Surinam maintains few economic relations with its neighbours, Guyana, Guyane and the

Caribbean territories. In the late 1960s relations with Guyana cooled off over a 9600 sq km border dispute regarding the New River triangle in the south-east of the country. However, in May 1970 the two governments agreed 'to discuss the matter in a civilized manner'. There is also a border dispute pending with Guyane.

On 25 February 1980, stimulated by military rather than political grievances, army sergeants seized power from Henck Arron, prime minister since 1977, in a military coup. In December 1982 Commander Desi Bouterse crushed an alleged plot to depose the military government during which period fifteen prominent Surinamese were executed at the military barracks. This resulted in the suspension of $1.5 billion economic assistance by the Dutch government. The present military-backed government under the prime minister-ship of the Dutch-trained sociologist, Errol Alibux, is working to bring about a return of stability and full normalcy to the country. A $50 million loan from the Inter-American Development Bank is helping to finance agricultural development projects.

GUYANE

Bounded on the east by Brazil and on the south and west by Surinam, Guyane – 'the Cinderella of the French colonial empire' – is the largest of France's overseas departments. Several off-shore islands form part of the colony. Among them, Devil's Island, for years a notorious penal settlement, once gave French Guiana a sinister reputation.

Like the other European nations the French were drawn towards the mythical 'El Dorado'. In 1568 Gaspar de Sostelle with 126 families from Spain attempted a settlement but was driven out by the Indian tribes. Laurence Keymis settled in a bay he called Port Howard in 1596 but the settlement was short-lived. In 1604 under Daniel de la Ravardière the French settled on the river where the capital, Cayenne, now stands. Throughout the seventeenth century there were abortive attempts at settlement by the French and the Dutch. These attempts had to be abandoned mainly because of the unfriendliness of the Indians. In 1626 the French erected and garrisoned a fort for protection, the remains of which the Dutch found in 1634. Later in the century the Dutch gave permission to David Nassy and other Jews to settle in Cayenne and provide slaves for the Guiana coast. The 1660s saw the return of the French – this time making peace with the Indians. During the Second Dutch War of 1665 the French colony and Sinamary were sacked. In 1667 the fort surrendered to the English who ravaged the country. The French complained against the attack and capture of Cayenne as contrary to the 1667 Peace Treaty. It was again recaptured from the Dutch for France in 1676.

Throughout the eighteenth and nineteenth centuries French attempts to colonize Cayenne proved fruitless and costly. Not only were bad management and an unrealistic approach to conditions responsible for failure but the political refugees who were deported there proved unwilling and unable to cope with the labour situation. Ten thousand out of an estimated 14,000 immigrants died of typhus. In 1794 after the National Convention abolished slavery, freed slaves fled to the hinterland refusing to work on the plantations. In 1808 Cayenne became an Anglo-Portuguese possession for eight years until, by the Treaty of Paris (1816), it became part of the now very small French colonial empire. During the 1820s a flourishing colony was founded at Mana by Mother Ann Marie Javouhay, Superior of the Sisters of St Joseph Cluny, for the freed slaves who had earlier left the plantations. When in 1848 slavery was irrevocably abolished, Cayenne faced severe financial crises. As in British and Dutch Guiana, immigrants were introduced from Asia to fill the labour gap. The discovery of gold in the 1850s brought an influx of immigrants but also lured labour away from agriculture and crippled development. The gold boom was, unfortunately, a brief interlude.

The 1848 decree had also brought the French Guianese full French citizenship and the right to vote. After 1854 Cayenne was governed by a senate decree of Napoleon III and in 1875 all French colonies became French departments with later representation in the French Assembly. A Minister for the Colonies took over the responsibility for the colonies in 1894. The economy, education and culture were modelled on French lines, for French policy was to turn all colonials into Frenchmen. In 1930 the country was divided into two – Guyane and the territory of Inini (the hinterland). Since 1946, Guyane, thoroughly Gallicized, has been an overseas department of France. There was a brief post-Second World War move for local autonomy. The Socialist Party under Justin Catayie urged autonomy in 1960 but was defeated in the 1961 elections.

There have been many attempts to increase the population (only 55,000) and thus fully colonize Guyane. A 1950 project to form a settlement of 'displaced persons' did not succeed – only 150 to 200 people of Czech, Polish and Hungarian origin remain. Another group-colonization scheme in 1961 failed through lack of discipline and finance.

With 90 per cent of impenetrable forest and poor navigability of rivers, commercial exploitation of Guyane's timber is difficult. However, the remoteness of its location has made it an admirable choice for a new French missile research centre. Integration of the economy with the EEC has given the country a much-needed boost.

MNM

Further reading

R. A. Glasgow, *Guyana. Race and Politics among Africans and East Indians* (The Hague, 1970)

G. K. Lewis, *The Growth of the Modern West Indies* (London, 1968)

R. A. van Lier, *Frontier Society: a Social Analysis of the History of Surinam*, 2nd edition (The Hague, 1971)

POLITICS AND SOCIETY

A political rally of the Popular Unity movement in Chile, 1972

Political traditions of Latin America

The colonial experience has been and still remains the most important single factor in the political tradition of Latin America. With the consolidation of the Spanish and Portuguese colonial empires between 1500 and 1650, it gave a degree of unity to the area unknown in any other part of the world, reinforced by the proselytization of the Catholic Church and (apart from Brazil and Haiti) the dissemination of the Spanish language. The colonies were regarded as co-equal kingdoms, owing direct allegiance to one overlord, the king of Spain, who administered them directly through the Council of the Indies at Seville, through peninsular-born officials, circumscribed in their powers by an elaborated code of law and practice, and subject to the institution of the *residencia* – a final evaluation of their administration – as a check on their activities while in office.

The traditions of this administrative structure were reinforced by its duration. The removal of Spanish royal authority at a stroke, by the forced abdication of Charles IV at Bayonne (1808) removed the keystone. But the empire fell apart only slowly, as conservatives sought to retain their position and privilege, professing their loyalty to his successor, Ferdinand. They distrusted above all the new nationalistic movement of the 'Liberales' in Spain, who with their new conception of the unity of the state drawn from the writers of the Enlightenment and the experience of the French Revolution, offered the colonies in a sense an inferior status to that to which they had hitherto been accustomed.

Liberalism moreover was associated with anti-clericalism and republicanism. By the early 1820s many conservatives were prepared to accept a republic as the alternative to Liberal interference from Spain, but they fought long and hard against any attempt to erode the traditional rights of the Church. Once independence was achieved, struggles between Conservatives and Liberals became the dominant feature of political life throughout the Spanish-speaking countries and, even in Brazil, where the retention of the monarchy until 1889 prevented its dissolution, Liberals came to be identified with the cause of provincial autonomy, and Conservatives with the goal of a strong state under centralized military–bureaucratic control. In former Spanish America, republican regimes became universal for the lack of possible monarchical candidates, and the mystique of Napoleon lent further support to the emergence of military generalship as the main qualification for political power. Hence, the first fifty years of independence are associated above all with the institutionalization of the military *caudillo*.

Caudillismo – the domination of politics by the caudillo – was thus a creole response to the crisis of decolonization. Being essentially personalist, its impact depended closely on the personalities involved. Simón Bolívar (1783–1830), liberator of Venezuela, Colombia, Ecuador, Peru and Bolivia, was asked to provide a constitution for Bolivia, named in his honour, and sought by his invention of the Areopagus, or board of censors, to reinstate that moral power of supervision which had inadvertently been swept away with the monarchy. His dilemma was that he would not use force to compel his people to be free. Dr José Gaspar Rodríguez de Francia (1766–1840) of Paraguay, an admirer of Benjamin Franklin's practicality, sealed off his country from the outside world to preserve its Rousseauesque, paternalistic society. But this was a solution hardly possible to the coastal South American states, and not at all in Central America, where José Cecilio del Valle (1776–1834) died while the votes electing him to the presidency were still uncounted, his plans for his people, discussed in correspondence with Jeremy Bentham, still unrealized. Bentham's belief in 'the greatest good for the greatest number' and his theories of law had a considerable influence on legal codes in Latin America even in the most dictatorial states, and the prison in Caracas is still called the Panóptico, his 'panopticon'.

Most caudillos, however, were military men who had little time for political ideas, and who owed their power to their constant vigilance, such as the ruler of the Argentine Confederation, Juan Manuel de Rosas (1793–1877). Rosas was the real target of Domingo Faustino Sarmiento's *Facundo* (1845), ostensibly a critique of a lesser caudillo of the interior. Sarmiento's contemporary, Juan Bautista Alberdi (1810–84) argued in 1852 that the true ends of government were to populate the national territory. Sarmiento (1811–88) wanted its population to be educated. Ironically, Rosas, who opposed formal unification, was by reaction the creator of the united Argentina of which Sarmiento was to serve as president (1868–74), under the US-influenced Constitution of 1853.

Argentina was distinctive in achieving constitutional shape so late; elsewhere the pattern was one of faction constitutionalism, under which constitutions were rewritten, suspended or simply ignored to suit the convenience of the group currently in power. New constitutions were written to legitimate seizures of power by force, or even the prolongation of a presidential term without resorting to election. Venezuela, the first state to write a constitution (1811), has since had more than twenty. It was assumed throughout the nineteenth century that this was a passing phenomenon that would vanish with 'maturity'. To some extent the establishment of the 'Conservative Republic' in Chile with the Constitution of 1833 and its peaceful political life for over fifty years seemed to confirm this assumption. Only in the 1870s was it realized in Peru by the *civilistas* that Latin American coups and dictatorships were integrally related to the root phenomenon of militarism. While still retaining the constitutional devices to restrain military ambition which had proved persistently useless in the past, they broke new ground in setting up a military academy to professionalize and so tame the military. This proved only a partial success. As time was to prove, an educated officer corps was more skilful in seizing, if not using, political power.

By 1857, the year of the Reforma in Mexico, in which the Church lands were confiscated and its privileges demolished, the first impetus of Liberalism was waning. It was soon to be reinforced by the doctrine of positivism originated in France by Auguste Comte, and introduced into Mexican education by Justo Sierra (1848–1912). Positivism, with its theory of stages of human development and in its belief in the certainty of the scientific understanding of society, was, shorn of its mystical origins and reinforced by the prevailing social Darwinism of Herbert Spencer, a strong justification of elite rule. As such it became the official doctrine of the Mexico of the Porfiriato (1876–1911) and, under the influence of Benjamin Constant Botelho de Magelhães (1830–91), found favour among the military leaders who created the Republic in Brazil in 1889 and placed Comte's slogan 'order and progress' on the national flag. Both native vigour and the inevitability of successful struggle was further implanted by Euclides da Cunha (1866–1909) in his quasi-novel of the 'inland sea', *Os Sertões* (1902). In Argentina, Agustín Alvarez (1857–1914) argued more explicitly that the examples of Brazil and Chile showed that stability lay in the forms of the past, and specifically in despotism. In Colombia, where a chair of sociology was established at the University of Bogotá as early as 1862, the Spencerian Rafael Núñez (1823–94), after a brief radical phase, became an evolutionary Conservative. And in Venezuela, after the dictatorship of Antonio Guzmán Blanco (1829–99) had given way to that of less enlightened successors, Laureano Vallenilla Lanz (1870–1936) in his *Cesarismo Democrático* (1919) not only provided an apt label for the system, but sought to defend it in a way that met the enthusiastic approval of Mussolini.

The year before, 1918, the 'University reform movement' which began at Córdoba, Argentina, disseminated a new impetus for revolt against despotism throughout the continent. Socialism, in its Saint-Simonian form, had been professed by Alberdi, but not until the last quarter of the nineteenth century did socialist writers find much favour in Latin America. Workers' movements were lacking on which to build, before the growth of the great railway, meat-packing and mining interests in Argentina, Uruguay, Chile, Peru and Mexico. The great organizing ideology for labour prior to 1914 was anarchism, also imported from Europe. Organized unionism was often met with armed intervention, as at Cananea in Mexico in 1906 and in Chile with the strike of 1907 in Iquique. In Mexico, where the reassertion of democratic rights by Francisco I. Madero (1877–

1913) brought the onset of the revolution (1910), the Casa del Obrero Mundial was permitted to organize in 1913, and workers, formed by Alvaro Obregón (1880–1928) into the so-called 'Red Battalions', found their spokesmen and won recognition of labour's position in the Constitution of 1917. As Obregón's Secretary of Education, José Vasconcelos (1871–1959) organized Latin America's first attempt at a mass literacy drive and gave state patronage to the arts a new social meaning. Under the presidency of Lázaro Cárdenas (1895–1970), the revolution was consolidated by the assimilation of workers' organizations to the ruling socialist National Revolutionary Party (PNR) and the mass distribution of land, to appease peasant demands for restitution of land, associated with the leadership of the guerrilla leader Emiliano Zapata (1879–1919), grew further in the 1920s.

Chilean Congress under Popular Unity. The painting on the wall shows a nineteenth-century parliament

Indigenismo, the revaluation of the Indian as opposed to the Hispanic contribution to Latin American life, had already had a cultural impact in Mexico and Peru in the 1890s. In part, it was a response to the prevailing dogmas of 'scientific racism' which denigrated all non-whites. In Mexico the young Peruvian student organizer Víctor Raúl Haya de la Torre (1895–1979), influenced by the *indigenista* values expressed in Vasconcelos's *La raza cósmica* (1925), sought to unify the continent on a programme of Indian values by the foundation of the American Popular Revolutionary Alliance (APRA). APRA, implanted in Peru after 1930, dominated Peruvian politics for a generation, though consistently denied the chance to take power by the army. The Marxist, José Carlos Mariátegui (1895–1930), author of the widely read *Siete ensayos de la realidad peruana*, founded in 1928 Peru's first Socialist Party. The views he expressed on the necessity for fundamental change, which in their *indigenista* influence departed noticeably from Marxist tradition, were rediscovered in the 1960s and found expression in the military-guided revolution of 1968 under General Juan Velasco Alvarado which nationalized heavy industries and expropriated the great coastal landholdings. In neighbouring Bolivia, the disaster of the Chaco War had forced a reappraisal earlier, and Bolivia had nationalized its oil (1937) before the revolution of 1952 brought land redistribution and nationalization of the tin mines. Establishing Quechua as an official language in each country in the 1970s was a symbolic step of great importance in practical terms to the millions otherwise pushed outside the national political culture.

Elsewhere, the main influence on the growth of left-wing ideas in this period was the impact of the Great Depression. Chile, after a period of disorder (including a short-lived 'Socialist Republic' in 1931 under colonel Marmaduque Grove and Carlos Dávila), evolved a 'Popular Front' government on European lines. But the usual outcome, as in Argentina, was a military seizure of power and a series of 'apolitical' rulers suppressing civil liberties for fear of left-wing influence. In El Salvador, Alberto Masferrer (1868–1932) had spoken of a peaceful road to socialism, but when a peasant rising occurred in 1932 thousands were shot down. The influence of the Atlantic Charter and allied wartime propaganda was to topple military governments all over Latin America in 1943–5, but, in the climate of the Cold War, even the 'spiritual socialism' of the Guatemalan Juan José Arévalo (president 1945–51) was suspect, and his successor, Jacobo Arbenz, was overthrown in 1954 trying to carry out a measure of land reform which met with the disapproval of the then government of the United States.

As early as 1900 *anti-yanquismo*, or hostility to the supposedly 'materialist' values represented by the United States, had received eloquent expression from the Uruguayan José Enrique Rodó (1872–1917). In his *Ariel*, Rodó, a positivist, reasserted the idealism which he considered the United States had lost, and which he believed

Che
Guevara

Latin America was destined to preserve. As United States power grew, some, like Vasconcelos, took refuge in traditional Hispanism. Alcides Arguedas (1870–1946) pessimistically argued that the Bolivians were a *pueblo enfermo*, a hopelessly sick people, incapable of development. While he was doing so, however, German military instructors were already implanting the ideas of fascism in his country, and the Chaco War was in part the result of military belief in their mission. Chile remained doubtful about the allied cause in the Second World War, and in Argentina, which remained aloof till 1945, Juan Domingo Perón (1895–1974) was after 1945 to use the inheritance of fascism in the service of a new populistic nationalism which was strongly anti-United States.

On the other hand, a young Argentine, Ernesto 'Che' Guevara (1928–67), who had visited Bolivia after the revolution of 1952, was radicalized by his experiences there and in Guatemala in 1954 into joining a group of Cuban exiles led by Fidel Castro Ruz (b. 1926) in an expedition to overthrow Cuba's dictator, President Fulgencio Batista. The traditional ascendancy which the United States had held in Cuba since sponsoring its independence made this movement increasingly anti-United States, and the Cuban revolution of 1959 took a Marxist–Leninist course in 1961 because it occurred just late enough to be able for the first time in forty years to call for help to a power outside the Americas, the Soviet Union.

Thus, the Cuban revolution, which at first drew its prime strength from the liberal independence tradition of the poet-revolutionary, José Martí (1835–95), changed traditional Latin American political assumptions. But its recipe for the capture of political power, advocated by Guevara himself in his book *La Guerra de Guerrillas* (1961), turned out to be impractical in most parts of the continent. Guevara himself was killed in Bolivia in 1967 in an unsuccessful attempt 'to make the Andes the Sierra Maestra of South America'. Worse still, fear of communism touched off a new round of reactionary coups. When the left turned to urban terrorism as an alternative, advocated by Carlos Marighela in Brazil and by the Tupamaros of Uruguay, military leaders followed the example of those in Brazil in 1964, of entrenching themselves in power for as long as seemed necessary to them to suppress dissent and work out a conservative counter-revolution. It seemed for a decade that even the gains of nineteenth-century liberalism might be wiped out in the process. In Chile, in 1973, President Salvador Allende, a Marxist socialist who had been freely elected in 1970, was overthrown by the armed forces, who refused to restore democracy and instituted repression on a massive scale. Another coup (the sixth there since 1930) brought military rule to Argentina in 1976. Uruguay, too, succumbed to military intervention, aided by Brazil. In all these countries the military justified their rule by invoking 'national security', a doctrine largely borrowed from US strategic thinking but which the Latin American officers applied to domestic politics. But in 1979 the return of the Andean countries to democracy was followed by an indigenous socialist revolution spearheaded by the Sandinistas in Nicaragua, and by a free election in Argentina in 1983, and it seemed to some as if Latin America might at last find some sort of reasonable course between militarism and revolutionism.

The enormous enthusiasm that greeted the Papal visits of Paul VI and John Paul II demonstrated that the Catholicism implanted by Spaniard and Portuguese alike still commanded an intense allegiance, which has enabled Christian Democratic parties to survive despite heavy pressure from both extremes. Democracy remains a vigorous ideal, notably in Costa Rica and Venezuela. The 1970s, under the influence of Vatican II, have seen Church leaders throughout the continent assuming the role of honest critics of authoritarianism, as in Chile after 1973, Brazil after 1964, and (to some extent) Argentina after 1976, and calling, often with success, for the restoration of basic human rights. Latin American thinkers, too, have been strong in the struggle for effective international law and organizations. Though the history of the Latin American political tradition shows so many examples of extreme partisanship, compounded by the frustration engendered by military intervention, the democratic spirit of independence against all comers has shown great resilience in the past and may be expected to do so in the future.

PARC

Further reading

R. J. Alexander, ed. and trans., *Aprismo: the Ideas and Doctrines of Víctor Raúl Haya de la Torre* (Kent State, 1973)
H. E. Davis, *Latin American Thought: a Historical Introduction* (New York, 1974)
C. Hale, *Mexican Liberalism in the Age of Mora 1821–1853* (New Haven, Conn., 1968)
J. L. Romero, *A History of Argentine Political Thought*, intro. and tr. T. F. McGann (Stanford, 1963)
A. Stepan, *The State and Society: Peru in Comparative Perspective* (Princeton, NJ., 1978)
C. Véliz, *The Centralist Tradition of Latin America* (Princeton, NJ., 1980)
L. Zea, *Latin America and the World* (Norman, Okla., 1969)

Caudillismo, coronelismo and caciquismo

Caudillo, caudillismo; coronel, coronelismo; cacique, caciquismo – these terms have had constant use in discussions of Latin American politics. What do they mean?

The term *cacique* derives from the Taino–Arawak word for chief, encountered by Columbus in Hispaniola on his first voyage. It is used throughout the Hispanic world for those who exercise local predominance. The Brazilian equivalent is *coronel*, colonel, which derives from the nineteenth-century militia ranks that in Brazil such men often enjoyed. *Cacique* is normally, though not always, used in a pejorative sense, implying one who perverts public institutions for private ends, abuses power and patronage to favour exclusively and excessively his own clientele, manipulates placemen in public office, interferes with justice and policing, controls elections through fraud, etc.

There are many descriptions of caciques in the *costumbrista* literature of the nineteenth century, most of which reflect a superior urban attitude to rural affairs, and a large number of peninsular Spanish works denouncing the phenomenon from the late nineteenth and early twentieth century. The best-known of these is Joaquín Costa's *Oligarquía y caciquismo como la forma actual de gobierno en España: urgencia y modo de cambiarla*, (Madrid, 1902). Detailed accounts of Latin American *caciquismo* begin with Victor Nunes Leal, *Coronelismo, enxada e voto* (Rio de Janeiro, 1948;

English translation, *Coronelismo: The Municipality and Representative Government in Brazil*, Cambridge, 1977). This is a fine historical–legal study that remains of fundamental importance. Nunes Leal conceived of *coronelismo* as the results 'of the superimposition of structural forms, evolved through the representative process, on an inadequate social and economic structure', and explored in detail the compromises between state and local power, the influence of fiscal scarcity, the organization of the police and judiciary and the role of elections in the system. Subsequent studies by historians and anthropologists of other parts of Latin America and the Mediterranean world as well as of Brazil have further explored the varieties and the evolution of *caciquismo* further. These investigations have abandoned denunciation in the style of Joaquín Costa, and have shown the underlying rationality of much of what occurs.

The power of the local cacique or coronel has diverse origins and will vary greatly from region to region. It should be noted that it is frequently false to assume that local power is exercised by landowners, either directly or through dependents, or that *caciquismo* rests either solely or predominantly on force and fraud. The role of local power-brokers has nowhere been rapidly reduced or extinguished by the exertions of central government or by the growth of modern national parties.

In Argentina the term *cacique* is usually confined to the chiefs of surviving indigenous groups, and the dominant local figure who controls votes is denoted a *caudillo*. Elsewhere in much of Spanish America the term *cacique* is also still used (with no pejorative connotation) for the indigenous chief.

The word *caudillo* simply means chief, or leader. Some historians have, however, sought to give the term a more particularly Spanish American definition, and one that applies specifically to the rulers of the decades immediately after independence: 'Caudillism may be defined as the union of personalism and violence for the conquest of power,' writes the American scholar Robert L. Gilmore. It is a means for the selection and establishment of political leadership in the absence of a social structure and political groupings adequate to the functioning of representative government. The practice and technique of caudillism, developed during the wars for independence, were based on those of the colonial oligarchies as modified by the regressive effects of irregular civil conflict. The 'typical caudillo' is depicted as dictatorial, as basing his power on personal control of informal military force, he himself and his followers being of rural origin. The term *caudillo*, while not necessarily derogatory, carries with it an aura of semi-barbarity that derives from the Argentine Domingo Faustino Sarmiento's celebrated polemic *Facundo* (1845), a work that has found many imitators, conscious and unconscious. A more carefully argued case for the persistence of a certain type of personal rule, based on tacit popular consent, is the Venezuelan Laureano Vallenilla Lanz's *Cesarismo Democrático* (1928). Vallenilla Lanz's title – 'democratic caesarism' – illustrates his key concept.

The historian and political scientist must conclude that the term is not a precise one, and both should take it with a pinch of salt and use it with caution. On closer examination the 'typical caudillos' do not share many characteristics. Juan Manuel de Rosas (Argentina), José Antonio Páez (Venezuela) and Antonio López de Santa Anna (Mexico) are all designated caudillos, but differed substantially in the origins and in the exercise of their power. Rosas's power-base was never exclusively rural, and in contemporary memoirs it was his subordinate clients of the interior, lesser men whose ambitions were essentially limited to their provinces, who were usually referred to as caudillos. (It is significant that in Argentina the term comes to be used to designate those who control votes at the provincial or municipal level – not such grand figures.) Like Rosas, Páez had been a horseman in his youth, though more warlike and of much humbler extraction; nevertheless, his ascendancy in Venezuela soon came to have more urban and institutional bases, and the backing of the *llaneros* of the central plains was supplanted by more conventional political skills. Santa Anna's intermittent power was not based on the control of any part of rural Mexico, but on his role as aribiter between factions, regions and institutions that included a sizeable regular army.

Recent historiography has begun to explore the political systems of post-independence Latin America in greater depth and detail. The results show a wide variety of political systems that reflect the region's varied social structure and the different circumstances of independence. Certain republics fail to produce figures that can be easily fitted into the caudillo mould: Chile, with its predominantly civilian politics, or Colombia, where frequent civil wars produced aspirants to the caudillo role but none for long successful against the civilian hegemony. The occasional references to such men as Diego Portales (Chile) or Rafael Nuñez (Colombia) as 'civilian caudillos' may be a measure of their ascendancy, but do not analyse or explain that ascendancy.

The term has survived the post-independence years not only in the more humble Argentine use (see above) but also as a convenient (often journalistic) label for any politician of stature, national or local. The most prominent twentieth-century figure in the Hispanic world who bore the title formally was not a Latin American at all, but Francisco Franco, who was, as Spanish coins minted in his long ascendancy remind us, 'by the Grace of God Caudillo of Spain'.

MD

Further reading

T. Halperín Donghi, *The Aftermath of Independence in Latin America* (New York, 1973)

R. L. Gilmore, *Caudillism and Militarism in Venezuela 1810–1910* (Athens, Ohio, 1964)

H. Hamill, Jr, ed., *Dictatorship in Spanish America* (New York, 1965)

R. Kern, ed., *The Caciques* (Albuquerque, NM, 1973)

The military in politics

In many Latin American countries the military has come to see itself as a natural ruling class. Nevertheless – as of the early 1980s – there are considerable variations between countries and six identifiable patterns of military behaviour in the area. In Brazil and Uruguay (the first pattern) there is still a military–civilian coalition with the military as the dominant partner in control of the presidency. In Bolivia and Argentina (the second pattern) the military is entrenched but military government, when it occurs, is highly unstable; the Argentine military in 1966 and 1976 attempted to move towards a more Brazilian pattern but did not succeed on either occasion. In Bolivia, where military intervention has been frequent since 1964, such a pattern has proved impossible to maintain in practice. The third pattern, which exists in Chile, Panama and Paraguay (and formerly in Nicaragua) is entrenched personalist rule by a military dictator; much depends on the personality of the dictator, but this pattern can be quite stable (as it proved in Franco's Spain) for as long as the dictator remains alive; succession problems are then likely. The fourth pattern (Peru and Ecuador) is one of alternating military and civilian government; coups give way to elections which themselves give way to coups. Until quite recently, this pattern was the usual one in Latin America but it has lately given way in several countries to long-term military rule. Fifth, there is in much of Central America a weaker form of the same pattern but here there are no genuine elections and military rule is based much less on the military institution and much more on personalism and simple gangsterism involving 'death squads' and the like. Finally, there are a number of countries (Mexico, Venezuela, Colombia, Costa Rica, Cuba and Nicaragua) in which civilians still rule. In most of these countries, however, the military remains a significant force which retains institutional privileges, commands a significant portion of the budget and acts independently of the civil authority in many fields.

The prominence of the military in politics can be explained in part by historical tradition. The armies that overthrew Spanish rule at the beginning of the nineteenth century were often left without any clear role in the new political order but with the means to compel attention and resources by resorting to force. In Peru, which finally became independent in 1824, the first civilian president did not take power until 1872. In some other countries, however, a civilian tradition was asserted for a time; Chile and Uruguay appeared to have evolved highly stable democratic systems by the end of the Second World War. Even so, the military moved in during the severe social and political crises which these countries faced in the 1970s. Historical explanations are of some value, therefore, but should not be relied upon too exclusively.

Military involvement in politics may be related, at a more general level, to the relative absence of international war in Latin America. There have been a few wars prior to 1945 and a few border skirmishes since; these tended to bring about a return to civilian rule although this did not happen in every case. Military governments are not especially aggressive in foreign policy terms – Argentina's occupation of the Falklands/Malvinas in 1982 being an exception – although it may well be that civilian governments have been forced to take a stronger line on border disputes than they would have wished for fear of military reaction.

Until very recently, all Latin American countries have looked abroad for arms supplies and military training. This has given the supplying power – most recently the United States – considerable opportunity to influence the behaviour of the military. At times (for example in Chile between 1970 and 1973) the United States has tried to encourage military intervention in politics and at others (for example in Venezuela after 1959) it has tried to discourage it, but US influence is rarely a decisive factor except in the small countries of Central America and the Caribbean where it continues to be preponderant. Some groups of army officers have developed strong pro-American views as a result of military collaboration with the United States; the most famous example of this is the position of the so-called 'Sorbonne' group of officers in Brazil. These officers fought alongside the Allies in Italy during the Second World War (the only army unit from Latin America to do so) and went on to form the core of the ESG (Escola Superior de Guerra, or Higher War College), a military–civilian training centre founded in 1949. Since then they have played a major part in Brazilian politics and provided three recent Brazilian presidents (Castello Branco, Ernesto Geisel and João Figueiredo). On the other hand, the United States has at times lost support by intervening too closely in Latin American military affairs. In both Peru and Bolivia anti-US regimes came to power shortly after an insurgency movement was put down; a part of the reason for this was that the CIA intervened directly in both countries, bypassing the conventional army structure which was antagonized in consequence.

More recently, the larger Latin American countries, notably Brazil, have emerged as important arms manufacturers and Brazil is now a significant arms exporter. Despite this, the Latin American military does not spend on weapons anything like their counterparts in the Middle East or Africa. Military spending is rarely more than 3 per cent of GNP although there has been some recent tendency for this to rise. Military regimes do not necessarily spend more on weapons than civilian governments, although some military presidents have (in the manner of some civilian presidents) sought to strengthen their political positions by a burst of military spending. This has some beneficial impact in the short term, but the long-term importance of military spending for political ends should not

Tanks in the streets of La Paz during the coup staged by Colonel Alberto Natusch, 1979

be exaggerated.

A good basis for comparing different kinds of military rule is the level of institutionalization within the military; here, it must be emphasized, one is speaking only of the military institution and not of the institutionalization of government as such. 'Institutional' military governments are characterized by high overlap between military rank and political office, the existence of an official or semi-official military ideology which serves to legitimize military rule, and relatively stable relationships between the military in government and certain civilian interest groups including economic technocrats, the business sector and the Church. All of this implies (although this is not part of the definition) that institutional military governments can maintain themselves in power despite considerable unpopularity, that they are highly effective in repressing left-wing or trade union opponents and that they are likely, at least in the short term, to try to control right-wing terrorist organizations.

Personalist military governments, in contrast, tend to be characterized by low overlap between military rank and political office. The original military coup was sometimes led by a relatively junior officer (notwithstanding that he called himself Colonel and later promoted himself General) or alternatively by a senior officer who gradually removed his various rivals from the scene. There are likely to be civilians in the government drawn from a range of interest groups. The regime is likely to seek to legitimize itself through controlled elections or a rigged plebiscite and is, therefore, bound to require a certain degree of popularity since a complete electoral farce may prove politically damaging. Popularity need not amount

to majority support but very unpopular personalist regimes may be vulnerable to middle-class discontent expressed through newspaper editorials or student demonstrations (as was Pérez Jiménez in Venezuela in 1957–8 and Odría in Peru in 1956). Personalist regimes will self-consciously present themselves as 'less military' than institutional ones; the president will often wear a suit rather than uniform.

Until around 1960, almost all military regimes in Latin America were of the personalist kind. These had the advantage of permitting close communication between military and civilian elites but were not always perceived as satisfactory by the military itself. For one thing, if the military president acted in an unpopular manner, the military itself would share in the obloquy without being in any position to influence the outcome; for this reason, military officers would at times refuse to defend a military president against popular demonstrations and would instead leave him to his fate. Secondly, the existence of a military caudillo would make it easier for revolutionary opponents of the regime to convert opposition to the ruler into opposition to the political system as a whole. The overthrow of General Batista by Fidel Castro in Cuba in 1956–9 convinced many military officers that something more flexible was needed. Thirdly, as the military institution became larger and its weaponry more sophisticated, it became increasingly difficult in the larger Latin American countries for an individual or a small group of officers to achieve complete personal ascendancy by means of an opportunist military coup; successful coups needed to involve progressively more people, they needed to be more carefully planned and to be more certain in their execution. This was the lesson drawn by military conspirators in Brazil who failed in 1961 but succeeded in 1964. Increasingly, therefore, coups came to be led by army commanders-in-chief rather than by rebellious colonels. These commanders, once in power, naturally sought to reinforce their positions by retaining control of the key power centres in the military institution. Finally, counter-insurgency experts, including the US government, came to the conclusion that an institutionalized military government would be more effective against revolutionaries than a personalist one because it would become more difficult for the latter to play off particular officers against each other and thereby split the military.

The first institutionalized military regime in Latin America took power briefly in Peru (1962–3). This was followed by regimes in Brazil (1964–), Argentina (1966–73 and also 1976–83), Peru (1968–80), Ecuador (1972–9) and Uruguay (1973–). The institutional structure was similar in each case. A senior military figure (often the army commander-in-chief) became president and was supported by a junta made up of the senior military commanders. In most cases, though not all, the junta was directly brought in to the government through the ministries of war, marine and air force. Usually, though not always, civilian technocrats would be brought in to the key economic positions of finance minister and head of the central bank. At all times, however, the military leadership would take soundings from the officer corps as a whole and would lay out the broad lines of policy which civilian technocrats would follow. The military would also retain effective institutional control of a number of matters; security and intelligence-gathering remained exclusively military preserves. Subsequently, in Brazil and Argentina, a fixed presidential term of office was set.

One of the factors which lay behind this transformation was the creation of a distinctive military ideology through the military schools of higher education. Given that the Latin American military has had few opportunities for prolonged armed combat, and that opportunistic coups are now more difficult to execute than formerly, the most important factor determining military seniority has become educational performance. Clearly military evaluations of education include emphasis on discipline as well as if not more than on creative thought. It, nevertheless, remains true that emphasis on education is highly significant. For one thing, the self-confidence which education brings has almost certainly been a key component in sustaining long periods of military rule and reduced the degree of civilian influence on the military outlook. One observer noted that in Peru in the 1930s a general trembled when he met an ambassador; now it is likely to be the other way round. Moreover, education in purely military matters came to be mixed increasingly – among the more senior officers and high-flyers – with education in economic and social questions. The Brazilian ESG, founded in 1949, and the

Peruvian CAEM (Centro de Altos Estudios Militares), founded in 1950, were pioneers in this regard. What was created by these institutions, and spread throughout Latin America, was an ideology of military rule. In the post-colonial era, it was asserted, communism was more likely to threaten a country through subversion than invasion. In order to defeat subversion (and, for that matter, to wage successful conventional war), it was necessary for the military to organize systematically and take on a far greater role in civil society than ever before. Subversion could also be weakened by some measure of social reform (as taught at CAEM) or alternatively by a period of rapid economic growth which would turn a weak and underdeveloped country into a developed one (the ESG perspective). In the interim, it was especially necessary to maintain tight political control. In either case, the military was given an agenda for action which might call for a long period of military rule and would certainly have the effect of reinforcing the ideological appeal of an existing military authority. 'Our duty as governors', General (and President) Velasco of Peru once told his men, 'is inseparable from our duty as military officers.'

These various institutional factors which we have considered suggest that the Latin American military can rarely be seen simply as representatives of a particular social class or group. Military officers in fact tend to be recruited from the lower-middle class. Since secondary education is normally a pre-requisite for admission, the lower class is generally excluded. The sons of the upper-middle class find it more agreeable in most cases to make their careers in less disciplined and demanding, and also better paid, occupations mainly in private companies, the law or banks. Social origin is rarely an important factor in military behaviour, particularly since successful officers are, socially speaking, upwardly mobile; indeed, one of the proudest claims of the Latin American military is precisely that it does facilitate such mobility. Moreover, the consciousness of discipline and occasional hardship plays an important part in creating a separate military consciousness and generating contempt for what is seen (often with justification) as the spoiled and cossetted existence of the upper-middle and upper classes. Finally, the hereditary element is an increasingly important factor in the Latin American military. A high proportion of military officers send their sons to follow them and these, in turn, frequently learn political as well as purely military ambition.

If one is to understand the behaviour of the military in politics, therefore, it is best to look directly at how they perceive their institutional interests. One underlying feature is hostility to excessive popular mobilization (often condemned as social indiscipline). Military regimes are sworn enemies of Marxist-led insurgencies and have destroyed these throughout South America with considerable ruthlessness; when engaged in putting down the MIR (a left-wing revolutionary group), Chilean President Pinochet reportedly told a questioner in 1974, 'Of course we torture people; we need the information.' Revolutionaries have had some success against personalist rulers such as Batista in Cuba and Somoza in Nicaragua, but none at all against institutional ones. Military governments are also likely to regard trade unions and critical newspapers with disfavour, but have not generally relied on total suppression. They have preferred to tolerate limited opposition activity on a discretionary basis, cracking down on opponents only if these 'go too far'. Some military governments, notably the Velasco Alvarado regime in Peru (1968–75) have actually encouraged limited popular mobilization, provided that this was kept within the bounds set by the government itself; this government, however, did find it increasingly difficult to channel popular demands in an approved manner and finally clamped down on its own creation. In general, military governments will react against strong popular organizations but may try to co-opt and foster weaker ones in the hope of being able to control them for their own objectives.

It is less easy to generalize about the economic policies pursued by military governments. The military in Brazil (1964), Chile (1973) and Argentina (1976) took power during severe economic crises, with inflation of 100 per cent per annum or more and economic growth falling. Each government responded with a classic IMF-style stabilization package which increased unemployment but also reduced the level of inflation; each government also went some way to dismantling a very high tariff structure. It is, however, hard to see what else they could have done under the circumstances. The Peruvian military, which found a very different situation when it took power in 1968, pursued a mildly expansionist fiscal policy at first, followed by a highly expansionist one which led to crisis in 1976–8. Over the longer term, there are some marked differences between military governments. In Chile after 1973, the Pinochet regime (which began 'institutionally' but later became more 'personalist' in character) pursued classic free market policies very firmly, and aimed to create a market society as well as a market economy. In Brazil, on the other hand, the aim of the military regime has been to develop a kind of state capitalism, with the main public enterprises playing a key role in capital formation. There is something of a military preference for state industry (except in the Chilean and to a lesser extent Argentine cases) and for the development of heavy industry under national control for security reasons, but this preference sometimes takes second place to the advice of civilian technocrats. The Peruvian military government did undertake some policies of social reform – notably a land reform – but few military governments have been interested in large-scale income redistribution (neither, it is fair to say, have many civilian governments).

Military governments are generally durable but not immortal. Until recently it was assumed that a military government would,

after a few years, either return directly to barracks and call elections or seek to transform itself into a civilian government by means of elections. One new feature of military governments is their longevity. The Peruvian military, which took power in 1968, only returned it to civilians in 1980 and the Ecuadorian military returned power after seven years (1972–9); General Pinochet, who took power in Chile in 1973, indicated that he would hold power until 1989 at the very least. The Argentine military, after its disastrous war in the Falklands/Malvinas, delivered power to an elected civilian government in 1983. In Brazil, the generals in 1982 allowed direct elections of state governors for the first time since 1965 and allowed indirect presidential elections in 1985. The military in Uruguay, also, allowed elections in 1984, eleven years after seizing power.

One factor making for a return to barracks in earlier times was the widely held assumption that civilian rule was 'normal' and military government an aberration, albeit a frequent one. This was no longer the case in the 1970s, when military governments throughout the continent made it clear that they intended if necessary to remain in power for long periods. Military disunity or economic failure may still undermine particular military regimes, but these may be handled simply by changes within the military itself. Whatever the short-run developments, few observers doubt that the military will continue to be a powerful force in Latin American politics.

GP

Further reading
S. P. Huntington, *Political Order in Changing Societies* (New Haven, Conn., 1968)
A. Lowenthal, ed., *Armies and Politics in Latin America* (Princeton, NJ, 1978)
G. Philip, *The Rise and Fall of the Peruvian Military Radicals 1968–76* (London, 1978)
A. Stepan, *The Military in Politics: Changing Patterns in Brazil* (Princeton, NJ, 1971)

Social structure and social change in Latin America

Introduction

It is dangerous to generalize about Latin American social structure. The reasons for this are important. First, although the region has a common cultural identity, stemming from Spanish and Portuguese colonization, some countries display much more 'Latin' qualities than others. The countries of the Southern Cone (Argentina, Uruguay, and to a lesser extent Chile) have the most European populations, made up largely of the descendants of European migrants. Other countries, such as those in the Andean zone and much of Central America, have large indigenous populations, or populations of mixed descent. In the Caribbean and Brazil the black population is more numerous, and its influence more important culturally.

Second, Latin American countries vary widely in their degree of economic development. This variation accounts not only for the proportion of people to be found in rural and urban areas, but also the kinds of employment and life-styles that different social groups exhibit in both settings. Only Cuba, among Latin American countries, is socialist, although the Sandinista government since 1979 in Nicaragua shows increasing evidence of moving leftwards. Socialist aspirations are mainly expressed by opposition groups in Latin America, unlike many other parts of the Third World.

Some countries, like Argentina and Brazil, have well-established industrial sectors and thus both a relatively large middle class and industrial working class. Other countries have experienced industrialization more recently; mainly since 1940 in the case of Mexico, or since 1970 in the case of some parts of the Andes and Central America. In these cases the internal market is smaller, and the population that makes up the 'market' has only acquired middle- or working-class values within the last couple of decades. It is important to recognize this fact when we look at Latin America from a Western European or North American perspective.

Third, because economic development in Latin America differs from that in the already industrialized countries, the social structure exhibits apparent contradictions that are perplexing to most outside observers. Traditional ways of life co-exist with the 'modern' world to a degree not found in North America, and rarely even in Europe. Poverty and riches live uneasily together. The city streets are given over to donkeys and beggars as well as to Cadillacs and Volkswagens. The modern department store, sometimes part of a multinational chain, shares urban space with countless thousands of street vendors, who form part of what economists term the 'urban informal sector' (meaning that they do not count in official statistics). Even in the countryside the peasant farmer is unlikely to pursue an unchanging, traditional pattern of agriculture, and often rubs shoulders with business farmers employing new agricultural technology, marketing co-operatives and government technicians. The co-existence of a modern capitalist class structure and a 'pre-capitalist' landlord and peasant society should serve to remind us that the former is dependent for its existence on the latter, while the existence of a modern sector in no way implies that the transition to industrial capitalist society will be completed on the European model.

Finally, it is important to emphasize that much that is important in Latin American social structure is not readily observed, and still less readily recorded, in the work of social scientists and statisticians. Some groups, especially women and children, are much more

'invisible' to governments and official experts than should ideally be the case. Like much of the Indian and black population, their status is a subordinate one, and what they think and feel is usually unrecorded.

Urbanization

Latin America is the most urbanized of Third World continents. Even two decades ago countries such as Chile, Argentina and Venezuela were more 'urban' than 'rural'. Today the picture is of a continent in which the majority live in cities and towns (see table 37). Even areas that are less developed, such as Central America, exhibit the same trend towards urbanization. Census data from 1970 suggests that in most of Central America, a region producing export crops such as bananas and coffee, and heavily dependent on imported manufactures, the urban population then made up over 40 per cent of the total (table 38).

The increase in the size and proportion of the population living in towns is attributable to two processes. First, migration from the countryside has swollen most cities in Latin America and a good many small towns and provincial centres of population. Much of this migration has occurred in stages, as people abandon their rural

Table 37. Urban population as percentage of total population

	1960	1980
Argentina	74	82
Brazil	46	65
Chile	68	81
Ecuador	34	45
Mexico	51	67

Source: International Bank for Reconstruction and Development (IBRD) *World Development Report, 1980* (Washington, DC, 1980).

Table 38. Central America: Urban and rural population totals, and percentage distribution patterns 1970[a]

Country	'Urban' segment by census definition			
	Populations (thousands)		Per cent	
	Urban	Rural	Urban	Rural
Costa Rica	760	1 112	41	59
El Salvador	1 405	2 144	40	60
Guatemala	1 878[b]	3 334[b]	36	64
Honduras	825[b]	1 829[b]	31	69
Nicaragua	883	995	47	53
Panama	679	749	48	52

[a] Data are for the actual census year for each country around 1970.
[b] Not adjusted for census under-enumeration.
Source: Interamerican Development Bank (IDB), *Population and Urban Trends in Central America and Panama* (Washington, DC, 1977).

livelihoods in favour of closer ties with the city. Research in provincial urban centres, such as Huancayo in Peru, suggests that urban links are often longstanding and close relations are maintained with cities hundreds of miles distant. Many of those who arrive in complex urban labour markets, as in the case of Monterrey in Mexico, have acquired training and 'credentials' *en route* to the city. So the image that many people have of the 'peasant' in the city is an inaccurate one; most migrants have long ceased to be peasants when they arrive in the city.

The second process which has contributed to urban growth is the net increase in the urban population itself. People establish themselves in urban environments remarkably quickly, begin to look around for somewhere secure to live and ways of earning a living. Since most of the migrant population is young, it is a relatively short time before their children are born, into urban homes. Cultural adaptation to the city is made easier by the fact that so many other urban residents have only lived there for a decade or less. Latin American cities are literally *being* created, in some cases almost overnight, and urban patterns of behaviour are learned in a pragmatic, highly adaptable way. Contrary to the myth that was current in the 1960s, when squatter settlements first became obvious to casual observers of Latin America, most urban squatters show every sign of knowing what they want and doing what they can to get it. Their 'life chances' may not be good, but this is because of the inequalities that exist in Latin American cities rather than the psychological handicaps imposed by an urban 'culture'.

Class structure

Most Latin American societies are extremely unequal by the standards of developed countries. The way that an individual is located within his society, in terms of his occupation and income, determines his access to educational opportunities and health

Tower blocks and shanties in São Paulo

provision, as well as his future social mobility. Since land is still an important factor in social status, especially in rural areas, the ownership and control of land is a major variable in the class structure. As we shall see, land ownership, like the ownership of capital, is concentrated in few hands throughout Latin America.

However, factors other than land ownership are of importance in discussing class. The concept of class refers not only to the ownership of the means of production but to the way that this pattern of ownership determines the individual's 'life chances'. The poor are not only materially poor, they also have more limited access to private and public services, worse health and nutrition standards, less educational opportunity and are at greater risk from political violence. Beginning with the occupational structure, table 39 shows the percentage distribution of the labour force in the three economic sectors of agriculture, industry and services. The 'service sector' is a notoriously ill-defined category, and we should recall that most service employment in Latin America is in poorly paid and often casual jobs, on the streets and in slum and squatter housing areas. It is clear from the table that, although industrial employment grew between 1960 and 1978 in Brazil, Ecuador and Mexico, this growth was largely at the expense of agriculture rather than services. Indeed, service sector employment grew in each country during this period; in Mexico by ten percentage points. In the case of Chile and Argentina industrial employment actually diminished as a proportion of total employment. The service sector, on the other hand, increased in both countries. These figures should serve to remind us that in the more industrially developed societies of Latin America there has been a limit to industrial expansion commensurate with the limited scale of the internal market.

Estimating the numbers of people outside 'formal' employment is always hazardous but table 40 provides some estimates from a population census undertaken in Brazil. In the more industrialized states like São Paulo and Rio de Janeiro under one-third of the labour force works in the 'informal economy'. However, in many states, including those of the south as well as the north-east, informal sector employment accounts for about two-thirds of the total. Similar figures could be produced for other Latin American countries.

The distribution of income is another indication of a country's class structure, pointing particularly to the different patterns of consumption available to the different social classes. Table 41 shows the percentage of total income received by the poorest 20 per cent of the population, and compares this figure with the share of household income received by the wealthiest 20 per cent. In four of the largest Latin American countries (Brazil, Mexico, Argentina and Chile) the wealthiest fifth of the population received over half the income in the late 1960s and early 1970s. By comparison the poorest fifth of the population received under 5 per cent of total household income.

Table 39. Labour force: percentage distribution of labour force by economic sectors

	Agriculture		Industry		Services	
	(1960)	(1978)	(1960)	(1978)	(1960)	(1978)
Argentina	20	14	36	29	44	57
Brazil	52	41	15	22	33	37
Chile	30	20	30	26	40	54
Ecuador	58	46	19	25	23	29
Mexico	55	39	20	26	25	35

Source: IBRD, *World Development Report, 1980.*

Table 40. Brazil (selected states), labour force outside the labour market and the market economy, 1970 (as a percentage of the economically active population)

States	%
Brazil	48.3
Federal District	14.5
São Paulo	29.7
Rio de Janeiro	30.8
Rio Grande do Sul	45.7
Pernambuco	56.0
Paraná	58.1
Minas Gerais	62.8
Paraíba	73.3

Source: FIBGE, *Censo Demográfico,* 1970.

Table 41. Income distribution: percentage share of household income by percentile groups of households: lowest and highest quintiles

	Lowest 20%	Highest 20%
Argentina (1970)	4.4	50.3
Brazil (1972)	2.0	66.3
Chile (1968)	4.4	51.4
Mexico (1977)	2.9	57.7
United Kingdom (1973)	6.3	38.8

Source: IBRD, *World Development Report, 1980.*

Particularly in the less industrially developed parts of Latin America landholding is an important element in the class structure. Control over land, usually linked with ownership, is the basis for political power and, inevitably, control over other social classes. Many parts of Latin America – and of Brazil – are less traditional than north-east Brazil, but table 42 illustrates a typical pattern of landholding in an area of large estates and smallholdings (latifundia/minifundia). In 1972 under 30,000 farms occupied over 41 million hectares of land, while 700,000 farms occupied only 10 million hectares. Much of the land in the large estates is unworked, or given over to extensive cattle-grazing, while the peasant farmers grow crops and raise a few animals on their small, intensively-worked plots.

Some indication of the distribution of resources in Latin American societies is provided by data on health and educational provision and nutritional standards. Table 43 illustrates the fact that most Latin Americans are less likely to visit a doctor or nurse than are North Americans. However, some countries, notably post-revolutionary Cuba, have made successful attempts to improve maternal and child health despite a shortage of doctors. This is reflected in the low infant mortality rate. The divergencies within Latin American countries are clearly seen in the figures for access to safe water. In Bolivia only one-third of the population has access to such a supply: in Uruguay almost everybody does.

Access to educational facilities is another indicator of socio-economic development. The figures in table 44 suggest that, although secondary school enrolments have increased, the majority of the school-age population does not attend secondary school. In

Latin America the middle and upper classes have privileged access to private universities through private preparatory and secondary schools. Nevertheless, it is important to record the phenomenal growth of the state universities, especially in countries such as Mexico and Peru, which has paralleled the expansion of secondary education.

In many Latin American societies, particularly those experiencing rapid industrial growth, the principal social division is no longer between a landed upper class, a small middle class and the popular masses. The division is between 'accommodated' groups in the middle and working classes and the mass of people, who are often very poor. In Mexico the population covered by a social security programme increased from 9.8 million in 1967 to 22.2 million in 1976. The increase in the proportion of newly-insured was no less impressive. In 1967 less than a quarter of the population were covered by social security. By 1976 it had increased to 35 per cent. These figures should give us cause for reflection. Latin American societies are very unequal, and the distribution of 'life-chances' is seriously prejudicial to the poor, but in some countries there is an emerging group of relatively secure working- and middle-class people whose principal benefactor, in many cases, is the state.

Social organization

Quantitative information on Latin American society provides an inadequate picture of the social structure, as it does not represent the important changes in values and behaviour that accompany economic development. It is necessary to look at the way that individuals and groups are organized to appreciate fully the more normative aspects of Latin American society. Perhaps the most ubiquitous social institution in Latin American, as in other societies, is the family.

The role of women, in the family as well as in the labour force, is closely associated with fertility and family size. Table 45 shows that in 1973 some Latin American countries were experiencing what amounted to a population explosion, as high birth rates were unchecked by natural mortality. In Mexico and the Dominican Republic women were giving birth to three times as many children per thousand as in the United States. In the more 'European' countries of the Southern Cone fertility was much lower than in countries with large Indian and black populations. This is true today, but accumulating evidence from some countries which have provided government backing for family planning, notably Mexico, suggests that the birth rate is coming under control. For the first time women are the major arbiters of their own fertility. The implications of this trend for male/female roles, the part played by the Roman Catholic Church, and the participation of women in the labour force, need to be given closer attention in the coming decades.

Table 42. Landholding in north-east Brazil (1972)

Size of property (ha)	No. of properties	Area (ha)
1–10	363 776	1 573 149
10–50	362 785	8 632 177
50–100	115 859	7 961 478
100–500	129 319	26 042 086
500+	27 209	41 821 384

Note: It is also worth observing that there are 15 latifundios in the north-east of more than 100 000 hectares, which occupy 2 659 135 hectares, considerably more land than that occupied by 363 776 small properties.
Source: INCRA Estatisticas Cadastrais, no. 1, 1972.

Table 43. Latin America: health and nutrition indicators

Country	Doctors[a]	Safe Water[b]	Infant mortality rate[c]
Argentina	21.7	66	55
Bolivia	4.7	34	158
Brazil	6.1	77	92
Colombia	4.8	64	98
Costa Rica	6.6	77	28
Cuba	8.9	—	25
Chile	4.5	84	55
Ecuador	4.7	42	66
El Salvador	2.7	53	60
Mexico	8.0	62	60
Uruguay	11.0	98	46
Venezuela	11.5	—	40
United States	16.3	—	14

[a] Number of doctors for each 10 000 inhabitants (1976).
Source: D. Lopez, La salud desigual en México (Mexico City, 1980), p. 122.
[b] Percentage of population with access to safe water (1975).
[c] Infant mortality rate (1978): number of infants who die before reaching one year per thousand live births.
Source: IBRD, World Development Report, 1980.

Table 44. Secondary school enrolments as percentage of age group

	1960	1977
Argentina	23	41
Brazil	11	24
Chile	24	50
Ecuador	12	44
Mexico	11	29

Source: IBRD, *World Development Report, 1980.*

Table 45. Crude birth rates for women aged 15 to 44 (1973) (Selected countries)

Country	Rate (per thousand)
Dominican Republic	226.9
Mexico	225.5
El Salvador	201.8
Guatemala	195.5
Nicaragua	189.4
Ecuador	183.7
Venezuela	170.6
Peru	167.5
Colombia	158.1
Chile	125.9
Cuba	122.3
Trinidad and Tobago	120.1
Argentina	101.9
United States	69.2

Source: Lopez, *La salud desigual en México*, p. 33.

Table 46. Mexican trade union membership (1970)

Sector	Total labour force	'Unionized' workers	% of unionized workers
Primary sector	5 103 519	149 101	3.0
Industry	2 973 540	1 148 032	38.6
Extractive	180 175	141 699	78.6
Manufacturing	2 169 074	803 316	37.0
Construction	571 006	150 830	26.4
Electricity	53 285	52 187	97.9
Transport	368 813	313 155	84.9
Commerce	1 196 878	37 181	3.0
Services	2 158 175	229 553	10.6
Others	1 154 132	101 328	
Totals	12 955 057	1 974 350	

Source: elaborated from *Anuario estadistico de los Estados Unidos Méxicanos, 1970–71,* Dirección General de Estadistica (Mexico City, 1971), pp. 59, 359–61.

Table 47. Mexico: structure of the manufacturing sector by type of firm (1970)

	No. of firms	Labour force	Capital investment (£)
Multinationals	1 016	281 029	1.2 billion
State owned	21	105 696	0.4 billion
Privately owned (Mexican)	117 770	1 160 487	1.7 billion

Source: ECLA *Principal Features of Industrailization Process and Industrial Policy in the 1970s* (Mexico City, 1979).

At one remove from the domestic unit are those organizations, such as trade unions, which articulate collective interests within the wider society. In some countries, especially those with a weak manufacturing base, trade union membership is low. In other countries it is relatively high, although in these cases trades unions are often virtually an extension of government, and even affiliated to government political parties. In Argentina, Chile, Uruguay and Brazil trade union activity has at times been curtailed by repressive military regimes. In Mexico, on the other hand, state paternalism (not always free from repression, it is true) has played a large part in union growth. Table 46 shows that the percentage of unionized workers is high in some Mexican economic sectors. In transport and the electricity industry most Mexican workers are members of a trade union, at least nominally, while only 10 per cent are unionized in the service sector, and even fewer in the 'primary sector' (principally agriculture).

For many Latin Americans the organizations to which they are affiliated serve both as instruments of individual self-advancement and the basis for solidarity with others. Thus movements to occupy land or gain land titles in squatter settlements have gained mass support in countries where such action is tolerated. At the same time cultural identity is important, blacks in Brazil and Cuba participate in Afro-Brazilian and Afro-Cuban religious cults; people of Indian origin join provincial clubs in Lima, Peru. The equivalent associations for the middle classes are similar to those in the industrialized countries: Rotary Clubs, Bar Associations and professional interest groups.

Looking at Mexico again, we see from table 47 that many more workers are employed in private Mexican-owned firms than in multinationals. Nevertheless, multinational companies play an increasingly important role in the most highly capitalized sectors of many Latin American countries such as Colombia, Brazil and Mexico. One important implication of the growth of multinational companies in Latin America is that their labour force acquires a dynamic which is more closely related to events in Europe or North America than to Latin America. Labour, as well as capital, becomes an international rather than a national commodity. The state in Latin American countries thus emerges as a mediating institution, seeking to legitimize and enforce its actions not only through its relations with national classes, but also with the representatives of international interests, including the multinationals.

Social change

We have already suggested various ways in which Latin American societies have changed during the last twenty years or so. The most notable changes have been felt throughout both rural and urban society, and it would be a mistake to attribute social change to urbanization alone. Rural society is no longer characterized by non-market relations. Indeed, it is doubtful whether non-market relations were ever quite as important as some writers on Latin American modernization suggested in the 1960s. Agricultural technologies have shifted the emphasis within rural society from the ownership of land to its control and use. Crop production is increasingly for animal consumption, for livestock and dairy products, many of which are exported, or for the vast masses that have congregated in the cities. Food policy has emerged as a key issue in Latin American society as the consumption habits and nutritional standards of the population are determined more and more by industrial food processing and sophisticated food distribution and marketing systems. It is a moot question whether these changes will herald an improvement in the diet of most people – indications are that the nutritional standards of the poorest people have actually declined.

The decade of the 1970s witnessed right-wing political repression throughout much of Latin America, making it difficult for opposition left-wing forces to organize politically in defence of living standards. For its part the Latin American left has not always shown a capacity to unite, and political rhetoric has sometimes been a substitute for planning concrete measures aimed at making improvements in living standards. At the same time a now very significant minority of the Latin American population, the middle class and some of the organized working class, has attained living standards comparable with those in Europe and North America. Their ascendancy has been closely related to the increasing intervention of the state in areas of life, such as education and family planning, which were traditionally the preserve of private institutions, notably the Church.

MRR

Further reading

H. Balan, J. Browning and E. Jelin, *Men in a Developing Society: Geographic and Social Mobility in Monterrey, Mexico* (Austin, Texas, 1963)
Interamerican Development Bank (IDB), *Population and Urban Trends in Central America and Panama* (Washington, DC, 1977)
International Bank for Reconstruction and Development (IBRD), *World Development Report* (Washington, DC, 1980)
N. Long, and B. Roberts, eds., *Peasant Cooperation and Capitalist Expansion in Central Peru* (Austin, Texas, 1978)
S. Mitchell, ed., *The Logic of Poverty: the Case of the Brazilian Northeast* (London, 1981)
D. Preston, ed., *Environment, Society and Rural Change in Latin America* (London, 1980)
M. R. Redclift, *Agrarian Reform and Peasant Organization on the Ecuadorian Coast* (London, 1978)

Social structure and social change in the Caribbean

Four features in combination – three historical and one geographical – give the Caribbean its regional coherence and distinguish it from neighbouring Latin America. The historical legacy involves the imprint of colonialism, the sugar plantation and slavery; geography is expressed by insularity. To understand the origin, and diversity, of Caribbean social structure and the developments it has undergone, it is necessary to explore the changing interrelationships between these key factors. Yet by no means all Caribbean societies have experienced insularity or the same chronology, nor have they all equally and completely evolved out of the mould of political dependence, sugar monoculture and social inequality in which they were set by the early nineteenth century.

Insularity, colonialism and decolonization

The Caribbean region embraces fifty-odd societies strung out in an archipelago which stretches for more than 2000 km from Cuba to Trinidad; it also includes the three Guianas on the shoulder of South America and Belize in Central America. The political, social and economic histories of these four mainland territories link them to the Caribbean rather than to Latin America. Moreover, although they are continental in location, their settlement pattern is coastal, and sandwiched, island-like, between the sea and an empty interior.

Social and political boundaries in the archipelago coincide with islands, each of which is a clearly demarcated living space, isolated from its neighbours by the sea. Only Hispaniola – occupied by Haiti and the Dominican Republic – and St Martin – partitioned between France and the Netherlands – are shared by two polities. Insularity implies smallness. Caribbean territories range in size from Cuba with 110,000 sq km and about 10 million inhabitants down to the Grenadines, each with a few hundred hectares and several score cultivators and fishermen. Most islands are smaller than Barbados, which has 250,000 persons on 430 sq km, and is approximately the same size as the Isle of Wight. Even the mainland territories, though large in area, record small populations. Guyana, despite its 215,000 sq km has barely more than 800,000 inhabitants.

Territorial fragmentation and small size – or small population – ensured that the most outstanding historical features of Caribbean societies would be their political dependence. The partitioning of the region by the Spanish, French, British, Dutch and Danish during the seventeenth and eighteenth centuries and United States intervention in the Greater Antilles since the nineteenth century, culminating in the annexation of Puerto Rico in 1898 and the purchase of the Danish Virgin Islands in 1917, have ensured that each territory's connections – political, economic and intellectual – have been forged almost exclusively with metropolitan countries in Western Europe or North America. Soviet Russian involvement in post-revolutionary Cuba has perpetuated this pattern.

Twenty years ago, only the three largest Caribbean units were independent, and two of them, Haiti and Cuba, have special symbolic significance for the others. Haiti's independence from France in 1804 was achieved in the aftermath of the area's only successful slave rebellion. Cuba, too, is a Caribbean anomaly. It is big and sophisticated by regional standards; and it fought two wars of independence in the nineteenth century before securing its freedom (although under *de facto* US control) from Spain in 1898.

Since the Second World War, however, metropolitan countries in Western Europe have been as anxious to decolonize as the islands have been to secure self-government and independence. Setting economic viability above political sovereignty, the French and Dutch West Indies have been decolonized by incorporation. Guadeloupe, Martinique and Guyane have become separate *départements* of France and send representatives to the Chamber of Deputies in Paris. Holland combined with its Caribbean possessions to form the Tripartite Kingdom of the Netherlands, but Surinam became independent in 1975 and the Dutch Antilles may also eventually secede, possibly atomizing into separate island states.

Fragmentation has already created a myriad of political entities in the Commonwealth Caribbean. British post-war policy aimed to launch all the Commonwealth units into independence through the West Indies Federation, but insular rivalries and fears of either subordination or financial burden led to its collapse in 1962. Jamaica, Trinidad, Barbados and Guyana became independent in the 1960s, the Windwards in the 1970s and Antigua and Belize and St Kitts–Nevis in the early 1980s. Yet Montserrat, the British Virgin Islands, the Caymans, the Turks and Caicos Islands and Anguilla remain self-governing British territories – indeed, the majority are colonies, and even in an era of independence many other small islands are still dependencies. Carriacou, subordinate to Grenada, boasts its own fief, Petite Martinique; and Barbuda, with

King Street, Kingston, Jamaica

1200 inhabitants, would have preferred the perpetuation of British colonialism to the perils of mismanagement and exploitation by recently independent Antigua, to which it is constitutionally tied.

Plantations, slavery and emancipation

Colonialism determined not only the historical subordination of Caribbean societies and their orientation towards distant metropoles, but their economic development as sugar plantations within the mercantilist systems of the north-west European powers. By the second half of the eighteenth century, when the West Indian sugar industry was at its peak, plantation cultivation had spread to virtually all the British, French, Dutch and Danish possessions, though the Spanish colonies remained either undeveloped – as in the case of Trinidad – or as revictualing stations on the route from the peninsula to the main.

Colonial plantations in the Caribbean created a grossly inegalitarian social hierarchy based upon legal estate. During the seventeenth century the major strata of Caribbean society were differentially incorporated as white free men and black slaves; and, when miscegenation became more prevalent in the mid-eighteenth century, an intermediate coloured element was formed through the manumission of the illegitimate offspring of the white elite. These legal estates determined that whites alone were fully-fledged citizens: the brown emancipated population enjoyed only limited civil rights, as did the increasing body of free blacks; slaves, whether black or the illegitimate, coloured offspring of poor whites, were non-persons, chattels to be bought and sold. Status and power were inversely related to group size. In Jamaica in 1825, for example, 25,000 whites legislated for a colony with 40,000 coloureds and 340,000 blacks.

A 'white bias' permeated all levels of the creole pigmentocracy. Possession of a white skin, aquiline nose, straight hair and thin lips became a badge of status, and gradations from the 'bad' features of the black to the 'good' features of the European, exemplified by mulattoes, quadroons, mustees and mustifinos (who were generally treated as white), formed stages on the road to whiteness and high rank. Moreover, the white bias carried cultural connotations: everything European was desirable; Africa was to be denigrated.

Caribbean legal estates during slavery determined not only the status of the constituent corporate categories – slaves, freemen, citizens – but the cultures they practised. African traits were largely eroded under the system of plantation slavery; the free people of colour (and the free blacks), while orientating themselves towards Europe, combined the behaviour of masters and slaves; and the whites practised a creole version of eighteenth-century European culture. Slaves were a pre-literate group and communicated in a creole version of English or French; their household structure was liable to continual disruption through sale or redeployment of individuals, and serial polygamy was the norm, with mothers rearing half-siblings; and their religious activity ran the gamut from witchcraft and African beliefs, through cults such as Vodún and Shango, to conversion to Catholicism or Protestant non-conformism – depending upon the norms of the colony's mother country.

Slave opposition to servitude took many forms – malingering, magico-religious activities, suicide, abortion – and rebellion. In Jamaica alone, twenty-nine rebellions took place over a period of 150 years, but only in Haiti did slave revolt generate revolution and independence. For, in the final analysis, the cohesion of these potentially unstable creole, slave societies in the Caribbean depended on force or the threat of force. The political and legal supremacy of the minority group of whites was reinforced by the whip, by metropolitan military detachments and by local militias, usually under white control and with free coloured non-commissioned officers.

Notwithstanding adamant elite opposition to change, the legal framework of the Caribbean creole societies was slowly dismantled in the nineteenth century. Slaves were emancipated in the British colonies in 1834, in the French islands in 1845, in Puerto Rico in 1873 and in Cuba as recently as 1886. The contrast between early British and French emancipation and late Spanish slave abolition was largely a reflection of economic differences: the sugar colonies of the north-west Europeans reached their apogee in the eighteenth century but were in decline by the early 1800s; the Spanish colonies developed as sugar monocultures only in the nineteenth century, and experienced their peak in the early twentieth century under US capitalism. Nevertheless, all Caribbean territories entered the twentieth century with a heritage of plantation slavery.

Nineteenth-century emancipation set in motion fewer changes than the planters had feared, largely because the landholding systems and property-restricted franchises – Haiti excepted – favoured the established order. Nonetheless, emancipated slaves were free to sell their labour, migrate, squat or purchase land. A substantial 'reconstituted' peasantry emerged in Haiti, Jamaica and the Windward Islands, though in the larger Leewards, Barbados and the Spanish-speaking islands the ex-slaves were unable to acquire land of their own and remained as plantation workers. In Trinidad, annexed by Britain from Spain in 1815, the small ex-slave population gravitated into farming or, more significantly, into urban occupations, notably in Port of Spain, the capital.

At the mid-point of the Caribbean's experiment with slave emancipation, the peasant-inspired Morant Bay Rebellion broke out in Jamaica in 1865. The white elite and its brown allies abandoned the old Assembly system in favour of Crown Colony Government, which had already been instituted in Trinidad. The Leeward Islands followed suit, and by the end of the nineteenth century virtually all the British colonies were under direct rule. The main effect was to place control of each island's destiny in the hands of white expatriate officials – and white creole planters and professionals. The rapid advance to power of the brown and black middle stratum after 1834 was halted, and the potential voting strength of the burgeoning group of black peasant freeholders was neutralized.

Persistence of economic and political elitism, bolstered by colonialism, shored up the framework of the culturally pluralistic Caribbean societies in the century after 1834. But the complexity of many societies was increased by immigration of East Indian and Chinese indentured labourers, and the arrival of free Chinese, Syrians, Lebanese and Spaniards; some islands, however, experienced a simplification of their creole stratification through racial extermination or outmigration.

By the end of the depression of the 1930s, it was possible to distinguish a number of distinct types of Caribbean society that had emerged out of the creole model based on plantation slavery. Jamaica perhaps most closely resembled that model, in that it consisted of three ranked cultural segments, correlated with colour, each with differential access to resources. Small, homogeneous folk societies, such as Barbuda and Anguilla were culturally similar to black Jamaican peasant communities. Haiti and the Windward Islands resembled Jamaica, but had lost their whites through genocide and emigration, respectively, and had brown elites instead. In Cuba and Puerto Rico massive white immigration over the previous fifty years for work on the sugar plantations had swamped the creole stratification and reduced the non-whites to enclaves in a class-based hierarchy.

Another example of late immigration disrupting the creole stratification – in contradiction to Jamaica, where the Chinese and

Syrians occupied status gaps within the social heirarchy – is provided by Trinidad and British Guiana (now Guyana). Between 1845 and 1919 tens of thousands of Indian indentured labourers were brought in to work on the nascent sugar estates. In Trinidad they accounted for over one-third of the population; in British Guiana they threatened soon to form the majority. Yet in both colonies the East Indians constituted an endogamous, spatially segregated and culturally distinct segment external to the creole stratification.

During the first four decades of the twentieth century adult suffrage existed in Haiti, Cuba and Puerto Rico, though none was considered a democracy. In the Commonwealth Caribbean, property restrictions meant that less than 10 per cent had the vote; politics remained an elite pastime, and the reins of government were held in expatriate hands. The conjunction of a restricted franchise with the international economic depression created severe labour disturbances in many Commonwealth islands, notably Jamaica and Trinidad. Pressure was mounted for universal adult suffrage and independence; political parties and trade unions were formed. Universal adult suffrage was gradually introduced into the British colonies after 1944, and a long period of constitutional decolonization began which lasted, in most cases, for almost twenty years before independence was finally granted.

Neo-colonialism

Despite adult suffrage and sovereignty, Caribbean societies remain culturally and racially stratified and economically dependent. Whites and mobile minority groups – the architects and beneficiaries of the old order – are everywhere under attack. Their residual identities, however strong, provide no basis for expressions of national solidarity. But black and East Indian electorates have been outmanoeuvred by 'brown' politicians, who have not hesitated to project overseas an Anglo-Saxon image of their island realms. Within the Caribbean, coloured political elites, supported by white commercial interests, have promoted a multi-racial ethic. Racial and cultural variations rarely receive public mention, and the official line everywhere emphasizes racial harmony.

The brown and black middle stratum which has filled the political and administrative vacuum left by the whites, has carefully created symbols of national unity. Local heads of state are usually black, local art forms receive government patronage, and annual celebrations of independence provide a holiday from the poverty which engulfs the lower stratum. In Jamaica, the British honours system, which co-opted local leaders, has been replaced by a new set of national awards. Trinidad's pre-lenten Carnival is promoted by the government to cast the national image in the mould of black creoles – as distinct from that of East Indians, who form the backbone of the political opposition.

Important though these changes have been, West Indian youth

dismisses them as mere tokens. During the last decade black power has become a vehicle for protest throughout the islands and its practitioners have advocated a break with economic imperialism and white racism. West Indian intellectuals, in particular, have protested at the penetration of each Caribbean economy by foreign enterprise. In their view, 'neo-colonialism' prevails, and each island remains dependent on overseas capital, decision-makers and technologies – and not solely in the traditional agricultural sector.

At the end of the growth decade of the 1960s, North American companies were pre-eminent in the Jamaican, Haitian, Dominican Republic and Guyanese bauxite industries; Texaco and Shell dominated Trinidad's oil economy; Tate and Lyle and Bookers were the giants of Commonwealth Caribbean sugar production; and Fyffes and Geest held a near monopoly in the marketing of West Indian bananas in Britain. But Caribbean nationalism during the 1970s, in the wake of Cuba's socialist revolution, created pressures to change the role of multinational corporations in the larger islands. The West Indies Sugar Corporation, a subsidiary of Tate and Lyle, divested itself of cane land in Jamaica and Trinidad; Jamaicans and Trinidadians, it was agreed, will eventually hold a 51 per cent share in foreign banks; Jamaica in 1974 extracted a tenfold rise in its bauxite revenues from the North American companies and contracted with Kaiser to purchase 51 per cent control of the local company together with all its holdings in land; Trinidad has purchased Shell's assets in the island. The cleanest sweep through state ownership occurred in Guyana, where the Co-operative Republic nationalized

A sugar factory in Hampden, Jamaica

the bauxite and sugar companies and now controls 80 per cent of the economy. Nevertheless, vital economic decisions are still made overseas, and the Lesser Antilles lack even these concessions to national ownership or popular involvement.

Special problems of economic development and diversification attach to islands with less than 100,000 inhabitants. In the Windwards and Leewards tourism has been embraced as a panacea, but it remains an enclave in the economic and spatial structure of the islands – as it does in larger Puerto Rico, Jamaica and Barbados – funded largely from overseas, imposing high infrastructural costs on island governments, employing few local workers, and consuming imported, rather than peasant-produced food.

Even more damaging than dependence has been the inability of the peripheral capitalist economies in the Caribbean to generate the economic growth and employment opportunities on which gradual social change has been predicated. Sugar and banana output have faltered; tourism is vulnerable to economic depressions, and, like bauxite mining and tax-incentive manufacturing, employs thousands where tens of thousands look for work. From oil-rich Trinidad to the Americanized Commonwealth of Puerto Rico, massive unemployment, underemployment and marginality characterize urban and rural dwellers alike. With the population doubling every forty years in many islands, it is not surprising that most Caribbean peoples are latent emigrants – and not a few are radicals.

Emigration and protest are linked in the cult of Rastafari which has diffused from Jamaica to most of the Commonwealth Caribbean. For Jamaican cultists, Rastafari – or Haile Selassie – is God.

Linden, Guyana: 'bauxite city'

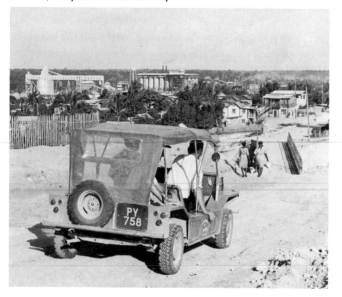

Not only is God black, but blacks are the true children of Israel, God's elect, who were carried into captivity in the Caribbean and placed under the yoke of white and brown Babylonians. Redemption depends on repatriation to Africa or, more specifically, to Ethiopia.

For many black power advocates of the 1970s West African tribal costume, Afro haircuts, American black power terminology and slogans such as 'black is beautiful' and 'Castro is the blackest man in the Caribbean' were adequate expressions of a new, post-colonial identity. But for socialists looking for structural change, it was Cuba's break with United States capitalism in the aftermath of Fidel Castro's revolution that was most appealing. Moreover, the 'New Man' and 'New Society', based not on material inducements but moral incentives, to which Cuba temporarily aspired in the 1960s, not surprisingly still appeals to Caribbean idealists, surrounded as they are on their own islands by materialism, poverty and racial disadvantage.

But most Caribbean societies have either not tried or have failed to make their social structures more radically egalitarian in the last twenty years, and the current economic recession (from 1981 onwards) is now undoubtedly widening the gap between rich and poor. Paradoxically, those islands that are most politically dependent – Puerto Rico and the French Antilles, have the highest standard of state welfare. And comparison between Cuba and the Commonwealth Caribbean shows that residents of the latter enjoy more personal freedom if less social equality. The only Commonwealth islands to emphasize social equality have been Jamaica under Michael Manley's Peoples' National Movement and Grenada under Maurice Bishop's Peoples' Revolutionary Government. Manley's programme of democratic socialism was overwhelmed by economic forces and the ballot box in 1980; Bishop's government came to an end in 1983 with his murder, followed in short order by American invasion.

Conclusion

This sketch of Caribbean society through time shows how the eighteenth-century colonial distinction between slaves, freemen and citizens subsequently became a temporal sequence of change experienced by blacks and browns. In Haiti, slave rebellion created black freemen who were simultaneously citizens; in Cuba, Puerto Rico and the British West Indies, the time lapse between emancipation and citizenship was wider and wider. Only in the last forty years have Commonwealth Caribbean blacks – and East Indians – enjoyed the political status of the eighteenth-century white elite. However, this tardy change from freemen to colonial citizens was closely followed by a change in the status of the societies as well – from island colonies to self-governing dependencies or independent states.

If most Caribbean units are no longer colonial, few Caribbean economies – Cuba and St Kitts excepted – are reliant on sugar plantations. Yet dependence on one or two primary products remains a hallmark of Caribbean societies, and under these conditions economic growth and related social change have been difficult to achieve, especially in the context of rapid population growth. Politics and awards for secondary and higher education have created non-white occupational mobility on a scale without parallel in the past. But the majority of West Indians find their social status and material standards remain disappointing and unacceptable. Nevertheless, the prospect of radical change along Cuban lines is no more appealing to most islanders than to the region's largest neighbour and self-appointed guardian, the United States.

Independence, so long awaited, ought to mean more than stuttering economic development based on dependence on external forces and the enactment of Westminster-style democracy under circumstances which encourage domination by conservative political elites. But, in view of the small-scale insularity of Caribbean societies and the glaring example of oppression and impoverishment in the black republic of Haiti, even these modest achievements could easily be undermined.

CC

Further reading

F. W. Knight, *The Caribbean: the Genesis of a Fragmented Nationalism* (New York, 1978)

D. Lowenthal, *West Indian Societies* (New York, London, Toronto, 1972)

D. Nicholls, *From Dessalines to Duvalier: Race, Colour and National Identity in Haiti* (Cambridge, London, New York, 1979)

A. Payne and P. Sutton eds., *Dependency under Challenge: the Political Economy of the Commonwealth Caribbean* (Manchester, 1984)

Political parties in Latin America

The variety of party types in Latin America is immense. Some are mass parties with long traditions and deep popular roots. Others are no more than cliques with only an episodic existence. Structurally, some are highly centralized, while others take decisions in an open and democratic fashion. And their ideological range is equally wide, from neo-fascist Catholic nationalism to extreme-left voluntarism.

This diversity is mirrored in their national political systems. In two cases (Cuba and Mexico), the civil power is well-established but monolithically so with, respectively, no opposition and only token opposition. In others (Costa Rica, Colombia and Venezuela, for example) rule by party is, at least for the present, intact, and the struggle for office remains highly competitive. In yet others (such as Guatemala and Honduras), political parties exist but at a rudimentary level, consisting of 'official' and 'tolerated' organizations which have little or nothing to do with political recruitment, the representation of interest, or the making of policy.

But the parties also have things in common. Doctrinally, most occupy the centre ground and are often difficult to distinguish in policy terms. Though formally (and some in happy contradiction) attached to various reformist positions, most accept the mixed-economy status quo and take a broadly similar nationalist position over key issues such as the public ownership of infrastructure and the character of foreign investment. The weakness of civil institutions, especially the judiciary and legislature, renders them similarly dependent on the executive branch, and in their internal organization they display like tendencies, notably towards elitism, factionalism, and personalism. And, as often as not, the dominant parties take decisions in ways which, though not democratic, are at least plural.

In many states their claim to rule is also disputed by other organized groups. For example, in Chile and Uruguay – once jointly hailed as models of stable parliamentary democracy – party government has been abruptly ended by the military and there are (at the time of writing) few signs of its early return. Conversely, in Peru and Ecuador (and there have been tentative moves in this direction in Brazil) rule by the military has recently given way to representative democracy, though one subject to veto. Argentina best illustrates the ambiguous status that parties acquire when power is so uncertainly located. Since the overthrow of Perón in 1955, the army has put an end to civilian governments of varying persuasions no less than four times but all of the major parties have survived. Since authoritarian military regimes also find it difficult to govern, it is hardly surprising that parties should so often be incapable of governing but also impossible to ignore.

A convenient way of organizing this diversity is to link party types to the evolution of their national political systems. Four stages can be identified: traditional party systems in the period of political reconstruction that followed independence; the rise of protest and access parties during the period of growth that followed reconstruction; the national popular phase linked to the reorientation of the international trading system after 1929; and the partial eclipse of civilian rule during the last two decades.

By the end of the nineteenth century a relatively uniform party configuration had emerged in Latin America. Politics in most states had ceased to be a matter of armed violence between regions and had come to be dominated by the conflict between Liberal and Conservative parties, each armed with borrowed doctrine. Liberals sought to promote national development, by which they meant the development of primary exports along with the infrastructure this required, through the promotion of free trade, a federal form of government, and the separation of Church and state. Conservatives, reflecting a more specifically colonial heritage, sometimes argued for the protection of domestic industry, for a powerfully endowed unitary state, and for a privileged position for the Church and other corporate groups. In some cases (for example, in Mexico under Díaz) the struggle was resolved through dictatorial rule and this had important consequences since it meant that neither access nor protest parties had the freedom to develop which they enjoyed elsewhere. But, even where party politics was competitive, it remained thoroughly oligarchic, thanks to a restricted franchise and (in many countries) the stifling of opposition.

Oligarchic politics has since collapsed but the practice of borrowing ideology has not. The development in this century of Socialist, Communist and reformist parties elsewhere has been mirrored throughout Latin America. Partly this reflects the political space created by the collapse of the old two-party system (where it existed) but also the fact that money as well as intellectual and moral support has been forthcoming from outside. But this is less important than has sometimes been claimed and the charge that many parties – especially those of the centre and left – are merely mimetic is hard to sustain. Only the most orthodox of the Communist parties have been willing to subordinate themselves to external direction and even they have suffered repeated splits in consequence. Whatever their doctrinal debts and however venal (as when accepting external help for electoral purposes), most remain stubbornly idiosyncratic.

Today the Conservative–Liberal two-party system survives only in Honduras (where it is of little importance) and in Colombia, where the parties have long since transformed themselves into mass patronage machines. However, vestigial Conservative parties, usually masquerading under less provocative names – such as the National Democrats (PDN) of Argentina or the National Action Party (PAN) of Mexico – survive though their influence everywhere is slight. No longer able to compete with the parties of the centre and left in electoral terms, the role of guardian of the right has been taken over by the military and by foreign and domestic technocratic elites. The Liberals, similarly undercut but also having had to confront the growth of nationalist sentiment as well, have fared even less well and survive only in the few states where the old system itself survives, and there in name only.

Along with the economic growth that accompanied this political reconstruction towards the end of the nineteenth century there emerged working-class and petty-bourgeois political interests that the old system could not satisfy. Some of these interests initially attempted to work through the system while others (notably the anarchists and syndicalists) rejected the parliamentary road altogether. But, in the face of continued intransigence, most turned either to the new parties that sought a wider distribution of power within the prevailing system or to the parties of protest, first Socialist and, after 1917, Communist.

Most of the Communist parties of Latin America developed as splinter groups from existing Socialist parties or anarchist movements and from that time on relations between Communists and socialists have rarely been harmonious. (The anarchists had lost all influence by the mid-1920s.) Divided by history, by real policy differences and by their struggle for the loyalties of the intelligentsia and workers, they, nevertheless, have more in common than either would want to admit. Both are, by their separate lights, democratically managed and both accept the necessity of a capitalist stage of development, the parliamentary road, and the convenience of co-operation with other progressive parties. As a result, both have suffered from splits by radicals tired of a policy of gradualism that, Chile aside, has so far brought few results and does not seem likely to do so in the future. The cases of Cuba and Nicaragua are not exceptions for their state power was won by military means and the dominance of state over party has been maintained.

These parties of the left have been vigorously attacked, more from the ultra-left than from the right, as elitist, academic and anti-nationalist, though they are less internationalist in practice than in rhetoric. There is some truth to these charges but it is hard to see how it could be otherwise. Both have had to work under conditions where the working class is poorly articulated and badly or paternalistically organized, and where the state seems ever ready to step in on behalf of those whom the left would seek to threaten.

A victory parade for Popular Unity in Chile, 1970

The experience of Chile indicates the difficulties involved. There, with the aid of a centre-right alternative and an electoral system that encouraged broad polarization, the Socialist and Communist parties were able to attract mass support and elect their Popular Unity (UP) coalition into power in 1970. But their very success along with their insistence upon a parliamentary and legal road to socialism when the opposition was not so constrained led to their overthrow and proscription. It seems that the more success such parties have, the more they are likely to fail, and, conversely, that continued impotence is the price of their survival.

Access parties are more difficult to categorize. Some developed like the Radical parties of Argentina and Chile towards the end of the last century. Others like Democratic Action (AD) in Venezuela or APRA in Peru evolved during the inter-war years as anti-dictatorial nationalist movements, but their early radicalism has since become much attenuated. Yet others, like Popular Action (AP) in Peru or the Christian Democrats (PDC) in Chile, are post-war developments. Their current status also varies. In Venezuela and Peru they are powerful. In Argentina the Radical Party staged a remarkable victory in the 1983 elections. In states where they have failed to develop (such as Mexico) many of their characteristics are found within the national popular parties.

The first of these characteristics is their lower-middle-class base. Though they also get support from the working class and, at the level of leadership, from upper-middle-class strata, they have a special appeal for those with something to lose but even more to gain from political mobilization. This accounts for their deliberately opaque but loosely reformist ideology which typically consists of support for increased expenditure on education and selective welfare and for high levels of public employment, but does not contemplate any serious alteration in the existing distribution of wealth and power. Above all – and this is why their attachment to civil institutions is so strong – they are dedicated to the provision of spoils for their supporters in the form of jobs, subsidies, entitlements and exemptions. This is often a matter of exchange between individuals but it can also involve obligation between the party and some work-specific group as was the case in the relationship between landless labourers and the Democratic Action party of Venezuela. Whichever characteristic predominates, it accentuates the tendency within such parties towards 'familistic' recruitment and informal decision-making.

The interest of access parties in spoils is not unique but is a persistent theme of almost all party life outside the left. Its roots lie in the overall scarcity, compounded by maldistribution, of desirable public and semi-public goods. Since only the state can supply these goods to those who have no access to them through the private sector (the lower-middle and working class), the struggle to control the state and its powers of patronage becomes highly competitive. The

exchange of influence-peddling in return for votes or other kinds of political support is a major factor in the ability of these otherwise ill-defined access parties to attract popular support. But it also has vicious consequences, namely high levels of partisan violence (which in Colombia reached civil war proportions in the 1950s), the erosion of public confidence in political institutions, and in wasteful and corrupt administration. Moreover, however well-developed and sensitive, spoils systems by their nature rest on reciprocity and so, for the most part, exclude the powerless and disorganized who have little with which to bargain.

It was to their needs that the *national popular movements* of the 1930s and 1940s addressed themselves. Power was seized by a *declassé* military in Argentina and Brazil and elsewhere through civilian protest (though in Peru APRA never succeeded), but the crisis of the old order was much the same everywhere: the collapse of export-led growth after 1929, the development in the more advanced economies of an industrial base and with it a better articulated working class, and the growing belief that the state could and should intervene more aggressively in the economy in order to better promote national development. Though rather too much has been made of it, structurally they inclined towards charismatic leadership (Perón in Argentina, Lázaro Cárdenas in Mexico, Getúlio Vargas in Brazil, Víctor Paz Estenssoro in Bolivia, Víctor Raúl Haya de la Torre in Peru, for example), towards an ideology of national redemption, and towards a corporate form of organization. Though their specific policies varied (for example, the substantial agrarian reforms that took place in Guatemala, Bolivia and Mexico were not matched in Brazil or Argentina), they generally involved the expropriation of foreign-owned infrastructure, the mobilization by the state of capital and labour organizations, the erection of tariff barriers and the introduction of large-scale consumption subsidies.

In most cases this not only led to significant growth and to a redistribution of income towards the working class and on occasion the peasantry but also to an inflated public sector, uncompetitive domestic industry and persistent inflationary and balance of payments crises. This might not have mattered had there been a transfer of power to the working class instead of to the state, but the alliance between the working class and national capital that had been orchestrated from the executive branch required continued growth if its contradictions were to be resolved. When this stopped and class polarization emerged in its place, none of the national popular regimes were able to withstand intervention by the military. This occurred in Guatemala in 1954, in Argentina in 1955, in Brazil in 1964 and in Bolivia in 1965, as often as not with backing from the United States. In the case of Argentina and Bolivia, where the transformation was deepest, working-class organization and with it a populist alternative has survived, but elsewhere it has been thoroughly dismantled. Certainly, the optimism of the period about the salutary effects of growth upon democratic culture and institutions was misplaced.

Only in Mexico did the regime survive, but this was largely because the radical stance taken by Cárdenas was abandoned in the 1940s by his successors. The Institutional Revolutionary Party (PRI) has held on to power precisely because of its contradictory attributes. It claims to be a creation of the people but was in reality organized by the state and remains part of it. Though highly centralized, it allows for modest dissent and the expression of regional peculiarities. Its nationalist and redistributive rhetoric give it a popular legitimacy of sorts, but it takes care not to endanger seriously the interests of the established and powerful. And, when threatened, it does not hesitate to join with the state in using violence.

At present (1984) competitive party rule exists only in Venezuela, Colombia, Costa Rica and, more tenuously, Argentina, Ecuador and Peru. But this is either because of extraneous good fortune (specifically oil in the case of Venezuela) or because the parties accept the constraints imposed by external dependence and corporate power at home. Even in Costa Rica, where liberal democratic institutions are strongest of all, not least because it has no army as

A PRI rally in Mexico, 1970

such, the future is far from certain. The experience of party rule that has been sensitive to the wishes of the people as a whole suggests that demands are created that lead inexorably to class conflict, political violence, and the overthrow of civilian government. But it also seems certain that the parties will survive, and continue to play a variety of roles in the future.

WL

Further reading

J.-P. Bernard, *et al. Guide to the Political Parties of South America* (Harmondsworth, 1973)
M. J. Blackman and R. G. Hellman, eds., *Terms of Conflict: Ideology in Latin American Politics* (Philadelphia, 1977)
J. A. Booth and M. A. Seligson, eds., *Political Participation in Latin America*, 2 vols. (New York, 1978–9)
M. L. Conniff, ed., *Latin American Populism in Comparative Perspective* (Albuquerque, NM. 1982)
J. Linz and A. Stepan, eds., *The Breakdown of Democratic Regimes: Latin America* (Baltimore, 1978)

Trade unions in Latin America

Although there are examples of trade unions forming in the midnineteenth century, and even instances of strikes not much later, it is in the last decade of that century that we must date the rise of modern labour movements in Latin America. Of course, there are wide differences between countries, but, in general, labour movements developed when industrial development had created a substantial urban labour force, when immigrant workers from Europe brought with them ideologies and models of union development (mostly anarchist and anarcho-syndicalist), when political elites realized that they had to come to terms with such movements if only to tame them, and when, in several countries at least, miners (in copper, nitrate and tin) provided a focus for working-class protest.

One must not exaggerate the militancy or ideological commitment of early labour movements. Conservative Catholicism was more important as an influence than militant anarchism. For every radical migrant from Europe, there were many more whose major aims had very little to do with politics and much more to do with self-advancement. Trade unions were influenced by, rather than influences on, the economic and political cycle. Unions could do little to arrest the decline of real wages during depression, or to protect their members at times of political authoritarianism.

The growth of trade unions reflected the overall development of Latin America in the twentieth century. Industrial development allowed the formation of stronger unions. The growth of the political left introduced new ideologies to the labour movement –

Communism replaced anarchism in importance, only to be challenged by the growth of socialist movements, of Christian democracy, and of other left-wing groups such as (in the 1960s) the Maoists, Trotskyists and Castroists. But the pattern of development was far from uniform – it could hardly have been so where some countries had a labour shortage and others a huge surplus. In some countries, Chile or Argentina for example, labour came to play a crucial political role; in others, such as Colombia or Venezuela, it remained subordinate to the major political parties; and in others, such as Paraguay, labour remained firmly controlled. In order to try to understand these developments we cannot simply describe the trade unions as such. We must look at the social structure of Latin American countries and at their political systems.

The nature of the working class

What *is* the working class in Latin American countries? Where does it end and the middle class begin? What is the relationship between a factory worker in a settled occupation, earning a reasonable income, and a street vendor, living in a shanty town and perhaps only recently arrived from the countryside? These questions are not merely statistical ones. They have great implications for the analysis of social class, and for political behaviour.

One immediate problem in trying to define the working class is the very small size of most industrial or manufacturing enterprises, and consequently the relatively small number of industrial workers employed in what is regarded as the 'modern sector'. In Chile close on half of all manufacturing workers are employed in firms of five workers or fewer; in Peru the average size of unions in manufacturing industry is about sixty members; and even in Brazil in the 1960s firms of fewer than five employees represented about 70 per cent of the total number of industrial firms. It is true that in some countries, such as Brazil, the manufacturing boom of the late 1960s and 1970s has increased very substantially the number of workers in large modern factories. In 1965, manufactured products accounted for 8 per cent of Brazil's exports, in 1979 this figure had risen to 35 per cent. Brazil is now the world's tenth largest exporter of cars. In Mexico between 1950 and 1976 the industrial labour force grew from 12 per cent to 18 per cent, while the agricultural labour force dropped from 58 per cent to 33 per cent. In Argentina 2 million people work in industry and only three quarters of a million in agriculture.

But it is a mistake to think of small or artisanal enterprises as residual or marginal, destined to disappear with economic progress. On the contrary, in many countries the number of artisanal firms is growing, often in a dependent relationship with large, often foreign-owned, capital-intensive plants. What is the class and political position of workers in these small enterprises? Their close relationship with an employer makes it easier for them to be controlled and

obviously far more difficult for them to organize a trade union. The size of this group and its economic importance mean that any trade union movement with claims to represent the working class as a whole would need to incorporate it; but there are few examples of any successful attempts to join together workers in large-scale enterprises with those at the other end of the scale.

Even more difficult to classify are workers who are self-employed, and who do not employ anyone else (apart from unpaid family labour). These people, neatly categorized as in the 'service' sector, lack stable employment and organizational structures, and often work immensely long hours for very little. Nor are their numbers insignificant. In Chile about 20 per cent of the urban labour force is classed as self-employed; in Brazil nearer 30 per cent. Yet their lack of involvement in trade unions does not mean that they cannot act with organized labour. On the contrary, as so much of union activity, as we shall see, has to be political, rather than industrial, these self-employed workers can often (though not always) act as the allies of the unions in a common struggle against government austerity policies that affect the whole community, or against miserable living conditions that affect all the urban poor. But their association with organized labour tends to be an activity of crisis, born out of desperation, as in the general strike in Peru in 1977 against an increasingly repressive government, or in the *cordones industriales* ('industrial belts' of worker-occupied factories) that developed in Chile in 1972–3 in order to defend the beleaguered Allende government. It is much more difficult to construct a continuing and permanent organization to involve all these sectors, especially as so many authoritarian governments in Latin America have prohibited party activity over recent years.

A third related difficulty is the often tense relationship between blue-collar and white-collar workers, between wage earners and salaried employees. Social status is important in Latin America. A white-collar worker feels superior to manual labourers; he enjoys a different and better social security system; he operates under a different labour code; and, though he can often act in a militant way, he does not necessarily support the political left. White-collar workers are numerically important, rarely less than a third of the urban labour force, and many of them will be employed by the government. Very often they will seek political distance from the working class by associating themselves with a distinct political party. In Chile, for example, while most manual workers were organized in the Socialist or Communist parties, the white-collar workers were associated with the Radical Party and later the Christian Democratic Party, and, of course, they played an important role in the middle-class opposition that did so much to bring down the Popular Unity government of President Allende. In Peru for a long time they provided a strong element in the APRA party, a party that started on the left in the 1930s but became more right-

Women workers at a Volkswagen factory in Brazil

types of rural worker. Plantation workers such as sugar workers in Peru, or banana workers in Central America are best seen as a rural proletariat working for a wage. These workers often form unions similar in nature and function to those of urban workers, whereas peasants mostly grow subsistence and sometimes cash crops on their own plots of land, tend to organize on the basis of locality and, if politically mobilized, are more likely to unite in a mass movement and engage in direct action rather than collective bargaining. Generally speaking, their contact with urban labour is slight, even in countries which had an advanced labour movement such as Chile. Their aims are different, their work styles and communities often have little in common with urban labour. Sometimes they can be united through common association with a political party, but that is nowadays rarer, given the widespread restrictions on party activity. A worker–peasant alliance may be theoretically necessary to make a successful revolution or even to construct a majority political party, but the practice of such an alliance looks remote for most of the countries of Latin America.

Differences between countries

The general point that will have emerged so far is the marked differentiation between the various groups that compose the working class in Latin America. But it would be superficial and misleading not to emphasize that there are also great differences between the various countries. Argentina, for example, has as modern an occupational structure as many European countries, with a large proportion of its work force in modern enterprises and only a small proportion working on the land. Argentine trade unions too, though they suffered from government repression after the coup of 1976, are often wealthy, bureaucratic, industry-wide federations quite similar to those of Europe. Chile needs to be singled out not because of the size or strength of its labour movement, but because of its radical political commitment, a commitment still strikingly alive in spite of strenuous government attempts to repress it after 1973. That radical commitment is the product of a long period of development of the left in which party and union activities were intertwined.

Although any generalizations really need to be hedged around with an enormous number of qualifications, it is possible to make the following points. (Although Cuban unions resemble others in Latin America in their dependence on the state, in most ways they are so different that they have not been considered.)

Only in Argentina are the majority of urban workers organized in independent, sector-wide unions with a powerful bureaucracy used to national collective bargaining. After 1976 the union movement suffered restrictions, but even then it was too powerful to be repressed in the way that it was, for a time at least, in Brazil, Uruguay or Chile.

wing and opportunistic in later decades. But one important group, the schoolteachers, who constitute the single largest (and perhaps most militant) union in Peru are now largely dominated by Maoist leaders. The political allegiance of white-collar workers is difficult to predict in advance; their militancy is often intense but their political sympathies show considerable inconsistency. The problem that this underlines is once again that of constructing a solid and unified labour movement with a clear strategy and a common political allegiance.

Two other points must be mentioned because they are crucial in affecting the labour market and in determining the political influence of the working class. There is, firstly, the very low rate of participation of women in the paid work force. Women generally constitute around 20 per cent of the active labour force and those who do work generally do so in domestic occupations or in agriculture or in the so-called service sector, which employs two-thirds of female labour, usually in low-paid, menial occupations. Wages for women are two or three times lower than those for men. Female participation in the rural labour force has increased partly because men migrate to better-paid jobs in the towns. Women, therefore, work in occupations that are normally not unionized, and their level of political participation is generally lower or more conservative than that of men.

Secondly, trade unions are not confined to urban and mining areas; they also exist in the countryside along with a whole host of other organizations such as leagues, movements, co-operatives, communal and ethnic associations. And in many Latin American countries the largest single occupational group are rural workers, and they are often the majority. There are, however, many different

A Chilean demonstrating for workers' rights, October 1972

Most other countries do have a number of powerful industry-wide federations but they organize only a small, sometimes privileged sector of the workforce, and can be rather detached from the general politics of labour (though that does not mean lagging behind; they can, in fact, be in advance). Petroleum workers or miners are, by the nature of their occupations, often isolated from the main urban centres. In Bolivia the tin miners have played a leading role in the politics of that country; but their militancy has hardly been typical of Bolivian labour, and neither has the miners' attachment to the politics of Trotskyism been widespread.

In Mexico and Brazil, economic development has recently seen the emergence of large and powerful unions – above all in the motor vehicle industry – but in these countries, until very recently, the structure of trade unionism was imposed by the government, and controlled by it, though not always easily, and with periods when unions threatened to break away from domination by the government.

Generally in Latin America trade unions are small, weak, poor and hamstrung with all sorts of regulations, legal and political, imposed by governments, and intended to inhibit the development of a free and independent labour movement. The bargaining agent is the small local plant union, more often than not engaged in a long process of trying to stop real wages falling even more behind the rate of inflation. Most workers, however, are employed in firms too small even to have a union, and so are not covered by the minimal guarantees that an active plant union can bring. Labour relations inside many factories or in many firms are, therefore, often paternalistic and the union, should one exist, is something of a company union. Unions fight to keep job turnover low, and in some countries it is much lower than in Europe, for example. The interest of employers, however, is in rapid turnover and this is often the case in sectors where unions are weak.

A general exception to this description are the state employees. The state in Latin America is often a very important source of employment and, although in most countries there are prohibitions against state workers forming unions, in practice this is ignored. State employees also have the advantage of being organized in large numbers and facing one employer – the government, which has power in theory to alter wage rates. State employees have emerged as some of the most militant groups in Latin America. Schoolteachers in a number of countries have often opposed government policy very violently.

Unions, politics and the state

It has been a persistent intention of governments in Latin America to curb the interests of the working class. Hence most countries have complex and elaborate labour codes, often promulgated before organized labour was in any sense a political threat. As labour has become a political threat, so the state has intensified its attempts to control or coerce labour movements.

Labour law regulates almost every aspect of union activity from collective bargaining to the way of selecting leaders. And, if there is legal conflict, Latin American judiciaries have shown themselves more likely to favour the government than the workers. But, apart from control over the activities of labour, some governments have even determined the structure of union organization, aiming particularly to prevent the emergence of a central national labour organization. The Brazilian labour code, for example, with the Ministry of Labour at the apex, lays down a very precise system of confederations, federations and local unions. Virtually all labour codes establish the difference between white- and blue-collar labour.

Apart from such open attempts to regulate labour, governments do not hesitate to employ other methods. The most notorious is that of repression, and instances are sadly too frequent of labour leaders removed from office, deported or even assassinated in the interests of 'national security'. However, it may be questioned whether this is as effective a method of control as co-option of labour leaders by a system of patronage and corruption and of unionists by an extensive system of government social welfare schemes. For many years

Mexican labour was led by men bought off by the government and notorious for their corruption (though this did not mean that they were inactive as union leaders, especially if confronting an employer unpopular with the government). Labour can co-operate with progressive or well-inclined governments as it did with President Cárdenas in Mexico in the 1930s. But the reality is that progressive governments of this type are rare in Latin America, and that what may start out as co-operation can end as manipulation.

The intention of such detailed regulation of unions was to remove labour from politics and to control their operations. Yet the consequences have been exactly the opposite. Because governments regulate so closely matters crucial to trade unions (incomes policies are an obvious example), unions must confront or try to influence governments if they are to achieve any of their basic objectives. Because legal regulation has made unions weak, they are forced to seek political allies to attempt to influence government policy. So in most countries in Latin America trade unions are associated with one or another political party – Socialists, Communists, or Christian Democrats in Chile; Peruvian sugar workers with the APRA, Peruvian schoolteachers with the Maoist left; Venezuelan peasant unions with AD (Democratic Action); the Mexican labour movement with the PRI (Institutional Revolutionary Party), and so on. The major exception, as always, is Argentina, where a political movement, Peronism, was dominated by the power of the trade unions, especially after 1955.

This close association with political parties brings advantages and disadvantages. The connection with a party can help to unify disparate occupational groups; it can articulate diffuse interests into a coherent strategy; it can aid and defend labour in crisis; and it can act as a source of funds and of legal advice. But there are disadvantages too. Because more than one party competes for the support of labour, there is the danger of sectarianism and the subsuming of the interests of the unions in those of the party (the best-known example of this is probably that of APRA in Peru). When a weak union movement needs an impetus towards unity, political differences can be a further dividing factor. And, when political parties are suppressed, then labour movements associated with such parties suffer as well. However, the North American model of apolitical unionism is totally misplaced in Latin America. Even the most basic expression of union activity is likely to be defined by the government as 'political'; and any attempt at collective action on behalf of the welfare of the poor is likely to be seen as subversive too.

An additional complication should be mentioned (though to explore its ramifications would be very complex) and that is the activities of international bodies. By this one means mostly North American influences whether directly through mutual involvement in the ORIT (Inter-American Regional Organization of Labour), or indirectly through American-based training institutes such as the

Demonstrators on a May Day march in Quito, Ecuador, 1976

AIFLD (American Institute for Free Labour Development), or more clandestinely through the CIA. A great deal of money is spent by these groups in Latin America; rather less, though still a great deal, is spent by various Christian groups channelled through CLAT (Latin American Confederation of Workers). How effective it is, is another matter. One should not underestimate the capacity of local labour movements to manipulate their much wealthier counterparts. But such activities are usually an intrusion into local politics and a force for division.

Conclusion

Popular protest, involving but not exclusively confined to trade unions, came to dominate the politics of many Latin American countries in the 1960s and 1970s. To attempt to contain that protest – in Chile, Uruguay, Argentina, Bolivia and Peru – the state resorted to more drastic measures of repression and control under the guidance of authoritarian military regimes. Indeed, so strongly was the threat felt in some countries, that a deliberate attempt has been made to restructure the economy in such a way that the working class is less likely to pose a challenge in the future. The monetarist policies pursued in Chile, by reducing the size of the manufacturing sector, obviously weaken industrial unions.

Yet the greatest obstacle to the consolidation of these authoritarian governments still remains the labour movement. After ten years of industrial peace, 1978 saw massive and impressive strikes in Brazil. A successful general strike in Peru hastened the military's decision to return the government to civilian hands. Even the repression obtaining in General Pinochet's Chile has not destroyed the political tradition of the union movement, aided to a very considerable extent by the Church.

As the most organized sector of the majority of the urban and rural poor, trade unions have been forced to speak for and to defend those interests. Trade unions have transcended their specific functions because the dominant system has made it extremely difficult to perform those functions with any degree of effectiveness. Unions therefore have to offer an alternative social and economic model that overcomes differences inside the working class.

This article has stressed the close relationship between the labour movement and the national political and economic system. Statistics on membership, density of union organization and so on are often inaccurate and misleading, and tell us very little about the nature and role of trade unions. The fortunes of labour movements are inextricably woven into national political systems, and while unions have changed in many ways during this century, this particular relationship has endured.

AEA

Further reading

A. Angell, *Politics and the Labour Movement in Chile* (London, 1972)
K. Erickson, *The Brazilian Corporative State and Working Class Politics* (California, 1977)
Latin America Bureau, *Unity is Strength: Trade Unions in Latin America* (London, 1980)
J. Nash, *We Eat the Mines and the Mines Eat Us: Dependency and Exploitation in Bolivian Tin Mines* (New York, 1979)
H. Spalding, *Organised Labour in Latin America* (New York, 1977)
E. Stevens, *Protest and Response in Mexico* (Cambridge, Mass., 1974)

Insurgency and terrorism

Twenty years lie between the two successful contemporary insurgencies in Latin America – Cuba in 1959 and Nicaragua in 1979. It is hard to look back to a time when insurgency was not dominated by the figure of Fidel Castro and by the ideas that crystallized around the rural guerrilla campaign which in 1959 wrested power from corrupt dictatorship in Cuba. Yet the very independence of South America owed much to guerrilla warfare, and further guerrilla campaigns were fought in Mexico, Cuba, Brazil and Nicaragua in the nineteenth and early twentieth centuries. Alongside these insurgencies the military more often than not played the dominant role in politics, the course of which was

punctuated by violent changes of power and by civil violence. Rural banditry, like urban crime, was endemic. Terror, employed as a tactic to intimidate rather than to seize power, was as much a part of life then as it is today.

In the wake of the Cuban revolution, these and other factors survived: the old and in many ways thoroughly unsatisfactory political order continued, regardless of the determined attempts by sincere but naive men to influence affairs for the better by resorting to political violence. Furthermore, in so far as events in Cuba stimulated insurgency elsewhere (Guatemala, Venezuela, Colombia, Peru, Bolivia, Dominican Republic), its failure appeared to reinforce the pattern of the past.

For instance, government in Bolivia, which had undergone more military coups than years of independence, remained for much of the time in the hands of a military clique, whose members, pursuing dreary and short-sighted barrack politics, followed one another in more or less corrupt succession. A long-standing caudillo, such as President Alfredo Stroessner of Paraguay, survived quite untouched by the new ideas, and was joined by new 'strong men' like President Pinochet of Chile, who overcame them. In Argentina and Uruguay the military felt compelled by the forthright attack of an unrepresentative minority upon the old order to intervene in the political process so as to restore safety to the streets. But in so doing they revived an old problem of how to return to barracks once they had eradicated the insurgent movements. In the early 1980s the problem still confronted military governments, and is likely to continue to do so until an alternative more suitable to Latin America than either Leninism or ineffective multiparty democracy is developed.

By placing the Cuban insurgency in context one must not rob it of its originality, nor deny the immense impact it has had. After Castro's victory, Cuba quickly became the first Marxist–Leninist state in the Americas, closely allied to the Soviet bloc. Thenceforth Castro improved the prospects of revolution in Latin America by giving potential insurgents a base, and later a haven. On occasions he supplied arms and provided training, but never sufficiently, in the 1960s, to decide the victory. Nor in 1979 were Cuban arms the decisive factor in the overthrow by insurgent forces of President Somoza in Nicaragua.

More particularly Castro internationalized the struggle by offering on radio and in the press a new dimension for insurgent pretensions. Such programmes were mostly couched in Marxist–Leninist terms, in their way as dated and pompous but as characteristic of their time as earlier liberal political rhetoric, and certainly as far removed from the facts. Yet they were essential, nonetheless, if the movement were to kindle the interest and the support of the 'socialist' world community led by Moscow.

In all, the Cuban interest in the 1960s and early 1970s probably had a greater effect upon the response to insurgency than on the guerrilla effort itself, for what was seen as communist influence generated extreme fear, causing governments to look abroad for remedies which might more properly have been found within the strengths and traditions of their own societies. Both the insurgency and the response outrageously restricted liberties and produced intense personal suffering. More widely, these campaigns contributed nothing to the lot of the common man.

The insurgencies of the 1960s failed outright; those of the early 1970s (Argentina, Uruguay) succeeded in destroying democratic freedoms and having them replaced by authoritarian restrictions. The outcome of the third insurgent complex in the late 1970s, which is being played out in Central America, has yet to be determined. But already in Nicaragua the revolution has come to power, and beyond its borders in El Salvador, Guatemala and Honduras the impact of the 1979 Sandinista victory has inspired revolt. The exact nature of the Nicaraguan revolution was still in question in 1984, but its survival did not seem in doubt.

Behind Castro, the guerrilla leader, was Ernesto 'Che' Guevara (1928–67), whose diaries and analysis of rural guerrilla warfare inspired men to fight and to think. Without doubt, the most original thinker who influenced rural tactics was Régis Debray (b. 1940), a French Marxist writer who accompanied Guevara to Bolivia, where he narrowly escaped death. Once released by the Bolivian authorities he returned to France to become, in 1981, an adviser to the

Régis Debray

socialist president François Mitterand. His principal contribution to insurgency was to stress the impact which a small band of guerrillas in the countryside, acting as a revolutionary nucleus, could have upon the revolutionary process. By pointing up this aspect, he reduced the role of the mass party, so crucial to Leninism; this change of priorities led to endless debate and even to splits in the increasingly fractionalized Marxist–Leninist political school.

But the establishment of a rural nucleus promised young men immediate action, and, in the light of Castro's success, there were those daring enough to venture their lives for their ideal of a more just political order. So it was in Paraguay, Argentina and the Dominican Republic (1959), in Venezuela and Colombia (1961), in Guatemala and Ecuador (1962), in Peru (1963), in Bolivia (1967) and in Brazil (1968). Often enough if the first attempt failed, a second and a third were tried, until the list of dead guerrilla leaders was long enough to convince the revolutionary faithful that on its own the rural nucleus would not bring about a change in the established order. Among the most memorable of these men were Luis de la Puente (d. 1965, Peru), Camilo Torres (d. 1966, Colombia), Fabricio Ojeda (d. 1966, Venezuela), Che Guevara (d. 1967, Bolivia), Guido 'Inti' Peredo (d. 1969, Bolivia), Carlos Marighela (d. 1969, Brazil) and Marco Antonio Yon Sosa (d. 1970, Guatemala).

The reasons for failure in large part stemmed from the hopelessly inadequate preparation and training of those involved and the indifference with which their efforts were met by the local peasantry. It is also true that US counter-insurgency training improved the performance of local special forces. This was particularly the case in Bolivia.

If the first complex of revolutionary activity failed, the idea of a continental revolution persisted, fortified by the notions of historical inevitability increasingly taught by orthodox Marxist–Leninists in Havana. At the time of the Vietnam War, it was thought that on the American mainland a number of fires might be lit, which would develop into a whole series of Vietnams. Che Guevara utterly failed to coordinate such a grand strategy on the ground. Castro was somewhat more successful politically with the creation in 1967 of the Organization for Latin American Solidarity (OLAS), which at least provided in Havana a meeting place for like-minded revolutionaries, even if nothing lasting came of its publications and more was heard of its quarrels than of its agreements.

In common with Guevara, the leaders of the second complex of insurgencies all held a belief that the armed struggle was more important than the vanguard party in bringing about the revolution. In this, like him, they were communist heretics. But rather than fight in the countryside, they sought to wage in the cities a campaign which embraced assassination, kidnap, bombings and sabotage, as well as the clandestine infiltration of the principal organs of the state.

Of greatest influence were the slim volume written by the long-standing Brazilian activist Carlos Marighela, *The Minimanual of the Urban Guerrilla*, and the work of the Spanish revolutionary Abraham Guillén. The new war in the cities was ugly and destructive: it was primarily played out in Brazil (1964–70), in Uruguay (1968–72) and in Argentina (1969–76), and caused the transformation of traditionally liberal societies into closed ones, where military rule was imposed upon all aspects of the state – on legislative, judicial and economic activities as well as upon labour, education and the press.

Elsewhere, attempts were made by existing rural guerrilla movements to set up urban bases. In Venezuela and Colombia rural activity was never entirely eradicated, although in the 1970s it never presented the same threat to the state as for a time, in the previous decade, it had succeeded in doing.

The protagonists in both insurgent complexes were drawn from identical backgrounds: they were young, middle-class, for the most part university-educated men and women, who from ideological conviction decided to embark upon the task of overthrowing the existing order. Nationalism did not play a dominant role in their motivation, although by attempting to identify the ruling orders with US imperialism they sought to stimulate national resentment.

But, in fact, it proved as impossible to arouse the masses in the cities as it had in the countryside, although the corrupt habits of weak democracy were tellingly exposed. As the normal powers of democracy proved unable to cope with terrorism, the security forces took matters into their own hands. The most terrible gangster practices developed. Responding to the cold-blooded terrorism by the subversive forces, paramilitary death squads eliminated individuals thought to be involved in the onslaught against the state.

To the outside world the Robin Hood image of the Uruguayan Tupamaros (MLN) was naturally appealing; so too was the daring approach they adopted in their tactics. But behind the apparent youthful middle-class decency and honesty lay a ruthless determination to disregard the electorate (they failed in 1971 to attract more than 20 per cent of votes as part of a Broad Front electoral alliance) and to destroy a democratic state. They never developed a clear political model as an alternative, and it would be wrong to think of them as orthodox Marxist–Leninists, although, had the Tupamaros come to power, Soviet-style communism might well have taken control, as it did in Cuba, and may still do in Nicaragua.

As it was, the military declared a state of internal war and uprooted the subversive network in 1972, when as many as 2800 members were jailed and sixty-two killed in shoot-outs. Raúl Sendic, the movement's founder was captured, and a decade later remained in jail in Montevideo. Many hundreds of his colleagues fled abroad, mostly to Europe. It was, indeed, a tragedy that so few could cause such fear as to change the course of politics, not momentarily through military intervention, but for a decade and more.

The Tupamaros had been helped by Cuba, but the reasons for their revolt lay deep within the Uruguayan economy and Uruguayan society. So it was in Argentina, where in the first half of the 1970s two political currents, Peronism and Trotskyism, contributed to an appalling growth of terrorism, on a scale hitherto unknown in the region. The reasons were complex but essentially had to do with the struggle for power.

General Perón (ousted 1955) had left behind him a trade union structure and political sympathizers within a national working-class movement known as 'justicialism'. From his exile in Spain he encouraged the younger members of the movement to adopt political violence as a tactic, but these acts of terrorism widened the gap between them and the older Peronist trade union bosses. As Perón's followers divided into a left wing and a right wing, the old man could hold the movement together only by refraining from condemning either side. In the end (1974) he backed the old-guard right, and Peronist fought Peronist in a bitter war of abduction, mutilation and murder.

From the various Peronist militias the Montoneros (1970) emerged as a left-wing movement using terrorist tactics against the government. Led by Mario Firmenich, the organization raised large sums of money by holding hostage business executives, and between 1974 and 1978 carried out a spectacular series of brutal assassinations of high-ranking government and security force members. They never developed an organization capable of waging a guerrilla campaign, but were rather concerned to inherit Peronist support and seize power on an extreme left-wing platform. As the Argentine military were drawn into the counter-insurgency campaign and eventually took over the government, the Montoneros went into exile in 1977, and from Europe and Havana sought to persuade social democrats of their spurious political credentials as an opposition exiled by military brutality.

In fact, their background was in part almost fascist, their tactics those of the worst kind of bully-boy and their pretensions utterly undemocratic. Nevertheless, Castro afforded Firmenich favours, and in 1979 the Montoneros were said to have contributed a portion of their ransom money to the Sandinista victory in Nicaragua.

Equally devastating to Argentine society was the growth in the early 1970s of the Trotskyist People's Revolutionary Army (ERP), set up in 1969 as a clandestine military apparatus with the purpose of waging a low-intensity war in town and country against the government. Like the Tupamaros, its leader Roberto Santucho (d. 1976) sought to promote the Robin Hood image by distributing expropriated food and clothes to the urban poor. ERP guerrillas were ruthless in the gunning down of their targets, whom they selected carefully from among the more prominent business executives and military hierarchy. Principally active in the larger cities, but especially in Buenos Aires and Córdoba, the ERP also promoted rural guerrilla warfare in the province of Tucumán.

The military responded to this threat in the same way as to the Peronists – an internal campaign was waged against them. The clandestine nature of the war chosen by the ERP led to terror tactics from paramilitary groups who disposed of several thousand people, leaving no trace of their whereabouts. To admit to these irregularities and to hold individuals responsible for such atrocities was deemed impossible by the military government, which when it had taken power in 1976 had been received with popular relief, but which subsequently proved lamentably weak in controlling the excesses of its own members.

In only one country (Nicaragua), and twenty years after the Cuban revolution, has insurgency contributed to the downfall of a despotic regime and the establishment of what was at first considered government by and on behalf of the people. But in Nicaragua a series of unique circumstances contributed to the Sandinista victory. First, President Carter finally proved unwilling to provide the support which the Somoza family had so far unquestioningly received from the United States. The struggle coincided, too, with a new determination on the part of Cuba to play host to insurgent movements and to strengthen not only their resolve but their arms supplies and their training. At the same time a sea change had been wrought in Latin American society by the new stance of the Catholic Church towards unjust government and poverty, a stand which manifested itself particularly in the growth of what became known as 'liberation theology'. Three priests, Ernesto Cardenal, Miguel d'Escoto and Edgar Parrales played prominent roles in the Sandinista movement and took office when it came to power. As moderates despaired of persuading Somoza to reform a government which had for long been little more than a family business, the Sandinistas picked up the support of the business and professional classes.

In the final analysis, however, it was a guerrilla force led by Edén Pastora that stretched the resources of a disciplined national guard, and engaged in a series of ragged military confrontations. Faced by a stalemate, once the United States had made clear that he was no longer wanted, Somoza withdrew rather than fight to the bitter end.

The precedent gave an enormous boost to the forces of revolution in Central America, but the circumstances of Nicaragua were peculiar, and are not mirrored in El Salvador, still less in Guatemala and Honduras. However, Cuban supplies to the Salvadorean insurgents, soon largely supplanted by arms captured from government troops, allowed them to hold their own in a military stalemate which cried out for political compromise in 1984. And in Guatemala César Montes (b. 1942) who had failed to raise the countryside in the 1960s as a leader of the Rebel Armed Forces (FAR) re-emerged in

A Salvadorean guerrilla kitted out in US-made equipment. It is estimated that nearly a quarter of all arms supplied to the Salvadorean army by the US government end up in guerrilla hands

the late 1970s as head of the Guerrilla Army of the Poor (EGP). Still further afield, Colombia felt the quickened Cuban revolutionary interest, which armed and supported Jaime Bateman's left-wing populist group known as M-19.

It may be that the resurgence of guerrilla activity in Central America prompts the medium-sized oil-rich powers of the region – Venezuela and Mexico – to act as a moderating influence and provide the initiative by helping to finance reform. Certainly the threat of revolution in Central America requires from the United States a thorough reappraisal of its foreign policy priorities and a rethinking of the style and manner in which it projects its strength.

PJ

Further reading

R. Debray, *A Critique of Arms* (London, 1977)

R. Gillespie, *Soldiers of Perón* (New York, 1983)

R. Gott, *Guerrilla Movements in Latin America* (London, 1970)

D. Hodges, *The Legacy of Che Guevara* (London, 1977)

J. Kohl and J. Litt, *Urban Guerrilla Warfare in Latin America* (London, 1974)

The Church in Latin America

From the earliest colonial times Roman Catholic values and practices have been an integral feature of Latin American society and culture. In large measure the region's religious history has been the history of Roman Catholicism. That Church's representatives entered the area, along with the earliest colonizers, as the ally and legitimator of Spanish and Portuguese colonial authorities. The latter effectively guaranteed the Church against ideological competition whilst the Church itself engaged in a process of mass conversion. The Church and colonial society were therefore viewed as essentially co-terminous communities.

By special Papal concession imperial authorities exercised unprecedented controls over the Church in the New World. The Spanish and Portuguese crowns controlled senior ecclesiastical appointments and co-opted churchmen into the imperial administration. The Church's spiritual authority was similarly exercised in defence of the status quo. In return the Church received such privileges as extensive landholdings and control over education. There were limited 'Church–state' conflicts over, for example, the rights of Indians, and the Jesuits even established paternalistically-run Indian communities largely free of secular control. The general picture, however, was of a Church wedded to the secular power and upholding the existing hierarchically structured social order. An orthodox Thomist theology, which perceived society in necessarily hierarchical terms, provided no basis for extensive social criticism; equally, the Church was conceived in clerical terms with the laity being accorded an essentially subordinate and passive role.

Given the Church's links with the imperial powers, only a handful of clergy, notably in Mexico, were actively associated with the independence struggle. After independence the new republics sought to maintain those controls over the Church once exercised by imperial authorities, whilst the Papacy sought to recover lost authority. Divisions within the governing elites of the new states further complicated the situation. Some, associated with Liberal parties and influenced by contemporary rationalism, liberalism or positivism, sought to curb clerical influence. In response the Church formed alliances with traditional upper-class interests generally associated with Conservative parties. In Chile and Colombia, for example, Liberal versus Conservative confrontations over the Church were a major source of ideological division.

Conflicts over the Church's social and political position had differing outcomes. At one extreme was Colombia where, in 1887, Church and state concluded a (still existing) Concordat that guaranteed to the Church a privileged and officially established position. At the other extreme was Mexico which, during the revolution, experienced a period of militant anti-clerical activity aimed at the definitive eradication of ecclesiastical influence. This gave way to a largely peaceful *modus vivendi* but one that still left the Church without much direct political influence. More striking, the Cuban Church, which had always lacked deep social roots, was driven to the margins of society as a consequence of revolution.

Elsewhere, in Chile for example (1925), the Church was ultimately disestablished but retained a *de facto* position of considerable significance. Throughout the region, however, the Church retained the hallmarks of its origins by remaining a more or less uniformly conservative institution generally united in support of established social structures.

The often seemingly secure nature of the Church's position tended to obscure the limited nature of its impact upon popular religious practice. The apparently successful mass conversion policy frequently left the indigenous population with a syncretic religion in which Catholic practices or values co-existed with beliefs and rites of pre-colonial origins. The later importation of slaves also, in reality, meant the introduction of African religious practices. The net result was a frequently tenuous link with official ecclesiastical structures. Equally, many apparently more orthodox Catholics shared in a popular 'cultural' religion which accepted Catholic symbolism and ritual as part of the prevailing culture but without high levels of religious understanding or explicit commitment. The higher levels of commitment tended to be disproportionately associated with middle- and, more especially, upper-class groups for whom formal religious practice was one part of a general upper-class life style. The commitment was generally individualistic and pietistic in character. Just as popular religion tended to promote passivity in face of prevailing inequalities, so more orthodox expressions of Catholicism continued to lack a socially critical component.

Socioeconomic and political changes in the area eventually exposed underlying weaknesses in the Church's position and, albeit gradually, constrained the institution to re-evaluate its relationship with the surrounding society. To some extent changes reflected fresh theological thinking percolating through from Europe but they also signified a response to changing realities. Thus, processes of economic development, some industrialization and, above all, urbanization in the late nineteenth and early twentieth centuries eroded the basis of the relatively static and largely rural society within which the Church had first developed and had cultivated its upper-class alliances. New middle- and lower-strata groups emerged, of a potentially more secularized kind. Equally, massive emigration from Europe to such countries as Argentina, Brazil, Chile and Uruguay meant the emergence of significant Protestant groups as well as of new secular ideologies.

Initial Church responses were of a generally defensive nature. They first took the form of working-class groups, run on paternalistic lines, for the promotion, for example, of mutual aid societies.

A Corpus Christi procession in Cuzco, Peru

Later, particularly from the 1920s onwards, serious efforts were made to mobilize Catholic laity, under clerical auspices, through such bodies as Catholic Action. Some union movements of Catholic inspiration were also created. For example, what is still the largest union confederation in Colombia, the UTC (Colombian Workers' Union) was established in 1946 at the instigation of local Jesuits. In Argentina and Brazil initial clerical reactions to fresh challenges sometimes took the form of alliances with ultra-nationalist or even fascist-type movements. In nearly all cases, however, the accent was on defending ecclesiastical institutions against perceived threats and on the possibility of pre-empting more radical change. The underlying presupposition was generally of a clerical triumphalism that envisaged an eventual return to the earlier 'neo-Christendom' position.

The difficulties and possible dangers inherent in such responses were indicated, for example, in Argentina where the hierarchy initially saw alliance with Perón's nationalist populist regime (1946–55) as an appropriate means of underwriting clerical influence within a menacing environment. At the outset Perón accepted such support as a useful source of legitimacy. Ultimately, however, he was constrained by political and economic crises to appeal to anti-clericalism, evidently widespread amongst his urban lower-strata following, as one means of rallying the latter's support. This tended, in practice, to reinforce the Argentine hierarchy's prevailing conservatism but also drew attention to the possibly inadequate nature of conventional responses to the Church's fundamental dilemmas.

During the 1950s support grew for initiatives of a less obviously defensive kind. Revised understandings, derived from such European theologians as Jacques Maritain, contributed to more positive evaluations of secular demands for greater political partici-

pation and the more equitable distribution of resources. Significantly enough, the Chilean Church was in the vanguard. It had felt particularly keenly the competition of secular left-wing parties and of Protestant groups and so had particularly strong incentives to revise traditional strategies. Thus, efforts were made to mobilize peasants and support was given to the cause of land reform. Of particular significance was the emergence of a reformist Christian Democratic Party committed to significant structural changes. The party (which had less successful counterparts elsewhere in Latin America) was not directly linked with the hierarchy and accepted Chilean society's pluralistic nature to the extent of deliberately appealing beyond the Catholic community's confines. It was, however, of avowedly Christian inspiration and ultimately aimed, in principle, at the construction of a society constituted in accordance with revised understandings of Catholic social doctrine.

On the theoretical plane Latin America's Christian Democrats have had the problem of relating general principles to the exigencies of daily political conflict. On the practical political plane, as shown by the fate of the Chilean government of Eduardo Frei (1964–70), they were unable to maintain an alliance between more conservative supporters who saw Christian Democracy as the best available defence against unwelcome changes and more radical activists positively committed to reform.

During the 1960s more radical and politicized understandings of Catholicism appeared on the Latin American Church's agenda and, to a significant extent, transformed the terms of religious debate. This was partly the consequence of long-germinating changes in the local Church and of the latter's response to an increasing sense of crisis in the region's economic, social and political life. Not least, the Cuban revolution led to a heightening of political expectations and tension. Notably in Brazil, this was reflected in some Catholic participation in attempts to mobilize previously quiescent groups, especially amongst the peasantry. The radical Catholic 'Movement for Basic Education' contributed to the general if limited radicalization process that preceded the 1964 military coup. Above all, the Brazilian, Paulo Freire, developed the influential concept of '*conscientização*' signifying the effort to raise the political consciousness of lower-strata groups in order to equip them for their own eventual political emancipation. Such developments had some support from the Brazilian hierarchy and, particularly, from the famous Archbishop Helder Câmara of Recife who played a major part in creating ecclesiastical bureaucratic structures capable of guiding the processes of change. Other parts of the hierarchy, however, were ambivalent or hostile. Nevertheless, precedents for further forms of radical Catholic political engagement had been established.

In the next two decades such forms of engagement became increasingly common. These developments often arose out of currents of Catholic thought associated with the Second Conference of Latin American Bishops held in Medellín (Colombia) in 1968. The first such conference had been held a decade earlier and had involved the creation of a permanent secretariat. The institutionalization of this body (CELAM – or Latin American Episcopal Conference) testified to growing awareness of the Latin American Church's shared problems. The Medellín Conference, more specifically, represented an attempt to spell out the implications, for Latin America, of changes in the wider Catholic community associated with the Second Vatican Council. The latter helped to foster and legitimize previously unorthodox positions running counter to the general trend of Latin American Church history. Thus, opposition was expressed to traditional alliances with privileged elites or the state. Their abandonment, it was suggested, would free the Church to fulfil a prophetic mission as an opponent of injustice and as the advocate of underprivileged groups. Such a re-alignment was taken to represent a more authentic presentation of the Christian tradition. Similarly, the individual conscience's inviolability was recognized together with a consequent acceptance of the legitimacy of religious and ideological pluralism. Indeed, the possibility opened up of some 'Christian–Marxist' dialogue and of practical cooperation between Catholics and representatives of other religious or secular traditions. Within the Church these were pointers to more collegiate and decentralized forms of authority and increased emphasis on the laity's responsibility for transforming secular society. There was a retreat from traditional concepts of an embattled 'fortress' Church and moves towards the notion of secular history as an arena of divine activity in which Catholics should participate, along with others of 'good will'. The Church's task, in this setting, becomes the sustenance of a prophetic ministry based

Crowds gather in the main plaza in front of the cathedral at Bogotá for the visit of Pope Paul VI in 1968

on correct discernment of 'the signs of the times'. Under the latter heading come contemporary demands for greater justice or equality between and within nations. Likewise, traditional images of the Church yielded to such communitarian, participatory and dynamic models as 'the Pilgrim People of God'.

Latin American ecclesiastical leaders and their advisers, associated with CELAM and already radicalized by their distinctive experiences, developed such thinking in the light of the region's particular problems. They prepared the Medellín gathering's agenda and kept the initiative during its discussions. The result was a watershed in Latin American Church history. The conference's official findings offered an authoritative interpretation of Latin American realities drawing on biblical (as opposed to traditional Thomist) understandings but also borrowing from such influential modes of political and economic analysis as 'dependency theory' that present the region's life in terms of patterns of international and national exploitation. Traditional, essentially individualistic concepts of sin were expanded to embrace the notion of 'structural sin' expressing itself through impersonal structures that prevent most Latin Americans from realizing their full human potential or from determining their own corporate destinies. Active participation in the transformation or eradication of these structures is seen as a necessary extension of the Church's witness.

Pope Paul VI, at Medellín, sought to preclude violence from the otherwise legitimate struggle for justice. This remains the prevailing official view of even such radical figures as Helder Câmara. However, a minority of radicalized Catholics have responded to the 'institutionalized violence' of entrenched opponents of radical change by presenting violence as a sometimes necessary and legitimate option. The analogy of 'the just war' is deployed. Camilo Torres, the Colombian priest, killed in a guerrilla operation in 1966, is cited as a possible model. In the 1970s some (though certainly not all) exponents of 'Liberation Theology' were in this category.

'Liberation Theology' is internationally known through the writings of figures such as Gustavo Gutiérrez, José Luis Segundo, Hugo Assman and Leonardo Boff. It partly represents an especially radicalized and politicized interpretation of the Medellín findings. In part it is also a product of a 'Christian–Marxist' dialogue. Certainly, its advocates have borrowed Marxist categories and analysed their situation in recognizably Marxist terms. It may be further viewed as both cause and effect of local-involvement, by Catholic activists, with such disadvantaged social sectors as urban shanty town dwellers and peasant groups.

These developments have shattered Latin American Catholicism's once conservative consensus and a new consensus has yet to emerge. Catholics, at all levels, including that of the official leadership, have divided responses to recent developments. Particularly in Central America some churchmen have been engaged in prolonged and even violent struggles with established military-backed regimes.

Some Nicaraguan priests have participated in the revolutionary Sandinista government. A Chilean 'Christians for Socialism' group, which played a prominent part in debate during Allende's regime (1970–3), acted as a model for similar radical groups committed to a peaceful evolutionary route to socialism. More common has been the espousal of reformist positions, though their advocates have been divided over the depth or speed of change. Portions of the Brazilian hierarchy, for example, have been bitterly critical of the general effects of capitalism on Brazilian society whilst others have tended to focus on specific injustices or violations of human rights. There are other, more traditional elements, whose chief priority is pastoral work conceived in conventional terms, who seek to limit political involvement to the enunciation of general principles. They fear that the importation of political divisions into the Church will damage the institution's cohesion and credibility. They also fear that politicization will ultimately lead to the loss of a distinctive Christian identity. Major concerns for them are the decline in priestly vocations, wavering on such issues as birth control and other symptoms of the crisis of authority, through which Roman Catholicism, in general, is passing.

Finally, a vociferous minority of influential ultra-conservatives has sought to co-opt the Church into the service of authoritarian regimes on the grounds that they are upholders of national security against a perceived Marxist threat. The 'Tradition, Family and Property' group is an example of such 'Integralist' pre-Vatican II Catholics.

For most Catholic spokesmen, experience of military government has had some radicalizing effects. In both Brazil and Chile, for example, much of the hierarchy initially acquiesced in or welcomed military intervention. Subsequent experience of repression generally solidified Church opposition. Churchmen were among the most articulate critics of systematic violations of human rights and Church organizations provided support for victims as well as for lower-strata victims of official economic policies. Within these contexts grass-roots 'Basic Christian Communities' have proliferated. These localized flexible structures have offered unprecedented opportunities for lay participation and have helped disadvantaged groups to acquire political consciousness and skills. In Brazil recruits from such quarters played a significant part in launching the Partido dos Trabalhadores (PT) – a political party created in 1979 under the auspices of labour leaders who have received considerable official Church support. Conversely, many opposition groups have turned to the Church as the most credible source of assistance and protection. It underlines the fact that no Latin American organization, apart from the state, has such a developed and extensive organizational network. The Basic Com-

munities give added depth and flexibility to already established parochial and diocesan structures. Equally, the Church can call on the resources of male and female religious orders, frequently drawn from abroad, who have provided the institution with often highly trained and readily disposable pastoral, intellectual and political leadership.

The above mentioned divisions also cut right across the once firm boundary dividing the Catholic from Protestant communities. The latter have both grown and divided along lines that, in some measure, correspond to divisions in the Catholic Church. Equally, there are growing instances of Catholic–Protestant co-operation. Thus, such long-established and mainly conservative middle-class groups as the Lutherans have seen the emergence of radical activists sharing many of the preoccupations of Catholic 'theologians of liberation'. One Brazilian Protestant theologian, Rubem Alves, has acquired an international reputation. On the other hand, charismatic Pentecostalist groups, with particularly extensive followings amongst the urban poor, generally eschew political involvement. Equally, ultra-conservative biblically fundamentalist groups, frequently of United States origin, remain largely uncritical of the established order. A recent Guatemalan military president, Efraín Rios Montt, belongs to such a group.

More traditional elements in the Roman Catholic Church, concerned about the general direction of post-Medellín changes, have actively sought to halt radicalizing tendencies. Led by Cardinal López Trujillo of Colombia such groups acquired control of CELAM's official apparatus and at the third conference of Latin American Bishops, held in Puebla (Mexico) in 1979 sought to re-emphasize the centrality of the Church's traditional evangelical or missionary task. They received some encouragement from the Vatican, and Pope John Paul II himself favoured an end to overt clerical involvement in politics. Puebla's eventual findings appeared to be something of a compromise. Renewed stress was placed upon the Church's traditional pastoral responsibilities but adherence to the cause of justice was also proclaimed. Debates about the appropriate religious responses to Latin America's problems are, therefore, bound to continue.

KM

Further reading

T. C. Bruneau, *The Church in Brazil: the Politics of Religion* (Austin, Texas, 1982)

A. Gheerbrant, *The Rebel Church in Latin America* (Harmondsworth, 1974)

P. Lernoux, *Cry of the People* (Garden City, 1980)

D. H. Levine, ed., *Churches and Politics in Latin America* (Beverly Hills, 1980)

B. H. Smith, *The Church and Politics in Chile* (Princeton, NJ, 1982)

CULTURE

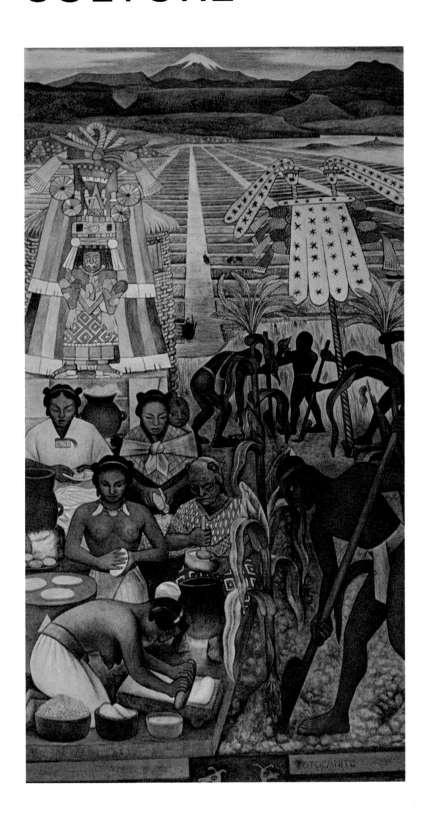

Diego Rivera, 'Valley of Mexico before the Conquest'

Literacy and education

Throughout the region, education systems vary considerably, reflecting differences in history, political institutions, levels of social and economic development, and patterns of urbanization and industrialization. Despite this, a number of major issues, trends and problems can certainly be detected. Education systems, despite rapid growth since the 1950s, have found their capacity to bring about social change and promote equity constrained by the prevailing economic and political order and social structure. Generally they have failed to effect a more equitable distribution of income and social services. Despite significant improvement in enrolment rates, the provision of education opportunities continues to be closely related to the social and economic status of the client population. The degree of individual advancement within the formal education systems is related, as before, to parents' socioeconomic background, place of residence and education history.

Formal education

At the 1979 Regional Conference of Education Ministers and those responsible for Economic Planning of Member States in Latin America and the Caribbean held in Mexico City, participants acknowledged the sustained effort that had been made by the countries of the region in the past decades to develop education and the very noteworthy achievements in the quantitative expansion of systems and in the improvement of educational content and processes. Such achievements should not be underestimated, given the

Schoolchildren in a remote Bolivian village

rapidly increasing school-age population in the region and the costs involved. Between 1960 and 1976 the total number of pupils in school increased from 30 to 75.2 millions. The increase was distributed in the following way: 31.5 million in primary, 10.4 million in secondary, and 3.3 million in higher education.

As table 48 shows, all the countries in the region have compulsory education ranging from five years to twelve years in length. Entrance ranges from four years to seven years of age. However, no countries in the region have been able to achieve the aim of universal basic education, due largely to high drop-out rates.

Table 49a illustrates the survival rates of the 1970 cohort (annual intake) of students in selected countries. In eight of the fourteen countries included in that table over 22 per cent of students fail to survive beyond grade 1. In Nicaragua and Brazil less than 60 per

Table 48. Duration of compulsory education and age limits

Country	Age limits	Duration (years)
Argentina	6–14	7
Bolivia	6–14	8
Brazil	7–14	8
Chile	6–15	8
Colombia	7–11	5
Cuba	6–14	6
Dominica	5–15	10
Dominican Republic	7–14	7
Ecuador	6–14	6
El Salvador	6–18	9
Falkland Islands (Malvinas)	5–15	10
Grenada	5–14	8
Guadeloupe	6–16	10
Guatemala	7–14	6
Guyana	6–15	8
Guyane	6–16	10
Haiti	6–12	6
Honduras	6–13	6
Jamaica	6–17	11
Martinique	6–16	10
Mexico	6–14	6
Montserrat	5–14	9
Netherlands Antilles	–	–
Nicaragua	7–13	6
Panama	6–15	9
Panama Canal Zone	6–14	
Paraguay	7–14	6
Peru	6–14	9
Puerto Rico	6–18	12
St Kitts/Nevis/Anguilla	5–14	9
St Lucia	5–15	10
St Pierre and Miquelon	7–14	7
St Vincent	5–15	10
Surinam	6–12	6
Trinidad and Tobago	6–12	7
Turks and Caicos Islands	4–14	9
US Virgin Islands	6–18	12
Uruguay	6–14	9
Venezuela	7–13	6

Source: UNESCO, *Statistical Year Book – 1980*.

cent of students continued into grade 2. Only in Chile, Costa Rica, Guyana and Uruguay did more than two-thirds of the 1970 cohort reach grade 5. The high wastage rate in the case of Brazil is clearly attested by the fact that even today only a quarter of the children in first-level school can hope to complete the course.

Table 49a. Survival rates of the 1970 cohort of students in selected countries
(percentage of students enrolled in grade 1 reaching higher grades)

	Grade 2	Grade 3	Grade 4	Grade 5	Grade 6
Brazil	58.8	50.6	43.2	38.2	33.2
Chile	90.1	85.3	81.8	76.7	71.6
Colombia	69.1	55.1	41.3	37.5	69.5
Costa Rica	94.2	89.2	83.8	77.7	73.2
Dominican Republic[a]	64.3	53.8	41.5	33.7	28.8
Ecuador	75.3	69.0	63.7	57.2	55.1
El Salvador	67.8	56.0	49.7	42.9	37.8
Guatemala	66.6	53.8	42.3	34.7	30.9
Guyana	99.9	99.9	95.0	86.4	86.4
Nicaragua	56.3	44.8	36.7	30.6	26.6
Paraguay	84.5	72.1	60.2	48.9	39.4
Peru[b]	77.6	67.7	64.0	57.7	52.6
Uruguay	100.0	98.7	98.6	94.8	94.2
Venezuela	90.2	85.1	71.9	65.5	61.7

[a] 1969
[b] 1971

Table 49b. Comparison of education efficiencies in urban and rural areas

A) Successful completers in primary education (as a percentage of entrances)

	Total country	Urban	Rural
Colombia	27.3	47.3	3.7
Dominican Republic	30.4	48.1	13.9
Guatemala	25.4	49.6	3.5
Panama	62.3	80.7	45.3
Average % completers	39	51	22

B) Efficiency of primary education

	Years taken to produce a successful completer				Input/output ratio		
	Ideal	Total country	Rural	Urban	Total country	Rural	Urban
Colombia	5	11	66	8	2.4	13.2	1.7
Dominican Republic	6	14	27	9	2.3	4.5	1.6
Guatemala	6	14	70	10	2.3	11.6	1.6
Panama	6	9	12	8	1.5	1.9	1.2

Source: Based on the UNESCO report, *The Statistical Measurement of Educational Wastage* (no date).

Drop-out

Studies suggest that the major reasons for these generally high drop-out rates are related to the poverty faced by large sectors of the population particularly in the rural areas. There, distances from school and financial constraints prevent parents from outfitting their children for enrolment and attendance. There is often parental pressure against children continuing their education because they are required to work in activities for which the primary school education lacks relevance. Poorer children from culturally deprived backgrounds frequently fail to adapt to the formal learning situation

Table 50. Brazil: distribution of enrolments in first-level education, 1971–3

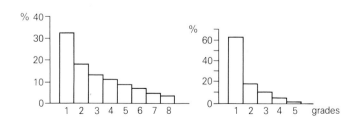

and rigid exam system. Many children have to abandon school to travel with their parents who are migrant labourers. Schools in many cases consist of only one room and do not offer a full primary school course.

Malnutrition and related illnesses also adversely affect achievement by reducing the child's ability to concentrate and learn. In four Latin American countries children miss more than fifty days of school a year because of illnesses related to malnutrition. This compares with an average of ten or less days per year lost in Western European countries. In Bahia, north-east Brazil, in 1973, only 6 per cent of primary school children reached the eighth grade. Hunger was responsible for half the drop-out in each grade.

Even in countries with a reputation for advanced educational achievements, such as Argentina, the percentage of children dropping out of primary school rose from 42.6 per cent to 49 per cent between 1970 and 1975. However, in north-eastern Argentine rural provinces, the drop-out rate ranged between 68 and 76 per cent. Table 49b, drawing on data from Colombia, the Dominican Republic, Guatemala and Panama illustrates very clearly the wide difference between the percentage of successful completers of primary education in urban and rural areas.

Non-enrolment

Problems of non-enrolment are much more acute in rural areas. Data for Brazil shows that of 19,326,100 children between seven and fourteen years of age 52 per cent lived in urban areas and 48 per cent in rural areas in the late 1970s. However, only 46.84 per cent of rural children were enrolled as against 87.98 of urban children.

Table 51 gives the adjusted school enrolment ratio for primary and secondary education for twenty-six countries in the region. Thirteen of these countries show ratios of over 100 for primary school enrolment in 1970. This is because the ratio expresses the enrolment of all ages in primary school as a percentage of the population of primary school age (all children, six to eleven). Enrolment in excess of 100 per cent is due to the fact that children over eleven years of age are still in primary school due to late entrance or repetition.

Repetition

Repetition is a serious problem in most Latin American countries as can be seen in table 52, and again particularly in the rural areas. In over half of the countries in the region over 20 per cent of pupils repeat their first year of education. Students generally have to sit an exam at the end of every year and promotion tends to be based entirely on the results of that exam, regardless of performance in class. Causes of repetition are similar to those outlined above to explain the drop-out rate. There is a distinct urban bias in most primary education systems. Very few primary or secondary cur-

ricula include agriculture, even though agriculture is still the basic activity of many of the countries in the region. Added to this are problems of shortage of materials, particularly books, unsuitable buildings, large class sizes, teacher absenteeism, and inadequate teacher training which means that teachers are often ill-equipped to handle the problems of slow learners. Repetition is more prevalent amongst pupils from low socioeconomic backgrounds and amongst girls.

Another explanation for poor performance and resulting dropout or repetition by children of low-income families can be found in the limited provision of pre-school education in the region. Except for Jamaica, Guyana and Mexico, which are attempting to expand state-provided pre-school education facilities, the service tends to be in the hands of private enterprises or charitable and church organizations restricted to urban areas and servicing privileged social classes. In Brazil, for example, in 1975 only 3.8 per cent of the 15 million children between the ages of two and six received any type of pre-school education and these were predominantly drawn from urban middle-class families. 70 per cent of children in that age range in addition to lacking pre-school education had inadequate nutrition and health care.

Primary education reform

Certain measures have been taken to improve the quality of primary education and reduce the high rates of drop-out and repetition. For example, the Chilean Education Reform (1964–70) and the Brazilian Education Reform (1971) attempted to introduce changes in the primary school curricula which would make the course of study more active, interesting and relevant for the students. The Brazilian Education Reform of 1971 doubled the length of free and compulsory primary education to eight years and also added compulsory vocational training courses to the last three years. Through this reform, the government is attempting to achieve the twin goals of preparing children for further education at secondary school while also giving those who will leave a minimum of vocational training.

A major criticism of formal education systems in the region refers to the lack of participation of the population in the design and provision of educational services. The Peruvian Education Reform set out in the General Education Law of 1972 addresses this problem by introducing community participation as an essential part of a decentralized education system. A key element in the new system is the NEC – Núcleo Educativo Comunal (Community Educational Nucleus) of which there were 650 in the country in 1980. At the level of each nucleus there is a Community Education Committee composed of parents, teachers, students and members of the community. These have not shown sufficient capacity to plan and programme curricula which respond to the needs and aspirations of

Table 51. Adjusted school enrolment ratio

| | Primary[a] | | | | | | Secondary[b] | | | | | |
| | Total | | | Female | | | Total | | | Female | | |
	1960	1970	MRE	1960	1970	MRE	1960	1970	MRE	1960	1970	MRE
Argentina	98	106	108	99	107	108	32	37	56	33	40	60
Bahamas	78	135	–	–	139	–	56	75	–	–	79	–
Barbados	95	100	108	92	98	110	39	65	78	33	58	81
Bolivia	64	68	80	50	56	72	12	21	32	9	18	27
Brazil	95	83	90	93	83	90	11	27	18	10	27	20
Chile	109	107	117	107	107	116	24	39	48	24	41	51
Colombia	77	100	106	77	102	109	12	23	35	11	22	35
Costa Rica	96	110	111	95	109	110	21	28	43	21	28	46
Dominican Republic	98	101	110	98	102	111	7	19	24	7	19	24
Ecuador	83	97	102	79	95	101	12	26	42	10	24	40
El Salvador	80	73	77	77	70	75	11	22	21	10	21	19
Grenada	93	99	–	159	147	–	21	42	–	19	26	–
Guatemala	45	58	–	39	52	–	7	11	–	6	9	–
Guyana	107	98	94	106	96	93	43	49	47	39	49	47
Haiti	46	49	–	42	43	–	4	6	–	2	4	–
Honduras	67	93	89	67	93	88	8	12	13	7	12	13
Jamaica	82	85	98	83	85	98	43	59	58	51	61	63
Mexico	80	104	116	77	102	114	11	22	37	8	17	34
Nicaragua	66	83	85	66	84	86	7	18	21	6	17	20
Panama	96	103	124	94	100	122	29	40	53	31	42	56
Paraguay	98	109	106	90	104	102	11	17	20	11	17	20
Peru	83	107	110	71	99	107	15	30	49	13	26	44
Surinam	110	100	105	106	96	101	28	38	42	27	38	42
Trinidad and Tobago	78	83	97	76	83	–	22	38	79	21	39	–
Uruguay	111	106	95	111	103	94	37	57	62	38	63	67
Venezuela	100	94	104	100	95	103	21	37	38	21	39	41

[a] Expresses enrolment of all ages in primary school education as a percentage of the population of primary school age (all children 6–11).
[b] Enrolment of all ages in secondary school education as a percentage of the population of secondary school age (12–17).
MRE = Most recent estimate (from later 1970s)
Source: *World Tables, 1980.* The World Bank, Washington 1980.

local communities, due to the lack of training for teachers in educational administration and planning, and the handling of community participation.

Such reform measures which attempt to develop education systems and programmes which are more closely suited to the problems, needs and sociocultural and economic characteristics of countries in the region appear to have met with only limited success. According to the conclusions of a meeting of education planners held in Venezuela in 1979, the emphasis within the formal education systems continues to be placed on conveying information to pupils through methods which tend to be abstract and have little practical content. Curricula tend to pay little attention to the discussion of local and national resource and environment problems or national and international social, economic and political questions.

Added to the internal factors limiting the effectiveness of reform measures are factors external to the education systems. The inequitable distribution of educational opportunities at all levels is closely related to inequalities in other production and service sectors. Unless radical attempts are made to achieve a more equitable distribution of housing, health and nutrition services and access to

Table 52. Rates of repetition in selected countries, 1970–6 (per cent)

| | Year | Grade in first cycle | | | | | |
		1	2	3	4	5	6
Argentina	1975	21	12	10	6	5	3
Brazil	1974	24	17	11	10	12	11
Chile	1974	19	15	13	10	9	8
Colombia	1974	20	16	13	11	8	–
Costa Rica	1975	–	13	14	–	8	3
Dominican Republic	1970	33	21	18	13	10	6
Ecuador	1973	17	14	11	11	10	9
El Salvador	1974	14	9	6	5	3	2
Guatemala	1972	26	14	12	7	5	2
Guyana	1973	18	7	7	6	8	14
Mexico	1965	22	14	13	11	9	4
Nicaragua	1973	16	11	9	8	6	3
Panama	1974	21	18	15	9	7	3
Paraguay	1974	25	20	16	11	7	3
Peru	1975	15	12	9	8	7	4
Uruguay	1973	30	18	16	14	13	7
Venezuela	1974	–	–	–	10	9	–

Source: Data from the Statistical Division of UNESCO.

productive employment, wastage rates in the formal education system will continue to be high.

Secondary education

Table 51 shows that in 1970 only four countries had more than 50 per cent enrolment ratio in secondary education. However, the most recent estimates show that this number has probably increased to six countries, Argentina, Barbados, Jamaica, Panama, Trinidad and Tobago, and Uruguay. Secondary education provision has expanded more rapidly than primary education since 1960. During the period 1960–75 primary school enrolments showed an average annual increase of 5 per cent while enrolments in secondary education rose to 9.3 per cent. As many females as males participate in secondary education though at the higher education level only 40 per cent of students are women.

During the decade 1965–75 one important trend, except in Argentina and Haiti, has been for private secondary schools to decline in importance relative to state secondary schools, largely resulting from increased government expenditure (see table 53). The number of countries with over 40 per cent of secondary school students enrolled in private schools dropped in this period from eleven to six. This trend has been particularly noticeable in Brazil where the percentage of students enrolled in private schools dropped from 49 to 25 per cent, largely as a result of the 1971 Education Reform Law which extended the period of primary school education and made it compulsory with free tuition.

Another noticeable trend has been the increase in attempts to relate secondary education to the job market by introducing more vocational training and technical and professional education either as options or compulsory subjects at secondary school level.

Higher education

Higher education enrolments increased more rapidly than both primary and secondary education during the period 1960–75, averaging 12.7 per cent per annum. Growth has been particularly rapid since 1970, the increase in the period 1970–8 being twice the figure for the period 1950–70.

In 1950 only two countries, Argentina and Uruguay, had twenty-five university students for every 1000 youths between the ages of twenty and twenty-five. Another four countries, Costa Rica, Panama, Peru and Bolivia, had between twenty and twenty-five, and the remainder less than twenty students for every 1000 youths. By 1975 the universities in the region could be divided into four groups as shown in table 54.

The rapid increase in higher education enrolments has been achieved largely as a result of greater public expenditure and at the expense of investment in primary education. In the region as a whole, public expenditure on higher education now constitutes

Table 53. Percentage of students enrolled in private schools by country and level, 1965 and 1975

	First level		Second level	
	1965	1975	1965	1975
Argentina	14	17	41	45
Barbados	–	9	26	21
Bolivia	26	9	26	24
Brazil	11	13	49	25
Chile	27	18	38	23
Colombia	14	15	58	38
Costa Rica	4	4	24	6
Dominican Republic	7	12	–	–
Ecuador	18	17	38	30
El Salvador	4	6	47	47
Guatemala	19	14	54	43
Haiti	26	42	43	76
Honduras	7	5	53	51
Jamaica	–	5	–	9
Mexico	9	6	29	25
Nicaragua	16	15	44	–
Panama	5	5	17	14
Paraguay	10	13	51	37
Peru	14	13	24	17
Surinam	–	65	57	52
Trinidad and Tobago	–	–	41	–
Uruguay	18	17	17	–
Venezuela	13	11	23	18

Source: Data from the Statistical Division of UNESCO.

Table 54. Number of higher education students for every 1000 youths between ages of twenty and twenty-four

Less than 80	80–100	100–50	150–280
El Salvador	Brazil	Peru	Argentina
Nicaragua	Dominican Rep.	Uruguay	Venezuela
Paraguay	Mexico	Bolivia	Panama
Honduras	Columbia		Costa Rica
Guatemala			Chile
Haiti			Ecuador

Source: Germán Rama, in UNICEF *Educación y sociedad en América Latina y el Caribe* (1981).

49 per cent of total government education expenditure.

Another major feature of this growth has been the expansion and proliferation of private universities, usually publicly supported by grants or student scholarships. Some of these private universities offer education of a high standard and are highly selective, while others lack the human and material resources to provide an adequate higher education. In Brazil, for example, 63 per cent of university students attend eleven Catholic universities and nine private secular universities while the remaining 37 per cent attend thirty-seven federal, state or municipally supported institutions. In addition there are five college federations and 786 single-purpose colleges, 77 per cent of which are private.

Mexico provides a good example of rapid expansion of higher education, particularly during the decade 1966–76. In 1965–6 there were 255,817 students enrolled in higher education: 112,717 were in university entrance courses, 141,194 in undergraduate, and 1906 in postgraduate-level courses. By 1975–6 the total number had increased to 970,248; 406,122 in university entrance, 545,182 in undergraduate, and 18,944 in the postgraduate-level courses. This constitutes a 279 per cent increase. In contrast to Brazil, 84.9 per cent of Mexican higher education students are enrolled in federal-funded universities and colleges.

In recent years many countries have introduced polytechnical institutes as an alternative to universities and others have established universities specializing in one subject area such as engineering, agricultural sciences and education in an attempt to relate higher education to specific employment opportunities. Yet the problems are increasing, due to lack of articulation between the teaching and research programmes carried out at universities and the needs of industry, agriculture and the social services. This rapid expansion in the number of students in higher education in response to increased demand for participation has not been accompanied by an equivalent expansion of appropriate job opportunities which accord with the level of education received. There is an increasing number of higher education graduates in low-status occupations in the tertiary sector, semi-employed or unemployed.

Education systems and policies closely reflect the dominant values and aspirations of each political system and can therefore change markedly with changes of regime. This fact is well illustrated in the case of the Southern Cone countries, where military intervention in Chile and Uruguay in 1973 and Argentina in 1976 led to radical changes at all levels of the education system. Prior to military rule these countries were recognized as being the most advanced in Latin America in educational terms, with a long tradition of non-religious and liberal education, high literacy rates and relatively high levels of enrolment in secondary education. Chile in particular possessed universities and research institutes of distinction, in which staff of diverse intellectual viewpoints could freely teach and write. These countries also had a background of progressive educational experiments together with well-developed systems of political participation.

The impact of authoritarian regimes upon intellectual and academic activities was pronounced. In their determination to wipe out activities labelled 'subversive' and silence all opposition, the regimes conducted purges which have affected not only higher education but also primary and secondary education. University autonomy has been abolished and university staff dismissed on a large scale. Over half the university staff in Uruguay have left or been dismissed since the early 1970s, while in Chile during its first few months in power the military government dismissed 30–5 per

cent of the teaching staff and 10–15 per cent of non-academic personnel. In Uruguay any teachers who were particularly active in any of the parties before 1973 are barred from holding posts. The governments ensure their control by appointing their own proven supporters to key positions in the university and educational administration.

According to observers, this system of control over education policy and practice has had a negative effect on the quality of education. The intervention of authoritarian governments in education planning has meant a reversion to earlier authoritarian teaching methods. As discussion and criticism are suspect, teachers rely on text-book teaching and a spirit of conformism prevails at all levels of education. There has also been a reduction in education budgets and in education enrolments (see table 53). Education expenditures in Chile declined from a high of 19.7 per cent of government expenditure under Allende to 10.9 per cent in 1975 and then rose again to 16.9 per cent in 1977, whilst between 1973 and 1979 university enrolment dropped an average of 3.4 per cent a year. In Argentina, the reduction in the education budget was more marked, falling from 17 per cent in 1965 to 11.6 per cent in 1979. Between 1976 and 1979 enrolment in universities declined from 532,525 to 389,249. However, in spite of the policies of authoritarian regimes in the 1970s, groups of educators and social scientists attached to small private institutions in the three countries were able to continue research and experiments in alternative education approaches.

Literacy

Though many governments have initiated literacy campaigns over the last twenty years and literacy rates have improved slowly in all countries except for Haiti, there has been little change in the overall number of illiterates and there are still 45.5 million in the region, representing almost 28 per cent of the population over fifteen years of age. As table 55 shows, there are wide differences in the rates of illiteracy between countries in the region. In 1970–5, Argentina and Trinidad and Tobago had illiteracy rates of less then 10 per cent, whilst at least 40 per cent of the adult population in Nicaragua, El Salvador, Guatemala and Haiti was illiterate. (Since then Nicaragua has reduced its illiteracy rate to 12.9 per cent as a result of the literacy crusade described below.) In all countries a larger percentage of women than men are illiterate due to the fact that men have better access to both formal and non-formal systems. For the region as a whole in the mid-1970s the illiteracy rate for men over fifteen was 24.8 per cent, and for women 31.3 per cent.

An examination of changes over the past twenty years reveals that in seven countries, namely Bolivia, Brazil, Costa Rica, the Dominican Republic, El Salvador, Haiti and Panama, the absolute number of illiterates has increased. Also in Argentina, Ecuador, Guatemala, Honduras, Mexico and Paraguay, the number of illiterates has not

Literacy and education

Table 55. Illiteracy rates, 1970–5
(percentage of population age fifteen and over)

Sex	Less than 10%		10% to 19.9%		20% to 29.9%		30% to 39.9%		40% to 59.9%		60% +	
BOTH	Argentina	7.4	Costa Rica	11	Panama	21.7	Dominican Republic	32.8	Nicaragua	42.5	Haiti	76.7
	Trinidad & Tobago	7.8	Chile	11.9	Venezuela	23.5	Brazil	33.8	El Salvador	42.9		
			Colombia	19.2	Mexico	25.8	Bolivia	37.3	Guatemala	53.9		
			Paraguay	19.9	Ecuador	26.6						
					Peru	27.6						
MEN	Trinidad & Tobago	5.3	Chile	11.1	Venezuela	20.3	Brazil	30.6	Nicaragua	42	Haiti	71.3
	Argentina	6.5	Costa Rica	11.4	Panama	21	Dominican Republic	31.2	Guatemala	46.1		
			Paraguay	14	Mexico	21.8	El Salvador	39.2				
			Peru	16.8	Ecuador	22.7						
			Colombia	18	Bolivia	24.8						
WOMEN	Argentina	8.3	Trinidad & Tobago	10.3	Colombia	20.2	Ecuador	30.4	Nicaragua	42.9	Guatemala	61.5
			Costa Rica	11.8	Panama	22.2	Dominican Republic	34.3	El Salvador	46.4	Haiti	81.6
			Chile	12.8	Paraguay	24.5	Brazil	36.9	Bolivia	49		
					Venezuela	26.6	Peru	38.2				
					Mexico	29.6						

Source: UNESCO, *Análisis de la situación educacional de la población de Bolivia* (Santiago, 1978).

decreased significantly.

Persistent high rates of illiteracy in some countries can be attributed to the highly dispersed nature of the rural population. As late as 1970, 35 per cent of the rural population lived in communities with less than twenty-five people per square mile. The consequences are evident. Illiteracy rates amongst rural youths are high in most countries whereas illiteracy amongst youths between fifteen and twenty-four years of age living in capital cities has almost been eliminated and has been greatly reduced in other urban centres. In some countries the rural illiteracy rate for adults over fifteen is four times greater than the urban figure.

Another explanation for high illiteracy rates in some countries (e.g. Guatemala, Bolivia) can be found in the high percentage of indigenous population. Discrimination against the indigenous population and their language has existed since the European conquest and, combined with difficulty of access, has had its effects on the high illiteracy rates amongst the 20 million or so indigenous inhabitants of the region. Indigenous languages have in some countries been ignored, pushed aside or banned by the official education systems. The emphasis has been on teaching the official language as a means of incorporating minorities into the national society.

Finally, other contributory factors are the absence of organized pressure for literacy from the rural population, the lack of political will to change and the lack of appropriate motivation and stimulation to acquire literacy skills.

Two countries which have carried out successful literacy campaigns in recent times, however, are Nicaragua and Cuba. In both cases a major characteristic was the emphasis on the achieve-ment of functional literacy as an essential means of achieving the participation of the masses in a process of sociopolitical transformation.

Nicaragua's literacy crusade, 1980

The Nicaraguan crusade is widely regarded as one of the most significant non-formal educational events in the region in the years since 1970. It constituted the first priority for the new government during its first year of office, following the fall of the Somoza regime.

The Nicaraguan literacy crusade shared many elements in common with its earlier Cuban counterpart. In addition to the eradication of illiteracy it had as major goals to raise the political awareness of the illiterate population, to raise the awareness of Nicaraguan youth of the life and problems of the rural poor and to organize and integrate the masses.

During the five-month crusade which started on 24 March 1980, scarcely eight months after the overthrow of the Somoza dictatorship, 130,000 volunteer youths were mobilized, trained and sent out to remote areas of the country to teach the illiterate rural population. They were known as *brigadistas* of the Popular Literacy Army and were assisted by smaller groups of qualified teachers and literate workers who worked mainly in the urban areas. *Brigadistas*, of whom 60 per cent were women, usually taught groups of less than ten for two hours a day. The remainder of the time they helped the farmers in agricultural production activities, conveyed preventive health concepts and participated in socioeconomic surveys. As a result of the campaign 400,000 people passed the final exam and the illiteracy rate fell from 50.3 per cent to 12.9 per cent.

Various reasons have been put forward for the success of the

The Nicaraguan literacy campaign

crusade. One important factor appears to have been the degree of decentralization achieved. The national literacy campaign staff was responsible for designing the reading, writing and mathematics text books, the teacher's guide and organizing the training programme. However, the major responsibility for running the campaign lay with the co-ordination teams and commissions in the 144 municipalities of the country. The co-ordination teams, consisting of specialists in fields such as pedagogy, logistics and statistics, provided the support for the commissions composed of part-time members drawn from the mass organizations, state industry and the private sector.

Another explanation for the success of the campaign can be found in the revolutionary struggle which preceded the fall of Somoza. It was necessary only to solidify and channel the already high political consciousness of the Nicaraguan people. It was evident that most illiterates were anxious to receive what was one of the first tangible benefits of the revolution.

According to a number of observers, the most important outcome of the campaign was the progress made in bridging the gap between urban middle-class youths and rural peasants. The Nicaraguan government is conscious of the fact that the literacy work did not end with the crusade and is engaged in literacy programmes with non-Spanish speaking Nicaraguans on the Atlantic coast, and a follow-up two-year popular basic education programme designed and run by the Vice-Ministry of Adult Education. The major

features of the post-literacy programme are that it emphasizes collective dialogue, is linked to production, and is flexible and active. The programmes are given in CEPs (Popular Education Collectives) by 10,000 voluntary popular co-ordinators who are drawn from the most outstanding of the new literates, *brigadistas*, literacy campaign teachers or members of mass organizations. Support for the co-ordinators is provided by popular promoters, who are usually teachers, and by a daily radio programme. Finally, weekly workshops are held in which promoters and co-ordinators evaluate their work and continue their training.

DW

Further reading

F. Cardenal and V. Miller, 'Nicaragua 1980: the Battle of the A.B.C.'s, *Harvard Educational Review* (February 1981)

R. F. Fagen, 'Cuba: the Political Content of Adult Education', *Hoover Institution Studies*, 4, (Stanford, Ca., 1964)

A. Prieto Morales, 'The Literacy Campaign in Cuba', *Harvard Educational Review* (February 1981)

T. G. Sanders, 'Education and Authoritarianism in the Southern Cone', American Universities Field Staff, Report 1981/no. 12, South America (Hanover, New Hampshire, 1981)

C. L. Stansifer, 'The Nicaraguan National Literacy Crusade', American Universities Field Staff, Report 1981/no. 6, South America (Hanover, New Hampshire, 1981)

The Spanish of Latin America

The speech of the Iberian peninsula came to the Americas through conquest: its carriers were conquistadors and missionaries, sailors and adventurers. At first, they came mainly from the south of Spain: a random sample of immigrants to what is now Panama tells us that before 1530 there came thirty-eight men from Castile, twenty-two from Extremadura, forty-four from Andalusia, seventeen from León and Asturias, one from Aragón, eleven from the Basque provinces and one from Galicia. Later the patterns changed, and the percentage of Galicians and Basques increased substantially. With the growth of townships, the rounding up of Indians on the plains into settlements, the establishment of missions and *encomiendas*, a very great number of indigenous people gave up their language in order to learn the speech of a new administration, a new law and a new culture. In parts of the new empire, too, the decline in numbers of the population indicates that resistance was at an end by the seventeenth century. By 1570, the indigenous population in Peru had fallen possibly by as much as 80 per cent and that of Mexico perhaps by even more.

The variants of Spanish introduced by the new overlords may well have indicated their points of origin in Spain, but they were modified later under the influence of indigenous languages where these survived and, above all, by geographical and ecological factors, such as altitude. The most important division in American Spanish has been pointed out by Angel Rosenblat: it is the division between highland and lowland speech.

Highland Spanish

Highland Spanish, or *serrano*, as heard in the Mexican uplands or the plateaus of the Andes tends to sound 'clipped', with vowels closing or being lost, and with certain consonants being more forcefully articulated than in lowland or coastal areas. Vowels, especially unstressed vowels, close or disappear particularly before a sibilant: *trátse, croksí* (*trátase, creo que sí*). Added to this is the confusion between /e/ and /i/ and between /o/ and /u/ where indigenous languages are spoken and bilingualism is common: *Pidro, comir* (*Pedro, comer*) and *decen, asé* (*dicen, así*); *ahura, culiflor* (*ahora, coliflor*) and *jogo, borro* (*jugo, burro*). Such confusion occurs in peninsular Spanish dialects as well, though to a much lesser extent. It may be due in part to the fact that indigenous languages such as Quechua have no /e/ or /o/ among their phonemes.

Amongs consonants, the devoicing of /b/, /d/ etc. seems to have been a feature of both highland and lowland Spanish where indigenous languages were spoken: thus *poscando, alcón* (*buscando, algún*) in a sixteenth-century Mexican text, *curato, vifs, ustets,* (*curado, vivos, ustedes*) in modern Peruvian but *nata, lloper* (*nada, llover*) in jungle Spanish, also from Peru. Final /n/ will velarize to [ng]: *bieng, imáng* (*bien, imán*); /r/ in initial, final or trilled pronunciation will become assibilated, giving a sound like *sh*, or *j* in French *je: ropa, amar, arriba* will sound *žopa, amarsh, ažiba*. Plosives /p/, /t/ and /k/, sibilant /s/ (or /z/), fricatives /f/, /v/ africates /ch/ are all pronounced with more force than in the lowlands or coastal areas.

In the matter of verbs, one of the most distinctive features of Andean highland Spanish is the influence of indigenous languages, e.g. the use of the gerundive in Spanish, *dice que va venir diciendo* ('he says he's coming') is a direct translation of Quechua *hamunqa nin, nispa*, literally, 'he says he's coming, saying'. Other examples are *los ninos eran jugándose* ('the children were playing') or even the Argentine *¿cómo le va yendo?* 'how are you?' The extended use of the gerund can also be found in fifteenth- and sixteenth-century Spanish, however, and some maintain that it also owes a lot to the influence of English, e.g. 'I am sending you a cheque' = *le estoy enviando un cheque*, heard in Colombia and elsewhere. But all three sources of influence are valid. Another trait of mountain speech or *serrano* is the use of diminutives: *así ahorito no más, todito molidito bonito, estito, agüita*, which is again due to indigenous influence but also a feature of mountain dialects in Spain, e.g. Asturian or Cantabrian.

Lowland Spanish

Here one finds most of the characteristics of Andalusian Spanish: the relaxation of consonants, often so extreme that the sound disappears altogether (*ecir* for *decir*) as well as a tendency to confuse: *ábrelo/áurelo, boñiga/moñiga, periódico/periólico, madre/magre, está observando/ehtá okservando, difunto/dihunto*. As in Andalusian, *bue-* often emerges as *güe-: güeno*, with its unvoiced version behaving similarly: *fue* pronounced *hue* or *jue: afuera = ajuera*. In general, then, plosives relax to fricatives (*b, d* give /b/, /u/, and /d/, and the point of articulation in the mouth goes back (*d* to *r/l, b* to *g, f* to *jota* or *h*). /r/ in initial or trilled use is pronounced as a uvular (i.e. as a French /r/), especially in Panama. This is thought to have originated in Puerto Rico. The major contrast with highland Spanish consonants occurs in the lowland aspiration or disappearance of /s/ at the end of a syllable or word (again an Andalusian characteristic): *ehtá, loh hombreh; la ciudade, la mamá* (*está, los hombres; las ciudades, las mamás*). The aspiration of /s/ to /h/ is typical of Chilean Spanish, and the complete disappearance of /s/ of Argentine, but it will not be long before all aspiration disappears, and all Latin American lowland Spanish will have followed the example of French in eliminating /s/ in these positions (cf. *tête* for old French *teste, forêt* for *forest*, etc.). The question often asked of how the plural is distinguished from the singular in e.g. *las mamás* and *la mamá* when the /s/ has disappeared is answered simply: often the quality of the final vowel is more open in the plural than in the singular. Otherwise the context will provide the clue.

The only other point to make about the sibilant is that in Latin America the Andalusian practice of *seseo* (substitution of the /s/ sound for /th/ common elsewhere in Spain) is followed in both lowland and highland Spanish, that is /s/ and /c/ are both pronounced as /s/, e.g. *cocer* (cook) and *coser* (sew) will both sound identical (like Castilian Spanish *coser*).

Of vowels in lowland Spanish there is less to say: in Colombian coastal areas as in Panama and other places one can sometimes detect a lengthening of *a: graande, yo las lleevo, bastaante*. There is also confusion of /e/ and /i/, /o/ and /u/ (e.g. *térmeno* for *término*) as in peninsular dialects, but not as pronounced as in highland speech.

Causes of difference between highland and lowland Spanish

Although factors such as the regional provenance of peninsular Spanish migrants as well as the influence of indigenous languages do affect types of Latin American Spanish (as for instance in the Yucatán peninsula of Mexico, where the Spanish is influenced by Mayan), the chief cause of divergence and differentiation is ecological. The effects of altitude on speech have, over the centuries, been profound. At 4000 metres there is 30 per cent less oxygen in the air than at sea level, and mountain dwellers have lung-capacities of 1600 cc more volume than have coastal peoples. Pulmonary ventilation (or the amount of air expelled and inhaled in breathing or speaking) is correspondingly greater. This affects the pronunciation of certain consonants. Medical Aerospace experiments made in altitude speech have shown that at 10,700 metres these consonants are articulated with no less than ten times more force than they are at coastal level, where vowels show no increase at all. At 6100 metres the force has only decreased to nine times, and at 3–4000 metres is still substantial. Indigenous mountain languages such as Quechua or Aymara (and elsewhere in the world Tibetan and Caucasian languages) have a richness of consonants which results from this increased ventilation. Thus Quechua has fifteen different phonemes where standard Spanish has four: /p/, /t/, hard /c/ (or q), /ch/. Furthermore, the 'strong' pronunciation of consonants at the expense of vowels stays with highland speakers long after they may have migrated to lowland or coastal areas: inhabitants of Guayaquil or Lima may keep their *serrano* speech for generations after coming from the mountains.

Standard and non-standard usage

As in every linguistic domain, both 'correct' and not-so-correct usage in Latin American Spanish can be heard. Colombia has long claimed to possess the purest form of Spanish, and its Academy has been called *El santuario de la lengua española* ('the sanctuary of the Spanish language'). But as time passes, there is doubt as to whether standard Spanish will survive much longer. This is not to say that a speech called Spanish will not continue for centuries, even as the hoariest pidgin English will still be called English. But there are signs of change: many are understandable slips common to all colloquial usage: *el radio* for *la radio*, *la idioma* for *el idioma*. But the breakdown of grammar goes hand in hand with the lessening of authority in schools and the growing of the prestige of the media, particularly of television programmes. *El conejo* gives *la coneja, el ratón, la ratona; el tigre, la tigra; el estudiante, la estudianta; Jesus, Jesusa*. Verbs, following the evolution of Vulgar Latin, simplify: *andó, andaron* for *anduvo, anduvieron*; the construction of *ir a +* infinitive: *voy a andar, vamos a ser*. These are forms that often occur in dialects of peninsular Spanish, but here they seem to have come to stay for good in the standard speech itself.

Voseo is another feature of Spanish in many parts of Latin America, though particularly in Argentina: it concerns the use of *vos* for the second-person singular, normally rendered by *tu: vos cantás, vos comés, vos sos*, with variants (*vos cantáis, vos coméis, vos sois* etc.). This extends to other tenses: *vos cantabas, vos has cantado, vos cantaste* or *cantastes, vos cantarás*.

Other phenomena are also shared with Andalusian: we have already mentioned *seseo*, and /ll/ as in *calle* emerges as [ž], *caže* (ž as *j* in French *je*). This is typical of Argentine Spanish; in the highlands of, say, Colombia or Ecuador, /ll/ is pronounced as it is written, whereas in other parts of the same countries it may be pronounced as [y].

Finally, archaisms still remain, e.g. *vido* for *vio* (Mexico), surviving from colonial days.

The most recognizable types of Latin American Spanish come from Mexico, Panama, Colombia, Chile and Argentina, though highland speech is also easily distinguishable from lowland or coastal. Many countries, such as Peru or Ecuador, vary greatly within their own boundaries, and the same could be said of Bolivia and Venezuela. So-called Andalusian patterns of speech are noticeable in the Central American republics, though less so in Costa Rica. Uruguayan Spanish is much like Argentine or *platense* (from the River Plate), and Paraguayan more like Chilean, and with an intriguing Guaraní influence.

The effects of bilingualism

One of the most interesting questions to be asked in the sphere of Latin American Spanish is that concerning the influence of the United States. Chicano, the Spanish of former Mexican provinces incorporated by the United States, as also the speech of immigrants from Mexico, may point the way in which the whole drift of the language is moving. Phenomena in Chicano such as code-switching (*se está brushing his teeth, tu miras funny*) reflect a facility of speech register manipulation that is apparent too in *engañol* or *spanglish* (as

347

spoken in Puerto Rico). These terms were once considered jokes, but are now seen to be variants of a universal speech as were those of Vulgar Latin in its day. They are constituted by the basic syntax or grammar of the one language heavily overlaid by the vocabulary of the other.

Creole and pidgin dialects based on Spanish should also be mentioned: two examples are *papiamentu* (the Spanish–Dutch speech of Curaçao) and *palenque*, an African-influenced dialect of the descendants of slaves in Colombia. Different criminal jargons and slangs also add to the sociolinguistic riches of Latin American Spanish: *lunfardo* (urban argot of Buenos Aires), *replana* (Lima), *coa* (Chile) and *caliche* (Mexico). An interesting Spanish–Italian hybrid was *cocoliche* (Argentina).

The future of American Spanish is anybody's guess: on one hand the severe simplifications in grammar which have already been touched on, the lessening authority of normative grammar, the colloquial and frequently very sub-standard language pouring through the media, the ubiquitous North American television programmes and cartoons – all these would suggest that as we move into a less literate society, where the schoolroom has less authority, so Spanish as we have known it may well change, simplifying its grammar on one hand, and indulging in wholesale importations of vocabulary on the other. However, the necessity of maintaining a commercial and cultural universal language in Latin America, the establishment's determined efforts to keep Spanish in its traditional state, the fact that Spanish is one of the great world languages of today with an immensely powerful status – all these give one pause for thought. Out of every ten people speaking Spanish today, eight will be from Latin America. Above all, the very likely emergence of a classical norm through the written word and the almost dizzy ascent of Latin American literature itself into being one of the most notable in the world, makes the eclipse of Spanish as we have known it far less certain than might be supposed from some of the examples mentioned earlier.

DG

Further reading

I. Amastae and L. Elias-Olivares, eds., *Spanish in the United States: Sociolinguistic Aspects* (Cambridge, 1982)

J. E. Davis, *The Spanish of Argentina and Uruguay* (Berlin, 1982)

C. E. Kany, *American-Spanish Syntax* (Chicago, 1945)
American-Spanish Euphemisms (California, 1960)
American-Spanish Semantics, (California, 1960)

T. Sebeok, ed., *Current Trends in Linguistics*, vol. 4 (Ibero-American and Caribbean Linguistics, The Hague, 1968)

Brazilian Portuguese

Portuguese ranks second only to Spanish among the Romance or neo-Latin languages spoken today, and over 90 per cent of its speakers are Brazilian. Interestingly, this New World Portuguese is perhaps more uniform, in spite of Brazil's geographical vastness, than the modes of speech frequently found in neighbouring valleys of northern Portugal, the very cradle of the Portuguese tongue.

Portuguese in the New World

Brazil was settled quite slowly during most of the sixteenth century. Certain language characteristics shared by Brazilian Portuguese with that of southern Portugal have led some linguists to conclude that early colonization of Brazil was accomplished predominantly by Portuguese from the south, although surviving evidence seems to refute that conclusion, and to show that the early settlers came from all corners of Portugal. As a possible explanation for this linguistic similarity, it has been suggested that a levelling of speech habits, akin to that which occurred in southern Portugal during the Reconquest, took place in Brazil among colonists of varied dialectal backgrounds.

Additionally, despite innovations introduced by intense and prolonged contact with Amerindian tongues and those of African slaves brought to work in Brazil, modern Brazilian Portuguese preserves many archaic features of the pre-eighteenth century metropolitan language. Indeed, many of the more obvious current differences between European and American Portuguese appear to be the result of changes in Lisbon speech of the eighteenth and nineteenth centuries which were not adopted in the New World.

The history of Brazilian Portuguese may be broadly divided into three periods. The first extends from the beginning of colonization up until the expulsion of the Dutch in 1654. Early communication among Portuguese colonists and the coastal indigenous tribes, because of the minuscule number of white settlers, often relied on the *língua geral*, a Tupi-based lingua franca the use of which the Portuguese crown forbade in 1727. Today, Tupi is spoken only in isolated areas of the Amazon valley and along the border with Paraguay. Even though the influence of Tupi on the Portuguese of Brazil has been overestimated by some, its contribution to the lexicon is undeniable. The national vocabulary of flora and fauna abounds in Tupi words, and if toponymics and personal names of indigenous origins are counted in, the list swells to over 10,000 words.

During the second period (roughly 1654–1808), the *língua geral* receded into the interior, losing ground to the creolized Portuguese arising from the interaction of mestizo, Indian, and African elements. While African influence on Brazilian Portuguese is lexically

MAJOR DIALECT DIVISIONS OF BRAZILIAN PORTUGUESE

less significant than that of Tupi, Brazilian speech may well owe its musical cadence to its earlier black-slave population. Of the two most important African languages brought to Brazil, that of the Yorubas was concentrated predominantly in the Bahian territory, while the Kimbundu tongue operated over a broader geographic area. It is believed that a Tupi–Kimbundu creole speech was the basis for the *caipira* dialect of Brazil, which at one time dominated all of old São Paulo province, reaching even to the hinterland of the north-east, and which, in the eyes of some linguists, explains the relative consistency of popular speech in the backlands today. Although the lexical presence of the Tupi and African languages is felt throughout the sociolinguistic gamut of modern Brazilian speech, its impact is clearly more pervasive among uneducated or rural speakers, in whose speech the elimination of the final plural -*s* of nouns and adjectives, as well as the massive reduction of conjugated forms in the verb engenders a most dramatic opposition between the educated or literary tongues and the rustic or popular varieties of the language.

The third period began with the transfer to Rio de Janeiro of the Portuguese court in 1808, after which urban Brazilian speakers came under renewed intense exposure to continental speech patterns, in turn causing city speech, even among the more modest social classes, to draw closer to the literary standard, while differences between urban and rural usage become more accentuated. After achieving political independence from Portugal, and especially with the advent of Romanticism, Brazilian writers, notably José de Alencar, strove to demonstrate Brazil's literary and *linguistic* independence from Lisbon through the artificial use of Indian

themes and terms. It is also during this period that exaggerated nationalism compelled a number of Brazilian intellectuals to proclaim the language of their nation to be separate from that of Portugal. Only after the initiation in 1922 of the literary movement known as modernism did Brazilian authors endeavour to accurately depict in their works the linguistic realities of their homeland, without denying the common bases of unity of the Portuguese idiom.

Dialects of Brazilian Portuguese

In the absence of a complete linguistic atlas of Brazil, the most acceptable dialectal partitioning yet proposed is that by Antenor Nascentes. According to his scheme (see map), Brazilian speech divides geographically into two major groups: north and south, the two being separated by a zone stretching from the mouth of the Mucuri River, between Espírito Santo and Bahia, to the city of Mato Grosso in the state of the same name, and passing through Minas Novas, Pirapora and Cuiabá. The north is further subdivided into two sub-dialects: *Amazonian*, which embraces the states of Acre, Amazonas, Pará, and north-western Goiás; and *north-eastern*, including the states of Maranhão, Piauí, Ceará, Rio Grande do Norte, Paraíba, Pernambuco, Alagoas, and north-eastern Goiás. There are in addition four southern sub-dialects: *Bahian*, which encompasses the states of Sergipe, Bahia, northern Minas Gerais, and east-central Goiás; *fluminense*, which includes the state of Rio, Espírito Santo, the Distrito Federal, and part of eastern Minas Gerais; *mineiro*, covering central, western, and part of eastern Minas Gerais; *southern*, bounding the states of São Paulo, Paraná, Santa Catarina, Rio Grande do Sul, southern Minas Gerais and its western triangle, southern Goiás and the southern half of Mato Grosso. The area from the Bolivian border extending across the northern half of Mato Grosso and including west-central Goiás, being sparsely populated, reveals no truly characteristic dialect traits, in the opinion of Nascentes.

Standard Brazilian Portuguese

Given its long-standing historical and cultural importance it is not surprising that Rio de Janeiro should set the modern standard for educated speakers of Brazilian Portuguese. The pronunciation of Rio, known as *carioca*, constitutes a sub-dialect of *fluminense* speech, and its status as the preferred linguistic model for the country has been confirmed officially by two norm-establishing congresses: that of the *Língua Nacional Cantada*, in 1937, and that of the *Língua Falada no Teatro* of 1956. The *carioca* accent, therefore, serves as the norm for theatre, radio, television, and instruction, and is currently gaining in extension, both geographically and socially.

Some of the more striking features of educated speech in Rio as compared with that of Lisbon, besides those of a lexical sort, include: the preservation of a slower and softer mode of intonation, with more evenly distributed stress patterns, once characteristic of Lisbon speech as well; the retention of vowel clarity in unstressed syllables in contradistinction to the muting or discoloration of such vowels in Portugal as the result of an intensification of stressed syllables; stronger nasalization in Brazil of accented vowels occurring before nasal consonants; the occlusive pronunciation of intervocalic *b*, *d*, and *g*, which are fricatives in Lisbon; the unvoiced aspiration and even loss of final *r*, especially of infinitives, in Rio; the preservation in Brazil of the *close* articulation of stressed *e* before a palatal consonant, which has *opened* to *a* in Lisbon; vocalization of word-final *l* [Brazi*u*], where it is velar in Portugal [Brazi*ł*]: though the palatalization of syllable-final *s*, *z*, and *x* is shared by both *carioca* and Lisbon speech, the more archaic, sibilated variety of these consonants is still prevalent throughout Brazil; perhaps the most obvious phonetic characteristic of Rio speech, however, is the palatalization of *d* and *t* before an *i* or unstressed *e*, where the *d* is pronounced as the voice affricate [ǰ] and the *t* as its voiceless counterpart [č].

While there have been several orthographic reforms and accords between Brazil and Portugal during the course of the twentieth century, certain phonetic differences between Old and New World Portuguese make total standardization impossible. Current Brazilian orthographic practices are regulated by a 1971 law, the particulars of which are set out in *A nova ortografia oficial* (Rio de Janeiro, 1972), published by the Brazilian Academy of Letters.

JJN

Further reading

J. Mattoso Câmara, *The Portuguese Language*, trans. Anthony Naro (Chicago, 1972)

H. W. Hoge and P. J. Lunardini, *Oral Brazilian Portuguese* (Wisconsin, 1965)

M. Merryman, *Portuguese: a Portrait of the Language of Brazil* (New York, 1945)

E. Thomas, 'Emerging Patterns of the Brazilian Language', in *New Perspectives of Brazil*, ed. Eric N. Baklanoff (Nashville, TN, 1966)

E. Thomas, *A Grammar of Spoken Brazilian Portuguese* (Nashville, TN, 1974)

Caribbean English

'Caribbean English' must be interpreted as applying to a number of different situations. The United States uses English as its vernacular and as its standard and official language, although the linguistic frontier between Spanish and English in the southern states is creeping northwards because of immigration from the Caribbean and Mexico, and varieties of both black English and of creole English (e.g. that of the Seminoles of Bracketville, Texas) are regarded by some as vernaculars distinct from Standard American. Around the western seaboard of the Caribbean there are creole English-speaking communities from Belize to Panama (e.g. in Bluefields, Limón, the Canal Zone) and in the islands off the coast (e.g. San Andrés and Providencia). In the case of Belize, the language of education is officially Standard English but a good deal of vernacular 'explanation' in fact takes place in classrooms, in creole English, Spanish, Maya or Carib for example; in the other countries of the isthmus Spanish is the official language. At the south-eastern boundary of the Caribbean three creole-speaking countries intrude into the officially Portuguese and Spanish-speaking enclaves of Brazil and Venezuela: the Guianas; with Standard English being the official language and creole English the most widely-used vernacular in Guyana, Dutch the official language and three English-related creoles the common vernaculars in Surinam (Sranan, Saramaccan and Djuka), and French and creole French the languages of Guyane or French Guiana.

In the Antilles, the former British West Indian islands all have Standard English as their official language, though the Standard in use is being modified by recognition – both tacit and explicit – of accepted differences between educated West Indian and educated British or American usage. In some of the islands the vernacular usage is a creole or modified creole English (e.g. the Bahamas, the Leewards, Jamaica, St Vincent, Barbados, Trinidad, Tobago) while in others the effect of French planter colonization is still evident in widespread or partial use also of a creole French vernacular, as in Dominica, St Lucia and – now dying out – in Grenada and in a very fragmentary way in Trinidad. English is also very commonly used in the Dutch Antilles, particularly the northern group of St Martin, St Eustatius and Saba, as it is in the Virgin Islands.

The differences between the creole vernaculars and more standard English are at all levels of linguistic organization: phonology, syntax, the lexicon and semantics. The precise processes by which creole (or 'locally-born') languages evolve are in dispute, but certainly in the Caribbean owe something to the regional and social provenance of British settlers in the seventeenth and eighteenth centuries, something to the systematic features of the languages of the West African slaves taken to the Caribbean, something to possibly universal processes which give rise to patterns of linguistic behaviour in contact situations, and something to the various models towards which different groups within the Caribbean have converged from time to time, whether those models were provided by Maroon (runaway slave) settlements dominated by West African speakers, or by urban free black and coloured creole society, or by the official language of the colonial power, e.g. Dutch, or English, or Spanish.

RBLeP

Further reading

F. G. Cassidy, *Jamaica Talk* (London, 1960)
F. G. Cassidy and R. B. Le Page, *Dictionary of Jamaican English*, 2nd edition (Cambridge, 1980)
J. Holm, ed., *Central American English* (Philadelphia, PA, 1983)
R. B. Le Page and David DeCamp, *Jamaican Creole* (London, 1960)
D. Taylor, *The Languages of the West Indies* (Baltimore, 1977)
J. Voorhoeve and U. M. Lichtveld, *Creole Drum* (Newhaven, Conn., 1975)

Caribbean French

The French linguistic presence in the Caribbean is manifold. Standard French is the official language of Haiti and the French Overseas Departments (Martinique, Guadeloupe with its dependencies, and Guyane). Only minor features of pronunciation (such as the quality of the nasal vowels or *r*), and some items of vocabulary (e.g. *morne* 'hill', *driver* 'to loiter', *béké* 'locally born white person', *figue* 'banana', *canari* 'earthenware pot'), many of them derived from creole (cf. below), distinguish the local variety. It lacks certain of the stylistic registers of metropolitan French, their function being carried out by creole

A French dialect, heavily influenced by that of Normandy, is used in daily conversation by the white inhabitants of St Barthélemy (a dependency of Guadeloupe), and by a small enclave of older speakers in St Thomas (US Virgin Islands). The most widespread French-based language in the region, however, is creole (French *créole*, in the English-speaking islands *patois*), which is the mother tongue of the majority of the population in the French territories (except for St Martin), Haiti, St Lucia and Dominica, as well as some older inhabitants of Grenada and Trinidad. French and its northern and western dialects, as spoken by the early settlers, provided creole with most of its vocabulary, but little of its grammar: e.g. creole has no grammatical gender distinctions, and the

verb does not change for person or tense (the latter being expressed by separate particles) – features which it shares not only with French-based pidgins and creoles elsewhere in the world, but also with lexically unrelated creole languages. (Such similarities have been variously explained, the theories currently most widely held being those which either draw parallels with the African languages spoken by the slaves, or point out the universality of such features in language contact situations.) The Caribbean French creoles are mutually intelligible, but not identical, that of Guyane being the most conservative, and that of Haiti distinguished from the others by numerous items of vocabulary and some major grammatical features. Nor are they uniform within themselves: Haitian presents three distinct regional varieties, and all the creoles living in contact with French are undergoing its influences, to a greater or lesser extent depending on socioeconomic factors, in a process of decreolization.

In Haiti and the French territories, French has traditionally been used for official and written communication, education, church services, newspapers and broadcasting, and has been the medium for writers such as Jacques Roumain, Aimé Césaire, Léon Damas and Edouard Glissant; whereas creole has been the spoken language of the masses, indispensable for intimate conversation and jokes for all classes, and the vehicle for a rich oral literature of stories, songs and proverbs. Sporadically written since the eighteenth century (poems, a Napoleonic proclamation, catechisms), creole now increasingly appears in the media and in written literature (F. Morisseau-Leroy's play *Antigone en créole*, 1953; Frankétienne's full-length novel *Dézafi*, 1975). In Haiti, creole has been the language for literacy campaigns, and is currently being used on an experimental basis as a medium of instruction in primary schools.

GA-B

Further reading

M. F. Goodman, *A Comparative Study of Creole French Dialects* (The Hague, 1964)
A. R. Highfield, *The French Dialect of St Thomas, US Virgin Islands* (Ann Arbor, 1979)
D. R. Taylor, *Languages of the West Indies* (Baltimore, 1977)
J. J. Thomas, *The Theory and Practice of Creole Grammar* (Port of Spain, 1869; repr. London and Port of Spain, 1969)

Amerindian languages

It has long been assumed that the indigenous peoples of the Americas originate from nomadic stock that crossed the Bering Straits from north-east Asia tens of thousands of years ago. These brought to the American continents an Asiatic type of man who formed the human core of waves of tribes. The languages they brought with them belonged to some 250 linguistic groups and have been estimated at well over 2000. Today, barely 100 groups remain covering some 800 languages. The condition of their speakers might suggest that their native speech will eventually disappear as the long fingers of technology and western civilization close over their cultures and their ways of life. Whether in mountain valleys or in the great jungle areas of the Amazon, the inroads made by mining companies, road builders and other 'developing' or 'acculturating' interests continue implacably the mopping-up operations started by the exploiters of the sixteenth century.

Even by 1600 Indians such as those on the plains and savanna land of modern Panama had been rounded up into manageable compounds and de-tribalized settlements, or had instead fled to outlawry in the mountains to the north. Places more difficult of access kept their indigenous cultures, for neither the high valleys of the Andes nor the steaming jungles of the Amazon basin have proved attractive for permanent European settlement. Either altitude or intense heat have been the salvation for many a native culture. Time alone will tell whether the contempt traditionally accorded the Indian by the majority of settlers, the creoles and the mestizos (those of mixed Indian and European blood) will work towards turning everyone into 'good' Peruvians or Mexicans, i.e. those speaking only Spanish, or whether the dogged adherence to their identity will in the end ensure their survival. Quechua was declared an official language of Peru in 1975 (with what effect remains to be seen), and Guaraní has long been spoken by over 90 per cent of Paraguayans. Yet it depends, as in so much language behaviour, on prestige factors, on the concept of 'getting on' in the mind of the migrant to the city and above all on being able to talk the language of commerce and technology. As urbanization increases and the countryside loses more and more of its population, one may well question the outcome.

Only the missionaries have been instrumental in actually encouraging the expansion of indigenous languages in the past, even as evangelizing bodies such as the Summer Institute of Linguistics encourage them today through their Bible-translating work.

It will be best at this juncture to indicate the areas where indigenous languages are still spoken. One word of caution: statistics of native speakers are notoriously difficult to acquire where a large part of the population of an area have never heard of the official name of their nation, and even when they have, feel not the slightest inclination to be entered into census lists where conscription, tax assessments and other strange tyrannies may well be the administrative outcome of having their village chief closeted in with some sinister-looking white men. Figures given – for the early 1980s – are therefore rather tentative.

Central America: Mexico and Guatemala

The language of the Aztecs, belonging to the Uto-Aztecan group, remains spoken for the most part on the great central plateau of Mexico. It has some 1 million speakers, 213,000 of whom are monolingual. Words such as *tomato*, *avocado* and *chocolate* are taken from their speech, today called Nahua or Nahuatl. The other great language of Mexico is Maya, which with the other thirty or so members of its family spreads from the Yucatán peninsula to the whole of highland Guatemala. It is thought that some 2 million speak one or another of the Maya languages. Yucatecan Maya has some 350,000 speakers, 50,000 of whom were monolingual until the middle of this century. Quiche, another of the family members, is spoken by approximately 500,000 in Guatemala, Cakchiquel 400,000, Mam 350,000 and Kekchi 300,000. Of these last Quiche is an important cultural medium: it has as literary monument the *Popol vuh*. Another Maya language is Huastec, spoken in Veracruz, but it lies some 2000 kilometres away from the main Maya area.

Apart from the two language areas of Aztec and Maya, Mixtec and Zapotec (south-east Mexico), as well as Otomi and Totonac all command over 100,000 speakers each. Sixty per cent of others such as Chatino, Mazatec and Tlapeneco were monolingual as late as the 1940s. The percentage is much lower now.

All in all, Mexico has some 2.5 million indigenous speakers among its 70 million inhabitants. Guatemala, with a total population of close on 7 million, is predominantly Indian and has consequently a far higher proportion.

Central America: El Salvador, Honduras, Nicaragua, Costa Rica and Panama

El Salvador (5 million people) has speakers from the Mísquito (or Mósquito) family as well as from the Lenca (Cacaopera and Chilanga respectively), but numbers are not more than a few hundred. The Lenca family is also represented in northern Honduras. Honduras itself in the mid-twentieth century had some 80,500 native speakers using Jicaque, Paya, Sumo, Zambo and Mísquito – these out of a total population of some 2.5 million. The area also includes black Carib speakers, as does also Belize. Mid-twentieth-century Nicaragua had some 21,500 indigenous speakers out of more than 2 million inhabitants, Mísquito being the principal native language with 20,000. Costa Rica's total is some 20,000 (around 1 per cent of the country's population). Some half dozen languages are spoken in north and south: one of these is Guaymí, which straddles the border with Panama, itself with native speakers in the mountainous west and also in the extreme east: the Cuna of the St Blas islands and the Darién mainland, and the Chocó. The total of indigenous speakers in Panama is estimated at 50,000 out of a population of around 1.8 million.

South America: the lowlands and coastal areas

In the north of the subcontinent, the Carib family is represented in lowland Colombia, but above all in the Guianas, Venezuela and north-east Brazil. Its centre of dispersal, however, would seem to have been between the upper Xingú and Tapajoz rivers. An interesting feature of Carib is that it has actually been extended in the last few centuries, as has Quechua. Black Carib, started by the fusion of Carib Indians with blacks when they were deported by the British after a rebellion in 1795, is spoken in Belize and Honduras, as already mentioned, but also in Nicaragua and Costa Rica.

Arawak, the first native language encountered by Columbus, had its centre of dispersal between the rivers Orinoco and Negro (i.e. in Venezuela and northern Brazil) and at one time is said to have covered an area reaching as far north as Florida. *Canoe*, *tobacco* and *hammock* are Arawak words. It is spoken, in one or other of its sixty· variant family members, in the Amazon basin towards the west and nearer the Andes.

Another important linguistic family is Gê, spoken at one time over most of the southern half of Brazil and especially on the table lands of the Mato Grosso and Goiás. There are three main groups of Gê speakers with at least eight major sublanguages.

The most extensive of all lowland family groups today is Tupi–Guaraní, spoken in one or other of its forty-nine variants from the Guianas down to northern Argentina. Because of the efforts of Jesuit missionaries in the seventeenth and eighteenth centuries,

THE TUPI–GUARANÍ LANGUAGE FAMILY

Guaraní was accorded a respect which – at least in Paraguay, where it is an official state language – has never diminished. (The Jesuits have been criticized for not preparing the Indians for the 'modern world' but one would be hard put to pretend that what came after the Jesuit expulsion from Paraguay at the end of the eighteenth century was from any point of view an improvement on what they had already achieved in the way of co-operation and productiveness.) In the Paraguayan capital, Asunción, today, the Guaraní spoken is strongly influenced by Spanish and is known as Yopará.

Other families of languages spoken by Brazilian Indians are Tucano, Catukina and Puinave. To the south and in the Argentine Chaco, a few languages still survive: Mataco, Chunupí, Chorote and Toba. In Paraguay, Lengua still flourishes in the Chaco missions.

South America: the highlands

The most powerful and extended language unit in highland South America is Quechua or Inca, a heritage of the vast empire which in the early fifteenth century had two capitals, in Cuzco (now south-east Peru) and Quito (now capital of Ecuador). Today, Quechua is spoken by some 8 million people, with dialect groups running the length of over 3000 kilometres of mountain ranges north to south, from southern Colombia to northern Chile and Santiago del Estero in central Argentina. Quechua is usually classified under eight dialects: Ecuadorian (in Ecuador, as in Argentina, it is called Quichua), Lamas, Ancash, Huancayo, Huanca or Ayacucho, Cuzco, Bolivian and Santiago del Estero. Of these, the Cuzco dialect has long been considered as 'classical' Quechua. The language in general has expanded since the conquest, as already mentioned, but immigrants to cities like Lima are often very eager to pretend they know nothing of it. On the other hand, one of the most identity-conscious groups within the Quechua linguistic empire are the Otavalo of northern Ecuador, who possess, furthermore, an enviable reputation as a commercially successful and industrious people. Other tribes in Ecuador with a comparable sense of pride in their identity are the Colorado of the north and the Jívaro, who live in the south-east of the country and continue over into Peru. These last two named are technically lowland peoples.

In Colombia, and north of the Quechua area, the Chibcha civilization is hardly represented any more by its language, though members of the family itself, like Guaymí and Cuna, are still spoken in Costa Rica and Panama. In Colombia the largest indigenous group (some 40,000) is that on the Guajira peninsula (the very northernmost tip of the subcontinent, on the Colombian-Venezuelan border) where the inhabitants speak one of the Arawak languages. Another interesting linguistic island is that of the Guambionos and Páez in southern Colombia.

Around Lake Titicaca, on the border of Peru with Bolivia, the Aymara language has over half a million speakers. It is thought to be

THE QUECHUA AND AYMARA LANGUAGE FAMILIES

the speech of the builders of the great centre of Tiahuanaco, a short distance to the south of the lake itself. Another group in this area are the Uru-Chipaya. The Uru islands are on Lake Titicaca, and though no islanders now speak the language, it still survives among the Chipaya villages to the west of Oruro. That there may be an interesting link between them and the Mayan language of Mexico and Guatemala has been suggested.

Further south, in what is now southern Chile, the Araucanian or Mapuche Indians still speak their language, though since the 1880s they have been confined to the reserves near Temuco and Nueva Imperial. In the north the Araucanians' language was known as Picunche, in the centre Mapuche and the south Huilliche. It is Mapuche that survives. Some quarter million of these speakers survive, out of a total Chilean population of 11 million. In Argentina the problem of Indians wanting to keep their traditional lands was solved simply by massacring many of them in the late nineteenth

century. There still remain numbers of Araucanians on the reserves in, for instance, the province of Neuquén. All in all, the Indian population of Argentina has been put at 130,000, out of a total population of 27 million. The northern Chaco has a few tribes such as the Mataco, to whom we have already referred.

As far as statistics can be found for countries north of Argentina and Chile, Bolivia is said to have 2.5 million indigenous people out of 5.7 million inhabitants, Paraguay 40,000 out of 3 million (this does not include Guaraní speakers, who constitute a huge percentage of the whole), Peru 3.5 out of 16.6 million, Colombia 200,000 out of 25 million, Venezuela 98,000 out of 15 million, the Guianas 16,000 out of 1.35 million. Brazil (total population 122 million) and Ecuador (8 million) have such widely differing indigenous statistics that it would only be adding confusion to confusion. As we have already said, moreover, numbers given are very tentative, and even the definition of an indigenous inhabitant varies from country to country and one census authority to another. Mestizos, who may speak an indigenous language (as very many do in Peru), may not qualify as Indians on the ground that they do not inhabit a specifically Indian community, or live in towns.

Quechua

A short article cannot easily give an adequate idea of some eighty to a hundred language families. A very brief description of the salient features of the largest and most widely spoken language, Quechua, may nevertheless be of interest as an introduction to the theme.

Quechua, or Inca, has a very rich consonantal phoneme-range. Thus, where Spanish or English have as phonemes /p/, /t/ and /k/ (or /q/), and Spanish has /ch/ – in other words four phonemes in all, Quechua has fifteen. In addition to the simple occlusive (p, t, k, ch) it has an aspirated version (ph, th, kh, ch) and a glottalized one (p', t', k', ch') and in addition /q/ is distinct from /k/ in pronunciation and forms distinct phonemes /q/, /qh/ and /q'/. There are, however, no voiced occlusives in Quechua, no /b/, /d/ or /g/. Vowels are limited to three, /a/, /i/ and /u/. Next to a /q/, however, /i/ will sound as /e/ and /u/ will sound as /o/. Thus what is in reality *Quichua* is pronounced more like *Quechua*.

There is no article as we know it, and no gender marker. The plural is marked by the suffix -kuna: *warmikuna* 'women', *wasikuna* 'houses'. Prepositions are also suffixed to the noun: *runa* 'man', *runapaq* 'for the man'; *wasi* 'house', *wasipa* 'of the house'. In verbs, the subject is indicated by suffixing a personal pronoun into the verbal root: *munay* 'to love' gives *munani* 'I love', *munanki* 'you love', *munan* 'he loves', *munanchis* 'we – that is, both you and I or we – love', *munaiku* 'we – that is *not* you, but I or we – love', *munankichis* 'you (plural) love', *munanku* 'they love'. Much Quechua is influenced by Spanish, and some estimates put Spanish in Quechua vocabulary at as much as 50 per cent. Still, most of the simple greetings or commonly used words are indigenous: *ari* 'yes', *manan* 'no', *paqarinkama* 'until tomorrow'.

Conclusions

Such a cursory glance at the indigenous languages spoken in what is now Latin America would be incomplete without certain conclusions: firstly, that the survival of indigenous languages has been greatest in the mountains or in the jungle. Coastal plains were 'civilized' or cleared almost completely by the Spanish, the Portuguese or other colonizers. Secondly, that two patterns of survival can be discerned: jungle languages tend to be many and varied because so many of the communities are insulated one from another by forest. Consequently, they grow apart from one another both socially and culturally. Rivers have along their banks a succession of indigenous communities which sometimes find it difficult to communicate with one another even when they belong to the same linguistic family. In the mountains, on the other hand, lines of communication are far easier and languages can travel more quickly either in the wake of a conquering army or through commerce and trade. There are thus fewer languages on the highland plateaus, and more assimilation of one language by another. Quechua absorbed many Indian languages less powerful than itself (and is still doing so). Thirdly, that the valleys leading down from the plateaus have as often as not been conquered from above, and not laboriously from down below. This gave the Incas, for example, a kind of herringbone pattern of conquest attacking valleys below as they moved along an axis at some 3000 metres. This again favoured linguistic expansion. As a result, the Inca system of communication and their highways often meant that their language would face little opposition. Their runner-team organization in particular was efficient, and it is said that a fish caught in the ocean could be served on the emperor's table in Cuzco the next day. What a fish can do a word might do as well, though it be from the emperor's table back to the coast.

DG

Further reading

D. J. Gifford and P. F. Hoggarth, *Carnival and Coca-Leaf* (Edinburgh, 1976)

M. J. Hardman, ed., *The Aymara Language in its Social and Cultural Context* (Florida, 1981)

Y. Lastra, *Cochabamba Quechua Syntax* (The Hague, 1968)

J. H. Steward and L. C. Faron, *The Native Peoples of South America* (New York, 1959)

J. A. Suárez, *The Mesoamerican Indian Languages* (Cambridge, 1983)

Native American literature

A great hidden chapter of world literature is that which belongs to the native peoples of the New World, especially those of present-day Latin America. It has stayed hidden for practical and ideological reasons. First there is the question of the recording systems used by native Americans, the matrix of their literature, which like the Inca quipu, appear alien and incompatible with the alphabet and are therefore dismissed as 'non-literary'. Then there is the question of deciphering these scripts, a task scholars still have to complete. Then again there is the question of the sheer availability of texts. Until recently classics in native script, like the precious screenfold books of Mesoamerica, could only be examined in inadequate reproductions; and only now are attempts being made even to catalogue the great corpus of pre-Columbian inscription in stone and wood, notably the hieroglyphic texts of the lowland Maya, several of which are of considerable length and literary interest. As for the alphabetic texts in major native languages recorded by native scribes after the European conquests, few have been adequately edited and translated into English, and the same is true of the major oral traditions subsequently collected in South America. In this respect such key works as the Nahua Cuauhtitlan Annals, the Quechua Huarochiri Narrative and the Guaraní *Ayvu Rapyta* have been scandalously neglected (especially since good versions exist in German and Spanish).

This state of affairs can be partly explained by an inherited reluctance to admit that the New World ever possessed anything equivalent to the script and scripture which in Christendom, as in Islam, have served as a chief ideological defence of empire. An allied difficulty has arisen from the fact that such accounts of its native literature as exist tend not to be literary but to obey anthropological and other criteria; and therefore the texts tend to be turned to some ulterior purpose rather than be respected for themselves, as specific and unique arrangements of symbols and words. This tendency began in the sixteenth century in the great ethnographic work of Friar Bernardino de Sahagún who, in gathering Nahua texts in Mexico, increasingly moulded them to his own Renaissance philosophy. And in our day it is typified in the work of Claude Lévi-Strauss who, in reporting on American cosmogonies in the four volumes of his *Mythologiques*, relies on French summaries of original texts in order to fit them into his 'structuralist' frame. Nonetheless, enough has been published to make feasible a survey of at least the classics in the major scripts and languages of the Latin American area, whose origins long antedate Columbus and whose grand themes point to a common ancestry.

The question of script

Before the Christians arrived with their alphabet, America possessed recording systems of its own, integral by origin with the calendars and tribute economics, the religions and social practices peculiar to that part of the world. Only one of these systems may be readily compared with the alphabet, insofar as it is phonetic and records speech graphically. This is the hieroglyphic writing sumptuously cut in panels and stelae at lowland Maya cities like Palenque, Tikal and Copan from about AD 300 to 900; especially noteworthy are the two trilogies of low-relief panels at Palenque, carved in the late seventh century. The one, in the Temple of Inscriptions, gives a biography of the king Pacal, buried there, and ranges far back into prehistory; the other deals more with the city itself, the ancestry of its rulers in the aristocratic 'tree-birth' that occurred at about the time of Christ, the tribute ensured by its warriors and the maize cultivated by its farmers. After the 'collapse' of the lowland cities hieroglyphic continued to be used in screenfold books, of which three examples survive, named after the cities that now house them: Dresden, Paris and Madrid. Ritual histories intricately bound up with astronomy and cosmogony, they bear dates which like those in the inscriptions go back millions of years. Furthering this long tradition, in the sixteenth century many lowland Maya authors adopted the alphabet, and used it to transcribe the hieroglyphic heritage. In the alphabetic Maya books particular to the towns of Yucatán and named collectively after Chilam Balam or Priest Jaguar, calendrical history and ritual chants follow the patterns established in the hieroglyphic texts. At the core of the Chilam Balam group is the Katun Count (*u kahlay katunob*) found at Tikal and in the Paris screenfold and transcribed in the Books of Tizimin, Chumayel, Mani, Oxcutzcab and Kaua. A time cycle of thirteen *katuns* (each of which lasts twenty years of 360 days) and the wheel of rotating government, this Count prompted an elaborate rhetoric of forecast and résumé in public affairs; it served as the basis, on the one hand, for personal prophecies (like those of Chilam Balam himself), and on the other for historical chronicles ranging back to the beginning of this era, Katun 4 Ahau or 3113 BC (as in the first chapter of the Book of Chumayel).

Within the same cultural region of New Spain or Mesoamerica, which in literary terms extends from Nicaragua in the east to Michoacán in the west, hieroglyphic co-existed with the closely related script often called 'Mixtec–Aztec' and here referred to as iconographic. Like hieroglyphic, it employs ritual sets of numbers and signs (9, 13, 20) and appears in inscriptions, which in this case date back well into the first millennium BC and extend past the Spanish arrival. And it appears likewise in screenfold books, of skin as well as paper, and in scrolls, of which several dozen survive in all, and was also extensively used in books of European paper and binding. Very variously named, these iconographic texts may in the

first instance be usefully grouped by genre: poetic and highly structured ritual histories to which cosmogony and esoteric dating are indispensable; political and migration histories, like that of Cuauhtinchan which traces over millennia the fortunes of the Toltecs and their Chichimec allies; year-by-year annals, with a more open boustrophedon or linear format, stemming from major centres like Tilantongo of Mixtlan and Tepexic of Anahuac, and from lesser towns like Tlapa and Huichapan; genealogies; biographies like that of Tilantongo's great hero Eight Deer; synoptic time-maps and *lienzos*; and tribute records like the gorgeous example from the Aztec capital Tenochtitlán, prepared for viceroy Mendoza.

Unlike hieroglyphic, iconographic script was not bound exclusively to the phonetics of any one Mesoamerican language and, outside the hieroglyphic zone, it was used internationally by speakers of Nahua like the Toltecs and Aztecs, Otomanguans like the Mixtec, Zapotec and Otomí, and highland Maya like the Quiche who describe the script of their forefathers as 'Toltec'. To convey meaning, iconographic script may rely on such pictorial factors as colour, precision of outline, and layout, as in complex page-designs that resemble modern Navajo sandpaintings and which in the ritual screenfolds may serve to give title-dates (for example, page one of the Fejérváry screenfold). And because of this pictorial quality iconographic texts have sometimes been assigned to the realm of fine art rather than literature. Nonetheless, they remain the classic antecedent to the many alphabetic texts written in Nahua and other Mesoamerican languages. This is obviously so with genre

The time-map title page of the Fejéváry screenfold

documents relating, say, to genealogy or tribute, and with annals like those of Cuauhtitlan and those incorporated into the work of such native historians as Chimalpahin, Tezozomoc, Castillo and Ixtlilxochitl. More intricate is the case of the ritual genre, for here iconographic script relies most on the techniques, peculiar to it, of multiple reading and of shifting between dimensions of time by means of ciphers and signs. In fact it is the key to alphabetic accounts of cosmogony, where the 'Suns' of creation encapsulate the past in the present, and of ceremonial esotericism. For example, in the *Twenty Sacred Hymns* collected by Sahagún in alphabetic Nahua, the rain god's persona is termed the 'Jaguar-Snake'. What is meant remains opaque without the help of the Laud screenfold, where the rain god's Jaguar is revealed as his thunder-roar and his Snake as his lightning; moreover, in the ritual set of Twenty Signs, Jaguar is XIV and Snake is V, which together make XIX, the number of the rain god's mask (or persona) in the same set of Signs.

Turning from New Spain to Peru and the Inca empire, Tawantin-suyu, we encounter another sort of recording system altogether, which in sheer physical and etymological terms bears little relation to usual European definitions of literature or letters. For the components of the Inca system are not marks on a page but knots made in the coloured cords of the object known by the Inca or Quechua term 'quipu'. With the Spanish invasion of the sixteenth century, quipus were burnt and scattered just like the paper and parchment books of Mexico, so that only 400 or so have survived; and they were long deemed mere 'mnemonic' devices, theoretically little more complex than knots in a handkerchief. Nowadays much more is understood of the quipu's pure and mathematical logic and of how in the actual working of the Inca state it could have had the function enjoyed by hieroglyphic and iconographic script in Mesoamerica. Hence in its turn the quipu may now be properly acknowledged as the literary antecedent to alphabetic texts written by Quechua- and Spanish-speaking authors, who indeed in several instances asserted that they were transcribing from quipu originals. A well-known case is Guamán Poma's *Nueva corónica* (a pun on 'crown' and 'chronicle') of pre-Hispanic Peru, whose chapters, each with its set of formulaic illustrations, reproduce the bureaucratic structure of the Inca state. Other examples can be found in the *Zithuwa Liturgy* with its patterns of set phrases and epithets, and in the kingship drama *Ollanta* where the quipu both serves as a means of communication and reflexively confirms the structure of the play itself, with its thrice five scenes.

Beyond the urban foci of Mesoamerica and Tawantinsuyu yet other recording conventions exist or have existed; but they have not been systematically related in this way or at any length to literary compositions in alphabetic script. Nonetheless, the *timehri* incised and painted by the Carib and Arawak, and once adapted by the ancient Chibcha to their ends, encapsulate the cosmogony of

northern South America; indeed they relate conceptually to the ritual sets of Mesoamerica like the Twenty Signs, the Thirteen Birds or Fliers, and the Nine Causes or Mothers of Creation. And among the Cuna of Panama a similar sort of pictograph, written in boustrophedon, serves to record the Ikala or therapeutic epic chants of their shamans. In all, the part of native Latin America where graphic and other recording conventions appear least essential to literature is precisely that which prompted Montaigne to pronounce that the New World was so young that it had 'yet to learn its ABC': the Tupi–Guaraní territories which stretch from the Amazon to Paraguay, to which may be added groups further south like the Mapuche or Araucanians of Chile.

A quipu, as depicted by Guamán Poma

Literary themes and genres

Among the great unifying themes of native American literature, the genesis story is paramount. For the same basic account recurs from southern Peru to northern Mexico and the Navajo; in Tawantinsuyu it is set out by Guamán Poma and the Quechua Huarochiri Narrative, and in Mesoamerica by such texts as the *Popol vuh* of the highland Maya, the Nahua Cuauhtitlan Annals, and the heavily glossed iconographic history from Tenochtitlán named after Huitzilopochtli. In this scheme the time we inhabit, far from existing independently, incorporates the four suns, 'sproutings' or lives of the past, in a way that recalls Hesiod's *Works and Days*. Some of the detail of what these lives were like and how they ended vary, but overall the structure remains the same. The first two lives ended respectively in the Flood and the Eclipse, both catastrophes resulting from malfunction in the sky or upper regions. In the Flood, also reported in the creation cycles of the Tupi-Guaraní (the *Ayvu Rapyta*; cf. the Makiritare *Watunna* and the Huitoto *Nainu-Ema*), the first race of men reverts to fish, while during the Eclipse the second race is set upon by its domestic creatures, dog and turkey in Mesoamerica, llamas in Peru. Higher up the evolutionary scale, the third life focuses on the struggle between scale-covered reptile and feathered bird on the one hand and the hairy mammals on the other. The fourth life is the epic story of man's ascent, of his difference from monkey and his capacity to inherit memory and to deceive. All this issues into the creation of contemporary man from maize, which is known archaeologically to have become a staple in Mesoamerica and elsewhere around 3000 BC, the date taken as the start of the present era in hieroglyphic dating and in iconographic annals like those of Tepexic.

Chronologically, this whole creation story lasts for a period commensurate with the millions of years spoken of by Guamán Poma and recorded hieroglyphically at Quirigua (Stela D, 400 million years) and in the Madrid screenfold (p. 57, 780 million years). Moreover, the iconographic screenfolds show us that the transition from one life to the next is equivalent to a shift between orders of time, the smallest of which is the astronomically derived precessional cycle of 26,000 years; as the fifth life or sun, our era conventionally equals a fifth of this period (5200 years). Recounting the development of maize from lesser cereals, the Huitzilopochtli History spells out the pre-era and era spans in lots of 400 years (52 plus 13 feathered turquoise in iconographic script, or 65 × 400 years).

When it comes to linking this genesis to the modern world a commonly used device is that of the culture hero and patron deity who champions the interests of a particular town or tribe. The thematic similarities between heroes of this kind from various parts of North and South America – Nanabush, Huitzilopochtli, Quetzal-Snake, the Twins, Bochica, Viracocha, Zume – attracted much attention in the late nineteenth century, as 'American Hero Myths', to quote D. G. Brinton's title. The motifs that recur in their respective life-stories invite close comparison, above all their parthenogenesis or miraculous conception. According to Cristóbal de Castillo, when the mother of Huitzilopochtli, who led the Axtecs to glory, conceived him ostensibly from a ball of down, her brothers grew angry and suspicious and they plotted to kill her only to be slain by the new-born hero who leapt from the womb fully armed. By contrast, the miraculously conceived Quetzal-Snake of Tula lived in obscurity until the age of nine, when he searched disconsolately for the bones of his father; the intellectual influence of his namesake on the early states of Mesoamerican civilization is reported in the Tepexic Annals and at Palenque. A different answer again to the social embarrassment of parthenogenesis is proposed by the highland Maya in the *Popol vuh*. For there the hero Twins engendered from their father's spittle after his death are brought into his first wife's family against the wishes of the grandmother; and they are fully accepted only when this matriarch involuntarily disowns her legitimate and first-born grandsons, the Twins' elder half-brothers, by laughing at the antics which the Twins make them perform with their music. In the Inca story of Viracocha told in the Huarochiri Narrative, it is he, the hero, who magically engenders; and the moral problem of fatherhood arises only when the child is weaned and the mother needs support. Then the young men of the village line up across the street and the one towards whom the child crawls is adjudged the father. In these four particular versions of the same literary motif, with their emphases on alacrity, inner searching, wit and paternalism, we may detect traces of the social ideologies which the texts in question defend.

Because of the different functions of literature within the various native societies of Latin America, it is mostly unhelpful to classify texts overall by genre. Yet in the case of performed literature, poetry and drama, some parallels can be drawn. In certain key respects the lyric poetry composed at Cuzco, the capital of Tawantinsuyu, has much in common with that of the Aztec capital Tenochtitlán. For in both places poetry became something acknowledged and produced in its own right, no longer closely tied to social function as a chant, say, for making rain, arousing warriors, consoling mourners or encouraging planters of maize. In Cuzco the *haravek* or court poets cultivated for their own sake the songs of warriors, planters and shepherds, with a skill that has left an enduring mark on Quechua, as the collection *Tarmap Pacha Huaray* (1905) testifies, and which survives in lyrics today, especially the pastoral *yaravi* (a term derived from *haravek* which has passed into the repertoire of Spanish American literature). At Tenochtitlán similar practices were followed among the brotherhood of court poets, which included King Nezahualcoyotl of Texcoco; many of their lyrics, preserved in the *Cantares mexicanos* and *Ballads of the Lords of New*

Spain manuscripts are divided into modes, according to the social function they once had.

In addition to this, as imperial courts and centres of four-part empires (which is what Tawantinsuyu means) Cuzco and Tenoch-titlán received the songs of their subjects literally as items of tribute, captured voices, according to a widespread American custom reported in the Cakchiquel History. Hence, from their privileged position the court poets came to appreciate the particular styles of the provinces around them, savouring them as something different from the metropolitan norm, with touches of the exotic. Guamán Poma defines the very geography of Tawantinsuyu through the songs and 'flowery music' typical of each of its four parts, all contributing to the wealth of the centre: large drums and quena flutes from Collasuyu; deer-horns and tambourines from Chin-chasuyu; wild topless dancers and pan-pipes from Antisuyu; and satirical singers with death-masks from Condesuyu. In the Tenoch-titlán collections, certain poems strive to capture the rough style of the Ŏtomi to the north-west while others imitate the aesthetic of the Gulf Coast and Cuextlan, renowned for its exquisite etching in shell.

A similar example of literary sophistication occurs in the highland Maya play *Rabinal Achi*, from the same Quiche region as the *Popol vuh*. The main speech in this work conveys, with huge rhetorical power, the defiance of a captured warrior facing death: as such it recalls the set speeches which captives were obliged to make by the code of war observed by the Tupi and neighbouring South Americans, the point being, the greater the defiance, the greater the victor's satisfaction. Known by the term *carbet*, these speeches attracted the attention of early European visitors to Brazil, who copied some out in their travel diaries, along with love-charms and other set pieces. This warrior defiance also forms an important part of the Inca play *Ollanta*, which as a kingship drama belongs to a whole cycle of plays extending from the first Inca *Manco Capac* to the last, *Atahuallpa*, whose tragedy is still performed annually in the Bolivian Andes. The speech in which the eponymous Ollanta defies the Inca Pachacuti (scene 4) resembles the *carbet*, it being the case that this hero stems from the Amazonian or north-eastern quarter of Tawantinsuyu, known as Anti-suyu (whence Andes). Historically, the Anti 'savages' bewildered the Inca with their knowledge of just the poisons and drugs used by Ollanta and his men in the play, and were reckoned especially wild and therefore satisfying to the metropolitan Cuzco audience. In an earlier scene (2), the same play provides a striking example of the framing of songs proper to the work-a-day world of Tawantinsuyu, when the song to scare birds from the crops ('Don't eat now, little bird, dove, dove of mine, in the lady's field') serves to warn Ollanta to keep away from the royal heroine; in fact the song is doubly framed, being performed before Pachacuti at his court, a small play within the play.

Relations with western literature

In invading America, Europeans imported not just the alphabet but a literary tradition, Christian and secular. Indeed they and their heirs on occasion went so far as to transpose this tradition directly into the major American languages, cases in point being the hymns composed in Tupi by Anchieta and in Nahua by Sor Juana, and the sermons in 'literary' Quechua composed by Spanish priests in Peru and quoted (with derision) by Guamán Poma. From their side, Indian converts helped in this task while others worked independently, adapting imported texts to their own ends. In Cuzco successors to the *haravek* like Medrano imitated the poetry of Góngora while the cycle of kingship plays was enriched with characters like the *gracioso* or buffoon typical of Spanish Golden Age drama, and the eponymous Faustian heroes of the plays *Yauri Tito Inca* and *Usca Pauccar*, who sell their souls in an effort to regain the lost royal power of the Inca.

In Mexico the lyric collection of Nahua *Cantares mexicanos* came to embrace Christian songs (and in turn began a line in Spanish Mexican poetry that extends through the Romantics to modern writers like José Emilio Pacheco). Also in Mesoamerica, the ritual bird and animal numbers and signs of iconographic script served as a rich local resource for the Nahua translators of Aesop's *Fables*. A yet more radical kind of translation can be found in the ritual screenfold histories, still made in Mexico, of native paper, whose shamanist iconography now includes animals of European origin and number sets like the twelve hours of night and day. To the north, when taking over a Spanish version of *Cinderella*, the Zuni respected the same shamanist priorities, focusing on the relationship between the heroine and her flock of turkeys who, neglected while she is away at the dance, revert to the wild and recover their own song and voice.

Fully aware of their role as transcribers of hieroglyphic texts, the lowland Maya authors of the Chilam Balam Books went to great lengths in reconciling this heritage with literature imported by the Spanish. The Books of Chumayel, Ixil and Kaua, for example, focus on the Biblical Genesis and commentaries by Christian scholars such as St John of Damascus and Alfonso X, which are integrated with Maya cosmogony to produce wholly ingenious accounts of the 'beginning of time'. The Book of Tusik contains hagiographical and apocryphal tales, while the Books of Kaua, Mani and Chan Kan translate into Maya the *Thousand and One Nights* story of the maid Tawaddud or Teodora. It was chosen because it concords so well with the chapter of riddles included in the Chilam Balam Books and used to examine candidates under the *katun* system of government in Yucatán.

Going in the opposite direction, the influence of native upon Latin American literature has been enormous, and forms but a recent chapter in a story that in Europe includes Montaigne, Vico's disciple Boturini, Herder, the Romantics Schiller, Lenau and Southey, as well as Antonin Artaud and D. H. Lawrence. As in English-speaking America, whose 'Indianist' writers extend from Longfellow to Charles Olson and Ed Dorn in the United States and include Wilson Harris in Guyana, the criterion here is not simply attention to native Americans as such but attention to their literature. It is this distinction which in the Andean area separates the novelist José María Arguedas, whose *Fox from Above* draws constantly on the Huarochiri Narrative, from predecessors like his Bolivian namesake Alcides Arguedas. In the case of the Guatemalan Miguel Angel Asturias it was the experience of reading and translating the *Popol vuh* and the Cakchiquel History which first helped him to understand his contemporary Maya compatriots and therefore to produce his masterpiece *Maize Men*. Then, in consciously updating Rubén Darío's ambition to be 'the poet of America', the Nicaraguan Ernesto Cardenal, at the crossroad of the continent, has composed his *Homage to the American Indians* through repeated quotation and reference to their literature (the Iroquois Book of Rites, *Cantares mexicanos*, Borgia screenfold, *Popol vuh*, Chilam Balam Books, hieroglyphic stelae at Quirigua and Uaxactun, the *Ikala* of the Cuna, a pastoral lament in Quechua, etc.). Lastly, it should be noted that American Indian texts may play a crucial role even in works not normally associated with them at all. For example, in Carpentier's novel *The Lost Steps* the answer to the hero's quest is provided by the *Popol vuh* and its account of the domestic revolt during the Eclipse, the Quiche text being singled out as 'the only cosmogony ever to have intuited the threat of the machine and the tragedy of the Sorceror's Apprentice'. In 'The handwriting of the god' by Jorge Luis Borges (whose sympathies are hardly known to be Indianist), this same passage from the *Popol vuh* informs the climactic vision of a Maya priest condemned by Alvarado to a hemispherical prison, which, the reader soon discovers, contains the hidden Indian mind of Latin America.

GB

Texts of Mesoamerica and Tawantinsuyu

Mesoamerica (numbers refer to the census by J. Glass et al., 1975)

Iconographic tradition
Annals: Tilantongo (240a, Nuttal), Tepexic (395a, Vienna), Tlapa (21–2, Azoyu), Tepechpan (317), Cuauhtitlán (1033)
History: Cuauhtinchlan (359), Huitzilopochtli (270), and (185), Fejéváry (118), Borgia (33), Cakchiquel (1172), *Popol vuh* (1179)
Biography: Eight Deer Bachelor (240b, Nuttall)
Tribute-record: Tenochtitlan (196, Mendoza)
C. de Castillo, *Fragments* (1021)
Chimalpahin, *Relations* (1023–7)
Tezozomoc, *Cronica mexicayotl* (1062)

Ixtlilxochitl, *Relaciones* (1043), *Historia chichimeca* (1044)

Hieroglyphic tradition
Inscriptions: Pacal Trilogy, Temple of Inscriptions, Palenque; City Trilogy, Temples of Cross, Sun and Foliated Cross, Palenque; Stela D, Quirigua
Screenfolds: Dresden (113), Madrid (187), Paris (247)
Chilam Balam Books: Chan Kan, Chumayel, Ixil, Kaua, Mani (1145–9), Tizimin (1157)

Drama and lyric
Rabinal Achi; Twenty Sacred Hymns; Cantares mexicanos; Ballads of the Lords of New Spain

Tawantinsuyu
Huarochiri Narrative
Guamán Poma, *Nueva corónica y buen gobierno*
Drama and lyric: *Ollanta, Atahuallpa, Yauri Tito Inca, Usca Pauccar, Zithuwa Liturgy, Tarmap Pacha Huaray*

Further reading

J. Bierhorst, *Four Masterworks of American Indian Literature* (New York, 1974)
G. Brotherston, *Image of the New World* (London and New York, 1979)
C. Burland, *Magic Books from Mexico* (Harmondsworth, 1953)
J. Glass et al., 'A Census of Native Middle American Manuscripts', *Handbook of Middle American Indians* (Austin, 1975), vol. 14, pp. 81–252, 253–80; vol. 15, pp. 322–99
M. León-Portilla, *Pre-Columbian Literatures of Mexico* (Norman, Okla., 1969)
N. Wachtel, *The Vision of the Vanquished* (London, 1977)

Spanish American literature

Colonial literature

Spanish American colonial literature (1492–1810) was an extension of Spanish literature of the same period, its variations explicable precisely in terms of the imperial relationship between America and Spain. Many of the best-known works are not formally literature at all, but historical chronicles written by priests, soldiers and explorers about the geography of the newly discovered region and the nature of its inhabitants. Of the Indian literatures of the continent there is only a faint trace in the imaginative poetry and prose of the colonial period. Their recuperation would have to await the twentieth century and the various national quests for identity.

In the Mexican ambit the best-known chronicles are those of Columbus, Cortés, Sahagún, Durán, Landa and Bernal Díaz del Castillo's *True History of the Conquest of New Spain* (1580), in an age when historical writing was still a branch of literature on the classical model. In Peru the foremost history was the *Comentarios reales* (1609; *Royal Commentaries of the Inca*, Texas, 1966) of the Inca Garcilaso de la Vega (1539–1616). A purely literary reaction to the experience of the conquest is found in poems such as *La Araucana* (1569) of Alonso de Ercilla (1534–94). The demands of the epic form made this account of the wars in Chile the first truly humane response in American literature to contact with the aboriginal population. Ercilla communicates the outlook of the Spanish ruling elite, a value system based upon honour and courage, which represents the dominant but ultimately less significant line of colonial literary production: military and aristocratic during the epic period of discovery and conquest, aridly ecclesiastical in the more sedentary age of the seventeenth and eighteenth centuries, a time of settlement and consolidation. The writers now remembered, therefore, are notable for their departure from these norms and for the elements of Americanist originality and protest in their works.

Bernal Díaz conveys traces of class conflict, the resentment of the lower ranks against their seigneurial commanders. 'Inca' Garcilaso is the first great mestizo writer, son of a Spanish hidalgo and an Inca princess. The taint of the illegitimate half-caste produces striking contradictions: a longing to be accepted, his elegant and noble style, bitter resentment at rejection, and a retrospective exaltation and vindication of the values and achievements of the Incas whom the Spaniards had subjugated. A century later, in the age of the baroque, dominated by the influence of the Spanish poet Góngora, colonial Latin America's greatest poet was a woman, Sor Juana Inés de la Cruz (1651–95), whose life and poetry were shaped by her implicit struggle against subservience, in a society now largely static. (It is also worth mentioning that the great Golden Age dramatist Juan Ruiz de Alarcón (1581–1639) was born and brought up in Mexico, and some critics see Mexican influences in his work.) The eighteenth century was equally barren in literary terms, reflecting the inquisitorial desolation of a still unenlightened mother country. But the continent was beginning to stir with creole resentment of colonial rule from Madrid and Seville, though the best-known literary work of the era, in an age of travellers (from La Condamine to Humboldt), is Concolorcorvo's *El lazarillo de ciegos caminantes* (1776; *El Lazarillo: a guide for Inexperienced Travelers*, Indiana, 1966), the semi-picaresque record of a journey from Montevideo to Lima by a disenchanted official of the Spanish colonial administration.

Increasingly the fundamental problem of the divorce between American contents and European forms becomes apparent, and conventional labels – the Baroque, the Enlightenment, etc. – should not be taken too literally. Perhaps the most significant facts about the colonial period are the Inquisition's prohibition of imaginative prose – this from the nation which had given Europe *The Spanish Bawd*, *Don Quixote* and the picaresque novel! – and of all works about the true Americans, the Indians.

The nineteenth century

Fittingly, the first famous work of the independence period in Spanish America (1810–30) was a picaresque novel, *El periquillo sarniento* (1816; The Itching Parrot), by the Mexican Fernández de Lizardi (1776–1827), a satirical look by a political journalist at opportunism and corruption in a society whose structures no longer conformed to the reality bursting out from below. This fascinating and contradictory era of enlightenment (whose essential antecedents are the American Revolution of 1776 and the French Revolution of 1789), later to be recalled in Alejo Carpentier's magnificent novel *El siglo de las luces* (1962; *Explosion in a Cathedral*, New York, 1963), is reflected in the transition between a neo-classical style founded on order, harmony and reason, and a romantic movement of political passion and private sentimentality which would make a particularly lasting imprint upon Spanish American literature precisely because it corresponds to the early decades in the history of the new nations. Even in the works of poets still constrained by the neo-classical mode, American themes revealed the direction of creole thought. Examples are the *Silva a la agricultura de la zona tórrida* (1826; Ode to the Agriculture of the Torrid Zone), by Andrés Bello (Venezuela, 1781–1865), a towering figure in nineteenth-century cultural history; *La victoria de Junín. Canto a Bolívar* (1825; The Victory at Junín. Song to Bolívar) and *Al general Flores, vencedor en Miñarica* (1833; To General Flores, Victor at Miñarica), by the Ecuadorean José Joaquín Olmedo (1780–1847), hymns respectively to the independence struggles and the period of anarchy and civil war which followed; and the celebrated romantic Americanist poems, *En el teocalli de Cholula* (1820; In the Temple of Cholula) and *El Niágara* (1824; Niagara), by José María Heredia (1803–39), whose native Cuba remained unliberated until 1898.

Spain's colonial monopoly in government and commerce was still overwhelmingly reflected in thought and literature in 1800. The centres of gravity were the two viceregal cities, Mexico City and Lima. The story of the nineteenth century is entirely different. Direct Spanish influences disappeared with astonishing rapidity; that of France, underground in the eighteenth century, became overt and took on an almost official status; while the focus of attention shifted to the River Plate region, especially Argentina. The nineteenth century was to be dominated by three essential themes: America and its landscapes (its history would take longer to assimilate); national politics, especially *caudillismo* and dictatorship; and later the Indian question. Many Spanish American personalities at this time were notable simultaneously in politics, thought and letters.

A photograph for an illustrated edition of *Martín Fierro*

An archetypal example is Esteban Echeverría (1805–51), a romantic by temperament and formation, who met Victor Hugo and others in Europe, and imported their themes and mannerisms into Latin America through Buenos Aires. He wrote the first true romantic poems of America, *Elvira o la novia del Plata* (1832; *Elvira, or the Argentine Bride*) and *La cautiva* (1837; *The Captive*) – hardly entertaining reading today – , the first brief anticipation of the naturalist genre, *El matadero* (1838; *The Slaughter House*, New York, 1959), many years before Zola; was a leader in the intellectual opposition to the Argentine dictator Rosas; and produced the influential *El dogma socialista* (1845). Rosas inspired other famous works. One, profoundly Latin American in its eclecticism and contradictory originality, was Domingo F. Sarmiento's *Facundo: civilización y barbarie* (1845; *Life in the Argentine Republic in the Days of the Tyrants*, New York, 1868), written, like much of Echeverría's work and so much literature of the continent from that time to this, in exile. Sociological tract, political manifesto, dramatic investigation into the nature of Argentine man in a romantic Americanist perspective, *Facundo* is one of the vertebral books of Latin American history. Less impressive an achievement, but still important as the first true 'dictator novel', is *Amalia* (1851), the work of another Argentine, José Mármol (1818–71). Elephantine, superficial, overblown, it is nonetheless essential for an understanding of Spanish American romanticism and the limits of its capacity, in such a different historical and social context, for absorbing the full philosophical, emotional and formal weight of the already con-

tradictory European model. A different example is *María* (1867), a tearful melodramatic novel by the Colombian Jorge Isaacs (1837–95), still much read today and filmed on several occasions.

The other major nineteenth-century contribution of Argentina and Uruguay to Spanish American literature was 'gauchesque' poetry. It was written not by gauchos, but by poets, sometimes rural but more usually city-reared admirers of the 'men on horseback', the most famous being Bartolomé Hidalgo (1788–1822), Hilario Ascasubi (1807–75), Estanislao del Campo (1834–80), and the great José Hernández (1834–86), whose long narrative poem *Martín Fierro* (1872), genuinely popular in inspiration and appeal, is another of the foundation works of Latin American literature. Hernández' gaucho is no amusing rustic, but an outsider, like Lorca's later Spanish gypsy; and whereas Sarmiento had seen him as an atavistic threat to developing civilization, Hernández defends him as the soul of Argentine nationhood. The pampa Indians, however, are seen as unredeemably barbarous and evil, in characteristic Argentine tradition.

In regions with different historical experiences, it was necessary to come to terms with Indian culture instead of suppressing it, and the last quarter of the nineteenth century sees the development of a dual treatment of the Indian: the exaltation of his past through 'Indianism', as in the long romantic poem *Tabaré* (1879) by the Uruguayan Juan Zorrilla de San Martín (1855–1931), or in *Cumandá* (1879), by Juan León Mera (Ecuador, 1832–94); and the 'indigenist' movement's condemnation of his unending subjugation and exploitation: *Enriquillo* (1879; *The Cross and the Sword*, London, 1956), by the Dominican Manuel de Jesús Galván (1834–1910), or, especially, *Aves sin nido* (1889; *Birds without a Nest*, London, 1904), by the redoubtable Peruvian authoress Clorinda Matto de Turner (1854–1909). The most important force behind the indigenist movement, however, was the formidable essayist and poet, Manuel González Prada (Peru, 1848–1918).

Many nineteenth-century novels from Spanish America seem indigestible today. There is no equivalent to a Galdós in Spain, an Eça de Queirós in Portugal, or a Machado de Assis in Brazil. If the novel is essentially a realist form tinged with all the 'impurities' that reality imposes upon art, the nineteenth-century Spanish American version is best understood as a transition from romantic–costumbrist elements ('creolism' or 'regionalism') to naturalism by the end of the century. For classical bourgeois realism in the mould of Stendhal, Balzac, Flaubert, or the mature Zola, we shall search in vain. The most representative novels of the period, after those mentioned, are *El fistol del diablo* (1845; *The Devil's Tiepin*), by the Mexican Manuel Payno (1810–94); *Martín Rivas* (1862; New York, 1918), by the Chilean Alberto Blest Gana (1830–1920); *Cecilia Valdés* (1882; New York, 1962), by the Cuban Cirilo Villaverde (1812–94); *Juan de la Rosa* (1885), by the Bolivian Nataniel Aguirre

(1843–88); *El zarco* (1888; *El Zarco, the Bandit*, London, 1957), by the Mexican Ignacio Manuel Altamirano (1834–93); and, in a mould at once more traditional and more original, the innumerable *Tradiciones peruanas* (*The Knights of the Cape*, New York, 1945) of Ricardo Palma (Peru, 1833–1919). The naturalist movement was well under way by the end of the century, and the legacy of *El matadero* was assumed by Eugenio Cambaceres (Argentina, 1843–88) with *Sin rumbo* (1885; Aimless), and extended by the best-known representative of the current, Federico Gamboa (Mexico, 1864–1939), with novels such as *Santa* (1903).

'Modernismo' to the Mexican revolution

But the crucial development at the end of the nineteenth century, in a remarkable shift of the centre of gravity away from the Southern Cone, was *modernismo*, which has sometimes unkindly been called French poetry written in Spanish. It continued the assimilation of European romanticism whilst absorbing the formalist lessons of parnassianism and symbolism. This came at a time when Latin America was being rapidly incorporated into the international economic system, its ruling elites were exporting raw materials in exchange for luxury consumer commodities, and a gradually emerging middle class was searching for its political and cultural expression. Despite the modernists' cry of art for art's sake and their lack of interest in politics, these realities were transparently encoded in their poetry, together with a contradictory rejection of bourgeois positivist values and a longing to escape from journalism, their new profession, to some purer version of the poet's calling.

The two giants of this period – both from small countries – are the Nicaraguan Rubén Darío (1867–1916), the more characteristic of the movement as a whole, and the Cuban José Martí (1853–95), whose life and work anticipated directions which Spanish American poets were to take once modernism was at an end. Darío, though less admired nowadays, was the most influential poet since Góngora, and the most effortless versifier in Spanish poetic history. Martí is the model of the committed poet and universal man: patriot and martyr, convinced Americanist, brilliant journalist and publicist, at once spontaneous and profound. He spent some time in Spain and more in North America. Darío lived in Chile and Argentina, where his influence was considerable, and then in France and Spain where, for the first time but not the last, disbelieving Spaniards had to accept the idea of their literature being revolutionized by the 'Americans'. *Modernismo* was characterized by cosmopolitanism, eclecticism, frequent references to other artistic modes, and a systematic juxtaposition and interweaving of the five senses in poetry which was skilful, supple and musical; though rarely profound. In prose it left little enduring work: typical were the *crónicas*, short pieces evoking people, places and 'sensations', of which the foremost exponent was the facile

Rúben Darío

Guatemalan expatriate Enrique Gómez Carrillo (1873–1927).

Modernismo began 'officially' in 1888 with Darío's book *Azul*, and faded during the First World War when the *belle époque*, of which it was a peripheral reflection, came to an end. Darío died in 1916. The outstanding writers of the dominant northern group were Darío himself, the Cuban Julián del Casal (1863–93), the Mexicans Manuel Gutiérrez Nájera (1859–95), Salvador Díaz Mirón (1853–1928), Amado Nervo (1870–1919), and Juan José Tablada (1871–1945); and the Colombians José Asunción Silva (1865–96), Guillermo Valencia (1873–1943), and Porfirio Barba Jacob (1883–1942); along with José Martí. Important poets from further south were José Santos Chocano (Peru, 1875–1934), another who pushed the movement in the direction of Americanism (or *mondonovismo*); the Bolivian Ricardo Jaimes Freyre (1868–1933), the Uruguayan Julio Herrera y Reissig (1875–1910); and the Argentine Leopoldo Lugones (1874–1938). From that day to this *modernismo*, obsessed with the rare and exotic, has been considered elitist, aestheticist and evasive, a not unfounded charge; but it undeniably transformed literary Spanish and prepared the assimilation of the European 1920s avant-garde and the transition from a regional to a universal literature. By 1920, however, only Hernández and Martí had approached solutions to the harmonization of form and content in

Spanish American literature. Only in the 1920s would this be regularly achieved by poets, and not until much later, with one or two exceptions, by novelists.

The post-war period saw two distinct currents in Spanish American literature: in the novel, the further development of a vigorous regional strain focusing on the inhabitants of the rural interior and their struggle with natural and social forces; and in poetry, the full integration of many poets into the international avant-garde, especially through the filter of Paris, where so many were in residence between the wars. The biggest single influence on art was the Mexican revolution (1910–20) which, through the cultural policies of José Vasconcelos, transformed the conception of America's historical identity and mission with its aggressive recuperation of the pre-Columbian heritage and rejection of the Hispanic legacy. If *modernismo* corresponds broadly to the integration of Spanish America into the world economy, the regionalist novel of the 1920s reflects the ensuing incorporation of the interior, a bifurcation once again of European form and American content; but the Mexican revolution offered the alluring image of a nation in search of American forms to express American realities, and nothing would have a comparable impact until the Cuban revolution of 1959.

One immediate result was the novel of the Mexican revolution itself, usually dated 1910–40, though of course authors have continued to write *about* the revolution to the present time. It is a regional subgenre, like the 'gauchesque'. The best-known example is *Los de abajo* (1915; *The Underdogs*, New York, 1963), by Mariano Azuela (1873–1952), which went unread until 1924: terse, cinematographic, sceptical, but exceptionally vivid, its most striking contribution to Latin American fiction is its remarkable grasp of popular speech. Other important works are Martín Luis Guzmán's *El águila y la serpiente* (1928; *The Eagle and the Serpent*, New York, 1930) and *La sombra del caudillo* (1929; The Shadow of the Caudillo), Gregorio López y Fuentes's *Mi general* (1934; My General), Rafael F. Muñoz's *¡Vámonos con Pancho Villa!* (1931; Ride with Pancho Villa!), and Mauricio Magdaleno's *El resplandor* (1937; Ablaze). Mexico's official indigenist policies also encouraged a vigorous committed current in other countries, such as *Raza de bronce* (1919; Race of Bronze) by the Bolivian Alcides Arguedas (1879–1946). A brilliant thinker who adopted the indigenist mantle of González Prada was José Carlos Mariátegui (1894–1930), founder of the Peruvian Communist Party and editor of the influential magazine *Amauta*; and another was his compatriot Victor Raúl Haya de la Torre, who founded the political movement APRA (American Popular Revolutionary Alliance) in Mexico in 1924. One of his followers, Ciro Alegría (1909–67), became the most successful indigenist novelist of the period to 1960, while another, Luis Alberto Sánchez, became the most prolific and enduring of Spanish American literary historians.

If poets after independence had vacillated between a neo-classical celebration of America's agricultural promise and a more spiritualistic romantic exaltation of its stupendous landscapes, the emphasis now was on the relation between men and the earth, with implicit contrasts in many writers between Indian collectivism and European individualism, or between materialist peasants and workers and a corrupt idealist oligarchy. *Los de abajo* had indicated this theme; other notable novels of the land were *La vorágine* (1924; *The Vortex*, New York, 1935), by the Colombian José Eustasio Rivera (1888–1928), who used his experiences on an Amazon boundary commission to create a narrative about the jungle and the capitalist exploitation of man and nature, with a fascinating blend of romantic and naturalist elements; *Don Segundo Sombra* (1926; New York, 1935), by Ricardo Güiraldes (1886–1927), a nostalgic and impressionistic view of the gaucho from the standpoint of a cosmopolitan Argentine landowner; and *Doña Bárbara* (1929; New York, 1931), by the Venezuelan Rómulo Gallegos (1884–1969), later briefly president of his country, who took his theme – the struggle between civilization and barbarism – from Sarmiento, to produce one of the most influential symbolic works of Spanish American fiction. Few novels have dated as badly; yet Gallegos's true objective was, as Alejo Carpentier has said, that of defining Latin American reality as a whole, pointing a finger and 'naming' things like Adam. Finally, no history, however brief, can overlook the unique short stories of the tortured Uruguayan writer, Horacio Quiroga (1878–1937), which relate men's struggles against the horrors of the American jungle.

Modern Spanish American poetry

In poetry the 1920s were the age of the avant-garde, continuing the cosmopolitan thrust of *modernismo*, but with an increasingly American perspective. The Mexican revolution had made the Spanish American republics less inclined to accept unconditionally the moral and cultural superiority of European civilization. The 1918 Córdoba (Argentina) student movement showed artists and intellectuals, for the first time, the possibility of an alliance between intellectual petty-bourgeoisie and workers; and the dizzying speed of the North American penetration of the Latin American economies, with dollar diplomacy, the Big Stick and the invasion of urban mass culture – jazz, the movies, radio, US-style journalism – made the defence of Spanish American culture an urgent and overtly political imperative. In Cuba, a logical development was black poetry, with Emilio Ballagas (1908–54) and the great mulatto poet Nicolás Guillén (b. 1902), whose work was vivid, straightforward, profoundly popular and politically aggressive; as well as black. Luis Palés Matos (1898–1959), a white Puerto Rican, was another inspired creator of Afro-American poetry.

In Paris the Chilean Vicente Huidobro (1893–1948), friend of

Apollinaire and so well integrated in the milieu that much of his work was written in French, originated a movement called creationism; while in Argentina, the Spanish 'ultraist' movement briefly captured a writer who had also lived in Europe and would later be more famous for his fiction, Jorge Luis Borges (b. 1899). But the two greatest names of the period, and of the century, are the haunted Peruvian, César Vallejo (1892–1938), poet of twentieth-century orphanhood, and Pablo Neruda (1904–73), a man by contrast always at home in the world, one of many outstanding Chilean poets and, in 1971, the second, after Gabriela Mistral (1945), to win the Nobel Prize. Both men became Communists, like Nicolás Guillén, working their different ways from an early post-*modernista* phase through avant-garde experimentalism – Surrealism is a fundamental influence in modern Spanish American poetry – and on to more openly defined political attitudes. Vallejo's best-known works are *Trilce* (1922), painful, disconcerting, unique, and the heart-rending *Poemas humanos* (1939; *Human Poems*, London, 1969); Neruda's, the *Primera residencia en la tierra* (1933; *Residence on Earth*, New York, 1946), and the immense if uneven *Canto general* (1950; General Song), including the magnificent 'Heights of Macchu Picchu'. Both can be compared with the great Spanish poets of the 1920s renaissance – Alberti, Lorca, J. Guillén, Aleixandre, then Hernández – , all influenced by Darío and two other great peninsular poets, Machado and Jiménez. A further crucial factor was the rehabilitation of Góngora. In 1936 most of these men experienced the Spanish Civil War as spectators or combatants, mainly with the Republicans. A somewhat younger participant was Octavio Paz (Mexico, b. 1914), whose best-known work is *Piedra de Sol* (1958; *Sun-Stone*, New York, 1963) and whose genius extends to essays and criticism. Whereas the Spanish American novel was by no means free of nineteenth-century regionalist and costumbrist elements, and still rudimentary in technique – a partial exception was *Don Segundo Sombra* – , Latin American poets, though not yet widely appreciated, were now fully up to date and able to compete on the world stage. The Spanish experience ensured that they would be committed.

In fact Latin American thought had been influenced since the early years of the century by the growing menace of the United States, and it was virtually impossible by the 1920s for a major thinker to admire that nation as Sarmiento had in the previous century. The best-known *pensador* was José Enrique Rodó (1871–1917), an Uruguayan essayist who counterposed Latin America's 'Arielist' inclinations to the barbarism of the North American 'Caliban'. Yet despite its immense influence, supported by the works of other ideologists like the Peruvian Francisco García Calderón (1883–1953) or the Argentine Manuel Ugarte (1878–1951), Rodó's spiritual message was at bottom no less elitist than the stance of the modernists. By the 1920s the undertaking was to

Pablo Neruda

redeem the Calibans – the masses – in Latin America itself, and it was now the often contradictory ideas of thinkers like José Vasconcelos (1882–1959), José Ingenieros (1877–1925), Haya and Mariátegui, which set the new tone. It was also an era of important cultural magazines: *Repertorio Americano* in Costa Rica (1920–58); *Martín Fierro* (1925–8) and *Sur* (1930–70) in Argentina; *Amauta* in Peru (1925–30); *Revista de Avance* in Cuba (1927–30); and *Contemporáneos* in Mexico (1928–31); followed later by *Marcha* in Uruguay (1938–74) and *Cuadernos Americanos* in Mexico (1942–).

The rise of the novel

The 1930s in Latin America, as elsewhere, appears a grim and even desolate period in literary production. Only one classic novel appeared, *Huasipungo* (1934; London, 1962), by Jorge Icaza (1906–78), one of a generation of radical Ecuadorean writers. This work gave a brutal 'socialist realist' slant to the treatment of Indians in highland Ecuador, and critics have persistently attempted to deny it classification as literature. Its power is undimmed, however. Amidst other anti-feudal and anti-imperialist works, Ciro Alegría produced a short novel *Los perros hambrientos* (1939; The Hungry Dogs), and a very famous long one, *El mundo es ancho y ajeno* (1941; *Broad and Alien is the World*, New York, 1941), which are among the last classics of the regionalist genre. Later fiction would require something more than exoticism or outrage to be accepted. It has become a critical cliché to see the moment in 1941 when Alegría's latter work beat *Tierra de nadie* (No-man's-land) by Juan Carlos Onetti (Uruguay, b. 1909) to a major prize in New York as a dividing of the waters. Onetti's grey, disenchanted urban novels, such as *El astillero* (1961; *The Shipyard*, New York, 1968), with overtones of Céline, Camus or Sartre and unostentatious but subtle mastery of techniques which communicate complex states of consciousness and moral ambiguity, were interpreted by many as a sign that Latin American fiction was moving at last from the country to the city and coming up to date. Gloomy metaphysics, relieved only by a somewhat desperate line in fantasy, remained a hallmark of River Plate fiction in such works as *Todo verdor perecerá* (1941; *All Green Shall Perish*, London, 1967), by Eduardo Mallea (Argentina, b. 1903); the vast *Adán Buenosayres* (1948; Adam Buenosayres) by Leopoldo Marechal (Argentina, 1900–70); the obsessive *Sobre héroes y tumbas* (1961; On Heroes and Tombs), by Ernesto Sábato (Argentina, b. 1911); and the tales of bureaucratic alienation penned by Mario Benedetti (Uruguay, b. 1920). Meanwhile in Mexico, Agustín Yáñez (1904–80), with *Al filo del agua* (1945; *The Edge of the Storm*, Texas, 1963), introduced certain Freudian insights and techniques into a novel which thus became the last work about the Mexican revolution from the period of consolidation and the first to apply new literary methods at a time when the revolution itself was perhaps 'dead'.

In reality, however, more had been happening in the 1930s than meets the eye, and a revision of the history of twentieth-century Latin American narrative is perhaps overdue. It is true that it takes longer for foreign developments to be incorporated in fiction than in poetry; equally, novelists themselves mature more slowly than poets and cannot respond as spontaneously to events. Nevertheless, three major writers, Miguel Angel Asturias (Guatemala, 1899–1974), Jorge Luis Borges and Alejo Carpentier (Cuba, 1906–80) – the

Jorge Luis Borges

'ABC' of twentieth-century Spanish American fiction – had begun in the late 1920s and 1930s to write works different from anything seen in the continent before. This is particularly true of Asturias and Borges, the first of whom would turn to pre-Columbian tradition and the relation between language, myth and consciousness among the popular masses, while the second would effect the same operation with regard to the structural connections between Latin American high culture and the masterworks of universal civilization. Asturias's best-known novel, *El señor Presidente*, completed by 1933, remained unpublished until 1946 (*The President*, London, 1963). Borges's stories – revolutionary in form – and essays appeared regularly from the 1930s, but were not influential until the 1960s (*Labyrinths*, New York, 1962; *A Personal Anthology*, London, 1968). The result, which has a lot to do with the sociology of readership, the economics of publishing and, in Asturias's case, problems of censorship, is that even when the Guatemalan launched *El señor Presidente* in 1946, followed in 1949 by his greatest work, *Hombres de maíz* (*Men of Maize*, New York, 1975), an interpretation of the entire span of Latin American history from the standpoint of the Indian, in the same year as Carpentier's 'magical realist' novel, *El reino de este mundo* (*The Kingdom of this World*, London, 1956), few critics realized that a new era was upon them. Yet it had even then been under way for many years, since in terms of composition *El señor Presidente*, Asturias's weird surrealist horror-movie, was virtually contemporaneous with *Doña Bárbara*, and Borges had begun writing his remarkable fictions not long after *Huasipungo* appeared. Such are the vagaries of an uneven development.

From about 1945, then, most Spanish American writers could begin to incorporate in their works the lessons of post-1914 Euro-American fiction – Proust, Kafka, Joyce, Woolf, Faulkner, Dos Passos – in a way that only a few, thanks to their acquaintance with Europe, had been able from the 1920s onwards. Yet when the Latin American novel finally 'boomed' in the early 1960s, critics claimed that only now had writers fully absorbed the innovations of their great European precursors. The same criticism has tended to see the 1950s as a kind of no-man's-land, yet a succession of books was written then as important as anything to be produced in the 1960s: Carpentier's *Los pasos perdidos* (1953; *The Lost Steps*, London, 1956), the baroque account of a modern city-dweller's confrontation with nature and the past; *Pedro Páramo* (1955; New York, 1959), a subtle Faulknerian evocation of the anonymous nightmares of rural Mexico by Juan Rulfo (b. 1918); *Los ríos profundos* (1958; *Deep Rivers*, Texas, 1978) followed later by *Todas las sangres* (1964; Everyone's Blood), a brilliant 'neo-indigenist' blend of native myth and contemporary class struggle by the half-Quechuan writer José María Arguedas (Peru, 1911–69); *Hijo de hombre* (1959; *Son of Man*, London, 1965), a moving epic of the Chaco War by another bilingual writer, Augusto Roa Bastos (Paraguay, b. 1918); and *La región más transparente* (1958; *Where the Air is Clear*, New York, 1960) by Carlos Fuentes (b. 1928), an X-ray of Mexico City reminiscent of Dos Passos; while Onetti continued to write prolifically and Julio Cortázar (Argentina, 1914–84) was becoming the continent's most original short-story writer after Borges.

The event which brought Latin America's image into sudden focus was the Cuban revolution of 1959, providing clearer political alternatives than ever before. In literature this confirmed the long swing to a militantly committed poetic current, conversational in tone, which continues today; and initially catalysed a succession of politically and morally ambiguous novels which, since ambiguity is an element on which the novel thrives, met with unprecedented critical and commercial success. A numerically and economically significant middle class now existed in several republics, and was prepared for the first time to read novels by its own writers. It seemed there was an inexhaustible supply of talented authors bursting to express the fertile promise of that historical conjuncture. And yet, if we exclude novelists already established and now rejuvenated – Asturias (Nobel Prize, 1967), Borges, Carpentier – , those who had been writing steadily before but were now more noticed – Onetti, Arguedas, Rulfo, Roa Bastos, José Donoso (Chile, b. 1924), author of *El obsceno pájaro de la noche* (1970; *The Obscene Bird of Night*, New York, 1974) – , and a number of one-novel writers like Cuba's José Lezama Lima (1910–76) with his astonishing erotic symphony *Paradiso* (1966; New York, 1974), we can see that the centre of this whirlwind was really four major talents: Julio Cortázar, himself really a member of an earlier generation, who had now started writing novels like *Los premios* (1960; *The Winners*, London, 1965), *Rayuela* (1963; *Hopscotch*, New York, 1966), a playful avant-garde tour-de-force on the relation between language, literature and reality, and *Libro de Manuel* (1973; Manuel's Book); Carlos Fuentes, author of *La muerte de Artemio Cruz* (1962; *The Death of Artemio Cruz*, New York, 1964), *Cambio de piel* (1966; *Change of Skin*, New York, 1968), and the blockbusting *Terra nostra* (1975; New York, 1976); Mario Vargas Llosa (Peru, b. 1936), phenomenally successful architect of *La ciudad y los perros* (1963; *The Time of the Hero*, New York, 1966), *La Casa Verde* (1966; *The Green House*, New York, 1969), an interpretation of Latin American history as ambitious as Asturias's *Hombres de maíz*, the obsessive, labyrinthine *Conversación en la Catedral* (1971; *Conversation in the Cathedral*, New York, 1974); and the majestic *La guerra del fin del mundo*; and also of course, Gabriel García Márquez (Colombia, b. 1928), author of the most famous novel of all, the magical *Cien años de soledad* (1967; *One Hundred Years of Solitude*, New York, 1970), which some critics compared with *Don Quixote* for the breadth of its perspective on the realities and illusions of Latin America's inhabitants. (García Márquez was awarded the Nobel Prize in 1982.) After these, and particularly after

Gabriel García Márquez

the hardening of the Cuban line on freedom of expression following Castro's dictum 'Inside the Revolution, everything; outside the Revolution, nothing' (1961), successive novelists quickly narrowed their focus, renounced general interpretations of Latin American reality, and turned to another 'new novel', the post-war French version, forcing critics to coin expressions like 'post-boom' or 'post-Modernist', to define the current situation.

One symbol of that era is the confrontation between the Cuban cultural review *Casa de las Américas*, edited by the poet Roberto Fernández Retamar, with its Marxist stance and inexorable espousal of 'socialist realism' and a Third World perspective, and the cosmopolitan *Mundo Nuevo*, directed from Paris by the liberal Uruguayan critic, Emir Rodríguez Monegal, which eventually turned out to have been financed by the CIA. The Cuban revolution recalled the tradition of José Martí, turned Nicolás Guillén into a living symbol of its identity, and awaited the birth of Che Guevara's socialist 'new man'. The difficulties of this for some intellectuals are gloomily conveyed in Edmundo Desnoes's novel *Memorias del subdesarrollo* (1967; *Memories of Underdevelopment*, New York, 1968). The 'boom' novelists meanwhile found themselves increasingly subject to the pressures of commercialism and the lure of an almost Hollywood-style adulation combined with a propaganda campaign that turned them into public figures on an international scale. The final parting of the ways came in 1971 with the celebrated 'Padilla affair', when Latin American writers and intellectuals were forced to choose sides. Interestingly and ironically, three of the most successful novelists typifying the era are Cuban exiles: Guillermo Cabrera Infante (b. 1929), whose *Tres tristes tigres* (1963; *Three Trapped Tigers*, New York, 1971) and *La Habana para un infante difunto* (1980; Havana for a Dead Prince) are brilliant exercises in linguistic pyrotechnics, humour and eroticism, all characteristic expressions of the 'post-boom'; Severo Sarduy (b. 1937), whose critical postures and fictional productions, like *De dónde son los cantantes* (1967; *From Cuba with a Song*, New York, 1973) and *Cobra* (1972), have made him a doyen of the French structuralists, especially the *Tel Quel* group; and Reinaldo Arenas (b. 1943), whose best-known work is the glittering *El mundo alucinante* (1969; *Hallucinations*, London, 1971).

Recent tendencies

The 1960s had been not only an age of – ultimately abortive – political ferment in the West, but also of pop culture and playfulness. This is reflected in the works of other young writers like the 'new-wave' Mexicans Salvador Elizondo (b. 1932), Fernando del Paso (b. 1935), Gustavo Saínz (b. 1940) and José Agustín (b. 1944), the Peruvian Alfredo Bryce Echeñique (b. 1939), and the Argentines Néstor Sánchez (b. 1935) and Manuel Puig (b. 1932). Puig is particularly interesting since his novels, such as *La traición de Rita Hayworth* (1968; *Betrayed by Rita Hayworth*, New York, 1971), tend not so much to celebrate pop culture as to reveal its alienating effect on the lives of ordinary people. The 1970s saw dictatorship return to much of the continent, and three established writers produced a now famous trio of novels on the phenomenon to add to Asturias's classic *El señor Presidente*: Carpentier, *El recurso del método* (1974; *Reasons of State*, London, 1976); García Márquez, *El otoño del patriarca* (1975; *The Autumn of the Patriarch*, New York, 1976); and Augusto Roa Bastos, *Yo el Supremo* (1974; I the Supremo), undoubtedly one of the most original and important recent works of Latin American literature.

If the novel has recently been influenced by the cinema and other forms of urban mass culture, poetry is increasingly shaped by oral forms, popular verse and the protest song movements of the late 1960s and 1970s, led by Cuba and Chile. As elsewhere, the quelling of old-style 'inspiration' has meant a dearth of labels for new trends; but one sees a diminution of traditional concepts of imagination and rhetoric and a concentration on less ambitious forms and everyday language (*sencillismo*). While there are positive reasons for this, one factor must be a simple loss of poetic insight into daily life characteristic of western poetry as a whole. Neruda and Paz remained the dominant poets long after the Second World War. Now the main influences are Nicanor Parra (b. 1914), the Chilean originator of the 'anti-poem', and the Nicaraguan revolutionary priest Ernesto Cardenal (b. 1925), who in 1980 became minister of culture in the Sandinista government, symbolizing the goal of those various young Spanish American poets of recent times – like Javier Heraud (Peru, 1942–63), Otto René Castillo (Guatemala, 1936–67), Roque Dalton (El Salvador, 1935–75), Francisco Urondo (Argentina, 1930–76) –

who have lost their lives in guerrilla struggles. Parra and Cardenal owe much to Vallejo's path-breaking use of popular idiom decades before. Curiously, though, Cardenal is also indebted to Ezra Pound's collage technique, juxtaposing the vulgarities of contemporary pop culture and ad-language with quotations from the classics, especially, in this case, those of pre-Columbian cultures.

When Octavio Paz optimistically declared in the 1950s that Latin Americans were 'now the contemporaries of all men', he was still speaking for only a select few. Today, however, when almost all the republics have a well-educated middle class subject to the daily barrage of international TV, radio and cinema, when the Cuban revolution presents a direct alternative to the European and North American way of life, and when many Latin American writers of both left and right appear regularly in the pages of even British magazines, the statement appears to have more meaning. With fiction becoming increasingly hermetic, convoluted and even narcissistic, and poetry ever more prosaic and matter-of-fact, the future is unusually difficult to predict. No doubt the Latin American literary New World has further surprises in store.

GM

Note: The titles of literary works referred to in this and subsequent articles are followed by the date of first publication and a translation of the title into English, where appropriate. Where an English translation has been *published*, the title is italicized and followed by the place and date of publication.

Further reading

G. Brotherston, *Latin American Poetry: Origins and Presence* (Cambridge, 1975)

G. Brotherston, *The Emergence of the Latin American Novel* (Cambridge, 1977)

E. Caracciolo-Trejo, ed., *The Penguin Book of Latin American Verse* (London, 1971)

J. Franco, *An Introduction to Spanish American Literature* (Cambridge, 1969)

D. Gallagher, *Modern Latin American Literature* (Oxford, 1973)

A. J. MacAdam, *Modern Latin American Narratives: the Dreams of Reason* (Chicago, 1977)

Brazilian literature

In the colonial period, the social and cultural characteristics that distinguished the five regions of Brazil – Bahia, Pernambuco, Minas Gerais, Rio de Janeiro and São Paulo – were reflected in the work of writers from those areas, thus creating definite regional trends and certain sets of values which added to the variety of Brazilian literature. Some Brazilian critics, like Wilson Martins, argue that Brazil did not possess a national literature 'in a general and specific sense before the end of the eighteenth century'. But the early works of the colonial period show an identifiable character of their own that cannot easily be dissociated from the Brazilian scene. The themes which have dominated Brazilian literature throughout – the Indian, the black, the sugar-cane, the drought, the *sertão* or backlands, the Amazon, Bahia, the sky-scraper – are the hallmarks of an original literary production. It has grown along consistent lines of development, even though the critical divisions adopted for changes in style may follow broadly European categories: the baroque era (1601–*c*.1770), neo-classicism (*c*.1760–1836), romanticism (1836–*c*.75), realism (*c*.1870–1922), and modernism (1922). These divisions are justified to a large extent by the fact that the main cultural currents that influenced the Brazilian intelligentsia came from Europe and were originally received through Portugal. Direct contacts with the wider world from the mid-nineteenth century onwards rendered this relationship far more diversified and led in our own time to a growing attachment to Brazilian oral literature.

The colonial era
The *Carta* (Letter) of Pero Vaz de Caminha on the discovery of Brazil, addressed to King Manuel and written between 22 April and 1 May 1500, is the first piece of literary merit to describe the new land. Caminha had sailed in the fleet of Pedro Alvares Cabral and in the *Carta* was informing the king about the results of the expedition. His description of the Amerindian reveals the illusions and dreams of the western mind in its search for an earthly paradise, but it also shows sound common sense. All the aspects described by Caminha, such as the apparent docility of the Indians, are those most suited to the convenience of the Portuguese explorers and project their image of themselves rather than that of the peoples they found. But there is also in this text a freshness of detail in the observation of the early contacts of the Portuguese with the Indians that reveals a spontaneous and immediate realism. This remains a characteristic of the literature of the colonial era, which cannot be dissociated from a tone of praise for the land and its resources. Pero de Maġalhães Gândavo, a Portuguese of Flemish origin whose dates of birth and death are unknown, produced around 1570 a *Tratado da Terra do Brasil* (published in 1826; Treatise on the Land of Brazil) and the

História da Província de Santa Cruz (1576; History of the Province of Santa Cruz). But, while striking a laudatory note, he shows clearly some aspects of Amerindian society, such as polygamy, inter-tribal wars and ritual revenges and anthropophagy, which detract from the paradisiacal vision given by Caminha. This kind of work of reportage constitutes a genre of its own; it was enriched by the experience and the missionary activity of the Jesuits in the new land.

Fr. Manuel de Nóbrega (1517–70) presents a balanced picture of Indian society, being less racially biased, though not free from prejudice, than his contemporaries in his *Diálogo sobre a conversão do gentio* (1577–9; Dialogue on the Conversion of the Heathen). Gabriel Soares de Sousa (1540?–91) provides in his *Tratado descritivo do Brasil em 1587* (Descriptive Treatise on Brazil in 1587) the most comprehensive description of the peoples, flora and fauna of the territory known to the Portuguese in the sixteenth century. But José de Anchieta, SJ (1534–97) was the first to combine the needs of religious indoctrination with literary quality, both in his religious poems and in his *autos* or morality plays. In these he followed the Iberian tradition in a rather innovatory way, by combining Portuguese and the native languages. Less successful was the attempt by Bento Teixeira (*c*.1560–?) to produce an epic poem, *A Prosopopéia* (1601), in praise of the Pernambuco ruler, Jorge de Albuquerque Coelho. His preoccupation with the form of poetic diction used by Camões in *The Lusiads*, whose pattern he tried to imitate, makes him a minor precursor of the new baroque style.

The logical and ordered syntax of the Renaissance was now giving way to sentences of conflicting meaning, to contradictory and problematic statements, such as those to be found in Hamlet's speeches. The north-eastern intelligentsia of Brazil, where the prosperity of the sugar-cane planters had created by 1600 an urban civilization, expressed its own complexity of thought, couched in the stylistic subtleties of Europe.

This change from old to new forms, and the solutions found in literary expression, did not conceal the existing conflicts. And these were nearly as acute in Brazil as in Europe. Portugal underwent Spanish domination (1580–1640), and had to fight the Dutch in Brazilian territory (1624–54). The towering figure of this period is Fr. Antônio Vieira, SJ (1608–97). His numerous sermons (published in Lisbon, 1679–1748, 16 vols.), are inextricably linked to his political and social crusades. Vieira attacks the Inquisition, defends the Indians from slavery, criticizes the presence and the religious ideas of the Dutch, and urges the people of Brazil to expel them (sermon preached in Salvador, 11 May 1640). His sermons are magnificent pieces of mannerist prose in which the power of his imagery is matched by flawless argument. These qualities of Vieira's style are present in all his writings, even in his voluminous correspondence, addressed to the king and to other influential people. Vieira was born in Lisbon and spent most of his life in Brazil. But the poet Gregório de Matos (1633–96) went from Bahia to Portugal, where he graduated in law at the university of Coimbra, and was made a judge before returning to his native town (1681), preceded by the fame of being a caustic satirical poet. Matos spares no one, nor any institution, in his satires. The Church, the colonial authorities, the new aristocracy of Indian blood, the menial classes, or whoever incurred his displeasure, was brutally, and often unfairly, castigated. His craftsmanship as a poet, where he introduced many indigenous words into his speech, is better shown in his religious and metaphysical verse. He exhibits here an outstanding mastery in the handling of conceits which serve the mood of his meditations on time and the human condition.

Between 1760 and 1840, Brazilian literature gradually adopted the neo-classical style. The most important writers of this tendency came from Minas Gerais. Cláudio Manuel da Costa (1729–80) in his *Obras* (1768; Works) praises his native land, which he says can vie in the excellence of its streams and hills with the Portuguese rivers and plains hallowed by literary tradition. Antônio Gonzaga (1744–1810) produced a fine collection of lyric poems, *Marília de Dirceu* (1792–99/1812), and published anonymously his *Cartas chilenas* (1789; Chilean Letters), a vigorous satire against the governor of Minas. The stand of Gonzaga and other Minas writers against the Portuguese authorities led to their arrest in 1789 under the accusation of being involved in a plot to overthrow the colonial government.

Independence and the nineteenth century

This dissatisfaction, stimulated by the events of the French Revolution (1789), culminated in the proclamation of independence on 7 September 1822. The opening up of Brazilian ports to international navigation, after the Portuguese court settled in Rio in 1808, favoured the growth of a national elite and created the economic and cultural conditions for the flowering of romanticism. The search for national origins, the expansion of imagination and individual freedom were the main characteristics of this complex movement. Gonçalves de Magalhães (1811–82) deals rather diffidently with romantic motives and moods in his *Suspiros poéticos e saudades* (1836; Poetic Sighs and Nostalgia). But he soon turns his attention to typical Brazilian themes, becoming one of the first *americanista* poets of the period. His impressive epic poem on the great Indian rebellion of 1506 against the Portuguese, *A confederação dos Tamoios* (1856; The Confederation of the Tamoyos), shows the Indian leader, Ambiré, and his wife, Iguaçu, giving their lives in the struggle for freedom. An artist far superior to Magalhães, however, is Gonçalves Dias (1823–64). His *Primeiros cantos* (1846; First Songs), *Segundos cantos* (1848; Second Songs) and *Últimos cantos* (1851; Last Songs) express in highly polished verse not only the beauty of Brazilian nature and the poet's nostalgia for the beloved country, but also the Indian protest against the occupation of the

land by the Portuguese (*O canto do Índio*, Song of the Indian). Dias tries also to see the inner conflicts that rend Indian society. In his poem, *Marabá*, he voices the anguish of a half-caste woman repudiated by her own tribe.

The epic and lyric tone so common in this Indianist poetry dominates also most of the fiction produced by José de Alencar (1829–77). He depicts magnificent frescoes of Indian life in *O Guarani* (1857; The Guarani), and *Iracema* (1865; *Iracema, the Honey-Lips*, London, 1886), two masterpieces of Indianist romantic literature. In *Iracema* he tries to create a new idiom, different from European Portuguese, by introducing a large number of Tupi expressions. But Alencar shows also in his novels the motley variety of Brazilian society. Whites and blacks, the ordinary working people and the bourgeois appear in his stories. He evinces a concern with social environment and psychological motivation that makes him a definite precursor of realism. His novels of city life – *Viuvinha* (1860; Little Widow) *Lucíola* (1862), *Senhora*; (1875; Lady) – are focused on the conflict between passion and the aspiration for social advancement. There is a remarkable shift in the tone and content of Brazilian Romanticism with Antônio de Castro Alves (1847–71), for the wide range of emotions he explores in his work and for the daunting vigour of his cosmic imagery. In his love poems he expresses an uninhibited sensuality that is only equalled by the majestic dignity of his social protest. In *Espumas flutuantes* (1870; Floating Foam) and *A cachoeira de Paulo Afonso* (1876; Paulo Afonso Falls) he lends a new and universal appeal to Indian themes. His condemnation of slavery, *Os escravos* (1883; The Slaves), still remains an unsurpassed piece of genuine poetic invective and human sympathy.

In the search for national inspiration with the *indianista* authors, Brazilian literature discovered the conflicts of subjectivity and attained a social awareness in the poetry of Castro Alves and his followers, that was soon to be strengthened by the abolitionist campaign coming from Recife and Rio de Janeiro. These conditions were favourable to the emergence of realism around 1880, a movement that was also shaped to some extent by Manuel Antônio de Almeida (1831–61) in his picaresque novel, *Memórias de um sargento de milícias* (1854–5; Memoirs of a Militia Sergeant).

The greatest realist novelist of Brazil, and one of its best short-story tellers, was J. Machado de Assis (1839–1908). His *Memórias póstumas de Brás Cubas* (1881; *Epitaph of a Small Winner*, New York, 1952) firmly established the new movement. The narrator of this book tells his own story after his death. In a detached and ironical vein, and after many philosophical digressions, he shows up the shallowness of a great love affair. In *Quincas Borba* (1891; *Philosopher or Dog?* New York, 1954; *The Heritage of Quincas Borba* London, 1954) he deals with a similar theme. But by revealing the growing madness of his main character, Machado exposes the

J. Machado de Assis

intelligentsia, now particularly receptive to the new European ideas, and beginning to recognize the character of their own industrial society. The Modern Art Week, held in São Paulo between 11 and 18 February 1922, introduced *modernismo* (not to be confused with the very different movement of the same name in Spanish America) in Brazil. By creating their own brand of futurism and by engaging a constant dialogue between literature and the plastic arts, by producing multiple styles and including oral language in the literary discourse, the modernists radically changed the character of Brazilian literature. Mário de Andrade (1893–1945) gives a critical vision of São Paulo in his poem *Paulicéia desvairada* (1922; *Hallucinated City*, Nashville, 1966), and deals with the question of a hero with a composite national character in his novel, *Macunaíma* (1928). Manuel Bandeira (1886–1968), in contrast, discovers modernism in the continuity of tradition. His poetic diction combines easily the colloquial and the ironical and succeeds admirably in turning personal fantasy into collective myth.

Bandeira was quite receptive to the *Manifesto regionalista* (1926; Regionalist Manifesto) issued by Gilberto Freyre (b. 1900), a sociologist who drew attention to the importance of the north-east, where recurrent drought emerges as an inescapable fate. But it is on the authors who chose that region as the background to their work that Freyre's influence was most enduring. After *A bagaceira* (1928; *Trash*, London, 1978) by J. Américo de Almeida (1887–1980), an old-fashioned novel on the sugar-cane theme, J. Lins do Rêgo (1901–57) produced a moving picture of the decline of a great estate in his sugar-cane cycle of novels, from *Menino do engenho* (1932; *Plantation Boy*, New York, 1966) to *Fogo morto* (1943; Dead Fire). The greatest writer of this group, however, is Graciliano Ramos (1892–1953), who shows perceptively in *Vidas sêcas* (1930; *Barren Lives*, Austin, 1965) the social roots of a natural calamity. He is also a shrewd analyst of personal disintegration (*Angústia*, 1936; *Anguish*, New York, 1946) and of the complex position of women in society. In João Cabral de Melo Neto (b. 1920), the north-east finds a demanding poet who treats the word with loving austerity (*Poesias completas*, 1968; Complete Poems), following the lesson of Carlos Drummond de Andrade (b. 1902), the greatest contemporary poet of Brazil. Drummond's search into the dialectic of reason and perception of the object has given superlative quality to his poetical work. And this quest is still at the root of all the experimental ventures of the *concretistas*, who have their main figure in Haroldo de Campos (b. 1929).

Brazilian literature was now to move into a deep exploration of language and ideas. Jorge Amado (b. 1912) began by writing populist novels on the cocoa planters and workers (*Cacau*, 1933; Cacao; *Suor*, 1934; Sweat), evolved to neo-realism (*Seara Vermelha*, 1946; Red Cornfield) and adopted in the 1950s the picaresque genre for his stories on Bahia. Yet, throughout all these changes, Jorge

assumptions of the romantic mind and the harsh materialism of society. He excels in this analysis of contrast and centres his observation on the development and ambiguity of social relations and their effect on his characters. Thus *Dom Casmurro* (1900; New York, 1953) explores the elusiveness of memory. And *Esaú e Jacó* (1904; *Esau and Jacob*, London, 1966) stands as an allegory of Brazilian society seen through the eyes of a young woman divided and confused in her love for twin brothers. Machado is a highly original author who very deliberately turned his back on regionalism.

Twentieth-century trends and writers

In 1897 the republican government violently crushed a religious movement in the backlands of Bahia led by the messianic figure of Antônio Conselheiro. The heroic resistance of the poor people of Canudos against the army made the problems of regionalism better known to the nation. And Euclides da Cunha (1866–1909) produced in *Os sertões* (1902; *Rebellion in the Backlands*, Chicago, 1944) an epic assessment of the rebellion that reveals a painful consciousness of the reality of the country.

The rebellion was a decisive factor in the minds of the São Paulo

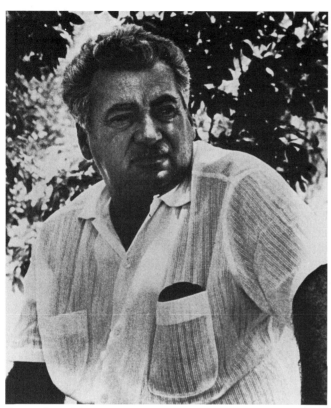

Jorge Amado

Amado remained the same inimitable story teller of his region, who has given us some admirable portraits of women (*Gabriela, Cravo e Canela*, 1958; *Gabriela, Clove and Cinnamon*, New York, 1962), making him the most popular Brazilian author at home and abroad. Érico Veríssimo (1905–75) introduced the *gaúcho* novel into Brazilian fiction and showed a remarkable psychological insight into his characters (*Clarissa*, 1933; *Música ao longe*, 1935; Faraway Music; and in the trilogy, *O tempo e o vento*, 1954–62; Time and the Wind). But the real change in Brazilian fiction dates from 1956, when J. Guimarães Rosa (1908–67) published an original novel, *Grande sertão: veredas* (*The Devil to Pay in the Backlands*, New York, 1963), in which the *sertão* becomes a metaphor for the whole world. The power of linguistic creation transcends geographic and national boundaries to make it a work of universal appeal and a true literary masterpiece. It is an extremely complex fable on the destiny of man and the essence of evil set against the symbolic background of the Minas *sertões*. This capacity to question the self and the sense of existence at all cultural levels is one of the most fascinating features of contemporary Brazilian literature. In *Quarup* (1967) by Antônio Callado (b. 1917) and *A pedra do reino* (1971; Stone of the Kingdom) by A. Suassuna (b. 1927) the quest for the self and national identity

is pursued as being one and the same through folklore and popular literature.

New directions in fiction are noticeable in the work of Osman Lins (1924–78), a demanding author who questions the limits of the narrative and the novel as a genre (*Nove novena*, 1966; *Avalovara*, 1973), and in the atmospheric novels of Autran Dourado (b. 1926), who evokes the decadence of Minas society. Dalton Trevisan (b. 1925) is a tormented observer in *A guerra conjugal* (1969; Conjugal Warfare) and *O vampiro de Curitiba* (1970; The Vampire of Curitiba) of erotic fantasies and domestic attrition.

LSR

Further reading

M. Bandeira, *Brief History of Brazilian Literature* (New York, 1954)

A. Coutinho, *An Introduction to Literature in Brazil* (New York, 1969)

D. Haberly, *Three Sad Races: Racial Identity and National Consciousness in Brazilian Literature* (Cambridge, 1983)

S. Putnam, *Marvelous Journey: a Survey of Four Centuries of Brazilian Literature* (New York, 1948)

English Caribbean Literature

In his novel *The Mimic Men* (1972) the Trinidadian V. S. Naipaul (b. 1932) writes: 'The empires of our time were short-lived, but they have altered the world for ever; passing away is their least significant feature.' The literature of the English-speaking Caribbean (i.e. the West Indies) has flourished only since 1950, but it is constantly and searingly marked by its awareness of a colonial history stretching back to the seventeenth century. Remarkably, thirteen years before the establishment of the first English colony in the West Indies, William Shakespeare's *The Tempest* (1611) put on stage a character called Caliban who in retrospect has provided one of the most potent self-images for the writers and intellectuals of the post-colonial Caribbean. Prospero, the European nobleman exiled on an unnamed island, had originally made much of the island's native inhabitant, but by the beginning of the play has reduced him to slavery. Caliban, forced into obedience by Prospero's magic art, can only rail against his master:

> You taught me language; and my profit on't
> Is, I know how to curse. The red plague rid you
> For learning me your language! (I.ii.365–7)

The paradox is acute. The quest that has been at the centre of modern Caribbean writing – the search to formulate a racial and cultural identity – takes place in the language of the colonizer and often involves a journey to or exile in the colonial metropolis. C. L. R. James (Trinidad, b. 1901) prefaces his extraordinary book on cricket (*Beyond a Boundary*, 1963) by speaking of the need to track down his ideas in England: 'To establish his own identity, Caliban, after three centuries, must himself pioneer into regions Caesar never knew.'

Unlike other post-colonial societies, the islands of the Caribbean have no indigenous culture to provide any ready-made locus of authentic (because non-colonial) values. Caliban is in fact an anagram of 'Canibal', Columbus's version of the name of the inhabitants of the eastern West Indies: it is the origin therefore both of the geographical term 'Caribbean' and that byword for the ultimate in savage behaviour: 'cannibalism'. The Caribs, as they are now referred to, had no writing and, though they survived longer than the neighbouring Arawaks – exterminated before English colonization began in the area – they left little cultural legacy and make only marginal appearances in Caribbean literature. Caribs and Arawaks still live in Guyana where Wilson Harris (b. 1921) has explored and elaborated their oral narratives in *The Sleepers of Roraima* (1970) and *The Age of the Rainmakers* (1971).

During the early colonial period little writing was done in the English Caribbean itself. The most significant literary form was the diary or journal of the English planter or visitor, a mode that begins with Sir Henry Colt's remarkable journal of 1631 and includes

works such as 'Monk' Lewis's *Journal of a West Indian Proprietor* (1834) and Lady Nugent's *Journal* (1839). The other book, set largely in the Caribbean, that has provided almost as powerful a set of literary references as *The Tempest*, is Daniel Defoe's *Robinson Crusoe* (1719).

The attempt to create a West Indian literature in English can be dated from the beginning of this century with the significant, if short-lived, *All Jamaica Library* whose first volume was *Becka's Buckra Baby* (1903) by Tom Redcam (pseudonym of T. H. MacDermot, 1870–1933). Exceptionally, the five volumes of this venture were published in Kingston. Most subsequent West Indian literature has been published in England, increasingly so in the last thirty years. The frequent pattern of literary and political involvement, emigration, and writing from and about exile, was early established. The Trinidadians Alfred H. Mendes (b. 1897) and C. L. R. James were instrumental in the establishment of a native

A sixteenth-century engraving depicting Caribs

C. L. R. James

cultural life in the late 1920s and early 1930s but their influential realist novels (Mendes's *Pitch Lake*, 1934, and James's *Minty Alley*, 1936) were published after they had emigrated. The pressure towards emigration has been described more recently by the novelist George Lamming (Barbados, b. 1927):

> This was the kind of atmosphere in which all of us grew up. On the one hand a mass of people who were either illiterate or if not, had no connection whatever to literature since they were too poor or too tired to read; and on the other hand a colonial middle class educated it seemed, for the specific purpose of sneering at anything which grew or was made in native soil.

James, like so many others after him, came to London (in 1932) as a necessary step in his literary career. He became instead a political theorist and commentator, and author (in 1938) of *The Black Jacobins*, the story of the Haitian revolution. Lamming himself came to London in 1950, in the footsteps of the Guyanan novelist Edgar Mittelholzer (1909–65) who had achieved rapid success with his *A Morning at the Office* (1950). He was followed shortly by almost a whole generation of the best West Indian writers, amongst them Roger Mais and Andrew Salkey, from Jamaica, Samuel Selvon and V. S. Naipaul from Trinidad, and Wilson Harris from Guyana.

If Caribbean literature is unified by the felt absence of a single cultural tradition, the breadth of responses to this absence has been enormously varied and has recently produced in English a tremendously vigorous and exciting literature. Only the main outlines can be indicated here.

Derek Walcott (St Lucia, b. 1930), the poet and playwright, who now lives in Trinidad, restates Caliban's dilemma by naming its horns Africa and the English language:

> I who am poisoned with the blood of both,
> Where shall I turn, divided to the vein?
> I who have cursed
> The drunken officer of British rule, how choose
> Between this Africa and the English tongue I love?
> Betray them both, or give back what they give?
> How can I face such slaughter and be cool?
> How can I turn from Africa and live?

> ('A Far Cry from Africa' in
> *Selected Poems*, 1964)

It is difficult to overestimate the importance of Africa for modern Caribbean writing as a whole. The sense that Caribbean culture can find its authentic voice as part of African tradition has always been strongest in French-speaking Haiti, but the shared awareness of a common past in slavery and a common origin in Africa led to early links between English-speaking West Indians and North American blacks. The Jamaican Claude McKay (1890–1948), author of one of the classic novels of Caribbean peasant life, *Banana Bottom* (1933), went to the United States in 1912 and was closely associated with the black literary movement known as the Harlem Renaissance. More recently West Indians have tested the potent ideal of 'Africa' against its contemporary reality by visiting and often living there. *The Leopard* (1958) by V. S. Reid (Jamaica, b. 1913) and *Other Leopards* (1963) by Denis Williams (Guyana, b. 1923) are just two of a series of fine and complex novels to come out of this encounter. Africa also figures prominently in the trilogy of long poems by the Barbadian Edward Brathwaite (b. 1930), *The Arrivants* (1973), perhaps the only West Indian poem comparable in scope and ambition to Aimé Césaire's magisterial *Cahier d'un retour au pays natal*.

English language and literature have been dominant influences, albeit ones handled with the ambivalence due to the culture of the colonizer. Caribbean speech patterns have been increasingly employed in much West Indian literature, and systematically in works like V. S. Reid's novel *New Day* (1949) and *Jamaica Labrish: Jamaica Dialect Poems* (1967) by Louise Bennett (b. 1919). Some of the finest West Indian writing has set out to rework English versions of colonial history. George Lamming uses *The Tempest* for his novel set in contemporary London, *Water with Berries* (1971). *Wide Sargasso Sea* (1966) by Jean Rhys (Dominica, 1890–1979) tells the story of Antoinette, the mad Mrs Rochester in Charlotte Bronte's *Jane Eyre* (1847). And Derek Walcott's poems in *The Castaway* (1965) draw imaginatively on the figures of Robinson Crusoe and Friday. Walcott is in fact notable for his superb command of the resources of the English poetic tradition but, typically, makes that command, his relationship with that tradition, into the subject-matter of his poetry, which often becomes a fraught and ambiguous meditation on the fragmented heritage of English culture.

As the earlier quotation from Naipaul suggests, the European colonial empires altered the world forever, and Walcott is by no means alone in his close inquiry into the enduring significance of the colonial past. Something of the varied unity of contemporary West Indian literature is suggested by the fact that four such different writers as George Lamming in *Natives of My Person* (1972), Wilson Harris in *Palace of the Peacock* (1960), Milton McFarlane (Jamaica, b. 1927) in *Cudjoe the Maroon* (1977) and V. S. Naipaul in *The Loss of El Dorado* (1969), should recently have written such accomplished works set in the colonial period. All of them in different ways concern quests. *Natives of My Person* is a remarkable novel about a seventeenth-century voyage of colonization from strife-torn Lime Stone (Europe) to the Caribbean island of San Cristobal, written in Lamming's extraordinary heightened prose. *Palace of the Peacock* (part of Harris's ambitious 'Guyana Quartet') moves between the sixteenth century and the twentieth as it tells of two related voyages into the interior, journeys of self-discovery, the 'deepening cycle of exploration' (the phrase is Harris's) with which

V. S. Naipaul

he attempts a reconstitution of the fragmented Caribbean psyche. Cudjoe was the Maroon guerrilla leader who led the resistance against a whole series of unsuccessful English attempts between 1655 and 1739 to destroy the towns established by runaway slaves in central Jamaica. McFarlane's quest is the recovery and dissemination of this history, passed down in secret oral traditions amongst the still largely autonomous Maroon communities, and part of the important process of rewriting Caribbean history from the perspective of the oppressed classes. Naipaul's *The Loss of El Dorado* similarly tells what he calls 'two forgotten stories', two moments when 'history' touched Trinidad: its part in Sir Walter Ralegh's search for El Dorado, and the later British attempt to foment revolution in Spain's American empire. Naipaul's is a carefully researched history but, like McFarlane's, consists in a powerful and imaginative recreation of crucial events in Caribbean history. In their different ways these four books all exemplify the remark made by the Martiniquan writer Aimé Césaire that the quickest way to the future is through the past.

Naipaul's career is almost a parody of West Indian exile in his complex trajectory through Trinidad, London, India, Africa and South America. Most of his work has been signally autobiographical, the major novels such as *A House for Mr Biswas* (1961), and *The Mimic Men* (1967) often following his initial explorations of these territories in journalism and travel-writing. Naipaul's quest in other words has been an acutely personal one which has taken him, his critics say, further and further from West Indian society as he becomes a universal traveller, ironically dissecting the decaying carcass of the modern world (*The Middle Passage*, 1962; *The Return of Eva Peron*, 1980).

Naipaul is, however, exemplary in the honesty with which he has confronted the problems of form. The West Indies has produced a whole series of classic novels since *A Brighter Sun* (1952) by Samuel Selvon (Trinidad, b. 1923) and George Lamming's autobiographical *In the Castle of My Skin* (1953), but the pressure to speak urgently and directly has tended (perhaps increasingly) to fissure the formal conventions of the European novel. Naipaul would here be in the company of his political opponents, *The Loss of El Dorado* resembling C. L. R. James's *The Black Jacobins* in its careful historical research presented with a novelist's imagination and narrative drive; *The Middle Passage* resembling the telling political diaries, *Havana Journal* (1971) and *Georgetown Journal* (1972) of the Jamaican Andrew Salkey (b. 1928) in their attempt to make sense, an honest and personal rather than fictional sense, out of the complexities of political and intellectual life in the contemporary Caribbean.

PH

Further reading

Anthologies
O. R. Dathorne, ed., *Caribbean Verse: an Anthology* (London, 1967)
K. Ramchand, ed., *West Indian Narrative* (London, 1966)

Critical writing
G. R. Coulthard, *Race and Colour in Caribbean Literature* (Oxford, 1962)
W. Harris, *Tradition, the Writer and Society* (London, 1967)
G. Lamming, *The Pleasures of Exile* (London, 1960)
B. King, ed., *West Indian Literature* (London, 1979)
K. Ramchand, *The West Indian Novel and its Background* (London, 1970)

French Caribbean literature

The native inhabitants of the Caribbean are as absent from the modern literature in French as from that in English. This was not always so. By far the most important Caribbean genre of the seventeenth and eighteenth centuries was the series of historical and anthropological works written by the Domincan and Jesuit missionaries. Phenomenally unsuccessful in their missionary activities, the fathers, often resident in the Caribbean for a large part of their lives, produced a series of valuable and influential books, none more so than *Histoire génerale des Antilles habités par les Français* (1667–71; General History of the French Antilles) by Jean-Baptiste du Tertre, which contains this classic description of the native inhabitants:

> The Savages of these islands are the most contented, happiest, least vicious, most friendly, least false, and the least tormented by sickness, of all the nations in the world. For they are still just as nature made them, that is to say living in great simplicity and natural naivety: they are all equal, with almost no form of superiority or servitude.

These Caribs, difficult to recognize in the cannibals that were later to horrify Robinson Crusoe, reappear nearly a hundred years later as living in what Rousseau called mankind's happiest and most stable epoch, the true youth of the world. By then (1754) the Caribs were fighting a desperate and soon-to-be-lost battle against the English and French colonists. In Aimé Césaire's powerful rewriting of Shakespeare's play, *Une Tempête* (1969; *The Tempest*, New York, 1974), Caliban is, despite his name, a black; and it is the black experience that forms the heart of modern Caribbean literature in French.

However, although properly belonging to the mainstream of French poetry, mention should first be made of the long tradition of poems of exile by French Caribbean writers, linking Nicolas-Germain Leonard (1744–93), who when in France wrote nostalgically about Guadeloupe and *vice versa*, with Saint-John Perse (pseudonym of Alexis Léger) whose eleven years in Guadeloupe (from his birth in 1887 to 1908) produced the stunning *Images à Crusoé* (1904; 'Pictures for Crusoe' in *Collected Poems*, trans. W. H. Auden *et al.*, Princeton, 1971).

Haiti, independent since 1804, has clear precedence in the development of a literature of its own, the first signs of this becoming apparent in the late nineteenth century with the publication of *De l'égalité des races humaines* (1885; On the Equality of Human Races) by Anténor Firmin (1850–1911). This riposte to the deepening racial prejudice of high imperialism affirmed the achievements of African civilizations and the place of blacks as the cultural equals of their oppressors. It is thus closely tied to the current that

only later became known as *négritude*. The US military occupation of Haiti from 1915 to 1930 – described in *Le choc* (1932), a novel by Léon Laleau (b. 1892) – led to a general cultural reassessment of which *Ainsi parla l'oncle* (1928; So the Uncle Said) by Jean Price-Mars (1876–1970) is the main document. Price-Mars urged the study of popular culture, the folklore, music, proverbs and religious practices of the Haitian people, ignored by the nineteenth-century intellectual elite: 'We have no chance of being ourselves unless we repudiate no part of our ancestral heritage. And indeed this heritage for eight-tenths of us is a gift from Africa.' Most contemporary Caribbean literature in French has been written under the influence of such formulations. In Haiti itself *La Revue indigène* (founded 1927) was a significant forum for such work, and it was the novelist and poet Jacques Roumain (1907–44) who founded the *Bureau d'ethnologie* in 1941.

In 1931 Léon Laleau wrote a poem, 'Trahison', which contained these lines:

> And this despair, equal to no other,
> for taming with words from France
> this heart which came to me from Senegal.

The dilemma – Africa with the words of France – is analogous to that faced by English-speaking West Indian writers, but Laleau's despair quickly gave way to an anger and assertion which have generally had little time for the meditative ironies of Naipaul or Walcott; whether in the famous collection *Pigments* (1937) by Léon-Gontran Damas (Guyane, 1912–78) with its absolute rejection of everything European; or in Carl Brouard (Haiti, 1902–65) already (in 'Nostalgie', 1927) writing of Africa as home. These works contain the language and sentiments of *négritude*. Although the word itself was only coined in 1939 by Césaire, the ideas themselves came to fruition in Paris in the early 1930s, stimulated by the meetings of French Caribbean and French African writers. The three great monuments to this collaboration are Leopold Senghor's influential anthology of black Caribbean and African poetry, *La nouvelle poésie nègre et malgache de langue française* (1948; The New Black and Malagasy Poetry in the French Language), the periodical *Présence Africaine* (founded 1947), and the extraordinary essays on the politics and psychology of colonialism and decolonization, *Peau noir, masques blancs* (1952; *Black Skin, White Masks*, New York, 1967) and *Les damnés de la terre* (1961; *The Wretched of the Earth*, London, 1967) by the Martiniquan Frantz Fanon (1925–61).

But the great poem of *négritude* is *Cahier d'un retour au pays natal* (1939; *Return to my Native Land*, London, 1969) by Aimé Césaire (Martinique, b. 1913). In 1942 Suzanne Césaire wrote: 'Martiniquan poetry will be cannibalistic or it will be nothing.' *Cahier* is fully cannibalistic: savage in its anger at imperialism, violent in its wrenching of French verse form and syntax. The poem begins by invoking in blistering prose poetry the poverty and despair of colonial Martinique. Soon the poet finds his voice

We shall speak. We shall sing. We shall shout.
Full voice, great voice, you shall be our good and our guide

and begins his hymn to blackness:

my negritude is not a stone,
nor deafness flung out against the clamour of the day
my negritude is not a white speck of dead water
on the dead eye of the earth
my negritude is neither tower nor cathedral.

Négritude is the dialectical opposite of white racialism; not a black racialism but rather an acceptance and affirmation of the identity of blacks as colonized peoples. Fanon puts it well:

The white man . . . desires the world and wants it for himself alone. He considers himself predestined to rule the world. He has made it useful to himself. But there are values which do not submit to his rule. Like a sorcerer I steal from the white man a certain world which he cannot identify.

So, in direct opposition to the colonial impulse, Césaire celebrates:

. . . those who have never invented anything
those who never explored anything
those who never tamed anything
those who gave themselves up to the essence of all things
ignorant of surfaces but struck by the movement of all things
free of the desire to tame but familiar with the play of the world.

The doctrines of *négritude* have been elaborated most extensively by the Senegalese poet Leopold Senghor. Césaire, meanwhile, has continued writing against colonialism in his poetry and plays, and in his lyrical essay *Discours sur le colonialisme* (1955; *Discourse on Colonialism*, New York, 1972).

While the poets of the 1930s were speaking with power and grandiloquence, the novelists were involved in the sort of documentary investigations that have their equivalents at this time in most parts of the continent. René Maran (Martinique, 1887–1960) had already written what has been called the first novel of *négritude*, *Batouala* (1921: *Batouala*, New York, 1972); but Jacques Roumain initiated a tradition of writing about the realities of Haitian proletariat and peasant life that culminated in the work of Jacques Stéphen Alexis (1922–61), killed leading an unsuccessful invasion of Duvalier's Haiti. Roumain's most important novels are *La montagne ensorcelée* (1931; The Enchanted Mountain) and *Gouverneurs de la rosée* (1944; *Masters of the Dew*, London, 1978). Alexis's masterpiece is *Compère Général Soleil* (1955; Old General Sun). Other prose

writers within this tradition include the Haitian Philippe Thoby-Marcelin (1904–75) (*Canapé Vert*, 1944; *Canapé Vert*, New York, 1944; *le Crayon de dieu*, 1951; *The Pencil of God*, London, 1952), the Martiniquan Joseph Zobel (b. 1915) (*La rue cases-nègres*, 1950; *Black Shack Alley*, New York, 1980), and the Guadeloupian Simone Schwartz-Bart (b. 1938) (*Pluie et vent sur télumée miracle*, 1972; *The Bridge of Beyond*, London, 1975).

The connection between politics and literature, always close in the Caribbean, has been especially so in the French-speaking areas. Roumain founded the Haitian Communist Party in 1934 and Césaire has for many years been a Deputy for Martinique to the French National Assembly – first as a Communist and then (after 1956) as a member of an independent revolutionary party. More recently, the exiled Haitian poet René Depestre (b. 1927) has, like the Uruguayan Mario Benedetti, expressed his support for the Cuban revolution by living and working in Cuba, and is now writing in Spanish as well as French. His early work in French remains notable; his recent *Poète à Cuba* (1976; Poet in Cuba) could prove to be one of the central intellectual and poetic works of the contemporary Caribbean.

PH

Further reading

G. R. Coulthard, *Race and Colour in Caribbean Literature* (Oxford, 1962)
N. Garrett, *The Renaissance of Haitian Poetry* (Paris, 1963)

Amerindian music

In the high civilization areas of both Mexico and Peru, much more complex instruments were in vogue before AD 1000 than in 1500. Among archaeological instruments excavated at c. AD 1000 sites in Tabasco and Veracruz (east coastal Mexico), clay multiple flutes of three or four pipes document harmonies not yet known by contemporary Europeans; the pipes blown from a single mouthpiece sounded chords such as $f\sharp$–a–c^1–e^1, $f\sharp$–a–c^1–d^1, and $f\sharp$–a–bb–e^1. Tabasco archaeological instruments included also 'goiter' flutes, the protuberance at the neck of the single vertical tube serving as an oscillating air chamber that changed the sound to a reedy quality. The most complex archaeological instruments excavated at Peruvian coastal sites are Nazca clay panpipes of as many as thirteen tubes. The adjacent tubes often sound microtone intervals. The cane panpipes still played in highland Peru require large breath supplies. Fortunately dwellers in the high altitudes of the Lake Titicaca area have long been adapted physically to their conditions, which have required large lung capacity.

Bolivian Indians playing native instruments: pututu horn, panpipes, drum

Vast cultural differences separated the less privileged Taino islanders met in the West Indies by Columbus during his four voyages (1492–3, 1498, 1502) from the more sophisticated mainlanders subdued by Cortés (Aztecs, 1521) and Pizarro (Incas, 1533). Nonetheless, all but a few Amerindians met by first-generation European explorers resembled each other in possessing drums, rattles, and other instruments to which they sang and danced.

The Aztecs' favourite pair of percussion instruments, each emitting two pitches, were the *huehuetl*, an upright barrel-shaped wooden drum covered at the top with animal skin and played with the bare hands; and the *teponaztli*, a horizontal cylinder wooden slit-drum, the two slabs of which (emitting pitches a third or fourth apart) were struck with rubber-tipped mallets. To enhance power, the blood of sacrificial human victims was poured into *teponaztli* interiors on important state occasions.

In addition to drums, the Incas favoured sexually significant vertical flutes and cane or clay panpipes joined in vertical rows. Although not addicted to human sacrifice as were the Aztecs, the Incas painted their drums vermilion to enhance their power.

Because eight was the most powerful number and size mattered, Inca men played eight large drums at accessions or at victory celebrations. Women played small concave hand drums for less imposing calendar observances.

Musical perfection counted so heavily in Aztec rituals that a drummer who missed a beat was summarily withdrawn from the ensemble and sacrificed to the offended deity. Training of the harshest kind forced Aztec youth in the *calmécac* ('seminary') to memorize lengthy sung narratives recounting Aztec cosmology and history. Men dominated bloody Aztec rituals. But at the Inca capital of Cuzco, maidens under eighteen years old provided musically high-pitched solace for warriors returning from battle in the four corners of the New World's largest pre-Columbian empire.

The earliest Amerindian melodies published anywhere were five Tupinambá chants included in Jean de Léry's *Histoire d'vn voyage faict en la Terre dv Bresil* (Geneva, 1585). A Calvinist visitor to the area of Rio de Janeiro in 1557–8, Léry, long after returning to Europe, certified having heard one of the five melodies sung to texts praising a beautiful bird of yellow plumage (*Canidé-iouue*), another in praise of a large succulent fish. The remaining three enter Léry's chapter 16 ('What can be called religion among the Brazilian Savages'). He heard them at a ceremony gathering 500 or 600 Tupinambá every third or fourth year. They repeated one chant of ten notes in a gradual crescendo lasting more than fifteen minutes. The next melody of fourteen notes covering a range of a fifth served as a refrain repeated intermittently during a three-hour men's circle dance. Women never joined this dance. To instill valour wizards leaped about blowing tobacco smoke into the dancers' nostrils. All Amerindians, wherever met by the first Europeans, used music and dancing in religious rituals designed to serve not as a mere entertainment but as appeasement of supernatural powers.

Tupinambás in Brazil, Caribs in the Antilles, Aztecs and Mixtecs in central Mexico, all mixed their sanguinary rites with music that terrorized such early European arrivals as Hans Staden, Jean de Léry, and Bernal Díaz del Castillo and his companions. On the other hand, Spanish writers such as Toribio Motolonía and Diego Durán greatly lauded ceremonial dances in Aztec courtyards performed in perfect time by scores of feather-adorned workers to the beat of *huehuetl* and *teponaztli*. *Cantares en idioma mexicano*, a Mexican National Library manuscript dating from 1551 to 1563 that contains Aztec language songs with interspersed *teponaztli* patterns, gives valuable clues to the drumming sequences in vogue as late as a generation after the fall of the Aztec capital.

What typified high culture expressions both before and after European contact differs considerably from Venezuelan and Brazilian tribal traits documented by 1911–13 sound recordings analysed by the ethnomusicological pioneer, Erich M. von Hornbostel. These twentieth-century recorded examples permitted his making the following oft-quoted generalizations concerning Venezuelan and Brazilian Indian style: so far as vocal timbre goes, singing gives the impression of the emphatic, entries are strongly accentuated, phrase beginnings are punctuated by strong exhaling, strong dynamic accents herald the first tone of each motive. A brief motive forms all the melody, its constant repetition the chant. Something severe and transcendental pervades all Indian chants. In the melodies, small descending intervals the approximate size of a minor third or major second abound. In dances, each quarter note is heavily accented, drumming never includes complex patterns but is always a steady uniform series of strikes sometimes not coordinated with the rhythm of the singing. Their music characteristically strings together equal-sized elements as if in a long necklace of equal-sized beads.

More recently (1975), the Hungarian Academy of Sciences has published a large collection of Nambicuara Indian melodies collected in the Brazilian Mato Grosso by Lajos Boglár and analysed by István Halmos that opens new vistas with its mention of globular nose flutes and intervallic series not known among the tribes familiar to Hornbostel. They rightly concluded that South American Indian music studies of the type concluded by them and by Isabel Aretz, Luis Felipe Ramón y Rivera and their disciples at the Instituto de Investigación Etnomusicológica y Folklórica at Caracas continue offering ever new insights into huge neglected areas.

RMS

Devil dancers at Oruro Carnival, Bolivia

Further reading

R. Stevenson, *Music in Mexico: a Historical Survey* (New York, 1952 and 1971)

The Music of Peru: Aboriginal and Viceroyal Epochs (Washington, DC, 1960)

Music in Aztec and Inca Territory (Berkeley and Los Angeles, 1968 and 1976)

'Aztec Music', 'Maya Music', 'Inca Music' in *The New Grove Dictionary of Music and Musicians*, 20 vols (London, 1980), I, 760–1; IX, 56–7; XI, 852–4

Folk and popular music

Latin American folk music derives from three major sources: the indigenous Indian, the colonizing Hispanic, and the transported African. Elements from all three are found in many combinations within musical form, structure, genre, instrumentation, vocal and performing style and practice, melody, rhythm, metre, scale (i.e. all musical and extra-musical parameters). In most places there is fusion into culturally mixed forms. Areas where archaic features, traced to a particular source, have been retained, reveal the crucial role of the type of contact between peoples, local and national political and cultural history, the use and function of music and the people's aesthetic.

The Spanish used music in their efforts to Christianize the indigenous population and the result was far from uniform. According to the musicologist Gérard Béhague, Inca culture seems to have resisted erosion rather better than Aztec culture: the former being influenced by the Hispanic, the latter mostly displaced. The result is a whole cycle of religious festivals, ostensibly Catholic, but with many native elements in music, dance and instrumentation accompanying the liturgical calendar of the Catholic Church. The most notable are the Carnival festivals which take place to mark the beginning of Lent in Brazil, Bolivia, the Caribbean area, northern Argentina and many other places. A whole body of folk song and dance is associated with such occasions, as are elaborate, ornate, highly decorated costumes (each of which have historical meaning).

While the structure of annual religious festivals may remain constant, the actual songs and dances performed within them show the changing taste of the participants in terms of genre, instrumentation and musical arrangement. The origin of such change is the city, for many participants will have returned to the country from urban areas bringing new popular songs with them, or will have migrated to the city taking their tradition with them. The Brazilian samba is most commonly associated with the annual Carnival in Rio de Janeiro for which working-class neighbourhood samba schools will prepare all year. It is also performed in the Capoeira (ritualized

An elaborate costume for Rio Carnival

Capoeira dancing in Bahia

martial art) cult in Bahia and in other cults and rituals in north-eastern Brazil. Its specific local identity can be traced to distinctive drum patterns which reveal the different African ancestry of those involved, as do other aspects of performing practice. Many dramatic dances with a religious central subject involve the bringing together of Catholic saints with deities brought from West Africa as do 'Voodoo' and possession cults in Cuba, Haiti, Jamaica, Trinidad and Brazil.

The development of many secular forms of music is traced back to the instrumentalists who accompanied Cortés on his first expedition. They brought with them the first string instruments (the lute, harp, violin, the guitar) and the Indians made their own variants: the Andean *charango*, a hybrid lute–small guitar, with five pairs of strings which uses an armadillo shell as a resonating case; the *tres* and *cuatro* (small three- and four-stringed guitars); the *guitarrón*, a twenty-five-string guitar found in Mexico today, used originally as accompanying instrument to traditional sung poetry in Chile, *Canto a lo poeta* (Song in the manner of the poet), based on the Spanish *décima*. The verse structure of the *décima*, *glosa* and *copla* (with their

prevailing syllabic line and stanza length and classic rhyme scheme – usually abbaaccddc) is found in many countries, not only in folk forms accompanying events of the cycle of life (birth, courting, marriage, death) but also, for example, in the *canción mexicana*. Song forms derived from the early Renaissance *romance* are widespread, most purely in Colombia and Chile, with structural traces in Argentina and Ecuador, and most notably in the *corrido*, the typical ballad of the Mexican revolution, which was revived in the 1940s. Other folk songs such as *tonadas* (Chile and Argentina) and *estilos* (Argentina and Uruguay) have maintained Spanish literary forms, as have many children's rhymes and songs, and Christmas songs which also show mestizo characteristics. The sung 'duel' using a variety of intricate forms is still found in Cuba, north-east Brazil, Chile, Argentina and Venezuela. Such forms have significant specific identifying traits generated by the particular cultural and political history of the area.

Apart from dances associated with religious occasions, secular circle and couple dances are also found today, the former more often in collective, peasant, communal areas (reminding us that the sung text was originally inseparable from dance movement), the latter in villages, towns, and urban areas: the structure and forms relating to social organization. Almost all important folk dances have their urban counterpart, for example, the *huayno*, *yaraví* and *taquirari* in the Andean area: the major distinguishing features of the urban forms are to be found in details of performing practice and instrumentation foreign to rural tradition.

From the Peruvian colonial dance of the first half of the nineteenth century, the *zamacueca*, have evolved the *zamba* and the *cueca* which through usage have developed as separate dances. The *cueca* is a couple dance in which both partners hold and use a handkerchief: imitative of the courtship of cock and hen, it is performed with much regional variation in such features as movement of the handkerchief, fingersnapping and footwork. In Chile the *cueca* is the national dance, in Argentina it is known as the *chilena*, while in Peru the name was changed from *chilena* to *marinera* at the time of the War of the Pacific. A rhythmic feature of this dance and many others (such as the Venezuelan *joropo*, the Mexican *son* and *huapango*, for example, 'La Bamba') is what is termed the 'hemiola' effect when bars of 6/8 and 3/4 are either in simultaneous use by singer and in the accompaniment or alternating; this rhythmic pattern is not only found in Spanish music where it is thought to have originated, but also in African music in cross-rhythmic patterns of the drum.

Nineteenth-century salon dances (waltz, mazurka, contradanse, polka) were brought to Latin America, influencing and fusing with folk and popular forms, for example the Mexican *jarabe*, most popular at the time of the War of Independence, and later on typically performed by Mariachi ensembles. European and North American twentieth-century dances have appeared in hybrid forms in local dance halls, for example, the *samba-fox*, and *rumba-fox*. Cuba, of all Latin American countries, has been the source of many influential popular genres: the *habanera*, *danza cubana*, bolero, mambo, conga, cha-cha-cha, all of which have strong Afro-Cuban features in rhythm, syncopation, metre and dance movements. The Colombian *cumbia* is today danced all over the continent and it too exhibits many African features in its choreography, and its frequent call and response structure.

Most song texts reveal the cultural attitudes and beliefs of the people amongst whom they originated, and many are spontaneously or consciously, directly or indirectly vehicles for political and social comment: for example, the Peruvian *vals*, the Argentine tango, the Brazilian *samba-canção*, the pre- and post-revolutionary *son* and *guaracha* of Carlos Puebla.

One of the most renowned of all Latin American popular dances is the Argentine tango. Scholars debate the origin of the name *tango*, which seems to have been the name for a drum used by black slaves, and was perhaps later used to refer to locale, accompaniment and then the dance itself. Three types of tango are usually differentiated: the mainly instrumental *tango-milonga* played by orchestras in the 1920s; the romantic, melodic, vocalized *tango-romanza* of the same era; and the *tango-canción*. It is the latter which, like the man who popularized it internationally, Carlos Gardel (1890–1935), has come to symbolize the tango. Like the dance, Gardel's background was in the poorer districts (*arrabales*) of Buenos Aires. He too rose to international fame and became the symbol of the dreams of the *porteño* of Buenos Aires as he sang film songs such as 'Mi Buenos Aires querido' (My Beloved Buenos Aires). The music of the dance brought together elements of folk and popular dances traced over the whole continent and beyond: the Andalusian tango, the Cuban *habanera*, the *milonga* of the River Plate area. Those who listened to its essentially sentimental and often pessimistic lyrics were the new immigrant population from all parts of Europe as well as the interior of Argentina. The tight choreographic structure, the mannerisms and movements of the dancing couple, the relationship between man and woman in the text have been related to the *compadrito* underworld culture of Buenos Aires and the stereotyped sex roles of that subculture – a subculture often evoked by tango lyrics.

The economic boom in the United States after 1945 stimulated much technological innovation (45 rpm and long-playing records, record players, radios); and the growth of the recording industry with its network of promoters and distributors, and the subsequent increase in the number of radio stations, had repercussions throughout the world which were no less significant in Latin America than elsewhere. From the beginning, popular musical forms have been produced locally in all countries: originally rock-and-roll had its own local imitators; today Argentina has its own 'rock nacional'.

Continental and national responses to the Cuban revolution and the activities of liberalizing governments promising much needed reforms in the 1960s influenced many musicians, who, because of their musical interests and political philosophy, were already involved in national folkloric movements, which were themselves sometimes encouraged by government economic and political policy, for example, the neo-folklore boom in Argentina in the 1950s and 1960s. The case of Chile is the most notable: here Violeta Parra and others travelled and collected rural folk songs and dances in the late 1950s, performing and teaching the material to urban audiences and, in the case of Parra, going on to write her own material in the folk idiom. This practical research influenced the next generation of musicians which included Violeta Parra's own children Angel and Isabel; it was a bridge between the older generation of popular poets and the new generation of what became known as *nueva canción* ('new song'). Student groups started, many of them involved in the struggle for university reform, and their continental political philosophy resulted in their choosing Indian names (as, for example, Inti-Illimani) and drawing on the music of the whole continent. Their use of indigenous instruments (the bamboo *quena* or flute, panpipes, drums, guitar variants such as the *charango*, *tres* and *cuatro*), African percussion instruments (güiro, maracas, claves), their professional concern with performance, their smooth singing style and harmonization, exhibit a new fusion of folk and popular; and some of their music (especially the longer pieces, the *cantatas*) is influenced by classical form. For performers and audiences such music is both folk and popular, for it is rooted in the indigenous tradition and yet feels free to call on the music of other traditions; much of it tells of the struggles of people for social and

Víctor Jara

political equality, for their everyday rights, and of their everyday experience, and those involved, in the case of Chile, were performing it within a dynamic political context.

Chile is a prominent case as much for the variety of music, the evidence of supportive festivals and a distribution network, as for the large number of musicians involved, who saw themselves as following a historical tradition, and who, as musicians, actively supported the election of Salvador Allende as president and his Popular Unity coalition as government. Following the military coup of 11 September 1973, Víctor Jara, the singer and theatre director, was brutally tortured and murdered, and other cultural activists tortured and imprisoned, and forced into exile. Their music today has by necessity become one of exile, solidarity and resistance. Similar music and musicians have existed in Uruguay and Argentina (with most of them forced into exile by military governments) and do exist in other countries (Mexico, Brazil); occasionally International Festivals are organized, as in Cuba in 1967 and Mexico in 1982. In Brazil, the *Bossa Nova* of the 1950s was later linked to the

Jovem Guarda movement which re-vitalized popular music with its new style of fluid subdued singing, integrating with harmonic, melodic and rhythmic elements.

JF

Further reading

Entries in the *New Grove Dictionary of Music and Musicians*, 20 vols. (London, 1980) by continent, ethnic group, country, song, dance and instrument

G. Béhague, 'Bossa and Bossas: Recent Changes in Brazilian Urban Popular Music', *Ethnomusicology*, 17 (1973), 209

G. Chase, *A Guide to the Music of Latin America* (Washington DC, 1962)

V. Chenoweth, *The Marimbas of Guatemala* (Lexington, Ky., 1964)

E. Grenet, *Popular Cuban Music* (Havana, 1939)

J. Jara, *Victor: an Unfinished Song* (London, 1983)

An increasing number of records and cassettes of Latin American folk and popular music are becoming available in record stores in Europe (especially France, Spain and Italy) and North America. Readers interested in acquiring such material are recommended to check the current stock in large record stores, or stores specializing in imports, in large cities.

Caribbean music

The musical life of the Caribbean islands is immensely rich and varied and much of it is similar to that found on the main continent of Latin America. The traditions of the African peoples who were brought in slavery to the sugar plantations have mixed with those of the colonizing groups from Spain, France and Britain and the result is a complex cultural spectrum. None of the aboriginal peoples survive and their cultures have been preserved only in archaeological remains and in certain elements of folklore.

African and Christian rituals have blended to produce cults such as Vodún (Voodoo) in Haiti, Santeria, Abakué, Congó and Lucumí in Cuba, Kumina in Jamaica, and Shango in Trinidad: Shango, for example, combines Nigerian Yoruba with Catholic and Baptist beliefs. Such cults are of particular importance in rural areas but are not only found there. They have evolved by combining similar or compatible elements from different belief systems: cult leaders, animal sacrifice, trance and spirit possession (of people or of one of the drums which play a fundamental role in the ritual), and worship of saints (which are typically an amalgamation of African deities with Christian saints) may be found alongside baptismal rites,

Bibles, candles and crosses. African features which permeate this and many other forms of music-making are leader–chorus alternation, body gestures, the movements and choreography of dances and the rhythms played by the various percussion instruments, such as drums (in various sizes and shapes), shakers and scrapers (these instruments vary in shape, size and materials, and are known by local names on different islands). The popular European misconception conveyed by the term 'black-magic' persists because many cult leaders practise folk-medicine and healing rites that outsiders are rarely permitted to observe.

The Spanish origin of music in rural areas (identified through elements of structure, form, scale, harmony) can be found in funeral songs, music for such festivals as Cruz de Mayo, and in forms of *décima* singing (such as *punto* in Cuba). The Spanish also brought string instruments and local variants have evolved: for example, the *tres* and *cuatro* (small three- and four-string guitars), or the three-stringed bamboo violin in Jamaica. The *tres* is used with the *tambora* drum to accompany the national dance of the Dominican Republic, the *merengue*.

The Trinidadian calypso (as sung, for example, by the Mighty Sparrow), popular throughout the Caribbean, forms part of the repertory of steel bands. New texts, which are typically social commentaries, are constantly re-set to established melodies and rhythmic forms. In Trinidad and Jamaica there also exists a separate musical tradition of the East Indian community (Hindu and Muslim).

Bob Marley

A steel band in Antigua

In Jamaica, the Rastafarians are a significant religious group who foster black consciousness, African identity, wear their hair in dreadlocks (tiny plaits) and smoke *ganja* (marijuana) as part of their religious practice, serving Jah (God), his representative on earth (Emperor Haile Selassie of Ethiopia) and closely reading the Bible. Their music, *reggae*, whose song texts transmit their philosophy, combines Afro-American and European elements and uses equipment familiar to modern rock groups. Their social significance was underlined by the musical intervention of its late representative, the internationally famous Bob Marley, in the political life of the island, and his state funeral in May 1981.

A whole multitude of continentally influential dances have originated in Cuba, including the rumba, the bolero, the cha-cha-cha, as have the *son* with its distinctive syncopated form, and the ironically humorous and lively *guarachas* and *guajiras* (especially those of Carlos Puebla whose four-man groups include a *marímbula* player). A host of other forms are performed by members of the *Trova*, the *Nueva Trova* (the self-critical song of the revolution) and by jazz and other bands. Their music embraces internationally contemporary trends in sound as well as the whole Cuban tradition.

JF

Further reading

R. Benmayor, 'La Nueva Trova, New Cuban Song', *Latin American Music Review*, 2, no. 1 (Spring 1981)

O. Lewin, *Forty Songs of Jamaica* (Washington, DC, 1973)

A. Pearse, 'Aspects of Change in Caribbean Folk Music', *Journal of the International Folk Music Council*, 7 (1955)

G. E. Simpson, *Religious Cults of the Caribbean: Trinidad, Jamaica and Haiti* (Puerto Rico, 1970)

Classical music and major composers

The colonial period

The cultivation of classical or 'serious' music, as opposed to folk or popular music, in Latin America began in the sixteenth century. European composers were appointed at that time to serve as chapel-masters in the churches that proliferated throughout the newly founded colonial cities. They produced sacred music, which followed the styles of the European masters, to accompany the celebration of the divine offices of the Church. Consequently, indigenous cultures exerted very little influence on this kind of music. It remained attached to European styles and methods of composition until long after the Spanish and Portuguese colonial period, unlike folk song which slowly revealed traces of a mestizo idiom as the colonial period progressed.

The founding of the first centre for music education by the Franciscan priest, Pedro de Gante, in Mexico, only five years after Cortés's conquest in 1519, set in motion an uninterrupted stream of developments. Significant achievements soon followed in the fields of composition, performance, and the manufacture of European instruments. Manuscript copies of the most outstanding examples of European music and the works of New World composers were made permanently available to the main cathedrals. Simultaneously, distinguished choir-masters, who were committed to the development of vocal and instrumental ensembles and qualified to perform such a repertoire, were appointed to the cathedrals. Music-printing quickly followed in 1556, when an Ordinary of the Mass containing chants in Gregorian notation was published in Mexico. The Spanish crown conferred a variety of musical privileges upon cities throughout its colonies, while Portugal provided for the early establishment of music instruction through the Conservatório dos Negros, a school run by the Jesuits in the sugar plantations of Santa Cruz, near Rio de Janeiro.

Among the treasures of early Church music in Mexico, the works of Hernando Franco (1532–85) certainly bespeak a composer of indisputable technical competence. His music partakes of the styles of his outstanding European contemporaries: Palestrina, Lassus, and Victoria. Franco was born in Europe, like most of the early composers appointed to the chapel-masterships of colonial churches. His career developed in Mexico City and Guatemala. From his works, as from those of his contemporaries such as Juan de Lienas (c.1585–1620) also active in Mexico, many traditions evolved that became significant for a host of native masters who succeeded them in the musical posts available in Hispanic America.

One of these masters was Gutierrez Fernández-Hidalgo (c.1555–1627), who held posts at cathedrals in Bogotá, Colombia, and Chuquisaca (now Sucre, Bolivia). Fernández-Hidalgo was one of the most outstanding Spanish Church composers of the late sixteenth century. Five volumes of his Masses, motets, hymns, and Magnificats have been preserved.

Composers following Fernández-Hidalgo in the seventeenth and eighteenth centuries included Francisco López Capillas (c.1615–74) in Puebla and Mexico City; Juan de Araujo (c.1646–1714), José de Orejón (c.1705–65), Tomás Torrejón y Velasco (1644–1728) in Peru; Esteban Salas (1725–1803) in Cuba; and José Mauricio Nunes Garcia (1763–1830) in Brazil. These composers were landmarks in the development of Church music. Their achievements were also supported by the active participation of many other skilful composers and by a musical life that, in many of the colonies, remained at all times open to the latest influences and achievements of Europe.

This period, sometimes known as the 'American baroque', is recognized for its splendid contributions in the fields of architecture, sculpture and poetry, as well as for its music. Along with the literary achievements of Sor Juana Inés de la Cruz, Mexico saw the development of a composer, Antonio de Salazar (1685–1715), who set some of her poems to music. While Aleijandinho (Antônio Francisco Lisboa) accomplished impressive sculptures in Minas Gerais, Brazil, Joaquin Emerico Lobo de Mesquita (c.1740–1805), one of a host of musicians who were affiliated to religious brotherhoods in that province, produced outstanding sacred compositions.

This predominance of sacred music was due to the centralization of musical activities around the Spanish and Portuguese Church, but towards the end of the colonial period, secular forms developed. Tomás Torrejón y Velasco contributed the oldest surviving example of an opera in Latin America, La Púrpura de la Rosa. This opera utilized a text of the Spanish dramatist Calderón de la Barca, and was produced in Lima in 1701 to celebrate the eighteenth birthday of King Philip V of Spain.

The villancico was another form of secular music that became increasingly cultivated by professional composers of the colonial period. This particular form, introduced by the Spaniards in the early stages of colonization, found its first fertile soil for New World development in the sphere of folk music. Soon musical examples showing traces of Indian and African influences were being sung by the populace. Shortly thereafter, the villancico reached the level of serious music. Settings were for two, three and four voices, as well as for solo voice with instrumental accompaniment. These compositions were similar in their technical approach to those of the Spanish composers of the period. Yet, at times, the use of certain rhythmic and melodic devices and the use of texts in local dialects linked them to either Indian or Afro-American traditions in music.

Other forms of secular music found their way into the repertory of serious composition by the end of the eighteenth century. One was the *contradanza* which, in Cuba, was the source for the development of forms such as the *habanera* and the *danzón*. Another was the *modinha*, a love song in two parts with a repetition of the first section at the end, popular in Brazil and Portugal alike. During the nineteenth century, the *modinha* was strongly influenced by Italian opera, especially when it was cultivated by composers as an art form.

Romanticism

Musical Romanticism in Latin America developed side by side with political independence. The stage of music development at this particular moment in Latin America was uneven. Some countries were at a pinnacle of their musical lives. Others had entered a phase of depression in which standards of performance had declined notoriously and composition appeared to be confined to weak imitations of Italian opera, to patriotic hymns, and to salon dances. As the New World disengaged itself from Spanish and Portuguese hegemony, other foreign influences entered the picture. For example, the Parisian tastes that ruled fashion, architecture, and home furnishings were matched by a wide repertoire of French dances found in upper-class households. By the end of the century, these dances had been assimilated by the mass of the people. Thus, local replicas of the mazurka, minuet, polka, waltz, tarantella, and contradanse became an important part of the popular heritage.

Many of these European dances also reached the repertoire of concert music in the form of short virtuoso pieces. Such pieces were written especially for the piano, by composers who seemed strongly influenced by Chopin, Liszt, and European Romantics of lesser stature. Outstanding among these were Ricardo Castro (1864–1907) and Felipe Villanueva (1862–1923) in Mexico; Ignacio Cervantes (1847–1905) and Nicolás Ruiz Espadero (1832–90) in Cuba; Leopoldo Miguez (1850–1902) and Henrique Oswald (1852–1931) in Brazil; José Maria Ponce de León (1846–82) in Colombia; Felipe Larrázabal (1816–73) in Venezuela; Amancio Alcorta (1805–62) and Juan Bautista Alberdi (1810–84) in Argentina; and Federico Guzmán (1837–85) in Chile.

Yet, in spite of the abundance of virtuoso instrumental music usually derived from the salon dances of the period, opera in the Italian style dominated art music throughout Latin America in the decades after independence. Elegant opera houses were built in the capital cities. The aristocracy gathered to hear the works of Paisiello, Pergolesi, Rossini and other Italian masters, or those of native composers who imitated the styles of their European counterparts – sometimes to the extent of setting their librettos in Italian. Carlos Gomes (1836–96) was Latin America's foremost opera composer of the Romantic period. Born in Brazil, he belonged to a host of over fifty composers active in that country between 1830 and the end of the century. Over 160 of their scores are extant.

Together with the production of opera and instrumental music by the composers of this period, nineteenth-century Latin America saw the rise to stardom of many of its first vocalists and virtuoso instrumental performers. Opera theatres in the New World received with frenzied enthusiasm the performances of such outstanding Italian prima donnas as Patti and Tetrazzini. Local examples included Luisa Pujol (1857–1907), the first Argentine soprano to sing at La Scala; Rosa Negri (1862–92), the aristocratic Chilean soprano; and Angela Peralta (1845–83) who starred in the first performance of numerous Mexican operas. String virtuosity was also carried to a high level of prestige by two Cuban mulattoes, Brindis de Salas (1852–1911) and José White (1836–1918). Pianists were represented by virtuosos of high calibre in various countries, as exemplified by the internationally recognized pianist/composer, Louis Moreau Gottschalk, from New Orleans, who frequently toured and even lived in Latin America. In Cuba, the composer Ignacio Cervantes was also a concert pianist and was considered a rival to von Bülow and the young Paderewsky. No less prestigious were Honorio Alarcón (1859–1920), the Colombian winner of international piano contests in Leipzig and Paris; Tomás León (1826–93) from Mexico; or the world-famous Teresa Carreño (1853–1917) from Venezuela, who was praised by Brahms, Liszt, and Grieg.

Nationalism

Before the nineteenth century was over, Latin America started developing musical styles that were more concerned with local and national traditions. Composers began to search in their own folk music for self-assertion and identification. They started drawing from traditional songs, dances, rhythmic and melodic materials. They applied these folk elements to the diverse forms and aesthetics of European music current at the time. The incorporation of folk and popular arts into the serious musical life of each country was accelerated by the rapid rise of the middle class and increased participation by the native sectors of society.

Nationalism in music developed before the turn of the century in works by Ignacio Cervantes, whose twenty *danzas* represent a parallel in Cuban music to Grieg's Norwegian Dances, and in works by Alberto Nepomuceno (1864–1920), author of a *Serie Brasileira* based on folk themes and rhythms from his native Brazil, completed in 1871. Such pioneering works were soon to influence other composers. One of them was the Mexican, Manuel Ponce (1886–1948), who received international recognition with his early popular song, *Estrellita*. He later became involved in developing a national idiom in composition, thus leading the way for his compatriots, Silvestre Revueltas (1899–1940) and Carlos Chávez (1899–1978).

These composers were only matched in their prestige in the years following the First World War by Heitor Villa-Lobos (1887–1959), a Brazilian who achieved a position of equality with the most outstanding European masters of his time.

Many Latin American composers participated in the early development of musical nationalism. Two composers from Cuba, Amadeo Roldán (1900–39) and Alejandro García Caturla (1906–40) depicted characteristic features of Caribbean-evolved Afro-American traditions. Other composers' works were nourished by both French Impressionism and the folk traditions of their own countries, as was evidenced in the music of Vicente E. Sojo (1887–1974) from Venezuela, Alberto Williams (1862–1952) from Argentina, Eduardo Fabini (1882–1959) from Uruguay, Pedro Humberto Allende (1885–1959) from Chile, and Guillermo Uribe-Holguín (1880–1972) from Colombia.

Until the time of the Second World War, composers in Latin America remained largely attached to the resources embodied in their folk music. Following in the steps of Villa-Lobos, Brazil produced such outstanding examples as Oscar Lorenzo Fernandez (1897–1948), Francisco Mignone (b. 1897), and Camargo Guarnieri (b. 1907). The disciples of Carlos Chávez in Mexico followed the

Heitor Villa-Lobos

nationalistic approach of their master in their early compositions. Outstanding among them is Blas Galindo (b. 1910). Outside Brazil and Mexico, national trends in serious music were perpetuated by many Latin American composers. Most of them were simultaneously open to the latest methods of composition developed in Europe, and allowed the traditions of their own countries to permeate their styles, for example, Juan José Castro (1901–68) and Carlos López Buchardo (1881–1948) in Argentina; Carlos Isamitt (1887–1978) in Chile; Juan Bautista Plaza (1898–1965) in Venezuela; Antonio Maria Valencia (1902–52) in Colombia; José Ardévol (b. 1908) and Harold Gramatges (b. 1918) in Cuba.

Contemporary styles

Nevertheless, exceptions to such nationalistic trends also existed. Some were sustained by the prevailing cosmopolitan cultural environments surrounding them, and others, by their deliberate opposition to the use of folk materials because of the alleged limitations that these imposed on their styles. These composers felt that their work could be strengthened by a freer handling of the aesthetics and methods of composition originating in Europe, which they considered as representative of their own heritage as classical composers, as folk music was of the ethnic sectors. One of these composers was the Mexican, Julián Carrillo (1875–1965), author and practitioner of a theory called *Sonido Trece*, involving the use of quarter, eighth and even smaller fractions of a tone. Another was Juan Carlos Paz (1897–1972) in Argentina, who pioneered the development of Schoenberg's twelve-tone serialism in Latin America. Domingo Santa Cruz (b. 1899) from Chile was yet another composer of music aloof from any folkloristic influences.

By the late 1940s, a number of composers who had either sponsored a type of self-imposed nationalism, or had been strongly influenced by the folk traditions of their countries, began gradually moving away from such tendencies. Simultaneously, a new generation emerged of musicians free from any need of deliberate borrowing from native music. They were plainly aware of their belonging to cultures that owed as much to Europe as to their own native environments. Musically, this trend is reflected in the works of a host of composers throughout Latin America, who come from areas either rich or poor in indigenous traditions, and who are all committed to a wide range of methods of composition. The work of the outstanding Argentine composer, Alberto Ginastera (1916–83), eloquently exemplifies the case of a composer who, after an early period of deliberate nationalism, moved to a position more concerned with the universal values of music than with forcing folk devices into classical composition.

The same historical forces that led Ginastera away from nationalism also stimulated similar developments in other composers of the same generation: Roque Cordero (b. 1917) from Panama, Claudio

Santoro (b. 1919) from Brazil, Alfonso Letelier (b. 1912) from Chile, Blas Galindo (b. 1909) from Mexico and Jorge Sarmientos (b. 1933) from Guatemala. Others of this generation of composers were only slightly touched by the spell of nationalism, for example, Juan Orrego-Salas (b. 1919) from Chile and Hector Tosar (b. 1923) from Uruguay.

The stylistic developments of a sequence of such musicians succeeded in putting Latin America on the map of world contemporary music by the early 1960s. Competent use of the most advanced techniques and methods of composition characterized this generation of Latin American composers. Atonality, serialism, aleatoric and electronic methods are used together with advances originating in composers' lack of dogmatism regarding the techniques employed.

These advances were employed by a group of Mexican composers who were stimulated by the cosmopolitan approach of the Spanish-born (and later naturalized-Mexican) composer, Rodolfo Halffter (b. 1900). Manuel Enríquez (b. 1926), Jorge de Elias (b. 1939), Hector Quintanar (b. 1936), and Mario Lavista (1943) share in redirecting their country's music away from the nationalistic trends that had prevailed until the early 1960s. Their use of improvisation as a tool of composition, of electronic sounds, and of new performance techniques employing traditional instruments, results in the replacement of conventional notation methods by a variety of 'graphisms' involving unprecedented symbols.

A number of other Latin American composers also utilize these techniques. In Chile, Gustavo Becerra (b. 1925), León Schidlowsky (b. 1931) and Alejandro Guarello (b. 1951) follow paths of evolution similar to those of the aforementioned Mexicans, while Juan Amenábar (b. 1922) and José V. Asuar (b. 1933) engage in creating electronic music. In Brazil, Edino Krieger (b. 1928), Marlos Nobre (b. 1939), Willi Correa de Oliveira (b. 1938), and Jorge Antunes (b. 1942) support similar advanced positions in music – especially when compared to that of Oswaldo Lacerda (b. 1928) who remains attached to a very subtle nationalism applied to a modern idiom. In Argentina, Ginastera's progressive stand in composition is emulated by a few of his contemporaries, for example, Roberto García-Morillo (b. 1911) and Roberto Caamaño (b. 1923), and a host of younger composers. Notable among these are Mario Davidowsky (b. 1934), Mauricio Kagel (b. 1931), Antonio Tauriello (b. 1931), Alcides Lanza (b. 1929), Gerardo Gandini (b. 1936), Armando Krieger (b. 1940); and in the field of electronic composition, Francisco Kröpfl (b. 1928). In Uruguay, the Italian-born Guido Santórsola (b. 1919) and Hector Tosar give a forward impulse to their compatriots León Biriotti (b. 1929), Antonio Mastrogiovanni (b. 1936) and Sergio Cervetti (b. 1941), conquering unprecedented international recognition for Uruguayan music.

Beyond Mexico, Chile, Brazil, Argentina, and Uruguay, other

Alberto Ginastera

Latin American countries are also making a name for themselves in modern music. These countries are characterized by either individual exponents, for example, Ecuador by Mesías Maiguaschca (b. 1938) and Bolivia by Alberto Villalpando (b. 1940), or by cohesive groups of composers sharing the same progressive views within a variety of approaches. The latter is the case for Peru if we consider the nature and quality of the achievements of a host of composers trained by the German-born Rodolfo Holzmann (b. 1910), for example, Enrique Iturriaga (b. 1918), Celso Garrido-Lecca (b. 1926), Enrique Pinilla (b. 1927), Cesar Bolaños (b. 1931) and Edgar Valcarcel (b. 1932). It also applies in Colombia and Venezuela. In the former, a very subtle concern for musical nationalism still persists in the works of Luis Antonio Escobar (b. 1925), while Fabio González Zuleta (b. 1920) adheres to serialism, Jesus Pinzón (b. 1928) and Blas Emilio Atehortua (b. 1933) represent the avant-garde. A similar pattern is encountered in Venezuela where the leading figure is Antonio Estevez (b. 1916), who, after an evolution that took him from an early nationalism to electronic music, works side by side with some who perpetuate musical folklorism and some representing more cosmopolitan approaches – composers such as Rhazes Hernández López (b. 1918) and Alfredo del Mónaco (b. 1938).

In the Caribbean area, both Cuba and Puerto Rico are contributers to the mainstream of recent developments with a variety of creative achievements as important as those of the rest of Latin America. Two outstanding Cubans living in the United States, Aurelio de la Vega (b. 1925) and Julian Orbón (b. 1925) share international recognition along with their compatriots active in Cuba itself, Juan Blanco (b. 1920), Carlos Fariñas (b. 1934), and Leo Brouwer (b. 1939). In Puerto Rico, the achievements of Hector Campos-Parsi (b. 1922) within aesthetics progressing from neoclassicism to atonality have been followed by those of the progressive Rafael Aponte-Ledée (b. 1938).

From this overview of Latin American music, we may conclude that countries which had remained creatively inactive until the

The Teatro Colón, Buenos Aires: the world's largest opera house

1950s were brought to the forefront of music by many qualified individuals or groups of composers. Simultaneously, the recent development of concert life in metropolitan centres and of musical education at all levels has opened the doors to a considerably wider exchange of conductors, instrumentalists and singers, both within Latin American countries and with the rest of the world. Cities like Mexico, Caracas, Rio de Janeiro, Buenos Aires and Santiago compete nowadays with important urban centres in the United States and Europe, both in the length and quality of their concert seasons. Each of these cities has at least one permanent orchestra. There are opera houses of world-wide prestige (such as the Teatro Colón of Buenos Aires) and chamber music ensembles of recognized competence scattered throughout Latin America.

JO-S

Further reading

G. Béhague, *Music in Latin America: an Introduction* (Englewood Cliffs, NJ, 1979)
G. A. Chase, *A Guide to the Music of Latin America*, 2nd edition (Washington, DC, 1962)
N. Slonimsky, *Music of Latin America* (New York, 1945)
The New Grove Dictionary of Music and Musicians, 20 vols. (London, 1980)

Apart from Heitor Villa-Lobos, Carlos Chávez and Alberto Ginastera, Latin American composers are less well represented in European and North American record catalogues than they deserve to be. Readers interested in hearing the works of Latin American composers on record are advised to check the appropriate catalogue and to keep an eye on new releases.

Pre-Columbian painting, sculpture and architecture

For it is one thing to read a description like mine of a city such as this and quite another to see it with one's own eyes, in all its strength and grandeur . . . (Bernal Díaz del Castillo, 1568)

When the Spanish arrived in the New World they encountered its two greatest empires, the Mexican Aztec in 1519 and then the Inca in 1531. Some, like Bernal Díaz, who described his wonder at the Aztec capital growing from the lake of Texcoco, appreciated their achievements. Yet most of the conquerors sought pure riches and thought nothing of melting down exquisite gold and silver craftsmanship, so that now little is left of the treasures adorning Incan cities. This confrontation between Old and New World pinpoints a central difficulty in understanding the art of native America; despite its glamour, the images express ideas and traditions which had evolved independently within the western hemisphere through successive cultures over more than two thousand years. Often they were, and still are, alien to outsiders' eyes.

The two great centres of civilization developed in Mesoamerica, including the highland and tropical forest zones of Mexico and Guatemala; and to the south along the narrow shelf of land between the Andes and the Pacific coast, especially in Peru. It has been shown that some goods filtered through Central America but direct contact between these two regions is not documented. Nonetheless, there are similarities in the art produced in these regions at a most fundamental level. In the quality of their workmanship the native craftsmen excelled in manipulating materials such as stone, clay and metals using the simplest of tools. Only the grandest schemes could have stimulated the technical invention and organized the labour necessary to erect massive stone buildings without use of the wheel, so it is no surprise to find that this work was overwhelmingly dedicated to the gods. In a sense this was a very practical objective since their deities were not abstract but the characterization of elements man depended on and were propitiated exclusively by ritual specialists. Over time the power of the elites who directed this work grew and they became akin to gods. Thus craftsmen were not free to vary the content or style of their work; locally this gave a firm pattern to building and craft, yet the variations over time and in diverse areas show how inventively different materials were used to express these relationships. The growing archaeological records help us to understand such qualities in native American art.

Mesoamerica

Cities and architecture

After 1000 BC society became increasingly centred on cities dominated by grand ceremonial building and two distinct types of architecture emerged in Mexico and among the Maya.

Among early societies, remains of the Olmec culture on the Gulf coast have caused avid speculation as they seem to anticipate major developments in Mexican civilization; in architecture the ceremonial centre of La Venta, dated 900–400 BC, was built up around two great pyramidal mounds setting the pattern of Mexican urban centres. This is seen at Teotihuacán in the Valley of Mexico where a powerful religious cult developed; at its greatest expansion (250–150 BC) the city covered more than 20 km with a population estimated at over 100,000 people; it was even rebuilt three times before meeting ruin around AD 900. Districts for traders, craftsmen and farmers were laid out on a grid plan and the courts of the elite flanked a ceremonial complex with the Pyramid of the Sun towering 61 m above. Each of its sides rose in four tiers encased in a type of stone façade known as *talud-tablero*. This gave the effect of distancing observers on the ground from ritual performed in a temple on

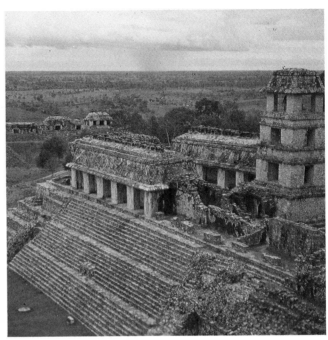

Palenque: one of the finest of all the Mayan centres

the summit. The main stairway, cut through the tiers, faces onto the Avenue of the Dead which links further temples and ornamented palaces.

Some of the finest lowland Maya architecture built in the Petén region of Guatemala shows the classic features preferred by this sophisticated people, although they experimented with refinements throughout their long history (400 BC–AD 1250). Unlike Mexican cities there is little evidence of rigid planning and the houses of lower classes must have clustered round the impressive complexes of palaces, courtyards and pyramids. Mayan temple-pyramids are tall and steep, rising to as much as 65 m, and embellished with masonry roof combs to emphasize the height. Rooms in the apical temple were roofed with overlapping stones forming a corbelled vault; the true arch does not appear in pre-Columbian building. The temple of the Giant Jaguar at Tikal is a good example of the type; it was built around AD 700 over an immensely rich tomb with the entire surface painted in vigorous colours, but it was used for ritual purposes rather than as a mausoleum.

Throughout Mesoamerica ball courts are found as a peculiar architectural feature. The game had a ritual significance: the object was to win by shooting a rubber ball through stone rings projecting from the walls of the 'I' shaped court. Spectators watched from lateral benches and in areas like El Tajín, Veracruz (AD 600–900), where the cult was most influential, they witnessed the sacrifice of the loser's life.

Friezes on the Temple of Quetzalcoatl: realistic snakes heads alternate with the stylized rain god

Sculpture and building decoration

Great skill was dedicated to stone sculpted into friezes or three-dimensional figures on a monumental or miniature scale. The Olmec sculpted free-standing heads from blocks of stone weighing up to 20 tons; by using dense jade the same proportions were transferred to miniature figures of 'baby-faced men' with 'jaguar mouths' beautifully carved without metal tools. Sculptural styles varied over time in different regions but a general idea was to portray the gods; they changed too, the most persistent being the rain god whose ringed eyes and fangs appear in many forms. At Teotihuacán each being in the pantheon took a conventional form, as in friezes on the Temple of Quetzalcoatl of realistic snakes' heads alternating with the stylized rain god. Important cult objects were also sculpted; all the paraphernalia of the ball game was found in stone at El Tajín. Later, the warlike Toltec introduced warriors as columns for altar stones at Tula around AD 900–1200, and their *chacmool* portray other warriors reclining with a sacrificial bowl held on the stomach. At the height of the sacrificial cult (from AD 1345 to the Spanish conquest), an Aztec sculpture of the goddess Coatlique decked in human skulls, hands and hearts is a potent example of their obsession with death.

The Maya covered their buildings with façades in a profusion of stylized ornaments and deities, but they also took special care to record the prowess of their dignitaries in life-like scenes on relief panels and stelae. The graceful yet detailed figures are among the most beautiful pieces of pre-Columbian sculpture and carved hieroglyphs document the celebrations, justly commemorating their patrons. There is even a record of the colour of such occasions surviving in frescoes painted in a similar style at Bonampak about AD 800.

Top: Toltec columns in the form of warriors at Tula. Above: Relief panel from a Mayan palace at Yaxchilan, Chiapas. A kneeling penitent makes a blood offering by drawing a rope studded with cactus spines through his tongue

Above left: A human skull adorned with mosaic of turquoise and jet. It is said to have been a gift to Cortés from the Aztec emperor Montezuma II. Above centre: Household talisman in the Tlatilco tradition. Right: Figure of a dancer in the 'laughing men' style of Las Remojadas

Ceramics

Pottery shows the inventive imagination of Mesoamerica better than any other medium. Work in clay served as an apprenticeship for sculpting stone; peculiar to the region are countless figurines of men, animals and deities sometimes doubling as jars or whistles. In the Tlatilco tradition, dated 1000–800 BC, little household talismans are energetically portrayed as humans with slanting eyes. They contrast with the laughing men of the later Las Remojadas, Veracruz style which, together with the quite independent dogs and men of west-coast ceramic styles, provide a uniquely light touch in Mesoamerican art.

Like the figurines, vessels were moulded or modelled by hand without use of the potter's wheel. The range of forms seems infinite, with curious variations on basic shapes of plates, bowls, bottles and jars; there are even 'teapot' forms and vessels with tripod legs were a particular favourite. Decoration is equally varied with a range of stamped, incised or applied designs; glazing was unknown but sheen was produced by burnishing or from the iridescence of metal in the clay-body. Exceptionally refined ceramics described as 'Thin Orange' were traded widely from Teotihuacán; the contemporary Monte Albán culture left more elaborate, increasingly baroque, ceramics. Within the Maya area grotesque urns were made with the same skill as fine Nebaj vessels of AD 700 decorated with polychrome painted figures similar to those in relief carving.

Jade, turquoise, feathers . . .

Jade was a prized material; nowhere are native and Spanish values better contrasted. Díaz saw his companions sink into Lake Texcoco with pillaged Aztec gold while he carried away four jade pieces which he exchanged for food and help among the Aztec. Jade and stones of similar quality had been traded since 900 BC. Both the Olmec and Maya excelled in lapidary work, producing calmly sophisticated masks, vessels, figures, ear-flares and belts smoothly polished with sand; sometimes these were buried unused in prestigious caches, a practice which increased the value of jade still further. The Mixtec–Puebla culture shows inspired craftsmanship from the tenth century, excelling in bone and wood carving, feather mosaics and painted screenfold books (the so-called 'codices'). Among the contents of native codices are records of all the luxurious materials, jewellery and costume sent in tribute from designated areas to the great city centres. In this way the Aztec collected Mixtec craft and learnt from their skill, but in Aztec hands delicate craftsmanship became tinged with a dread and gloom especially evident in skulls and masks inlaid with turquoise or in obsidian knives flaked to a sharp edge for cutting out human hearts.

. . . and gold

Since techniques of metalwork were introduced to the west coast from Peru and Ecuador around AD 800–900, they were used almost exclusively for ornament, rarely for tools. The Mixtec perfected the art in golden filigree rings, necklaces dangling with pendants, masks and bells; and it is a curious tribute to their skill that the finest native jewels sent to the Emperor Charles V were made by them.

The Andes
Architecture and stone-carving

The most complete archaeological record in South America falls within the boundaries of Peru. Monumental building in the valleys of the arid coastal belt and in the high Andes shows a distinctive split in cultural tradition. Stone was a primary building material in the highlands, while sun-baked mud adobes were used on the coast. In comparison with Mesoamerica, sculpture was not as developed an art form though its content, often religious, was important.

In the site of Chavín de Huántar built about 600 BC in the northern highlands, the influence of earlier grand building projects like Cerro Sechín on the coast can be seen. Chavín was primarily a religious site and the spreading temple complex consists of vast rectangular pyramids of two or three levels enclosing a central court. The plan is complicated by subterranean passages and stairways. These elements did not form an architectural type and the importance of Chavín culture, evident between 1100 and 300 BC, lies in relief designs sculpted in the stone façades and friezes which covered the building. One free-standing stele called the Raimondi Stone incorporates some important motifs. A fanged being is portrayed with a staff in each hand and a headdress embellished with serpents and feline heads; in other friezes they appear alongside condors or eagles. Essentially Chavinoid, these stylized emblems recur throughout Peru so that at times the study of Peruvian iconography seems like 'hunt the cat' because the motifs have been identified in other areas as evidence of the cult's spread.

At the southern highland site of Tiahuanaco on the shores of Lake

Drawing from the Raimondi Stone

Titicaca in Bolivia, a similar figure holding two staffs and wearing a headdress (now very damaged) forms the centrepiece of a monolithic 'Gateway of the Sun'. This mysterious civilization is not well understood; even the site reconstruction is disputed; but between 800 BC and AD 1200 a cult in which feline motifs appear spread into the Bolivian highlands and through a sister-site at Pucara in Peru to the southern coast.

On the coast, independent cultures flourished in productive river valleys, with the working population segregated from the secular or religious centre to live on the land above the level of irrigation. At the site of Moche on the northern coast, flourishing between AD 150 and 800, only the ruling dynasty and their civil and religious administrators lived in a complex dominated by two flat-topped pyramidal mounds of adobe. The larger Pyramid of the Sun must have reached almost 100 m in height and required the organization of a massive workforce to build it. The successor to Moche, in AD 900, was the Chimú site of Chan Chan where there are ten high-walled enclosures with an average span of 390 by 200 m. Each became a mausoleum in which a deified ruler was buried with his property. As the power of living kings increased, they continued to be worshipped after death as gods.

The extent of Incan architecture and engineering was unprecedented in the Andes and was designed by the Inca, a living god in charge of a massive military and political organization. Cuzco, the capital, was planned in the shape of a puma with the great fortress of Saccshuamán at its head. The style of their monolithic building is well appreciated in the three zig-zag terraces of Saccshuamán with perfectly matched blocks of stone weighing up to 60 tons. Temples, palaces, storehouses and roads with posthouses were built with skilled speed by thousands of workers throughout the vast empire, stretching from Colombia to Argentina by the time of the Spanish conquest. Pure engineering in stone is balanced by a sensitive use of natural rock to sculpt haunting abstract forms.

Ceramics

From their appearance in 1500 BC, Peruvian ceramics document the shift of successive cultures. Known techniques were similar to those of Mesoamerica although there was less variation in form; but in the inventive vitality of painted or moulded decoration their ceremonial ware excels. Among north-coast cultures a favoured form used a bridge or stirrup-handle and the Moche moulded them perfectly with portraits of dignitaries and scenes of daily life such as weavers, curing practices, musicians and even explicit copulation. Ceremonial events are painted with black line cartoon-like characters on a white ground. The snakes and condors of Tiahuanaco and Pucara pottery are defined in colours like designs taken from weavings; often the most realistic element is a moulded puma head. The early polychrome motifs of south-coast Nazca potters during

A Moche
stirrup-spout
bottle

Top: A Colombian gold mask. Above: Weaving of the present-day Salasaca Indians of Ecuador. Traditional methods and designs are used

the first centuries AD show birds and fish in the most lyrical of all Peruvian designs; later, about AD 600, they adopted Tiahuanacoid designs. White slipped figurines with black line adornment were made by the central-coast Chancay around AD 1200; their crude homeliness indicates the relative isolation of this culture. Incan pottery was mass-produced; the classic forms, like a water jar with pointed base, lugs and long neck with flaring lip, are elegant but the geometric designs are restrictive.

Metalwork

The myth of Incan silver and gold reached the Spanish in the Caribbean, giving a powerful incentive to explore southwards. Years after the event the Inca Garcilaso de la Vega wrote about the Spaniards' impressions of Cuzco; they saw gardens in the Inca's palace where all manner of birds and animals were set in their natural landscape. The scene was made entirely of gold and silver; for once the explorers' dreams were overwhelmed. The craft, which the Inca inherited, had been developed since 900 BC; by the first century AD various metals and alloys could be worked in many techniques, including some unknown to the Old World. The Moche used them to make tools and jewellery of quality, but the first real excess of wealth and status displayed in metal can be attributed to the Chimu who were integrated into the Incan empire in the late fifteenth century.

Textiles

One of Peru's greatest treasures lay buried in subterranean tombs on the south coast until 1925. Hundreds of mummies interred by the people of the Paracas culture, between 500 and 100 BC, had been wrapped in layers of the most exquisite cloth perfectly preserved by the arid desert. The finest hand-spun threads of cotton and wool of native camelids were woven in a variety of techniques including weft and warp-stripe, brocade, embroidery and lace. But it is the colours defining figures of fantastic monsters, birds, serpents and animals that are truly astounding. Natural dyeing had obviously been perfected with hundreds of colour gradations. It is likely that the south coast particularly excelled in weaving; but superb textiles of pile and tapestry from Tiahuanaco and the most delicate gauze and painted cloth from Chancay have also survived, suggesting that humid conditions in the highlands have destroyed many other examples. Cloth is easily transported and the cross-currents in iconography of distinct cultures may partly be attributed to textile designs. Examples of Incan weaving have survived and from discussions in early Spanish chronicles their importance is known quite precisely. Cloth was classified and the finest was specially woven and reserved for the Inca himself; it was piled high in storehouses which were a wonder to the Spanish. Religious and secular symbols were woven into cloth and no gift between dignitaries was complete without it. Small wonder, then, that this most versatile of all pre-Columbian arts has actively survived to the present.

FN

Further reading

Mesoamerica
N. Hammond, *Ancient Maya Civilisation* (Cambridge, 1982)
M. Porter-Weaver, *The Aztecs, Maya and their Predecessors: Archaeology of Mesoamerica*, 2nd edition (London, 1981)
G. C. Vaillant, *The Aztecs of Mexico* (Harmondsworth, 1965)

South America
G. Bawden and G. W. Conrad, *The Andean Heritage* (Cambridge, Mass., 1982)
A. Kendall, *Everyday Life of the Incas* (London, 1973)
L. G. Lumbreras, *The Peoples and Cultures of Ancient Peru* (Washington, DC, 1974)

Latin American painting, sculpture and architecture to 1830

Aftermath of conquest

Within a few years of the conquest the Spaniards had effected in their American territories an artistic revolution the scale and speed of which is probably unique in the history of art. Construction of the massive stone temples and palaces of the Aztecs and Incas ceased immediately; objects with ritual connotations were destroyed, and many traditions of exquisite craftsmanship disappeared almost overnight. There were, of course, survivals, even revivals, but these were restricted to the minor arts, or, in the major arts, to decorative details and occasionally to technical innovations. The entirely new range of art and architecture required by the conquerors left little room for anything but stylistic influence to spread across from native traditions. This influence certainly played a part in producing a distinctive colonial style, but it should not be confused with a true survival.

It is also important to be aware that, while differing profoundly from indigenous art, colonial art also differs from that of the Iberian metropolis. Some differences were deliberate, others not, but they were all products of the new situation. The lack of European-trained craftsmen and of traditional European materials, or different climatic and geographical features – frequent earthquakes, for example – necessitated modifications from European norms. Crucial too is the fact that, throughout the colonial period, art's primary role was as a servant of the Church: in the early years this was not an established Church, as in Europe, whose members had been familiar with Christian images and symbolism for centuries, but a Church involved above all in a massive missionary enterprise. It was recognized by churchmen that there was much in Christian doctrine that could confuse the neophyte, and so they enforced, principally through the medium of the Inquisition, a restricted range of subject matter: only Christ, the Virgin, the more respectable saints and stories from the New Testament are commonly represented. Another change was that new architectural forms had to be devised to cope with the huge congregations of Indians.

As well as such modifications in subject matter and type, there were considerable modifications in style. An often miscellaneous selection of European examples served as models, not exclusively nor even predominantly Iberian. From Seville came large numbers of paintings and sculptures hurriedly and often shoddily made specifically for the American market; from Italy, France, Germany and especially the Low Countries came engravings and popular prints, and even a few architectural plans. The copying and recopying of such models – often copies themselves – resulted in simplifications, misinterpretations and a flattening of the forms in architectural decoration as well as in painting and sculpture. This last was particularly true of those areas where the most developed indigenous cultures had flourished: Central America and the Andean region. The convincing representation of the three-dimensional world on a two-dimensional plane played little or no part in native artistic traditions, and in these areas, where to begin with the art and architecture was largely produced by retrained native craftsmen, this loss of contour resulted in a distinctive decorative style. Those areas where there were smaller, less culturally sophisticated indigenous populations tended to remain more closely dependent on European models.

In the areas of greater density of native population it is useful to recognize, at least during the first 150 years or so after the conquest, a distinction between art produced for the native population, largely by anonymous native craftsmen, and art produced for the colonists. The latter lived in the newly founded towns, where the cultural orientation remained firmly European; European artists and craftsmen who emigrated to America settled in these towns, and tended to form themselves into guilds whose membership was restricted to those of European blood. Not surprisingly, the art produced in this context consciously emulated European models. One of the functions of such art was to reinforce the colonists' sense of their own European identity, whereas the primary function of the art produced for the Indians was, at least to begin with, to encourage their conversion to Christianity, for which the adherence to current European artistic styles was irrelevant.

Architecture

Christian churches were usually the first permanent signs of the European colonization of America: for the colonists their churches, situated prominently at the centre of their newly laid-out grid-plan towns, were symbols of their secure foundations in the New World; for the Indians, the missionary churches which they were required to build in their own towns and villages were the material manifestations of the new order.

It was decreed that the construction of churches should be financed by the settlers, the crown and the native population in equal proportions; in practice what tended to happen was that the settlers, and often the crown representatives too, paid their shares from profits from the various tributes collected from the Indians, while the Indians contributed their own share in the form of labour. The native involvement in these buildings was therefore considerable, but in the sixteenth century at least this was rarely evident. The tens of thousands of Christian missionary churches built during the sixteenth century were immediately recognizable as such, however simple their construction. The essential elements which turned a barn-like structure into a church were a bell-tower, and a definition of the entrance or entrances by some reference to the architectural system known in Europe as 'classical': columns or

Façade of the Augustinian church at Acolman, Mexico

pilasters surmounted by an entablature and perhaps a triangular pediment. Churches in this plain but unmistakably European style continued to be built throughout the colonial period, and examples survive in many places.

Not all the early churches were so rudimentary. In Mexico in particular the three mendicant orders initially authorized to work in the New World – the Franciscans, the Dominicans and the Augustinians – were quick to establish a series of substantial monastic houses with imposing vaulted churches alongside. These buildings were not designed by architects but by the friars themselves, and executed almost entirely by the Indians. It is interesting that although the true arch and therefore also roofing by means of stone vaults were unknown in America before the conquest, the Indian masons, under the guidance of the friars, grasped the principle almost immediately. Good examples of sixteenth-century Franciscan monastery churches survive at Huejotzingo and Tepeaca, and of Augustinian churches at Acolman and Ixmiquilpan, all in Mexico.

As well as these churches and monasteries, in areas of great missionary activity a new architectural form appeared during the early colonial years: the open chapel, or *capilla de indios*. This, a simple vaulted structure, open on one or more sides, and facing on to a large open space, was probably developed to cope with the huge Indian congregations. Crowds could gather in front to hear the prayers and teachings of the priests within, who were thus afforded both shelter and distinction. Several examples survive, as at Teposcolula and Tlahuelilpa in Mexico. The space in front of both churches and open chapels was often enclosed by a wall to form an atrium, so in effect extending the jurisdiction of the church, and in the corners of these atria small oratories called *posas* were often built, where temporary altars were erected during religious festivals. This emphasis on exterior ritual may have been a concession to indigenous practices: Indian worship had traditionally taken place in the open air.

In Central America during the sixteenth century the favoured style of architectural decoration, resources permitting, was that of the plateresque, the Spanish version of the architectural style of the Italian Renaissance. The first American cathedral, Santo Domingo on the island of Hispaniola, built between 1512 and 1541, boasts a splendid double-arched west portal in this style, which must have been executed by Spanish masons. So too must have been the façade of the Augustinian church at Acolman (1560) which served as the prototype for other Augustinian façades, including that at Yuririapúndaro (1566). These two make an interesting comparison as in the latter, while clearly a copy of that at Acolman, the architectural members are subordinated to the flat, decorative carving, betokening Indian craftsmanship. In South America the substantial churches which survive from the sixteenth century are more austere in appearance, the Colombian cathedrals of Cartagena (1585) and Tunja (1600) being closer to the Italian Renaissance pattern, while San Francisco in Quito, Ecuador (1580s?), echoes the severe style of the Escorial in Spain.

Most of the major American cathedrals, although founded in the sixteenth century, were built during the seventeenth and eighteenth centuries, when the then secure and increasingly prosperous settlers could turn their attention to the adornment of their cities. The history of these cathedrals is long and complicated, often stretching from the late sixteenth century when ambitious (often over-ambitious) plans were drawn up, through various stages of con-struction during the seventeenth century, to final completion sometimes in the eighteenth or even the nineteenth century. Mexico City cathedral is an extreme case: begun in 1563, by 1615 the main walls were only half built; it was dedicated in 1656 although the interior was not completed until 1667, the bell-towers not until 1791, and some other details not until 1813. Several cathedrals suffered badly from earthquakes both during and after their con-struction, as for example those of Antigua (Guatemala), Lima (Peru), and Santiago de Chile (this last was also burnt down in 1769, shortly after having been rebuilt to new designs after repeated earthquake damage); others, for example at Bogotá (Colombia) and Córdoba (Argentina), fell down as a result of the inexperience or lack of training of the builders in charge.

Nevertheless, the majority of cathedrals surviving today whose foundation dates back to the sixteenth century present an internal arrangement which is closely related to the original design. Most are large, gothic-vaulted structures in the hall-church mode of three or more aisles of equal height. The massive gothic-vaulted cathedral of Seville (completed 1506) was often the model, but the old-fashioned gothic vaults were also popular because they were simpler and cheaper to construct than domical or barrel vaults, and also, being lighter, they were more resistant to damage by earthquakes.

It is with the façades that designers had the greatest chance to experiment. The predominant type in larger Spanish American churches is the retable-façade, similar in format to a retable, the elaborate sculptural altarpiece so common in Spain and Latin America. A basic architectural framework surrounds the main portal, and a series of niches is filled with statues and/or relief panels depicting saints or scenes from the life of Christ. In the seventeenth century some of the most imaginative retable-façades were produ-ced in Peru. Cuzco cathedral was planned in 1582 by Francisco Becerra (who also designed Lima and Puebla cathedrals), but the façade design dates from about 1650. The clusters of columns and sweeping segments of pediment suggest a strong upward movement towards the delicate pinnacles and scrolls at the top. The façade of the Jesuit church in Cuzco was built at the same time (1651–68) and in deliberate rivalry with the cathedral across the square. Here the

Façade of the Compañía, Cuzco

lateral portals are dispensed with, and the bell-towers appear to be squeezing the façade into an even more pronounced vertical thrust. The upward curvings of the broken pediments are emphasized by those of the entablature which bulges up into a tri-lobed arch above the whole façade, an extraordinarily imaginative device which prefigures similar developments in Europe. The influence of these two designs can be found over a wide area; good examples are San Francisco, Lima (pre-1664), Lampa near Lake Titicaca (1685), and Sucre cathedral side portal (1693).

During the eighteenth century façades became increasingly elaborate: the twisted Salomonic column seems almost obligatory, and all the architectural members are encased in a riot of shallow-relief carving of a generally organic nature. Influential examples include La Merced in Antigua, Guatemala (1760), the Compañía, Quito (1765) and San Agustín, Lima (1720). The carving of the façade of the Compañía in Arequipa (1698) was the prototype of the sculptural style known as 'mestizo' which spread through southern Peru, Bolivia and northern Argentina, and which is characterized by a *horror vacui* and by the inclusion of indigenous plants and animals. In the mid-eighteenth century, in Mexico in particular, the sculptural forms tended to become three-dimensional, sometimes actually replacing the traditional architectural members. An excel-lent example that combines both two- and three-dimensional sculp-ture is the façade of the cathedral of Zacatecas in Mexico (1752): the columns of the first storey are wreathed in leaves and fruit, while in the upper storeys the columns are replaced by shells, bunches of grapes, masks and scrolls arranged in vertical bands. When this sculptured column-substitute has anthropomorphic features it is called an *estípite*, and as such becomes one of the hall-marks of the baroque in Latin America. The *Sagrario*, Mexico City, with façades

Baroque façade
of the Sanctuary,
Ocotlán, Mexico

completed in 1768 by Lorenzo Rodríguez (c.1704–74), may perhaps be seen as the *estípite*'s most outstanding victory.

The use of colour was another common feature of Latin American baroque architecture. Brightly coloured glazed tiles were often used with striking effects in Mexico, as at San Francisco, Acatepec (c.1730), and in the Sanctuary, Ocotlán (c.1750), where the frothy white sculpture of the portal (which includes *estípites*) is set off to advantage by the red-tiled bases of the flanking bell-towers. In Peru the carved church façades were sometimes painted in bright colours.

Ecclesiastical architecture dominates the Spanish colonial record in America. Secular architecture, whether public or domestic, was always less important. Despite this, many examples of colonial houses and larger buildings survive in all the cities which in their day were focal points of the Spanish empire. Among the finest civic buildings still to be seen are the School of Mines in Mexico City, designed by the architect and sculptor Manuel Tolsá; the Torre-Tagle mansion in Lima, Peru, which now houses the Peruvian foreign ministry; and the austere neo-classical Royal Mint (Casa de la Moneda) in Santiago, Chile, designed by the Italian architect Joaquín Toesca and used after 1846 as the Chilean presidential palace.

Brazilian architecture only came into its own in the eighteenth century, notably in the rich mining province of Minas Gerais. In contrast with the architecture of the Spanish colonies, it demonstrates less concern for external ornament (an important exception is the façade of São Francisco, Salvador, of 1703) and

concentrates on internal spatial arrangements. The aisled hall-church form, so popular elsewhere, is rejected in favour of the inventive use of a single spatial unit, often oval or octagonal in plan. Good examples are N. S. do Pilar (1720–33) and the Rosario (completed by 1785) both in Ouro Preto, and São Pedro in Recife (1728–82). One such church, São Francisco, Ouro Preto, was designed and executed between 1766 and 1794 by the remarkable Aleijadinho (Antônio Francisco de Lisboa), better known as a sculptor.

The political tensions of the late eighteenth and early nineteenth centuries were paralleled in America, as in Europe, by a reaction against the artistic styles of the previous two centuries. For the intellectual elite the fantastic elaborations of Latin American baroque became equated with the corruption and decadence of the old colonial order, but the neo-classical movement in America was not strong enough to effect radical changes of taste in any but the major Spanish American colonial cities: the love of ornament was too deep-rooted. In Mexico the first architect to reintroduce relatively plain columns into his façades was Francisco Antonio Guerrero y Torres (c.1740–92); he built the elegant Pocito chapel at the famous sanctuary of Guadalupe (1777–91), which is also interesting for its ground plan, reminiscent more of Brazilian than Spanish American designs. The purest neo-classical architecture was produced, not surprisingly perhaps, by Spaniards: Manuel Tolsá (1757–1816) in Mexico City and Matías Maestro in Lima. Both had some success in changing the prevailing style, but by and large the period of greatest architectural activity in Latin America coincided with a taste for rich elaborations and baroque effects.

Painting and sculpture

The successful 'spiritual conquest' of the New World required more than an appropriate architectural setting: it needed a new Christian iconography to replace the images of the various deities to whom the Indians had traditionally offered their prayers, and this need was initially met in two ways. Works of art were imported from Europe, and workshops were created in the monasteries where the friars could train Indians to execute suitable works in an approximately European representational mode, usually by setting them to copy imported engravings. The most famous of these schools were established by Franciscans, by Pedro de Gante in Mexico City in 1527, and by Pedro Gosseal in Quito, Ecuador, in about 1550. Fresco provided a cheap and easy way of producing Christian images, as well as of simulating sculptured altars, coffered ceilings and architectural mouldings, and it had the added advantage of being familiar to Indian craftsmen from pre-conquest times. In Mexico at the Franciscan monastery of Huejotzingo (1550–60) the black and white murals are based on Flemish engravings, while the brightly coloured contemporary works at Ixmiquilpan demonstrate

Detail from a fresco at Ixmiquilpan

Painting by Echave Orio, 'La Porciuncula'

a strong native influence. Frescoes survive from the late sixteenth century in village churches around Cuzco, Peru, and the technique continued to be used in this area for over 200 years.

As with architecture, the Church remained the chief artistic patron throughout the colonial period for both the Indian and European populations. Religious art was the dominant, almost the only, genre to be practised. Of the other subjects open to artists in Europe – landscape, still-life, history, mythology and portraiture – only the last was of any importance; the others were virtually non-existent. By the later sixteenth century the demand for religious art was being supplied from a third source: craftsmen from several different countries had established workshops in the new Latin American towns and were producing works of art in a more consciously European style than most of that produced in the monastic workshops. Their sources, however, are often very heterogeneous: their own European training, imported paintings and sculptures, mostly from Seville and rarely of the highest quality, and engravings and illustrated books, most of which came from the Netherlands. Thus in 1566 Simon Pereyns (active 1566–88) arrived in Mexico from Antwerp and worked largely from engravings after Flemish artists, while Spaniards, such as Andrés de la Concha (active 1575–1612) and Balthasar de Echave Orio (c.1548–1620), worked in the Italian-influenced Sevillian style. Someone with a knowledge of French art must have been involved in the unique series of secular frescoes that decorated colonial mansions in Tunja, Colombia, around 1590–1610, and in the later sixteenth century

several Italians were attracted to Lima: Bernardo Bitti (1548–c.1620), Mateo Pérez de Alesio (1547–c.1628), a follower of Michelangelo, and Angelino de Medoro (c.1567–c.1631), who arrived in about 1600 having already worked in Bogotá, Tunja and Quito.

During the seventeenth century the influence of the flourishing Sevillian schools of painting is evident everywhere. During the 1640s and 1650s Zurbarán's workshop exported hundreds of canvases to America, and their powerful tenebrism was widely imitated. A few years later the soft, sweet style of Murillo was adopted by several notable painters, including Cristóbal de Villalpando (c.1652–1714) in Mexico, Gregorio Vázquez Ceballos (1638–1711) in Colombia, and Miguel de Santiago (c.1625–1706) in Ecuador. In the southern Andes, however, the influence of Flemish prints remained strong, as in the work of the Indian Diego Quispe Tito (1611–after 1681) in Cuzco, and of Melchor Pérez de Holguín (b. c.1660) and his followers in Bolivia.

During the eighteenth century few of the many documented painters stand out except in Mexico, where a lively school of portraiture challenged the supremacy of religious art. Portraits of nuns were especially popular: Sor Juana Inés de la Cruz, the nun–

poetess, was depicted several times, serene and beautiful, surrounded by books, as in the paintings of 1750 by Miguel Cabrera (1695–1768). Cabrera is also remembered for his plans to found an Academy in Mexico City which would exclude anyone who taught Indians to paint.

Genuine survivals of indigenous forms and techniques are most common in the field of pictorial representation, although only outside the jurisdiction of the stricter guilds, of course. In Mexico pre-conquest-style painted books containing information about native history and beliefs, as well as about the tributes due from different localities, continued to be produced, with some modifications, into the eighteenth century. Fine examples are the Codex Mendoza (c.1520) and the curious, deliberately archaizing Techialoyán manuscripts of the eighteenth century. In Peru in 1612 the mestizo Guamán Poma de Ayala completed an extensive history of the Incas, which he illustrated throughout with drawings that are a pleasing synthesis of European forms with Incan themes, while in the Mexican feather paintings of Christ and the Virgin, indigenous techniques are applied to new subject matter.

Indigenous influence is present in one of the most interesting schools of colonial painting, that of Cuzco, which by the eighteenth century was exporting works all over South America. Contemporaneously with the Europe-oriented Quispe Tito, a more provincial school of largely anonymous mestizo and Indian artists developed, which, although generally indebted compositionally to European sources, is quite distinct in style. An evident lack of concern for depth and contour is balanced here by an emphasis on decorative detail: the Holy Family, the angels and saints are dressed in richly embroidered costumes with magnificent lace trimmings, over which gold leaf is liberally applied in flat repeating patterns. The backgrounds are often little Andean landscapes with numerous local plants and birds dotted around, and sometimes with scenes of village life or figures tending flocks of llamas.

This obvious pleasure in the multiplication of decorative detail for its own sake is a common feature of the cult images which enjoyed (and enjoy) such popularity all over Latin America. Once a painting or sculpture was recognized as having special powers, like for example the seventeenth-century wooden crucifix, Cristo de los Temblores, in Cuzco cathedral, which was believed to be efficacious against earthquakes, or the sixteenth-century painting of the Virgin of Guadalupe in Mexico, the protectress of the Indians, then it would be copied to enable devotees to venerate it elsewhere. Statues were often copied on to canvas or panel with the addition of the candles, curtains and flowers that adorned the altar of the original. These copies were then often copied themselves, each time becoming stiffer and more icon-like, but with richer costumes and with ever more jewellery and floral tributes.

In the field of European-style figure sculpture, only a handful of

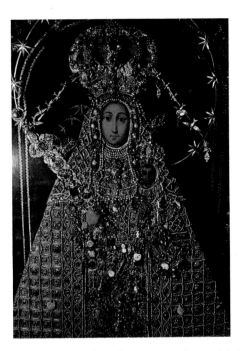

Virgin of Guadalupe, Sucre cathedral. The costume is richly embroidered with pearls

the documented craftsmen are of especial interest. The main influence throughout the colonial period was the Sevillian school, and Martínez Montañéz (1568–1649) in particular, who specialized in stark crucifixions and passion figures in polychromed wood. He exported a few such statues to America (although many more are attributed to him) and the type was repeated again and again, by, for example, Pedro de Lugo (active 1626–56) in Colombia, and Bernardo de Legarda (active 1731–73) and Manuel Chili, known as Caspicara (active late eighteenth century) in Quito. Christ's Passion offered colonial artists a rare chance to depict the naked body and they made the most of it, stressing the beauty of the long limbs and smooth white skin and the ugliness of the wounds and rivulets of scarlet blood.

In the eighteenth century, Brazil was to produce the finest individual artist of the whole colonial period: the mulatto Antônio Francisco Lisboa (1738–1814), called 'O Aleijadinho' ('the little cripple'). Both architect and sculptor, he has left ample testimony in the province of Minas Gerais of his outstanding ability to manipulate space in a dramatic and powerful way. The most famous of his many works are the sculptural groups in wood of the Stations of the Cross in the church of Bom Jesus, Congonhas do Campo (1797–9) and, above all, the twelve rugged stone prophets (1800–5) which watch over the monumental staircase that leads up to the same church.

Aleijadinho's genius apart, the most striking sculptural creations of the colonial period are the church interiors: the furnishings (choir-stalls, pulpits and retables), and the gold and polychromed

Main altar of the church of São Francisco, Salvador

stucco-work on the walls and ceilings, all largely anonymous. From as early as 1600 moulded stucco, particularly in the form of grotesques and entwined plants, predominantly in red, white and gold, was a special feature of the Dominican chapels of the Rosary, as for example at Puebla and Oaxaca in Mexico, both early seventeenth century. About fifty years later, the Jesuits used stucco to decorate many of their churches with flatter, more geometric forms, as in Quito and Córdoba, and by the eighteenth century the practice is widespread. The general tendency is towards increasing unity between the stucco decorations of the walls and ceiling, and the church furnishings, especially the retables.

A retable can include paintings and sculpture in the round and in relief, all organized within an architectural framework, usually of gilded wood. The central image is often an earlier work, a treasured sculpture from Spain, for example, or a popular miraculous image, and this forms the iconographical starting point for the figures and biblical scenes arranged around it. The stylistic development of the retable follows a similar pattern throughout Latin America from, to cite only one or two of the most splendid examples, one of the earliest surviving, that at Huejotzingo, with paintings by Simon Pereyns of 1586, through that in San Francisco, Bogotá, designed by Ignacio García de Ascucha in 1623, which is still fundamentally classical in style, to the splendid baroque example in the Compañía, Cuzco, designed by Diego Martínez de Oviedo in 1670, and finally to the overwhelming richness of such eighteenth-century examples as that at São Francisco, Salvador, Brazil (1730s?) and San Martín, Tepotzotlán, Mexico of c.1755. It is interesting that the tendency throughout the seventeenth and eighteenth centuries to even more fanciful elaborations of the architectural framework of these retables in Latin America, as in Spain, often predates similar developments in the architecture of church façades. It is as if the designers

Top: Aleijadinho's sculpture of the prophet Isaiah outside the church of Bom Jesus, Congonhas do Campo. Above: Figures of the Last Supper by Aleijadinho in the chapel of the church of Bom Jesus, Congonhas do Campo

working on a smaller scale and in less durable materials felt freer to experiment than those working in masonry.

By the end of the eighteenth century there was a reaction against this elaborate form of interior, led by the same men who were responsible for introducing the new taste in architecture: Manuel Tolsá in Mexico City, and Matías Maestro in Lima. In these two cities many churches were stripped bare, their retables burnt in an excess of neo-classical enthusiasm. Many more such interiors have been damaged or destroyed by earthquakes but enough survive in all their glittering splendour to make them among the most impressive monuments to colonial artistic achievement.

VF

Further reading

G. Kubler and M. Soria, *Art and Architecture of Spain and Portugal and their American Dominions* (Harmondsworth, 1959)

P. Kelemen, *Baroque and Rococo in Latin America* (New York, 1951)

H. E. Wethey, *Colonial Architecture and Sculpture in Peru* (Cambridge, Mass., 1949)

Painting and sculpture since 1830

Academicism and local colour

From the viewpoint of art, the period after independence in Latin America was somewhat poor in achievement. Painting and sculpture tended to be strongly derivative, with European (above all, French) models well to the fore. This was reinforced by the predominance of 'the academy', – i.e. the academies or schools of fine arts established in the various cities – where imported neo-

classicism was the main orthodoxy. Yet even at this period local, 'national' influences were bound to seep into Latin American art, as painters strove to adapt neo-classicism or other European academic styles to the real world that surrounded them. The appearance of distinctively Latin American themes, the acceptance of features of 'creole' life as proper subjects for art – such tendencies gradually became more noticeable, especially in Mexico, Brazil and the countries of the Southern Cone (Argentina, Chile, Uruguay).

The portraiture of the period, for instance, inevitably reflected local society (not least the Europeanizing aspirations of the creole elites, as shown, for instance, in their styles of dress). Works of art that evoked the growing national traditions of the new states – depictions on canvas of the battles of independence, statues of heroes, monumental sculptures – also bore an obvious Latin American stamp. The natural world of the American continent, in all its prodigality, was a further theme soon taken up by artists: this subject was affectionately cultivated by a number of foreign painters who lived and worked in the region – the most talented of these being a Bavarian, Johann Moritz Rugendas (1802–58) – and whose example proved contagious. Another foreigner who depicted Latin American (in this case, Ecuadorian) landscapes in an extraordinarily vivid way was the North American, Frederick Edwin Church (1826–1900), though he did not stay long enough to influence local artists. In paintings by foreigners and Latin Americans alike, it is easy to sense the special emotion with which exotic New World landscapes, typical rural characters, and the expanding urban scene were presented and interpreted on canvas. The three painters often considered as nineteenth-century Latin America's finest – Prilidiano Pueyrredón (Argentina, 1823–70), Juan Manuel Blanes (Uruguay, 1830–1901), and the remarkable José María Velasco

José María Velasco, 'Mexico' (1877)

(Mexico, 1840–1912) – all succeeded admirably in incorporating persuasive elements of 'local colour' into basically international styles.

Despite the achievements of talented individuals such as these, the general artistic panorama remained somewhat conservative. But new influences gradually put in their appearance. Towards the end of the nineteenth century, French Impressionism began to leave its mark on certain Latin American artists. Among its most interesting exponents were a Mexican, Joaquín Clausell (1866–1935), a prolific Chilean, Juan Francisco González (1853–1933) – whose Impressionism was most pronounced during a productive twelve-year period (1888–1900) of residence at Limache, near Valparaíso – and, somewhat later on, the Venezuelan, Armando Reverón (1889–1954), whose later development was altogether remarkable. Some of Reverón's later canvases combine a luminosity reminiscent of Turner with the delicate allusiveness of some kinds of Chinese art.

It must also be remembered that a 'popular' tradition of 'naive' or 'primitive' art always existed alongside that of 'the academy' in the nineteenth century, and, indeed, beyond. (Twentieth-century Haiti was to see a particularly flourishing development of these forms.) From the mid-nineteenth century onwards, advances in lithography also provided artists with a definitely non-academic outlet for their talents. Easily the most extraordinary figure in this particular line was the Mexican, José Guadalupe Posada (1851–1913), the author of at least 15,000 prints and satirical woodcuts, whose compelling images of animated skeletons and skulls gave his art an utterly special stamp.

Soon after 1900, challenges to nineteenth-century academicism grew sharper. A notable part here was played by the Mexican artist (and energetic publicist) Gerardo Murillo (1875–1964), who

José Guadalupe Posada, 'Don Quijote and Sancho Panza'

changed his name to 'Dr Atl' ('atl' being the Nahuatl word for 'water'). Dr Atl and other rebel artists from the Academy of San Carlos – Mexico's main artistic institute, founded as far back as 1785 – mounted a highly successful exhibition of 'dissident' art in Mexico City in September 1910. The effects of this initiative were delayed by the start, a few weeks later, of the Mexican revolution, which, quite apart from its political importance, was to prove a decisive turning point for modern Latin American art.

Mexican muralism and its influence

The revolution shook Mexico to its foundations. Artists found that they had a choice of three courses of action: to become active combatants; to take part in the struggle through propaganda efforts; or to leave the country altogether for a while. Once the violent years of upheaval were over, once thought was given to rebuilding the shattered nation, Mexican artists joined forces in pursuit of a common ideal: to contribute their art to a great programme of popular education. This programme, supported by the intelligentsia and by the governments of the day (especially that of President Alvaro Obregón, whose education minister was the philosopher José Vasconcelos), certainly had its roots in Dr Atl's pre-revolutionary criticisms of academic art. Following on from the dissident movement of 1910, artists now drew consciously on pre-Columbian and Spanish colonial traditions, and on the popular art of figures such as Posada; these indigenous elements were blended with the modern influences radiating from Europe to create a new and unique artistic trend – an essentially didactic pictorial language designed to further popular education, but one which soon transcended that simple aim. The result was a rich artistic movement, unprecedented and in many ways still unequalled in Latin America, in which a host of talented individuals played their part.

The key feature of the Mexican Renaissance (as it has been called) was its emphasis on *the painting of murals* – something that sets it apart, for instance, from post-revolutionary Soviet Russian art, which had similar didactic purposes. The three acknowledged 'giants' of Mexican muralism were Diego Rivera (1886–1957), José Clemente Orozco (1883–1949), and David Alfaro Siqueiros (1898–1974). It is difficult to exaggerate the importance of this trio – the first Latin American painters to enter the pantheon of modern art. All three were obsessed with large-scale nationalist visions of history and society (tinged with exuberant Marxism in the cases of Rivera and Siqueiros, with moralism and even mysticism in the case of Orozco), with the Spanish conquest and the revolution itself as major and recurring themes in their work. This was an original, authentic Latin American form of art. Important differences of style are to be noted within the mainstream of muralism. Rivera's infatuation with Marxism, for instance, was given increasingly systematic expression, while Orozco's work was tinged with

Diego Rivera, detail from 'The Night of the Rich'

Detroit Institute of Arts, appropriately enough on the theme of the automobile industry. (Another Rivera mural, for the Rockefeller Center in New York, proved too controversial, and was later obliterated, an unforgivable act of philistinism.) Orozco and Siqueiros, too, worked at times outside Mexico. This tradition has continued. As recently as the mid-1960s, to mention only one example, a later representative of the great tradition, Jorge González Camarena, executed a powerful mural ('Presence of Latin America') for the University of Concepción in Chile. The Mexican imprint, in fact, is to be found on numerous stretches of wall throughout the western hemisphere.

The Mexican muralist school was at its height in the 1920s and 1930s – years of unsurpassed achievement – and it has continued to inspire artists ever since. Its immediate impact on the rest of Latin America was considerable. Artists in several countries (sometimes through direct contact with Mexico) were prompted to develop their own 'indigenist' schools of modern painting. This trend was perhaps most conspicuous in the Andean republics (notably Ecuador, Peru and Bolivia), where strong indigenous traditions were to be found, and it clearly affected the work of modern Ecuador's most famous painter, Osvaldo Guayasamín (b. 1919). Guayasamín's work, which includes murals, strikes a rich vein of social protest while incorporating, also, the influence of Picasso. It would be hard to deny that the Latin American penchant for mural-painting – including perhaps the propagandistic 'impromptu muralism' that has flourished during certain political episodes, for example the Allende government in Chile – stems to a large extent from the

Osvaldo Guayasamín, 'Tears of Blood'

ambiguity and irony. A comparison could also be drawn between Rivera's crowded realism, relying sometimes on stock caricatures, and Orozco's increasingly dramatic and loose style (which became a significant influence on Abstract Expressionism in the United States).

The achievement of the muralists can best be studied, obviously, in Mexico – in Rivera's notable sequence in the National Preparatory School, the Secretariat of Education, and the National Palace, all in Mexico City, and in Orozco's magnificent series of frescoes in various public buildings in Guadalajara. Siqueiros's major Mexican works are to be found in the National Palace of Fine Arts, the University City, and the National History Museum in the Mexican capital. For lovers of modern art, pilgrimages to these places are obligatory. The great muralists were also sometimes in demand outside Mexico. Rivera himself did several major commissions in the United States, including some impressive murals in the

Mexican example, even where different styles have been used. Mexican influence was indirect in the work of the great Brazilian painter Cândido Portinari (1903–62), but this superb artist's quest for a genuinely national, Brazilian art *was* often expressed in large murals, although his style, traditional and modern at one and the same time, was all his own.

Nationalism and internationalism

Mexican muralism, the single most notable phenomenon in modern Latin American art, was far from being the only effort made in the region to renew artistic traditions. In the early part of the twentieth century, various 'rebellions' against academicism took place in other countries. The most famous of these, undoubtedly, was the *Semana de Arte Moderna* (Modern Art Week) held in São Paulo, Brazil, in February 1922. This event, accompanied by noisy controversy, brought together writers and musicians as well as painters and sculptors, but its protagonists were all deeply committed to coming to terms with the twentieth century. Unlike the Mexicans with whom they were contemporary, the Brazilian promoters of the *Semana de Arte Moderna* did not have a precise or doctrinaire programme, over and above a keen desire for innovation. In this respect they can be seen to have set the tone for modern Latin American art as a whole, which has certainly shared in the extraordi-

nary diversity of the present century's artistic endeavour. For while many Latin American artists have continued to emphasize the quest for authentic local values, others have eagerly embraced more cosmopolitan attitudes, striving to assert themselves (and Latin America) in the increasingly international marketplace of contemporary art.

The period after the *Semana de Arte Moderna* in Brazil – a country of key importance for modern Latin American art – was long dominated by the gentle nationalist genius Cândido Portinari. But there were others, like Tarsila do Amaral (1886–1973) and Emiliano di Cavalcanti (1897–1976) who also aimed at reflecting Brazilian realities in their art. (Brazil was large enough, too, to accommodate flourishing 'regionalist' schools of painting, based especially on Recife and Bahia.) In their very different ways – too varied to allow for instant classification – Pedro Figari (Uruguay, 1861–1938), Carlos Mérida (Guatemala, b. 1891), Raquel Forner (Argentina, b. 1902), Antonio Berni (Argentina, b. 1905) and Alejandro Obregón (Colombia, b. 1920) can, similarly, be regarded as representative artists who assimilated key features of early twentieth-century European styles – post-Impressionism, Fauvism, Cubism, Expressionism, and so on – in their distinctive explorations of Latin American, national, social and political (in Berni's case, left-wing) themes.

Roberto Matta, 'Against You, Dove Assassins' (1949)

In Mexico, a possibly understandable reaction to the programmatic nationalism of the muralists was embodied in the work of a very distinguished painter, Rufino Tamayo (b. 1899), in which the early influence of Picasso and Braque was soon transcended in a constantly developing personal style. Tamayo's rejection of the philosophical underpinnings of the muralist school was shown in his simple dictum: 'Painting is painting.' A further break with muralism came through Surrealism, whose principal French apologist, André Breton, visited Mexico in 1938. Among the Surrealists Breton 'discovered' in Mexico – though she had never heard of the movement before his visit – was a remarkable woman painter, Frida Kahlo (1910–54), at one time married to Diego Rivera. Kahlo's tiny autobiographical paintings were based on the native tradition of the *retablo* (the naive, often anonymous paintings on tin made as offerings after miraculous deliverance). It cannot really be argued that Surrealism became a full-blooded Latin American school, but its influence, though diffuse, was strong. Two of the region's internationally most famous modern painters, the Cuban, Wilfredo Lam (b. 1902), and the expatriate Chilean, Roberto Matta (b. 1912), were fundamentally influenced by the Surrealist aesthetic during their formative periods, and remained so thereafter. Lam's totemic canvases often express the magic 'primitivism' which Surrealists were always seeking.

Increasingly from the Second World War onwards, modern art's most radical innovation – abstract or non-figurative art – began to exercise a strong appeal throughout Latin America, with representatives in every country. An early figure in preparing the ground for this approach was the great Uruguayan, Joaquín Torres-García (1874–1949). In the 1920s Torres-García was active in Paris, where he was the co-founder of the Cercle et Carré group – responsible for organizing the world's first major international exhibition of abstract art (Paris, 1930). Torres-García returned to his native Montevideo in 1934. His extensively expounded theory of 'constructivist universalism' and his angular, geometrical style (using muted earth colours and retaining certain vaguely figurative aspects) had an immense influence in Uruguay. It was duly noted in neighbouring Argentina – a country where, following an early lead given by painters such as Emilio Pettoruti (1892–1971) and Xul Solar (1887–1963), abstractionism in all its successive forms was to gain a particularly strong following. This was also to prove true in Venezuela, where Alejandro Otero (b. 1921) developed, in his 'colour-rhythms' (first shown in 1955), a striking version of Op Art.

Yet by no means all Latin American painters adopted abstractionism. An extraordinary Colombian, Fernando Botero (b. 1920), struck out in a very different direction, elaborating a highly original, neo-figurative style based on exaggerated, parodistic reworkings of old masters. In Mexico, José Cuevas (b. 1933) has produced neo-figurative drawings of superb quality, rejecting the muralist school

Bruno Giorgi, 'The Meteorite' (Brasília)

while acknowledging his debt to Orozco. Rafael Coronel (b. 1932) and (especially) Alberto Gironella (b. 1929) are two further Mexican artists whose striking neo-figurative work can be said to have anticipated – though in a lighter way, and with something of the 'bite' of Dada and Surrealism – the recent controversial German trend known as neo-expressionism.

The development of twentieth-century Latin American sculpture parallels that of painting in important respects, with modern figurative styles existing alongside a trend (increasingly powerful after the 1940s) towards the abstract. Among modern sculptors in the figurative tradition, Vítor Brecheret (Brazil, 1894–1956), Bruno Giorgi (Brazil, b. 1905) and Joaquín Roca Rey (Peru, b. 1923) all won considerable reputations both inside and outside their respective countries. Giorgi's work can be seen to good effect in Brasília. Sculptors and sculptresses who moved away from representation towards abstract, symbolic or 'totemic' forms include Edgar Negret (Colombia, b. 1920), who found a highly personal style, Marina Núñez del Prado (Bolivia, b. 1910), creator of powerful semi-abstract 'interpretations of the Bolivian soul', María Martins (Brazil, 1900–73), Noemi Gerstein (Argentina, b. 1910) and Alicia Peñalba (Argentina, b. 1918). Latin American sculpture in recent times has sometimes attempted to reinterpret pre-Columbian forms in a modern idiom – with what degree of success is a matter of debate. Sculpture has also been imaginatively used to enhance some of the superb modern architecture of the region. Conspicuous examples of this 'integration of the plastic arts' are to be seen in Mexico City and Brasília.

The institutional framework for modern art in Latin America was greatly strengthened in the middle decades of the twentieth century. The opening of museums of contemporary art in major cities, combined with the proliferation of private galleries, did much to reinforce the triumph of the modern movement. The São Paulo Biennale (first held in 1951) quickly developed a well-deserved reputation as one of the important dates in the world's artistic calendar – a rival, indeed, to its European counterpart at Venice. In Argentina, in the 1960s, the Torcuato di Tella Institute for the Arts did much to promote experimentalism and to add to the cultural liveliness of Buenos Aires during that lively decade, though it fell a victim to the altogether harsher climate of the 1970s. Latin American art, whether consciously nationalist or consciously internationalist, or neither, continues to share in the general ferment of the artistically agitated twentieth century. As contemporary art has become more international, Latin America has participated fully in universal trends, and yet, at the same time, its artists (or some of the most distinguished) have maintained a distinctive ability to reaffirm, in unusual ways, the vitality of the figurative tradition.

MD/SC

Further reading

L. Castedo, *A History of Latin American Art and Architecture* (London, 1969)

J. Charlot, *The Mexican Mural Renaissance, 1920–1925* (New Haven, Conn., 1963)

G. Chase, *Contemporary Art in Latin America* (New York, 1970)

A. Rodríguez, *A History of Mexican Mural Painting* (London, 1969)

B. D. Wolfe, *The Fabulous Life of Diego Rivera* (New York, 1963)

Bienal de São Paulo. Catalogues (1951–)

Modern architecture in Latin America

Modern architecture in Latin America is perhaps best understood when seen in contrast with its nineteenth-century counterpart. In general that was a lacklustre period, bearing little comparison with colonial times or with the twentieth century. The most cursory survey reveals that by the second quarter of the nineteenth century the early Mexican neo-classical style of Manuel Tolsá (1757–1816) and Francisco Eduardo Tresguerras (1759–1833) had been turned into one of the most sterile academic movements on record. Circum-

stances were similar in Brazil, where the work of two French architects, Grandjean de Montigny (1776–1850) and Louis Vauthier (c.1810–77), helped to encourage academic taste. With a greater or lesser degree of intensity, sooner or later comparable events unfolded throughout most of the continent. Conditions did not improve as the century progressed. By the late 1870s and early 1880s a new preference had set in for rendering effusively the more ornate aspects of French Second Empire architecture, and this did little to improve architectural character in general. 'Europeanization' as a means of equating conspicuous splendour with a standard of urban decorum, as for instance in Manaus (on the River Amazon) in the 1890s, scarcely allowed for an opportunity to develop an architecture proper to the region. It was almost exclusively in rural dwellings and in the anonymous residences of the provincial middle class that nineteenth-century Latin American builders remembered some of the lessons of their colonial past and showed some degree of sympathy for local conditions of climate, building tradition, and way of life in general. But these excellent and reasonable examples were shunned for the most part as hopelessly unfashionable, and there remained, well into the twentieth century, much enthusiasm for designs slavishly derived from a European high-bourgeois tradition. Better academic aesthetic standards, however, eventually replaced earlier and more exuberant ones. Thus, the early twentieth-century remodelling of Carlos Enrique Pellegrini's Teatro Colón in Buenos Aires, originally built in 1855–7, and Adamo Boari's Palacio de Bellas Artes in Mexico City, of 1904–34, find a place among the better examples of twentieth-century academic neo-classicism in Latin America.

In spite of the strength of the academic tradition, the architectural climate began to change in a most remarkable manner in the early 1930s. At that time, when most European modern architects were attempting to create a universal style, an important group of avant-garde Latin American architects became concerned with expressing the specific character of their respective cultures. Such an interest in nationalism gives a particular flavour to modern Latin American architecture, and in general marks its importance. Although some of the objectives of avant-garde architecture in Latin America parallel similar ones in painting and literature, a modern nationalist architecture developed later than other arts. During the late 1920s and early 1930s the first examples of modern architecture in the area tended to follow stylistic patterns that Le Corbusier had developed earlier.

One of the earliest expressions of modern architecture in Latin America occurred in Brazil in 1925. That year Gregori Warchavchik, a young Russian émigré architect, published an important manifesto, 'Apropos of Modern Architecture', and subsequently built houses in a contemporary style in Rio de Janeiro and São Paulo in 1927 and in 1931. Shortly thereafter, Warchavchik entered into a partnership with the 28-year-old Lúcio Costa, who had just been forced to resign after only one year in office as Director of the National Academy of Fine Arts for having replaced a standard Beaux-Arts curriculum of instruction with Bauhaus teaching methods. As a result of these events, the centre of avant-garde architecture in Brazil shifted almost exclusively to the office of Warchavchik and Costa, where students gathered to discuss the latest theories of the International Style.

In 1936, partly to advance the cause of modern architecture in Brazil, Gustavo Capanema, who was at the time Minister of Education, asked Costa to submit a design for a new building for the Ministry of Education and Health in Rio (designed in 1937 and finished in 1943). Costa was allowed to secure the consulting services of Le Corbusier, who came to Brazil for a second time after a first trip in 1929. The result of that association was a design of such quality that it brought modern Brazilian architecture to worldwide prominence. More importantly, with the design of this building Costa taught Brazilian architects how to turn Le Corbusier's plasticity into a means for evoking essential native rhythms without doing violence to a contemporary style.

Besides having an interest in creating a modern Brazilian architecture, Costa's circle worked also to record and restore colonial buildings, which they saw as a source of the national tradition they wished to continue. After its inception in 1936, the National Service of Historical and Artistic Patrimony (SPHAN) was headed by Costa himself. Pursuing their nationalist interests further, avant-garde architects came to consider that a modern Brazilian architecture should parallel colonial developments, and worked towards an integration of the visual arts to evoke what had occurred in the eighteenth-century national baroque. It was partly to fulfil such an aim of subsuming all the arts into architecture that in his Ministry of Education Building Costa made use of sculpture by Bruno Giorgi, Antonio Celso, and Jacques Lipchitz, and commissioned two murals from Cândido Portinari. With such a decision Costa started a trend which became characteristic not only of modern Brazilian architecture, but of the whole of twentieth-century Latin American architecture.

Oscar Niemeyer, by far the most outstanding student in Costa's circle, was allowed to collaborate in designing the building for the Ministry of Education. Moreover, he became Le Corbusier's draughtsman for three months. Such splendid beginnings led in time to a remarkable independent practice. By adding his own sensuous curvilinear rhythms to the spatial conceptions and methods of construction of Le Corbusier and Costa, Niemeyer established a new trend in Brazilian architecture that was fresher, more mature, and more characteristically national than Costa's. This early period in Niemeyer's career included among other designs the Brazilian Pavilion for the New York Fair, 1938 (in

Top: The Ministry of Education and Health, Rio de Janeiro. Above: The Presidential Palace, Brasília

collaboration with Costa), the Casino at Pampulha (Minas Gerais), 1942, and the Church of Saint Francis of Assisi, also at Pampulha, of 1943. Adopting Costa's principle of integrating the visual arts and architecture, Niemeyer included in his work of this period murals by Portinari, by Roberto Burle Marx, and by himself. Just as it had been the case in his choice of architectural forms, art in his buildings always had a strong Brazilian flavour.

Brasília was undoubtedly the most important architectural event of the 1950s in Latin America. In 1956 an international jury awarded first prize to Lúcio Costa's scheme, which adopted the shape of a bird with outspread wings. Concurrently, President Juscelino Kubitschek appointed Niemeyer technical advisor to NOVACAP, the governmental authority for the new capital of Brazil. In his new capacity, Niemeyer designed the buildings for the Congress, the presidential palace, the cathedral, a housing complex, and other major structures. His design for the Congress building was as forcefully symbolic as Costa's plan for the city; it included a concave dome for the Senate and a convex bowl for the Chamber of Deputies. He also made use of curvilinear forms for his cathedral, which he designed as a sheath of outward-opening concrete parabolas held together at their apex and forming a cone underneath. For the presidential palace, on the other hand, he chose an elongated parallelepiped as an overall shape, and relieved it with a colonnade in the shape of inverted parabolas. Brasília was supposed to be the crowning achievement in the development of modern Brazilian architecture, a cause that had the wholehearted support of President Kubitschek, who had been Niemeyer's friend since the early 1940s. On paper Costa's and Niemeyer's designs had created a complex of extraordinary elegance, but reality was different. The scale of the city turned out to be too vast to be harmonious and, moreover, Brasília has not aged well. Nevertheless, at the time that the designs were made known to the international architectural community, Brasília was hailed as one of the outstanding designs of the century.

Mexico was another important leader in the development of modern Latin American architecture. Its early avant-garde architecture, however, was different from that of Brazil. During the 1930s Mexican architects, such as Juan O'Gorman and Luis Barragán, followed a stern international functionalist line exhibiting large expanses of glass and taut planes of white stucco. But already by the 1940s Barragán was investigating the possibilities of using vernacular elements of architecture in his residential work in the subdivision of El Pedregal in Mexico City.

By the end of the decade Mexican architecture was well on the way to creating a style that was as national as it was modern. This fact is clearly indicated in the design of the buildings of the University of Mexico (UNAM), which became a joint venture of gigantic proportions. In the incredibly short span of three years, from 1950 to 1953, more than 150 young architects, engineers, and technicians completed the basic portion of the overall plan for the University City, designed by Mario Pani and Enrique del Moral. This project made manifest an extraordinarily strong surge of nationalist sentiment. Not only did some of the shapes reproduce forms of pre-Columbian buildings, as was the case of Alberto Arai's handball courts in the shape of Toltec pyramids, but also, and for the first time, the work of Mexican muralists, with their powerful Indian themes, was extensively used for the exterior decoration of buildings. The Central Administration Building, by Mario Pani, Enrique del Moral, and Salvador Ortega, carried two murals by Siqueiros; the Central Library, by Juan O'Gorman, Gustavo Saavedra, and Juan Martínez de Velasco, was covered by murals by O'Gorman; and the Medical and Biological Sciences Building had murals by Francisco Eppens. The University of Mexico, with its vast scale, marked a new step in the development of Latin American architecture in the early 1950s, one that pointed to new possibilities of an almost heroic breadth. Brasília, it will be remembered, came but a few years later.

Félix Candela, a Spaniard who fought on the Nationalist side during the Civil War and who arrived in Mexico in 1939, represents a different trend within the scope of Mexican architecture. Candela's work has always been coloured by an influence from Eduardo Torroja's sense of structure. As such, his work is characterized by the use of the *cascarón*, or concrete shells in the shape of hyperbolic paraboloids. The Pavilion for Cosmic Ray Research at the University of Mexico, the Church of Santa Mónica in Mexico City, of 1966, and the Sports Palace for the 1968 Olympics, in Mexico City, are among his outstanding works.

University of Mexico, Central Library

The example of Mexico and Brazil was soon followed in other countries. In Venezuela, Carlos Raúl Villanueva, who had studied at the Ecole des Beaux-Arts in Paris and whose use of concrete has been greatly influenced by Auguste Perret, designed for Caracas the first low-cost public housing project in Latin America, El Silencio, of 1941–3. This was followed by El Paraíso, of 1952–4, and by the 23 de Enero Housing Complex, of 1955–7. But the University of Caracas is Villanueva's best known work by far. There, his Olympic stadium (1950), and his Olympic swimming pool (1957), make a daring use of reinforced concrete. The unit of the Aula Magna (Great Hall) and the covered plaza is Villanueva's most famous work in the university complex. Alexander Calder, who designed the 'flying saucers' that not only decorate the interior of the hall, but more importantly regulate its acoustics to perfection, has said of it: 'None of my mobiles has met with a more extraordinary environment – more effective or more grandiose.'

In Havana, the Plaza de la República, designed in 1950–1, was a Cuban response to the new Latin American trend of vast monumental projects in a contemporary style. The Office of the Comptroller, by Aquiles Capablanca, of 1952, with murals by Amelia Peláez, is usually accepted as the best building in the complex. The Tropicana Night Club, by Max Borges, Jr, of 1952, essentially consisting of a series of eccentric concrete arches and semicircular glass curtain walls telescoping down to a stage, was a very successful attempt at linking sensuous modern forms with the lush vegetation of a tropical garden. On another level, the residential work of Mario Romañach, especially the Alvarez Residence, of 1957, is a remarkable example of an important trend in Cuban architecture of the 1950s. It endeavoured to create a national style that would express an avant-garde mode at the same time that it would evoke the rhythms and

colour of native colonial buildings. The composition is ordered about a central courtyard, a feature that Cuban architecture had abandoned for a good seventy years. Romañach put it to work not merely as a way of evoking the past but also, and more importantly, as a means of bringing the prevailing breezes into the house, which thus required no air-conditioning. Air would flow from the courtyard into the rooms and would then escape through an upper clerestory after having been deflected by the reinforced concrete hyperbolic paraboloids that constituted the roof. The design of this house thus reflected an evocation of national culture and a clever use of local climatic conditions. Moreover, the sensuality of its forms was brought under control by a consistent use of the golden mean as a system of proportion – one example of the influence of Le Corbusier's *Modulor* in Cuban architecture.

After the Revolution of 1959, the complex of buildings for the teaching of the plastic and performing arts in the former Country Club of Havana is the one important attempt the government has made to continue the earlier nationalist style. Designed by Ricardo Porro as a school of plastic arts in 1961–2, the complex consists of a

The Alvarez Residence, Havana

University of Caracas, Aula Magna

series of sensuous breast-like domes developing along sinuous contours. After Porro's defection in 1963, the project was finished in 1965 by Vittorio Garatti, who added to it a school of performing arts in Porro's style.

But not all important modern architecture in Latin America responds to nationalistic trends. In Colombia, for instance, the building for the Bank of Bogotá (1959), by Pablo Lanzetta and Reinaldo Valencia, followed the strict pattern of a North American skyscraper, and in fact, Skidmore, Owings and Merrill were retained as consultants for the project.

In the Southern Cone, architects generally followed the canons of the International Style during the 1940s and 1950s. Such is the case, for instance, of Jorge Ferrari and Amancio Williams, of Argentina. Among the outstanding modern buildings of Buenos Aires, the San Martín Municipal Theatre, (1953–61), by Mario Roberto Alvarez and Macedonio Oscar Ruiz, and the Bank of London and South America Building (1960–6), by Clorindo Testa, Santiago Sánchez, and Alfredo Agostini, are to be especially noted. Of these, the latter already points to Brutalist sources. Earlier, in 1949–54, Le Corbusier had designed and built a residence in Argentina, the Curuchet House, in Mar del Plata.

Mainly because of economic conditions, and at times because of political developments, the unfolding of Latin American architecture during the 1970s and 1980s has not paralleled the brilliant achievements of earlier decades. No new names have emerged to dazzle the international architectural community, and only a few architects from the earlier generation remain in practice. Of these, the most distinguished today is Luis Barragán, of Mexico, who continues to employ native forms of architecture to create extraordinarily clean spaces decorated with a magnificent play of warm and pastel colours. For his achievements he received the Pritzker Prize in 1980. By this act the whole of the Latin American nationalist architectural movement received a belated but important accolade.

NM

Further reading

F. Bullrich, *New Directions in Latin American Architecture* (New York, 1969)

M. L. Cetto, *Modern Architecture in Mexico* (New York, 1961)

P. Goodwin, *Brazil Builds: Architecture New and Old* (New York, 1943)

H. R. Hitchcock, *Latin American Architecture Since 1945* (New York, 1955)

S. Moholy-Nagy, *Carlos Raul Villanueva and the Architecture of Venezuela* (London, 1964)

O. Niemeyer, *Oscar Niemeyer* (Milan, 1975)

Spanish American theatre

The theatre in Spanish America has been the Cinderella of the arts. While the subcontinent has produced poets of worldwide fame, such as Pablo Neruda and Octavio Paz, and writers of fiction as distinguished as Jorge Luis Borges and Gabriel García Márquez, no Spanish American dramatist has as yet achieved international recognition.

It seems to have been the case that something akin to theatre existed in pre-Columbian Indian cultures in Spanish America, but after the conquest the stage was taken over for a while as a means of spreading the Gospel. The Mexican nun, Sor Juana Inés de la Cruz (1648–95) is remembered as a prolific playwright within the conventions of the Spanish baroque theatre, but other dramatists from the colonial period and the nineteenth century are only of interest to specialists. In our own century we perceive a gradual acceleration of theatrical activity to a point at which in the mid-1980s there are probably about 150 working dramatists in Spanish America as well as a very large number of groups writing and staging 'collective' theatre.

From the turn of the last century we can postulate three fairly clearly defined generations of Spanish American dramatists, with a fourth now making its presence felt. The first of these generations was the pioneer group of men born approximately in the decade 1865–75. At this time, although Lima and one or two other capital cities had some sort of theatrical tradition, the main centres of dramatic activity were Buenos Aires and Mexico City. The year 1903 saw the success of the first really significant modern Spanish American play *M'hijo el dotor* (My Son, the Lawyer) in Buenos Aires by the Uruguayan dramatist Florencio Sánchez (1875–1910). Sánchez and his Argentine contemporary Roberto Payró (1867–1928) can be regarded as the founders of the theatre in the River Plate region. Theirs was a social theatre with a strong didactic and critical element designed to stir the awareness of their audiences to the rapidly changing reality of their countries and to the need for newer, less traditional attitudes among the middle class. Similarly in Mexico, Federico Gamboa (1864–1939) in *La venganza de la gleba* (1905; The Vengeance of the Serfs) seems to forecast the peasant uprising which was to be at the heart of the Mexican revolution a decade later. Unfortunately this pioneering activity was followed by a decline in drama production for some twenty years.

The second generation of twentieth-century Spanish American dramatists was composed of men born roughly between 1895 and 1905. It included in Argentina Samuel Eichelbaum (1894–1967), Roberto Arlt (1900–42) and Conrad Nalé Roxló (1898–1970), and in Mexico Xavier Villaurrutia (1903–50), Celestino Gorostiza (1904–67) and especially Rodolfo Usigli (1904–79). With their appearance in the 1930s we begin to see the emergence of fully professional dramatists, conscious of the evolution of the European theatre in their own time, and in some cases producing a large output. Between the two World Wars, Spanish American theatre was seeking to respond to two different imperatives. One was to explore new areas of specifically Spanish American reality; the other was to keep abreast of technical innovations, especially those which came in the aftermath of Surrealism. These imperatives can be seen clearly at work in Mexico where they produced a strongly nationalist tendency centred on the Comedia Mexicana (Mexican Theatre) group in the late 1920s and early 1930s, and alongside it the more important and innovatory Teatro Orientación (Orientation Theatre) group. The latter introduced Pirandello, Chekhov, Shaw, O'Neill, Strindberg and other influential European playwrights to Mexican audiences. Usigli, Bernard Shaw's greatest disciple in Spanish America, attempted to bestride both tendencies, but his most famous play *El gesticulador* (1937; The Impersonator) was so politically subversive that it could not be publicly performed for ten years and even then provoked a Cabinet crisis. Usigli was still having his plays prohibited in his old age. In contrast, Villaurrutia's *Invitación a la muerte* (1940; Invitation to die) is almost a 'black comedy' and was strikingly novel in its time. In Buenos Aires we see a similar split between the basically realist theatre of observation represented by Eichelbaum in *Un guapo del 900* (1940; A Tough of the Past) and the curiously distorted Pirandellianism of Arlt's theatre of ideas on the one hand and Nalé Roxló's fantasy and poetic drama on the other.

The third generation of modern Spanish American playwrights comprised writers born roughly between 1920 and 1930. They now form the dramatic Establishment. By the 1950s Buenos Aires and Mexico City had begun to lose their predominance as centres of dramatic activity and at the same time a fresh set of European influences was beginning to be felt. The theatre in Peru began a new phase with the appearance of Sebastián Salazar Bondy (b. 1924). René Marqués (1919–79) founded the experimental Ateneo theatre company in Puerto Rico. In Chile two famous university theatre groups, the University of Chile Theatre Institute and the University of Chile Experimental Theatre were founded in 1941 and 1943 respectively. Elsewhere, too, the theatre began to come to life. For the first time in the 1950s we can begin to talk meaningfully about a Spanish American theatre in the full geographical sense of the term.

If the output of the dramatists of this third generation has not made a significant impact outside Spanish America, the chief reason is undoubtedly its prevailing tone of rebellious and even revolutionary social commitment. As also happened with Spanish American novels and poetry of social protest, the tendency is to privilege 'message' by the use of often crude symbolism and deliberately loaded conflicts, so that even where an attempt is made at the same time to exploit new dramatic techniques the literary quality of the plays is usually severely compromised. Thus, whether we look at a play like *Por los caminos van los campesinos* (1946; Along the Roads go the Peasants) by the Nicaraguan Pablo Antonio Cuadra (b. 1912), or more famous plays like the Argentine Carlos Gorostiza's *El puente* (1949; The Bridge), René Marqués's *Là muerte no entrará en Palacio* (1957; Death Must not Get into the Governor's Palace) and the Chilean Egon Woolf's *Los invasores* (1962; The Invaders), we feel uneasily that as the sociopolitical situation changes these works will be in danger of becoming mere museum pieces.

This danger does not deter many younger Spanish American dramatists. For them the essential problem since the 1950s has been to combine commitment with increasingly complex vanguardist techniques. Here Brecht has been far and away the greatest influence. The solutions to the problem have taken various forms. Luis Rafael Sánchez of Puerto Rico in his play *La pasión según Antígona Pérez* (1968; The Passion of Antigone Pérez) uses the model of Sophocles's *Antigone* to attack political oppression in Spanish America. The Mexican Vicente Leñero's *Pueblo rechazado* (1968; The Rejects) uses German 'documentary theatre' techniques similar to those of Peter Weiss and Rolf Hochhuth to dramatize the real-life story of Prior Lemercier of Cuernavaca who came into conflict with reactionary Church authorities. Similarly Jorge Díaz, Alejandro Sieveking and Sergio Vodonovic in Chile strive towards a radical but innovatory style of playwriting. In Argentina Osvaldo Dragún's *Historias para ser contadas* (1957; Stories for Telling) portended what has been called the 'theatre of dissent' of Victor de los Solares, Guillermo Gentile and Ricardo Monti, all of whom emerged in 1970. Their work moves away from documentalism towards symbolic stage-parables but the socio-political thrust remains. In a sense the climax of this tendency is to be seen in 'collective' theatre. Here a group studies a certain amount of material relating to a given episode and then uses it to improvise dramatic situations which may produce a collectively created text or one which is written *post facto* by a member of the group. The subject matter is almost always some very recent event. 'Collective' theatre is certainly the supreme example of 'living theatre' in contemporary Spanish America. In Chile, for instance, in the early 1970s there were some 600 such groups operating.

At the opposite extreme is the theatre of the absurd in the tradition of Ionesco, Beckett, Adamov and Albee, together with the shock-effect theatre of cruelty influenced by Artaud and Genet. A number of the most striking plays of the 1960s combine both absurdist and cruel elements. In the Chilean Jorge Díaz's *El cepillo de dientes* (1961; The Toothbrush) the two characters play a very elaborate game in order to avoid communicating with each other, symbolically destroy the set and ritually 'kill' each other. The Cuban José Triana's *La noche de los asesinos* (1966; The Night of the

Assassins) again involves a monstrous and horrifying game, while his fellow Cuban Antón Arrufat's *Todos los domingos* (1965; Every Sunday) involves successive re-enactments of the same grotesque love-scene until, just as it becomes reality, one of the partners is stabbed to death. More consistently brutal is Griselda Gambaro's *El campo* (1967; The Camp). It is actually set in a prison camp and makes its impact through the representation of systematic degradation and terror. The problem of this kind of theatre is less its minority interest than its derivativeness. As Brecht took over from Pirandello as a major influence, so more recently Gotowski's ideas came into vogue after a period of avant-garde theatre which took its orientations from Genet, Beckett or Albee.

At the end of the 1970s the Spanish American theatre was still feeling its way forward in three radically different directions. For one of these, that of extreme social and political commitment, we might point to the post-Allende Chilean theatre of Victor Torres, Jorge Díaz, Alejandro Sieveking and Sergio Vodanovic which rested on a mood of angry indictment of Chilean society (for example, Sieveking's *Pequeños animales abatidos*, 1975; The Beavers). The second, that of popular 'collective' theatre, is seen in the work of such a group as the Grupo Teatro Escambray operating in the backwoods among the peasant hill farmers of Cuba and dramatizing, for example, the problems of collectivizing the land. The third, that of uncompromising experimentalism, might be represented by the Centro de Cultura Experimental in Buenos Aires and the 'play' *El pan nuestro* (1977; Our Daily Bread) by its director Bruno Bert, in which the scenes or 'situations' alter from performance to performance. It remains to be seen whether a dramatist of international stature will emerge from this constantly expanding dramatic activity.

DLS

Further reading

L. F. Lyday and G. W. Woodyard, *Dramatists in Revolt: the New Latin American Theatre* (Austin and London, 1976)
The Latin American Theatre Review, University of Kansas (especially no. 13/2, supplement for Summer 1980, a general survey)

Brazilian theatre

The first manifestations of a dramatic character appear in Brazil in the Jesuit missions of the sixteenth century. José de Anchieta S.J. (1534–97) wrote *autos* or medieval morality plays with the intention of gaining converts to the Christian religion among the Amerindian population. The propaganda motive is so obvious that the plays are bilingual with passages both in Portuguese and Tupi to make them easily understood by a mixed audience. The oldest theatre in Brazil is located in Vila Rica (Ouro Preto) and dates from the early eighteenth century. But it was only after 1808 that the first permanent theatre, Teatro Real de S. João, was built in Rio de Janeiro by order of the Prince Regent João, who had moved his court from Portugal to Brazil to escape the French invasion of the country. In 1855 the Ginásio Dramático was founded in Rio, where French drama was shown to the public. Gradually the emerging bourgeoisie of merchants, businessmen and landowners began to join the aristocracy and a lower middle class of civil servants in regular visits to the theatre. It was, however, only after the end of the Second World War, when many experimental theatres were born in São Paulo and Rio de Janeiro, that a larger urban public felt the attractions of the theatre.

The founder of the Brazilian theatre was J. Gonçalves de Magalhães (1811–82) – the first author to show in his work the influence of romanticism. He lived in Paris, where he came in contact with the new ideas and launched there with a group of friends a literary magazine, *Niterói* (1836), in order to promote a complete change from the neo-classic to the romantic style. On his return to Brazil, he was greatly assisted in his plans by the distinguished actor João Caetano, who had organized in Rio de Janeiro, in 1833, the National Drama Company. João Caetano staged Gonçalves de Magalhães's drama, *Antônio José ou o poeta e a inquisição* (1836; Antônio José or the Poet and the Inquisition). The play takes as its subject the story of Antônio José (1705–39), born in Rio of Jewish parents, who became a famous playwright in Lisbon and was burnt at the stake by the Inquisition, because of his pointed attacks on physical and intellectual repression. In accordance with the principles of romantic aesthetics, Magalhães chose a national subject for his play, but he still bowed to the neo-classical tradition by writing a tragedy in blank verse. A large variety of themes, developed with great skill, is to be found in the twenty-six plays written by L. C. Martins Pena (1815–48). His one-act comedies are the best part of his dramatic production, in which he captures the mood and explores the imbroglios of ordinary life, using the colloquial language of the lower-class districts where he sets the action. Some of his most famous plays are *Os três médicos* (1845; Three Doctors), *O cigano* (1845; The Gipsy), and *O inglês maquinista* (1845; The English Engineer). The genre created by Pena was successfully continued by Artur Azevedo (1855–1980), whose plays – *Horas de humor* (1876; Humorous Hours), *A princesa dos cajueiros* (1880; The Cashewnut Princess), *A viúva Clark* (1900; The Widow Clark), *O dote* (1907; The Dowry) – were successfully staged until 1907. His comedies deal with domestic situations of bourgeois family life.

A dramatic poetic style was attempted by Gonçalves Dias (1823–64), who improved on the model left by Gonçalves de Magalhães.

Among his well-polished plays, *Leonor de Mendonça* (1847) takes pride of place, as a sensitive drama in verse that portrays the conflict between passion and intolerance, showing that fate is determined by men's actions rather than by God's will. Machado de Assis (1839–1908), the novelist, was also fascinated by the theatre. He translated French drama and wrote his own comedies – *O caminho da porta* (1862; The Way Out), *Os deuses de casaca* (1866; Gods in Dinner Jackets) – but his civilized plays did not seem to stir the public, who preferred Artur Azevedo.

The audiences of Rio and São Paulo were bourgeois or upper-class and were content with a pure form of entertainment that made no intellectual demands. The modernist movement of the 1920s left the theatre untouched, and the dramas of Oswald de Andrade (1890–1954), such as *O homem e o cavalo* (1934; Man and Horse), were never staged, due to the technical limitations of the Brazilian theatre at the time.

The great renewal of the texts written for the theatre, and of staging techniques, started only in 1943, with the arrival of theatre experts among the European refugees from the Second World War. Brazilian theatre then experienced a radical change and soon achieved an extraordinary vitality and diversity of styles in the plays produced between 1943 and 1978. In the same period there was an increase in the number of small experimental theatres in Rio and São Paulo, in spite of the negative effects of official censorship. While Guilherme de Figueiredo (b. 1915) produced dramatic parables (*A raposa e as uvas*, 1949; The Fox and the Grapes), and Pedro Bloch (b. 1914) reworked Pirandello's techniques (*As mãos de Eurídice*, 1951; The Hands of Eurydice), a brilliant group of playwrights appeared on the scene. Nelson Rodrigues (1912–80) stripped bare the unconscious tensions of the upper-middle classes in expressionist plays, *Vestido de noiva* (1943; The Wedding Gown), *A serpente* (1978; The Serpent). Jorge Andrade (b. 1922) centred on the conflicts of a declining 'aristocracy' of coffee-planters – *A moratória* (1955; Moratorium), *Pedreira das almas* (1958; Quarry of Souls) – and dealt courageously with the question of torture and political persecution in *Milagre na cela* (1977; The Miracle in Jail).

All this theatre exposed and condemned poverty and social oppression. João Cabral de Melo Neto (b. 1920) rebelled against poverty and famine in his *auto* on the north-east, *Morte e vida Severina* (1956; Severino's Life and Death), and A. Suassuna (b. 1927) addressed the same problems from a Christian viewpoint, in a mocking vein, in his morality plays. The revolt in the city, in the megalopolis of São Paulo or Rio, was shown by Gianfrancesco Guarnieri (b. 1936) in his *Eles não usam black tie* (1958; They Don't Wear Black Tie) and *A semente* (1963; The Seed). Meanwhile Augusto Boal (b. 1931) staged a political play that revealed the anguish and the hopes of an oppressed continent in *Revolução na América do Sul* (1960; Revolution in South America). And in 1970,

Chico Buarque de Holanda (b. 1944) achieved great success with his *Opera do Malandro* (The Villain's Opera), where music, song, acting and mime were combined to achieve an experience of 'total theatre'. Experimentation and audacious originality are thus the main features of the present-day Brazilian theatre.

LSR

Further reading
L. Kirschenbaum, *History of the Brazilian Drama* (Los Angeles, 1954)

Latin American cinema

Spanish America
Cinema made an early appearance in Spanish America. Some months after Lumière first showed his historic 'cinématographe' in Paris in 1895, moving pictures could be seen in Mexico City, Buenos Aires and Havana. Picture houses soon spread through the various republics and attracted what would become one of the largest cinema audiences in the world. Figures for Cuba in the mid-twentieth century reveal that out of a population of 7 million, 1.5 million went to the cinema every week. (These figures have doubled since the revolution partly due to the increased access of the rural population.) Such numbers reveal a profitable market for distributors and exhibitors and, more importantly, point to film (before the advent of television) as being the most important artistic medium for influencing and shaping values and ideas. It was not just Lenin who understood film to be 'the most important of all the arts'. Hollywood, especially after the First World War, was to monopolize film production and distribution throughout the continent.

Early production in Spanish America was limited to newsreels and documentaries. The first fictional films, Mario Gallo's *El fusilamiento de Dorrego* (1909; The Shooting of Dorrego) in Argentina or *El grito de Dolores* (1908; The Cry of Dolores) in Mexico, presented historical dramas, which became refined in Argentina with the popular *Nobleza gaucha* (Gaucho Nobility) by Eduardo Martínez in 1915. Documentaries, historical reconstructions and contemporary social themes provided the main subject matter up to the 1920s – the work of Enrique Díaz Quesada in Cuba was exemplary in this respect. As yet there were no really national film industries, for the products were diffuse and sporadic, although the Mexican government made good use of film propaganda during the revolutionary period: Pancho Villa, in particular, became a film star in North America after signing an exclusive contract with Mutual Film Corporation to film 'him and his war'. Tastes in Spanish

Carlos Gardel, greatest of all Argentine tango singers, starred in films made in the United States and France in the early 1930s

America were to change with the advent of Hollywood cinema in the 1910s, and especially after the First World War.

The Argentine writer (and occasional film critic) Jorge Luis Borges has remarked 'To enter a cinema in Lavalle Street [Buenos Aires] and find myself (not without surprise) in the Gulf of Bengal or Wabash Avenue seems preferable to entering the same cinema and finding myself (not without surprise) in Lavalle Street.' The national product became increasingly replaced by the magic, but also the marketing of Hollywood. In 1925, Hollywood supplied nearly all the feature films shown in Latin America: 90 per cent in Argentina, 95 per cent in Mexico, taking the two countries with the most developed film culture. This dependence had been slightly reduced by 1937 (70 per cent in Argentina, 80 per cent in Mexico). The history of Spanish American cinema is that of small national industries trying to compete for markets with North American distributors and in some cases exhibitors. North American companies could undercut local producers and offer a range of films made with lavish budgets. This problem became more acute when the relatively cheap and easy-to-make silent movies were replaced by talking pictures. Few republics had the money to invest in the new technology. Chile, which had produced a large number of feature films in the 1920s could not sustain this development, and Cuba became the exotic site for North American and Mexican film companies.

The extent of Hollywood cultural penetration was to be analysed in the 1960s by a group of Latin American film-makers and theoreticians who saw their task as opposing the Hollywood model and recovering 'national' culture. The system they sought to reject

was established in this early period: the local market was saturated by foreign films which imposed their own styles and values. Control of the market could also be kept at government level. In 1944, during the Second World War, the United States attempted to put pressure on the then neutral Argentine government by imposing a package of measures which included cutting supplies of raw film stock to Argentina, while continuing to supply Mexico, thus damaging production. At the same time, the office of the Co-ordinator of Inter-American Affairs under Nelson Rockefeller provided a grant to help modernize the Mexican motion picture industry 'to support the war effort and hemispheric solidarity'.

In these conditions, only Argentina and Mexico developed viable film industries. Both were aided by the advent of sound, which had crippled other, smaller industries. Hollywood adopted a policy which varied between dubbing its films ('Hollywood proposes monsters which combine the illustrious features of Greta Garbo with the voice of Aldonza Lorenzo', wrote Borges), using sub-titles, which excluded a large number of illiterates, or replacing its 'stars' with Spanish actors, none of which could successfully hamper local industries. By exploiting the market for 'talkies' and musical comedies, Latin America made fifty-six features in 1936 and ninety in 1937. In 1937 Mexico made fifty-two, Argentina thirty, Brazil four, Peru two and Uruguay and Cuba one each. Mexico and Argentina also exported features to other Latin American republics and benefited from the war years. By 1948, each industry had more than 10 per cent of the local market in Bolivia, Cuba, Chile, Ecuador, Paraguay, Uruguay and Venezuela.

Mexican cinema received state aid from Camacho, who set up the Banco Cinematográfico. Early productions included melodramas starring the Chilean singer José Bohr, and the more sophisticated productions of the director Fernando de Fuentes who shot historic themes (*El Compadre Mendoza*, 1933; Compadre Mendoza; and *Vámonos con Pancho Villa*, 1935; Let's Go with Pancho Villa), literary classics (*Doña Bárbara*, 1943), and inaugurated a succession of *comedias rancheras* with *Allá en el rancho grande* (1936; Down on the Farm). The directors Emilio Fernández and Alejandro Galindo produced bucolic 'indigenous' films with local stars such as Dolores del Río, who appeared in all the productions of El Indio Fernández, including the famous *Maria Candelaria*. There were some successes (the comedies of Cantinflas and the influential films of the Spanish exiles Buñuel and Alcoriza) but also a welter of mediocre 'local colour' comedies, musicals and drama. The situation deteriorated with the unionization of the industry in 1945, which became increasingly monolithic and effectively barred new talent and new ideas. In 1951, the industry produced over 100 films, but by 1964 this was down to less than fifty. In Argentina a similar pattern emerged. Tango musicals and comedies predominated, with local stars such as Luis Sandrini, Libertad Lamarque and Pepe Arias.

A scene from *La última cena* (1977)

(The great tango singer Carlos Gardel was a star in films made in 1931–5 by Paramount, in France and the United States.) Some directors of note emerged – Luis Saslavsky, Mario Soffici and Lucas Demare whose nationalist *Guerra gaucha* (1942; Gaucho War) was a great success. From 1946 President Perón protected the local industry, yet enforced censorship, and the industry went into a long decline and only revived again (briefly) in the early 1970s.

The 1950s saw the emergence of 'cine clubs' which began to create the conditions for the theoretical and practical 'break' with the dominant forms which occurred in the 1960s. One example is the development in Cuba of the groups Nuestro Tiempo and Visión, from which Tomás Gutiérrez Alea and Julio García Espinosa, amongst others, emerged. Guillermo Cabrera Infante began writing film criticism at this time and his subsequent novels contain numerous references to film and film techniques. The 1960s produced what has loosely been called the 'new cinema' of Latin America, reflecting the mood of political and social optimism in those years. The film-makers also became the theoreticians of the movement. Influential essays such as Julio García Espinosa's 'Imperfect Cinema', Getino and Solanas's 'Third Cinema' and Glauber Rocha's 'Aesthetics of poverty' all criticized the dominant Hollywood model and in some cases the European *auteur* movement, and proposed in its place 'cinema as "process"', in which the relations of production and reception would be changed. Instead of passive 'mass' audiences, the film-makers sought to promote active popular participation, for, as Mattelart has pointed out, one cannot change the

mass media just by inverting the message, making heroes revolutionaries rather than John Wayne.

Theory is often better developed than practice, though in these years there was a widespread cultural offensive. Cuba offered one model. The film industry ICAIC was founded within months of the seizure of power by Fidel Castro's revolutionary government and despite having to start from nothing, acquiring equipment and training directors after the flight of North American technology, it produced from 1959 to 1977 nearly one hundred features, 600 documentaries and more then 800 weekly newsreels. Documentaries have a special significance in a revolutionary context and the work of Santiago Alvarez has been exemplary. Feature films have covered a wide range of historical and contemporary themes and in a great variety of styles. Notable feature films produced include Julio García Espinosa's *Adventuras de Juan Quin Quin* (1967; Adventures of Juan Quin Quin), Tomás Gutiérrez Alea's *La muerte de un burócrata* (1966; Death of a Bureaucrat), *Memorias del subdesarrollo* (1968; Memories of Underdevelopment) and *La última cena* (1977; The Last Supper), Manuel Octavio Gómez's *La primera carga al machete* (1968; The First Machete Charge) and *Los días del agua* (1971; Days of Water), Humberto Solás's *Lucía* (1968) and *Cantata de Chile* (1976; Song of Chile), Pastor Vega's *Retrato de Teresa* (1979; Portrait of Teresa) and Sarah Gómez's *De Cierta Manera* (1974/77; One Way or Another). There is no dominant orthodoxy – the filmmakers (Alea, García Espinosa, Solás, Octavio Gómez, Pastor Vega amongst others) act as a co-operative and are free to work within the limits of a budget. Audiences have increased and the rural population has been integrated for the first time through the mobile cinema. Chile under Allende was less successful in using film in its ideological struggle. Few films were produced in the Popular Unity period and the state corporation Chile Films was split by factionalism. In fact, the most productive period in Chile occurred in the late 1960s with Raúl Ruíz's *Tres tristes tigres*, Helvio Soto's *Caliche sangriente* (Bloody Nitrate), Aldo Francia's *Valparaíso mi amor* (I Love Valparaiso) and Miguel Littin's *El chacal de Nahualtoro* (The Jackal of Nahualtoro), which was seen by over 250,000 people in Chile. In the River Plate region, Mario Handler and Ugo Ulive made *Elecciones* (1967; Elections), an analysis of the corrupt Uruguayan political system, and Solanas's marathon *La hora de los hornos* (Hour of the Furnaces) explored the neo-colonial conditions of Argentina, and traced the history of Peronism. This had to be shown in clandestine sessions. When Perón returned, there was a brief burst of creativity with the national epic *Juan Moreira* and *La Patagonia rebelde* (Rebel Patagonia) being shown in major film theatres.

In Bolivia at this period Jorge Sanjines and his film co-operative Ukamau made films on the exploitation of the Indians and the miners. (*Ukamau*, 1966; *Yawar Mallku*, 1969, Blood of the Condor; *El coraje del pueblo*, 1971; The Courage of the People). They lived with indigenous communities, learned Quechua and Aymara and attempted to convey this cultural difference in an appropriate language. The winds of change even reached Mexico, when young directors protested against the monolithic union structure and eventually received state support under President Echeverría. All these different groups met in festivals such as that of Viña del Mar (Chile) in 1967, but theirs was a 'permitted' cinema, caused by the expansive optimism of the 1960s and could not be sustained in the very different political climate of the mid-1970s.

Today some industries continue uninterrupted. Cuba and Mexico are the most stable, state-supported industries. In Mexico since Echeverría, cinema is now largely controlled by the state and, as in Brazil, radical film-makers work within the interstices of this system, or else support Third World 'epics'. The Mexican Octavio Paz has called the state a 'philanthropic ogre', a phrase which accurately describes the uneasy relationship between the state and the independent film-maker in Brazil and Mexico. Venezuela is beginning to promote its own industry and Peru and Colombia have produced some interesting independent film-makers – Marta Rodríguez and Jorge Silva in Colombia and Nora de Izcué in Peru. In Central America films are beginning to appear which deal with the revolutionary movements in Nicaragua and El Salvador. Most of the talented directors of the Southern Cone had to go into exile in the 1970s and adapted to these different conditions. There has been a lively 'exile' Chilean cinema since 1973, but all the directors look

forward to different conditions in Latin America where they might produce not just an image (in Jean-Luc Godard's words) but a just image of their societies.

Brazil

Cinema came early to Brazil, and in the first decade of the century a great number of feature films and documentaries were produced, including a series on famous contemporary crime (Antonio Leal's *Os estranguladores*, 1908; The Stranglers), historical documentaries and local-colour realism. This vigorous industry could not, however, compete with the Hollywood films which entered the country in the 1910 and 1920s. As in Spanish America, the home market was saturated: Hollywood supplied 95 per cent of the market in 1925, and 85 per cent in 1928 and 1937. National production was sustained in the 1920s in various regional groups, so called 'ciclos' (cycles) in Recife, Campinas, Manaus and most significantly Cataguazes, under Humberto Mauro. Mauro has been acclaimed as the pioneer of 'cinema novo' ('new cinema') in his critical portrayal of regional life, using low budget, 'anti-industrial' techniques.

The advent of sound caused more money to be injected into the industry. Adhemar Gonzaga set up the Cinédia studios and allowed Mauro to produce his most eclectic and influential film *Ganga Bruta* (1933) but this success was not sustained. The Atlántida studios produced a series of films in the 1930s and 1940s, the *chanchadas*, which were a form of farce, interspersed with songs by popular entertainers. Carmen Miranda starred in features such as *Alô, alô carnaval* (1936; Hello, Carnival!), before leaving for Hollywood. The films were idealized and exotic, but attracted a mass audience who could listen to local songs and jokes. Another attempt to set up a studio system in São Paulo in the late 1940s – the Vera Cruz Company – failed, despite having Alberto Cavalcanti as director and producing the occasional popular success (Lima Barreto: *O cangaceiro*, 1953, reviled by later directors for its 'false' treatment of the north-east).

A clear national focus was offered by the directors of the *cinema novo* a movement which grew up in the brief optimistic years of Kubitscheck and Goulart. A precursor and 'father' of the movement, Nelson Pereira Dos Santos, made *Rio 40 Graus* (Rio 40 Degrees) in 1955 about poverty and social inequality in Rio. This led to a series of films which Glauber Rocha, the movement's main theoretician, has divided into three phases. The first, between 1960 and 1963, focused on the north-east, describing the feudal conditions, poverty and mystic religion of that region. Directors' styles ranged from the extravagance of Glauber Rocha's *Deus e o diabo na terra do sol* (Black God, White Devil), to the neo-realism of Ruy Guerra's *Os fuzis* (The Guns) and Pereira Dos Santos's *Vidas sêcas* (Barren Lives). The second phase, between 1964 and 1967, dealt with political disillusionment after the coup and included Glauber Rocha's *Terra em transe* (Land in Anguish) and Gustavo Dahl's *O bravo guerreiro* (Brave Warrior). In 1968, repression became more severe and directors were forced to work in more indirect, allegorical modes, in what has been called the 'tropicalist' phase. At the same time they attempted to reach a wider popular audience, setting up their own distribution network Difilm and producing such popular successes as *Macunaíma* and the 'cannibalist' nationalist *Como era gostoso o meu francês* (How Tasty my Little Frenchman Was). This period is said to have ended when a number of directors left the country in 1972.

Since 1974, conditions have improved for film-makers. The state has played an increasing role, supporting Embrafilme, which gives grants and has established an extensive distribution network. Legislation has meant that cinemas must show Brazilian films for at least a third of the year. The result is a relatively healthy climate in which quality films vie with commercial mediocrity and *pornochanchadas* (porno-farces). With the revolution at a distance, even radical film-makers such as Ruy Guerra make critical films (*A Queda*, 1977; The Fall) within the system. The successes and limitations of such a strategy are the subject of lively debate.

JK

Further reading

E. Bradford Burns, *Latin American Cinema: Film and History* (Los Angeles, 1975)
J. Burton, *The New Latin American Cinema: an Annotated Bibliography of English Language Sources 1960–1976* (Cineaste Pamphlet 4, New York, 1976)
R. Johnson and R. Stam, eds., *Brazilian Cinema* (New Jersey, 1982)
C. Mora, *Mexican Cinema: Reflections of a Society, 1896–1980* (Los Angeles, 1982)
Z. Pick, ed., *Latin American Film Makers and the Third Cinema* (Ottawa, 1978)
B. R. Nevares, *The Mexican Cinema: Interviews with Thirteen Directors* (New Mexico, 1976)

Film magazines: see in particular, the special issues dedicated to Latin American or Third World Cinema
Afterimage, no. 3 (Summer, 1971)
Framework, no. 10 (Spring, 1979) and 12 (Autumn, 1979)
Image et Son, no. 340 (1979)
Jump Cut, nos. 19, 20, 21, 22 (1979–81)
Screen, vol. 24, no. 2 (March–April 1983)

The press

Many Latin American countries can trace back the history of their press to the appearance of commercial gazettes in the late colonial period. Of the existing newspapers, however, the oldest date back to the early years of independent life – the first half of the nineteenth century. Chile's *El Mercurio* – still the country's leading newspaper – and Brazil's *Jornal do Comércio* were founded in 1827; Peru's *El Comercio* in 1839, Panama's English-language *The Star and Herald* in 1849 (and its Spanish-language offshoot, *La Estrella de Panamá*, in 1853). In the Caribbean, Jamaica's *Daily Gleaner* dates back to 1834.

In several countries, major political upheavals interrupted this continuity. In Mexico (the country with the second-largest number of newspapers) the 1910 revolution led to a complete break with the past: the oldest existing newspapers (all still leading the field) are *El Universal* (1916), *Excelsior* (1917) and *La Prensa* (1928). In Bolivia, three successive breaks left few survivors from the past: *El Diario* (1904) from when the tin barons emerge on the scene as the new dominant force in the economy, *Ultima Hora* (1939) from the days of the populist experiment led by President Germán Busch, and *Presencia* (1952) from the revolution led by Victor Paz Estenssoro's *Movimiento Nacionalista Revolucionario*. Similarly, in Cuba the revolution headed by Fidel Castro in 1959 led to the disappearance of all pre-revolutionary newspapers: the oldest in existence is *Granma*, founded in 1965.

In many other cases, political upheavals, while not causing such complete breaks, have been responsible for the birth and demise of journalistic booms, some of which have left a lasting mark on the development of the Latin American press. In Argentina, the country with the third-largest number of newspapers even today, and with the highest indices of circulation per thousand inhabitants, the rise of *Yrigoyenismo* in the early twentieth century coincided with a publishing boom of which the best-remembered exponent was the newspaper *Crítica* – a remarkable experiment with a large-circulation 'popular' daily whose writers included the leading intellectual lights of the time; Peronism in the late 1940s and early 1950s saw the creation of a huge state-controlled network of press media which was swept away by the military coup of 1955; and the boom of the late 1960s and early 1970s – which at one point made Buenos Aires the city with the largest number of magazines in the world – was dealt a crippling blow by the political violence of the mid-1970s, in which many journalists were killed and most of the leading talents in the field were driven into exile. In post-war Uruguay, 'the Switzerland of the Americas' saw the appearance of *Marcha*, once the most prestigious magazine of political analysis in the hemisphere, which vanished with the creeping military takeover of government in the early 1970s.

The fact that most countries in the region share a common language (Spanish) and a common cultural heritage has repeatedly kindled the aspiration of developing region-wide publications. Only one lasting success has been registered in this field: the fortnightly newsmagazine *Visión*, founded in 1950 and currently printing over 200,000 copies – a low figure by comparison with its peers in the main capitals. Better fortune has accompanied some more recent (1970s) ventures with a more limited, sub-regional scope. Leading exponents in the field are the Lima-based *Andean Report* (an English-language monthly covering economic news in the Andean countries) and the Guatemala-based *Inforpress Centroamericana* (with its English-language companion, *Central America Report*), a weekly covering economic and political events in the isthmian countries.

If the common bond of the Spanish language has not provided strong enough foundations for the development of a region-wide press, historical links with Britain and the United States have stimulated the growth of high-quality newspapers and journals in English. As mentioned above, Panama's oldest extant newspaper is the English-language *Star and Herald*. In Argentina, *The Buenos Aires Herald*, founded in 1876, occupies a position of enormous prestige, gained mainly by its editorial independence, maintained even through periods in which most other publications had fallen prey to censorship, self-censorship or the fear of violent reprisals. Also in Argentina, *The Review of the River Plate*, founded in 1891, has long been considered an authoritative journal of economic and commercial information. Venezuela's *Daily Journal* has equally long been considered one of the best exponents of the Caracas press. The above-mentioned *Andean Report* and *Central America Report* are also leading examples, and most capitals also have excellent examples of the classical newsletter (such as *Economic Survey* in Buenos Aires and *This Week in Guatemala*). Paradoxically, in terms of news-gathering techniques and sophistication, the English-language press is far more developed on the Spanish-speaking mainland than in the English-speaking Caribbean.

A side-effect of the political upheavals which have so marked the development of the Latin American press has been the prevalence of constraints on press freedom in most countries. These, varying according to time and place, have ranged from outright censorship to subtler methods of economic coercion and even institutionalized bribery. Argentina in the mid-1970s presented the extreme case of physical repression of the press: as a professional group, journalists and publishers were leading targets of the campaign of assassinations, abductions ('disappearances'), imprisonment and enforced exile unleashed by the extreme right – and its counterpart, widespread self-censorship out of fear in the surviving media. The editor of the *Buenos Aires Herald*, Robert Cox, was forced to leave the country after threats were made against his life; the publisher and editor of *La Opinión*, Jacobo Timerman, was abducted, tortured and expelled from the country after having been stripped of his citizenship and his newspaper – his book *Prisoner Without a Name, Cell without a Number* made his case known throughout the world.

Mexico has traditionally provided the best example of institutionalized 'indirect' constraints: compliance by publishers is ensured by the government monopoly of newsprint imports (and the permanent threat to restrict them as a punitive measure), while the allegiance of journalists has been traditionally 'bought' by bribery, in the form of a second paypacket from government institutions or agencies (this latter practice has been banned by the government of Miguel de la Madrid). A combination of outright censorship and 'indirect' pressures has been used by the Sandinista regime in Nicaragua against the only opposition newspaper, *La Prensa*, while in Cuba all press organs are controlled by the state, the party or their agencies.

The Survey of Press Freedom in Latin America, published in 1984 by the Council of Hemispheric Affairs and The Newspaper Guild, offers the following panorama:

Argentina: Constraints on the press began to be relaxed by the military government in 1982. However, seizures and temporary closures of newspapers and magazines continued right up to the installation of the elected government of President Raúl Alfonsín in December 1983. Since then, formal and informal restrictions have been lifted.

Bolivia: Since the military handed power to the civilian government of President Hernán Siles Zuazo, the press has been formally protected by constitutional guarantees that had been laid aside since 1967.

Brazil: Since 1982, the political *abertura* has brought greater freedom for the printed media, though government control of key supplies and government advertising are still used 'to keep journalists and publishers in line'. Stricter control continued to be enforced on the electronic media.

Chile: The 1980 constitution allows the ministry of the interior to ban the publication of newspapers and magazines which present 'a risk of disturbance to public order'. Self-censorship is the norm.

Colombia: Censorship was formally ended in July 1982, towards the end of President Julio César Turbay Ayala's term of office.

Cuba: The government and the Communist Party manage news by hiring ideologically 'correct' journalists and by setting official guidelines for periodicals and broadcasts. Some freedom is allowed for criticism on domestic issues.

Dominican Republic: Since May 1982 the government of President Salvador Jorge Blanco has re-established free expression. However, the government has continued to manipulate official advertising to favour pro-government publications.

El Salvador: Violence by right-wing groups and self-censorship imposed by newspaper proprietors have contributed to the maintenance of conservative news policies and the elimination of editorial slants which challenge the status quo.

Guatemala: Apart from legal constraints on reporting, violence and intimidation against journalists have silenced criticism.

Haiti: Apart from legal constraints, physical violence against journalists has contributed to making self-censorship the norm.

Mexico: Government control of the press subsists through bribery, control of newsprint and use of the government's advertising budget as an incentive to favourable coverage.

Nicaragua: Formal constraints on the press were eased, but not eliminated, in the period leading up to the general elections of November 1984.

Panama: There are no formal constraints, but strong-arm tactics have been used against overtly critical journalists. The appearance of *La Prensa* in 1980 signalled a break in the uniform pro-government slant of most of the press.

Paraguay: Since 1970 the law establishes penalties including prison sentences for advocating 'hatred among Paraguayans or the destruction of social classes'. The government also resorts to arrests, beatings and closure of media organizations. Despatches of foreign news agencies are monitored by the state telecommunications agency.

Peru: Since 1981, an anti-terrorist law allows the government to take action against vaguely defined actions of the media deemed incitements to terrorism. Journalists can be jailed for 'offending the dignity of an official'.

Uruguay: Since December 1983 the military government has subjected to prior censorship all party-political, trade-union and humorous publications. Orders have been issued, on specific occasions, banning all coverage of political or strike-related events.

Venezuela: The only formal laws susceptible to abuse are the requirement that journalists be licensed and vaguely defined libel laws.

It is only in the past twenty years that Latin American journalism has begun to break away from the traditional 'literary' style – wordy and not too concerned with factual reporting. The change was pioneered in the mid-1960s, in Argentina, by Jacobo Timerman, who introduced the first newsmagazines on the lines of the US publications *Time* and *Newsweek*. Timerman founded, first, *Primera Plana*, then its competitor, *Confirmado*. Though both of these have since disappeared, their 'newsier' style, hallmarked by a more economic use of the Spanish language, has lived on in Argentina, and soon found imitators in neighbouring countries, mainly in the Southern Cone.

In Chile, Emilio Filippi switched the already existing magazine *Ercilla* to the new style and managed to maintain its tradition of (relative) editorial independence well into the years of Pinochet's rule. When forced to relinquish the editorship of *Ercilla* in the late 1970s, Filippi founded the award-winning *Hoy* as its even more outspoken successor.

At about the same time, similar changes were taking place in Brazil, which spawned a string of excellent newsmagazines such as *Veja*, *Exame* and *Isto E*. In spite of having to cope with the restrictions imposed by the military regime which came to power in 1964, the Brazilian press continued to develop professionally and technically, to the current position in which its quality is by far the highest in Latin America. This is in sharp contrast to Argentina, where the interruption of the press boom of the 1970s by the military coup of 1976 led many of the country's best journalists into exile and caused a dramatic fall in quality from which the press had not recovered when democracy was restored in 1983.

Daily newspapers took longer than the magazines to adapt to modern journalistic techniques and styles. Here again the pioneer was Argentina's Jacobo Timerman, who in 1971 founded *La Opinión*, a daily newspaper devised on lines similar to those of France's *Le Monde*. *La Opinión* was a casualty of the 1976 coup, but its influence was felt in several other Spanish-speaking countries: its mark, and that of some of its shortlived Argentine followers, is recognizable in Spain's *El País* and *Diario 16* and in Mexico's *Unomásuno*.

Another landmark in the modernization of the region's daily press was the appearance in Venezuela, in 1979, of *El Diario de Caracas*, founded by Rodolfo H. Terragno, an exiled Argentine publisher who had earlier broken new ground in his home country with the magazine *Cuestionario*.

It is difficult to discern any clear pattern in the correlations between the development of the press and social indicators throughout the region. The three countries with the largest populations (Brazil, Mexico and Argentina, in that order) are also those with the largest number of daily newspapers (in the same order). Thereafter, however, the correlation breaks down: Uruguay, for example, ranks ninth in number of newspapers but sixteenth in size of population. When attention turns to the circulation of these newspapers per thousand inhabitants, Argentina moves up to the top of the list, and Uruguay shoots up to second place (while Mexico falls to sixth place, Venezuela to eighth, Peru to ninth and Brazil all the way down to twenty-first place).

Literacy rates do not offer any clearer correlation with circulation: though Argentina and Uruguay rank, respectively, first and second on the literacy scale, matching their position regarding circulation, Venezuela is in fifth place (eighth in circulation), Mexico in tenth (sixth in circulation) and Brazil in twelfth (twenty-first in circulation). Chile has the third-highest literacy rate and ranks twelfth in circulation.

EC

Radio and television in Latin America

Radio stations proliferate throughout Latin America and television also has a firm hold. According to the latest available estimates (*c*.1980) there are over 62 million radio receivers and close on 23 million TV sets in the eighteen Spanish-speaking countries of Latin America. For Brazil the figures are 35 million radio receivers and 15 million TV sets.

Both in the vast, thinly populated areas and in the great conurbations like Mexico City, São Paulo and Buenos Aires, broadcasting holds a commanding position as a vehicle of information and of entertainment. The penetration of radio and television is aided by several factors, including the generally low level of newspaper readership, the vigorous thrust of commercial interests, and the efforts of some governments to use the media for purposes of education and national integration.

In most Latin American countries broadcasting is under the control of a government department that is responsible for granting concessions for radio stations and television channels. In Mexico, for instance, this is the Directorate-General of Radio, Television and Cinematography, generally known as RTC. All commercial radio and TV stations in Mexico are compelled by law to cede one-eighth of their broadcasting time to the government and it is the RTC that is responsible for planning and producing the material designed to fill that allocation, though it has not yet succeeded in taking up all the air and screen time to which it is entitled. RTC is also in charge of Radio Mexico, the short-wave external service, as well as 'La Hora Nacional', an official government bulletin carried on Sunday evening by all the radio stations in the country. In Brazil, broadcasting is under the supervision of the Federal Ministry of Communications. Through Radiobrás, a state holding company established in 1976, the ministry co-ordinates the operation of all the government-owned radio and TV stations. Radiobrás is also designed to build up radio and TV coverage in the north-east and in the Amazon region, both areas which have hitherto been poorly served by the Brazilian media. In October 1981 Radiobrás announced the installation of a new radio station in the city of Manaus to cover the entire Brazilian Amazon area, and to broadcast on a tropical wave band, with a power output of 250 kW. All radio stations in Brazil are compelled to broadcast a daily programme called 'A Voz do Brasil' (The Voice of Brazil), a bulletin of news and current affairs which is compiled by the Agência Nacional, a government agency subordinated to the office of the presidency. In Argentina – to take a third example – there is a Directorate of Radio and a Directorate of Television, two government agencies run by the Secretary of Public Information. These directorates are responsible for devising the regulations which govern all broadcasting; and an advisory body, the Federal Broadcasting Committee (COM-FER), which includes representatives of the Communications Secretariat and the radio and television stations, and deals with matters of administration. There are also private organizations, formed to further the interests of the commercial radio and TV stations.

Radio

There are many thousands of radio stations in Latin America. Even the Dominican Republic – one of the smallest countries – has over one hundred. In Brazil – the biggest country in Latin America – there are well over one thousand. Argentina and Venezuela have about 150 each.

The vast majority of stations throughout the area are small commercial enterprises, in many cases virtually built around one man playing records – or cassettes – interspersed with jingles and advertising slogans. But there are also, in most of the larger cities, sophisticated organizations which operate several different programme streams, each designed to appeal to a particular section of the listening audience. Such a network is likely to include a news-type station which carries frequent short bulletins and perhaps three times a day – at breakfast time, at noon and in the evening – lengthy programmes of international and local news and comment; an FM station – in all probability fully automated – presenting the latest music from the international hit parade; and a medium- or long-wave station devoted to interminable soap operas (*radionovelas*) or the local brand of popular music, for example, brassy ranch style (*música ranchera*) in the case of Mexico and Central America, tangos and milongas in the case of Argentina. Advertising is selected to suit the appropriate stream. The first two types of station described (news and FM) will carry commercials aimed at the Class A – that is, the more affluent – consumer sector of society. The commercial message of the soap opera or local music type of station will be addressed to the Class B or Class C consumer.

National radio. In most countries there is also the National Radio or the official state network. Often under-financed and ill-equipped, these stations are subject to the whim of the current political establishment and the staff's often altruistic ideals are a poor defence against insecurity of tenure. With few exceptions – Brazil's Radiobras is one – these stations do not make a great impact.

University stations. In several Latin American countries universities are active in the field of broadcasting. Though by their very nature directed to the more discriminating minority audiences, university stations are sometimes run by enthusiasts who are able to offer surprisingly rich fare to listeners seeking refuge from the commercial battle of the air. Apart from broadly educational programmes supported by their own academic resources and classical music presented without concession, they tend to include in their output the choicest cultural programmes supplied by the leading international broadcasters such as the BBC (whose English by Radio series get particularly wide usage), West Germany's Deutsche Welle, Netherlands Radio and the Voice of America.

The most well-endowed university station, and the one with the most ambitious output, is undoubtedly Radio UNAM, the broadcasting service of the National Autonomous University of Mexico.

Religious stations. There are in Latin America numerous religious broadcasting organizations, both Roman Catholic and Protestant. Leading the field – and heard throughout the American continent and beyond – is HCJB (La Voz de los Andes), founded in Quito, Ecuador, in 1931. HCJB is a (Protestant) World Radio Missionary Fellowship station (of Florida, USA) which provides a wide-ranging service of news, cultural and evangelical material in sixteen different languages.

Of the Roman Catholic stations one of the most important is Radio Sutatenza of Colombia which, as part of an organization known as 'Acción Cultural Popular', aims to improve standards of literacy and self-reliance among the rural population of the country. Similar objectives are pursued on a somewhat more limited scale by Radio San Gabriel of La Paz, Bolivia, whose entire output, educational and religious, is in Aymara, the predominant language of the Indians in the area surrounding Lake Titicaca. Radio San Gabriel seeks also to promote in its audience an awareness of Aymara culture and nationhood.

Television

There are about 400 TV stations in Latin America, and most countries now transmit in colour. The largest TV organization in the Spanish-speaking world is Mexico's Televisa, a privately owned commercial chain with four television channels which dominates Mexico City as well as covering virtually the whole country with the aid of over eighty repeater stations. Televisa's immense output of home-produced *telenovelas* (drama serials) and dubbings of foreign originations are marketed throughout Spanish-speaking America and give Mexico an unrivalled preponderance in the medium.

Also noteworthy is the penetration of Televisa into the sizeable and fast-growing Spanish-language broadcasting market in the United States which it has achieved by means of two US-based subsidiaries: the Spanish International Network (SIN) and the Spanish International Communications Corporation (SICC), a SIN subsidiary which controls five of the eleven TV stations broadcasting full-time in Spanish in the United States. SIN began operations in the United States in 1961, when it opened a station in Texas, the state with the biggest concentration of Spanish speakers. Today it links more than sixty cities through all but three of the ninety or so TV stations that broadcast in Spanish in the United States.

In Brazil, the most powerful TV organization is the Rede Globo (Globo Network), a Rio-based conglomerate which comprises TV, radio, the influential newspaper *O Globo*, a leading record company and various show business interests. Globo claims the lion's share of TV audiences in Rio and São Paulo. It has stations in several other leading cities and regularly places its programmes in over twenty associated stations throughout the country. It has offices in New York, Paris and London, and has exported its programmes to many countries in Europe and Africa. (In Great Britain, Channel 4, established in 1982, has shown a variety of Brazilian material.)

International broadcasting organizations

Of the various international bodies designed to promote co-operation between different broadcasting organizations and to represent their interests, the leading one in Latin America is AIR (Asociación Inter-Americana de Radiodifusión), which has its central office in Montevideo, Uruguay. Argentina, Brazil, Chile, Colombia, Mexico and Venezuela are also associate members of EBU, the European Broadcasting Union, which was founded in 1950 to support the interests of members and to assist the development of radio and television worldwide. Cuba is a member of OIRT, the International Radio and Television Organization, which groups together the radio and television organizations of mostly Eastern-bloc countries. The radio and TV organizations of the English-speaking Caribbean are grouped within the CBU, the Caribbean Broadcasting Union, an association of national broadcasting systems formed to promote interchange between member countries.

AMAP

Science in Latin America

Science in early colonial times

The scientific enterprise in Latin America has been closely linked to that of the western world from the Spanish conquest to the present. The Aztecs, Mayas and Incas had protoscientific accomplishments similar to those of the other high civilizations of antiquity (for example, numeration and astronomical observations related to calendrical computation, descriptive botany, pharmacology, metallurgy), elements of which were quickly assimilated by the Spaniards into the corpus of European science. The great expedition of Francisco Hernández (1517–87) to New Spain from 1570 to 1577 was designed to recover and preserve Aztec natural history, particularly materia medica, towards which end Hernández learned

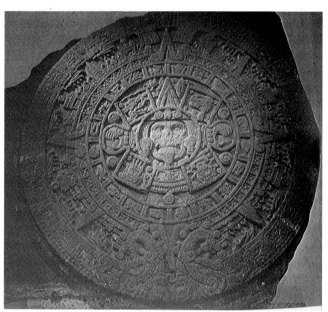

The Aztec calendar stone. Its symbols epitomize the Aztec ideas of the universe

Nahuatl. The result of his labours was a massive natural history of New Spain, unpublished in his lifetime. Prior to the Hernández expedition, a great store of New World natural history had already been transferred to Europe in such treatises as the *Natural and General History of the Indies* (1535, a summary of which had appeared in 1526) of Gonzalo Fernández de Oviedo (1478–1557) and the *Medicinal History of the Indies* (1565) by Nicolás Monardes (*c.*1493–1588), whose principal focus was the medicinal use of New World plants, animals and minerals.

At the same time, the geography of the New World was being integrated into the modified classical scheme based on the fifteenth-century recension of Ptolemy's geography. A conceptual breakthrough was achieved by Pedro Mártir de Angleria (1457–1526) who first posited the existence of a 'New' World as distinct from that which had been known to the ancients. The earliest general geography to synthesize a vision of old and new worlds conjoined was the *Suma de geografía* (1519) of Martín Fernández de Enciso. Early cartographic representations of the New World were found on maps drawn by Sebastian Cabot (1474–1557), Juan de la Cosa (d. 1510) and Francisco Domínguez, a Portuguese cartographer assigned to the Hernández Expedition.

The New World section of the manuscript world map attributed to Juan de la Cosa (1500)

In the seventeenth century, scientific activity domiciled in Latin America grew in importance, in part because of the growth of universities in the Spanish empire and in part a reflection of the density of urban populations and the growth of local economies which required technical personnel. Colonial men of science shared the age's characteristic enthusiasm for celestial observation, owing to the vogue of the telescope. Particularly noteworthy were Diego Rodríguez's (1596–1668) *Observation of the New Comet*, an astrological study of the comet of 1652 which cites observations by Galileo, and the observation of the comet of 1680 by Carlos Sigüenza y Góngora (1645–1700), another Mexican scientist, probably a student of Rodríguez. Siguenza was greatly influenced by the Spanish *novatores*, scientists who attempted to come to grips with the new science without breaking openly with official dogma. Accordingly, Sigüenza utilized elements of Copernican cosmology without championing it openly.

The accrued Spanish experience in practical metallurgy was synthesized in the work of seventeenth-century authors, particularly in the *Arte de los metales* (1640) of Alvaro Alonso Barba (*c*.1569–1662) which discusses amalgamation, founding and other processes used in the Peruvian silver mines.

The eighteenth century

Science in eighteenth-century Latin America was characterized by a number of well-defined processes: first, the slow percolation of the New Science – represented by Copernicus, Galileo, Newton and Harvey – a process which took more than a century owing to the scholasticism of official institutions of learning; second, the surveying of the natural history of Spanish America by a succession of expeditions sponsored by the crown, large-scale enterprises characteristic of the scientific programme of enlightened despotism and which reflected the period's zeal for taxonomy, typified by Linnaeus and his worldwide network of scientific informants; and third, the association of men of science with scientific nationalism and, later, the movement for political independence.

In general, the open teaching of Copernicanism and Newtonian physics was delayed in Latin America by a full century or more. José Celestino Mutis (1732–1808) espoused heliocentrism at the Colegio Mayor del Rosario in Bogotá in the 1770s and his disciple Juan Eloy Valenzuela (d. 1834) taught Newtonian physics there from 1777. Cosme Bueno (1711–98) had taught the doctrines of Newton at the University of San Marcos in Lima from 1758. There, as in Bogotá, however, the new science was mainly diffused outside the universities, where scholasticism was still entrenched. The Real Convictorio de San Carlos, founded in 1774, was Newtonian in orientation. In the University of Mexico, Newtonian physics was not regularly taught until the first decades of the nineteenth century.

The circulation of the blood, another touchstone of the New

University of San Marcos, Lima. An important centre of learning in the eighteenth century

Science, also arrived late, one of the earliest sources being a treatise on 'Evidence of the Circulation of the Blood' published in Lima in 1723 by Federico Bottoni, a Sicilian physician who had been in contact with Spanish *novatores* familiar with William Harvey. The great generation of Peruvian physicians of the end of the eighteenth century was introduced to Harvey through Bottoni's volume.

The first major expedition of the eighteenth century, one with primarily geodesic aims, was that of Charles Marie La Condamine to South America in 1735–44. This expedition was organized by the French government, but under strict controls imposed by the Spanish crown and with the participation of Spanish personnel. Its purpose was to measure the length of a degree in order to test Newton's assertion that the earth was not absolutely round. The group which carried out most of the geodesic measurements included La Condamine, Jorge Juan (1713–73), Antonio de Ulloa (1716–95) and Pedro Vicente Maldonado (b. 1704). The triangulation was completed in June 1739 when 3° of latitude had been covered. At the same time meteorological observations were made, as were studies of Newtonian attraction and the length of the beat of Huygens's pendulum at different altitudes above sea level. In Lima, La Condamine exchanged astronomical data with Pedro Peralta (1663–1743) and other members of the expedition (in particular, Joseph de Jussieu and Louis Godin) were instrumental in diffusing the ideas of Copernicus and Newton among the Peruvian intelligentsia. This expedition also produced botanical results, including the first accurate description of cinchona.

The persistent problem of establishing accurate boundary demarcations between Spanish and Portuguese territory produced a number of important expeditions in the eighteenth century. The northern boundary, in the region of the Orinoco River, was explored beginning in 1753 by a group led by José de Iturriaga (b. 1699) and which included Eugenio de Alvarado (b. 1715), Vicente Doz (c.1736–81), the instrument maker Apolinar Diez de la Fuente and José Solano (b. 1726), the latter a disciple of Jorge Juan. Linnaeus's disciple, Pehr Lofling (1729–56) was attached to the expedition as a botanist but the natural history component was largely forgotten after his premature death. Among the significant achievements of the expedition were Alvarado's expedition to Guayana, Solano's reconnaissance of the upper Orinoco and La Fuente's search for the source of that river. Solano, Doz and La Fuente all produced maps of the area which considerably clarified the geography of northern South America.

More varied was the work of demarcation teams in the River Plate, which included the geographers Juan de Aguirre (d. 1811), Diego de Alvear (1749–1830) and Francisco Millau (1728–1805), as well as Félix de Azara (1746–1821), whose studies of flora and fauna resulted from, although were not officially part of, his service on the boundary commission.

First of the three great botanical expeditions was that to Peru, led by Hipólito Ruíz (1752–1816), José Pavón (1754–1840) and the French botanist Joseph Dombey (1742–94). The expedition arrived in Lima in April 1778 and by the time its work ended in 1788 the botanists had amassed 589 drawings, 3000 plant descriptions and a herbarium of 1980 dried specimens. The most interesting scientific aspect of the Ruíz–Pavón expedition was its explicitly Linnaean character. The decree establishing the expedition explicitly imposed the Linnaean system of classification, and Ruíz and Pavón personally diffused Linnaean concepts when they lectured on botany at the University of San Marcos in 1780.

The botanical expedition to New Granada was established in 1783 in Mariquita, under the direction of Mutis and his assistant Valenzuela. In 1791 the expedition moved to Bogotá where Mutis involved a number of young naturalists, including the geographer Francisco José de Caldas (1768–1816), the botanist Antonio Zea (1766–1822) and the zoologist Jorge Tadeo Lozano (1771–1816) in his labours and where in the first several years of the nineteenth century it was transformed into a genuine scientific institution, with the leadership passing to Mutis's nephew Sinforoso in 1808. The expedition's work included production of 6849 plates, of which 5393 survive. Mutis's preoccupation with cinchona has overshadowed the rich variety of the expedition's work, which included physical observations and the establishment of an observatory directed by Caldas.

The last of the great botanical expeditions, that to New Spain, was established in 1787 as an explicit continuation of the sixteenth-century enterprise: 'with the general and important objective of promoting the progress of physical science, banishing doubts and adulterations in medicine, dyeing and other useful arts, and to augment commerce, and also with the special end of supplementing, illustrating and perfecting the original writings which Dr Francisco Hernández left in accord with the present state of these natural sciences' (Royal Order of 20 March 1787). The expedition included the director Martín de Sessé (1751–1808) and the creole botanist José de Mociño (1757–1819). Unlike the other botanical expeditions, that to New Spain was institutionalized immediately with the establishment of a botanical garden in Mexico City and a chair of botany, inaugurated in 1788 by Vicente Cervantes (1755–1829). The Linnaean spirit was also in evidence in colonial Brazil where the Franciscan José Mariano de Vellozo (1748–1811) collected a large herbarium and described around seventeen hundred plant species, published in 1827 as the *Flora fluminensis*.

Another expedition, headed by the Italian Alessandro Malaspina (1754–1809) was primarily hydrographic in aim, although its personnel included the naturalists Thaddaeus Haenke (1761–1817), Luis Née (1734–1803) and Antonio Pineda (1753–92). The expedition sailed in July 1789 and explored in the River Plate, Central America, Mexico and the Philippines, returning to Spain in 1795. A botanical expedition to western Cuba (1795–9) was organized by the Count of Mompox (1769–1807), with Baltasar Boldó as chief botanist. All these expeditions lent themselves to making astronomical observations, of which the most noteworthy were the observations of the transit of Venus across the solar disc by Doz and Joaquin Velázquez de León (1732–86) in Baja California (1769) and that of the transit of Mercury by Dionisio Alcalá Galiano (1762–1805) in Montevideo in 1789. A major expedition, with different aims, was the Royal Maritime Expedition of Vaccination, led by the physician Francisco Javier de Balmis (1753–1819), which visited the Caribbean, Mexico and the Philippines in 1803–6 to inoculate citizens against smallpox.

Colonial science was, by definition, dependent upon Europe. But scientists in Lima, Mexico City and Bogotá had, by the end of the eighteenth century, weaned themselves from dependence on Spain and were acquiring books and instruments from England and France. According to Alexander von Humboldt (1769–1859), only

Drawings of *Cinchona lanceifolia* (left) and *Aristolochia cordiflora Mutis* (right) from Mutis's *Expedición botánica*

Joseph Banks, director of Kew Gardens in London, had a botanical library better than that of Mutis. Increasing participation in the mainstream of science tended paradoxically to heighten the creole naturalists' sense of isolation. An example is Caldas's confession that when he invented a barometric instrument, he was unsure whether or not it might already have been invented. Nevertheless, by the end of the century Spanish American naturalists had begun to think in terms of fully autonomous national schools of science, conducting research on a European level but without the necessity of direct European tutelage.

As a result, many of the creole scientists associated with Bourbon expeditions were later involved in the independence movements, particularly in New Granada, New Spain and Peru. When Humboldt toured Latin America (in 1799–1804) he stimulated naturalists there to examine the resources of their own countries with a view towards social and political reform. At the same time, creole scientists such as the Peruvians José Hipólito Unánue (1755–1833) and José Manuel Dávalos (1758–1821) sought to defend the New World against charges of biotic and climatic inferiority levelled by the Count de Buffon and Cornelius de Pauw. This was the rationale of Unánue's famous *Observations on the Climate of Lima* (1802), whose exaggerated conclusions regarding the singularity of Lima's climate may actually have impeded the introduction of European medicaments which he believed to be inappropriate to Peruvian conditions. The nationalistic impulse in science was particularly strong in Mexico where members of the botanical expedition sought to revive Aztec botany, so that 'Mexico might glory in having its own materia medica', in Mocino's words. Such impulses were easily

converted into political ideology and scientists were highly visible in the independence movements, particularly in New Granada, where Caldas, Lozano and other disciples of Mutis were executed for revolutionary activities. The image of physical science among enlightened creoles was highly coloured by Benjamin Franklin, admired not only as a Newtonian and experimentalist, but also as a political example. Political leaders like Antonio Nariño of New Granada not only idealized Franklin and tinkered with electrical machines but also felt akin to the ideals of democracy which he represented.

The aftermath of independence

Science was a major casualty of the trauma of independence and although certain colonial institutions, such as the Observatory of Bogotá and the Real Seminario de Minería of Mexico, survived into the independence period, they did so at an impoverished level. The latter case is typical. Instruction at the Seminar, in the two decades prior to independence, had been at a European level, thanks to such professors as Fausto de Elhuyar (1754–1833) and Andrés Manuel del Río (1765–1849), discoverers of tungsten and vanadium respectively. As director, Elhuyar had introduced the new chemistry into the curriculum by commissioning a Spanish translation (1797) of Lavoisier's *Elementary Treatise of Chemistry*. During the war of independence mining engineers flocked to the Mexican side and lost their lives. The Seminar itself fell into decay after 1810 and classes were not resumed until 1827, with only a handful of students.

Even European exploration declined, with but a few efforts such as that of Jean Baptiste Boussingault (1802–87), who had gone to Latin America at the behest of Humboldt, Charles Darwin's notable voyage on HMS *Beagle* (1831–5) and, later, the Spanish Pacific Commission (1862–6) which achieved interesting results in descriptive taxonomy.

The reception of Darwinism provides some insight into the status of the natural sciences in Spanish America in the late nineteenth century. With the exception of Argentina, Darwinism was received and discussed by physicians and social scientists, rather than naturalists, and the evolutionary debate was centred in medical schools and academies, anthropological societies and the literary lyceums and clubs where positivist social thinkers gathered. Although historians have promoted the notion that Spencerian positivists favoured Darwinism while Comtians opposed it, the actual situation was more complex. Spencerians did indeed raise Darwin's banner in Argentina and Uruguay (where positivist political control over education was strong enough to provide official support for Darwinism and to force Catholics to counterattack in the Congress) and in Mexico Comtians with strong links to France were, on the whole, opposed. In Venezuela, however, Comtian positivism and Darwinism were allied. Darwinian biology was first taught in the medical schools as, for example, by José Arechevaleta in Uruguay and in Venezuela by the anatomist Luis Razetti (1862–1932), who in 1905 manoeuvred the Academy of Medicine of Caracas into declaring itself in favour of Darwinism.

Argentina was the only country where naturalists bore the brunt of the Darwinian debate, because only in that country was there a large enough concentration of palaeontologists and other naturalists to foment a broad-based, informed discussion of Darwin's evidence. The natural history museums of Buenos Aires, La Plata and Paraná all had important collections of fossils whose contents were analysed in articles both in European and national journals, such as the *Revista Argentina de Historia Natural* (1891). At the centre of the Argentine debate was the palaeontologist Florentino Ameghino (1854–1911), author of a famous treatise on fossil mammals and a convinced evolutionist who waged a quixotic crusade to establish Argentina as the original home of the human species.

The recuperation of science in Latin America towards the end of the nineteenth century is associated with the influence of French science and scientific institutions. The Colombian botanist José Triana (1826–90) collaborated with French and other European botanists on the flora of New Granada, published most of his research in France, and resided there from 1857 until his death. Later in the century, Paris became the pole of attraction for Latin American medical researchers. The Venezuelan José Gregorio Hernández (1864–1919) studied with Mathias Duval and Charles Richet in 1889–91, and imported a complete histological laboratory from France upon his return to Caracas. In Brazil, around the turn of the century, Osvaldo Cruz (1872–1917) established an Institute of Experimental Pathology explicitly modelled on the Pasteur Institute where he had studied from 1896 to 1899. His associate, Carlos Chagas (1879–1943), discovered an endemic parasitic

'*Beagle* at the foot of Mount Sarmiento in Tierra del Fuego' by Conrad Martens (1834)

disease, which now bears his name, caused by a trypanosome infesting the huts of Brazilian villagers. Other physicians such as the Cuban Carlos Juan Finlay (1833–1915), who identified the vector of yellow fever, were educated in the United States.

The twentieth century

The early twentieth century witnessed the efforts of several Latin American governments both to improve the quality of scientific education and to vastly broaden the scope of scientific activities. In Argentina the government sought to implant German science directly at the University of La Plata where the physicist Emil Bose was installed as director of the Faculty of Exact Sciences in 1909. There he established a well-equipped institute of physics and lured from Germany a corps of distinguished faculty, including Richard Gans, an authority on electromagnetism, and Jakob Laub, Einstein's first collaborator who gave the first lectures on relativity in the New World. The institute produced a number of very talented Argentine physicists, yet after its initial burst of activity, the effort to establish German physics failed. To the north, the Mexican revolution stimulated the renaissance of some old institutions (such as the National Astronomical Observatory) and the creation of a host of new ones: the School of Chemistry, the Office of Geographical and Climatological Studies, and the Office of Biological Studies, the latter under the direction of Alfonso L. Herrera (1868–1942), an outstanding biologist, evolutionist and pioneer researcher into the origins of life.

The Spanish Civil War (1936–9) produced a substantial migration of Republican Spanish scientists to Latin America, where they had a positive impact. Indeed, in many countries Spanish refugees were responsible either for the founding or renovation of entire disciplines or sub-fields. Representative figures were Gustavo Pittaluga (1876–1955), for parasitology in Cuba; Emilio Mira y López (1890–1946), for clinical psychology in Brazil; Pau Vila (1881–1980), for geography in Venezuela; José Royo Gómez (1895–1961), for geology in Colombia and Venezuela. The Argentine Psychoanalytic Association was founded by another Spanish exile, Angel Garma (b. 1904), together with two Argentines and a Jewish refugee. Medical research in Venezuela was put on a modern footing by three refugees: the Catalan physiologist August Pi i Sunyer (1879–1965) and two German Jews, Martin Meyer and Werner Jaffe.

The period after the Second World War really constitutes a sharply different phase in the history of Latin American science, marked by the massive influx of students from Latin countries into universities in the United States, the problems attendant upon their return to Latin America (including the 'brain drain'), and the establishment of major new research entities such as the Instituto Venezolano de Investigaciones Cientificas (1959) in Venezuela and national councils for higher scientific research, with both policy and

research roles, in many other countries. Related to governmental efforts was the formation by scientists of national associations for the advancement of science: Peru (1920), Argentina (1933), Brazil (1948), Venezuela (1950).

A full range of scientific institutions, of inevitably varying size and quality, now exists across the region. Scientists and technologists are in increasing demand for a great variety of national projects, including significant nuclear power programmes in several countries. Governments, in the most recent period, have played a greater part in stimulating scientific research and in expanding education. The number of universities in Latin America approximately doubled between the end of the Second World War and the close of the 1960s. Both the natural sciences and engineering have benefited from this process of expansion, an important feature of which has been the creation of institutes for technology and applied science – the formation of Chile's State Technical University (1947) being an early example. Scientists, like other members of the academic community, have not always been able to escape the effects of political upheaval. General Juan Carlos Onganía's heavy-handed (and quite gratuitous) intervention in Argentine universities after the military coup of 1966 drove hundreds of well-qualified scientists into exile and virtually destroyed the departments of mathematics and physics at the University of Buenos Aires. Latin American scientists, like their counterparts elsewhere, often lament the inadequacy of laboratory facilities or of funding. There has also, at times, been debate as to the role of pure science in relation to the tasks of economic and social development. In general, however, the most recent phase has been marked by a growing awareness of science and technology as valuable components in the development of Latin America. Scientists themselves have been active in moves towards a greater degree of regional co-ordination of scientific activity.

Three Latin American scientists have won Nobel Prizes: the Argentine, Bernardo Houssay (1887–1971), in 1947, and the Venezuelan, Baruj Benacerraf, in 1981, both in medicine; and Luis F. Leloir of Argentina in chemistry (1970).

TFG

Further reading
I. H. W. Engstrand, *Spanish Scientists in the New World: the Eighteenth Century Expeditions* (Seattle, 1981)

R. Hilton, *The Scientific Institutions of Latin America* (Standford, 1970)

R. R. Miller, *For Science and National Glory: the Spanish Scientific Expedition to America, 1862–1866* (Norman, Oklahoma, 1968)

A. R. Steele, *Flowers for the King: the Expedition of Ruiz and Pavon and the Flora of Peru* (Durham, 1981)

N. Stepan, *Beginnings of Brazilian Science* (New York, 1976)

CHILE: OBSERVATORY AREA

La Silla observatory, in the Norte Chico of Chile

Astronomy in the Norte Chico of Chile

The dry, semi-desert region of Chile known to Chileans as the Norte Chico possesses atmospheric conditions almost ideally suited to astronomical observation: 'the seeing,' as astronomers say, is as good in this particular area as anywhere on the earth's surface. The mountains in the vicinity of La Serena – the region's main city, situated at 30°S, some 400 km north of the Chilean capital, Santiago – have an average of 280 clear nights each year. Tucson, Arizona, the best place in the northern hemisphere from this standpoint, has no more than 200. Given the intrinsic interest of southern hemisphere skies – which contain, among other things, the galactic centre region and the two Magellanic Clouds (small galaxies near our own, invisible from northerly latitudes) – it is not surprising that astronomers should have taken advantage of the favourable conditions of the Norte Chico. A number of important observatories have been installed there since the mid-1960s.

The INTER-AMERICAN OBSERVATORY has the largest telescope in the southern hemisphere, the 4 m reflector opened in 1976. The decision to build this observatory was taken in 1962, and it was dedicated in 1967. Used primarily by astronomers from the United States and Latin America, it is run by the US Association of Universities for Research in Astronomy (AURA), and stands on a dramatic mountain site at Cerro Tololo, some 35 km from the small town of Vicuña in the Elqui Valley – a valley traditionally celebrated for its production of good-quality pisco, a clear brandy. In addition to the 4 m instrument, the equipment at Cerro Tololo includes 1.5 m, 1 m, 0.9 m and 0.4 m reflectors.

The EUROPEAN SOUTHERN OBSERVATORY (ESO), operated by the Organisation Européene pour des Recherches Astronomiques dans l'Hémisphère Austral (whose member countries are France, West Germany, Italy, the Netherlands, Belgium, Denmark, Sweden and Switzerland), is located at Cerro La Silla, some 100 km north of La Serena. (The spot was chosen in 1964.) Its striking mountain-top position can be glimpsed unforgettably (in the distance) from Chile's main north–south highway. The largest of Cerro La Silla's thirteen telescopes is a 3.6 m reflector (like Cerro Tololo's largest, opened in 1976), the remaining instruments covering a range from 0.4 m to 2.2 m.

Other large telescopes in the area are maintained by the CARNEGIE INSTITUTION of Washington (2.5 m and 1 m) and the UNIVERSITY OF TORONTO (0.61 m).

In less than two decades, in fact, the sleepy provincial city of La Serena (founded 1544, pop.: 120,000) has become one of the astronomical capitals of the world.

SC

Index

Headings other than proper names indicate main references, but the reader should also seek references under countries, places and regions.

Acknowledgements

The publishers gratefully acknowledge permission to reproduce the illustrations listed below. Every effort has been made to obtain permission to use copyright material; the publishers trust their apologies will be accepted for any errors or omissions.

J. Allan Cash Photolibrary 383r; Allison and Busby Ltd 373r; Archive Pictures Inc. 285; BBC Hulton Picture Library 293; Dr George Bankes 173l, 174; Elizabeth Baquedano 130, 166, 168, 389, 390l, tr, 391l, c; Dr Harold Blakemore 161, 184, 322, 403r (poster reproduction of painting by Guayasamín); Trustees of the British Museum 390br, 391r; Dr Colin Clarke 65, 100, 202, 292, 317, 319; Dr Simon Collier 145, 182, 247, 251; Dr Peter Coy 170, 324, 408; Cuban Embassy 279, 304; André Deutsch Ltd 375; Dr J. P. Dickenson 276, 380r; European Southern Observatory 428; Jan Fairley 382; Dr Valerie Fraser 395, 397, 398; Mike Goldwater/Network Photographers 332; Dr R. N. Gwynne 66, 70; Keystone Press Agency Ltd 297r, 330, 366, 383l; Abel Lagos 275; J. C. Langley 169; Latin America Bureau 327, 328; Barry Lewis/Network Photographers 43, 103; Lloyds Bank International Ltd 114; Manchester Museum/photo: Wilf Thomas 393l; Mansell Collection 229; Jenny Matthews/Format Photographers 231, 232; Professor Narciso Menocal 409r; Mexican Embassy 217, 219, 221, 222; Tony Morrison/South American Pictures 11, 22, 23, 25, 27l, 28, 29, 30, 31, 32, 35, 36, 38, 41, 45, 46, 48, 49, 51, 53, 72, 79, 84, 86, 99, 108, 127, 129, 131, 149, 158, 159, 160, 173r, 175 176, 183, 195, 200, 242, 243r, 254, 265, 266, 286l, 293l, 298, 334, 335, 338, 379, 380l, 393, 396, 399, 400, 405; John Moss/United Society for the Propagation of the Gospel 61, 63, 273r, 302, 312, 326, 388; Ian Mursell 301, 378; Museo Histórico Nacional de Uruguay 262; Museo Maritimo, Barcelona 177; Museo Naval, Madrid 422b; Sister Mary Noel-Menezes 297l, 320; Organization of American States 204, 208, 209, 228, 232, 237, 238, 250, 253, 255l, 260, 263, 269, 270, 273l, 277, 284, 286r, 363, 365, 367, 371, 372, 386, 387, 407, 409, Palacio Nacional, Mexico City 337; Peruvian Times 243l, 423; Paul Popper Ltd 27r, 255r; Edward Ranney/photo: Martin Chambi 241; Secretariat of Education, Mexico City 403l; US National Archives 283.